Houghton Mifflin
Mathematics

HOUGHTON MIFFLIN

BOSTON • MORRIS PLAINS, NJ

California • Colorado • Georgia • Illinois • New Jersey • Texas

ISBN 0-618-08178-X

4 5 6 7 8 9 VH 06 05 04 03 02 01

Authors

Senior Authors

Dr. Carole Greenes
Professor of Mathematics Education
Boston University
Boston, MA

Dr. Miriam A. Leiva
Distinguished Professor of
Mathematics, Emerita
University of North Carolina
Charlotte, NC

Dr. Bruce R. Vogeli
Clifford Brewster Upton Professor
of Mathematics
Teachers College, Columbia University
New York, NY

Program Authors

Dr. Matt Larson
Curriculum Specialist for Mathematics
Lincoln Public Schools
Lincoln, NE

Dr. Jean M. Shaw
Professor of Mathematics Education
University of Mississippi
Oxford, MS

Dr. Lee Stiff
Professor of Mathematics Education
North Carolina State University
Raleigh, NC

Content Reviewers

Lawrence Braden (Grades 5–6)
Mathematics Teacher
St. Paul's School
Concord, NH

Dr. Don Chakerian (Grades 3–4)
Emeritus Professor of Mathematics
University of California
Davis, CA

Dr. Kurt Kreith (Grades 3–4)
Emeritus Professor of Mathematics
University of California
Davis, CA

Dr. Liping Ma (Grades K–2)
Visiting Scholar
Carnegie Foundation for the
Advancement of Teaching
Menlo Park, CA

Dr. David Wright (Grades 5–6)
Professor of Mathematics
Brigham Young University
Provo, UT

Reviewers

California Math Teacher Advisory Board

Doug Hedin

Park Oaks Elementary
  School
Thousand Oaks, CA

Vicky Holman

Mount Pleasant Elementary
  School
San Jose, CA

Jennifer Rader

Desert Trails Elementary
  School
Adelanto, CA

Fran Range-Long

Alice Birney Elementary
  School
Fresno, CA

Sylvia Kyle

Chester Nimitz Elementary
  School
Cupertino, CA

Karlene Seitz

Citrus Glen Elementary
  School
Ventura, CA

Grade 4

Beth Holguin

Graystone Elementary
  School
San Jose, CA

Marilyn Higbie

Jane Addams Elementary
  School
Long Beach, CA

Tarie Lewis

Melrose Elementary School
Oakland, CA

Sandra Jo McIntee

Haynes Street School
West Hills, CA

Mike Tokmakoff

Hoover Street Elementary
  School
Los Angeles, CA

Nancy Yee

Valhalla Elementary School
Pleasant Hill, CA

Grade 5

Patty Jernigan

Santa Susana
Simi Valley, CA

Joe Koski

Nu-View Elementary
  School
Nuevo, CA

Bill Laraway

Silver Oak Elementary
San Jose, CA

Steve Monson

Castro Elementary School
El Cerrito, CA

Sherri Qualls

Weibel Elementary School.
Fremont, CA

Arlene Sackman

Earlimart Middle School
Earlimart, CA

Robyn Suskin

Sierra Madre School
Sierra Madre, CA

Grade 6

Herb Brown

Lake Gregory Elementary
  School
Crestline, CA

German Palabyab

Harding Elementary School
El Cerrito, CA

Carole Patty

West Riverside Elementary
  School
Riverside,CA

Maureen Smith

Patterson Elementary
  School
Fremont, CA

Jeff Varn

Sierra Madre Elementary
  School
Sierra Madre, CA

Family Letter

Dear Family,

Every parent hopes his or her child will be confident and successful in school. *Houghton Mifflin Mathematics* is designed to provide children with a solid foundation in mathematics that will help lead to such success.

This program is based on the Mathematics Content Standards for California. The goals of this program are

- Providing a curriculum that balances skills, conceptual understanding, and problem solving

- Providing instruction and practice to help children become proficient in computational skills

- Helping children become good mathematical problem solvers

- Enabling children to use correct mathematical terms to communicate their understanding of math concepts

Look for the standards box in each lesson.

The notation in this box represents the following standard.

Number Sense 3.0 **Students solve problems involving addition, subtraction, multiplication, and division of whole numbers and understand the relationships among the operations.**

On pages vi–ix you will find a full listing of all the Mathematics Content Standards for California for Grade 4.

As you work with your child throughout the year, the listing of these standards will help you understand what he or she is learning in each lesson.

We trust your child will have a successful year!

Sincerely,
Houghton Mifflin Company

California

MATH STANDARDS

By the end of grade four, students understand large numbers and addition, subtraction, multiplication, and division of whole numbers. They describe and compare simple fractions and decimals. They understand the properties of, and the relationships between, plane geometric figures. They collect, represent, and analyze data to answer questions.

Number Sense (NS)

1.0 Students understand the place value of whole numbers and decimals to two decimal places and how whole numbers and decimals relate to simple fractions. Students use the concepts of negative numbers:

1.1 Read and write whole numbers in the millions.

1.2 Order and compare whole numbers and decimals to two decimal places.

1.3 Round whole numbers through the millions to the nearest ten, hundred, thousand, ten thousand, or hundred thousand.

1.4 Decide when a rounded solution is called for and explain why such a solution may be appropriate.

1.5 Explain different interpretations of fractions, for example, parts of a whole, parts of a set, and division of whole numbers by whole numbers; explain equivalents of fractions (see Standard 4.0).

1.6 Write tenths and hundredths in decimal and fraction notations and know the fraction and decimal equivalents for halves and fourths (e.g., 1/2 = 0.5 or .50; 7/4 = 1 3/4 = 1.75).

1.7 Write the fraction represented by a drawing of parts of a figure; represent a given fraction by using drawings; and relate a fraction to a simple decimal on a number line.

1.8 Use concepts of negative numbers (e.g., on a number line, in counting, in temperature, in "owing").

1.9 Identify on a number line the relative position of positive fractions, positive mixed numbers, and positive decimals to two decimal places.

2.0 Students extend their use and understanding of whole numbers to the addition and subtraction of simple decimals:

2.1 Estimate and compute the sum or difference of whole numbers and positive decimals to two places.

2.2 Round two-place decimals to one decimal or the nearest whole number and judge the reasonableness of the rounded answer.

3.0 Students solve problems involving addition, subtraction, multiplication, and division of whole numbers and understand the relationships among the operations:

3.1 Demonstrate an understanding of, and the ability to use, standard algorithms for the addition and subtraction of multidigit numbers.

3.2 Demonstrate an understanding of, and the ability to use, standard algorithms for multiplying a multidigit number by a two-digit number and for dividing a multidigit number by a one-digit number; use relationships between them to simplify computations and to check results.

3.3 Solve problems involving multiplication of multidigit numbers by two-digit numbers.

3.4 Solve problems involving division of multidigit numbers by one-digit numbers.

4.0 Students know how to factor small whole numbers:

4.1 Understand that many whole numbers break down in different ways (e.g., $12 = 4 \times 3 = 2 \times 6 = 2 \times 2 \times 3$).

4.2 Know that numbers such as 2, 3, 5, 7, and 11 do not have any factors except 1 and themselves and that such numbers are called prime numbers.

Algebra and Functions (AF)

1.0 Students use and interpret variables, mathematical symbols, and properties to write and simplify expressions and sentences:

1.1 Use letters, boxes, or other symbols to stand for any number in simple expressions or equations (e.g., demonstrate an understanding and the use of the concept of a variable).

1.2 Interpret and evaluate mathematical expressions that now use parentheses.

1.3 Use parentheses to indicate which operation to perform first when writing expressions containing more than two terms and different operations.

1.4 Use and interpret formulas (e.g., area = length x width or $A = lw$) to answer questions about quantities and their relationships.

1.5 Understand that an equation such as $y = 3x + 5$ is a prescription for determining a second number when a first number is given.

2.0 Students know how to manipulate equations:

2.1 Know and understand that equals added to equals are equal.

2.2 Know and understand that equals multiplied by equals are equal.

Measurement and Geometry (MG)

1.0 Students understand perimeter and area:

1.1 Measure the area of rectangular shapes by using appropriate units, such as square centimeter (cm²), square meter (m²), square kilometer (km²), square inch (in²), square yard (yd²), or square mile (mi²).

1.2 Recognize that rectangles that have the same area can have different perimeters.

1.3 Understand that rectangles that have the same perimeter can have different areas.

1.4 Understand and use formulas to solve problems involving perimeters and areas of rectangles and squares. Use those formulas to find the areas of more complex figures by dividing the figures into basic shapes.

2.0 Students use two-dimensional coordinate grids to represent points and graph lines and simple figures:

2.1 Draw the points corresponding to linear relationships on graph paper (e.g., draw 10 points on the graph of the equation $y = 3x$ and connect them by using a straight line).

2.2 Understand that the length of a horizontal line segment equals the difference of the x-coordinates.

2.3 Understand that the length of a vertical line segment equals the difference of the y-coordinates.

3.0 Students demonstrate an understanding of plane and solid geometric objects and use this knowledge to show relationships and solve problems:

3.1 Identify lines that are parallel and perpendicular.

3.2 Identify the radius and diameter of a circle.

3.3 Identify congruent figures.

3.4 Identify figures that have bilateral and rotational symmetry.

3.5 Know the definitions of a right angle, an acute angle, and an obtuse angle. Understand that 90°, 180°, 270°, and 360° are associated, respectively, with 1/4, 1/2, 3/4, and full turns.

3.6 Visualize, describe, and make models of geometric solids (e.g., prisms, pyramids) in terms of the number and shape of faces, edges, and vertices; interpret two-dimensional representations of three-dimensional objects; and draw patterns (of faces) for a solid that, when cut and folded, will make a model of the solid.

3.7 Know the definitions of different triangles (e.g., equilateral, isosceles, scalene) and identify their attributes.

3.8 Know the definition of different quadrilaterals (e.g., rhombus, square, rectangle, parallelogram, trapezoid).

Statistics, Data Analysis, and Probability (SDP)

1.0 Students organize, represent, and interpret numerical and categorical data and clearly communicate their findings:

   1.1 Formulate survey questions; systematically collect and represent data on a number line; and coordinate graphs, tables, and charts.

   1.2 Identify the mode(s) for sets of categorical data and the mode(s), median, and any apparent outliers for numerical data sets.

   1.3 Interpret one-and two-variable data graphs to answer questions about a situation.

2.0 Students make predictions for simple probability situations:

   2.1 Represent all possible outcomes for a simple probability situation in an organized way (e.g., tables, grids, tree diagrams).

   2.2 Express outcomes of experimental probability situations verbally and numerically (e.g., 3 out of 4; 3/4).

Mathematical Reasoning (MR)

1.0 Students make decisions about how to approach problems:

   1.1 Analyze problems by identifying relationships, distinguishing relevant from irrelevant information, sequencing and prioritizing information, and observing patterns.

   1.2 Determine when and how to break a problem into simpler parts.

2.0 Students use strategies, skills, and concepts in finding solutions:

   2.1 Use estimation to verify the reasonableness of calculated results.

   2.2 Apply strategies and results from simpler problems to more complex problems.

   2.3 Use a variety of methods, such as words, numbers, symbols, charts, graphs, tables, diagrams, and models, to explain mathematical reasoning.

   2.4 Express the solution clearly and logically by using the appropriate mathematical notation and terms and clear language; support solutions with evidence in both verbal and symbolic work.

   2.5 Indicate the relative advantages of exact and approximate solutions to problems and give answers to a specified degree of accuracy.

   2.6 Make precise calculations and check the validity of the results from the context of the problem.

3.0 Students move beyond a particular problem by generalizing to other situations:

   3.1 Evaluate the reasonableness of the solution in the context of the original situation.

   3.2 Note the method of deriving the solution and demonstrate a conceptual understanding of the derivation by solving similar problems.

   3.3 Develop generalizations of the results obtained and apply them in other circumstances.

Contents

Remembering Your Facts

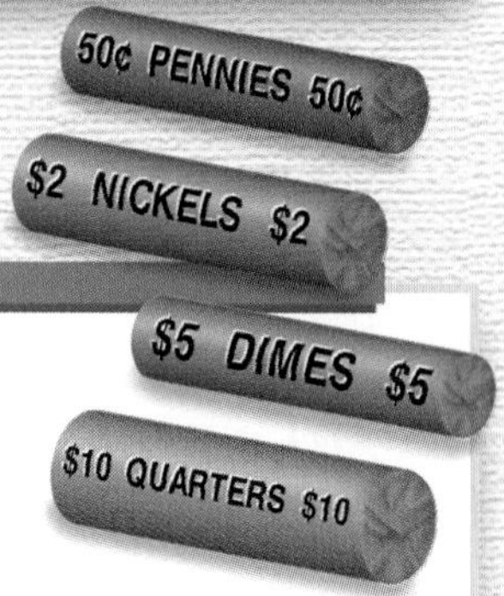

50¢ PENNIES 50¢
$2 NICKELS $2
$5 DIMES $5
$10 QUARTERS $10

CHAPTER 1 Place Value and Money

Addition and Subtraction

CHAPTER 3

Relating Multiplication and Division

Multiplication of Whole Numbers

Division by One-Digit Divisors

CHAPTER 6 — Measurement and Negative Numbers

CHAPTER 7 Fractions and Mixed Numbers

CHAPTER 8

Decimals

CHAPTER 9 Statistics and Probability

Geometry and Measurement

CHAPTER 11 Graphing and Algebra

Division by Two-Digit Divisors

Book Resources

Addition Facts

Add.

1. $2 + 2$	**2.** $2 + 7$	**3.** $3 + 5$	**4.** $4 + 4$	**5.** $4 + 8$
6. $3 + 7$	**7.** $7 + 7$	**8.** $9 + 5$	**9.** $2 + 5$	**10.** $5 + 9$
11. $5 + 5$	**12.** $6 + 9$	**13.** $9 + 8$	**14.** $2 + 6$	**15.** $3 + 4$
16. $4 + 6$	**17.** $5 + 6$	**18.** $7 + 8$	**19.** $8 + 8$	**20.** $2 + 8$
21. $3 + 6$	**22.** $4 + 5$	**23.** $5 + 7$	**24.** $6 + 7$	**25.** $8 + 9$
26. $9 + 9$	**27.** $2 + 3$	**28.** $2 + 9$	**29.** $3 + 8$	**30.** $2 + 4$
31. $5 + 8$	**32.** $6 + 6$	**33.** $7 + 9$	**34.** $9 + 6$	**35.** $4 + 7$
36. $3 + 3$	**37.** $3 + 9$	**38.** $6 + 8$	**39.** $9 + 7$	**40.** $4 + 9$

Subtraction Facts

Subtract.

1. $4 - 2$	**2.** $14 - 7$	**3.** $17 - 9$	**4.** $16 - 8$	**5.** $17 - 8$
6. $11 - 4$	**7.** $13 - 6$	**8.** $15 - 7$	**9.** $15 - 6$	**10.** $14 - 5$
11. $10 - 5$	**12.** $15 - 9$	**13.** $12 - 5$	**14.** $11 - 3$	**15.** $6 - 2$
16. $12 - 4$	**17.** $11 - 5$	**18.** $11 - 2$	**19.** $9 - 4$	**20.** $10 - 4$
21. $9 - 3$	**22.** $5 - 2$	**23.** $16 - 7$	**24.** $16 - 9$	**25.** $14 - 6$
26. $12 - 6$	**27.** $18 - 9$	**28.** $13 - 5$	**29.** $12 - 3$	**30.** $6 - 3$
31. $13 - 4$	**32.** $8 - 4$	**33.** $10 - 3$	**34.** $7 - 3$	**35.** $8 - 3$
36. $7 - 2$	**37.** $9 - 2$	**38.** $14 - 9$	**39.** $8 - 2$	**40.** $10 - 2$

Multiplication Facts

Multiply.

1. 8×4	**2.** 7×9	**3.** 8×6	**4.** 9×3	**5.** 3×3
6. 4×2	**7.** 6×9	**8.** 9×7	**9.** 6×6	**10.** 8×5
11. 7×4	**12.** 8×3	**13.** 9×2	**14.** 3×2	**15.** 9×9
16. 9×8	**17.** 7×6	**18.** 7×5	**19.** 5×4	**20.** 6×3
21. 8×2	**22.** 8×8	**23.** 8×7	**24.** 6×5	**25.** 6×4
26. 4×3	**27.** 6×2	**28.** 8×9	**29.** 9×6	**30.** 5×5
31. 7×3	**32.** 5×2	**33.** 5×9	**34.** 7×7	**35.** 9×5
36. 9×4	**37.** 4×4	**38.** 5×3	**39.** 7×2	**40.** 2×2

Division Facts

Divide.

1. 25 ÷ 5	**2.** 54 ÷ 9	**3.** 35 ÷ 5	**4.** 24 ÷ 3	**5.** 8 ÷ 2
6. 32 ÷ 4	**7.** 30 ÷ 5	**8.** 18 ÷ 2	**9.** 20 ÷ 4	**10.** 24 ÷ 4
11. 18 ÷ 3	**12.** 6 ÷ 2	**13.** 63 ÷ 7	**14.** 63 ÷ 9	**15.** 48 ÷ 6
16. 36 ÷ 6	**17.** 81 ÷ 9	**18.** 40 ÷ 5	**19.** 27 ÷ 3	**20.** 9 ÷ 3
21. 36 ÷ 4	**22.** 16 ÷ 4	**23.** 21 ÷ 3	**24.** 12 ÷ 3	**25.** 10 ÷ 2
26. 15 ÷ 3	**27.** 14 ÷ 2	**28.** 45 ÷ 9	**29.** 12 ÷ 2	**30.** 16 ÷ 2
31. 72 ÷ 8	**32.** 64 ÷ 8	**33.** 72 ÷ 9	**34.** 49 ÷ 7	**35.** 4 ÷ 2
36. 45 ÷ 5	**37.** 54 ÷ 6	**38.** 56 ÷ 7	**39.** 42 ÷ 6	**40.** 28 ÷ 4

CHAPTER 1

Place Value and Money

Why Learn About Place Value and Money?

You use place value to help you understand how large or small a number is. Your family uses money to buy food and clothes.

When you count things you have collected, such as marbles or stamps, you are using place value. When you buy lunch or a movie ticket, you are using money.

You can count the number of children that are building the sand castle, but it would be difficult to count how many grains of sand are in the castle.

Reviewing Vocabulary

Understanding math language helps you become a successful problem solver. Here are some math vocabulary words you should know.

place value	the value of a digit determined by its place in a number
digit	one of the symbols used to write numbers
standard form	a number written with commas separating groups of three digits
expanded form	a number written showing the value of each digit
word form	a number written in words

Reading Words and Symbols

When you read mathematics, sometimes you read words, sometimes you read words and symbols, and sometimes you read only symbols.

Look at the different ways you can show the same number.

▶ **standard form:** 45,620

▶ **word form:** forty-five thousand, six hundred twenty

▶ **expanded form:** 40,000 + 5,000 + 600 + 20

Try These

1. Write the standard form of each number.

   a. three hundred eight

   b. one thousand, four hundred sixty-three

   c. 80,000 + 1,000 + 400 + 50 + 2

   d. 60,000 + 500 + 4

2. Tell whether the 4 is in the *hundreds, thousands,* or *ten thousands* place.

   a. 2,476   b. 46,880   c. 4,711

   d. 94,752   e. 46,308   f. 405

3. Write the numbers in order from least to greatest.

   a. 65 73 45   b. 175 204 192   c. 1,973 1,745 1,945

4. Write *true* or *false.*

   a. You can write forty-five cents as $0.45 or 45¢.

   b. You can use two different coins to give someone 31¢.

   c. The value of two quarters and one nickel is less than the value of five dimes.

   d. The value of one $5 bill is equal to the value of five $1 bills.

Upcoming Vocabulary

Write About It Here are some other vocabulary words you will learn in this chapter. Watch for these words. Write their definitions in your journal.

ones period	**estimate**
thousands period	**round**
millions period	

Place Value Through Hundred Thousands

You will learn how to read and write numbers through hundred thousands.

New
Vocabulary
period

Learn About It

Michigan Stadium in Ann Arbor is the largest stadium in the United States. It has 107,501 seats!

A place-value chart can help explain what this number means.

THOUSANDS			ONES		
hundred thousands	ten thousands	thousands	hundreds	tens	ones
1	0	7	5	0	1

The value of the 1 is 100,000.   The value of the 7 is 7,000.   The value of the 5 is 500.   The value of the 1 is 1.

Each group of 3 digits separated by a comma in a number is called a **period**.

There are different ways to write 107,501.

Different Ways to Write a Number

You can use standard form.	107,501
You can use expanded form.	100,000 + 7,000 + 500 + 1
You can use short word form.	107 thousand, 501
You can use word form.	one hundred seven thousand, five hundred one

Use a comma to separate the periods.

Explain Your Thinking

▶ Why are zeros important in the ten thousands and tens places of 107,501?

▶ In 444,444, which 4 has the greatest value? Tell how you know.

Guided Practice

For Exercises 1–3, write each number three other ways.

1. 104,002   **2.** 104,020   **3.** 104 thousand, 200

4. What is the value of the 5 in 405,044?

Ask Yourself

• What is the value of each digit?

• Do I need a comma?

Standards NS **1.0**   MR **2.4**

Independent Practice

Write each number in standard form.

5. 700,000 + 30,000 + 800 + 90

6. 405 thousand, 603

7. 900,000 + 10,000 + 6,000 + 500 + 3

8. twenty thousand, eight hundred

9. 8 hundred thousands, 9 ten thousands, 7 thousands, 5 tens, 6 ones

Write each number in short word form and word form.

10. 201

11. 8,973

12. 89,001

13. 99,909

14. 320,000

15. 300,200

16. 302,000

17. 332,332

18. 500,000 + 20,000 + 1,000 + 600 + 30

19. 70,000 + 4,000 + 100 + 3

**Write each number in expanded form.
Then write the value of the underlined digit.**

20. 7<u>0</u>1

21. 5,<u>2</u>60

22. 63<u>9</u>,572

23. <u>7</u>07,321

24. 89,2<u>2</u>5

Problem Solving • Reasoning

Use Data Use the table for Problems 25–27.

25. How many seats are there in Memorial Stadium? Write this number in two ways.

26. **Estimate** Which stadium has more than eighty thousand seats?

27. **Write About it** Look at the number of seats for Memorial Stadium and Dodd Stadium. In which number does the digit 6 have the greatest value? Explain.

Stadium Seats	
Stadium	**Number of Seats**
Roberts Stadium	33,000
Memorial Stadium	75,662
Stanford Stadium	85,500
Dodd Stadium	46,000

Mixed Review • Test Prep

Use skip counting. Find the next number.

28. 2, 4, 6, 8, ____

29. 10, 20, 30, 40, ____

30. 3, 6, 9, 12, ____

31 Which number sentence belongs to the same family of facts as 12 − 9 = 3?

A 3 + 9 = 12

c 9 − 3 = 6

B 12 + 3 = 15

D 3 + 6 = 9

Extra Practice See Set A on page 40.

Compare and Order Numbers

You will learn how to compare and order numbers through 999,999.

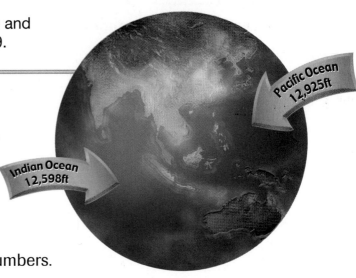

Pacific Ocean
12,925ft

Indian Ocean
12,598ft

Learn About It

Ocean depths vary from place to place. Which is greater, the depth shown in the Pacific Ocean or the one shown in the Indian Ocean?

You can use place value to compare numbers.

Step 1 Line up the digits in the numbers. Begin at the greatest place value. Find the place where the digits are different.	**Step 2** Compare the digits that are different. Write > or <.
1 2, **9** 2 5 1 2, **5** 9 8 ↑ ↑ same different	1 2, **9** 2 5 1 2, **5** 9 8 ↑ 9 hundreds > 5 hundreds < is less than > is greater than

Since 900 > 500, 12,925 > 12,598 and 12,598 < 12,925.

Solution: The depth in the Pacific Ocean is greater.

Order 150,031 and 83,901 and 83,445 from greatest to least.

You can use place value to order numbers.

Step 1 Line up the digits in the numbers. Begin at the greatest place value. Find the first place where the digits are different.	**Step 2** Compare the other numbers. Find the first place where the digits are different. Write > or <.
1 5 0, 0 3 1 8 3, 9 0 1 8 3, 4 4 5 ↑ 150,031 is the greatest number. It is the only number with hundred thousands.	1 5 0, 0 3 1 **8 3, 9** 0 1 **8 3, 4** 4 5 ↑ 9 hundreds > 4 hundreds so 83,901 > 83,445

Solution: The numbers in order from greatest to least are 150,031 > 83,901 > 83,445.

Standards NS 1.0, 1.2   MR **1.1, 2.3, 2.4**

Explain Your Thinking

▶ When you compared 83,901 and 83,445, did you need to compare the digits in the tens place? in the ones place? Why or why not?

▶ When you compare and order numbers, explain why you line up the digits in the numbers by place value.

Guided Practice

Compare. Write >, <, or = for each ⬤.

1. 1,001 ⬤ 999

2. 19,009 ⬤ 19,009

3. 102,309 ⬤ 102,409

4. 303,113 ⬤ 330,113

Write the numbers in order from least to greatest.

5. 1,209 12,909 9,999

6. 69,541 689,541 68,541

7. 999 1,009 199 19,009

8. 441,876 421,876 42,876

Ask Yourself

• Which digits do I compare first?

• What do I do when digits in the same place have the same value?

• Which number is the least? the greatest?

Independent Practice

Compare. Write >, <, or = for each ⬤.

9. 909 ⬤ 990

10. 1,207 ⬤ 1,207

11. 1,009 ⬤ 999

12. 4,901 ⬤ 14,901

13. 75,704 ⬤ 75,074

14. 2,347 ⬤ 2,487

15. 92,876 ⬤ 101,001

16. 54,932 ⬤ 54,932

17. 89,621 ⬤ 73,991

18. 135,734 ⬤ 55,724

19. 879,566 ⬤ 869,566

20. 101,902 ⬤ 671,110

Write the numbers in order from greatest to least.

21. 101 99 80

22. 98 999 908

23. 404 440 400

24. 1,021 1,008 1,111

25. 10,912 9,980 11,001

26. 890 12,908 1,299

Write the numbers in order from least to greatest.

27. 234 879 87

28. 110 237 908

29. 5,773 5,785 5,783

30. 3,199 2,233 887

31. 190,909 180,909 170,909

32. 102,000 12,000 100,200

Problem Solving • Reasoning

Use Data Use the table for Problems 33–35.

33. Which is deeper, the Atlantic Ocean or the Indian Ocean?

34. Which ocean is between 11,000 and 12,000 feet deep?

35. Analyze Lake Baykal in Asia is the deepest lake in the world. It is 5,315 ft deep. Which is deeper, Lake Baykal or the Arctic Ocean? Did you need to compare the digits in the hundreds place? Explain.

36. Measurement Sarah and Tina are using blue felt to make ocean pictures. Tina's piece of felt is 2 inches longer than Sarah's piece. Sarah's piece is 34 inches long. How long is Tina's piece of felt?

Average Ocean Depths	
Ocean	Feet
Atlantic Ocean	11,730
Arctic Ocean	3,407
Pacific Ocean	12,925
Indian Ocean	12,598

Mixed Review • Test Prep

Multiply or divide. *(pages xxiv–xxv)*

37. $35 \div 5$ **38.** $32 \div 4$ **39.** 2×6 **40.** $49 \div 7$ **41.** 4×9 **42.** 3×4

43 Which expression equals five? *(pages xxii–xxiii)*

A $6 - 2$ **B** $2 + 3$ **C** $4 - 1$ **D** 4×3

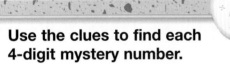
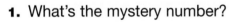

Logical Thinking

Use the clues to find each 4-digit mystery number.

1. What's the mystery number?
- Its tens digit is 2.
- Its thousands digit is 4.
- Its hundreds digit is the sum of its ones digit and its tens digit.
- Its ones digit is two times its tens digit.

2. What's the mystery number?
- Its thousands digit is three times its ones digit.
- Its hundreds digit is two times its ones digit.
- Its tens digit is four less than its hundreds digit.
- Its ones digit is 2.

3. Which of the mystery numbers is greater?

Number Sense

How Big Is Big?

100,000 is big if you are waiting that many minutes for a ferry.

100,000 is small if you are filling a bucket with that many grains of sand.

Try These

Choose the best number for each situation.

1. The time it takes to watch a TV show.

100,000 minutes   10,000 minutes   100 minutes

2. The number of people that live in a town.

10,000 people   100 people   10 people

3. The time it takes to brush your teeth.

1,000 minutes   100 minutes   1 minute

4. The number of school days in two weeks.

100 days   10 days   1 day

5. The height of a 10-story building.

10,000 feet   100 feet   1 foot

6. The number of people you could fit in an elevator.

1,000 people   100 people   10 people

Rounding Numbers

You will learn how to round numbers.

New
Vocabulary
estimate
round

Learn About It

This giraffe weighs 2,868 pounds!
Stephen wants to **estimate** this weight by
rounding to the nearest 100 pounds.
You can **round** a number to estimate.

**2,868
POUNDS**

Different Ways to Round

You can use a number line.

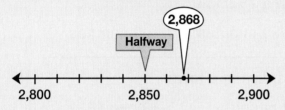

2,800   2,850   2,900

2,868 is closer to 2,900.
So, round 2,868 to 2,900.

You can follow these steps.

Step 1 Circle the digit in the place you
want to round to.

2,8̂68

hundreds
place

Step 2 Underline the digit to the right of
the circled digit.

2,8̂6̲8

digit to
the right

Step 3 • If the underlined digit is 5 or greater,
increase the circled digit.

• If the underlined digit is less than 5, do not
change the circled digit.

• Then change all digits to the right of the
circled digit to zeros.

2,8̂6̲8

6 > 5
Change 8 to 9.
Write zeros to
the right.

2,868   rounds to   2,900

Solution: Rounded to the nearest 100 pounds, the giraffe weighs 2,900 pounds.

Explain Your Thinking

▶ Can a 3-digit number round to 1,000?
Use an example to explain why or why not.

Standards NS **1.0, 1.3**   MR **2.3, 2.4**

Guided Practice

Round each number to the place of the underlined digit.

1. <u>7</u>53,812   **2.** 7<u>5</u>3,812   **3.** 75<u>3</u>,812

Ask Yourself

• What is the digit to the right of the rounding place?

• Is this digit 5 or greater, or is it less than 5?

Independent Practice

Use the number line to round each number to the nearest ten.

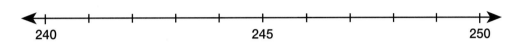

```
240          245          250
```

4. 241   **5.** 247   **6.** 243   **7.** 245   **8.** 242   **9.** 249

Round each number to the place of the underlined digit.

10. <u>6</u>6   **11.** <u>1</u>42   **12.** 4<u>1</u>7   **13.** 7,<u>8</u>93   **14.** 2,<u>3</u>66   **15.** 5,9<u>9</u>8

16. 9,8<u>8</u>1   **17.** 6,0<u>5</u>4   **18.** 33,<u>5</u>01   **19.** 12,4<u>0</u>3   **20.** 114,<u>7</u>72   **21.** 196,<u>9</u>72

Problem Solving • Reasoning

22. Estimate A baby giraffe weighed 113 pounds when it was born. To the nearest ten pounds, how much did it weigh?

23. Analyze Each day a giraffe's heart pumps about 23,000 gallons of blood. What is the greatest whole number that rounds to 23,000? the least?

24. Suppose a giraffe ate 8 pounds of leaves each hour for 6 hours. Did the giraffe eat more or less than 40 pounds of leaves in that time? Explain how you got your answer.

Math Is Everywhere!

SOCIAL STUDIES The area of Serengeti National Park in Tanzania, Africa, is 5,702 square miles. It's one of the largest wildlife preserves in the world!

Is the size of the Serengeti closer to 5,000 or 6,000 square miles? Explain.

Mixed Review • Test Prep

Add or subtract. *(pages xxii–xxiii)*

25. $7 + 8$ **26.** $18 - 9$ **27.** $15 - 6$

28 Which is most likely the height of a building?

    A 50 inches   **C** 50 miles

    B 50 feet   **D** 50 pounds

Extra Practice See Set C on page 41.

11

Problem-Solving Skill: Estimated or Exact Amounts

You will learn how to decide if a number is being used to show an estimate or an exact amount.

When you read numbers in a newspaper or magazine, you need to decide if the numbers are being used to show an estimate or an exact amount.

Read the newspaper article below.

Around the World

Brian Jones and Bertrand Piccard just flew around the world in a hot-air balloon! It took them 19 days to travel 29,054 miles. Their balloon reached heights of almost 40,000 feet. At times, they traveled faster than 100 miles an hour. They flew over 23 different countries. Before this flight, the longest distance ever flown in a balloon was about 14,000 miles.

Sometimes numbers are used to show estimates.

Words such as *about* or *almost* tell you that a number is being used to show an estimate.

Do you know the exact height the balloon reached?

• No, the article says the balloon reached heights of *almost* 40,000 feet.

• The word *almost* lets you know that 40,000 feet is an estimate.

Sometimes numbers are used to show exact amounts.

A number is being used to show an exact amount if it is clear that the amount has been counted.

Do you know exactly how many countries the two men flew over?

• Yes, the article says that they flew over 23 different countries.

• The number of countries was counted. So 23 is being used to show an exact amount.

Look Back Why does thinking about how a number is used help you decide whether it shows an estimate or an exact amount?

 **Standards** MR **1.0, 2.0**

Bertrand Piccard from Switzerland and Brian Jones from Great Britain spent 19 days in a hot-air balloon as they traveled around the world.

Guided Practice

Use the newspaper article on page 12 to help solve each problem. Give a reason for your answer.

1. What was the longest distance ever flown in a balloon before Jones and Piccard's flight? Is this an exact amount or an estimate?

   Think: Is there a clue that tells whether the number was rounded?

2. A Web site has 14 pictures of Jones and Piccard's balloon that were taken during the flight. Is this an exact amount or an estimate?

   Think: Is this an amount that was counted?

Choose a Strategy

Solve.

Problem-Solving Strategies

- Use Logical Thinking
- Write an Equation
- Find a Pattern
- Draw a Picture

3. In Carrie's first 4 balloon flights, she flew 8 miles, 11 miles, 14 miles, and 17 miles. If she continues this pattern, how far is she likely to fly on her 10th flight?

4. A deflated hot-air balloon weighs about 500 pounds. About how much would 3 deflated hot-air balloons weigh? Is your answer an exact amount or an estimate? Explain.

5. Three people will share the cost of a balloon ride. Each will pay the same amount. The cost of the ride is $600. Can they determine the exact amount each should pay? Why or why not? How much will each pay?

6. Gary, Ruel, Micala, and Beth are standing in line waiting for a balloon ride. Ruel is not first. Gary is behind Micala. Gary is not last. Beth is first. In what order are they standing in line?

7. Look at the numbers in the ad at the right. Which numbers are being used to show estimates? exact amounts? Explain how you know.

FOR SALE: More than 100 hot-air balloons available. Each balloon is 55 ft. wide. Over 20 designs to choose from. Only $8,750 each!

Extra Practice See Set 1–4 on page 43.

Quick ✔ Check

Check Your Understanding of Lessons 1–4

Write each number in expanded form. Then write the value of the underlined digit.

1. 5<u>2</u>,489
2. 2<u>7</u>5,672
3. <u>5</u>47,463

Write the numbers in order from least to greatest.

4. 53,862   3,674   5,674
5. 187,412   378,527   278,527

Round each number to the place of the underlined digit.

6. 2,5<u>7</u>8
7. 4<u>2</u>,327
8. <u>5</u>61,691

Solve.

9. A modern jet airliner can travel at speeds of about 600 miles an hour. Is this an estimated amount or an exact amount? How do you know?

10. One version of a 747 jumbo jet can carry 374 passengers. Is this an estimated amount or an exact amount? How do you know?

How did you do?

If you had difficulty with any items in the Quick Check, you can use the following pages for review and extra practice.

California Standards	ITEMS	REVIEW THESE PAGES	DO THESE EXTRA PRACTICE ITEMS
Number Sense: **1.1, 4.1**	1–3	pages 4–5	Set A, page 40
Number Sense: **1.1, 1.2**	4–5	pages 6–8	Set B, page 40
Number Sense: **1.1, 1.3**	6–8	pages 10–11	Set C, page 41
Number Sense: **1.4** Math Reasoning: **1.4, 2.4, 3.1**	9–10	pages 12–13	1–4, page 43

Test Prep • Cumulative Review

Maintaining the Standards

Choose the letter of the correct answer.

1 How is three hundred sixty thousand, four hundred written in standard form?

A 3,604

B 36,400

C 364

D 360,400

Use the table to answer Questions 2–3.

California Cities	
City	**Population**
Fresno	354,091
Laguna Beach	23,170
Oakland	372,242
Riverside	226,546

2 Which city has the greatest population?

F Fresno

G Oakland

H Laguna Beach

J Riverside

3 If the population of Fresno is rounded to the nearest ten thousand, what is the rounded number?

A 300,000

B 350,000

C 354,000

D 400,000

4 Which fact would most likely be an estimate?

F the population of your state

G the number of students in your class

H a checkbook balance

J your teacher's paycheck

5 Which lists the numbers in order from least to greatest?

A 762   7,420   7,416

B 7,420   7,416   762

C 7,416   7,420   762

D 762   7,416   7,420

6 Which fact would most likely be exact?

F the number of players on a team

G the distance to the moon

H the population of the world

J the distance to the sun

7 The newspaper has a circulation of 100,000. What words mean 100,000?

A one hundred

B ten thousand

C one thousand

D one hundred thousand

8 The population of Bassville is 389,946. What is 389,946 rounded to the nearest thousand?

Explain How did you find your answer?

Internet Test Prep
Visit **www.eduplace.com/kids/mhm**
for more *Test Prep Practice.*

15

How Big Is 1 Million?

You will learn how big 1 million is.

Learn About It

Use a newspaper to find out how big 1 million is.

Look at a page of a newspaper. If you read a newspaper from cover to cover, do you think you would read 1 million words? How large is 1 million?

Divide your class into 10 teams to find out.

Materials

For each group:
10 pages of a
newspaper

Step 1 Count and circle 100 words in an article. Write "100 Words" on the circle. Continue to circle groups of 100 words until you have 1,000 words circled.

• How many groups of 100 words did you circle?

Whole Class		
Number of Teams	**Pages Altogether**	**Words Altogether**
1	10	10,000
2		
3		
10		

Step 2 Use estimation to circle 1,000 words on each of the nine remaining pages.

• About how many words did you circle altogether? Make a table like the one above. Fill in the first row.

Step 3 Put your 10 pages together with the 10 pages from another team. Fill in the second row of your chart.

• About how many words did the two teams circle altogether?
Now combine all of the newspaper pages with the other 8 teams in your class. Complete your table.

Standards NS 1.0, 1.1   MR 1.0, 1.2

Step 4 Suppose your class combined pages with 9 other classes. Use a table like the one below to answer the following questions.

- How many pages would there be altogether?

- How many words would there be altogether?

Ten Classes		
Number of Classes	Pages Altogether	Words Altogether
1	100	100,000
2	200	200,000
3		
10		

Try It Out

Use your tables to answer each question.

1. How many thousands are there in 10,000?

2. How many thousands are there in 100,000?

3. How many thousands are there in 1,000,000?

4. How many hundreds are there in 1,000,000?

5. Describe the patterns you see in your charts.

Write about it! Talk about it!

Use what you have learned to write about these questions.

6. **Estimate** It takes about 1,000,000 one-inch cubes to fill a minibus. How many minibuses could be filled using 1,000,000 two-inch cubes? Explain.

7. Would you use millions to count the following things? Explain your reasoning for each.

    a. the people in a state

    b. the students in your school

    c. the grains of sand on a beach

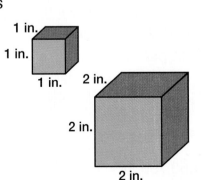

Place Value Through Hundred Millions

You will learn how to read and write numbers through 999,999,999.

Learn About It

Earth's path around the Sun is called its orbit. The length of Earth's orbit is about 603,765,000 miles!

A place-value chart can help explain what this number means.

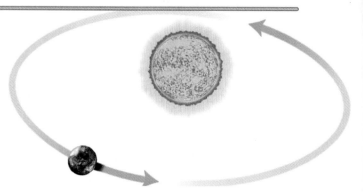

MILLIONS			THOUSANDS			ONES		
hundred millions	ten millions	millions	hundred thousands	ten thousands	thousands	hundreds	tens	ones
6	0	3	7	6	5	0	0	0

The value of the 6 is 600,000,000.

The value of the 3 is 3,000,000.

There are different ways to write 603,765,000.

Remember: Write a comma between periods.

Different Ways to Write a Number

You can use standard form.	603,765,000
You can use expanded form.	600,000,000 + 3,000,000 + 700,000 + 60,000 + 5,000
You can use short word form.	603 million, 765 thousand
You can use word form.	six hundred three million, seven hundred sixty-five thousand

Explain Your Thinking

▶ What pattern do you see in place-value names?

Guided Practice

For Exercises 1–3, write each number three other ways.

1. 560,790,341   2. 506,709,341   3. 500,000 + 200

4. Write 2<u>3</u>0,207,090 in expanded form. Then write the value of the underlined digit.

Ask Yourself

• What is the value of each digit?

• Do I need a comma?

Independent Practice

Write each number in three other ways.

5. 6,007,002   **6.** 6,070,020   **7.** 60,070,200   **8.** 606,707,202

9. 900,000 + 1,000 + 800 + 50 + 3   **10.** 80,000 + 400 + 80 + 9

11. 16 million, 201 thousand, 856   **12.** twenty-five thousand, three hundred sixty

13. 8 hundred millions, 7 ten millions, 4 millions, 9 hundred thousands, 4 tens, 9 ones

14. sixty-three million, seven hundred twenty-five thousand, nine hundred forty-three

Write the place of the 7 in each number. Then write its value.

15. 708,993,040   **16.** 37,990,841   **17.** 16,007,845   **18.** 122,799

19. 20,895,227   **20.** 78,901   **21.** 107,912   **22.** 19,870,001

Problem Solving • Reasoning

Use Data Use the table for Problems 23–25.

23. How far is Earth from the Sun? Write this number in two other ways.

24. How far is Mercury from the Sun? In this number, does the digit 5 or the digit 7 have a greater value? Explain.

25. **Estimate** Mars is about 100,000,000 miles farther from the Sun than Mercury is. About how far is Mars from the Sun?

26. **Write Your Own** Write a 9-digit number that has a 3 in the ten millions place, a 5 in the hundred thousands place, and a 2 in the ones place.

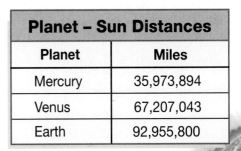

Planet – Sun Distances	
Planet	Miles
Mercury	35,973,894
Venus	67,207,043
Earth	92,955,800

Mixed Review • Test Prep

Find the number that is likely to come next in each pattern.

27. 0   5   10   15 ____   **28.** 94   90   86   82 ____   **29.** 987   876   765   654 ____

30 Which expression should go in the ■ to make the number sentence true? 8 + 5 = ■ *(page xxii)*

     A 8 + 13   **B** 5 × 8   **C** 13 + 8   **D** 5 + 8

Extra Practice See Set D on page 41.

Compare and Order Greater Numbers

You will learn how to compare and order numbers through millions.

Learn About It

Which do you think has more people, a city or a state? In a recent year, 1,201,134 people were living in New Hampshire and 1,220,665 people were living in San Diego, California. Which had more people?

New Hampshire

San Diego

You can use place value to compare numbers.

Step 1 Line up the digits in the numbers. Begin at the greatest place value. Find the place where the digits are different.

New Hampshire: **1,2 0** 1, 1 3 4
San Diego: **1,2 2** 0, 6 6 5
↑ ↑
same different

Step 2 Compare the digits that are different. Write > or <.

1,2 0 1, 1 3 4
1,2 2 0, 6 6 5
↑
2 ten thousands > 0 ten thousands

So 1,220,665 > 1,201,134 and 1,201,134 < 1,220,665.

Solution: That year more people lived in San Diego than in New Hampshire!

You can use place value to order greater numbers.

Order 4,688,239 and 6,715,039 and 4,593,712 from greatest to least.

Step 1 Line up the digits. Begin comparing at the greatest place value.

4, 6 8 8, 2 3 9
6, 7 1 5, 0 3 9
4, 5 9 3, 7 1 2
↑
6 million > 4 million

So 6,715,039 is the greatest number.

Step 2 Continue comparing. Then order the numbers.

4, 6 8 8, 2 3 9
6, 7 1 5, 0 3 9
4, 5 9 3, 7 1 2
same ─── ↑ ↑
6 > 5

So 4,688,239 > 4,593,712

Solution: 6,715,039 > 4,688,239 > 4,593,712

Standards NS 1.0, 1.1, 1.2   MR 1.1, 2.0

Explain Your Thinking

▶ How does looking at the number of digits in each number help you order the numbers? Explain.

Guided Practice

Compare. Write >, <, or = for each ●.

Ask Yourself

• How do I line up the digits?

• Which digits do I compare first?

• What do I do when digits in the same place have the same value?

1. 7,968,305 ● 7,968,305

2. 2,300,062 ● 2,030,062

3. 38,472,152 ● 384,721,520

Write the numbers in order from least to greatest.

4. 123,908   111,908   133,998

5. 9,999,999   101,200,011   874,987

6. 134,908,784   13,493,093   101,999,908

7. 1,202,334   1,220,334   12,233,000

Independent Practice

Compare. Write >, <, or = in the ●.

8. 45,679,043 ● 9,987,483

9. 2,301,934 ● 2,301,934

10. 99,902,234 ● 112,311,011

11. 98,760,032 ● 98,790,032

12. 404,004,004 ● 444,440,004

13. 190,098,181 ● 99,090,870

Write the numbers in order from greatest to least.

14. 85,407,363   8,407,363   85,073,630

15. 225,522,145   25,522,145   252,522,145

16. 112,110   190,911   222,345

17. 993,457,601   994,574,601   993,574,601

n **Algebra • Patterns** Find the number that is likely to be the next number in each pattern.

18. 444,010   444,020   444,030   _____

19. 32,000   32,200   32,400   _____

20. 1,234   2,345   3,456   _____

Problem Solving • Reasoning

Use Data Solve. Choose a method. Use the table for Problems 21–26.

Computation Methods

• Estimation   • Paper and Pencil   • Mental Math

21. Does New York or Los Angeles have the greater population?

22. Does Jacksonville or San Jose have the smaller population?

23. **Compare** Use only the number of digits in the populations. Which city has fewer people, San Jose or Phoenix? Explain how you know.

24. About 1,000,000 more people live in Houston than in Jacksonville. About how many people live in Houston?

City Populations	
City	Population
New York, NY	7,420,166
Los Angeles, CA	3,597,556
San Jose, CA	861,284
Phoenix, AZ	1,198,064
Jacksonville, FL	693,630

25. **Analyze** One of the numbers in the table is between 1,000,000 and 4,000,000 and has a 6 in the tens place. Which is it?

26. **Write Your Own** Use the table to write a problem about comparing and ordering numbers.

Mixed Review • Test Prep

Add or subtract. *(pages xxii–xxiii)*

27. $6 + 9$ **28.** $7 - 2$ **29.** $9 + 4$ **30.** $13 - 5$

31. $15 - 7$ **32.** $12 - 8$ **33.** $7 + 8$ **34.** $7 + 5$

35 The arrows around this box show that it is being turned upside down. Which shows the box after it is turned upside down?

  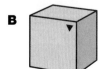

Extra Practice See Set E on page 41.

Number Names

Complete each sentence by writing the correct number of ones or tens.

1. 35 = 2 tens and _____ ones

2. 215 = _____ tens and 5 ones

3. 200 = _____ tens

4. 75 = 5 tens and _____ ones

5. 150 = 1 hundred and _____ ones

6. 290 = 28 tens and _____ ones

Comparing and Ordering

For each exercise, use the given digits to make as many 3-digit numbers as you can. Then put the numbers you made in order from least to greatest.

1. 3 4 1

2. 6 9 5

3. 5 7 6

4. 0 2 9

5. 9 4 1

6. 0 4 8

Number Match

Use each number once to complete the sentences below so they make sense.

2	20	200
2,000		20,000

1. Yesterday I practiced piano for _____ minutes.

2. More than _____ people came to the stadium for the baseball game.

3. Our new computer cost about _____ dollars.

4. I have _____ sisters.

5. I'm reading a book that has almost _____ pages.

Rounding Greater Numbers

You will learn to round greater numbers.

Learn About It

Ty plays soccer. He found out that 12,369,321 children under the age of 18 played soccer this year. Ty wants to round this number to the nearest million.

What is 12,369,321 rounded to the nearest million?

Round 12,369,321 to the nearest million.

Step 1 Find the place you want to round to.	**Step 2** Look at the digit to its right.	**Step 3** Round.
1 2, 3 6 9, 3 2 1 ↑ millions place	1 2, 3 6 9, 3 2 1 ↑ digit to the right	1 2, 3 6 9, 3 2 1 ↑ 3 < 5 Don't change 2. Write zeros to the right.

12,369,321 **rounds to** 12,000,000

Solution: Rounded to the nearest million, 12,369,321 is 12,000,000.

Another Example

Round to the Nearest Hundred Thousand

9,9**6**2,940
↑
hundred thousands place

6 > 5.
Change 9 to 10.
Write zeros.

9,962,940 **rounds to** 10,000,000

Explain Your Thinking

▶ How could you change one digit in 7,856,041 so that it rounds to 7,800,000?

▶ Can a 6-digit number round to the nearest million? Why or why not?

Guided Practice

Round each number to the nearest million.

1. 5,472,361
2. 38,510,219
3. 72,604,299
4. 8,299,675
5. 102,334,989
6. 99,980,221

Ask Yourself

• What digit is in the rounding place?

• What is the digit to its right?

• Do I change the digit in the rounding place?

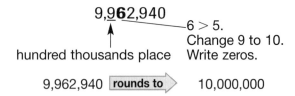 **Standards** NS **1.0, 1.3**   AF **1.0**   MR **2.4**

Independent Practice

Round each number to the place of the underlined digit.

7. 2<u>9</u>,300   **8.** 5<u>0</u>5,113   **9.** 47<u>3</u>,264   **10.** 3<u>0</u>3,449

11. 9,<u>5</u>77,211   **12.** <u>2</u>,554,319   **13.** <u>1</u>,020,890   **14.** 7,<u>4</u>25,333

15. 19<u>3</u>,704,119   **16.** 209,<u>1</u>21,456   **17.** 7<u>8</u>,901,223   **18.** <u>5</u>7,304,600

**Mental Math Which place was each number rounded to?
Write *ten thousands*, *hundred thousands*, or *millions*.**

19. 36,768,401 → 37,000,000   **20.** 879,463 → 1,000,000

21. 403,2 85 → 400,000   **22.** 52,023,864 → 52,000,000

23. 9,345,099 → 9,000,000   **24.** 135,877,980 → 136,000,000

Problem Solving • Reasoning

25. Estimate Suppose a store sells 398,111 balls each year. To the nearest hundred thousand, how many balls is this?

26. It is estimated that about 18,000,000 people play tennis a year. To which place was this number probably rounded? Explain.

27. Write About It Ninety-nine thousand, six hundred three footballs are made each day at a football factory. Round 99,603 to the nearest ten thousand. Then round it to the nearest thousand. What do you notice about your answers? Explain.

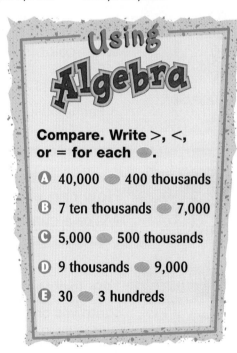

Using Algebra

Compare. Write >, <, or = for each ●.

Ⓐ 40,000 ● 400 thousands

Ⓑ 7 ten thousands ● 7,000

Ⓒ 5,000 ● 500 thousands

Ⓓ 9 thousands ● 9,000

Ⓔ 30 ● 3 hundreds

Mixed Review • Test Prep

Compare. Write >, <, or = for each ●.

28. 4 + 4 ● 0 + 8   **29.** 9 × 10 ● 9 × 7

30. 8 hundreds ● 12 tens   **31.** 8 × 7 ● 9 × 6

32 Which sign would go in the ● to make this number sentence true? *(page xxv)*

$$24 \; ● \; 8 = 3$$

A +   **C** ×

B −   **D** ÷

Extra Practice See Set F on page 42.   **25**

Problem-Solving Strategy: Use Logical Thinking

You will learn how to solve a problem by using logical thinking.

Sometimes you can use logical thinking to solve a problem.

Problem Al, Ron, Jo, and Di live in different houses. Each house is a different color. Di's house is white. Al's house is not blue. Ron's house is not green. Jo's house is not yellow or blue. What color is each person's house?

Understand

What is the question?
What color is each person's house?

What facts do you know?
- Each house is a different color.
- Di's house is white.
- Al's house is not blue.
- Ron's house is not green.
- Jo's house is not yellow or blue.

Plan

How can you solve the problem?
Make a chart and use logical thinking to complete it.

Solve

Use logical thinking to complete a chart.
Write *yes* or *no* for the facts you know. When you write *yes* in a row or column, you can write *no* in the rest of the row or column.

- Di's house is white, so it is not blue, green, or yellow.
- Jo's house is green, because it is not white, blue, or yellow.
- Al's house is yellow, because it is not white, blue, or green.
- Ron's house is the remaining color, blue.

	White	Blue	Yellow	Green
Di	yes	no	no	no
Jo	no	no	no	yes
Al	no	no	yes	no
Ron	no	yes	no	no

Look Back

Look back at the problem.
Do the answers match the facts in the problem?

Standards MR **1.0, 1.1, 2.0, 2.3, 3.0, 3.2**

Guided Practice

Solve.

① Rita, Gail, Rae, and Barb each has a different-colored bike. The bikes are red, blue, green, and black. No one has a bike in a color that begins with the first letter of her name. Barb's is not red. Rita's is not blue. What color is each person's bike?

Think: What are the heads of each column and row in my table?

② Four people get off an elevator at different floors. Going up, it stops at the 3rd, 4th, 6th, and 10th floors. Mia says goodbye to Earl as she gets off. Su is the last person to get off. Ray gets off one floor after Mia. At which floor does each person get off?

Think: Which two floors are only one floor apart?

Choose a Strategy

Solve. Use these or other strategies.

Problem-Solving Strategies

- Find a Pattern
- Use Logical Thinking
- Draw a Picture
- Make a Table

③ Joni calls two friends to meet her at the city park. Each of those friends calls two other friends to join them, and each of those friends calls two other friends. If Joni and all her friends come to the park, how many people will be there?

④ Four cars are parked on a street. They are blue, green, silver, and white. The white car is between the blue and the green cars. The blue car is next to the silver car but not next to the white car. What is the order of the four cars?

⑤ Sandy, Pedro, Gina, and Yoshio have different colored swim goggles. Their goggles are purple, orange, green, and pink. No one has goggles in a color beginning with the same letter as his or her name. Sandy and Gina's are not orange or pink. What color is each person's goggles?

⑥ Ian, Choi, and Ann are playing a ring-toss game. Everyone has thrown three rings except Ann. She has scored 60 and 70 points. Ian has scored 50, 40, and 80 points. Choi has scored 60, 30, and 50 points. How many points does Ann need to tie for first place?

Extra Practice See 5–8 on page 43.

Quick ✓ Check

Check Your Understanding of Lessons 5–9

Write the place of the 4 in each number. Then write its value.

1. 104,371   **2.** 403,879,673   **3.** 14,659,702

Use >, <, or = to compare each pair of numbers.

4. 76,570,046 ⬤ 76,590,040   **5.** 530,078,960 ⬤ 503,078,960

Round each number to the place of the underlined digit.

6. 274,605,119   **7.** 503,978   **8.** 55,192,370

Solve.

9. Mark, Emma, Bob, and Carol each have different-colored bicycles. The colors of their bicycles are red, blue, yellow, and green. Mark does not have a blue or yellow bicycle. Emma's bike is not red or blue. Bob does not have a yellow or red bike. Carol's bicycle is green. What color is each person's bicycle?

10. Four friends ride the bus home together. The bus stops at Oak, Elm, Hickory, and Pine streets in that order. When Dan gets off, he says goodbye to Meg. Nari is the last person to get off. Ben gets off one stop before Dan. Which friends get off the bus at which stop? Explain how you got your answer.

How did you do?

If you had difficulty with any items in the Quick Check, you can use the following pages for review and extra practice.

California Standards	ITEMS	REVIEW THESE PAGES	DO THESE EXTRA PRACTICE ITEMS
Number Sense: **1.1, 1.4**	1–3	pages 16–19	Set D, page 41
Number Sense: **1.1, 1.2**	4–5	pages 20–22	Set E, page 41
Number Sense: **1.1, 1.3**	6–8	pages 24–25	Set F, page 42
Math Reasoning: **1.1, 1.2, 2.3, 3.1, 3.2**	9–10	pages 26–27	5–8, page 43

Test Prep • Cumulative Review
Maintaining the Standards

Choose the letter of the correct answer.

1 Which statement is true?

  A 6,851 > 6,861

  B 499 < 4,500

  C 420,016 < 1,216

  D 17,548 <1,754

2 How is sixteen million, five hundred two written in standard form?

  F 16,502

  G 160,502

  H 1,652

  J 16,000,502

3 A computer company donated $1,520,625 to a national charity. What is $1,520,625 rounded to the nearest hundred thousand?

  A $1,000,000

  B $1,500,000

  C $1,521,000

  D $2,000,000

4 Which fact would most likely be an estimate?

  F the number of miles from Earth to the moon

  G the number of teachers in your school

  H the number of people in your family

  J the number of days in a week

5 Termites can lay up to 30,000 eggs in a day. What words mean 30,000?

  A thirty hundred

  B thirty thousand

  C thirty

  D thirty million

Use the table to answer Questions 6–7.

Doll Making Factories	
Factories	**Number of Dolls Made**
Factory A	10,522,305
Factory B	10,498,612
Factory C	9,875,402
Factory D	10,502,345

6 Which factory made the most dolls?

  F Factory A   **H** Factory C

  G Factory B   **J** Factory D

7 If the number of dolls made by Factory C is rounded to the nearest thousand, what is the rounded number?

  A 9,000,000   **C** 9,876,000

  B 9,875,000   **D** 9,880,000

8 Write a problem where an exact answer is necessary, and a problem where an estimate is appropriate.

Explain Tell how to solve each problem.

Safe Site

Compare Money Amounts

You will learn how to count and compare amounts of money.

Learn About It

Eliza wants to buy this model horse. She has 1 twenty-dollar bill, 1 ten-dollar bill, 2 five-dollar bills, and 2 one-dollar bills. She also has 1 quarter, 2 dimes, 1 nickel, and 1 penny. Does she have enough money?

To find out, first count the money she has.

$40.00

Find the total value of the bills by counting on. Start with the bill with the greatest value.

$20.00	➡	$30.00	➡	$35.00	➡	$40.00	➡	$41.00	➡	$42.00

Find the total value of the coins by counting on. Start with the coin with the greatest value.

25¢	➡	35¢	➡	45¢	➡	50¢	➡	51¢

Write the total amount as $42.51.

Then compare $42.51 to $40.00.

Solution: Yes, she has enough money, since $40.00 is less than $42.51.

Another Example

Other Bills and Coins

$100.00	➡	$105.00	➡	$105.50	➡	$105.65

Total: $105.65

Standards NS **1.2**   MR **2.4**

Explain Your Thinking

▶ Why is it usually easier to count the bills or coins with the greatest value first?

Ask Yourself

- In what order will I count the bills?
- In what order will I count the coins?

Guided Practice

Write each amount.

1.

2.

3.

4.

5.

6.

7. Look at Exercises 1–6. Write the greatest amount. Then write the least amount.

Independent Practice

Write each amount. Then write which is the greater.

8.    **or**

9.  **or**

10. 6 dimes, 2 quarters, 4 nickels **or** 7 nickels, 2 half-dollars

11. 1 hundred-dollar bill, 2 fifty-dollar bills **or**
    2 hundred-dollar bills, 1 ten-dollar bill

Problem Solving • Reasoning

Use the prices and items shown at the right for Problems 12–15.

12. Which item costs the most?

13. List the prices from greatest to least.

14. Eliza has a ten-dollar bill. She wants to buy 2 items. Which items can she buy? Explain.

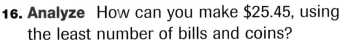

15. Write Your Own Use the items and prices at the right to make up a problem about money.

16. Analyze How can you make $25.45, using the least number of bills and coins?

17. Amiel has 4 pennies, 1-ten-dollar bill, 2 five-dollar bills, 5 nickels, 3 one-dollar bills, and 1 dime. In what order would you count the coins and bills?

Mixed Review • Test Prep

What time is shown on each clock?

18.

19.

20.

21.

22.

23.

Choose the letter of the correct answer. *(pages 10–11)*

24 Rounded to the nearest hundred, which number rounds to 700?

   A 988   **C** 760

   B 772   **D** 688

25 Rounded to the nearest thousand, which number rounds to 2,000?

   F 989   **H** 2,989

   G 1,989   **J** 3,989

Dollar Dunk

Practice using money by playing this game in a small group.
Try to be the first to get rid of all your cards!

What You'll Need

- *40 index cards or*
- *Teaching Tool 1*

Players
2 – 4

1¢   5¢   10¢

10 cards   10 cards   8 cards

25¢   50¢

8 cards   4 cards

Here's What to Do

1. Make a deck of cards like those shown.

2. Shuffle and deal 5 cards to each player. Stack the rest of the cards face down.

3. The object is to get rid of the cards by making $1.00 with some or all of the cards. One player asks another player for a card. If that player has the card, they give it to the first player. If not, the player "dunks" into the deck by taking the top card.

4. Whenever players can make $1.00, they place those cards face up in front of them.

5. Repeat Steps 3 and 4. The first player with no cards is the winner.

Share Your Thinking What are the best cards to have in your hand? Explain why.

Make Change

You will learn how to make change.

Learn About It

Kim and her dad are buying a bicycle helmet that costs $24.93. They give the clerk $30.00. What are the fewest coins and bills the clerk should give them in change?

One way to find their change is to count on from the cost of the helmet.

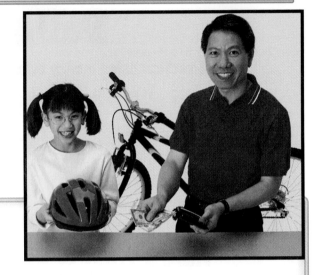

- Start with the cost of the helmet.

- Count coins and bills until you reach the amount they paid.

Cost of helmet				Amount they paid
$24.93 ⇨	$24.94 ⇨	$24.95 ⇨	$25.00	$30.00

$5.07 is the change.

- Finally, count the bills and coins used to make the change.

Solution: They should get $5.07 in change.

Explain Your Thinking

▶ Suppose 2 twenty-dollar bills are used to pay for the helmet. If change is given with the least number of bills and coins, what bills and coins are used? Explain.

Guided Practice

A $10.00 bill was used to buy each item below.
List the coins and bills you would use to make change.

1.  $ 6.75

2. $ 4.39

3.  $ 7.99

Ask Yourself
- What amount do I start with?

- What coins and bills do I need?

Standards | Extends Grade 4 Standards

Independent Practice

A $20 bill was used to buy each item below. List the coins and bills you would use to make change.

4.  $ 12.95

5.  $ 15.88

6.  $ 9.77

7. cost of item: $6.89

8. cost of item: $1.05

9. cost of item: $4.44

10. cost of item: $10.19

11. cost of item: $13.99

12. cost of item: $18.70

Write the names of the coins and bills you would use to make change for each of the following.

13. You bought an item worth $1.93. You paid with 2 one-dollar bills.

14. You bought an item worth $7.74. You paid with 2 five-dollar bills.

15. You bought an item worth $2.03. You paid with 3 one-dollar bills.

16. You bought an item worth 79¢. You paid with 2 half-dollars.

Problem Solving • Reasoning

17. A padlock costs $8.69. Dan gives the clerk $20. What coins and bills should he get in change?

18. **Analyze** Sean gives the clerk a ten-dollar bill and a dime to pay for a bicycling magazine that costs $5.05. What coins and bills should the clerk give Sean in change?

19. **Patterns** Biking post cards cost 50¢ each or 3 for $1. What is the least amount Tina can pay for 12 post cards? Use patterns to decide.

Mixed Review • Test Prep

Round each number to the nearest ten. (pages 10–11)

20. 78

21. 111

22. 179

23. 235

24. 874

25. 895

26 Which number has an 8 in the hundred thousands place? (pages 4–5)

   A 81,990

   c 8,990

   B 819,900

   D 899

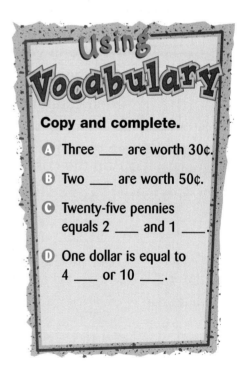

Using Vocabulary

Copy and complete.

A Three ____ are worth 30¢.

B Two ____ are worth 50¢.

C Twenty-five pennies equals 2 ____ and 1 ____.

D One dollar is equal to 4 ____ or 10 ____.

Extra Practice See Set H on page 42.

LESSON 12
Problem-Solving Application: Use Money

You will learn how to solve problems that involve money.

Sometimes you need to use money to solve word problems.

Problem Michelle just got a puppy. She has $15.00 to buy a collar and a water bowl. If she buys a large bowl and a cloth collar, how much change will she get?

PET SUPPLIES

Small bowl	$4.49
Large bowl	$6.99
Cloth collar	$5.49
Leather collar	$7.49
ID tag	$3.89
Dog shampoo	$4.49
Brush	$5.09
Comb	$3.29

Understand

What is the question?
How much change will Michelle get?

What do you know?
- Michelle has $15.00.
- The large bowl costs $6.99.
- The cloth collar costs $5.49.

Plan

What can you do to find the answer?
Add the cost of the large bowl and the cloth collar.

Then count on to find the change.

Solve

Add the cost of the items.

```
    $6.99  ←——large bowl
 +  $5.49  ←——cloth collar
   $12.48  ←——total cost
```

Then find the change from $15.00.

Cost of Items						

$12.48 ⇨ $12.49 ⇨ $12.50 ⇨ $12.75 ⇨ $13.00 ⇨ $14.00 ⇨ $15.00

$2.52 is the change.

Look Back

Look back at the problem.
Is the answer reasonable? Explain.

Standards MR **1.0, 1.1, 1.2, 2.0, 3.0, 3.2**

Guided Practice

Solve. Use the sign from page 36.

Solve. Use the sign from page 36.

① Michelle bought a brush for her new puppy. Her change was a penny, a nickel, a dime, and a quarter. How much money did she give the clerk?

Think: How should I start to count the total amount of money?

② Rosa buys one bottle of dog shampoo. She pays with two $1 bills, seven quarters, and eight dimes. How much change should she get?

Think: How can I find the amount she gave the clerk?

$3.89 $7.49 $6.99 $4.49 $5.09

Choose a Strategy

Use the sign from page 36 for Problems 3, 4, and 6.
Use these or other strategies.

Problem-Solving Strategies

• Use Logical Thinking   • Write an Equation   • Find a Pattern   • Act It Out

③ Nahim has coupons for $2.00 off the leather collar, $1.00 off a brush, and $1.00 off the cloth collar. Which collar costs less with a coupon?

④ Ryan wants to buy a brush, a comb and a bottle of dog shampoo. Will he be able to buy all of them if he has only a $10 bill? Explain your answer.

⑤ One bag of dog treats costs $5.35, 2 bags cost $10.00, 3 bags cost $15.35, 4 bags cost $20.00, 5 bags cost $25.35. What is the cost of 7 bags of dog treats likely to be?

⑥ Eilene buys an ID tag for her new kitten. She pays with a $5 bill. The clerk gives her the least number of bills and coins possible. What bills and coins will she get as change?

⑦ Daniel earns $2, $3, $2.50 and $3.50 for walking dogs after school. The dogs' names are Bo, Spot, Pup, and Red. Red's owners pay $1 more than Pup's owners do. Bo's owners pay the least. How much does each dog's owner pay?

⑧ Jane and Tom are both saving to buy a doghouse. Jane has $15 in the bank now. Every 3 months she puts $8 in her account. Tom has $20 in the bank now. Every 3 months he puts $9 in his account. Whose account will have more after one year? Explain.

Check Your Understanding of Lessons 10–12

Write each amount. Then write which is the greater amount.

1. 3 one-dollar bills, 2 dimes, 3 pennies   **or**   1 five-dollar bill, 2 nickels

2. 5 dimes, 2 nickels, 2 one-dollar bills   **or**   2 quarters, 1 dime, 1 nickel

Write the names of the coins and bills you would use to make change for each of the following.

3. You bought items worth $2.84. You paid with 3 one-dollar bills.

4. You bought an item worth $6.74. You paid with 1 ten-dollar bill.

5. You bought an item worth 89¢. You paid with 4 quarters.

6. You bought items worth $13.98. You paid with 2 ten-dollar bills.

Solve.

7. Kelly bought 1 bag of potting soil and 1 bag of mulch. She paid with one $5-bill, three $1-bills, and 2 quarters. How much change should she get?

8. Lee had some money. Then he earned $10 more cutting grass. He used some of the money to buy a hoe and a trowel. He had $5.25 left. How much money did he start with?

Garden Supplies	
hoe	$7.99
rake	$8.79
trowel	$3.79
mulch	$2.68
potting soil	$5.49

How did you do?

If you had difficulty with any items in the Quick Check, you can use the following pages for review and extra practice.

California Standards	ITEMS	REVIEW THESE PAGES	DO THESE EXTRA PRACTICE ITEMS
Number Sense: **1.2**	1–2	pages 30–32	Set G, page 42
Math Reasoning: **1.1, 2.2, 2.6**	3–6	pages 34–35	Set H, page 42
Math Reasoning: **1.1, 1.2, 2.2, 2.4, 2.6, 3.1**	7–8	pages 36–37	9–11, page 43

Test Prep • Cumulative Review
Maintaining the Standards

Choose the letter of the correct answer.

1 How is fifty million, three thousand written in standard form?

 A 50,003 C 50,300

 B 50,003,000 D 503,000

2 Which shows the prices of these items in order from least to greatest?

 F $3.98 $3.76 $3.70 $5.00

 G $3.76 $3.70 $3.98 $5.00

 H $5.00 $3.98 $3.76 $3.70

 J $3.70 $3.76 $3.98 $5.00

3 What is 2,159 rounded to the nearest hundred?

 A 2,000 C 2,200

 B 2,100 D 2,259

4 Which fact would most likely be an estimate?

 F the number of girls in your class

 G the number of inches in a yard

 H the grocery bill

 J the amount of water in a lake

5 What is 5,461,305 rounded to the nearest hundred thousand?

 A 5,000,000 C 5,500,000

 B 5,461,000 D 5,550,000

6 Which shows the greatest amount of money?

 F

 G

 H

 J

7 Which fact would most likely be exact?

 A the distance around the world

 B the number of stories in a building

 C the population of California

 D the number of fish in the ocean

8 The headline was "25,000 People See Game." The announcer said "There were about 20,000 people at the game." Both are correct.

 Explain How can both the headline and the announcer be correct?

Safe Site

Internet Test Prep
Visit **www.eduplace.com/kids/mhm**
for more *Test Prep Practice.*

Extra Practice

Set A

Write each number in standard form. *(Lesson 1, pages 4–5)*

1. 800,000 + 50,000 + 400 + 70

2. 604 thousand, 309

3. 500,000 + 20,000 + 3,000 + 800 + 6

4. thirty thousand, nine hundred

5. 3 hundred thousands, 2 ten thousands, 5 thousands, 6 tens, 4 ones

Write each number in short word and word form.

6. 230,000

7. 400,300

8. 403,000

9. 554,554

10. 600,000 + 30,000 + 2,000 +700 + 40

11. 80,000 + 5,000 + 100 + 3

Write each in expanded form. Then write the value of the underlined digit.

12. 72<u>8</u>,683

13. 6,<u>1</u>70

14. 5<u>0</u>,862

15. <u>5</u>05,432

16. 78,3<u>3</u>7

Set B

Compare. Write >, <, or = for each ●. *(Lesson 2, pages 6–9)*

1. 808 ● 880

2. 1,409 ● 1,409

3. 5,802 ● 15,802

4. 64,805 ● 64,850

5. 147,689 ● 47,689

6. 88,961 ● 88,651

Write the numbers in order from greatest to least.

7. 108   98   82

8. 97   989   907

9. 505   550   500

10. 1,032   1,003   1,322

11. 11,653   9,879   12,002

12. 980   11,807   1,197

Write the numbers in order from least to greatest.

13. 354   978   89

14. 5,399   4,522   978

15. 150,808   152,008   150,088

16. 120   249   807

17. 4,879   4,891   4,886

18. 645,704   645,804   6,580

Extra Practice

Set C

Use the number line to round each number to the nearest ten. *(Lesson 3, pages 10–11)*

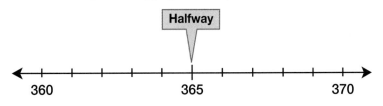

1. 366   **2.** 362   **3.** 368   **4.** 363   **5.** 361   **6.** 369

Round each number to the place of the underlined digit.

7. 8<u>8</u>   **8.** <u>1</u>37   **9.** 5<u>1</u>6   **10.** 9,<u>8</u>73   **11.** 3,<u>4</u>75   **12.** 7,8<u>8</u>9

13. 18,9<u>7</u>2   **14.** 34,<u>0</u>53   **15.** 44,<u>5</u>07   **16.** 13,7<u>0</u>2   **17.** 121,<u>6</u>61   **18.** 18<u>7</u>,863

Set D

Write each number in three other ways. *(Lesson 6, pages 18–19)*

1. 4,005,000   **2.** forty-six thousand, two hundred seventy-two

3. 15 million, 304 thousand, 794

4. 700,000 + 2,000 + 600 + 40 + 7

5. seventy-six million, two hundred fifty-seven thousand, four hundred forty-two

Set E

Compare. Write >, <, or = for each ⬤. *(Lesson 7, pages 20–23)*

1. 8,796,206 ⬤ 8,769,432   **2.** 3,105,896 ⬤ 3,105,896

3. 98,908,135 ⬤ 111,422,033   **4.** 79,860,041 ⬤ 79,890,041

Write the numbers in order from greatest to least.

5. 98,604,232   9,604,347   98,134,323   **6.** 6,012,009   8,652,913   10,276,411

7. 578,419,152   58,844,167   587,419,152   **8.** 7,462,198   76,462,198   76,624,198

Extra Practice

Set F

Round each number to the place of the underlined digit. *(Lesson 8, pages 24–25)*

1. 7̲4,320

2. 5,8̲90,643

3. 1̲85,279

4. 3̲6,241,588

5. 197̲,264,335

6. 5̲,237,709

7. 1̲,205,890

8. 90̲5,203

9. 4̲04,557

10. 30̲7,232,689

11. 8̲7,109,322

12. 8,6̲99,322

Set G

Write each amount. Then write the greater amount. *(Lesson 10, pages 30-33)*

1.   or

2.  or

3. 5 nickels, 6 dimes, 3 one-dollar bills or 2 one-dollar bills, 5 quarters, 5 dimes

4. 2 ten-dollar bills, 1 five-dollar bill, 2 quarters or 1 ten-dollar bill, 3 five-dollar bills, 1 quarter, 2 dimes.

Set H

A $20.00 bill was used to buy each item below. List the coins and bills you would use to make change. *(Lesson 11, pages 34–35)*

1.  $ 19.95

2.  $ 9.25

3.  $ 6.89

4. Cost of item: $8.96

5. Cost of item: $12.77

6. Cost of item: $3.48

Extra Practice • Problem Solving

Solve. Give a reason for your answer. *(Lesson 4, pages 12–13)*

1 Abraham Lincoln received 2,216,067 votes for President. Is this an estimated or an exact amount?

2 Mount Everest is the highest mountain in the world. It is about 29,000 feet above sea level. Is this an estimated or an exact amount?

3 A baseball stadium seats more than 48,000 fans. Is this an estimated or an exact amount?

4 A baseball player hits 53 home runs during a season. Is this an estimated or an exact amount?

Solve. *(Lesson 9, pages 26-27)*

5 Tina, Ron, Lucy, and Jeff each have different pets. Jeff's pet is not a cat. Ron's pet is not a cat or a gerbil. Lucy's pet is not a canary. Tina has a dog. What pet does each person have?

6 Four friends each ride the bus to a different stop. Carlos gets off the bus after Elaine. Sue gets off the bus last. Greg gets off the bus after Carlos. In what order do the friends get off the bus?

7 Joe, Tom, Hal, and Bob are standing in line. Tom is first. Hal is not last. Joe is behind Tom and Hal. Bob is in front of Hal. In what order are the boys in line?

8 Three girls each have 20, 25, and 30 beads. Mai does not have the most. Lu has more beads than Jo. Jo does not have the fewest. How many beads does each girl have?

Solve. Use the table. *(Lesson 12, pages 36-37)*

9 Ms. Ruiz bought a pair of tennis shoes. She paid for them with five $10-bills. How much change should she receive?

10 Jo bought a headband and a water bottle. She had 55¢ left. How much did she start out with?

11 Mr. Gray bought three pairs of sports socks and a headband. His change was $4.55. How much money did he give the clerk?

Sports Equipment	
Tennis shoes	$42.50 pair
Sport socks	3 pairs for $7.95
Headbands	$2.50 each
Water bottles	$1.95 each

Chapter Review

Reviewing Vocabulary

1. In which period are the digits 456 in the number 123,456,789?

2. In the number 7,523,548, what digits are in the ones period?

3. What is the difference between an exact amount and an estimate?

4. In the number 98,125,467, in which period are the digits 98?

Reviewing Concepts and Skills

Write Exercises 5 and 6 in standard form. Then write Exercises 7–10 in expanded form. *(Lesson 1, pages 4–5)*

5. 600,000 + 20,000 + 900 + 50

6. two million, two hundred seven

7. 3,270

8. 43,872

9. 523,837

10. 87,137

Compare. Write >, <, or = for each ●. *(Lessons 2, 7 pages 6–7, 20–22)*

11. 908 ● 980

12. 2,409 ● 2,409

13. 9,798,206 ● 9,789,206

14. 48,605 ● 48,650

15. 8,502 ● 15,802

16. 4,125,896 ● 4,125,897

Write the numbers in order from least to greatest.

17. 654   578   87

18. 2,302,424   2,203,424   22,342,424

19. 132   259   817

20. 7,777,777   801,300,002   981,342

Round each number to the place of the underlined digit. *(Lessons 3, 6, 8 pages 10–11, 18–19, 24–25)*

21. 4̲37

22. 73̲6

23. 9,5̲83

24. 5,6̲75

25. 9,28̲9

26. 186̲,264,335

27. 4̲,837,709

28. 1̲,605,890

29. 31̲5,203

Write each number in three other ways. *(Lesson 6, pages 18–19)*

30. 800,000 + 3,000 + 500 + 40 + 7

31. thirty-six thousand, seventy-five

Write each amount. Then write the greater amount. *(Lesson 10, pages 30–33)*

32.  **or**

33.  **or**

Find the correct change, using the least number of coins and bills. List the coins and bills used. *(Lesson 11, pages 34–35)*

34. You bought a book for $6.39. You paid with a $10 bill.

35. You bought a toy for $3.15. You paid with a $5 bill.

Solve.

36. In 1980, Caspar, Wyoming, had a population of 51,016. Is this an exact amount or an estimate?

37. Jupiter is more than 500,000,000 miles from the Sun. Is this amount exact or estimated?

38. Ali, Jim, Sue, and Pam each play a different sport. Ali doesn't play soccer or baseball. Jim doesn't play soccer or swim. Sue doesn't play hockey or swim. Pam swims. What sport does each person play?

39. Jim's dad had two $10 bills and one $5 bill. He bought Jim a shirt for $7.95 and a pair of jeans for $14.98. Jim's dad gave the clerk all three bills. How much money did Jim's dad receive as change?

Brain Teasers Math Reasoning

DIGITS

A number is between 100 and 1,000.
- The sum of its digits is 11.
- The tens digit is 2 less than the hundreds digit.

What could the number be? List all possible answers.

WHAT DID YOU SAY?

You include the words "two thousand" and the word "fifteen" when you read this 4-digit number. What could the number be? List all the answers.

Safe Site

Internet Brain Teasers
Visit **www.eduplace.com/kids/mhm** for more *Brain Teasers.*

Chapter Test

Write each number in standard form.

1. 500,000 + 20,000 + 600 + 90   **2.** 315 thousand, 278

Write each number in short word form and word form.

3. 715,730   **4.** 75,302   **5.** 2,311,618   **6.** 93,002,850

Compare. Write >, <, or = for each ●.

7. 47,689 ● 47,651   **8.** 2,123,816 ● 2,123,816   **9.** 8,765,664 ● 80,755,664

Write the numbers in order from greatest to least.

10. 10,898,824   1,089,884   1,809,824   **11.** 97,989   907,888   9,879

Write the numbers in order from least to greatest.

12. 3,679   31,691   3,886   **13.** 7,399,123   75,223   6,978

Round each number to the place of the underlined digit.

14. <u>1</u>8   **15.** 14,<u>3</u>87   **16.** <u>1</u>6,899   **17.** 9,<u>0</u>83   **18.** 1,<u>4</u>85

19. 2<u>8</u>,782   **20.** 6,2<u>5</u>9   **21.** <u>5</u>0,123   **22.** 24,<u>9</u>97   **23.** 32,0<u>4</u>6

Write the place of the 5 in each number. Then write its value.

24. 607,574,020   **25.** 35,790,643   **26.** 19,405,293   **27.** 261,568

Write each amount. Then write the greater amount.

28. 1 fifty-dollar bill, 2 twenty-dollar bills, 2 quarters **or** 7 ten-dollar bills, 5 five-dollar bills, 4 dimes

29. 3 ten-dollar bills, 4 five-dollar bills, 8 quarters **or** 1 twenty-dollar bill, 2 ten-dollar bills, 12 quarters

Write the names of the coins and bills you would use to make change for each of the following.

30. You bought an item worth $1.92. You paid with a five-dollar bill.

31. You bought an item worth $8.49. You paid with a ten-dollar bill.

Solve.

32. There are 435 members of Congress in the United States House of Representatives. Is this an exact or an estimated amount?

33. There are 4 fish tanks on a pet store shelf. Each tank has a different kind of fish. There are no betas in the second tank. There are no guppies or tetras in the first tank. The guppies are not in the third tank. The neons are in the fourth tank. What kind of fish are in each tank?

Write About It

Solve each problem. Use correct math vocabulary to explain your thinking.

1. Tino writes the number six hundred eight million, four hundred twelve thousand, nine like this:

608,400,129

   a. What mistake did Tino make? Why do you think he made that mistake?

   b. Write the number correctly in standard form. Then tell the value of the digit 9.

   c. Write the number in expanded form.

2. A roll of pennies contains $0.50. A roll of nickels holds $2.00. A roll of dimes holds $5.00. A roll of quarters holds $10.00.

   a. You want to know how many coins are in each kind of roll. Explain how you could find the answers.

   b. You have two rolls of each kind of coin. You want to exchange the coins for bills. If you want only $20 bills, $10 bills, $5 bills, and $1 bills, what is the least number of each bill you can get?

50¢ PENNIES 50¢

$2 NICKELS $2

$5 DIMES $5

$10 QUARTERS $10

Another Look

Use the map to solve the problems. You can use what you know about place value, rounding, and comparing numbers.

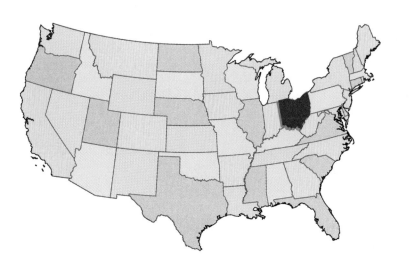

Toledo
312,174

Cleveland
495,817

Akron
215,712

Columbus
670,234

Cincinnati
336,400

1. List the cities and their populations in order from greatest to least. Round the population of each city to the nearest hundred thousand. List the cities and their rounded populations.

2. Find the city using these clues for its population: It has a 5 in the thousands place, a 7 in the hundreds place, and twice the number in the hundred-thousands place as in the ten-thousands place.

3. **Look Back** Compare the rounded populations of Cincinnati and Toledo. Can you tell which city is larger from the rounded numbers? What could you do to find rounded populations that would show which of these two cities is larger?

4. **Analyze** Write the greatest number you can make using each digit from the population of Columbus only once.

Standards NS 1.2, 1.3, 1.4   MR 1.1

Enrichment

Clocks and Roman Numerals

The short hand on a clock is the hour hand. The long hand is the minute hand. It takes 5 minutes for the minute hand to move from one number to the next.

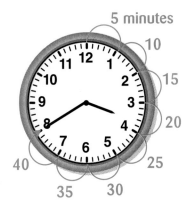

This clock shows 3:40 or

40 minutes after 3 or

20 minutes before 4.

Some clocks have Roman numerals.

- Roman numerals use different letters for different numbers.

  I = 1   V = 5   X = 10

- For most Roman numerals, you *add* the value of the letters to find the value of the numeral.

  III = 1 + 1 + 1 = 3   VI = 5 + 1 = 6

- When I appears before V or X, you *subtract* the value of I from the value of V or X.

  IV = 5 - 1 = 4   IX = 10 - 1 = 9

Write the standard numeral for each Roman numeral.

1. II   **2.** IX   **3.** XI   **4.** VIII   **5.** IV   **6.** VII

Write the time shown on each clock in two ways.

7.

8.

9.

10.

Explain Your Thinking

How are Roman numerals different from standard numerals? Explain.

CHAPTER 2

Addition and Subtraction

Why Learn About Addition and Subtraction?

You use addition to find how many in all, and you use subtraction to find a part of a whole or to compare amounts.

When you play a game in which you can both win and lose points, you use addition and subtraction to keep score.

These girls and boys are buying several items. The clerk will add the price of each item to get the total. The children can use subtraction to check that their change is correct.

Reading Mathematics

Reviewing Vocabulary

Understanding math language helps you become
a successful problem solver. Here are some math
vocabulary words you should know.

addend	a number that is added to another number
sum	the answer in an addition problem
difference	the answer in a subtraction problem
estimate	to find an approximate answer rather than an exact answer
regroup	to use 1 ten for 10 ones, 1 hundred for 10 tens, 15 ones for 1 ten 5 ones, and so on
number sentence	a sentence that uses symbols to show how numbers are related

Reading Words and Symbols

When you read mathematics, sometimes you read only
words, sometimes you read words and symbols, and
sometimes you read only symbols.

There are different ways to
read addition.

$$\begin{array}{r} 368 \\ +\ 57 \\ \hline 425 \end{array}$$

$$\underset{\text{addend}}{368} + \underset{\text{addend}}{57} = \underset{\text{sum}}{425}$$

▶ Three hundred sixty-eight plus
fifty-seven equals four hundred
twenty-five.

▶ The sum of three hundred
sixty-eight and fifty-seven is
four hundred twenty-five.

There are different ways to
read subtraction.

$$\begin{array}{r} 221 \\ -\ 5 \\ \hline 216 \end{array}$$

$$221 - 5 = \underset{\text{difference}}{216}$$

▶ Two hundred twenty-one minus
five equals two hundred sixteen.

▶ The difference of two hundred
twenty-one and five
is two hundred sixteen.

Try These

1. Write *true* or *false* for each statement about arithmetic.

   a. You can use addition to check subtraction.

   b. When the number of tens in a sum is greater than 10, you regroup the 10 tens as 1 hundred.

   c. When zero is subtracted from a number, the difference is always zero.

2. Tell if each 9 is an *addend, sum,* or *difference.*

   a. $4 + 5 = 9$ b. $17 - 8 = 9$ c. $9 + 2 = 11$ d. $12 - 3 = 9$

   e. $\begin{array}{r} 7 \\ + 9 \\ \hline 16 \end{array}$ f. $\begin{array}{r} 13 \\ - 4 \\ \hline 9 \end{array}$ g. $\begin{array}{r} 6 \\ + 3 \\ \hline 9 \end{array}$ h. $\begin{array}{r} 9 \\ + 1 \\ \hline 10 \end{array}$

3. Write a number sentence for each exercise.

   a. Eight hundred twenty-four minus three hundred nineteen equals five hundred five.

   b. Thirty-nine plus forty-five plus seventy-two equals one hundred fifty-six.

   c. The difference of forty-three and eighteen is twenty-five.

Upcoming Vocabulary

Write About It Here are some other vocabulary words you will learn in this chapter. Watch for these words. Write their definitions in your journal.

expression	**inequality**	**Commutative Property**
algebraic expression	**variable**	
	two-variable equation	**Associative Property**
evaluate		
equation	**Zero Property**	

Addition Properties

You will learn about the properties of addition.

Learn About It

Here are three properties you can use when you add.

Addition Properties

Zero Property

When you add zero to a number, the sum is that number.

$$6 + 0 = 6$$

Commutative Property

When you change the order of the addends, the sum stays the same.

$$5 + 7 = 12$$
$$7 + 5 = 12$$

Associative Property

When you change the way addends are grouped, the sum stays the same.

Parentheses tell you which addends to add first.

$$(387 + 950) + 50 = 387 + (950 + 50)$$

$$1{,}337 + 50 = 387 + 1{,}000$$

$$1{,}387 \qquad 1{,}387$$

Explain Your Thinking

▶ Which of the groupings of $387 + 950 + 50$ do you think makes it easier to add? Why?

Guided Practice

Copy and complete each number sentence. Tell which property of addition you used.

1. $11 + 0 = \blacksquare$

2. $45 + 34 = \blacksquare + 45$

3. $(4 + 6) + 8 = \blacksquare + (6 + 8)$

4. $\blacksquare + 0 = 0 + 18$

5. $20 + (\blacksquare + 5) = (20 + 30) + 5$

6. $0 + \blacksquare = 55$

Ask Yourself

• Is one of the addends zero?

• If there are parentheses, which addends do I add first?

Standards NS 3.0   AF 1.0, 1.1, 1.2, 1.3   MR 2.3, 2.4, 3.2

Independent Practice

Find each sum.

7. $0 + 789$ **8.** $(5 + 5) + 15$ **9.** $45 + 32$ **10.** $32 + 45$

Copy and complete each number sentence.
Tell which property of addition you used.

11. $34 + 99 = \blacksquare + 34$ **12.** $342 + 0 = \blacksquare$ **13.** $(14 + 9) + 5 = 14 + (\blacksquare + 5)$

Group the addends so that you
can add mentally. Then find each sum.

14. $648 + 392 + 8$ **15.** $995 + 421 + 5$ **16.** $75 + 25 + 67$

Problem Solving • Reasoning

Use Data Use the table for Problems 17 and 18.

17. **Compare** Is the total number of children who signed up for beginner lessons greater than the total number who signed up for advanced lessons? How can you use one of the properties of addition to help you decide?

Swim Lesson Sign-Ups		
Class	Boys	Girls
Beginner	65	49
Intermediate	83	72
Advanced	49	65

18. **Write About It** Are more boys than girls signed up for swimming lessons? How can you answer the question without adding?

19. **Analyze** Do you think there is a Zero Property for subtraction? Why or why not?

20. **Analyze** Do you think there is a Commutative Property for subtraction? Why or why not?

Mixed Review • Test Prep

Write the number. *(pages 18–19)*

21. Four hundred seven thousand, sixty-six

22. Twenty-eight million, three hundred one

23. Nine million, three hundred five thousand, nine hundred ten

24 Round 34,567 to the nearest hundred. *(pages 24–25)*

    A 34,000   **B** 34,500   **C** 34,600   **D** 35,000

Add Whole Numbers

You will learn how to add numbers using regrouping.

Review
Vocabulary
regroup

Learn About It

The Navajo use the wool from sheep for many different crafts. Suppose a family had one flock of 129 sheep and another flock of 97 sheep. How many sheep did they have in all?

Add.   **129 + 97 =** ■

Find 129 + 97.

Step 1 Add ones. 9 + 7 = 16	**Step 2** Add tens. 1 + 2 + 9 = 12	**Step 3** Add hundreds. 1 + 1 = 2

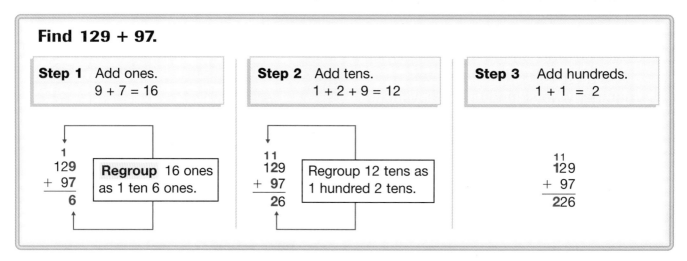

$$\begin{array}{r} \overset{1}{129} \\ +\ 97 \\ \hline 6 \end{array}$$ **Regroup** 16 ones as 1 ten 6 ones.

$$\begin{array}{r} \overset{11}{129} \\ +\ 97 \\ \hline 26 \end{array}$$ Regroup 12 tens as 1 hundred 2 tens.

$$\begin{array}{r} \overset{11}{129} \\ +\ 97 \\ \hline 226 \end{array}$$

Solution: They had 226 sheep in all.

Other Examples

A. Add Large Numbers

$$\begin{array}{r} \overset{11}{5{,}293} \\ +\ 2{,}048 \\ \hline 7{,}341 \end{array}$$

B. Add More Than Two Addends

$$\begin{array}{r} \overset{1\ \ 1}{3{,}642} \\ 1{,}903 \\ +\ \ \ 305 \\ \hline 5{,}850 \end{array}$$

Explain Your Thinking

► Why is it important to line up digits correctly when you add?

► How can adding numbers in a different order help you check that your answer is correct?

Standards   NS **3.0, 3.1**   AF **1.0, 1.4**   SDP **1.0**   MR **1.1, 2.4**

Guided Practice

Add.

1. $\begin{array}{r} 362 \\ + 517 \\ \hline \end{array}$

2. $\begin{array}{r} 283 \\ + 55 \\ \hline \end{array}$

3. $\begin{array}{r} 6,562 \\ + 298 \\ \hline \end{array}$

4. 625 + 248

5. 319 + 1,270

6. 34,621 + 3,195

Ask Yourself

• Are the digits lined up correctly?

• Do I need to regroup?

• How can I check that the answer is reasonable?

Independent Practice

Add.

7. $\begin{array}{r} 652 \\ + 145 \\ \hline \end{array}$

8. $\begin{array}{r} 345 \\ + 172 \\ \hline \end{array}$

9. $\begin{array}{r} 732 \\ + 88 \\ \hline \end{array}$

10. $\begin{array}{r} 5,195 \\ + 3,261 \\ \hline \end{array}$

11. $\begin{array}{r} 6,714 \\ + 8,600 \\ \hline \end{array}$

12. $\begin{array}{r} 3,431 \\ + 768 \\ \hline \end{array}$

13. $\begin{array}{r} 5,182 \\ + 3,957 \\ \hline \end{array}$

14. $\begin{array}{r} 9,832 \\ + 761 \\ \hline \end{array}$

15. $\begin{array}{r} 894 \\ + 4,717 \\ \hline \end{array}$

16. $\begin{array}{r} 52,391 \\ + 17,402 \\ \hline \end{array}$

17. $\begin{array}{r} 81,295 \\ + 15,848 \\ \hline \end{array}$

18. $\begin{array}{r} 67,218 \\ + 6,326 \\ \hline \end{array}$

19. $\begin{array}{r} 3,621 \\ + 1,893 \\ \hline \end{array}$

20. $\begin{array}{r} 14,231 \\ + 5,628 \\ \hline \end{array}$

21. $\begin{array}{r} 28,547 \\ + 6,348 \\ \hline \end{array}$

22. $\begin{array}{r} 8,132 \\ + 1,659 \\ \hline \end{array}$

23. $\begin{array}{r} 21,296 \\ + 17,542 \\ \hline \end{array}$

24. $\begin{array}{r} 13,984 \\ + 56,688 \\ \hline \end{array}$

25. $\begin{array}{r} 72,576 \\ + 9,785 \\ \hline \end{array}$

26. $\begin{array}{r} 43,157 \\ + 16,921 \\ \hline \end{array}$

27. 482 + 553

28. 1,765 + 440

29. 36,373 + 2,605

30. 15,862 + 53,021

31. 54,186 + 1,983

32. 13,421 + 7,899

Use the Associative and/or Commutative Property to help you find each sum.

33. 75 + 25 + 46

34. 78 + 53 + 47

35. 179 + 345 + 1

36. 2,990 + 654 + 10

37. 8,354 + 291 + 9

38. 1,820 + 178 + 80

Algebra • Functions Copy and complete each function table or find the rule.

Rule: Add 50

	Input	Output
39.	360	■
40.	■	490
41.	2,000	■
42.	■	3,100

Rule: Add 100

	Input	Output
43.	46	■
44.	■	375
45.	105	■
46.	328	■

47. Rule: ■

Input	Output
30	105
194	269
75	150
22	97

Problem Solving • Reasoning

Use Data Use the price list for Problems 48–51.

48. Analyze Is $200 enough to buy 1 piece of pottery and 2 necklaces? Why or why not?

49. How many rain sticks did Julie buy if she got back $2 in change when she paid with a $20 bill?

50. What is the cost of 1 rug, 2 pieces of pottery, and 1 necklace?

51. Write Your Own Use the information in the price list to write a word problem. Have a classmate solve your problem.

Navajo Craft Shop	
Item	**Price**
Woven rugs	$2,450
Pottery	$164
Necklaces	$23
Rain sticks	$9

Mixed Review • Test Prep

Find the values of these groups of coins and bills. *(pages 30–31)*

52.

53.

54.

55.

56 Which number is greater than 8,994? *(pages 26–27)*

   A 8,239   **B** 8,608   **C** 8,949   **D** 9,002

Extra Practice See Set B on page 92.

Add Consecutive Whole Numbers

Consecutive whole numbers are whole numbers that increase by 1 at each step. For example, 7, 8, 9, and 10 are consecutive whole numbers.

When you add an even number of consecutive whole numbers, there is an interesting pattern. Look at these examples.

Find 7 + 8 + 9 + 10.

7 + 8 + 9 + 10

→17←

→17←

17 + 17 = 34

The sum is 34.

Find 10 + 11 + 12 + 13 + 14 + 15.

10 + 11 + 12 + 13 + 14 + 15

→25←

→25←

→25←

25 + 25 + 25 = 75

The sum is 75.

Try These

1. 16 + 17 + 18 + 19

2. 4 + 5 + 6 + 7 + 8 + 9

3. 30 + 31 + 32 + 33

4. 97 + 98 + 99 + 100

5. 4 + 5 + 6 + 7 + 8 + 9 + 10 + 11

6. 3,105 + 3,106 + 3,107 + 3,108

7. What is the sum of the first ten counting numbers (1, 2, 3, . . . , 10)?

Explain Your Thinking

▶ Which four consecutive whole numbers have a sum of 90? Explain how you found your answer.

Subtract Whole Numbers

You will learn how to subtract whole numbers.

Learn About It

In the United States, some cat breeds are more popular than others. The table shows how many cats of certain breeds were registered in one year.

How many more Siamese cats were registered than ocicats?

Popular Cat Breeds in the United States

Breed	Number of Cats Registered
Persian	42,578
Siamese	2,865
American shorthair	1,032
Ocicat	868

Subtract.   **2,865 − 868 = ■**

Find 2,865 − 868.

Step 1 Subtract ones.

$$\begin{array}{r} \overset{515}{2{,}86\!\!\!/5} \\ -\ \ 868 \\ \hline 7 \end{array}$$
Regroup a ten as 10 ones.

Step 2 Subtract tens.

$$\begin{array}{r} \overset{15}{}\ \ \ \\ \overset{7\,5\!\!\!/15}{2{,}86\!\!\!/5} \\ -\ \ 868 \\ \hline 97 \end{array}$$
Regroup a hundred as 10 tens.

Step 3 Subtract hundreds.

$$\begin{array}{r} \overset{1715}{}\ \\ \overset{1\,7\,5\!\!\!/15}{2{,}86\!\!\!/5} \\ -\ \ 868 \\ \hline 997 \end{array}$$
Regroup a thousand as 10 hundreds.

Step 4 Subtract thousands.

$$\begin{array}{r} \overset{1715}{}\ \\ \overset{1\,7\,5\!\!\!/15}{2\!\!\!/{,}86\!\!\!/5} \\ -\ \ 868 \\ \hline 1{,}997 \end{array}$$

Solution: There were 1,997 more Siamese cats registered than ocicats.

You can use addition to check subtraction.

$$\begin{array}{r} \overset{1\ \ 1\ 1}{} \\ 1{,}997 \\ +\ \ \overset{}{868} \\ \hline 2{,}865 \end{array}$$

Add the difference to the number you subtracted. If the sum matches the number you subtracted from, your answer is correct.

Standards   NS **2.1, 3.0, 3.1**   SDP **1.0**   MR **2.4**

Other Examples

A. Subtract Without Regrouping

$$\begin{array}{r} 864 \\ -\ 302 \\ \hline 562 \end{array}$$

B. Subtraction with 5-Digit Numbers

$$\begin{array}{r} {\scriptstyle 1\ 13} \\ 82,396 \\ -\ 21,584 \\ \hline 60,812 \end{array}$$

Explain Your Thinking

▶ Look back at Example B. How can you use addition to check that the answer is correct?

Guided Practice

Subtract.

1. $\begin{array}{r} 483 \\ -\ 262 \\ \hline \end{array}$

2. $\begin{array}{r} 4,674 \\ -\ 1,833 \\ \hline \end{array}$

3. $\begin{array}{r} 86,724 \\ -\ 70,862 \\ \hline \end{array}$

4. $839 - 45$

5. $75,359 - 5,248$

> ### Ask Yourself
> • Are the digits lined up correctly?
> • Do I need to regroup before I subtract?
> • How can I check that the answer is correct?

Independent Practice

Subtract. Use addition to check that your answer is correct.

6. $\begin{array}{r} 967 \\ -\ 815 \\ \hline \end{array}$

7. $\begin{array}{r} 757 \\ -\ 486 \\ \hline \end{array}$

8. $\begin{array}{r} 324 \\ -\ 77 \\ \hline \end{array}$

9. $\begin{array}{r} 8,397 \\ -\ 5,067 \\ \hline \end{array}$

10. $\begin{array}{r} 5,188 \\ -\ 1,434 \\ \hline \end{array}$

11. $\begin{array}{r} 8,452 \\ -\ 1,826 \\ \hline \end{array}$

12. $\begin{array}{r} 7,927 \\ -\ 2,639 \\ \hline \end{array}$

13. $\begin{array}{r} 7,829 \\ -\ 3,487 \\ \hline \end{array}$

14. $\begin{array}{r} 5,381 \\ -\ 2,173 \\ \hline \end{array}$

15. $\begin{array}{r} 9,634 \\ -\ 4,976 \\ \hline \end{array}$

16. $\begin{array}{r} 6,325 \\ -\ 2,776 \\ \hline \end{array}$

17. $\begin{array}{r} 5,584 \\ -\ 492 \\ \hline \end{array}$

18. $\begin{array}{r} 97,488 \\ -\ 46,273 \\ \hline \end{array}$

19. $\begin{array}{r} 35,295 \\ -\ 17,489 \\ \hline \end{array}$

20. $\begin{array}{r} 75,849 \\ -\ 6,406 \\ \hline \end{array}$

21. $\begin{array}{r} 47,283 \\ -\ 32,657 \\ \hline \end{array}$

22. $\begin{array}{r} 24,522 \\ -\ 7,165 \\ \hline \end{array}$

23. $\begin{array}{r} 42,176 \\ -\ 11,348 \\ \hline \end{array}$

24. $\begin{array}{r} 28,137 \\ -\ 9,241 \\ \hline \end{array}$

25. $\begin{array}{r} 14,621 \\ -\ 5,835 \\ \hline \end{array}$

26. $583 - 291$

27. $875 - 782$

28. $1,376 - 429$

29. $8,522 - 5,046$

30. $58,361 - 36,175$

31. $88,526 - 9,410$

32. $6,432 - 3,829$

33. $11,768 - 4,382$

34. $39,221 - 14,823$

Problem Solving • Reasoning

Use Data Use the table for Problems 35–39.

German shepherd (*left*)

Labrador retriever (*right*)

35. How many more Labrador retrievers than poodles are registered?

36. How many more beagles than poodles are registered?

37. The number of rottweilers registered is 10,784 more than the number of German shepherds registered. How many rottweilers are registered?

38. Write Your Own Write a problem using the data from the table. Have a classmate solve your problem.

39. Analyze If the numbers in the table were rounded to the nearest thousand, would you be able to tell if more beagles than poodles were registered? Explain why or why not.

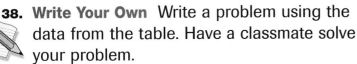

Popular Dog Breeds in the United States

Breed	Number of Dogs Registered
Labrador retriever	149,505
German shepherd	79,076
Beagle	56,946
Poodle	56,803

Beagle (*top*)

Poodle (*bottom*)

Mixed Review • Test Prep

Answer each question. *(pages 34–35)*

As the clerk gave Mark his change, she said, "Here's your change: $2.79, $2.80, $2.90, $3.00, $4.00, $5.00."

40. What was the price of Mark's purchase?

41. How much money did Mark give the clerk?

42. What coins and bills did Mark get as change?

43. How much money did Mark get back?

Choose the letter of the correct answer. *(page 49)*

44 Where should the minute hand point to show 10:30?

A 12
B 9
C 6
D 3

45 What time does the clock below show?

F 1:40
G 1:20
H 2:40
J 2:20

Extra Practice See Set C on page 92.

Get the Least

Practice subtracting whole numbers by playing this game.
Try to get the least difference!

What You'll Need

- *playing board for each player (Teaching Tool 2)*
- *a number cube labeled 1 to 6*

Players 2 or more

Here's What to Do

Players take turns.

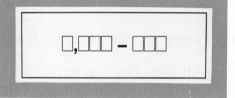

$$\square,\square\square\square - \square\square\square$$

1. For each turn, a player rolls the number cube and then writes the digit rolled in one of the boxes on the playing board. Once a digit has been written in a box, it may not be changed.

2. After the players' boards have been filled, players find the difference between their two numbers.

   The player with the least difference is the winner.

Share Your Thinking Describe the strategy you used to try to get the least difference.

Estimate Sums and Differences

You will learn how to use rounded numbers to estimate sums and differences.

Review
Vocabulary
estimate

Learn About It

Amanda wants to buy a personal pizza for $3.89 and a large drink for $1.59. She has exactly $5.75. Does Amanda have enough money?

You do not need to know the exact cost. You only need to know if the total is less than $5.75. So you can **estimate** the sum.

Estimate the total cost.

Estimate the sum of $3.89 and $1.59.

Try rounding each addend to the nearest dollar. Then add the rounded numbers.

$3.89	**rounds to**	$4.00
+ $1.59	**rounds to**	+ $2.00
		$6.00

Since both addends were rounded *up*, the actual cost will be *less than* $6.00. But will it be more or less than $5.75?

Try rounding to the nearest ten cents. Then add.

$3.89	**rounds to**	$3.90
+ $1.59	**rounds to**	+ $1.60
		$5.50

Since both addends were rounded *up*, and the sum of these numbers is *less than* $5.75, then you know the exact amount is also *less than* $5.75.

Solution: Amanda has enough money.

Other Examples

A. Round to the Nearest Hundred

5,629	**rounds to**	5,600
+ 448	**rounds to**	+ 400
		6,000

So 5,629 + 448 is *about* 6,000.

B. Estimate a Difference

478	**rounds to**	500
− 318	**rounds to**	− 300
		200

So 478 − 318 is *about* 200.

Explain Your Thinking

▶ If both addends are rounded down, will the sum of the rounded numbers be greater than or less than the actual sum?

Standards NS **1.3, 2.1, 2.2** MR **1.1, 2.4**

Guided Practice

Round each number to the nearest ten. Then estimate.

1. 45 + 32

2. 586 − 98

3. 4,567 + 1,111

Round each number to the nearest hundred or dollar. Then estimate.

4. $4.67 + $2.35

5. $8.34 − $3.97

6. 7,824 + 4,136

7. 8,432 − 356

Ask Yourself
- Which place am I rounding to?
- Am I finding a sum or a difference?

Independent Practice

Round each number to the nearest ten. Then estimate.

8. 347 + 128

9. 543 + 221

10. 187 + 362

11. 876 + 112

12. 587 + 321

13. 234 + 98

14. 4,876 + 678

15. 5,467 + 3,789

Round each number to the nearest hundred or dollar. Then estimate.

16. 396 + 123

17. $6.99 − $2.34

18. 5,822 − 321

19. $67.78 + $19.88

20. $5.38 + $3.29

21. 987 − 432

22. $45.89 − $6.42

23. 34,564 + 1,089

Problem Solving • Reasoning

Use Data Use the menu for Problems 24 and 25.

24. Ramon bought a chicken sandwich and a small drink. About how much change should he get back if he paid with a $10 bill?

25. Write About It Emma estimated the cost of a salad and a small drink by rounding each price to the nearest dollar. Was her estimate more or less than the actual amount? By how much?

Menu

LUNCH
Chicken Sandwich ... $2.79
Personal Pizza $3.89
Salad $1.39
Grilled Cheese $2.49

DRINKS
Small $1.29
Large $1.59

Mixed Review • Test Prep

Write the value of the underlined digit. *(pages 4–5)*

26. 7<u>4</u>1

27. 3<u>2</u>,156

28. 5,<u>9</u>03

29. <u>4</u>7,302

30. 1,08<u>4</u>

31. Which number is sixty thousand, nine hundred five? *(pages 4–5)*

A 6,905 **B** 6,950 **C** 60,905 **D** 60,950

Problem-Solving Skill: Estimated or Exact Answers

You will learn how to decide whether an exact answer or an estimate is needed to solve a problem.

Before you solve a problem, you must decide whether you need an estimate or an exact answer.

Students sold fruit to raise money for a trip. The table shows how many of each fruit the students sold each week.

Amount of Fruit Sold		
Week	Fruit	Number Sold
Week 1	Apples	123
Week 2	Pears	216
Week 3	Oranges	236
Week 4	Mangoes	105

Sometimes you can estimate to solve a problem.

About how many apples and pears were sold?

Since the question asks you to find *about* how many pieces of fruit were sold, you can estimate the sum. Estimates can be made quickly and easily.

Round to the nearest hundred.

$$123 \xrightarrow{\text{rounds to}} 100$$
$$+ 216 \xrightarrow{\text{rounds to}} + 200$$
$$\overline{ 300}$$

They sold *about* 300 apples and pears.

Sometimes you need an exact answer to solve a problem.

How many more oranges than mangoes did they sell?

Since the question asks you to find how many more, you need to find the exact difference. An exact answer gives you precise information.

Find 236 − 105.

$$\begin{array}{r} 236 \\ - 105 \\ \hline 131 \end{array}$$

They sold 131 more oranges than mangoes.

Look Back When is an exact answer better than an estimate? When is an estimate better than an exact answer?

Standards NS **1.3, 1.4**   MR **1.0, 1.1, 2.0, 2.5, 3.0, 3.2**

Guided Practice

Use the table on page 66. Decide whether you need an estimate or an exact answer. Then solve.

1 How many oranges and mangoes were sold altogether?

Think: Is the question asking for an exact amount?

2 Did the students sell more than 700 fruits during the sale?

Think: Can you use an estimate to solve the problem?

Choose a Strategy

**Solve. Use the table on page 66 as needed.
Use these or other strategies.**

Problem-Solving Strategies

- **Work Backward**
- **Guess and Check**
- **Write an Equation**
- **Use Logical Thinking**

3 Students raised $193 by selling apples and $212 by selling pears. About how much money did students raise in the first two weeks of the sale?

4 A bag of McIntosh apples has 4 more apples than a bag of Empire apples. There are 18 apples altogether in both bags. How many apples are in the bag of McIntosh apples?

5 A mango was sold for 5¢ more than an orange and 5¢ less than a pear. Oranges were sold for 90¢ each. How much did a pear cost?

6 There are 103 students going on the trip. Each student spent 2 hours working at the fruit sale. How many hours did students work in all?

7 Ed, Tasha, Katie and Jerry each sold fruit during a different week. Tasha sold fruit before Ed but after Jerry. Katie sold mangoes. During which week did each student sell fruit?

8 The students raised $885 during the fruit sale. They had raised $217 for the trip before the sale. Now they need to raise only $105 more for the trip. About how much will the trip cost?

Extra Practice See 1–3 on page 95.

Subtract Across Zeros

You will learn how to subtract when some digits are zero.

Learn About It

Look at the fourth grade's read-a-thon poster. How many more books do the fourth-graders need to read to reach their goal?

700

Annual Read-a-thon

317 books read so far!

Subtract.   **700 − 317 =** ▪

Find 700 − 317.

Step 1 7 > 0, so you need to regroup. There are no tens to regroup. So regroup hundreds. Regroup 1 hundred as 10 tens.	**Step 2** Regroup 1 ten as 10 ones.	**Step 3** Subtract.
$$\begin{array}{r}\overset{6\ 10}{\cancel{7}\cancel{0}0}\\-3\,1\,7\\\hline\end{array}$$	$$\begin{array}{r}\overset{9}{\overset{6\ \cancel{10}10}{\cancel{7}\cancel{0}\cancel{0}}}\\-3\,1\,7\\\hline\end{array}$$	$$\begin{array}{r}\overset{9}{\overset{6\ \cancel{10}10}{\cancel{7}\cancel{0}\cancel{0}}}\\-3\,1\,7\\\hline 3\,8\,3\end{array}$$

Solution: The fourth graders need to read 383 more books.

Another Example

Find 78,000 − 16,566.

$$\begin{array}{r}\overset{\ \ \overset{9}{}\ \overset{9}{}}{\overset{7\ \cancel{10}\ \cancel{10}\ 10}{7\,8,\cancel{0}\,\cancel{0}\,\cancel{0}}}\\-1\,6,5\,6\,6\\\hline 6\,1,4\,3\,4\end{array}$$

Explain Your Thinking

▶ How can you check that an answer is reasonable?

▶ How can you check that an answer is correct?

Guided Practice

Subtract. Estimate to check that the answer is reasonable.

1.   802
  − 488
	2. 306
	  − 94
		3. 4,055
		  − 1,572
			4. 7,030
			  − 2,381

5. 500 − 156   **6.** 9,070 − 2,404   **7.** 67,046 − 22,315

Standards NS **2.1, 3.1**   MR **2.1**

Independent Practice

Subtract.

8. 306 − 159	**9.** 710 − 572	**10.** 900 − 748	**11.** 605 − 94	**12.** 7,038 − 3,251
13. 806 − 181	**14.** 304 − 234	**15.** 500 − 178	**16.** 350 − 98	**17.** 7,007 − 2,772
18. 2,004 − 1,413	**19.** 8,080 − 637	**20.** 7,000 − 5,294	**21.** 50,509 − 35,267	**22.** 29,000 − 17,007

23. 10,055 − 8,215   **24.** 66,000 − 44,120   **25.** 98,009 − 25,506

Problem Solving • Reasoning

26. This year the school's goal for the read-a-thon is 7,000 books. The students have read 5,690 books. How many more books do they need to read to reach the goal?

27. Compare Last year, the goal was 6,500 books. If 6,221 books were read, how many more books needed to be read for the school to reach its goal?

28. Analyze The school increases its goal by 500 books each year. What will the school's goal be in 5 years if its goal this year is 7,000 books?

29. Martha read 9 books more than Jim. Together they read 43 books. How many books did Jim read?

READING National Children's Book Week takes place the third week of November each year. Libraries often celebrate by holding reading and story writing contests.

National Children's Book Week was first held in 1919. How many times has it been celebrated so far?

Mixed Review • Test Prep

Write > or < for each ⬤. *(pages 6–7)*

30. 2,591 ⬤ 2,159   **31.** 58,439 ⬤ 54,839   **32.** 361,005 ⬤ 316,006

33 Which time is quarter past 2? *(page 49)*

A 1:45   **B** 2:45   **C** 2:15   **D** 2:30

LESSON 7

Problem-Solving Application: Use Operations

You will learn how to use addition and subtraction to solve problems.

Maine

After you understand a problem, you need to plan which operation to use.

Problem The United States has 88,633 miles of shoreline. Maine has 3,478 miles of shoreline! How many miles of shoreline in the United States are not in Maine?

Understand

What is the question?

How many miles of shoreline in the United States are not in Maine?

What do you know?

• The United States has 88,633 miles of shoreline.
• Maine has 3,478 miles of shoreline.

Plan

How can you find the answer?

Since you want to know how many of the miles of shoreline in the United States are not in Maine, you need to subtract.

Remember:
Add to find how many there are altogether.
Subtract to find a part of the total or to compare amounts.

Solve

Find 88,633 − 3,478.

$$\begin{array}{r} {\scriptstyle 12} \\ {\scriptstyle 5\ 2\ 13} \\ 88,6\cancel{3}\cancel{3} \\ -\ \ 3,4\ 7\ 8 \\ \hline 85,1\ 5\ 5 \end{array}$$

85,155 miles of shoreline in the United States are not in Maine.

Look Back

Look back at the solution.

Tell how you can use either estimation or addition to check your answer.

Standards MR **1.0, 1.1, 2.0, 2.1, 3.0, 3.2**

The shoreline along the Pacific coast includes the Marin Headlands in northern California.

Remember:
▶ Understand
▶ Plan
▶ Solve
▶ Look Back

Guided Practice

Solve. Use addition and subtraction to solve each problem.

1. There are 17,141 miles of shoreline along the Gulf coast. There are 40,298 miles of shoreline along the Pacific coast. What is the total number of miles along these coasts?

   Think: Do I need to find the total amount or part of the total amount?

2. Georgia has 2,344 miles of shoreline. The 15 states on the Atlantic coast have 28,673 miles of shoreline. How many miles of shoreline along the Atlantic coast are not in Georgia?

   Think: Do I need to find the total amount or part of the total amount?

Choose a Strategy

Solve. Use these or other strategies.

> **Problem-Solving Strategies**
>
> • Draw a Picture   • Write an Equation   • Solve a Simpler Problem   • Use Logical Thinking

3. There are 261,914 square miles of land and 5,363 square miles of water in the state of Texas. What is the total area of the state of Texas in square miles?

4. The highest recorded temperature in Hawaii was 100°F in 1931. The lowest recorded temperature was 12°F in 1979. What is the difference between the two temperatures?

5. Maine was part of Massachusetts until 1820 when Maine became the twenty-third state. In what year will Maine have been a state for 200 years?

6. The Mississippi River is 898 miles longer than the Colorado River. The Colorado River is 1,450 miles long. How long is the Mississippi River?

7. Rhode Island, the smallest state, became a state in 1790. Alaska, the largest state, became a state in 1959. How many years after Rhode Island did Alaska become a state?

8. The area of California is 158,869 square miles. This area includes both land and water. The land area is 155,973 square miles. What is the water area?

Quick ✓ Check

Check Your Understanding of Lessons 1–7

Add.

| 1. | 347
+ 569 | 2. | 4,208
+ 3,986 | 3. | 58,763
+ 3,409 |

Subtract.

| 4. | 735
− 369 | 5. | 5,602
− 3,745 | 6. | 70,236
− 9,537 |

Round each number to the nearest hundred. Then estimate.

7. 3,345 − 895

8. 6,672 + 3,215

Solve.

9. Tara's class is collecting bottles for recycling. During the first week the class collected 245 bottles. During the second week it collected 382 bottles. About how many bottles did the class collect?

10. There are 28,673 miles of shoreline along the Atlantic coast. There are 40,298 miles of shore line along the Pacific coast. How many more miles of shoreline are along the Pacific coast than the Atlantic coast?

How did you do?

If you had difficulty with any items in the Quick Check, you can use the following pages for review and extra practice.

California Standards	Items	Review These Pages	Do These Extra Practice Items
Number Sense: **1.3, 3.1**	1–3	pages 56–57	Set A and B, page 92
Number Sense: **3.1**	4–6	pages 60–62	Set C, page 92
Number Sense: **3.1**	7–8	pages 64–65	Set D, page 93
Number Sense: **1.4, 3.1** Math Reasoning: **1.1, 2.5**	9	pages 66–67	1–3, page 95
Number Sense: **3.1** Math Reasoning: **1.1, 2.6**	10	pages 70–71	4–7, page 95

Test Prep • Cumulative Review
Maintaining the Standards

Choose the letter of the correct answer.
If a correct answer is not here, choose NH.

1 Lincoln School held a fundraiser. Grade 4 sold 325 plants, and Grade 5 sold 390 plants. How many plants were sold in all?

A about 300   **C** about 700

B about 500   **D** about 900

Use the table to answer Questions 2–4.

Zoo Attendance	
Month	**Number of Visitors**
June	1,475
July	2,507
August	3,709

2 How many people visited the zoo from June through August?

F 7,591   **H** 7,691

G 7,592   **J** NH

3 How many more people visited the zoo in August than in June?

A 2,233   **C** 2,374

B 2,234   **D** NH

4 How many people visited the zoo in June and July?

F about 3,000

G about 4,000

H about 5,000

J about 6,000

---

5 What number should go in the box to make the number sentence true?

$$5{,}675 = 5{,}000 + \blacksquare + 70 + 5$$

A 6

B 60

C 600

D 6,000

---

6 Which number sentence is an example of the Associative Property of Addition?

F $(3 + 5) + 6 = 3 + (5 + 6)$

G $4 + 7 = 7 + 4$

H $7 - 7 = 7 - 7$

J $8 + 0 = 8 + 0$

---

7 Which of the following is equal to 10?

A $(15 - 3) + 2$ **C** $(15 - 2) + 3$

B $15 - (2 + 3)$ **D** $(15 + 2) - 3$

---

8 What is the rule?

Input	Output
125	75
350	300
575	525
700	650

Explain How did you find your answer?

Safe Site

Internet Test Prep
Visit **www.eduplace.com/kids/mhm**
for more *Test Prep Practice.*

73

Expressions and Equations

You will learn how to write and simplify expressions and how to write equations and inequalities.

Learn About It

Here are some examples of **expressions** in mathematics.

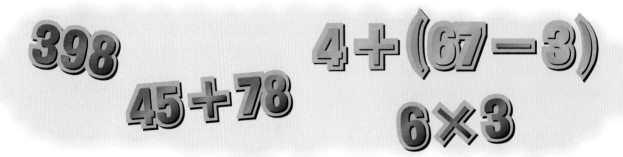

An expression may be just one number,
or it may consist of numbers and operation symbols.
Sometimes an expression contains parentheses.

When you simplify an expression, you do all of
the operations and write the result.

Simplify the expression (87 − 57) + (85 − 65) − 10.

- First, do the operations inside
  the parentheses.

- Then do the rest of the operations
  from left to right.

$$(87 - 57) + (85 - 65) - 10$$
$$30 \quad + \quad 20 \quad - \quad 10$$
$$50 \quad - \quad 10$$
$$40$$

Other Examples

A. Parentheses at End

$$15 + (27 - 7)$$
$$15 + 20$$
$$35$$

B. Add Inside Parentheses

$$30 + (150 + 140) - 20$$
$$30 + 290 - 20$$
$$30 + 270$$
$$300$$

Standards AF **1.0, 1.1, 1.2, 1.3**   MR **2.3**

Sometimes two different expressions
have the same value.

When you simplify **(10 + 20) − 5**, the result is **25**.

When you simplify **18 + (2 + 5)**, the result is **25**.

In this case, you can write an **equation**.

$$(10 + 20) − 5 = 18 + (2 + 5)$$

or

$$18 + (2 + 5) = (10 + 20) − 5$$

A number sentence that says two expressions have the same value is called an equation.

Sometimes simplifying two expressions
gives different results.

When you simplify **(2 + 13) + 30**, the result is **45**.

When you simplify **(10 + 4) − (3 + 1)**, the result is **10**.

In this case, you can write the two expressions with a
symbol (≠) that means "is not equal to" between them.

$$(2 + 13) + 30 \neq (10 + 4) − (3 + 1)$$

or

$$(10 + 4) − (3 + 1) \neq (2 + 13) + 30$$

You can also write an **inequality**.
Use the symbol (>) that means "is greater than" or the
symbol (<) that means "is less than" to write an inequality.

$$(2 + 13) + 30 > (10 + 4) − (3 + 1)$$

or

$$(10 + 4) − (3 + 1) < (2 + 13) + 30$$

A number sentence that says two expressions do not have the same value is called an inequality.

Explain Your Thinking

▶ Does 48 − (16 − 6) equal (48 − 16) − 6? Why or why not?

Guided Practice

Simplify each expression.

1. $(18 - 7) + 3$

2. $(83 - 3) + (14 + 6)$

3. $(19 - 6) + 32$

4. $(64 - 37) + (29 - 17)$

Ask Yourself

• Which operation should I do first?

Copy and complete by using = or ≠.

5. $(16 - 8) + 2$ ⬤ 10

6. $(18 + 5) - 1$ ⬤ $20 + 3$

7. $(7 - 3) + (8 - 2)$ ⬤ 18

Copy and complete by using >, <, or =.

8. 82 ⬤ $48 + (39 - 1)$

9. $16 - (3 + 8)$ ⬤ 42

10. $(50 + 15) + 1$ ⬤ 66

Independent Practice

Simplify each expression.

11. $(15 + 3) + (20 - 10)$

12. $(52 - 2) - 15$

13. $(25 + 75) + (6 + 9)$

14. $(48 - 2) + 18$

15. $(16 - 1) - (13 + 2)$

16. $(14 + 10) - (8 - 3)$

Copy and complete by using = or ≠.

17. $78 + (15 - 10)$ ⬤ $(15 - 10) + 78$

18. $38 + (24 + 9)$ ⬤ $38 - (24 + 9)$

19. $(23 - 10) + 7$ ⬤ $23 - (10 + 7)$

20. $(44 + 29) + 17$ ⬤ $44 - (29 - 17)$

Copy and complete by using >, <, or =.

21. $6 + (145 - 18)$ ⬤ $(145 - 18) + 6$

22. $(17 - 10) + 3$ ⬤ $(100 + 90) - 1$

23. $8 + (140 - 10)$ ⬤ $100 + 24$

24. $6 + (86 + 9)$ ⬤ $(6 + 86) + 9$

Write *true* or *false* for each number sentence.

25. $78 = 56 + (43 + 1)$

26. $65 < (50 + 10) + 5$

27. $68 - 1 \neq (67 + 1) - 1$

28. $85 > (80 + 10) - 5$

29. $13 + 13 < (25 + 1) + 0$

30. $16 - 1 \neq 14 + 1$

Copy and complete.

31. $24 = (20 + \underline{\hspace{1cm}}) - 6$

32. $15 + 1 = (10 - \underline{\hspace{1cm}}) + 7$

33. $(3 + \underline{\hspace{1cm}}) + (6 - 4) = 5 + 1$

34. $18 + \underline{\hspace{1cm}} = 56 - (20 + 10)$

Insert parentheses to make the equation true.

35. $87 - 25 + 5 = 56 + 1$

36. $65 - 3 + 2 = 70 - 10$

37. $18 = 16 - 13 + 15$

Problem Solving • Reasoning

38. Analyze Alyssa bought two books, one for $6 and the other for $8. She gave the cashier a $20 bill. Which expression shows the amount of change in dollars that Alyssa should receive?

a. $(20 - 6) + 8$ **b.** $20 - (6 + 8)$

39. Look back at Problem 38. Simplify the expression you chose to find how much change Alyssa should receive.

40. Write Your Own Write a word problem that can be solved by simplifying the expression $(18 - 2) + 6$.

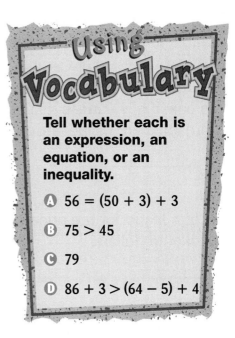

Using Vocabulary

Tell whether each is an expression, an equation, or an inequality.

A $56 = (50 + 3) + 3$

B $75 > 45$

C 79

D $86 + 3 > (64 - 5) + 4$

Mixed Review • Test Prep

**Round each number to the nearest hundred.
Estimate each sum or difference.** *(pages 10–11)*

41.
$\begin{array}{r} 548 \\ - 325 \\ \hline \end{array}$

42.
$\begin{array}{r} 674 \\ + 318 \\ \hline \end{array}$

43.
$\begin{array}{r} 563 \\ - 341 \\ \hline \end{array}$

44.
$\begin{array}{r} 5,280 \\ + 1,044 \\ \hline \end{array}$

45.
$\begin{array}{r} 6,535 \\ + 270 \\ \hline \end{array}$

Choose the letter of the correct answer. *(page 49)*

46 What time does the clock show?

A 2:10
B 2:50
C 3:10
D 3:50

47 What time does the clock show?

F quarter past 8
G quarter past 9
H quarter to 8
J quarter to 9

Extra Practice See Set F on page 94.

Write and Evaluate Algebraic Expressions

You will learn how to write and evaluate addition and subtraction expressions containing variables.

New Vocabulary
variable
algebraic expression

Learn About It

A child's ticket for the Wizard roller coaster is $2 less than an adult's ticket. You don't know the price of an adult's ticket, so you can use a variable to stand for the price.

A letter or a symbol used to stand for a number is called a **variable**. Expressions that contain variables are called **algebraic expressions**.

• Let n stand for the price of an adult's ticket in dollars.

• Then the expression $n - 2$ can stand for the price of a child's ticket in dollars.

How much is a child's ticket for the Wizard if an adult's ticket costs $3?

To find the cost of a child's ticket, you can evaluate the expression $n - 2$ when $n = 3$.

$3 - 2 = 1$

Solution: If an adult's ticket costs $3, a child's ticket costs $1.

Standards AF 1.0, 1.1

Write an expression that shows the price of an adult's ticket if it is $3 more than a child's ticket.

- Let s stand for the price of a child's ticket.
- Then the price of an adult's ticket is $s + 3$.

How much is an adult's ticket if a child's ticket is $2?

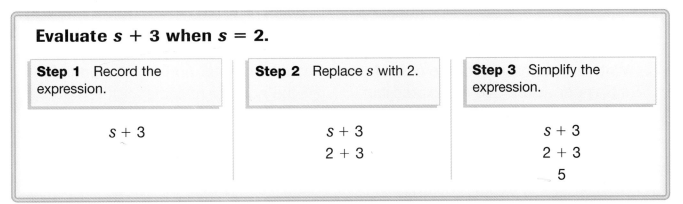

Evaluate $s + 3$ when $s = 2$.

Step 1 Record the expression.	**Step 2** Replace s with 2.	**Step 3** Simplify the expression.
$s + 3$	$s + 3$ $2 + 3$	$s + 3$ $2 + 3$ 5

Solution: An adult's ticket is $5 if a child's ticket is $2.

Explain Your Thinking

▶ Look at the above problem. How can you find the price of a child's ticket if the price of an adult's ticket is $4?

Guided Practice

Name the variable in each algebraic expression.

1. $w + 2$ **2.** $p - 3$ **3.** $4 + z$

Evaluate each expression when $x = 8$.

4. $x + 9$ **5.** $x - 2$ **6.** $x + x + 6$

> ### Ask Yourself
> - What is the value of the variable?
> - Do I add or subtract to evaluate the expression?

Independent Practice

Evaluate each expression when $n = 7$.

7. $n + 3$ **8.** $n - 2$ **9.** $n + 10$ **10.** $15 + n$

11. $16 - n$ **12.** $62 - n$ **13.** $(n + n) - 1$ **14.** $n + (n + 2)$

Evaluate each expression when $p = 5$.

15. $p + 3$ **16.** $p - 4$ **17.** $56 + p$ **18.** $19 - p$

19. $8 - p$ **20.** $p + 12 + p$ **21.** $(p + 15) + 4$ **22.** $(15 - p) + 14$

Problem Solving • Reasoning

Solve. Choose a method.

Computation Methods

• **Mental Math**   • **Estimation**   • **Paper and Pencil**

23. A ticket for the Spinner costs $1 more than a ticket for the Maze. Write an expression for the cost of a Spinner ticket. Use the expression to find the cost of a Spinner ticket if a Maze ticket is $3.

24. **Compare** Suppose n stands for the number of seats on the Wizard roller coaster and $n - 6$ stands for the number of seats on the Maze roller coaster. Which roller coaster holds more people?

25. **Measurement** The park is open from 11 A.M. to 10 P.M. each day of the weekend. How many hours is it open on the weekend?

26. On Saturday, 572 children and 324 adults rode the Wizard roller coaster. About how many people rode the Wizard on Saturday?

Mixed Review • Test Prep

Find the value of each group of coins. *(pages 30–33)*

27. 2 quarters, 1 dime

28. 1 quarter, 3 nickels

29. 4 dimes, 9 pennies

Choose the letter of the correct answer. *(pages 30–33)*

30 Which is worth more than 3 dimes, 2 nickels, and 4 pennies?

   A $0.36   **C** $0.44

   B $0.39   **D** $0.49

31 Which amount shows four thousand, three hundred three dollars?

   F $433   **H** $4,303

   G $4,033   **J** $4,330

Logical Thinking

Suppose p is greater than 0. Tell whether the expression will have a value greater than, less than, or equal to p.

1. $p + 10$ **2.** $p + p$ **3.** $p - 0$ **4.** $(2 \times p) - p$

Extra Practice See Set G on page 94.

Show What You Know

Changing the Order

Use the Commutative Property to match expressions.

1. $x + 5$
2. $3 + (x - 5)$
3. $(x - 3) + 5$
4. $3 + x$

    a. $x + 3$
    b. $5 + x$
    c. $(x - 5) + 3$
    d. $5 + (x - 3)$

Using Vocabulary

Match each statement with the correct algebraic expression.

1. When n is 6, the value of this expression is 8.
2. When n is 6, the value of this expression is 2.
3. When n is 2, the value of this expression is 6.
4. When n is 8, the value of this expression is 6.

    a. $n - 4$
    b. $n + 2$
    c. $n - 2$
    d. $n + 4$

Always, Sometimes, or Never?

Use *always*, *sometimes*, or *never* to answer each question.

1. Choose a number for n. When does the value of $n + 0$ equal the value of $0 + n$?

2. Choose a number for x. When does the value of $x + 1$ equal the value of $x - 1$?

3. Choose a number for r. When does the value of $r + 5$ equal the value of $5 + r$?

4. Choose a number for z. When does the value of z equal the value of $2z$?

Write and Solve Equations

You will learn how to write and solve algebraic equations.

Learn About It

There are 4 more strings on a large puppet than on a small puppet. A large puppet has 7 strings. You can write two different expressions to show the number of strings on a large puppet.

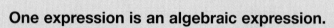

One expression is an algebraic expression.

- Let *p* stand for the number of strings on a small puppet.
- Then **p + 4** is the number of strings on a large puppet.

The other expression is the actual number.

7 is the number of strings on a large puppet.

You can use the two expressions to write an equation.

$$p + 4 = 7$$

How many strings are on a small puppet?
Solve the equation $p + 4 = 7$.

To find the number of strings on a small puppet, you need to find the value of *p*. When you find the value of a variable that makes an equation true, you solve the equation.

Different Ways to Solve an Equation

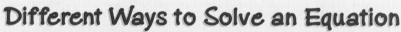

You can use a number sentence.

$p + 4 = 7$

Think: $3 + 4 = 7$.
So *p* must be 3.

$p = 3$

You can find a missing number.

$p + 4 = 7$

Think: $p = 7 - 4$.
So *p* must be 3.

$p = 3$

Check the solution.

$p + 4 = 7$
$3 + 4 = 7$
$7 = 7$

Both sides of the equals sign are the same, so the solution is correct.

Solution: There are 3 strings on a small puppet.

Standards AF **1.0, 1.1, 1.5** SDP **1.3** MR **1.1, 2.4**

Explain Your Thinking

▶ What does "solve the equation" mean?

Guided Practice

Match each equation with its solution.

1. $n + 6 = 10$
2. $9 = n - 3$
3. $8 + n = 14$

   a. $n = 12$
   b. $n = 6$
   c. $n = 4$

> **Ask Yourself**
> - Can I add to solve the equation?
> - Can I subtract to solve the equation?

Independent Practice

Solve each equation. Check the solution.

4. $m + 10 = 35$
5. $r + 7 = 43$
6. $5 = k - 5$
7. $c - 10 = 10$

8. $n + 7 = 19$
9. $15 = k + 8$
10. $m + m = 8$
11. $x + (x + 4) = 18$

Problem Solving • Reasoning

Use Data Use the graph for Problems 12 and 13.

12. **Estimate** About how many people saw puppet shows at the spring festival?

13. About how many more people went to see *Magic Land* than went to see *Mystery Island*?

14. **Analyze** There are 5 more puppets in *The Funny Forest* than are in *The Happy Sea*. There are 12 puppets in *The Funny Forest*. Write and solve an equation to find the number of puppets in *The Happy Sea*.

Mixed Review • Test Prep

Add or subtract. *(pages 56–63; 68–69)*

15. $8{,}943 - 416$
16. $5{,}106 + 3{,}719$
17. $10{,}355 - 4{,}092$
18. $36{,}274 + 16{,}372$

19. Estimate the sum by rounding to the nearest dollar: $\$18.85 + \$4.89$. *(pages 64–65)*

   A $25
   B $24
   C $23
   D $22

Solving Addition Equations

You will learn that equals added to equals are equal.

Learn About It

See what happens when you add the same number to each side of an equation.

Step 1 Solve this equation.

$x + 6 = 15$

Think: $9 + 6 = 15$.
So $x = 9$.

Step 2 Add 4 to each side of the original equation. Then solve the new equation.

$x + 6 + 4 = 15 + 4$

$x + 10 \quad = \quad 19$

Think: $9 + 10 = 19$.
So $x = 9$.

• What do you notice about the solution to both equations?

Step 3 Choose any number. Then add the number to each side of the original equation $x + 6 = 15$.

• What do you notice about the solutions to all of the equations?

See what happens when you subtract the same number from each side of an equation.

Step 1 Solve the equation.

$x + 7 = 19$

Think: $12 + 7 = 19$.
So $x = 12$.

Step 2 Subtract 4 from each side of the original equation. Then solve the new equation.

$x + 7 - 4 = 19 - 4$

$x + 3 \quad = \quad 15$

Think: $12 + 3 = 15$.
So $x = 12$.

• What do you notice about the solution to both equations?

Step 3 Choose any number less than or equal to 7. Then subtract the number from each side of the original equation $x + 7 = 19$.

• What do you notice about the solutions to all of the equations?

Standards AF **1.0**, 1.1, **2.0**, 2.1 MR **2.3**

Try It Out

1. Solve the equation $x + 8 = 15$.

   Copy and complete the tables below.

Start with $x + 8 = 15$.

	Add this number to each side of the equation.	Write the new equation.	Solve the new equation.	Is the solution the same as the solution for $x + 8 = 15$?
2.	4	$x + 8 + 4 = 15 + 4$ $x + 12 \ = \ 19$	$x = 7$	
3.	5			
4.	8			

Start with $x + 8 = 15$.

	Subtract this number from each side of the equation.	Write the new equation.	Solve the new equation.	Is the solution the same as the solution for $x + 8 = 15$?
5.	7	$x + 8 - 7 = 15 - 7$ $x + 1 \ = \ 8$	$x = 7$	
6.	3			
7.	8			

8. Begin with the equation $x + 4 = 12$. What number could you subtract from both sides of the equation to get the new equation $x + 0 = 8$?

Write about it! Talk about it!

Use what you have learned to answer these questions.

9. What happens to the solution to an equation when you add the same number to each side of the equation?

10. What happens to the solution of an equation when you subtract the same number from each side?

11. What is a quick way to solve the equation $x + 12 = 25$?

Equations with Two Variables

You will learn about how equations with two variables relate to function tables.

New Vocabulary
two-variable equation

Learn About It

Adam is 3 years younger than Ben. If Ben is 10 years old, how old is Adam?

Remember that an equation is a statement that shows that two expressions are equal.

My age is 10

My age is Z

You can use two expressions to write a two-variable equation for Adam's age.

Let n stand for Ben's age in years.	Then $n - 3$ is an expression for Adam's age in years.
Let z stand for Adam's age in years.	Then z is an expression for Adam's age in years.
Use the two expressions to write an equation.	$n - 3 = z$

You know the value of n, so you can substitute to find the value of z.

Substitute 10 for n in the equation.	$n - 3 = z$
	$10 - 3 = z$
Adam's age $\longrightarrow$	$7 = z$

Solution: If Ben is 10 years old, then Adam is 7 years old.

A function table is a table of ordered pairs that follow a rule. The rule tells you how to find the value of one variable if you know the value of the other one.

Rule: $n - 3 = z$

n	z
9	6
10	7
11	8

Explain Your Thinking

▶ Look at this equation: $y = x + 10$. Suppose you know that the value of y is 15. How can you find the value of x?

Standards AF **1.0, 1.1, 1.5** MR **2.3**

Guided Practice

Find the values of the variables and complete.

Ask Yourself
- Which value do I know?
- Which value do I need to find?

1. $y = x - 3$

x	y
6	▨
9	▨

Think: $6 = y + 3$
$9 = y + 3$

2. $m - 2 = n$

m	n
▨	7
▨	12

Think: $m - 2 = 7$
$m - 2 = 12$

3. $m = w - 13$

w	m
18	▨
▨	20

Think: $m + 13 = 18$
$20 + 13 = w$

Independent Practice

Copy and complete each function table or the rule.

4. $b = a + 4$

a	b
6	▨
3	▨
2	▨

5. $y = x - 5$

x	y
5	▨
6	▨
▨	10

6. $m = 7 + n$

n	m
6	▨
3	▨
▨	10

7. ▨

x	y
10	5
16	11
13	8

8. ▨

p	q
3	5
5	7
10	12

Problem Solving • Reasoning

9. Sean's mother is 3 years older than his father. His mother is 39 years old. How old is Sean's father?

10. Analyze Mia is 8 years older than Sue Ellen. Let x stand for Sue Ellen's age. Let y stand for Mia's age. Write an equation using x and y that shows this relationship. Then use the equation to find Mia's age when Sue Ellen is 12.

11. Write Your Own Write a two-variable equation in which the value of x is less than the value of y.

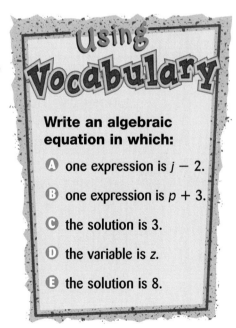

Using Vocabulary

Write an algebraic equation in which:

Ⓐ one expression is $j - 2$.

Ⓑ one expression is $p + 3$.

Ⓒ the solution is 3.

Ⓓ the variable is z.

Ⓔ the solution is 8.

Mixed Review • Test Prep

Add or subtract. *(pages 56–57, 60–61)*

12. $3,416 + 255$

13. $56,290 - 3,211$

14. $10,004 + 8,203$

⑮ Solve the equation $n + 8 = 24$. *(pages 82–83)*

A 32 **B** 16 **C** 6 **D** 3

Extra Practice See Set I on page 94.

Problem-Solving Strategy: Guess and Check

You will learn how to solve problems by using the Guess and Check strategy.

Sometimes a good way to solve a problem is to guess and check.

Problem A nature photographer took some pictures of puffins and otters. She told a friend that she photographed 43 animals with 102 legs. How many puffins and otters did she photograph?

What is the question?

How many puffins and otters did she photograph?

What do you know?

• The 43 animals have 102 legs.

• Puffins have 2 legs and otters have 4 legs.

How can you solve the problem?

Guess two numbers. Check to see if they are correct. If not, continue until you find numbers that work.

Solve

1st Guess:	2nd Guess:	3rd Guess:
40 puffins → 80 legs	30 puffins → 60 legs	35 puffins → 70 legs
3 otters → 12 legs	13 otters → 52 legs	8 otters → 32 legs
Check: **92 legs**	Check: **112 legs**	Check: **102 legs**
Too few. Guess again.	Too many. Guess again.	This is the answer.

She photographed 35 puffins and 8 otters.

Look back at the problem.

How do you decide when to use Guess and Check to solve a problem?

Standards MR **1.0, 1.2, 2.0, 2.6, 3.0, 3.1, 3.2**

Guided Practice

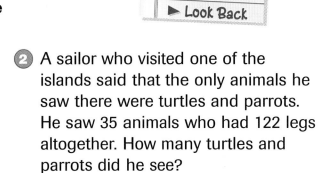

Use the Guess and Check strategy to solve each problem.

1 The tour boat that travels along the three islands collected $250 in fares. The captain had 24 bills in all. He had only $20 bills and $10 bills. How many of each kind of bill did the captain have?

Think: What numbers would be a reasonable first guess?

2 A sailor who visited one of the islands said that the only animals he saw there were turtles and parrots. He saw 35 animals who had 122 legs altogether. How many turtles and parrots did he see?

Think: What should the sum of the two numbers be?

Choose a Strategy

Solve. Use these or other strategies.

Problem-Solving Strategies

• Make a Table   • Write an Equation   • Guess and Check   • Use Logical Thinking

3 Tim and Jared collect cards of rare birds. Tim has 8 more cards than Jared has. Together they have 104 cards. How many cards does Tim have?

4 Tina's pet parakeet cost $4 more than Cory's pet canary. If Tina's pet parakeet cost $18, how much did Cory's pet canary cost?

5 The sailor said that only lizards and peacocks live on another island. There are 66 animals with 220 legs on that island. How many are peacocks?

6 Mike has saved $43 to buy binoculars. The 13 bills he has are $1 bills, $5 bills, and $10 bills. How many of each kind of bill does he have?

7 The average life span of the great horned owl is 12 years longer than the average life span of the elf owl. If the average life span of the great horned owl is 17 years, what is the average life span of the elf owl? Explain your reasoning.

8 Lee, Ned, Joe, and Kim each saw one of these 4 different birds: a cardinal, a duck, a hawk, and an owl. Joe did not see a cardinal or a duck. Kim did not see a duck or an owl. Ned did not see an owl, a hawk, or a duck. Which bird did each person see?

Quick ✓ Check

Check Your Understanding of Lessons 8–13

Evaluate each expression when $n = 8$.

1. $(n + 13) + 6$ **2.** $n + 32 + n$ **3.** $n + (n - 4)$

Solve each equation. Check the solution.

4. $m + 6 = 24$ **5.** $x + (x + 7) = 25$ **6.** $p - 25 = 15$

Write the rule for each function table.

7.

x	y
3	7
9	13
15	19

8.

r	s
16	7
28	19
20	11

Solve.

9. Michael sells birdhouses for $4 more than bird feeders. A birdhouse and a bird feeder can be purchased for $20. How much does each item cost?

10. Michael sold 17 birdhouses. He sold five more birdhouses in April than he did in March. How many birdhouses did he sell each month?

How did you do?

If you had difficulty with any items in the Quick Check, you can use the following pages for review and extra practice.

California Standards	Items	Review These Pages	Do These Extra Practice Items
Algebra: **1.1, 1.2**	1–3	pages 78–80	Set G, page 94
Number Sense: **1.1, 1.2**	4–6	pages 82–83	Set H, page 94
Number Sense: **1.1, 1.2 1.5**	7–8	pages 86–87	Set I, page 94
Math Reasoning: **1.1, 2.2, 3.1, 3.3**	9–10	pages 88–89	8–9, page 95

Test Prep • Cumulative Review

Maintaining the Standards

Choose the letter of the correct answer. If a correct answer is not here, choose NH.

1 What number should go in the box to make the number sentence true?

$$12,908 = 12,000 + 900 + \blacksquare$$

A 8   C 800

B 80   D 8,000

---

2 Which expression is not equivalent to $(28 - 10) - 8$?

F $18 - 8$

G $28 - (10 - 8)$

H $(28 - 8) - 10$

J $28 - 10 - 8$

---

3 To which equation does the table correspond?

x	y
1	3
2	4
3	5
4	6

A $y = x + 2$

B $y = x + 4$

C $y = x - 2$

D $y = x + 3$

---

4 What is the value of n?

$$(2 + 9) - (6 + 3) = n$$

F 0   H 2

G 1   J 3

Use the table to answer Questions 5–6.

Road Mileage Between Cities	
Los Angeles to	**Number of Miles**
Boston	2,979
Chicago	2,054
Dallas	1,387
Detroit	2,311

5 How much farther is it from Los Angeles to Boston than it is from Los Angeles to Chicago?

A 25 miles   C 935 miles

B 924 miles   D NH

---

6 Mr. Richman traveled from Los Angeles to Detroit and then back to Los Angeles. How many miles did he travel in all?

F 2,311

G 4,611

H 4,622

J NH

---

7 What number should go in the box to make the number sentence true?

Explain How did you find your answer?

$$(3 + 5) + 2 = 8 + \blacksquare$$

Safe Site

Internet Test Prep
Visit **www.eduplace.com/kids/mhm**
for more *Test Prep Practice.*

91

Extra Practice

Set A (Lesson 1, pages 54–55)

Find each sum.

1. 0 + 834
2. (4 + 4) + 10
3. 35 + 23
4. 42 + 34
5. 45 + (6 + 4)
6. 62 + 36
7. 36 + 62
8. 356 + (0 + 10)

Copy and complete each number sentence. Tell which property of addition you used.

9. 27 + 88 = ■ + 27
10. 467 + 0 = ■
11. (11 + 7) + 6 = 11 + (■ + 6)

Group the addends so that you can add mentally. Then find each sum.

12. 127 + 491 + 9
13. 693 + 283 + 7
14. 80 + 20 + 39

Set B (Lesson 2, pages 56–58)

Add.

1. 373
    + 421

2. 294
    + 74

3. 7,486
    +   74

4. 2,447
    + 5,598

5. 13,684
    + 6,467

6. 567 + 348
7. 2,974 + 340
8. 7,236 + 6,482
9. 67,482 + 3,489
10. 13,953 + 44,031
11. 32,287 + 21,243

Set C (Lesson 3, pages 60–62)

Subtract. Use addition to check that your answer is correct.

1. 875
    − 723

2. 768
    − 485

3. 435
    − 87

4. 9,488
    − 6,048

5. 4,297
    − 2,745

6. 5,427
    − 2,798

7. 7,675
    − 592

8. 88,596
    − 57,382

9. 54,386
    − 37,579

10. 64,738
    − 7,304

11. 464 − 182
12. 587 − 494
13. 1,265 − 838
14. 7,733 − 4,058
15. 69,472 − 25,187
16. 65,938 − 7,820

Extra Practice

Set D (Lesson 4, pages 64–65)

Round each number or amount to the nearest hundred or the nearest dollar. Then estimate the sum or difference.

1. 285 + 219   **2.** $8.79 − $2.88   **3.** 876 − 433   **4.** 497 + 231

5. 6,418 − 307   **6.** 72,663 + 1,194   **7.** 83,462 + 2,076   **8.** 7,722 − 581

9. 5,325 + 631   **10.** 54,823 − 3,898   **11.** 27,215 − 5,085   **12.** 4,138 + 387

Is each answer correct? Write *yes* or *no*.
Use estimation to help you decide.

13.	**14.**	**15.**	**16.**	**17.**
77	521	8,852	$4.47	$4.17
+ 21	− 382	+ 107	− 0.66	+ 7.20
16	139	8,959	$4.53	$11.37

18.	**19.**	**20.**	**21.**	**22.**
$7.26	841	$8.40	71	4,561
− 0.69	− 457	+ 3.15	+ 58	+ 203
$6.57	184	$11.55	129	4,358

Set E (Lesson 6, pages 68–69)

Subtract. Estimate to check that the answer is reasonable.

1.	**2.**	**3.**	**4.**	**5.**
508	610	800	807	6,046
− 269	− 434	− 643	− 93	− 2,383

6.	**7.**	**8.**	**9.**	**10.**
4,008	9,070	9,000	70,608	39,000
− 1,527	− 528	− 4,393	−47,377	− 16,004

11.	**12.**	**13.**	**14.**	**15.**
7,090	8,002	64,009	50,038	81,070
− 4,562	− 3,497	− 35,857	− 19,754	− 38,123

16. 600 − 460   **17.** 6,300 − 643   **18.** 5,004 − 4,702

19. 20,076 − 7,332   **20.** 44,000 − 22,350   **21.** 87,005 − 34,602

22. 30,702 − 6,488   **23.** 15,900 − 10,172   **24.** 78,060 − 23,587

Extra Practice

Set F (Lesson 8, pages 74–77)

Simplify each expression.

1. $(16 + 3) + (30 - 20)$ **2.** $(19 - 6) - 9$ **3.** $(45 + 55) + (7 + 8)$

Copy and complete by using = or ≠.

4. $67 + (17 - 11)$ ⬤ $(17 - 11) + 67$ **5.** $(39 + 7) + 23$ ⬤ $(39 - 7) + 23$

Copy and complete by using >, <, or =.

6. $(19 - 10) + 4$ ⬤ $(100 + 40) - 2$ **7.** $6 + (150 - 30)$ ⬤ $100 + 14$

Set G (Lesson 9, pages 78–81)

Evaluate each expression when $n = 6$.

1. $n + 5$ **2.** $n - 3$ **3.** $n + 12$ **4.** $12 + n$

5. $18 - n$ **6.** $78 - n$ **7.** $(n + n) - 4$ **8.** $n + (n + 5)$

Evaluate each expression when $p = 8$.

9. $p + 5$ **10.** $p - 3$ **11.** $67 + p$ **12.** $17 - p$

13. $9 - p$ **14.** $p + 17 + p$ **15.** $(p + 12) + 6$ **16.** $(18 - p) + 11$

Set H (Lesson 10, pages 82–83)

Solve each equation. Check the solution.

1. $m + 15 = 65$ **2.** $r + 8 = 35$ **3.** $6 = k - 6$ **4.** $c - 20 = 20$

5. $n + 6 = 15$ **6.** $17 = k + 10$ **7.** $m + 3 = 10$ **8.** $x + 9 = 15$

Set I (Lesson 12, pages 86–87)

Copy and complete each function table or write the rule.

1. Rule: $b = a + 6$

a	b
7	▧
4	▧
1	▧

2. Rule: $y = x - 4$

x	y
8	▧
9	▧
10	▧

3. Rule: _____

n	m
4	8
6	10
10	14

Extra Practice • Problem Solving

Use the table. Decide whether you need an estimate or an exact answer. Then solve. *(Lesson 5, pages 66–67)*

Sneakers and Stuff is having a sale. The table shows how many pairs of sneakers have been sold each day of the sale.

1 The storeowner gives her salespeople a bonus each day more than 200 pairs of sneakers are sold. How many times did the salespeople get bonuses?

2 For each pair of sneakers purchased, a discount coupon was given. How many coupons were given out on the last two days of the sale?

3 During the first two days, were more than 300 pairs of sneakers sold?

Sneaker Sale	
Day	**Pairs Sold**
Monday	134
Tuesday	221
Wednesday	243
Thursday	137
Friday	198

Solve. Use addition or subtraction to solve each problem. *(Lesson 7, pages 70–71)*

4 Virginia has 3,315 miles of shoreline. All 15 states on the Atlantic coast make up 28,673 miles of shoreline. How many miles of shoreline along the Atlantic coast are not in Virginia?

5 There are 28,673 miles of shoreline along the Atlantic coast. There are 40,298 miles of shoreline along the Pacific coast. How many miles of shoreline are along the Atlantic and Pacific coastlines?

6 The Gulf coast has 17,141 miles of shoreline and the Arctic coast has 2,521 miles of shoreline. How many miles of shoreline are there altogether?

7 Alaska has 31,383 miles of shoreline. The Pacific coast has 40,298 miles of shoreline. How many miles of the Pacific coast shoreline are not in Alaska?

Solve these problems, using the Guess and Check strategy. *(Lesson 13, pages 88–89)*

8 Karen sold 19 of her tropical fish. She sold three more fish to Fish Pond than she did to Something's Fishy. How many fish did she sell to Fish Pond?

9 A football team buys T-shirts and sweatshirts. A sweatshirt costs $8 more than a T-shirt. Together they cost $40. How much does a sweatshirt cost?

Chapter Review

Reviewing Vocabulary

Answer each question.

1. Does the statement $(457 + 8) + 50 = 50 + (457 + 8)$ make use of the Commutative Property or the Associative Property?

2. Is $4 + (67 - 3)$ an expression or an equation?

3. Is $n + 3 = 12$ an expression or an equation?

4. Which is the variable in the algebraic expression $n + 3$?

Reviewing Concepts and Skills

Complete each number sentence. Tell which property of addition you used. *(pages 54–55)*

5. $23 + 76 = \blacksquare + 23$ 6. $586 + 0 = \blacksquare$ 7. $(12 + 9) + 7 = 12 + (\blacksquare + 7)$

Add. *(pages 56–59)*

8. $\begin{array}{r} 639 \\ + 257 \\ \hline \end{array}$ 9. $\begin{array}{r} 7{,}537 \\ + 2{,}026 \\ \hline \end{array}$ 10. $\begin{array}{r} 27{,}637 \\ + \quad 183 \\ \hline \end{array}$ 11. $\begin{array}{r} 35{,}347 \\ + 54{,}530 \\ \hline \end{array}$

Round each number to the nearest hundred. Then estimate the sum or difference. *(pages 64–65)*

12. $396 + 408$ 13. $759 - 278$ 14. $8{,}312 - 406$ 15. $83{,}772 + 2{,}287$

Subtract. Use addition to check that your answer is correct. *(pages 60–63, 68–69)*

16. $577 - 393$ 17. $7{,}006 - 3{,}903$ 18. $7{,}080 - 649$ 19. $9{,}867 - 782$

Simplify each expression. *(pages 74–77)*

20. $(12 + 8) + (40 - 20)$ 21. $(14 + 11) - (9 - 3)$ 22. $(47 - 3) + 12$

23. Complete using = or ≠. $56 + (13 + 9) \bullet 56 - (13 + 9)$

24. Complete using >, <, or =. $(24 - 15) + 5 \bullet (40 + 20) - 12$

Evaluate each expression when $n = 7$. (pages 78–81)

25. $n + 9$ **26.** $n - 2$ **27.** $76 + n$ **28.** $5 + (19 - n)$

Copy and complete each function table or write the rule. (pages 86–87)

29. Rule: Add 50

Input	Output
420	■
■	620
2,042	■

30. Rule: ■

Input	Output
50	75
190	215
298	323

Solve each equation. Check the solution. (pages 82–83, 86–87)

31. $r + 20 = 35$ **32.** $19 = k + 12$ **33.** $8 = m - 8$ **34.** $b + 2 + 4 = 18$

Solve each problem. (pages 66–67, 70–71, 88–89)

35. At a department store, a hat and a pin are $22. The hat costs $12 less than the pin. How much does the hat cost at the department store? How much does the pin cost?

36. The school library and the town library together have a total of 55,608 books. There are 42,897 books in the town library. How many books are in the school library?

Brain Teasers Math Reasoning

MISSING DIGITS

Choose digits from 4 to 9 to fill in the boxes. Do not use any digit twice.

```
  1 ■ 3        1,■5■
+ ■ 2 ■      +  4 ■ 6
-------      --------
  8 1 2        2,0 0 3
```

SUM AND DIFFERENCE

When you add two numbers, the sum is 148. When you subtract them, the difference is 20. What are the numbers?

Safe Site

Internet Brain Teasers
Visit **www.eduplace.com/kids/mhm**
for more *Brain Teasers*.

Chapter Test

Complete each number sentence. Tell which property of addition you used.

1. 41 + 53 = ▓ + 41   **2.** 595 + 0 = ▓   **3.** (14 + 7) + 3 = 14 + (▓ + 3)

Add or subtract. You can estimate to check that your answer is reasonable.

4. 668 − 492	**5.** 8,759 + 683	**6.** 700 − 320	**7.** 4,008 + 1,802	**8.** 50,609 − 27,584

Round each number to the nearest hundred. Then estimate the sum or difference.

9. 698 + 212   **10.** 859 − 347   **11.** 9,215 − 507   **12.** 7,647 + 6,572

13. 7,438 + 6,257   **14.** 5583 + 4298   **15.** 785 − 640   **16.** 4,682 + 3,749

Simplify each expression.

17. (14 + 6) + (50 − 10)   **18.** (42 − 2) + (56 + 4)   **19.** (12 + 14) − (8 − 1)

20. Complete, using = or ≠.   49 + (19 − 3) ● (19 − 3) + 49

21. Complete, using >, <, or =.   (35 − 15) + 12 ● (40 − 10) + 8

Evaluate each expression when $n = 9$.

22. $n + 9$ **23.** $n + (14 − 9)$ **24.** $4 + (20 − n)$

25. $n − 4$ **26.** $n − (8 + 0)$ **27.** $5 + (10 − n)$ **28.** $7 − (n − 3)$

Complete each function table.

29. Rule: $b = a + 8$

a	b
4	▓
5	▓
7	▓

30. Rule: $p = q + 6$

p	q
▓	8
▓	7
▓	10

Solve.

31. There were 128 dogs and 63 cats in the animal shelter. Twenty-five more cats were brought in today. The shelter has room for 300 animals. Is there room for the 25 cats?

32. Jim bought a pair of jeans and a pair of shorts. The jeans cost $8 more than the shorts. Together the jeans and the shorts cost $42. How much did the jeans cost?

33. A video store tracked how many videotapes were rented during a five-day week. How many fewer videotapes were rented on the day of fewest rentals than on the day of greatest rentals?

Video Rentals

Day	Number Rented
Monday	134
Tuesday	221
Wednesday	243
Thursday	137
Friday	198

 Write About It

Solve each problem. Use correct mathematical vocabulary to explain your thinking.

1. The students at Watson Elementary School wanted to collect 1,000 soda cans for the local fire department's fundraising drive. The table shows how many cans have been collected.

a. Michael wrote a short report telling why he thinks the students met their goal. Do you agree with Michael's work as shown? Explain.

b. Is the number of cans collected on Monday and Wednesday greater or less than the number of cans collected on Tuesday, Thursday, and Friday?

2. Susan completed this subtraction problem.

a. Explain what she did wrong.

b. Show how to find the correct answer.

Fundraising Drive

Day	Cans Collected
Monday	189
Tuesday	98
Wednesday	279
Thursday	192
Friday	189

I rounded the number of cans collected each day to the nearest hundred and then added 200 + 100 + 300 + 200 + 200 = 1,000 So the children made their goal.

$$\begin{array}{r} 9{,}372 \\ -\ 3{,}291 \\ \hline 6{,}121 \end{array}$$

Another Look

Use the map to solve the problems. You can use what you know about addition, subtraction, and equations.

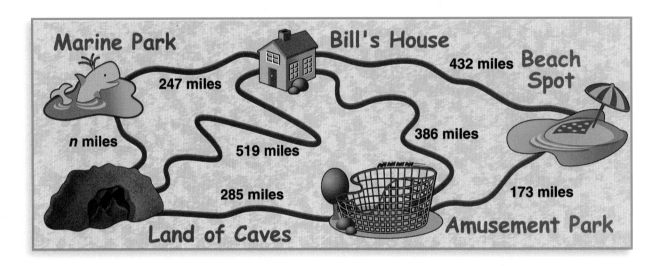

1. How many miles is it from Bill's house to each vacation spot and back?

2. The total distance from Bill's house to Marine Park and then to the Land of Caves is 501 miles. Write and solve an equation to find the distance from Marine Park to the Land of Caves.

3. **Look Back** What ways could you use to check that your answers to Problem 1 are correct?

4. **Analyze** Bill wants to visit two places this summer before returning home. Which two places could he visit and travel the shortest possible distance?

| Standards | NS **3.0** | MR **1.0, 2.0** |

Enrichment

Venn Diagrams

Venn diagrams are used to show how two or more groups are related.

The fourth-graders in Ms. Kelliher's class did writing or art projects for social studies. Each student did at least one project.

The first Venn diagram shows students who did writing projects. Some wrote a story, some wrote a poem, and some wrote both.

These students only wrote a story.

These students wrote a story *and* a poem.

These students only wrote a poem.

Use the first Venn diagram to answer these questions.

1. Which students wrote both a story and a poem?

2. Which students wrote a poem?

Use the second Venn diagram to answer these questions.

3. How many students made a diorama?

4. How many students made a flip book?

5. How many students did all three projects?

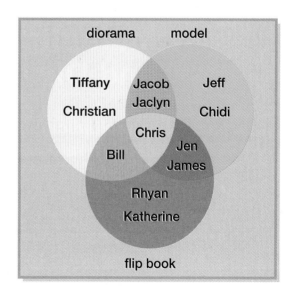

Make a Venn diagram.

6. Use this information.

Chess Club Members		Math Club Members		Science Club Members	
Emily	Alex	Andrew	Liz	Andrew	Liz
Andrew	Eric	Alex	Matt	Emily	Katy

Standards SDP **1.0, 1.1**   MR **3.2**

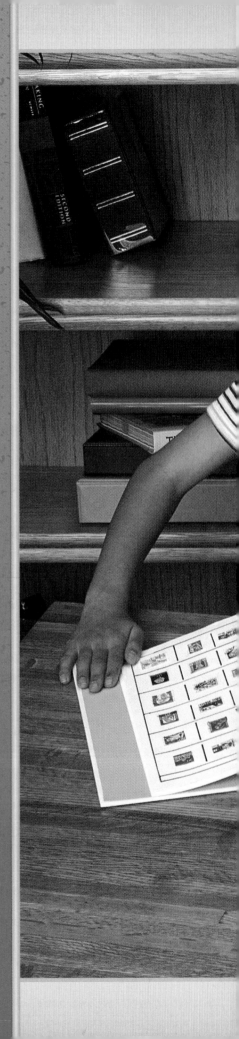

CHAPTER 3

Relating Multiplication and Division

Why Learn About Relating Multiplication and Division?

Learning multiplication facts will help you learn related division facts.

If you want to display action figures, rocks, or coins in equal rows, you can use multiplication or division to find different ways to arrange them.

These students are placing stamps in a book. Each page of their book has 6 rows with 5 boxes in each row. They can use multiplication to figure out how many stamps will fit on a page.

Reading Mathematics

Reviewing Vocabulary

Understanding math language helps you become a successful problem solver. Here are some math vocabulary words you should know.

multiply	to find the total number of objects that are in equal groups
fact family	related facts that use the same numbers
array	a group of objects arranged in rows and columns
divide	to separate objects into equal groups
remainder	the number that is left over after dividing

Reading Words and Symbols

When you read mathematics, sometimes you read only words, sometimes you read words and symbols, and sometimes you read only symbols.

You can use multiplication or division sentences to describe an array.

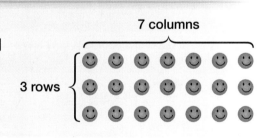

7 columns

3 rows

$$3 \times 7 = 21$$

factor   factor   product

$$21 \div 3 = 7$$

dividend   divisor   quotient

$$
\begin{array}{r}
7 \leftarrow \text{factor} \\
\times\ 3 \leftarrow \text{factor} \\
\hline
21 \leftarrow \text{product}
\end{array}
$$

divisor → 3)21   7 ← quotient   ← dividend

Try These

1. For each tell whether 8 is a *factor, product, dividend, divisor,* or *quotient.*

   a. $16 \div 8 = 2$ **b.** $8 \times 4 = 32$ **c.** $4 \times 2 = 8$ **d.** $24 \div 3 = 8$

   e. $2\overline{)8}$ with 4 **f.** $\begin{array}{r} 9 \\ \times\ 8 \\ \hline 72 \end{array}$ **g.** $6\overline{)48}$ with 8 **h.** $8\overline{)40}$ with 5

2. Write a multiplication or division example for each.

   a. The dividend and the quotient are the same number.

   b. The product is 0.

   c. Both factors are the same number.

   d. The divisor is 1.

3. Write a number sentence for each exercise.

   a. Sixty-four divided by eight equals eight.

   b. Seven times six equals forty-two.

   c. The product of four and three is twelve.

   d. The quotient of sixty-three divided by seven is nine.

Upcoming Vocabulary

Write About It **Here are some other vocabulary words** you will learn in this chapter. Watch for these words. Write their definitions in your journal.

Commutative Property	**Associative Property**
Property of One	**two-step function**
Zero Property	

LESSON 1

Use Doubles to Multiply

You will learn how doubles can help you multiply.

New Vocabulary
factor
product

Learn About It

Callie collects stamps and keeps them in an album.
She puts 9 stamps on each page of her album.

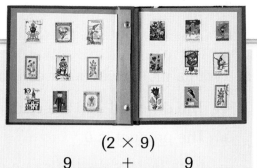

How many stamps are on 2 pages?

$$2 \times 9 = n$$

$$2 \times 9 = 18$$

factor   factor   product

$$\begin{array}{r} 9 \leftarrow \text{factor} \\ \times\, 2 \leftarrow \text{factor} \\ \hline 18 \leftarrow \text{product} \end{array}$$

There are 18 stamps on 2 pages.

(2×9)

9   +   9

How many stamps are on 4 pages?

$$4 \times 9 = n$$

| **Since** $2 \times 9 = 18$ |
| **then** $4 \times 9 = 18 + 18.$ |
| $18 + 18 = 36$ |

So $4 \times 9 = 36.$

Think:
4 is the double of 2.

There are 36 stamps on 4 pages.

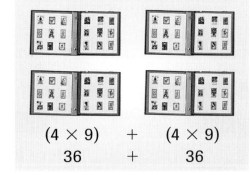

(2×9) + (2×9)

18   +   18

How many stamps are on 8 pages?

$$8 \times 9 = n$$

| **Since** $4 \times 9 = 36$ |
| **then** $8 \times 9 = 36 + 36.$ |
| $36 + 36 = 72$ |

So $8 \times 9 = 72.$

Think:
8 is the double of 4.

There are 72 stamps on 8 pages.

(4×9) + (4×9)

36   +   36

How many stamps are on 3 pages?

$$3 \times 9 = n$$

| **Since** $2 \times 9 = 18$ |
| **then** $3 \times 9 = 18 + 9.$ |
| $18 + 9 = 27$ |

So $3 \times 9 = 27.$

Think:
3×9 is double 9 plus one more 9.

There are 27 stamps on 3 pages.

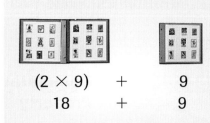

(2×9) +   9

18   +   9

Standards | NS **3.0**   MR **1.1, 2.3, 2.4**

How many stamps are on 6 pages?

$$6 \times 9 = n$$

Since $3 \times 9 = 27$
then $6 \times 9 = 27 + 27$
$27 + 27 = 54$

So $6 \times 9 = 54$.

There are 54 stamps on 6 pages.

Think:
6 is the double of 3.

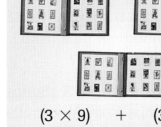

(3×9) + (3×9)
27 + 27

Explain Your Thinking

▶ How can knowing that $3 \times 3 = 9$ help you find 6×3?

▶ Can knowing that $2 \times 5 = 10$ help you find 8×5? Explain.

Guided Practice

Find the first product. Then use the first product to help you find the second product.

Ask Yourself
• Which doubles fact can I use to help me find the product?

1. 1×8
2×8

2. 3×4
6×4

3. 2×7
4×7

4. 1×6
2×6

5. 3×6
6×6

6. 4×8
8×8

7. 2×8
4×8

8. 3×2
6×2

Independent Practice

Multiply. Use doubles to help you.

9. $\begin{array}{r} 7 \\ \times 6 \\ \hline \end{array}$

10. $\begin{array}{r} 6 \\ \times 8 \\ \hline \end{array}$

11. $\begin{array}{r} 6 \\ \times 6 \\ \hline \end{array}$

12. $\begin{array}{r} 10 \\ \times 4 \\ \hline \end{array}$

13. $\begin{array}{r} 10 \\ \times 8 \\ \hline \end{array}$

14. $\begin{array}{r} 8 \\ \times 4 \\ \hline \end{array}$

15. 2×6

16. 6×5

17. 4×6

18. 3×6

19. 8×5

20. 4×5

21. 6×8

22. 3×6

23. 1×9

24. 8×4

25. 7×8

26. 9×6

n **Algebra • Expressions** Compare. Write >, <, or = in the ⬤.

27. 3×10 ⬤ 6×4

28. 4×6 ⬤ 8×3

29. 6×6 ⬤ 3×10

30. 3×5 ⬤ 4×4

31. 6×8 ⬤ 6×6

32. 4×9 ⬤ 6×6

Problem Solving • Reasoning

Use the sign for Problems 33–35.

33. Callie bought 6 stamps from South America and 8 stamps from Europe. How much did she spend?

34. **Money** Trish bought 3 stamps from Europe and 4 stamps from Africa. How much change should she get back from $20?

35. **Compare** Danny bought 10 stamps from Asia. How many stamps from Australia could he have bought with the same amount of money?

36. Steve has a stamp album with 9 stamps on each page. How many stamps are on 8 pages?

37. **Analyze** Together, Callie, Santos, and Trish have 80 stamps from Australia. Callie has twice as many stamps as Santos. Trish has 20 stamps. How many stamps does Callie have?

38. **Logical Thinking** When you multiply a number by an even number, is the product odd or even? Give examples to support your answer.

INTERNATIONAL STAMP SALE

Continent	Price per Stamp
Africa	$3
Asia	$2
Australia	$4
Europe	$2
South America	$3

Mixed Review • Test Prep

Find each sum or difference. *(pages 56–63)*

39.	**40.**	**41.**	**42.**	**43.**
8,362 − 2,925	6,413 + 2,877	5,185 − 3,876	3,821 + 4,398	7,344 − 4,827

44. 183 + 47 + 6   **45.** 295 + 38 + 159   **46.** 4,623 − 3,519   **47.** 3,828 − 1,769

Choose the letter of the correct answer. *(page 49)*

48 What time does the clock show?

A 8:05
B 1:20
C 1:40
D 2:40

49 To which number should the minute hand point to show 5:15?

F 12
G 9
H 6
J 3

Factors

When you multiply whole numbers to find a product, the numbers multiplied are called factors of the product.

$$\text{factor} \times \text{factor} = \text{product}$$

To find factors of a whole number, think of all the ways to break down that number as a product of other whole numbers.

- You can multiply by one to express 12 as the product of two factors.

$$1 \times 12 = 12$$

- You can use basic facts to find other factors of 12.

$$2 \times 6 = 12 \qquad\qquad 3 \times 4 = 12$$

- You can express 12 as a product of more than two factors by using basic facts to find other factors.

$2 \times 6 = 12$	$3 \times 4 = 12$
Think: $6 = 2 \times 3$	**Think:** $4 = 2 \times 2$
So $2 \times 2 \times 3 = 12$.	So $3 \times 2 \times 2 = 12$.

Try These

Find all the factors of each number. Then write each number as a product of more than 2 factors.

1. 8   **2.** 16   **3.** 18   **4.** 20

Explain Your Thinking

▶ How does knowing basic facts help you write a number as a product of more than 2 factors?

Multiplication Properties

You will learn how multiplication properties can help you find products.

New
Vocabulary
Commutative Property
Property of One
Zero Property
Associative Property

Learn About It

Multiplication properties can help you find products.

Commutative Property

 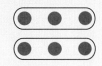

$3 \times 2 = 6$ $2 \times 3 = 6$

When you change the order of the factors, the product stays the same.

$$a \times b = b \times a$$

Property of One

$1 \times 6 = 6$

When you multiply any number by 1, the product is equal to the other factor.

$$1 \times n = n$$

Zero Property

◯ ◯ ◯ ◯

$0 \times 4 = 0$

When you multiply any number by 0, the product is 0.

$$0 \times n = 0$$

Associative Property

When you group factors in different ways, the product stays the same.

$$(a \times b) \times c = a \times (b \times c)$$

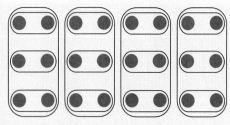

$(3 \times 2) \times 4$

$6 \times 4 = 24$

$3 \times (2 \times 4)$

$3 \times 8 = 24$

Standards NS **3.0**   AF **1.0, 1.1, 1.2**   MR **2.3**

Explain Your Thinking

▶ Why is it helpful to know about the Commutative Property when you multiply?

Guided Practice

Use multiplication properties to help you find the products.

1. 8×0

2. 1×934

3. 0×56

4. $6 \times (0 \times 10)$

5. $(2 \times 2) \times 4$

6. $3 \times (3 \times 4)$

Ask Yourself

• Is one of the factors 0 or 1?

• Did I multiply what is in the parentheses first?

Independent Practice

Solve. Name the property that you used.

7. $1 \times 4 = n$

8. $6 \times 8 = m \times 6$

9. $(3 \times 3) \times 2 = 3 \times (v \times 2)$

10. $75 \times 1 = h$

11. $0 \times 72 = r$

12. $(4 \times 2) \times n = 4 \times (2 \times 6)$

13. $0 \times 10 = g$

14. $(4 \times p) \times p = 4$

15. $5 \times (s \times 2) = (5 \times 1) \times 2$

Problem Solving • Reasoning

16. When the product of two numbers is 0, what do you know about the numbers?

17. Analyze When the product of two numbers is equal to one of the factors, what do you know about the other factor?

18. Logical Thinking In the equation $n \times 0 = 0$, what can you say about n? Explain.

19. The product of three whole numbers is 8. Their sum is 7. What are the numbers?

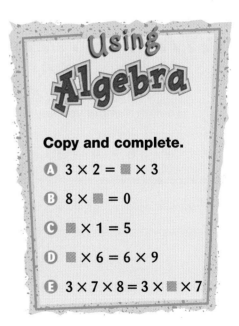

Using Algebra

Copy and complete.

Ⓐ $3 \times 2 = \blacksquare \times 3$

Ⓑ $8 \times \blacksquare = 0$

Ⓒ $\blacksquare \times 1 = 5$

Ⓓ $\blacksquare \times 6 = 6 \times 9$

Ⓔ $3 \times 7 \times 8 = 3 \times \blacksquare \times 7$

Mixed Review • Test Prep

Name the value of each underlined digit. *(pages 10–11)*

20. 16,9<u>4</u>2

21. 98,4<u>1</u>7

22. 7<u>6</u>0,354

23. <u>4</u>31,695

24. 8,5<u>1</u>2

㉕ What is the value of the 7 in 173,462? *(pages 10–11)*

A 700

B 7,000

C 70,000

D 700,000

Use Patterns to Multiply

You will learn how to use patterns to multiply by 5, 9, and 10.

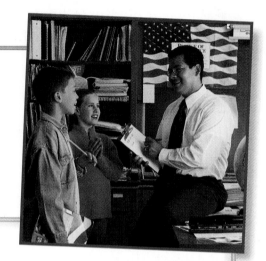

Learn About It

The school is holding a T-shirt sale to raise money for a trip to the science museum. Mr. Lopez kept a tally of the number of students who have returned their permission forms for the museum trip.

Multiplying by 5

Think about counting by 5s when you multiply by 5.

5	10	15	20	25	30	35	40	45	50

- The ones digits follow a pattern: 5, 0, 5, 0, 5, 0, 5, 0, 5, 0
- The tens digits follow a pattern: 1, 1, 2, 2, 3, 3, 4, 4, 5

Multiply. $5 \times 4 = n$

Think: 5, 10, 15, 20
The 4th number you say is 20.

$$5 \times 4 = 20$$

Multiply. $5 \times 7 = n$

Think: 5, 10, 15, 20, 25, 30, 35
The 7th number you say is 35.

$$5 \times 7 = 35$$

Multiplying by 10

Look at the patterns when you multiply by 10.

- The product always has a zero in the ones place.
- The underlined factor is the same as the other digit in the product.

$$10 \times \underline{1} = 10$$
$$10 \times \underline{2} = 20$$
$$10 \times \underline{3} = 30$$
$$10 \times \underline{4} = 40$$
$$10 \times \underline{5} = 50$$

Standards   NS **3.0**   AF **1.1**   SDP **1.0**   MR **1.1, 2.3**

Multiplying by 9

Look at the patterns when you multiply by 9.

- The sum of the digits of each product is 9.

  $9 \times 2 = 18$ $9 \times 3 = 27$
      $(1 + 8 = 9)$ $(2 + 7 = 9)$

  $9 \times 4 = 36$ $9 \times 5 = 45$
      $(3 + 6 = 9)$ $(4 + 5 = 9)$

- The tens digit of the product is one less than the underlined factor.

  $9 \times \underline{2}$ =   18 $9 \times \underline{3}$ =   27
        1 less   1 less

  $9 \times \underline{4}$ =   36 $9 \times \underline{5}$ =   45
        1 less   1 less

$9 \times \underline{1} = 9$		
$9 \times \underline{2} = 18$		
$9 \times \underline{3} = 27$		
$9 \times \underline{4} = 36$		
$9 \times \underline{5} = 45$		
$9 \times \underline{6} = 54$		
$9 \times \underline{7} = 63$		
$9 \times \underline{8} = 72$		
$9 \times \underline{9} = 81$		
$9 \times \underline{10} = 90$		

Explain Your Thinking

▶ How can patterns help you find the product of 9 and 4?

▶ Can doubles help you find the same product of 9 and 4? Explain.

▶ How can the Associative Property help you find the product of $3 \times 5 \times 2$ mentally?

Guided Practice

Multiply.

1.   10
     $\times\ 4$

2.   8
     $\times\ 9$

3.   5
     $\times\ 5$

4.   6
     $\times\ 9$

5.   9
     $\times\ 4$

6.   4
     $\times\ 5$

7.   2
     $\times\ 9$

8.   10
     $\times\ 8$

9. 9×10 **10.** 5×8 **11.** 6×5 **12.** 3×9

13. 5×7 **14.** 10×7 **15.** 9×5 **16.** 5×10

Ask Yourself

- What pattern can I use?
- What multiplication property can I use?

Independent Practice

Multiply.

17. 4 ×9		**18.** 10 ×6		**19.** 8 ×5		**20.** 7 ×5		**21.** 9 ×4		**22.** 10 ×7	

23. 9 ×9		**24.** 5 ×8		**25.** 10 ×9		**26.** 9 ×8		**27.** 10 ×10		**28.** 5 ×9	

29. 4×10 **30.** 10×0 **31.** $3 \times 2 \times 10$ **32.** $5 \times 7 \times 2$

Algebra • Functions Follow the rules. Copy and complete the tables.

Rule: Multiply by 5

	Input	Output
33.	0	▪
34.	6	▪
35.	7	▪
36.	8	▪
37.	10	▪

Rule: Multiply by 9

	Input	Output
38.	▪	36
39.	5	▪
40.	6	▪
41.	8	▪
42.	9	▪

Rule: Multiply by 10

	Input	Output
43.	▪	0
44.	▪	20
45.	5	▪
46.	7	▪
47.	▪	90

Problem Solving • Reasoning

Use Data Use the graph for Problems 48–49.

48. How many T-shirts were sold?

49. Analyze How many more extra large shirts than medium shirts were sold? Tell two ways to decide.

50. Large T-shirts are $9 each, and baby T-shirts are $5 each. If you spent $38 to buy 6 shirts, how many of each did you buy?

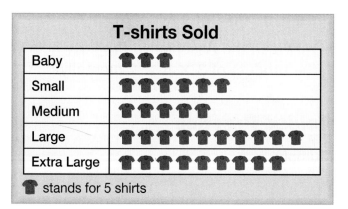

T-shirts Sold

Baby	👕👕👕
Small	👕👕👕👕👕
Medium	👕👕👕👕
Large	👕👕👕👕👕👕👕👕👕
Extra Large	👕👕👕👕👕👕👕👕

👕 stands for 5 shirts

Mixed Review • Test Prep

Find each difference or sum. *(pages 56–57; 68–69)*

51. $700 - 45$ **52.** $9,098 + 734$ **53.** $5,006 - 3,456$ **54.** $7,564 + 1,698$

55 Evaluate $n + 4$ when n is 6. *(pages 78–81)*

A 2   **B** 10   **C** 24   **D** 64

Number Sense

Multiples

A multiple of a number is a product of that number and any other whole number.

Some multiples of 10 are 10, 20, 30, 40, 50, 60, 70, 80, 90, 100

Some multiples of 8 are 8, 16, 24, 32, 40, 48, 56, 64, 72, 80

You can use multiples to solve a problem like this one.

Hot dogs are sold in packages of 10, and hot-dog rolls are sold in packages of 8. What is the least number of packages of hot dogs and rolls that you need to buy to have the same number of hot dogs and rolls?

To solve the problem, make two tables.

Packages of hot dogs	1	2	3	4	5	6	7	8	9	10
Number of hot dogs	10	20	30	**40**	50	60	70	**80**	90	100

Packages of rolls	1	2	3	4	5	6	7	8	9	10
Number of rolls	8	16	24	32	**40**	48	56	64	72	**80**

Now look for numbers that are in both tables. 40 and 80 are in both. Because you want the least number of packages of hot dogs and rolls, look above the 40 in each table. You need to buy 4 packages of hot dogs and 5 packages of rolls.

Both 40 and 80 are common multiples of 10 and 8. We say that 40 is the *least* common multiple of 10 and 8 because it is the smallest number that is a multiple of both 10 and 8.

Try These

List the first 10 multiples of the numbers in each pair. Then underline the common multiples and circle the least common multiple.

1. 2, 6   **2.** 3, 4   **3.** 4, 9   **4.** 3, 7   **5.** 5, 8

Quick ✓ Check

Check Your Understanding of Lessons 1–3

Find each product. Use doubles to help you.

1. $8 \times 7 = n$ **2.** $6 \times 9 = n$

Solve. Name the property that you used.

3. $1 \times 27 = n$ **4.** $3 \times 5 = 5 \times n$

5. $78 \times 0 = n$ **6.** $(4 \times 3) \times 3 = 4 \times (n \times 3)$

Multiply.

7. $\begin{array}{r} 8 \\ \times\, 9 \\ \hline \end{array}$ **8.** $\begin{array}{r} 6 \\ \times\, 7 \\ \hline \end{array}$ **9.** $\begin{array}{r} 8 \\ \times\, 8 \\ \hline \end{array}$

Solve.

10. The product of three whole numbers is 24.
The sum of the numbers is 9.
What are the numbers?

How did you do?

If you had difficulty with any items in the Quick Check, you can use the following pages for review and extra practice.

California Standards	ITEMS	REVIEW THESE PAGES	DO THESE EXTRA PRACTICE ITEMS
Number Sense: **3.0** Algebra: **1.1**	1–2	pages 106–108	Set A, page 152
Number Sense: **3.0** Algebra: **1.1, 1.2**	3–6	pages 110–111	Set B, page 152
Number Sense: **3.0**	7–9	pages 112–114	Set C, page 152
Math Reasoning: **1.1, 2.4**	10	pages 109–111	Sets B and C, page 152

Test Prep • Cumulative Review

Maintaining the Standards

Choose the letter of the correct answer. If a correct answer is not here, choose NH.

1 Seth has a collection of 989 stickers and 316 stamps. About how many more stickers than stamps does Seth have?

A 500

B 700

C 800

D 1,300

2 What is the sum of 6,747 and 21,105?

F 14,358 **H** 27,852

G 27,842 **J** NH

3 The art teacher collected 4 buttons from each student in her class. There are 8 students in her class. Which answer shows the number of buttons the teacher collected in all?

A 8 + 4

B 8 ÷ 4

C 8 × 4

D 8 − 4

4 Which expression is equal to 13?

F $(3 \times 2) + 7$

G $3 \times (2 + 7)$

H $(3 \times 7) + 2$

J $3 \times (7 + 2)$

Use the table to answer Questions 5–6.

x	y
3	1
5	3
7	5
9	?

5 Which equation does the table show?

A $y = x + 2$ **C** $y = x + 0$

B $y = x - 2$ **D** $y = x - 1$

6 What number is missing from the table?

F 0 **H** 7

G 2 **J** 11

7 What number should go in the box to make the number sentence true?

$$(2 + 3) \times 4 = 5 \times \blacksquare$$

A 2 **C** 4

B 3 **D** 5

8 What is the value of n in the following equation?

$$16 - (4 \times 3) = n$$

Explain Tell how you found your answer.

Relate Multiplication and Division

You will learn how knowing multiplication facts can help you divide.

Review
Vocabulary
array
fact family

Learn About It

Darren arranged 27 coins from Canada in a rectangular **array** with the same number of coins in each row.

Darren wrote two multiplication equations about the array of coins.

$$9 \times 3 = 27$$

columns   coins in   coins
each column   in all

$$3 \times 9 = 27$$

rows   coins in   coins
each row   in all

Darren also wrote two division equations about the array of coins.

$$27 \div 9 = 3$$

coins   columns   coins in
in all   each column

$$27 \div 3 = 9$$

coins   rows   coins in
in all   each row

The multiplication and division equations that can be written by using the numbers 3, 9, and 27 form a **fact family**. Fact families show how multiplication and division are related.

$$9 \times 3 = 27 \qquad 27 \div 9 = 3$$
$$3 \times 9 = 27 \qquad 27 \div 3 = 9$$

Other Examples

A. Fact Family for 2, 8, and 16

$$2 \times 8 = 16 \qquad 16 \div 2 = 8$$
$$8 \times 2 = 16 \qquad 16 \div 8 = 2$$

B. Fact Family for 5, 5, and 25

$$5 \times 5 = 25 \qquad 25 \div 5 = 5$$

Explain Your Thinking

▶ Why does the fact family for 5, 5, and 25 have only two equations?

▶ How can knowing that $4 \times 7 = 28$ help you find $28 \div 4$?

▶ Can you form a fact family by using 2, 7, and 27? Explain.

Guided Practice

Write the fact family for each array or set of numbers.

1. ●●●
●●●

2. ●●●●
●●●●
●●●●

3. 3, 3, 9

4. 6, 7, 42

Ask Yourself

• Do I know a fact family that can help me find the answer?

Independent Practice

Complete each fact family.

5. $4 \times 6 = $ ▩　　$24 \div 4 = $ ▩
$6 \times 4 = $ ▩　　$24 \div 6 = $ ▩

6. $8 \times 9 = $ ▩　　$72 \div 8 = $ ▩
$9 \times 8 = $ ▩　　$72 \div 9 = $ ▩

Write the fact family for each set of numbers.

7. 2, 2, 4

8. 3, 6, 18

9. 4, 9, 36

10. 5, 8, 40

11. 5, 9, 45

12. 6, 8, 48

13. 2, 9, 18

14. 4, 8, 32

15. 8, 8, 64

16. 7, 9, 63

17. 7, 7, 49

18. 9, 9, 81

Problem Solving • Reasoning

19. If you know that $6 \times 5 = 30$, what other facts do you know?

20. **Analyze** There are two fact families that contain the numbers 3 and 6. Write the equations for both fact families.

21. **Write About It** Darren has 16 coins from England. How many different rectangular arrays can he make with the coins? Tell how you decided. Draw the arrays and write the equations.

Math Is Everywhere!

Social Studies
The Royal Mint in England produces 20,000 tons of coins each year!

The Royal Mint operates 24 hours a day, 7 days a week, for 51 weeks each year. How many days does the Royal Mint not operate each year?

Mixed Review • Test Prep

Add or subtract. *(pages 56–63)*

22. $2,729 - 401$

23. $4,537 + 8,657$

24. $8,119 + 6,999$

25 Which number is the best estimate of $2,978 + 9,163 + 10,870$? *(pages 64–65)*

　A 21,000　　**B** 22,000　　**C** 23,000　　**D** 24,000

Extra Practice See Set D on page 152.

119

Use Doubles to Divide

You will learn how doubles can help you divide.

New Vocabulary
dividend
divisor
quotient

Learn About It

Randi keeps her 12 old movie posters rolled in tubes. She puts 2 posters into each tube. How many tubes does she use?

Divide.   **12 ÷ 2 = n**

Find 12 ÷ 2.

$12 ÷ 2 = n$ **Think:** $2 × n = 12$
                              $2 × 6 = 12$

So   12   ÷   2   =   6.
      ↑   ↑   ↑
   dividend   divisor   quotient

$\overset{6}{2\overline{)12}}$ ← quotient

divisor ↑   ↘ dividend

Solution: She uses 6 tubes.

If Randi doubles the number of posters she puts into each tube, how many tubes will she use?

Divide.   **12 ÷ 4 = n**

Different Ways to Divide

You can use doubles.

$12 ÷ 4 = n$

Think: 4 is the double of 2.
So the quotient will be half of 12 ÷ 2.

$12 ÷ 2 = 6$ Half of 6 is 3.

So $12 ÷ 4 = 3$.

You can use a multiplication fact.

$12 ÷ 4 = n$

Think: $4 × n = 12$
              $4 × 3 = 12$

So $12 ÷ 4 = 3$.

Solution: She will use 3 tubes.

Explain Your Thinking

▶ When the divisor is doubled, what happens to the quotient?

Standards NS **3.0**   SDP **1.0**   MR **2.3, 2.4**

Guided Practice

Divide.

1. 8 ÷ 2
   8 ÷ 4

2. 18 ÷ 3
   18 ÷ 6

3. 20 ÷ 2
   20 ÷ 4

4. 24 ÷ 3
   24 ÷ 6

5. 40 ÷ 4
   40 ÷ 8

6. 24 ÷ 4
   24 ÷ 8

Ask Yourself

- Can I use doubles to help me divide?
- Do I know a related multiplication fact?

Independent Practice

Divide.

7. 2)‾20‾

8. 2)‾18‾

9. 3)‾27‾

10. 6)‾30‾

11. 4)‾32‾

12. 8)‾24‾

13. 6)‾24‾

14. 3)‾24‾

15. 8)‾32‾

16. 4)‾16‾

17. 18 ÷ 2

18. 30 ÷ 6

19. 21 ÷ 3

20. 20 ÷ 4

Problem Solving • Reasoning

Use Data Use the graph for each problem.

21. Randi put all of her movie posters in 2 tubes with the same number in each tube. How many posters were in each tube?

22. **Money** Randi purchases tubes for $3 each. How much will she spend for tubes for her circus posters if she puts 6 posters into each tube?

23. **Write About It** Can Randi divide the number of travel posters equally into 4 tubes? Explain.

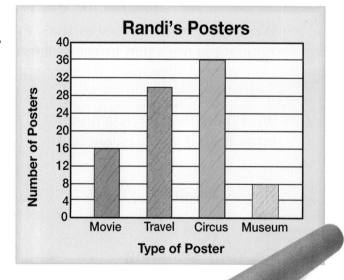

Mixed Review • Test Prep

Write each number in words. *(pages 4–5)*

24. 1,789

25. 3,054

26. 2,906

27. 5,470

28 Which number shows eight thousand, nine hundred four? *(pages 4–5)*

A 89,004   **B** 80,904   **C** 8,940   **D** 8,904

LESSON 6

Division Rules

You will learn how to use certain rules for finding quotients.

Learn About It

To celebrate National Teacher Day, Nina bought 5 flowers for her 5 teachers. She gave 1 flower to each teacher.

5 ÷ 5 = 1

Division Rules

Here are some rules that can help you solve division problems with 1 or 0.

- When you divide a number by itself, the quotient is 1. This is true for all numbers except 0.

  5 ÷ 5 = 1   or   5)$\overline{5}$ = 1

- When you divide a number by 1, the quotient is the same as the dividend.

  5 ÷ 1 = 5   or   1)$\overline{5}$ = 5

- When you divide 0 by a number other than 0, the quotient is 0.

  0 ÷ 5 = 0   or   5)$\overline{0}$ = 0

- You cannot divide a number by 0.

Explain Your Thinking

▶ Which numbers in a division problem can be 0? Explain.

▶ When the divisor is 1, what do you know about the quotient?

Guided Practice

Use the division rules to help you solve each equation.

1. $0 \div 3 = n$ **2.** $9 \div 9 = s$ **3.** $2 \div p = 1$

4. $4 \div r = 4$ **5.** $v \div 7 = 0$ **6.** $6 \div k = 6$

Ask Yourself

- Is 0 the dividend?
- Are the divisor and the dividend the same?
- Is the divisor 1?

122   **Standards** | AF **1.0, 1.1**   MR **2.3**

Independent Practice

Solve. If an equation has no solution, tell why.

7. $4 \div 1 = n$ **8.** $6 \div 0 = p$ **9.** $m \div 8 = 0$ **10.** $j \div 1 = 9$

11. $k \div 1 = 1$ **12.** $5 \div m = 5$ **13.** $0 \div 5 = t$ **14.** $m \div 3 = 1$

n **Algebra • Expressions Compare. Write >, <, or = in the ●.**

15. $7 \div 1 \, ● \, 6 \div 1$ **16.** $0 \div 4 \, ● \, 4 \div 4$ **17.** $6 \div 6 \, ● \, 6 \div 1$

18. $0 \div 19 \, ● \, 0 \div 7$ **19.** $0 \div 9 \, ● \, 8 \div 8$ **20.** $24 \div 24 \, ● \, 692 \div 692$

Problem Solving • Reasoning

Use Data Use the sign for each problem.

21. How many tulips can you buy for $7? How many roses can you buy for $2?

22. Compare How many more carnations than roses can you buy for $8?

23. Analyze Alan bought 5 flowers and spent $6. He bought at least one of each kind of flower. What flowers did he buy?

24. Write Your Own Use the information in the sign to write your own problem. Give your problem to a classmate to solve.

Mixed Review • Test Prep

Find each sum or difference. *(pages 54–63; 68–69)*

25. $\begin{array}{r} \;^{7.3} \\ \$6.43 \\ -\;2.78 \\ \hline 3.65 \end{array}$ **26.** $\begin{array}{r} ^{11} \\ \$5.29 \\ +\;3.71 \\ \hline 1200 \end{array}$ **27.** $\begin{array}{r} ^{4} \\ \$9.50 \\ -\;5.24 \\ \hline 4.26 \end{array}$ **28.** $\begin{array}{r} \$18.76 \\ -\;9.25 \\ \hline 1151 \end{array}$ **29.** $\begin{array}{r} ^{11} \\ \$13.25 \\ +\;28.84 \\ \hline 4209 \end{array}$

Choose the letter of the correct answer. *(pages 54–59; 68–69)*

30 What is the sum of 1,758 and 87?

    A 1,735   **C** 1,835

    B 1,745   **D** 1,845

31 What is $6,004 − $935?

    F $5,179   **H** $5,069

    G $5,171   **J** $5,061

Extra Practice See Set F on page 153.

Divide by 5, 7, 9, or 10

You will learn how to use related multiplication facts to help you divide by 5, 7, 9, or 10.

Learn About It

A music store is displaying 42 kazoos in 7 boxes. The same number of kazoos is in each box. How many kazoos are in each box?

Divide.   **42 ÷ 7   or   7)42**

Find 42 ÷ 7.

Think of a related multiplication fact.

$$7 \times k = 42$$
$$7 \times 6 = 42$$

So 42 ÷ 7 = 6.

Solution: There are 6 kazoos in each box.

Other Examples

A. Divide by 5

$$40 \div 5 = n$$
Think: $5 \times n = 40$
$$5 \times 8 = 40$$
So 40 ÷ 5 = 8.

B. Divide by 9

$$63 \div 9 = z$$
Think: $9 \times z = 63$
$$9 \times 7 = 63$$
So 63 ÷ 9 = 7.

C. Divide by 10

$$80 \div 10 = m$$
Think: $10 \times m = 80$
$$10 \times 8 = 80$$
So 80 ÷ 10 = 8.

Explain Your Thinking

▶ How does knowing that $7 \times 10 = 70$ help you find 70 ÷ 10?

▶ Which related multiplication fact would you use to help you find 35 ÷ 7?

Guided Practice

Divide.

1. 9)81

2. 10)80

3. 7)63

4. 5)45

5. 42 ÷ 7

6. 90 ÷ 9

7. 40 ÷ 5

8. 49 ÷ 7

Ask Yourself

• Do I know a related multiplication fact that can help me find the quotient?

Standards NS **3.0, 3.4**   MR **2.3**

Independent Practice

Divide.

9. $10\overline{)40}$ **10.** $9\overline{)36}$ **11.** $7\overline{)49}$ **12.** $5\overline{)25}$ **13.** $9\overline{)54}$

14. $9\overline{)72}$ **15.** $9\overline{)90}$ **16.** $9\overline{)63}$ **17.** $7\overline{)70}$ **18.** $5\overline{)50}$

19. $9 \div 9$ **20.** $35 \div 7$ **21.** $27 \div 9$ **22.** $40 \div 5$ **23.** $42 \div 7$

24. $60 \div 10$ **25.** $9 \div 1$ **26.** $56 \div 7$ **27.** $81 \div 9$ **28.** $45 \div 5$

29. $35 \div 5$ **30.** $72 \div 8$ **31.** $63 \div 7$ **32.** $50 \div 10$ **33.** $63 \div 9$

Problem Solving • Reasoning

34. At the music store, 81 harmonicas are on display. The harmonicas are arranged in 9 equal rows. How many harmonicas are in each row?

35. **Money** Kazoos are on sale. You can buy 5 kazoos for $25. How much is each kazoo?

36. **Write About It** The music-store owner has 45 maracas. She wants to display all of the maracas in equal rows. Can she put 5, 7, 9, or 10 maracas in each row? Explain your reasoning.

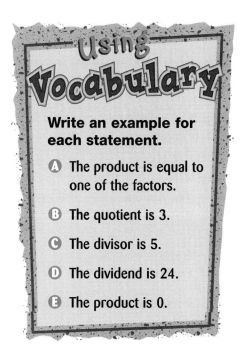

Using **Vocabulary**

Write an example for each statement.

Ⓐ The product is equal to one of the factors.

Ⓑ The quotient is 3.

Ⓒ The divisor is 5.

Ⓓ The dividend is 24.

Ⓔ The product is 0.

Mixed Review • Test Prep

Round each number to the nearest thousand. *(pages 10–11)*

37. 3,762   **38.** 112,154   **39.** 876   **40.** 16,023   **41.** 7,863

Choose the letter of the correct answer. *(pages 30–35)*

42 Which is equal to 3 quarters, 1 dime?

    A $0.85   **B** $0.80   **C** $ 0.90   **D** $0.75

43 Which group of coins is equal to $2.00 − $1.87?

    F 1 dime, 3 pennies   **H** 1 dime, 7 pennies

    G 1 nickel, 3 pennies   **J** 1 nickel, 7 pennies

Extra Practice See Set G on page 153.

Division With Remainders

You will learn how to divide when there are remainders.

New Vocabulary
remainder

Learn About It

Megan and Rachel bought 15 used books at a yard sale. They want to share the books equally. How many books will each girl get? How many books will be left?

When you divide, the **remainder** tells how many are left. The remainder must always be less than the divisor.

Divide. $15 \div 2$ or $2\overline{)15}$

Find $15 \div 2$.

Step 1 Think of multiplication facts that have products close to 15.

$2 \times n = 15$
$2 \times 7 = 14$
$2 \times 8 = 16$

8 is too many.
Try 7 as the quotient.

Step 2 Divide.

$$\begin{array}{r} 7 \\ 2\overline{)15} \\ -14 \\ \hline 1 \end{array}$$ ← Multiply. 2×7
← Subtract. $15 - 14$

Step 3 Show the remainder.

$$\begin{array}{r} 7 \text{ R1} \\ 2\overline{)15} \\ -14 \\ \hline 1 \end{array}$$ ← remainder

Solution: Each girl will get 7 books. There will be 1 book left.

Other Examples

A. Remainder of 2

$$\begin{array}{r} 6 \text{ R2} \\ 3\overline{)20} \\ -18 \\ \hline 2 \end{array}$$ ← Multiply. 3×6
← Subtract. $20 - 18$

B. Remainder of 0

$$\begin{array}{r} 7 \\ 5\overline{)35} \\ -35 \\ \hline 0 \end{array}$$ ← Multiply. 5×7
← Subtract. $35 - 35$

Explain Your Thinking

▶ What will the remainder be when you divide 12 by 5? How do you know?

▶ What must you do if the remainder is greater than the divisor?

Standards NS **3.0** MR **2.4**

Guided Practice

Divide.

1. $4\overline{)7}$ 2. $6\overline{)19}$ 3. $2\overline{)11}$ 4. $3\overline{)13}$

5. $25 \div 7$ 6. $53 \div 8$ 7. $34 \div 9$ 8. $25 \div 3$

Ask Yourself
- Do I know multiplication facts that can help me?
- Did I show the remainder? Is it less than the divisor?

Independent Practice

Divide.

9. $2\overline{)3}$ 10. $4\overline{)6}$ 11. $5\overline{)12}$ 12. $2\overline{)9}$ 13. $4\overline{)21}$

14. $8\overline{)15}$ 15. $5\overline{)19}$ 16. $2\overline{)17}$ 17. $4\overline{)23}$ 18. $9\overline{)27}$

19. $7 \div 2$ 20. $9 \div 4$ 21. $15 \div 5$ 22. $16 \div 3$ 23. $26 \div 8$

24. $24 \div 5$ 25. $20 \div 8$ 26. $31 \div 6$ 27. $26 \div 9$ 28. $61 \div 9$

Problem Solving • Reasoning

Solve. Choose a method.

Computation Methods

- **Mental Math**   • **Estimation**   • **Paper and Pencil**

29. **Measurement** The yard sale took place over a weekend. It was held from noon to 5 P.M. each day. How many hours was the yard sale?

30. Bobby bought 53 old CDs. He put the same number of CDs into each of 8 boxes. What is the greatest number that he could put into each box?

31. Half as many sweaters as coats were for sale. There were 49 sweaters. About how many coats and sweaters were for sale in all?

32. **Money** Anna bought 2 used tennis racquets for $7 each and a used volleyball for $5. She paid with a $20 bill. What was her change?

Mixed Review • Test Prep

Solve each equation. *(pages 82–83)*

33. $p + 2 = 34$ 34. $12 = 17 - x$ 35. $n + n + 5 = 29$ 36. $m + 6 = 78$

Choose the letter of the correct answer. *(pages 4–5)*

37 Which number is 10,000 greater than 273,485?

    A 373,485   **B** 283,485   **C** 274,485   **D** 273,585

Problem-Solving Skill: Multistep Problems

You will learn how to solve problems that have more than one step.

Sometimes it takes more than one step to solve a problem. You must decide what the steps are and in what order to do them.

The drama teacher rented costumes for the school play. He rented 21 soldier costumes that came in boxes with 3 costumes in each box. He also rented 2 boxes of clown costumes with 5 costumes in each box. How many boxes of costumes did he rent?

Decide what to do.

You know that he rented 21 soldier costumes that came in boxes with 3 costumes in each box. You also know he rented 2 boxes of clown costumes. First, find the number of boxes of soldier costumes. Then find the total number of boxes.

Do each step in order.

Step 1 Divide to find the number of boxes of soldier costumes.

$$n = 21 \div 3$$

number of boxes of costumes   number of soldier costumes   number in each box

$$n = 7$$

There are 7 boxes of soldier costumes.

Step 2 Add to find the total number of boxes.

$$T = 7 + 2$$

total number of boxes of costumes   number of boxes of soldier costumes   number of boxes of clown costumes

$$T = 9$$

The total number of boxes is 9.

The drama teacher rented 9 boxes of costumes.

Look Back Could you have done the steps in a different order? Explain why or why not.

Standards NS **3.0, 3.4**   MR **1.0, 1.1, 1.2, 2.0, 3.0, 3.2**

Colorful masks are made by artists from all over the world.

Guided Practice

Solve each problem.

1. The costume shop sells masks for $2 each or 5 for $6. You want to buy 7 masks. What will be the total cost?

   Think: For how many masks will you have to pay $2 each?

2. Clown noses are $4 a bag. There are 3 noses in a bag. How many clown noses can you buy for $12?

   Think: How many bags can you buy for $12?

Choose a Strategy

Solve. Use these or other strategies.

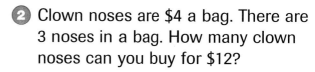

Problem-Solving Strategies

• Make a Table   • Guess and Check   • Write an Equation   • Use Logical Thinking

3. Teachers and parents helped out backstage. Half as many teachers as parents were backstage. If 5 teachers helped out backstage, how many parents were backstage?

4. The costume shop buys funny eyeglasses for $1 a pair. It sells each pair for $3. How many pairs of eyeglasses does the shop have to sell to make a profit of $16?

5. The school play has two acts. Each act is 40 minutes long. There is a 15-minute break between the two acts. The play begins at 4:00 P.M. What time will the play end?

6. The regular price of a wig is $10. Each wig is on sale for $4 less than the regular price. With $60, how many more wigs can you buy at the sale price than at the regular price?

7. Mr. Hark bought twice as many wigs as eyeglasses. He bought half as many eyeglasses as noses. He bought 16 noses. How many wigs did Mr. Hark buy?

8. There are 35 students in the school play. There are 3 more boys than girls in the play. How many boys are in the school play? How many girls are in the school play?

Extra Practice See Set 1–4 on page 155.

Quick ✓ Check

Check Your Understanding of Lessons 4–9

Write the fact family for each set of numbers.

1. 7   9   63

2. 8   6   48

Solve each equation.

3. $32 \div 32 = n$

4. $26 \div 1 = n$

5. $0 \div 16 = n$

Divide.

6. $8\overline{)16}$

7. $9\overline{)72}$

8. $9\overline{)39}$

Solve.

9. An electronics store sells videotapes for $3.00 each or 3 for $8.00. What will be the total cost of 5 tapes?

10. A package of 4 blank audiocassettes costs $8.00. How many cassettes can you buy with $24.00?

How did you do?

If you had difficulty with any items in the Quick Check, you can use the following pages for review and extra practice.

California Standards	ITEMS	REVIEW THESE PAGES	DO THESE EXTRA PRACTICE ITEMS
Number Sense: **3.0**	1–2	pages 118–119	Set D, page 152
Number Sense: **3.0** Algebra: **1.1**	3–5	pages 122–123	Set F, page 153
Number Sense: **3.2**	6	pages 120–121	Set E, page 153
Number Sense: **3.2**	7	pages 124–125	Set G, page 153
Number Sense: **3.2**	8	pages 126–127	Set H, page 153
Math Reasoning: **1.1, 1.2, 2.6, 3.1, 3.2**	9–10	pages 128–129	1–4, page155

Test Prep • Cumulative Review
Maintaining the Standards

Choose the letter of the correct answer. If a correct answer is not here, choose NH.

1 A gym class of 45 students is divided into groups. There are 9 students in each group. How many groups are there?

A 2　　　**C** 5

B 4　　　**D** 9

2 What number should go in the box to make the number sentence true?

$$(3 + 6) + 5 = 9 + \blacksquare$$

F 0　　　**H** 5

G 3　　　**J** 6

3 Three thousand, one hundred forty-two tickets were sold for the game on Monday night. Two thousand, nine hundred five tickets were sold for Tuesday night. About how many tickets were sold in all?

A 3,000　　　**C** 5,000

B 4,000　　　**D** 6,000

4 Sandy has 72 trading cards. She wants to divide her cards evenly among 8 friends. Which answer shows the number of cards each friend will receive?

F 72×8　　　**H** $72 \div 8$

G $72 + 8$　　　**J** $72 - 8$

5 What is the difference between 12,008 and 6,549?

A 5,349　　　**C** 5,569

B 5,459　　　**D** NH

6 Which expression does not equal 12?

F 4×3

G 2×6

H $2 \times 2 \times 3$

J $3 \times 3 \times 2$

7 What is the rule?

Input	Output
18	6
12	0
16	4
13	1

A Input + 12 = Output

B Input − 12 = Output

C Input ÷ 3 = Output

D Input × 3 = Output

8 What number should go in the box to make the number sentence true?

$$(7 + 3) \times 2 = 10 \times \blacksquare$$

Explain How did you find your answer?

Safe Site

Internet Test Prep
Visit **www.eduplace.com/kids/mhm**
for more *Test Prep Practice.*

131

Write and Evaluate Expressions

You will learn to write and evaluate multiplication and division expressions containing variables.

Learn About It

Todd and Kerry are building model cars. Kerry wants to build twice as many model cars as Todd. How many cars does she want to build?

Since you don't know how many model cars Todd plans to build, you can use a **variable** and write an **algebraic expression** for the number of cars that Kerry wants to build.

• Let w stand for the number of model cars Todd plans to build.

• Then the number of model cars Kerry wants to build can be expressed as

$2 \times w$ or $2 \cdot w$ or $2w$

You read all of these algebraic expressions as "2 times w."

To evaluate the expression, replace w with some number of cars and then simplify the expression.

Suppose that Todd plans to build 6 model cars. How many cars does Kerry want to build?

Evaluate $2w$ when $w = 6$.

Step 1 Record the expression.	**Step 2** Replace w with 6.	**Step 3** Simplify the expression.
$2w$	$2w$ 2×6	$2w$ 2×6 12

Solution: If Todd plans to build 6 model cars, Kerry wants to build 12 model cars.

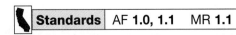

Standards AF **1.0, 1.1** MR **1.1**

Todd wants to buy cases to display his model cars. Each case holds 4 model cars. How many cases should he buy?

- Let *r* stand for the number of model cars Todd has built.

- Then *r* ÷ 4 stands for the number of cases Todd should buy.

If Todd has 16 model cars, how many cases should he buy?

Evaluate *r* ÷ 4 when *r* = 16.

Step 1 Record the expression.	**Step 2** Replace *r* with 16.	**Step 3** Simplify the expression.
r ÷ 4	*r* ÷ 4 16 ÷ 4	*r* ÷ 4 16 ÷ 4 4

Solution: If Todd has 16 cars, he should buy 4 cases.

Explain Your Thinking

▶ Does 3*m* mean 3 + *m*?

▶ How can you use a variable to show "some number divided by 2"?

▶ If *y* = 8, what will you do to evaluate the expression 6*y*?

Guided Practice

Evaluate each expression when *n* = 6.

1. 5*n*   **2.** *n* ÷ 3   **3.** *n* × 4   **4.** 2*n* + 4

Match each description with an algebraic expression. Let *p* stand for the number of model cars Tom has.

5. 5 times the number of cars Tom has   **a.** *p* ÷ 2

6. half as many cars as Tom has   **b.** *p*

7. the number of wheels on all of Tom's cars   **c.** 5*p*

8. the total number of steering wheels on all of Tom's cars   **d.** 4*p*

> **Ask Yourself**
> - What is the variable?
> - What is the value of the variable?
> - Should I multiply or divide to evaluate the expression?

Independent Practice

Evaluate each expression when $p = 9$.

9. $3p$ **10.** $p \div 3$ **11.** $p + 3$ **12.** $p - 3$ **13.** $5 \cdot p$

14. $p + 10$ **15.** $p \div 9$ **16.** $6 \cdot p$ **17.** $p \div 1$ **18.** $12 - p$

Evaluate each expression when $n = 5$.

19. $n \times 5$ **20.** $n - 4$ **21.** $35 \div n$ **22.** $n \div 5$ **23.** $65 \div n$

24. $8n$ **25.** $8n + 3$ **26.** $10n$ **27.** $4 \cdot n$ **28.** $n + 8$

Let s stand for the number of model airplanes in Jodi's collection. Write an algebraic expression for each description.

29. 5 fewer model airplanes than in Jodi's collection $s - 5$

30. 3 more model airplanes than in Jodi's collection

31. half as many model airplanes as in Jodi's collection

32. 6 times as many model airplanes as in Jodi's collection

Problem Solving • Reasoning

33. Ashley and Rodney collect model boats. Ashley has half as many as Rodney. Let b stand for the number of boats Rodney has. Write an expression to show the number of boats Ashley has.

34. Look back at Problem 33. If Rodney has 12 model boats, how many does Ashley have?

35. **Analyze** How can you use the expression you wrote in Problem 33 to find the number of boats Rodney has if Ashley has 8?

Mixed Review • Test Prep

Add or subtract. *(pages 60–69)*

36. $3,218 - 1,754$ **37.** $21,324 + 7,432$ **38.** $9,000 - 659$ **39.** $87,654 + 13,498$

40 Which number is 5,578 rounded to the nearest thousand? *(pages 10–11)*

     A 5,000   **B** 5,500   **C** 5,600   **D** 6,000

Expression Matchup

Practice evaluating expressions by playing this game.
Try to get more matches than the other player!

What You'll Need

- *16 index cards or (Teaching Tool 3)*

Here's What To Do

1. Make 16 cards like the ones shown.

2. Shuffle the cards. Place them facedown in any order in a 4 × 4 array.

3. A player turns over any two cards. If the cards show an expression and its value, the player keeps both cards. If not, the player turns the cards over and places them in the same positions.

4. Players take turns repeating Step 3 until all 8 matches have been made. The player with the greater number of cards is the winner.

$x + 6$ $x = 3$	9	$m \div 8$ $m = 24$	3
$4 + y$ $y = 2$	6	$2p$ $p = 4$	8
$z - 8$ $z = 10$	2	$5q$ $q = 2$	10
$9 - m$ $m = 4$	5	$d \div 6$ $d = 24$	4

Share Your Thinking Describe the strategy you used to try to get a match.

Write and Solve Equations

You will learn how to write and solve algebraic equations.

Learn About It

The art teacher bought some boxes of colored pencils with 10 pencils in each box. She got 40 pencils. How many boxes did the art teacher buy?

Since she got 40 colored pencils, you can write an equation.

- Let *y* stand for the number of boxes the art teacher bought.

- Then the expression 10*y* stands for the number of colored pencils.

$$10y = 40$$

number of ⎯ number ⎯ total number
colored pencils   of   of colored
in each box   boxes   pencils

To solve the equation, you have to find the value of *y* that will make the equation true. This value is called the solution of the equation.

Solve for *y*. **10*y* = 40**

Different Ways to Solve an Equation

You can use a related multiplication fact.	You can use a related division fact.
10*y* = 40	10*y* = 40
10 × ■ = 40	10 × ■ = 40
10 × 4 = 40	■ = 40 ÷ 10
	4 = 40 ÷ 10

The only value of *y* that will make the sentence true is 4.

The solution of the equation is *y* = 4.

Solution: The art teacher bought 4 boxes of colored pencils.

Standards AF **1.0, 1.1, 1.5** MR **2.4**

To check that the solution of an equation is correct, replace the variable with the solution and simplify.

Check the solution $y = 4$.

$$10y = 40$$
$$10 \times 4 = 40$$
$$40 = 40 \leftarrow$$

The same number appears on each side of the equals sign, so the solution is correct.

Three students bought some markers and shared the cost equally. Each student's share was $2. What was the total cost of the markers?

Use an equation to find the cost of the markers.

Step 1 Write an equation.

Each student's share was $2.

- Let T stand for the total cost.

- Then the expression $T \div 3$ stands for each student's share.

$T \div 3 = 2$ or $2 = T \div 3$

Step 2 Solve the equation.

Use a related multiplication fact.
$$T \div 3 = 2$$
$$\blacksquare \div 3 = 2$$
$$\blacksquare = 2 \times 3$$
$$T = 6$$

Solution: The total cost was $6.

Explain Your Thinking

▶ How can you check that $T = 18$ is the solution of $T \div 3 = 6$?

▶ Is $4z$ an equation?

▶ If $q \div 5 = 10$, what would you do to find the value of q?

▶ If $3k = 21$, how can you solve for k?

Guided Practice

Match the equation with its solution.

1. $5n = 15$
2. $5 = n \div 3$
3. $15 \div n = 3$

a. $n = 5$
b. $n = 3$
c. $n = 15$

Ask Yourself

- Do my equations have two expressions and an equals sign?

- What related multiplication or division fact can I use to solve the equation?

Independent Practice

Solve each equation. Check the solution.

4. $6m = 18$

5. $r \div 7 = 7$

6. $5 = 5q$

7. $6 = 12 \div n$

8. $n \div 7 = 3$

9. $15 = 5n$

10. $4m = 10 + 6$

11. $7 + 2 = m \div 3$

Problem Solving • Reasoning

12. A box of crayons contains 8 crayons. Suppose Tony has 72 crayons. Write two different equations that you could use to find the number of boxes he has.

13. Solve one of the equations you wrote in Problem 12 to find the number of boxes Tony has. Check your solution.

14. **Analyze** Olivia has 7 pencils in her pencil case. This is half as many as Sam has. How many pencils does Sam have? Write an equation that represents the problem. Then solve the equation to find how many pencils Sam has.

Mixed Review • Test Prep

Name the value of each underlined digit. *(pages 4–5)*

15. 56,<u>7</u>84

16. 1<u>1</u>2,498

17. 4,8<u>3</u>4

18. <u>36</u>,234

19 What is the value of 2 quarters, 2 dimes, and 1 nickel? *(pages 31–32)*

A $0.65 **B** $0.75 **C** $0.80 **D** $1.00

Write *true* or *false* for each statement.
Explain your answer.

20. The equation $6 = 3x$ has the same solution as the equation $3x = 6$.

21. The equation $4n = 0$ has the same solution as the equation $0 \div 4 = n$.

22. The equation $5k = 5$ has the same solution as the equation $k \div 5 = 5$.

23. The equation $y + 3 = 9$ has the same solution as the equation $3y = 9$.

Patterns in Data Tables

Disk-O-Tech sells computer disks. The table shows the number of disks in 1, 2, 3, 4, and 5 boxes. How is the number of disks related to the number of boxes?

There are several ways you can show the relationship.

- **You can describe the relationship by saying:** "The number of disks is 8 times the number of boxes."

- **You can use algebraic expressions.** If n stands for the number of boxes, then $8n$ stands for the number of disks in the boxes.

- **You can use a two-variable equation.** Let n stand for the number of boxes and m stand for the number of disks in the boxes. The equation $m = 8n$ shows the relationship.

Computer Disks	
Number of Boxes	Number of Disks
1	8
2	16
3	24
4	32
5	40
n	$8n$

Try These

Use the table at the right to solve the problems.

1. Look for patterns in the table. How many mouse pads would be in 9 boxes? Tell how you decided.

2. You buy some boxes of mouse pads and get 40 mouse pads. How many boxes did you buy? Tell how you decided.

3. Use words to describe the relationship between the number of mouse pads and the number of boxes.

4. Let x stand for the number of boxes. Write an expression to show the number of mouse pads in x boxes.

5. Let x stand for the number of boxes and y stand for the number of mouse pads. Write an equation using both x and y to show the relationship.

Mouse Pads	
Number of Boxes	Number of Mouse Pads
1	4
2	8
3	12
4	16
5	20
x	y

Problem-Solving Application: Using Patterns

You will learn how to use variables to describe and solve problems.

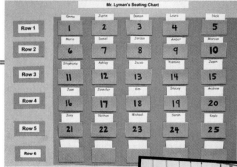

Sometimes you can use patterns to help solve problems.

Problem Look at Mr. Lyman's seating chart. What is the number of the last seat in Row 6?

Understand

What is the question?
What is the number of the last seat in Row 6?

What do you know?
• Each row has 5 seats.

• The numbers of the last seats in the first 5 rows.

Plan

How can you find the answer?
You can use a pattern to write an expression.

• The number of the last seat in each row is 5 times the row number.

• Let r represent the row number. Then the number of the last seat in each row is $5 \cdot r$ or $5r$.

Solve

Replace the variable r with 6.
Then simplify.

$5r$

5×6

The number of the last seat in Row 6 is 30.

30

> Since the row number is 6, $r = 6$.

Look Back

Look back at the problem.
How can you use counting by 5s to check your answer?

| **Standards** | AF **1.0, 1.1**   MR **1.0, 1.1, 2.0, 2.4, 2.6, 3.0, 3.2, 3.3** |

Guided Practice

**Use the seating chart on page 140
for Problems 1 and 2.**

Use the seating chart on page 140

1. David sits in the first seat of a row in Mr. Lyman's class. His seat number is 26. In which row does David sit?

   Think: How is the first number of a row related to the last number of the row before it?

2. The number of the last seat of the last row is 40. How many rows are there in Mr. Lyman's classroom?

   Think: How can you use the expression $5r$ to help you solve the problem?

Choose a Strategy

**Solve. Use Miss Benton's seating chart.
Use these or other strategies.**

Problem-Solving Strategies

- **Use a Table**
- **Write an Equation**
- **Guess and Check**
- **Use Logical Thinking**

3. Eric, Josh, Becky, and Tina sit in the first four seats of the fourth row. Tina does not sit in the first seat. Josh sits next to Tina and Becky. Eric sits next to Becky only. What is each student's seat number?

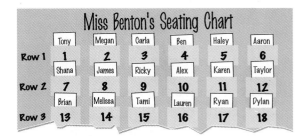

Miss Benton's Seating Chart

	Tony	Megan	Carla	Ben	Haley	Aaron
Row 1	1	2	3	4	5	6
	Shana	James	Ricky	Alex	Karen	Taylor
Row 2	7	8	9	10	11	12
	Brian	Melissa	Tami	Lauren	Ryan	Dylan
Row 3	13	14	15	16	17	18

4. The number of the first seat of the last row in Miss Benton's classroom is 31. How many rows are there in Miss Benton's class? How many seats are in the classroom?

5. There are 33 students in Miss Benton's class. There are 5 more girls than boys. How many girls are in Miss Benton's class? How many boys are in the class?

6. Lauren sits in the fourth seat of the third row. Her friend Joey sits in the fourth seat two rows behind her. What is Joey's seat number?

7. When the homework club meets, the students fill all the seats in the first $2\frac{1}{2}$ rows of the room. How many students are in the homework club?

Extra Practice See 5–6 on page 155.

1

Solve Multiplication Equations

You will learn that equals multiplied by equals are equal.

Learn About It

See what happens when you multiply both sides of an equation by the same number.

Step 1 Rewrite this equation with a multiplication sign.

$$3f = 6$$

$$3 \times f = 6$$

Step 2 Now multiply each side of the original equation by 2.

$$2 \times 3 \times f = 2 \times 6$$

Step 3 Write the new equation.

$$6f = 12$$

Step 4 Solve the two equations: $3f = 6$ and $6f = 12$.

$$3f = 6 \qquad 6f = 12$$
$$f = 2 \qquad f = 2$$

• What do you notice about the values of f?

Step 5 Choose any number. Multiply both sides of the equation $3f = 6$ by that number.

Then solve the new equation.

• What do you notice?

Step 6 Repeat Step 5 four times, choosing a new number each time.

- What do you notice?

Try It Out

Solve the equation 2s = 4. Then complete the table below.

	Start with the equation 2s = 4. Multiply each side by this number.	Write the new equation.	Solve the new equation.	Is the solution to the new equation the same as the solution to 2s = 4?
1.	3	$(3 \times 2) \times s = 3 \times 4$ $6s = 12$	$s = 2$	
2.	5			
3.	7			
4.	9			

Begin with the equation 5v = 10.

5. What is the solution of the equation?

6. By what number would you have to multiply both sides to get the equation $30v = 60$?

7. **Analyze** Can you get the equation $15v = 40$ by multiplying both sides by the same number?

Write about it! Talk about it!

Use what you have learned to answer these questions.

8. What happens to the solution of an equation when you multiply both sides by the same number?

9. The solution of the equation $3m = 9$ is $m = 3$. How does this help you find the solution of $9m = 27$?

Two-Step Functions

You will learn how to describe functions with two operations and solve for one variable when you have the value of the other.

Learn About It

The sign shows the fees for renting a canoe and a life jacket. The table below shows the charges for renting a canoe and a life jacket for 1 through 5 hours.

BIRCH LAKE
RENTAL FEES

Canoe $9 an hour

Life Jackets $5 a trip

This equation represents the cost of renting a canoe and a life jacket for a 1-hour trip.

$$(\$9 \times 1) + \$5 = \$14$$

   hourly   number of   charge for   total cost
   cost   hours   life jacket

Remember
to perform the operation inside the parentheses first.

This equation represents the cost of renting a canoe and a life jacket for a 4-hour trip.

$$(\$9 \times 4) + \$5 = \$41$$

   hourly   number of   charge for   total cost
   cost   hours   life jacket

This equation represents the cost of renting a canoe and a life jacket for any number of hours.

$$9n + 5 = T$$

   hourly   number   charge   total
   cost   of   for life   cost
          hours   jacket

| Rental Charge for Canoe and Life Jacket ||
Number of hours	Rental charge
1	$14
2	$23
3	$32
4	$41
5	$50

To describe the relationship, say, "The total cost in dollars is equal to 9 times the number of hours plus 5."

 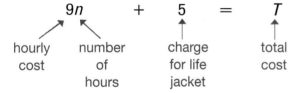 **Standards** | AF **1.0, 1.1, 1.2, 1.3, 1.4, 1.5**   MR **1.1, 1.2**

You can use the equation $9n + 5 = T$ to find the total rental cost when you know the number of hours.

Carl rented a canoe and a life jacket for a 6-hour trip. What was the total cost?

Solve $9n + 5 = T$ when $n = 6$.

Step 1 Write the equation.	**Step 2** Replace n with 6.	**Step 3** Solve.
$9n + 5 = T$	$9n + 5 = T$ $(9 \times 6) + 5 = T$	$9n + 5 = T$ $(9 \times 6) + 5 = T$ $54 + 5 = T$ $59 = T$

Solution: The total cost was $59.

You can also use the equation $9n + 5 = T$ to find the number of hours when you know the total rental cost.

Kim rented a canoe and a life jacket for a total cost of $77. For how many hours did she rent the canoe?

Solve $9n + 5 = T$ when $T = 77$.

Step 1 Write the equation.	**Step 2** Replace T with 77.
$9n + 5 = T$	$9n + 5 = T$ $9n + 5 = 77$

Step 3 Use the Guess and Check strategy to solve.

Try $n = 7$.	Try $n = 9$.	Try $n = 8$.
$(9 \times 7) + 5 = 68$ $68 < 77$	$(9 \times 9) + 5 = 86$ $86 > 77$	$(9 \times 8) + 5 = 77$ $77 = 77$ $n = 8$
Try a larger value for n.	Try a smaller value for n.	

Solution: Kim rented the canoe for 8 hours.

Explain Your Thinking

▶ Look back at the equation $9n + 5 = T$. How would you change the equation if the rental charge for the life jacket was increased to $7 a trip?

Guided Practice

Copy and complete each function table.

$y = 2x + 5$

	x	y
1.	3	■

$m = 3n + 1$

	n	m
2.	■	16

$5s - 1 = t$

	s	t
3.	2	■

Ask Yourself

- Which variable's value do I know?
- Which variable's value do I want to find?

Independent Practice

Copy and complete each function table.

$m = 2n - 4$

	n	m
4.	3	■
5.	2	■
6.	■	6

$y = 4x - 3$

	x	y
7.	4	■
8.	1	■
9.	■	9

$z = 3q - 1$

	q	z
10.	1	■
11.	3	■
12.	■	20

$p = 3m + 1$

	m	p
13.	10	■
14.	5	■
15.	■	25

Problem Solving • Reasoning

16. Ed has $9. He then saves $10 each week. Let w stand for the number of weeks. Let s stand for the total amount Ed saved. Which equation shows the total amount Ed will have saved after w weeks?

a. $s = 10w - 9$ **b.** $s = 9w + 10$ **c.** $s = 9 + 10w$

17. Use the equation you chose in Problem 16 to find out how much Ed will have after 4 weeks. Then use the equation to find out how many weeks it will take him to have a total savings of $89.

18. Analyze Ali has $12 and saves $4 a week. Karyn has $10 and saves $5 a week. Who will have more money after 3 weeks? How much more? Tell how you found your answer.

Mixed Review • Test Prep

Estimate each sum or difference. *(pages 56–57)*

19. $3,765 + 836$ **20.** $5,612 - 453$ **21.** $$23.45 + 11.99 **22.** $$78.11 - 34.52

23 Which number shows eight thousand, twenty-two? *(pages 5–6)*

A 8,220 **B** 8,202 **C** 8,022 **D** 822

Show What You Know

Number Puzzles

Match each number puzzle with an equation. Then solve.

1. If you multiply me by 3 and then add 2, the sum is 14. What number am I?

2. If you multiply me by 2 and then subtract 3, the difference is 13. What number am I?

3. If you multiply me by 2 and then add 3, the sum is 13. What number am I?

4. If you multiply me by 3 and then subtract 2, the difference is 10. What number am I?

a. $2p - 3 = 13$ **b.** $2x + 3 = 13$ **c.** $3n + 2 = 14$ **d.** $3y - 2 = 10$

Yes or No?

Tell whether the values for the variables make each equation true. Write *yes* or *no*.

1. $y = 2x + 1$
$x = 7$
$y = 15$

2. $m = 2 + 4n$
$n = 4$
$m = 18$

3. $z = 7q - 5$
$q = 2$
$z = 7$

4. $g = 3h - 1$
$h = 7$
$g = 19$

5. $r = 6 - 4s$
$s = 1$
$r = 2$

6. $y = 7x - 5$
$x = 1$
$y = 12$

Guess My Rule

Write an equation that shows how the two variables are related.

1.

n	m
1	5
4	11
5	13
7	17

2.

x	y
0	2
3	11
4	14
8	26

3.

k	m
3	6
4	8
5	10
7	14

4.

p	q
3	13
5	21
6	25
7	29

Problem-Solving Strategy: Write an Equation

You will learn how to write equations to represent and solve problems.

BLOOM'S FLOWERS

Sometimes you can use an equation to solve a problem.

Problem At Bloom's Flowers, spring flowers cost $2 each and vases cost $9 each. What is the total cost for a vase with 8 spring flowers?

Understand

What is the question?
- What is the total cost of a vase with 8 spring flowers?

What do you know?
- Each flower costs $2.
- A vase costs $9.

Plan

How can you find the answer?

You can write an equation.

Let b stand for the number of flowers ordered.
Then $2b$ stands for the cost of those flowers.

Let T stand for the total cost of the flowers with the vase.

Then the total cost can be represented by $T = 2b + 9$.

Solve

Replace b with 8. Then solve the equation.

$T = 2b + 9$
$T = (2 \times 8) + 9$
$T = 16 + 9$
$T = 25$

Since there are 8 flowers, $b = 8$.

The total cost is $25.

Look Back

Look back at the problem.
Does your answer match the information given in the problem?

| **Standards** | AF **1.0, 1.1, 1.2, 1.3, 1.5**   MR **1.0, 1.2, 2.0, 2.6, 3.0, 3.2**

Guided Practice

Use the Write an Equation strategy to solve each problem.

1 Roses cost $5 each. The delivery charge for any order is $12. Mr. Kelley had 10 roses delivered to his wife. What was the total cost?

Think: What expression could you use to show the cost of the roses?

2 Amber bought lilies in a glass vase. She paid $28 for a vase with 5 lilies. The vase cost $8. What was the cost of each lily?

Think: How can you show the cost of the lilies without the vase?

Choose a Strategy

Solve. Use these or other strategies.

Problem-Solving Strategies

• Use a Pattern   • Write an Equation   • Guess and Check   • Use Logical Thinking

3 At Bloom's Flowers, the price of an orchid is twice as much as the price of a tulip. Together a tulip and an orchid cost $18. What is the price of a tulip?

4 On Monday at Bloom's Flowers, eleven more ivy plants than mum plants were sold. 24 mum plants were sold. In all, how many ivy and mum plants did the shop sell on Monday?

5 A large flowerpot costs $5 more than a medium pot. A medium pot costs $4 more than a small pot. A small pot costs $2. If you bought one of each size flowerpot, what would the total cost be?

6 There are four plants in a row. The ivy is between the fern and the jade plants. The jade is between the ivy and the spider plants. The fern is the plant farthest to the left. Which plant is farthest to the right?

7 To feed the plants, 7 drops of plant food are added to a quart of water. There are 4 quarts in a gallon. How many drops of plant food are needed for a gallon of water?

8 Look at the pattern.

BLOOMBLOOMBLOOMBLOOM

If the likely pattern continues, how many *O*'s are in the first 100 letters?

Quick ✓ Check

Check Your Understanding of Lessons 10–15

Evaluate each expression when $p = 6$.

1. $p \times 7$ **2.** $36 \div p$ **3.** $p + 24$

Solve each equation. Check the solution.

4. $n \div 9 = 4$ **5.** $3x = 15 + 6$ **6.** $5 + 3 = r \div 4$

Copy and complete each function table.

7. $m = 3n - 2$

n	m
3	?
?	4
1	?

8. $y = 3x + 3$

x	y
?	9
4	?
3	?

Solve. Use the array for Problem 9.

9. What expression shows the relationship between the last number in a row and the row number?

10. A bag of sand costs $7. The delivery charge for an order is $10. Write an equation that shows the total cost for delivery of 4 bags of sand.

Row 1	2 4 6 8 10
Row 2	12 14 16 18 20
Row 3	22 24 26 28 30
Row 4	32 34 36 38 40
Row 5	▪ ▪ ▪ ▪ ▪
Row 6	▪ ▪ ▪ ▪ ▪

How did you do?

If you had difficulty with any items in the Quick Check, you can use the following pages for review and extra practice.

California Standards	ITEMS	REVIEW THESE PAGES	DO THESE EXTRA PRACTICE ITEMS
Algebra: **1.1**	1–3	pages 132–134	Set I, page 154
Algebra: **1.1**	4–6	pages 136–138	Set J, page 154
Algebra: **1.1, 1.4, 1.5**	7–8	pages 144–146	Set K, page 154
Algebra: **1.1, 1.4** Math Reasoning: **1.1, 2.3, 2.4, 3.1, 3.2**	9,10	pages 140–141, 148–149	5–10, page 155

Test Prep • Cumulative Review
Maintaining the Standards

Choose the letter of the correct answer. If a correct answer is not here, choose NH.

1 A store sells pencils in packages of 8 pencils per pack. If Mrs. Hermida needs 56 pencils, how many packs must she buy?

A 5   **C** 7

B 6   **D** NH

2 Which expression does not equal 16?

F 4×4

G $2 \times 2 \times 4$

H $2 \times 2 \times 2 \times 3$

J 2×8

3 What is the value of *n*?

$$n \div 7 = 6$$

A 32

B 35

C 36

D 42

4 Which number should go in the box to make the equation true?

$$(4 \times 4) + 3 = 16 + \blacksquare$$

F 1

G 2

H 3

J 4

5 Which expression is equal to 38?

A $5 \times (9 - 7)$ **C** $(5 \times 7) - 9$

B $(5 \times 9) - 7$ **D** $(7 \times 9) - 5$

Use the table to answer Questions 6–7.

x	y
1	6
2	12
3	18
4	?

6 Which equation does the table show?

F $y = x + 6$

G $y = x - 6$

H $y = 6x$

J $y = x \div 6$

7 Which number is missing from the table?

A 6   **C** 24

B 22   **D** 32

8 Lynn, Beth, and Mark are trading baseball cards. Lynn trades 5 of her cards for 4 of Beth's cards, and 7 of her cards for 9 of Mark's cards. If Lynn started with 50 cards, how many does she have now?

Explain How did you find your answer?

Extra Practice

Set A *(Lesson 1, pages 106–109)*

Multiply. Use doubles to help you.

1. 2×8
2. 3×7
3. 8×5
4. 8×3

5. $\begin{array}{r} 7 \\ \times\ 4 \\ \hline \end{array}$
6. $\begin{array}{r} 4 \\ \times\ 8 \\ \hline \end{array}$
7. $\begin{array}{r} 8 \\ \times\ 8 \\ \hline \end{array}$
8. $\begin{array}{r} 10 \\ \times\ 6 \\ \hline \end{array}$
9. $\begin{array}{r} 10 \\ \times\ 7 \\ \hline \end{array}$

Compare. Write >, < or = in the ●.

10. 4×10 ● 6×8
11. 3×4 ● 6×2
12. 5×5 ● 3×10

Set B *(Lesson 2, pages 110–111)*

Solve. Name the property that you used.

1. $1 \times 7 = n$
2. $5 \times 7 = m \times 5$
3. $(4 \times 5) \times 6 = 4 \times (v \times 6)$

4. $83 \times 1 = h$
5. $0 \times 92 = r$
6. $p = 3 \times (5 \times 1)$

Set C *(Lesson 3, pages 112–115)*

Multiply.

1. $\begin{array}{r} 3 \\ \times\ 9 \\ \hline \end{array}$
2. $\begin{array}{r} 10 \\ \times\ 7 \\ \hline \end{array}$
3. $\begin{array}{r} 6 \\ \times\ 5 \\ \hline \end{array}$
4. $\begin{array}{r} 10 \\ \times\ 0 \\ \hline \end{array}$
5. $\begin{array}{r} 7 \\ \times\ 5 \\ \hline \end{array}$

6. 10×9
7. 8×5
8. 4×9
9. $5 \times 5 \times 2$

Set D *(Lesson 4, pages 118–119)*

Complete each fact family.

1. $4 \times 7 = \blacksquare$
   $7 \times 4 = \blacksquare$
   $28 \div 4 = \blacksquare$
   $28 \div 7 = \blacksquare$

2. $5 \times 6 = \blacksquare$
   $6 \times 5 = \blacksquare$
   $30 \div 5 = \blacksquare$
   $30 \div 6 = \blacksquare$

3. $7 \times 6 = \blacksquare$
   $6 \times 7 = \blacksquare$
   $42 \div 6 = \blacksquare$
   $42 \div 7 = \blacksquare$

4. $6 \times 9 = \blacksquare$
   $9 \times 6 = \blacksquare$
   $54 \div 6 = \blacksquare$
   $54 \div 9 = \blacksquare$

Write the fact family for each set of numbers.

5. 2, 7, 14
6. 3, 5, 15
7. 4, 5, 20
8. 7, 8, 56

Extra Practice

Set E *(Lesson 5, pages 120–121)*

Divide.

1. $16 \div 2$ **2.** $42 \div 6$ **3.** $45 \div 5$ **4.** $32 \div 8$

5. $4\overline{)20}$ **6.** $6\overline{)48}$ **7.** $4\overline{)28}$ **8.** $4\overline{)24}$

Set F *(Lesson 6, pages 122–123)*

Solve. If an equation has no solution, tell why.

1. $9 \div 1 = n$ **2.** $7 \div 0 = p$ **3.** $m \div 6 = 0$ **4.** $j \div 1 = 8$

5. $0 \div 3 = k$ **6.** $4 \div m = 4$ **7.** $t \div 1 = 1$ **8.** $m \div 5 = 1$

Compare. Write >, < or = in the ●.

9. $5 \div 1$ ● $6 \div 1$ **10.** $0 \div 7$ ● $7 \div 7$ **11.** $32 \div 32$ ● $521 \div 521$

Set G *(Lesson 7, pages 124–125)*

Divide.

1. $7 \div 7$ **2.** $35 \div 5$ **3.** $28 \div 7$ **4.** $42 \div 7$

5. $70 \div 7$ **6.** $14 \div 7$ **7.** $40 \div 4$ **8.** $90 \div 9$

9. $7\overline{)63}$ **10.** $9\overline{)54}$ **11.** $9\overline{)18}$ **12.** $5\overline{)40}$

Set H *(Lesson 8, pages 126–127)*

Divide.

1. $2\overline{)7}$ **2.** $4\overline{)5}$ **3.** $5\overline{)13}$ **4.** $2\overline{)11}$ **5.** $7\overline{)32}$

6. $4\overline{)9}$ **7.** $6\overline{)10}$ **8.** $7\overline{)24}$ **9.** $7\overline{)16}$ **10.** $4\overline{)29}$

11. $13 \div 2$ **12.** $13 \div 4$ **13.** $17 \div 5$ **14.** $14 \div 3$

15. $27 \div 8$ **16.** $18 \div 4$ **17.** $34 \div 7$ **18.** $43 \div 6$

Extra Practice

Set I (Lesson 10, pages 132–135)

Evaluate each expression when $p = 8$.

1. $4p$ **2.** $p \div 4$ **3.** $p + 5$ **4.** $p - 2$

5. $p + 10$ **6.** $p \div 8$ **7.** $64 \div p$ **8.** $p \div 1$

Let n stand for the number of model airplanes in Jill's collection. Write an algebraic expression for each description.

9. half as many model airplanes as in Jill's collection

10. 3 times as many model airplanes as in Jill's collection

11. 6 fewer model airplanes than in Jill's collection

12. 5 more model airplanes than in Jill's collection

Set J (Lesson 11, pages 136–139)

Solve each equation. Check the solution.

1. $7m = 21$ **2.** $r \div 7 = 6$ **3.** $8 = 8q$ **4.** $9 = 18 \div n$

5. $n \div 7 = 4$ **6.** $18 = 3n$ **7.** $5m = 20 + 5$ **8.** $5 + 3 = x \div 4$

Set K (Lesson 14, pages 144–146)

Copy and complete each function table.

$m = 3n - 2$

	n	m
1.	4	
2.	6	
3.		4

$y = 5x - 4$

	x	y
4.	3	
5.	6	
6.		36

$z = 4q - 1$

	q	z
7.	1	
8.	3	
9.		23

$p = 2m + 1$

	m	p
10.	9	
11.	7	
12.		11

Extra Practice • Problem Solving

Solve. *(Lesson 9, pages 128–129)*

1 A toy store sells action figures for $3 each or 4 for $11. You want to buy 10 action figures. What will be the total cost?

2 Marbles are $4 a bag. There are 30 marbles in a bag. How many marbles can you buy for $12?

3 Robert buys baseball trading cards that cost $2 a pack. There are 8 baseball cards in each pack. How many baseball cards can Robert buy for $10?

4 Maya spent $32 on trading card packs and marbles. She spent 3 times as much money on marbles as she did on trading cards. How much money did she spend on each?

Use the array of consecutive whole numbers for Problems 5–6. *(Lesson 12, pages 140–141)*

5 The last number in a row is 42. What is the row number?

6 Copy and complete the array. Start at 1. Underline 1 and 2 and circle the next number. Then underline the next two numbers and circle the following number. Continue this pattern to the end. Describe the circled numbers.

Row 1	1 2 3 4 5 6
Row 2	7 8 9 10 11 12
Row 3	13 14 15 16 17 18
Row 4	19 20 21 22 23 24
Row 5	25 26 27 28 29 30
Row 6	▪ ▪ ▪ ▪ ▪ ▪
Row 7	▪ ▪ ▪ ▪ ▪ ▪

Use the Write an Equation strategy to solve each problem.

(Lesson 15, pages 148–149)

7 A bakery sells apple turnovers for $2 each. The delivery charge for any order is $4. Mr. Kelly would like 12 apple turnovers delivered to his office. What will the cost be?

8 A bakery sells loaves of rye bread in baskets. A basket of 6 loaves of rye bread sells for $14. The basket alone costs $2. What is the cost of each loaf of bread?

9 A dozen bagels costs twice as much as a dozen onion rolls. Together they cost $9. What is the cost of a dozen bagels?

10 To make poppy-seed rolls, 2 eggs are needed for each dozen rolls. How many eggs are needed for 6 dozen poppy-seed rolls?

Chapter Review

Reviewing Vocabulary

1. When the dividend is 0, what do you know about the quotient?

2. Write a multiplication equation and label the factors and product.

3. What remainders are possible when you divide by 5?

4. Show an example of the Commutative Property of Multiplication.

Reviewing Concepts and Skills

Multiply. *(pages 106–109, 112–115)*

5. 4×8
6. 6×5
7. 8×6
8. 10×4

9. 10×6
10. 7×5
11. 3×9
12. 8×9

Solve. Name the property that you used. *(pages 110–111)*

13. $1 \times 29 = n$
14. $(7 \times 6) \times 8 = 7 \times (m \times 8)$
15. $8 \times 9 = y \times 8$

Write the fact family for each set of numbers. *(pages 118–119)*

16. 5, 7, 35
17. 7, 9, 63
18. 3, 7, 21

Divide. *(pages 120–121, 124–125)*

19. $24 \div 6$
20. $64 \div 8$
21. $36 \div 4$
22. $27 \div 3$

23. $25 \div 5$
24. $45 \div 9$
25. $42 \div 7$
26. $70 \div 10$

Solve. If an equation has no solution, tell why. *(pages 122–123)*

27. $8 \div 1 = n$
28. $5 \div 0 = t$
29. $9 \div m = 9$
30. $m \div 1 = 7$

Divide. *(pages 126–127)*

31. $17 \div 2$
32. $21 \div 4$
33. $27 \div 5$
34. $29 \div 8$

Evaluate each expression when $n = 6$. *(pages 132–135)*

35. $7n$
36. $n + 12$
37. $48 \div n$
38. $3n + 7$

**Let *n* stand for the number of cats in Sophia's collection.
Write an algebraic expression for each description.**

39. 7 fewer cats than in Sophia's collection

40. 4 times as many cats as in Sophia's collection

Solve each equation. Check the solution. *(pages 136–139)*

41. $9m = 27$ **42.** $7 = 7r$ **43.** $7 = 42 \div x$ **44.** $n \div 8 = 7$

Copy and complete each function table.

45. $m = 3n + 2$

n	m
5	▪
7	▪
2	▪

46. $y = 4x - 5$

x	y
3	▪
7	▪
11	▪

Solve. *(pages 128–129, pages 148–149)*

47. A sports shop sells T-shirts for $5 each or 5 for $22. What will be the total cost of 8 T-shirts?

48. The zoo gift shop sells posters for $6 each or 3 for $15. What will be the total cost of 5 posters?

49. The sports shop sells baseball caps for $4 each. The delivery fee is $6 for each order. What will it cost to have 12 caps delivered?

50. The zoo gift shop makes $2 on each animal mask sold. How many masks must be sold to make a profit of $24?

Brain Teasers Math Reasoning

FILL THEM IN

Copy and complete. Use each of the digits 1–9 once.

$$▪ \times 4 = 2▪ \qquad 6 \times ▪ = 54$$
$$6 \times ▪ = ▪0 \qquad ▪ \times 4 = 1▪$$
$$8 \times ▪ = ▪6$$

WHO DOESN'T BELONG?

Think about multiplication. Which number doesn't belong? Explain why.

18   63   90   25

Safe Site

Internet Brain Teasers
Visit **www.eduplace.com/kids/mhm**
for more *Brain Teasers.*

157

Chapter Test

Multiply.

1. 4×6 **2.** 8×7 **3.** 10×9 **4.** 5×7 **5.** 9×8

6. 6×3 **7.** 9×2 **8.** 8×7 **9.** 7×7 **10.** 6×5

Solve each equation. Name the property that you used.

11. $1 \times 37 = n$ **12.** $(9 \times 7) \times 3 = 9 \times (m \times 3)$

Write the fact family for each set of numbers.

13. $8, 7, 56$ **14.** $9, 6, 54$

Solve. If an equation has no solution, tell why.

15. $9 \div 0 = t$ **16.** $m \div 1 = 4$

Divide.

17. $24 \div 8$ **18.** $48 \div 8$ **19.** $45 \div 5$ **20.** $63 \div 9$

21. $33 \div 5$ **22.** $53 \div 7$ **23.** $41 \div 8$ **24.** $70 \div 9$

Evaluate each expression when $n = 6$.

25. $n + 15$ **26.** $48 \div n$ **27.** $6n + 7$

Solve each equation. Check the solution.

28. $7m = 42$ **29.** $9 = 72 \div x$ **30.** $n \div 4 = 8$ **31.** $4m = 20$

Solve.

32. A large shirt costs $4 more than a medium shirt. A medium shirt costs $3 more than a small shirt. The small shirt costs $8. If you bought one shirt of each size, what would be the total cost?

33. The balloon shop sells balloons in bunches of 7. The delivery cost for one bunch of balloons is $6. The total cost for a bunch of balloons to be delivered is $20. What is the cost of each balloon?

 Write About It

Solve each problem. Use correct mathematical vocabulary to explain your thinking.

1. Joan has 18 stamps from Germany.

   a. How many different rectangular arrays can she make with the stamps? Draw the arrays.

   b. Write the fact family that corresponds to each array.

   c. A fact family contains the numbers 4 and 8. What other number belongs in the fact family? Is there another number for a different fact family? Write the equations for both fact families.

2. Amy completed the following division:

   a. Explain what she did wrong.

   b. Show how to find the correct answer.

$$\begin{array}{r} 6 \text{ R3} \\ 2\overline{)15} \\ \underline{12} \\ 3 \end{array}$$

Another Look

Mrs. Johnson is grading a math test. She puts the number of correct answers on each student's test into the Shrinker. Then she puts the number that comes out of the Shrinker into the Expander. The number that comes out of the Expander is the student's test grade.

Use the Shrinker and the Expander to solve the problems. You can use what you know about multiplication and division.

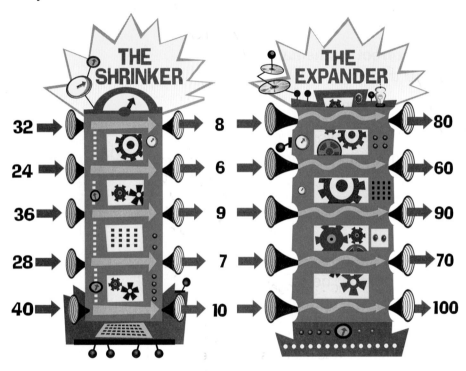

1. Write a division fact for each input-output number pair shown for the Shrinker.

2. Write a multiplication fact for each input-output number pair shown for the Expander.

3. **Look Back** Describe the rule for each machine. Then write an expression for each machine output that uses a variable for its input.

4. **Analyze** Find the final grade a student with 34 correct answers would get. *Hint:* Look at the final grades for 32 and 36 correct answers.

Enrichment

Sieve of Eratosthenes

A **prime number** is a whole number that has exactly two factors, itself and 1. When a prime number is divided by any whole number other than itself or 1, the remainder will not be zero.

Eratosthenes was an ancient Greek mathematician who discovered the following way to find prime numbers. Follow these steps to find all prime numbers less than 50.

> **New Vocabulary**
> prime number
> multiples
> composite number

Step 1 Make a table like this one to show all whole numbers from 1 to 50.

1	2	3	4	5	6	7	8	9	10
11	12	13	14	15	16	17	18	19	20
21	22	23	24	25	26	27	28	29	30
31	32	33	34	35	36	37	38	39	40
41	42	43	44	45	46	47	48	49	50

Draw a box around the number 1. The number 1 is not prime because it has only one factor, 1.

Step 2 Circle the 2. Cross out all **multiples** of 2 that are greater than 2.

To find multiples of 2, count by 2s.
2, 4, 6, 8, 10, 12, 14, . . .
(You add 2 more each time.)

Step 3 Go back to the beginning of the table. Circle the least number that is not circled or crossed out. (This should be 3.) Cross out all multiples of 3 that are greater than 3 and have not already been crossed out.

Step 4 Go back to the beginning of the table again. Circle the least number that is not circled or crossed out. Cross out all multiples of that number that are greater than that number and have not already been crossed out.

Step 5 Keep repeating Step 4 until all the numbers have been circled or crossed out.

Step 6 List all numbers that have been circled. These are the prime numbers less than 50.

The numbers that have been crossed out are called composite numbers.

A **composite number** has more than two factors.

Explain Your Thinking

When you circled the 7, the only multiple you could cross out was 49. Why?

CHAPTER 4

Multiplication of Whole Numbers

Why Learn About Multiplication of Whole Numbers?

Multiplication of whole numbers is the same as repeated addition. When you multiply, you can quickly find the total amount of a number of equal groups.

If someone agrees to pay you $2.50 an hour to rake leaves for 3 hours, you can use multiplication to figure out how much money you will earn.

These teenagers are charging $5.00 for each car they wash. They can multiply $5.00 by the number of cars they will wash to find how much money they will earn.

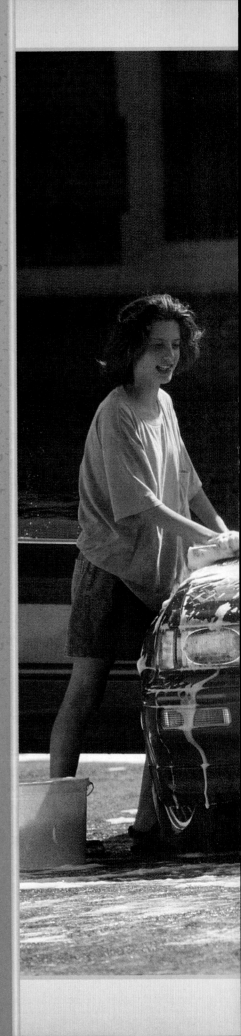

Reading Mathematics

Reviewing Vocabulary

Understanding math language helps you become a successful problem solver. Here are some math vocabulary words you should know.

multiply   to find the total number of objects that are in equal groups

product   the answer in multiplication

factor   a number that is multiplied

Reading Words and Symbols

When you read mathematics, sometimes you read only words, sometimes you read words and symbols, and sometimes you read only symbols.

The properties of multiplication can help you multiply.

Commutative Property You can change the order of the factors and the product stays the same.

$6 \times 8 = 48$
$8 \times 6 = 48$
$6 \times 8 = 8 \times 6$

Property of Zero When you multiply any number by 0, the product is 0.

$0 \times 9 = 0$
$9 \times 0 = 0$

Property of One When you multiply any number by 1, the product is the other factor.

$1 \times 5 = 5$
$5 \times 1 = 5$

Associative Property You can group factors in different ways and the product stays the same.

$$(4 \times 2) \times 3 = 4 \times (2 \times 3)$$
$$8 \times 3 = 4 \times 6$$
$$24 = 24$$

Try These

1. Name the multiplication property you could use to help solve each pair of equations. Then solve each equation.

   a. $9 \times 5 = n$
   $5 \times 9 = n$

   b. $(2 \times 2) \times 3 = n$
   $2 \times (2 \times 3) = n$

   c. $1 \times 8 = n$
   $8 \times 1 = n$

   d. $6 \times 0 = n$
   $0 \times 6 = n$

2. Write *true* or *false* for each sentence.

   a. The product is always greater than the factors.

   b. Both factors cannot be the same number.

   c. A product can be the same number as a factor.

   d. You can use a pattern to multiply by 5.

3. Use the clues to find each number.

   a. The product of its digits is 24.
   It is odd.
   The difference between its digits is 5.

   b. It is even.
   The product of its digits is 18.
   The sum of its digits is 9.

   c. The difference between its digits is 1.
   The product of its digits is 20.
   It is odd.

   d. The product of its digits is 6.
   The difference between its digits is 5.
   It is odd.

   e. The sum of its digits is 5.
   The product of its digits is 6.
   It is even.

   f. It is odd.
   The product of its digits is 9.
   The difference between its digits is 0.

Mental Math: Multiply Multiples of 10, 100, and 1,000

You will learn how to use basic facts and patterns to help you multiply mentally.

Learn About It

Duane is learning about the number of calories burned while doing different activities. How many calories will Duane burn playing tennis for 3 hours?

Activity	Calories Burned in One Hour
Swimming	300
Horseback riding	350
Bike riding	400
Playing tennis	400
Playing basketball	450
Hiking	200

Multiply. $3 \times 400 = n$

Find 3×400.

You can use basic facts and patterns of zeros to help you multiply.

$3 \times 4 = 12$ (3×4 ones)

$3 \times 40 = 120$ (3×4 tens)

$3 \times 400 = 1,200$ (3×4 hundreds)

Think: What do you notice about the number of zeros in the factors and in the product?

Solution: Duane will burn 1,200 calories.

Another Example

Multiple of 1,000

Find $5 \times 8,000$.

$5 \times 8 = 40$
$5 \times 80 = 400$
$5 \times 800 = 4,000$
$5 \times 8,000 = 40,000$

Why It Works

$5 \times 8,000 = 5 \times (8 \times 1,000)$
$= (5 \times 8) \times 1,000$
$= 40 \times 1,000$
$= 40,000$

Explain Your Thinking

▶ What basic fact and pattern of zeros were used in the example?

Guided Practice

Use basic facts and patterns to find each product.

1. 5×7
5×70
5×700
$5 \times 7,000$

2. 8×6
8×60
8×600
$8 \times 6,000$

Ask Yourself

• What basic fact can I use?

• How many zeros should be in the product?

166   **Standards**   NS 3.0   MR 1.1, 2.3

Independent Practice

Use basic facts and patterns to find each product.

3. 4 × 4
4 × 40
4 × 400
4 × 4,000

4. 7 × 3
7 × 30
7 × 300
7 × 3,000

5. 6 × 9
6 × 90
6 × 900
6 × 9,000

6. 9 × 8
9 × 80
9 × 800
9 × 8,000

7. 6 × 5

8. 6 × 50

9. 6 × 500

10. 6 × 5,000

11. 2 × 80

12. 4 × 50

13. 6 × 70

14. 9 × 90

15. 3 × 200

16. 7 × 700

17. 9 × 300

18. 5 × 900

19. 6 × 4,000

20. 2 × 5,000

21. 4 × 4,000

22. 3 × 6,000

Problem Solving • Reasoning

Use Data Use the table on page 166 for Problems 23–25.

23. Sam swam for 1 hour and rode his bike for 2 hours. How many calories did Sam burn?

24. **Compare** Tina says she burned as many calories on a 3-hour hike as she did on a 2-hour horseback ride. Is she right? Explain.

25. **Analyze** Duane did 3 different activities for 1 hour each. He burned a total of 1,250 calories. What activities did he do?

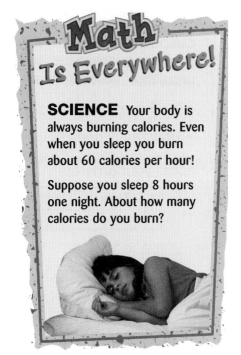

SCIENCE Your body is always burning calories. Even when you sleep you burn about 60 calories per hour!

Suppose you sleep 8 hours one night. About how many calories do you burn?

Mixed Review • Test Prep

Compare. Write >, <, or = in the ⬤. *(pages 6–9)*

26. 1,280 ⬤ 1,208

27. 700 + 30 + 6 ⬤ 30,000 + 20

28. 500,000 + 4,000 + 900 ⬤ 799,901

Choose the letter of the correct answer. *(pages 10–11)*

29 What is 3,295 rounded to the nearest ten?

A 3,300   **C** 3,200
B 3,290   **D** 3,000

30 What is 53,922 rounded to the nearest hundred?

F 50,000   **H** 53,920
G 53,900   **J** 54,000

Modeling Multiplication by One-Digit Numbers

You will learn how to multiply numbers by using base-ten blocks.

Learn About It

Use base-ten blocks to help you multiply a two-digit number by a one-digit number.

The fourth-graders at Smith School are going on a field trip. There are 32 students on each of 3 buses. How many students are there altogether?

Find 3 × 32.

Materials

For each pair: base-ten blocks

Use base-ten blocks to show 3 groups of 32.

Each row shows 3 tens 2 ones, or 32.

- How many tens blocks did you use?
- How many ones blocks did you use?

Record your answers in a chart like this one.

Tens	Ones
9	6

What is 3 × 32?

How would you find the total number of students if there were 2 classes with 26 students in each class?

Find 2 × 26.

Step 1 Use base-ten blocks to show 2 groups of 26.

- How many tens blocks did you use?
- How many ones blocks did you use?

Standards NS 3.0 MR 2.3, 2.4

Step 2 When the number of ones blocks is 10 or greater than 10, you need to regroup 10 ones as 1 ten.

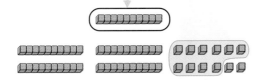

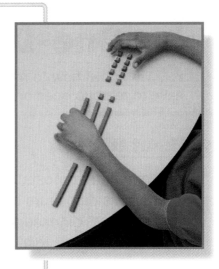

- How many tens blocks and how many ones blocks do you have now?

What is 2 × 26?

Try It Out

Tell what multiplication sentence is shown by the blocks.

1.

2.

Use base-ten blocks to find each product.

3. 3 × 31

4. 2 × 18

5. 4 × 21

6. 3 × 22

7. 5 × 15

8. 2 × 27

9. 7 × 13

10. 4 × 16

11. Write About It Look back at Exercises 3–10. In which exercises did you have to regroup ones as tens? How can you tell if you will have to regroup just by looking at a problem?

Write about it! Talk about it!

Use what you have learned to answer these questions.

12. Which is less, 2 × 31 or 2 × 32? Explain how you can tell without multiplying.

13. How could you use addition to find 3 × 35?

Multiply Two-Digit Numbers by One-Digit Numbers

You will learn how to multiply when you have to regroup ones or regroup tens.

Learn About It

Joseph has a miniature dinosaur collection. He has arranged his dinosaurs on 3 shelves in his room. There are 26 dinosaurs on each shelf. How many dinosaurs does Joseph have?

Multiply.   **3 × 26 = *n***

Find 3 × 26.

Step 1 Think: 3 groups of 26. Use base-ten blocks to show 3 groups of 26.

$$\begin{array}{r} 26 \\ \times\ 3 \\ \hline \end{array}$$

Step 2 Multiply the ones.

3 × 6 ones = 18 ones

Regroup 18 ones as 1 ten 8 ones.

$$\begin{array}{r} 1 \\ 26 \\ \times\ 3 \\ \hline 8 \end{array}$$ 18 ones

Step 3 Multiply the tens.

3 × 2 tens = 6 tens

Add the 1 ten.

6 tens + 1 ten = 7 tens

$$\begin{array}{r} 1 \\ 26 \\ \times\ 3 \\ \hline 78 \end{array}$$ 7 tens

---

Solution: Joseph has 78 dinosaurs.

Other Examples

A. No Regrouping

$$\begin{array}{r} 43 \\ \times\ 2 \\ \hline 86 \end{array}$$

B. Regrouping Tens as Hundreds

$$\begin{array}{r} 71 \\ \times\ 4 \\ \hline 284 \end{array}$$ 4 × 7 tens = 28 tens or 2 hundreds 8 tens

Explain Your Thinking

▶ What is the greatest number of ones you can have before you need to regroup? Explain.

| **Standards** | NS **3.0**   AF **1.1, 1.2**   MR **2.3**

Guided Practice

Find each product.

1. 2 × 14

2. 5 × 21

Ask Yourself

- What do I multiply first?

- Do I need to regroup ones? tens?

- Do I need to add any tens?

Multiply.

3. 41 × 7	**4.** 11 × 8	**5.** 19 × 5	**6.** 31 × 4	**7.** 52 × 3	**8.** 61 × 6

Independent Practice

Find each product.

9. 3 × 15

10. 4 × 23

11. 2 × 12

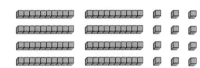

Multiply.

12. 73 × 2	**13.** 11 × 6	**14.** 92 × 3	**15.** 13 × 5	**16.** 46 × 2	**17.** 31 × 9
18. 63 × 3	**19.** 82 × 4	**20.** 61 × 8	**21.** 12 × 7	**22.** 18 × 5	**23.** 24 × 3
24. 31 × 3	**25.** 92 × 2	**26.** 11 × 9	**27.** 72 × 4	**28.** 16 × 2	**29.** 36 × 2

30. 29 × 2 **31.** 25 × 3 **32.** 29 × 3 **33.** 12 × 3 **34.** 42 × 2 **35.** 16 × 4

36. 51 × 7 **37.** 34 × 2 **38.** 12 × 6 **39.** 16 × 3 **40.** 22 × 2 **41.** 33 × 3

𝑛 Algebra • Expressions Write >, <, or = in the ⬤.

42. 81 × 3 ⬤ 3 × 81

43. 2 × 3 × 7 ⬤ 5 × 6

44. 8 × 92 ⬤ (8 × 90) + (8 × 2)

45. 98 × 0 ⬤ 98 × 1

Problem Solving • Reasoning

Use the picture at the right for Problems 46 and 47.

46. Stephen and Margo have toy bug collections. Stephen has 2 tubes filled with bugs. Margo has 2 packages of bugs. How many bugs does Stephen have?

47. Compare Lei and Mary also have toy bug collections. Lei has 5 tubes of bugs. Mary has 4 packages of bugs. Who has more bugs? Explain.

48. Toy bugs are on five shelves in a toy store. The first shelf has 10 bugs. The second has 20. The third has 40. The fourth has 80. How many bugs do you predict to be on the fifth shelf? Why?

49. Analyze A storage container has 8 drawers that can hold 10 bugs each, 6 drawers that can hold 15 bugs each, and 4 drawers that can hold 20 bugs each. How many bugs can the container hold in all?

Mixed Review • Test Prep

Estimate by rounding to the greatest place value. *(pages 64–65)*

50. 8,445 − 5,999 **51.** $43.99 + $79.81 **52.** 87¢ − 34¢ **53.** 91,925 + 12,778

Choose the letter of the correct answer. *(pages 56–58, 60–62)*

54 What is the difference between 4,906 and 2,194?

A 2,892 **C** 2,712
B 2,812 **D** 1,812

55 What is the sum of 10,080 and 733?

F 11,813 **H** 10,713
G 10,813 **J** 10,347

Logical Thinking

Look at the way the first pair of words is related. Choose the letter that shows a similar relationship for the second pair.

56. Multiplication is to division as

    A. subtraction is to multiplication
    c. addition is to subtraction
    B. multiplication is to subtraction
    D. division is to addition

Number Sense

Multiplying in a Different Way

When people multiply, they often multiply the ones digit and then the tens digit. But there are other ways to multiply.

Morgan discovered another way to multiply. Study how he completed the multiplication.

Multiply 29 by 4 in the way you have been taught. Did you get the same answer?

$$29 \times 4 = (20 + 9) \times 4$$
$$= (20 \times 4) + (9 \times 4)$$
$$= 80 + 36$$
$$= 116$$

▶ How does thinking of 29 as 20 + 9 help Morgan multiply?

Angelica used still another way to multiply. Study how she completed the multiplication.

Multiply 29 by 4 in the way you have been taught. Did you get the same answer?

$$29 \times 4 = (30 - 1) \times 4$$
$$= (30 \times 4) - (1 \times 4)$$
$$= 120 - 4$$
$$= 116$$

▶ How does thinking of 29 as 30 − 1 help Angelica multiply?

Try These

Use Morgan's method to complete each multiplication.

1. $17 \times 9 = (10 + \blacksquare) \times 9$
$= (10 \times 9) + (\blacksquare \times 9)$
$= 90 + \blacksquare$
$= \blacksquare$

2. $98 \times 7 = (\blacksquare + \blacksquare) \times 7$
$= (\blacksquare \times 7) + (\blacksquare \times 7)$
$= \blacksquare + \blacksquare$
$= \blacksquare$

Use Angelica's method to complete each multiplication.

3. $39 \times 8 = (40 - \blacksquare) \times 8$
$= (40 \times 8) - (\blacksquare \times 8)$
$= 320 - \blacksquare$
$= \blacksquare$

4. $59 \times 9 = (\blacksquare - \blacksquare) \times 9$
$= (\blacksquare \times 9) - (\blacksquare \times 9)$
$= \blacksquare - \blacksquare$
$= \blacksquare$

Estimate Products

You will learn how to estimate products.

Learn About It

Danny's town is celebrating Cinco de Mayo. Last year there were 419 people at the celebration. About twice as many people are expected this year. About how many people are expected this year?

You can estimate products by rounding factors to their greatest place value.

- First, round 419 to the nearest hundred.

    419 **rounds to** 400

- Then multiply.

    $2 \times 400 = 800$

    2×419 is close to 2×400.

Solution: The estimate shows that about 800 people are expected this year.

More Examples

A. Estimate to the Nearest Thousand

Estimate $3 \times 7{,}901$.

7,901 **rounds to** 8,000

$3 \times 8{,}000 = 24{,}000$

$3 \times 7{,}901$ is close to 24,000.

B. Estimate With Money

Estimate $8 \times \$21.95$.

$21.95 **rounds to** $20

$8 \times \$20 = \$160$

$8 \times \$21.95$ is about $160.

Explain Your Thinking

▶ How can estimating a product help you to check whether the answer to a multiplication problem is reasonable?

Guided Practice

Estimate each product by rounding to the greatest place value.

Ask Yourself

- What does the greater number round to?

- Do I need to write a dollar sign in the product?

| 1. | 82 × 5 | 2. | $4.23 × 9 | 3. | 781 × 6 | 4. | $8.49 × 8 |

5. $2 \times \$28$ **6.** 4×180 **7.** $7 \times \$19.95$

Standards NS **1.3, 3.0**   MR **2.5**

Independent Practice

Estimate each product.

8. 55
      × 4

9. 639
      × 2

10. 4,598
       ×   3

11. $8.74
       ×   6

12. 6,317
       ×   4

13. 73
       × 7

14. 298
       × 5

15. 1,901
       ×   2

16. $7.35
       ×   3

17. 993
       × 6

18. 8 × 46

19. 9 × 663

20. 5 × 5,294

21. 7 × $86.32

22. 6 × 487

23. 7 × 7,890

24. 9 × 9,409

25. 4 × $79.98

Problem Solving • Reasoning

26. Patterns The first 5 people to arrive at the celebration will get a paper lantern. After that, every 5th person will get a lantern until there are no lanterns left. If Sally is the 30th person to arrive, and there are 10 lanterns to give away, will she get one? Explain.

27. The food booth sold 102 tacos, three times as many burritos as tacos, and two times as many enchiladas as burritos. To the nearest hundred, how many of each kind of food was sold?

28. Analyze A Mexican dance program will run from 1:30 P.M. to 2:15 P.M. Each group will dance for 5 minutes. Is there enough time for 7 groups to dance? Explain.

Using Vocabulary

Copy and complete.

Ⓐ The product of a non zero 1-digit number and a 2-digit number has at least _____ digits.

Ⓑ The answer in a multiplication problem is called the _____.

Ⓒ Numbers that are multiplied are called _____.

Mixed Review • Test Prep

Add or subtract. *(pages 56–58, 60–62, 68–69)*

29. $336.30
       + 15.32

30. 81,426
       −20,351

31. 900,001
       −399,873

Choose the letter of the correct answer. *(pages 4–8)*

32 Which number is less than 5,019?

A 5,111   **C** 5,020

B 5,009   **D** 5,100

33 Which is another name for 8 hundreds 18 tens?

F 1,980   **H** 980

G 998   **J** 818

Extra Practice See Set C on page 204. **175**

Problem-Solving Strategy: Find a Pattern

You will learn how to solve problems by finding a pattern.

Sometimes you can use a pattern to solve a problem.

Problem Matt wants to solve the math club's problem of the week. The bulletin board shows the first seven numbers of a pattern. Matt needs to find the next two numbers.

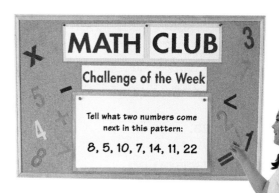

MATH CLUB

Challenge of the Week

Tell what two numbers come next in this pattern:

8, 5, 10, 7, 14, 11, 22

Understand

What is the question?
What are the next two numbers in the pattern?

What do you know?
The first seven numbers are 8, 5, 10, 7, 14, 11, 22.

Plan

How can you find the pattern?
Find a rule that describes how each number is related to the number that comes before it.

Solve

Find the pattern.

8   5   10   7   14   11   22

−3   ×2   −3   ×2   −3   ×2

Rule: Subtract 3 and record the number.
Multiply by 2 and record the number.

Use the rule to find the next two numbers.

$22 - 3 = 19$ $19 \times 2 = 38$

The next two numbers in this pattern are 19 and 38.

Look Back

Look back at the problem.
Suppose Matt had to find the next four numbers.
What two numbers would come after 38?

Standards MR **1.0, 1.1, 1.2, 2.0, 3.0, 3.2**

Guided Practice

Solve.

① Look at the pattern.

1   5   10   14   28   32

What is the likely rule? Use that rule to find the next number in the pattern.

Think: How do I get from the first number to the second? the second number to the third?

② Look at the pattern.

A   C   E   G   I   K

What rule would give this pattern? Use that rule to find the next letter.

Think: How do I get from the first letter to the second? the second letter to the third?

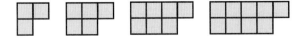

Choose a Strategy

Solve. Use these or other strategies.

Problem-Solving Strategies

• Write an Equation   • Use Logical Thinking   • Guess and Check   • Draw a Picture

③ Erin and Juan are in a computer club. They are buying 15 computer disks. Each disk costs $2. Erin paid $14 and Juan paid the rest. How much did Juan pay?

④ Look at the pattern.

1,000   900   810   730   660

What rule would give this pattern? Use that rule to find the next number.

⑤ Amy lives in the eighth house on Elm Street. The first house on Elm Street is numbered 1. The second is 5. The third is 9. The fourth is 13. If this pattern continues, what is Amy's house number likely to be?

⑥ Five students hold cards with the numbers 1 to 5 in order. Bob is as far from Kim as Tara is from Ethan. Tara is in the middle. Russ has number 1. Neither Ethan nor Bob has number 5. Which students hold which cards?

⑦ Look for a pattern in the figures below. Then draw the next figure in the pattern.

⑧ Rita buys butter for the cooking club. She buys less than 15 lb of butter each week. She bought 12 lb last week. The difference between the amounts she bought last week and this week is 10 lb. How much butter did Rita buy this week?

Quick ✓ Check

Check Your Understanding of Lessons 1–5

Find each product.

1. 6 × 400   **2.** 3 × 7,000   **3.** 8 × 800   **4.** 7 × 6,000

Multiply.

5.
$$\begin{array}{r} 22 \\ \times 3 \\ \hline \end{array}$$

6.
$$\begin{array}{r} 34 \\ \times 4 \\ \hline \end{array}$$

7.
$$\begin{array}{r} 25 \\ \times 9 \\ \hline \end{array}$$

8.
$$\begin{array}{r} 53 \\ \times 6 \\ \hline \end{array}$$

Estimate each product.

9. 6 × 45   **10.** 3 × 297   **11.** 4 × 8,321   **12.** 7 × $28.43

Solve.

13. Look at the pattern.

5, 2, 6, 3, 9, 6 . . .

What rule would give this pattern? Use that rule to find the next number.

14. The letters below form a pattern.

A, Z, B, Y, C, X, D

What is the likely rule? Use that rule to find the next letter.

How did you do?

If you had difficulty with any items in the Quick Check, you can use the following pages for review and extra practice.

California Standards	Items	Review These Pages	Do These Extra Practice Items
Number Sense: **3.0** Math Reasoning: **1.1**	1–4	pages 166–167	Set A, page 204
Number Sense: **3.0**	5–8	pages 170–172	Set B, page 204
Number Sense: **1.3**	9–12	pages 174–175	Set C page 204
Math Reasoning: **1.1, 3.0, 3.2**	13–14	pages 176–177	1–4, page 207

Test Prep • Cumulative Review
Maintaining the Standards

Choose the letter of the correct answer. If a correct answer is not here, choose NH.

1 Which number sentence is an example of the Associative Property?

A $517 + 345 = 345 + 517$

B $98 + (57 + 16) = (98 + 57) + 16$

C $3 \times (5 + 6) = (3 \times 5) + (3 \times 6)$

D $(87 - 15) + 3 \neq 87 - (15 + 3)$

2 If $8 \times 4 = \blacksquare$, then which equation is true?

F $4 \times \blacksquare = 8$

G $8 \times \blacksquare = 4$

H $\blacksquare \div 8 = 4$

J $8 \div \blacksquare = 4$

3
$$207$$
$$-68$$

A 139

B 141

C 149

D 239

4 Marsha needs 9 beads to make one bracelet. If she has 54 beads, how many bracelets can she make?

F 5

G 7

H 9

J NH

5 About how many students are enrolled in the three schools?

School Enrollment	
School	**Number of Students**
Jefferson	5,947
Washington	3,015
Lincoln	4,118

A 10,000   **C** 12,000

B 11,000   **D** 13,000

6 Which expression does not equal 42?

F $2 \times 2 \times 2 \times 2 \times 2$

G $2 \times 3 \times 7$

H 6×7

J 2×21

7 There are 20 rows of chairs with 8 chairs in each row. How many chairs are there?

A 28   **C** 160

B 150   **D** 208

8 What number should go in the box to make the number sentence true?

$$(16 \div 8) \times 5 = (\blacksquare) \times 5$$

Explain. Tell how you found your answer.

Safe Site

Internet Test Prep
Visit **www.eduplace.com/kids/mhm**
for more *Test Prep Practice.*

LESSON 6

Multiply Three-Digit Numbers by One-Digit Numbers

You will learn how to multiply three-digit numbers by one-digit numbers.

WATER SLIDE
295 ft

Learn About It

The water slide at the park is 295 feet long. A new water slide will be 3 times as long. How long will the new water slide be?

Multiply. $3 \times 295 = n$

Find 3 × 295.

Step 1 Multiply the ones.

$3 \times 5 = 15$ ones

$$
\begin{array}{r}
\overset{1}{2}95 \\
\times \quad 3 \\
\hline
5
\end{array}
$$
Regroup 15 ones as 1 ten 5 ones.

Step 2 Multiply the tens.

$3 \times 9 = 27$ tens

Add the 1 ten.

$27 + 1 = 28$ tens

$$
\begin{array}{r}
\overset{21}{2}95 \\
\times \quad 3 \\
\hline
85
\end{array}
$$
Regroup 28 tens as 2 hundreds 8 tens.

Step 3 Multiply the hundreds.

$3 \times 2 = 6$ hundreds

Add the 2 hundreds.

$6 + 2 = 8$ hundreds

$$
\begin{array}{r}
\overset{21}{2}95 \\
\times \quad 3 \\
\hline
885
\end{array}
$$

Solution: The new water slide will be 885 ft long!

Check your work. Estimate.

295 rounds to 300

$300 \times 3 = 900$

885 is close to 900, so the answer is reasonable.

Other Examples

A. Regrouping Ones

$$
\begin{array}{r}
\overset{1}{6}23 \\
\times \quad 4 \\
\hline
2{,}492
\end{array}
$$

B. Multiplying With Money

$$
\begin{array}{r}
\$1.32 \\
\times \quad 3 \\
\hline
\$3.96
\end{array}
$$

Remember:
Place a dollar sign and a decimal point in the answer.

Explain Your Thinking

▶ When multiplying, what must you remember to do with the numbers that you regroup?

▶ When you multiply a 3-digit number by a 1-digit number, will your answer always be a 3-digit number?

Standards NS **3.0**   MR **2.1**

Guided Practice

Find each product. Estimate to check.

1. 215
× 4

2. $1.84
× 2

3. 621
× 3

4. $5.98
× 7

Ask Yourself
• Do I need to regroup the ones, tens, or hundreds?
• Do I need to add any regrouped tens or hundreds?

Independent Practice

Find each product. Estimate to check Exercises 5–10.

5. 321
× 2

6. $1.13
× 5

7. 197
× 4

8. 214
× 6

9. 715
× 3

10. 291
× 9

11. $1.24
× 8

12. 398
× 2

13. 514
× 5

14. $9.21
× 8

15. 122
× 7

16. 135
× 6

17. 929 × 3

18. 199 × 4

19. 791 × 8

20. 277 × 2

21. 982 × 4

Problem Solving • Reasoning

Use Data Use the sign at the right for Problems 22–24.

22. How many hours is the water park open each week?

23. **Analyze** Danielle's family paid $41 for admission to the water park. How many children and adults are there in Danielle's family?

24. Two hundred twenty-five people can go down the water slide every hour. How many people can go down the slide in one day?

WELCOME TO THE WATER PARK

Open 7 Days a Week

Hours Open:
1:00 P.M. – 10:00 P.M.

Admission:
Children $7 Adults $10

Mixed Review • Test Prep

Solve each equation. *(pages 82–83)*

25. $16 - n = 9$

26. $8 + n = 13$

27. $23 = n + 19$

28. $18 = 25 - n$

Choose the letter of the correct answer. *(pages 78–80, 132–134)*

29 Which expression shows three less than a number?

A $n - 3$ **C** $n + 3$

B $3 - n$ **D** $3 + n$

30 Which expression has the same value as $5 × 4 × 6$?

F $20 × 4$ **H** $24 × 6$

G $30 × 5$ **J** $24 × 5$

Extra Practice See Set D on page 205.

Multiply Greater Numbers

You will learn how to multiply greater numbers.

Learn About It

Sierra traveled with her family to her grandmother's house for a family reunion. A few days later, she traveled back home. How many miles did she travel in all?

Multiply. **2 × 1,956 = _n_**

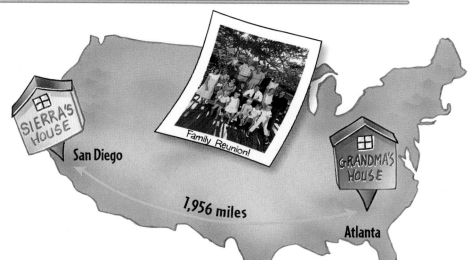

SIERRA'S HOUSE

San Diego

Family Reunion!

GRANDMA'S HOUSE

1,956 miles

Atlanta

Find 2 × 1,956.

Step 1 Multiply the ones.

2 × 6 = **12 ones**

$$\begin{array}{r} 1 \\ 1{,}956 \\ \times \quad 2 \\ \hline 2 \end{array}$$

Regroup 12 ones as 1 ten 2 ones.

Step 2 Multiply the tens.

2 × 5 = **10 tens**

Add the 1 ten.

10 + 1 = **11 tens**

$$\begin{array}{r} 11 \\ 1{,}956 \\ \times \quad 2 \\ \hline 12 \end{array}$$

Regroup 11 tens as 1 hundred 1 ten.

Step 3 Multiply the hundreds.

2 × 9 = **18 hundreds**

Add the 1 hundred.

18 + 1 = **19 hundreds**

$$\begin{array}{r} 1\ 11 \\ 1{,}956 \\ \times \quad 2 \\ \hline 912 \end{array}$$

Regroup 19 hundreds as 1 thousand 9 hundreds.

Step 4 Multiply the thousands.

2 × 1 = **2 thousands**

Add the 1 thousand.

2 + 1 = **3 thousands**

$$\begin{array}{r} 1\ 11 \\ 1{,}956 \\ \times \quad 2 \\ \hline 3{,}912 \end{array}$$

Check your work. Estimate.

1,956 rounds to 2,000

2 × 2,000 = 4,000

3,912 is close to 4,000, so the answer is reasonable.

Solution: She traveled 3,912 miles.

182 **Standards** NS **1.2, 3.0** AF **1.0** MR **2.0, 2.1**

Other Examples

A. Regrouping Twice

$$\begin{array}{r} \overset{3\ 4}{1,6\overset{}{1}9} \\ \times\ \ \ \ 5 \\ \hline 8,095 \end{array}$$

B. Multiplying a Five-Digit Number

$$\begin{array}{r} \overset{1}{12,3}94 \\ \times\ \ \ \ \ \ 2 \\ \hline 24,788 \end{array}$$

C. Multiplying Money

$$\begin{array}{r} \$62.21 \\ \times\ \ \ \ \ \ 4 \\ \hline \$248.84 \end{array}$$

Explain Your Thinking

▶ How do you know when you need to regroup?

▶ Is $4,000 or $400 a reasonable estimate for
8 × $52.71? Explain your reasoning.

Guided Practice

Find each product. Estimate to check.

1.	1,112 × 2	2.	4,126 × 8	3.	3,988 × 5

4. 2,211 × 6   **5.** 3,986 × 5   **6.** 1,984 × 3

Ask Yourself

• Do I need to regroup the ones, tens, or hundreds?

• Do I need to add any tens, hundreds, or thousands?

Independent Practice

Write each product. Estimate to check Exercises 7–11.

7.	2,128 × 4	8.	3,123 × 6	9.	4,132 × 2	10.	2,969 × 7	11.	5,987 × 3
12.	5,496 × 5	13.	1,312 × 8	14.	8,367 × 3	15.	3,196 × 9	16.	4,517 × 2

17. 7,871 × 6   **18.** 399 × 9   **19.** 1,299 × 3   **20.** 2,973 × 2   **21.** 1,211 × 8

22. 2,133 × 4   **23.** 5,911 × 4   **24.** 9,121 × 5   **25.** 1,634 × 4   **26.** 489 × 8

Algebra • Expressions Estimate to compare. Write > or < for each ⬤.

27. 697 × 5 ⬤ 1,244 × 2

28. 2,987 + 3,980 ⬤ 387 × 7

29. 2,000 ⬤ 3 × 945

30. 2 × 999 ⬤ 10,000

31. 5,978 − 879 ⬤ 2 × 912

32. 79 × 9 ⬤ 1,111 × 2

33. 256 × 7 ⬤ 20,911 − 11,001

34. 3,987 × 2 ⬤ 997 + 5,112

Problem Solving • Reasoning

Solve. Choose a method. Use the map for Problems 35–39.

Computation Methods

• Mental Math   • Estimation   • Paper and Pencil

35. Measurement Fran takes the train from Savannah to Birmingham and back twice a year. How many miles does she travel during both trips?

37. Compare Gavin travels from Birmingham to Jacksonville. Troy travels from Birmingham to Charleston. Who travels farther? How much farther?

38. Analyze Sierra's cousin lives in Atlanta. On one round trip, he travels 1,680 miles and visits 3 of the cities shown on the map. What cities does he visit?

39. Write Your Own Use the map to write a multiplication problem.

36. Terry's family lives in Jacksonville. The family travels to Florida City and back, then to Pensacola and back and, finally, to Birmingham and back. How many miles does the family travel in all?

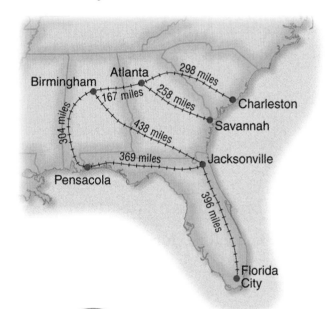

Mixed Review • Test Prep

What time is shown on each clock?

40.

41.

42.

43.

44.

45.

46 Which group shows the numbers in order from greatest to least? *(pages 6–8)*

A 4,500   405,000   45,000

B 405,000   45,000   4,500

C 4,500   45,000   405,000

D 45,000   405,000   4,500

Extra Practice See Set E on page 205.

Show What You Know

Greatest Product

Arrange each set of digits into a one-digit number and a three-digit number whose product is the greatest possible.

1. 9, 0, 2, 3 **2.** 7, 8, 9, 0 **3.** 2, 6, 4, 9

4. 0, 1, 5, 9 **5.** 5, 1, 3, 9 **6.** 7, 3, 5, 1

Ordering Products

Order these products from greatest to least without multiplying. Explain how you can tell without doing the multiplication.

1. 6 × 129; 8 × 945; 1 × 97 **2.** 0 × 1,255; 8 × 45; 1 × 234

3. 9 × 121; 2 × 34; 0 × 569 **4.** 5 × 67; 4 × 67; 7 × 67

5. 7 × 45; 7 × 42; 7 × 43 **6.** 4 × 17; 9 × 117; 5 × 20

Greater Than or Less Than?

Choose the correct answer. Explain how you can tell without doing the multiplication.

1. Which product is less than 1,500?

2 × 812 or 4 × 369

2. Which product is greater than 2,500?

3 × 875 or 6 × 275

3. Which product is greater than 1,000?

5 × 220 or 9 × 99

4. Which product is less than 3,000?

4 × 701 or 5 × 689

Multiply With Zeros

You will learn how to multiply with zeros.

Learn About It

The students at Cedar Hill are collecting boxtops from cereal boxes to earn points for a new computer. There are 2,007 students at Cedar Hill. If each student collects 6 boxtops, how many boxtops will be collected?

Multiply. $6 \times 2,007 = n$

Find 6 × 2,007.

Step 1   Multiply the ones.
   $6 \times 7 = 42$ ones

$$\begin{array}{r} \overset{4}{2,007} \\ \times \quad 6 \\ \hline 2 \end{array}$$

Regroup 42 ones as 4 tens 2 ones.

Step 2   Multiply the tens.
   $6 \times 0 = 0$ tens

Add the 4 regrouped tens.
   $0 + 4 = 4$ tens

$$\begin{array}{r} \overset{4}{2,007} \\ \times \quad 6 \\ \hline 42 \end{array}$$

Step 3   Multiply the hundreds.
   $6 \times 0 = 0$ hundreds

$$\begin{array}{r} \overset{4}{2,007} \\ \times \quad 6 \\ \hline 042 \end{array}$$

Step 4   Multiply the thousands.
   $6 \times 2 = 12$ thousands

$$\begin{array}{r} \overset{4}{2,007} \\ \times \quad 6 \\ \hline 12,042 \end{array}$$

Regroup 12 thousands as 1 ten thousand 2 thousands.

Check your work. Estimate.

2,007 rounds to 2,000

$6 \times 2,000 = 12,000$

12,042 is close to 12,000, so the answer is reasonable.

Solution: There will be 12,042 boxtops collected.

Other Examples

A. Three-Digit Number

$$\begin{array}{r} \overset{3}{304} \\ \times \quad 8 \\ \hline 2,432 \end{array}$$

B. Zeros in the Ones and Tens Places

$$\begin{array}{r} \overset{1}{9,500} \\ \times \quad 3 \\ \hline 28,500 \end{array}$$

Standards   NS **3.0**   MR **2.1**

Explain Your Thinking

▶ Look back at Example *A*. If 8×0 tens = 0 tens in the product, why is the tens digit 3?

Guided Practice

Multiply. Estimate to check.

1.	790	2.	205	3.	3,070	4.	4,900
	× 3		× 4		× 2		× 9

Ask Yourself

• Do I need to do any regrouping?

• Do I need to add any regrouped numbers?

Independent Practice

Multiply. Estimate to check Exercises 5–9.

5.	109	6.	705	7.	6,003	8.	3,860	9.	5,900
	× 2		× 5		× 8		× 3		× 6

10. 908×8　　**11.** $1,076 \times 6$　　**12.** $6,040 \times 5$　　**13.** $8,900 \times 7$　　**14.** $9,095 \times 9$

Problem Solving • Reasoning

Use Data Use the table for Problems 15–17.

15. Estimate To the nearest hundred, how many more labels did the fourth grade collect than the third grade?

16. The high school students collected 5 times the number of labels as the third, fifth, and sixth grades combined. How many labels did the high school students collect?

17. Write Your Own Using the data in the table, write a multiplication problem. Give it to someone to solve.

Soup–Label Collection	
Class	**Number of Labels**
Third Grade	105
Fourth Grade	316
Fifth Grade	150
Sixth Grade	275

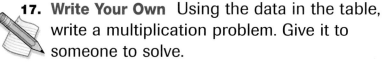

Mixed Review • Test Prep

Add or subtract. *(pages 56–58, 60–62, 68–69)*

18. $983 - 334$　　**19.** $3,423 + 8,923$　　**20.** $9,004 - 3,192$　　**21.** $\$52.18 + \$51.94$

22 What is $9,634 - 967$? *(pages 60–62)*

　　A 7,677　　　**B** 8,667　　　**C** 8,777　　　**D** 10,601

Problem-Solving Skill: Choose the Operation

You will learn when to use addition, subtraction, multiplication, or division to solve a problem.

Sometimes you need to decide which operation to use to solve a problem.

Thirty-six boys and 36 girls signed up for karate classes this year. That is 10 more students than signed up last year. There will be 6 karate classes this year, and the same number of students will be in each class.

You can add or multiply to find how many altogether.

How many students signed up for karate classes this year?

$$\begin{array}{r} 36 \\ +36 \\ \hline 72 \end{array}$$ or $$\begin{array}{r} 36 \\ \times\ 2 \\ \hline 72 \end{array}$$

72 students signed up this year.

You can subtract to find a part of the total amount.

How many students signed up for karate classes last year?

$$\begin{array}{r} 72 \\ -10 \\ \hline 62 \end{array}$$

62 students signed up last year.

You can divide to find the number in each group.

How many students will be in each karate class?

$72 \div 6 = 12$

12 students will be in each class.

Look Back Why can you add or multiply to find out how many students signed up for karate class this year?

Standards NS **3.0**   MR **1.0, 2.0, 3.0, 3.2**

Left: Expert karate students earn black belts.

Right: Eric Holland is a black belt karate student. He won first place in a black-belt championship.

Guided Practice

Tell whether you would add, subtract, multiply, or divide. Then solve.

 There were 350 students who signed up for the state karate tournament. Only 39 of them were 10 years old. How many were not 10 years old?

> **Think:** Do I need to find a part of a total amount?

 Three brothers shared the cost of a gift for their karate instructor. The gift cost $27. If each brother paid the same amount, how much did each pay?

> **Think:** Do I need to find a part of an amount or a total amount?

Choose a Strategy

Solve. Use these or other strategies.

Problem-Solving Strategies

- **Write an Equation**
- **Guess and Check**
- **Draw a Picture**
- **Work Backward**

3. John collected some money for his team. He spent $6 of it. Then he spent $3 of it. He collected $7 more. Then he had $10 in all. How much money did he collect to start with?

4. At the Soccer Store, a pair of soccer shoes costs $45.59. At Sports R Us, the same pair costs $57.98. How much will you save if you buy the shoes at the Soccer Store?

5. Only fourth-grade and fifth-grade students are in a gymnastics club. There are 20 students in the club altogether. There are 3 times as many fourth-graders as fifth-graders. How many fourth-graders are in the club?

6. Monica read about three different sports for a total of 100 minutes. She read about the first and second sport for 45 minutes each. How much time did she spend reading about the third sport?

7. Eliza plays on a rectangular soccer field that is 100 yards long and 50 yards wide. The field has a yellow line painted around its edge. What is the total length of the yellow line?

8. Tamara plays basketball. Last week her team traveled 155 miles. This week they traveled 126 miles. How many miles has the team traveled in the last two weeks?

Extra Practice See 5–8 on page 207.

Quick ✓ Check

Check Your Understanding of Lessons 6–9

Multiply.

1. 216
× 3

2. $4.71
× 6

3. 327
× 8

Multiply.

4. 2,146
× 4

5. $32.14
× 6

6. 2,421
× 7

Multiply.

7. 4,060
× 4

8. 5,009
× 6

9. 2,400
× 7

Solve.

10. Four friends shared the cost of a computer game. The game cost $32. If each person paid the same amount, how much did each person pay? Explain.

11. There are 11 players on a soccer team. Enough children signed up to make 4 teams. How many children signed up to play soccer? Explain.

How did you do?

If you had difficulty with any items in the Quick Check, you can use the following pages for review and extra practice.

California Standards	ITEMS	REVIEW THESE PAGES	DO THESE EXTRA PRACTICE ITEMS
Number Sense: **3.0**	1–3	pages 180–181	Set D, page 205
Number Sense: **3.0**	4–6	pages 182–184	Set E, page 205
Number Sense: **3.0**	7–9	pages 186–187	Set F, page 205
Math Reasoning: **1.0, 2.0, 2.4**	10–11	pages 188–189	5–8, page 207

Test Prep • Cumulative Review
Maintaining the Standards

Choose the letter of the correct answer. If a correct answer is not here, choose NH.

1 Which expression does not equal 40?

A 2×20

B $2 \times 4 \times 5$

C 5×8

D 3×15

2 Seventy-two chairs are placed around tables. Each table seats 8 people. How many tables are there?

F 7

G 8

H 9

J NH

3 What is the value of n?

$(46 \times 3) - 6 = n$

A 122

B 128

C 132

D 138

4 A grocery store received 9 crates with 12 oranges in each crate. How many oranges were there in all?

F 60

G 100

H 108

J 120

5 What number should go in the box to make the number sentence true?

$(412 \times 6) + 5 = \blacksquare + 5$

A 2,252   **C** 2,462

B 2,372   **D** 2,472

6 If $40 \div \blacksquare = 8$, then which equation is true?

F $8 \times \blacksquare = 40$

G $\blacksquare \times 40 = 8$

H $40 \times 8 = \blacksquare$

J $\blacksquare \div 40 = 8$

7
$$\begin{array}{r} 156 \\ \times \quad 4 \\ \hline \end{array}$$

A 604   **C** 628

B 624   **D** NH

8 *About* how many more points did Grade 4 score than Grade 5?

Explain What method did you use to estimate?

Math Competition	
Grade	**Number of Points**
4	395
5	205
6	317

Internet Test Prep
Visit **www.eduplace.com/kids/mhm**
for more *Test Prep Practice.*

191

Mental Math: Multiply Multiples of 10 and 100

You will learn how to use patterns and basic facts to multiply mentally.

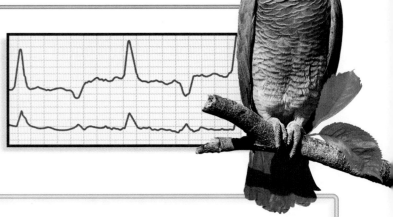

Learn About It

The small African parrot's heart beats 500 times a minute. How many times does the parrot's heart beat in 30 minutes?

Multiply.   **30 × 500 = _n_**

Find 30 × 500.

You can use basic facts and patterns of zeros to multiply.

$$3 \times 5 = 15$$
$$3 \times 50 = 150$$
$$30 \times 50 = 1,500$$
$$30 \times 500 = 15,000$$

Use the basic fact 3 × 5 = 15. Count the number of zeros in the factors. Write that number of zeros to the right of 15.

Solution: The parrot's heart beats about 15,000 times in 30 minutes.

Another Example

Multiple of 10

Find 50 × 60.

$$5 \times 6 = 30$$
$$5 \times 60 = 300$$
$$50 \times 60 = 3,000$$
$$50 \times 600 = 30,000$$

Why It Works:

$$50 \times 60 = (5 \times 10) \times (6 \times 10)$$
$$= (5 \times 6) \times (10 \times 10)$$
$$= 30 \times 100$$
$$= 3,000$$

Explain Your Thinking

► How many zeros are in the product of 50 and 800? Explain how you know.

Guided Practice

Use basic facts and patterns to find each product.

1. 70 × 8
   70 × 80
   70 × 800

2. 40 × 5
   40 × 50
   40 × 500

Ask Yourself

• What basic fact can I use?

• How many zeros should be in the product?

Standards NS **3.3**   MR **1.1**

Independent Practice

Use basic facts and patterns to find each product.

3. 3 × 40
30 × 40
30 × 400

4. 7 × 30
70 × 30
70 × 300

5. 6 × 90
60 × 90
60 × 900

6. 9 × 80
90 × 80
90 × 800

7. 30
× 2

8. 30
×20

9. 300
× 20

10. 200
× 30

11. 300
× 90

12. 60
×60

13. 600
× 60

14. 70
×90

15. 300
× 80

16. 900
× 20

17. 80
×40

18. 600
× 70

19. 200
× 50

20. 400
× 90

21. 600
× 10

Problem Solving • Reasoning

22. Suppose a small African parrot costs $90. How much does a pair of small African parrots cost?

23. **Money** Kim bought a bag of birdseed for her small African parrot for $5.95. The clerk gave her four $1 bills and a nickel in change. What bill did Kim use to pay for the birdseed?

24. **Write About It** A small African parrot's cage is about 20 in. long. Describe how you could find how long a pet-store shelf would have to be to hold 20 of these cages placed side by side.

Math Is Everywhere!

SCIENCE Small African parrots are also known as "lovebirds." Since their natural habitat is near the equator, they are used to 12 hours of nighttime.

If a lovebird slept 12 hours a day for every day in May, how many hours would it sleep in May?

Mixed Review • Test Prep

Add or subtract. *(pages 56–58, 60–62, 68–69)*

25. 2,345
+8,625

26. 48,075
−15,905

27. 13,860
− 532

Choose the letter of the correct answer. *(pages 64–65)*

28 To the nearest thousand, how much is 83,026 − 81,903?

A 160,000   **C** 2,000

B 10,000   **D** 1,000

29 To the nearest hundred, how much is 634 + 13,773?

F 15,300   **H** 14,400

G 14,600   **J** 13,100

Extra Practice See Set G on page 206.

Multiply Two 2-Digit Numbers

You will learn how to multiply two 2-digit numbers.

Learn About It

Harvest Acres runs hayrides. The hayride cart can hold 14 passengers. In one day the cart makes 13 trips to the pumpkin patch. How many passengers can ride in one day?

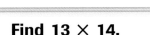

Multiply.   **$13 \times 14 = n$**

Find 13×14.

Step 1 Multiply 14 by 3 ones.	**Step 2** Multiply 14 by 1 ten.	**Step 3** Add the products.	The **Distributive Property** shows why this way of multiplying works.
$\begin{array}{r} 1 \\ 14 \\ \times 13 \\ \hline 42 \end{array}$	$\begin{array}{r} 1 \\ 14 \\ \times 13 \\ \hline 42 \\ 140 \end{array}$	$\begin{array}{r} 1 \\ 14 \\ \times 13 \\ \hline 42 \\ +140 \\ \hline 182 \end{array}$ $\leftarrow 3 \times 14$ $\leftarrow 10 \times 14$ $\leftarrow (3 \times 14) + (10 \times 14)$	$13 \times 14 = (10 + 3) \times 14$ $13 \times 14 = (10 \times 14) + (3 \times 14)$

Solution: There are 182 passengers who can ride in 1 day.

When you multiply by multiples of 10, you can use the Associative Property.

Find 25×30.

You can think of 30 as 3×10.

$$\begin{aligned} 25 \times 30 &= 25 \times (3 \times 10) \\ &= (25 \times 3) \times 10 \\ &= 75 \times 10 \\ &= 750 \end{aligned}$$

The **Associative Property** says that changing the grouping of the factors does not change the product.

$$25 \times (3 \times 10) = (25 \times 3) \times 10$$

Explain Your Thinking

▶ How does the Distributive Property show how each step works when you multiply?

Standards   NS **3.2, 3.3**   AF **1.0, 1.1, 1.2**

Guided Practice

Multiply.

1. $\begin{array}{r} 31 \\ \times 23 \\ \hline \end{array}$

2. $\begin{array}{r} 49 \\ \times 17 \\ \hline \end{array}$

3. $\begin{array}{r} 52 \\ \times 36 \\ \hline \end{array}$

4. $\begin{array}{r} 22 \\ \times 45 \\ \hline \end{array}$

Ask Yourself

• What numbers are multiplied first?

• What numbers are multiplied next?

• What do I add to find the product?

Copy and complete. Use the Associative Property to multiply.

5. $33 \times 20 = 33 \times (\blacksquare \times 10)$
$= (\blacksquare \times 2) \times \blacksquare$
$= \blacksquare \times \blacksquare$
$= \blacksquare$

6. $74 \times 20 = \blacksquare \times (\blacksquare \times 10)$
$= (\blacksquare \times \blacksquare) \times \blacksquare$
$= \blacksquare \times \blacksquare$
$= \blacksquare$

7. $51 \times 50 = 51 \times (\blacksquare \times \blacksquare)$
$= (\blacksquare \times \blacksquare) \times 10$
$= \blacksquare \times 10$
$= \blacksquare$

8. $62 \times 30 = \blacksquare \times (\blacksquare \times 10)$
$= (\blacksquare \times \blacksquare) \times \blacksquare$
$= \blacksquare \times \blacksquare$
$= \blacksquare$

Independent Practice

Multiply.

9. $\begin{array}{r} 26 \\ \times 16 \\ \hline \end{array}$

10. $\begin{array}{r} 21 \\ \times 31 \\ \hline \end{array}$

11. $\begin{array}{r} 34 \\ \times 24 \\ \hline \end{array}$

12. $\begin{array}{r} 84 \\ \times 42 \\ \hline \end{array}$

13. $\begin{array}{r} 71 \\ \times 63 \\ \hline \end{array}$

14. $\begin{array}{r} 52 \\ \times 25 \\ \hline \end{array}$

15. $\begin{array}{r} 63 \\ \times 53 \\ \hline \end{array}$

16. $\begin{array}{r} 89 \\ \times 92 \\ \hline \end{array}$

17. $\begin{array}{r} 65 \\ \times 29 \\ \hline \end{array}$

18. $\begin{array}{r} 25 \\ \times 78 \\ \hline \end{array}$

19. 14×13

20. 27×33

21. 19×91

22. 34×39

23. 39×34

Multiply. Use the Associative Property.

24. 18×30

25. 41×50

26. 93×70

27. 55×60

28. 98×90

29. 68×20

30. 15×40

31. 27×70

32. 54×90

33. 16×30

Algebra • Equations Find each value of _n_.

34. $(10 \times n) + 9 = 349$

35. $25 \times 19 = 500 - n$

36. $34 \times 21 = n + 34$

37. $39 \times 20 = n - 20$

38. $25 \times (n \times 3) = 750$

39. $60 \times n = 120$

Problem Solving • Reasoning

Use Data Use the graph for Problems 40–42.

40. Estimate In an average week, about 3 times as many pumpkins are picked than were picked on Friday. About how many pumpkins are picked in an average week?

41. On which day was the greatest number of pumpkins picked? How many more pumpkins were picked on this day than on Thursday?

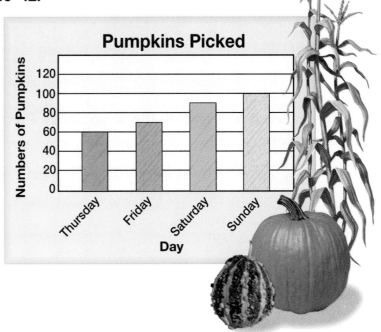

Pumpkins Picked

42. Write About It The number of pumpkins picked on Sunday is 5 times the number of pumpkins Julia's class picked. Describe how you could find the number of pumpkins Julia's class picked.

43. During the festival this year, Harvest Acres made $65 on candy-apple sales. It made 16 times that amount selling apple cider. How much did Harvest Acres make on apple-cider sales?

44. Analyze Jason read about harvest festivals for 10 minutes, pumpkin recipes for 15 minutes, and hayrides for 45 minutes. If he finished reading at 12:15 P.M., at what time did Jason start to read?

Mixed Review • Test Prep

Simplify each expression. *(pages 78–80, 132–134)*

45. $(4 + 6) \times 4$

46. $8 + 9 \times 2$

47. $18 - (2 + 12)$

Choose the letter of the correct answer. *(pages 30–32)*

48 Which group of coins represents $1.21?

A

C

B

D

Multiplying Does It!

Practice what you have learned about multiplication by playing this game.
The player who gets the greatest product wins.

What You'll Need

- *2 sets of number cards labeled 0 to 9 (Teaching Tool 4)*

**Players
2–4**

Here's What to Do

1. One player shuffles the number cards and places them facedown in a stack.

2. Each player draws four cards from the stack to make a multiplication problem. Each player decides to make either two 2-digit factors or a 1-digit factor and a 3-digit factor and then multiplies.

3. The players compare their products. The player who has the greatest product is the winner.

4. Players shuffle the cards and play again.

   Try adding a twist to the game by playing to get the least product instead of the greatest product!

Share Your Thinking What are the best numbers to have if you want to make the greatest product? How would you place these digits in the numbers? Explain.

Multiply Three-Digit Numbers by Two-Digit Numbers

You will learn how to multiply a three-digit number by a two-digit number.

Learn About It

The table shows the number of miles that some people in one town walk every month while working at their jobs. How many miles does the police officer walk on his job in a year?

Miles Walked in a Month	
Police officer	136
TV reporter	84
Salesperson	67
Mail carrier	60
Teacher	116

Multiply. $136 \times 12 = n$

Find 136×12.

Step 1 Multiply 136 by 2 ones.

$$
\begin{array}{r}
1 \\
136 \\
\times\ \ 12 \\
\hline
272 \leftarrow 2 \times 136
\end{array}
$$

Step 2 Multiply 136 by 1 ten.

$$
\begin{array}{r}
1 \\
136 \\
\times\ \ 12 \\
\hline
272 \\
1360 \leftarrow 10 \times 136
\end{array}
$$

Step 3 Add the products.

$$
\begin{array}{r}
1 \\
136 \\
\times\ \ 12 \\
\hline
272 \\
+\ 1360 \\
\hline
1{,}632
\end{array}
$$

Solution: The police officer walks 1,632 miles in a year!

Other Examples

A. Zero in the Tens Place

$$
\begin{array}{r}
2 \\
4 \\
205 \\
\times\ \ \ 59 \\
\hline
1845 \\
10250 \\
\hline
12{,}095
\end{array}
$$

B. Zero in the Ones Place

$$
\begin{array}{r}
5 \\
2 \\
490 \\
\times\ \ \ 63 \\
\hline
1470 \\
29400 \\
\hline
30{,}870
\end{array}
$$

C. Multiple of 10

$$
\begin{array}{r}
24 \\
937 \\
\times\ \ \ 70 \\
\hline
000 \\
65590 \\
\hline
65{,}590
\end{array}
$$

Explain Your Thinking

▶ What are the least and the greatest number of digits possible in the product when you multiply a three-digit number by a two-digit number?

Guided Practice

Multiply.

1.	241 × 14	2.	305 × 32	3.	132 × 60

Ask Yourself

• What numbers are multiplied first?

• What numbers are multiplied next?

• What do I add to find the product?

Independent Practice

Multiply.

4.	132 × 20	5.	121 × 43	6.	208 × 52	7.	496 × 71	8.	500 × 85

9.	430 × 50	10.	734 × 24	11.	260 × 65	12.	109 × 72	13.	482 × 39

14. 30×149 **15.** 46×544 **16.** 94×263 **17.** 81×719

18. 68×610 **19.** 83×753 **20.** 75×906 **21.** 90×885

Problem Solving • Reasoning

Use Data Use the table on page 198 for Problems 22–24.

22. Estimate Mr. Lee teaches for 9 months and works as a salesperson for 3 months. About how many miles does he walk in a year on his two jobs?

23. Analyze In 6 months, Ms. Crawford walks about 480 miles on her job. What is Ms. Crawford's job?

24. Logical Thinking In her job, Ms. King walks one mile more in 4 months than a sales person walks in 5 months. What is Ms. King's job?

Using Algebra

Compare. Write >, <, or = for each ●.

Ⓐ 56×24 ● 25×56

Ⓑ $16 + 14 \times 3$ ● 900

Ⓒ 2×425 ● 2×400

Ⓓ 300×6 ● 600×4

Ⓔ 678 ● 70×9

Ⓕ 250 ● 20×15

Mixed Review • Test Prep

Multiply. *(pages 110–111)*

25. $2 \times 9 \times 5$ **26.** 0×33 **27.** 184×1 **28.** $5 \times 15 \times 0$

29 Which is represented by $5n$? *(pages 136–138)*

　　A five plus a number 　**C** a number minus five

　　B five times a number 　**D** five divided by a number

Problem-Solving Application: Use a Pictograph

You will learn how to use a graph to solve problems.

Sometimes you need to use a graph to solve a word problem.

The pictograph shows the five favorite animals of the students in Faber Elementary School. How many more students chose dogs than cats as their favorite animal?

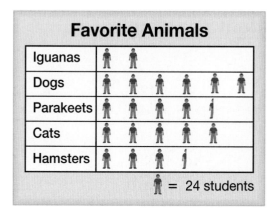

Favorite Animals

Iguanas	
Dogs	
Parakeets	
Cats	
Hamsters	

= 24 students

What is the question?
How many more students chose dogs than cats?

What do you know?
Each stands for 24 students.
Each stands for 12 students.

How can you find the answer?
Use the graph. Find the total votes for dogs.
Find the total votes for cats. Then subtract.

Find the total votes for dogs.	Find the total votes for cats.	Then subtract.
Dogs have 6 .	Cats have 5 .	144
		− 120
$24 \times 6 = 144$	$24 \times 5 = 120$	24

24 more students chose dogs than cats.

Look back at the problem. Explain how you can solve this problem without any calculation.

Standards NS **3.0** SDP **1.0** MR **1.0, 1.2, 2.0, 3.0, 3.3**

Guided Practice

Use the pictograph on page 200 to solve each problem.

Remember:
► Understand
► Plan
► Solve
► Look Back

1 One hundred forty-four students chose which animal as their favorite?

Think: How does the number of 👤 help me solve this problem?

2 How many more students chose parakeets than iguanas as their favorite animal?

Think: How many students does a half of a 👤 represent?

Choose a Strategy

Use the pictograph below to solve each problem.
Use these or other strategies.

Problem-Solving Strategies

- **Use Logical Thinking**
- **Write an Equation**
- **Draw a Picture**
- **Find a Pattern**

3 How many chocolate cones were sold?

4 Four times as many cookie crunch cones as vanilla cones were sold. How many cookie crunch cones were sold?

5 How many vanilla cones and chocolate cones were sold in all? Explain how you got your answer.

6 Suppose 132 more strawberry cones were sold. How would this change the pictograph?

7 Soft serve ice cream cones were also sold. There were 12 times the number of soft serve ice cream cones sold as there were strawberry cones sold. How many soft serve ice cream cones were sold? How could you show this on the pictograph?

Best-Selling Ice-Cream Flavors

Chocolate	🍦 🍦 🍦 🍦 🍦 🍦
Vanilla	🍦 🍦 🍦 🍦
Strawberry	🍦 🍦
Chocolate Chip Mint	🍦 🍦 🍦

🍦 = 132 cones.

Extra Practice See 9–12 on page 207.

Quick ✓ Check

Check Your Understanding of Lessons 10–13

Find each product.

1. 60 × 90   **2.** 40 × 700   **3.** 30 × 500

Multiply.

4.　　41
　　× 23

5.　　74
　　× 42

6.　　24
　　× 52

Multiply.

7.　　304
　　× 38

8.　　632
　　× 23

9.　　874
　　× 60

Solve.

10. The pictograph shows the number of plastic bottles each grade brought in for recycling. Did the fourth grade or the sixth grade bring in more bottles? How many more?

11. Which class brought in 99 bottles? How can you tell?

Plastic Bottles for Recycling

Third Grade	🍾🍾🍾
Fourth Grade	🍾🍾🍾🍾🍾🍾🍾
Fifth Grade	🍾🍾🍾🍾🍾
Sixth Grade	🍾🍾🍾🍾🍾

🍾 = 18 bottles.

How did you do?

If you had difficulty with any items in the Quick Check, you can use the following pages for review and extra practice.

California Standards	ITEMS	REVIEW THESE PAGES	DO THESE EXTRA PRACTICE ITEMS
Number Sense: **3.3** Math Reasoning **1.1**	1–3	pages 192–193	Set G, page 206
Number Sense: **3.2, 3.3**	4–6	pages 194–196	Set H, page 206
Number Sense: **3.2, 3.3**	7–9	pages 198–199	Set I, page 206
Data Analysis: **1.0, 1.3** Math Reasoning: **1.1**	10–11	pages 200–201	9–12, page 207

Test Prep • Cumulative Review

Maintaining the Standards

Choose the letter of the correct answer. If a correct answer is not here, choose NH.

1 What is the product of 49×65?

A 114 **C** 845

B 539 **D** 3,185

2 The students of Memorial School traveled to Washington, D.C., for their class trip. Each of 12 buses carried 32 students. How many students went on the class trip?

F 60 **H** 382

G 380 **J** NH

3 Tommy has 36 photos. He wants to put the photos into an album. If he puts 4 photos on each page, which equation can be used to find the number of pages he will need?

A $36 \div 4 = \blacksquare$

B $36 \times 4 = \blacksquare$

C $36 + 4 = \blacksquare$

D $36 - 4 = \blacksquare$

4 Which expression does not equal 30?

F 5×6

G $5 \times 3 \times 2$

H 2×16

J 3×10

5 Phyllis drove 235 miles each day for 14 days. How many miles did she drive in all?

A 2,290 **C** 3,390

B 3,290 **D** 3,920

6 Which equation does the table show?

x	y
10	5
20	15
30	25
40	35

F $y = x - 5$

G $y = x + 5$

H $y = x \div 2$

J $y = x \times 2$

7 What is the quotient of $36 \div 6$?

A 5 **C** 7

B 6 **D** 8

8 Forty-eight students lined up in 8 equal rows to get a picture taken. How many students were in each row?

Explain Tell how you found your answer. Use a diagram if it helps.

Safe Site

Internet Test Prep
Visit **www.eduplace.com/kids/mhm**
for more *Test Prep Practice.*

203

Extra Practice

Set A (Lesson 1, pages 166–167)

Use basic facts and patterns to find each product.

1. 2×6
   2×60
   2×600
   $2 \times 6,000$

2. 6×5
   6×50
   6×500
   $6 \times 5,000$

3. 8×7
   8×70
   8×700
   $8 \times 7,000$

4. 9×3
   9×30
   9×300
   $9 \times 3,000$

5. 6×2

6. 6×20

7. 6×200

8. $6 \times 2,000$

9. 3×30

10. 8×60

11. 7×70

12. 4×90

13. 7×400

14. 2×800

15. 3×600

16. 9×600

17. $8 \times 4,000$

18. $6 \times 7,000$

19. $4 \times 8,000$

20. $5 \times 6,000$

Set B (Lesson 3, pages 170–172)

Multiply.

1. $\begin{array}{r} 12 \\ \times\ 6 \\ \hline \end{array}$

2. $\begin{array}{r} 37 \\ \times\ 2 \\ \hline \end{array}$

3. $\begin{array}{r} 28 \\ \times\ 3 \\ \hline \end{array}$

4. $\begin{array}{r} 61 \\ \times\ 7 \\ \hline \end{array}$

5. $\begin{array}{r} 84 \\ \times\ 2 \\ \hline \end{array}$

6. $\begin{array}{r} 48 \\ \times\ 2 \\ \hline \end{array}$

7. $\begin{array}{r} 29 \\ \times\ 3 \\ \hline \end{array}$

8. $\begin{array}{r} 21 \\ \times\ 8 \\ \hline \end{array}$

9. $\begin{array}{r} 93 \\ \times\ 3 \\ \hline \end{array}$

10. $\begin{array}{r} 12 \\ \times\ 3 \\ \hline \end{array}$

11. 9×41

12. 2×39

13. 2×43

14. 4×23

Set C (Lesson 4, pages 174–175)

Estimate each product.

1. $\begin{array}{r} 22 \\ \times\ 5 \\ \hline \end{array}$

2. $\begin{array}{r} 81 \\ \times\ 3 \\ \hline \end{array}$

3. $\begin{array}{r} 547 \\ \times\ 7 \\ \hline \end{array}$

4. $\begin{array}{r} 2,986 \\ \times\ 4 \\ \hline \end{array}$

5. $\begin{array}{r} \$37.84 \\ \times\ 9 \\ \hline \end{array}$

6. 6×777

7. $9 \times \$19.95$

8. $3 \times 7,485$

9. 9×83

10. 4×39

11. 8×29

12. 6×41

13. $5 \times \$55.83$

Extra Practice

Set D *(Lesson 6, pages 180–181)*

Find each product. Estimate to check.

1. 138 $\times$ 3	**2.** 295 $\times$ 2	**3.** 143 $\times$ 6	**4.** 312 $\times$ 5	**5.** 292 $\times$ 7
6. $6.25 $\times$ 4	**7.** $7.36 $\times$ 2	**8.** 475 $\times$ 3	**9.** 423 $\times$ 6	**10.** $2.33 $\times$ 8

11. 8 $\times$ 312   **12.** 3 $\times$ 671   **13.** 2 $\times$ $8.33   **14.** 4 $\times$ 717

15. 5 $\times$ 329   **16.** 9 $\times$ 117   **17.** 6 $\times$ $4.59   **18.** 5 $\times$ 242

19. 6 $\times$ 198   **20.** 3 $\times$ 684   **21.** 7 $\times$ $1.87   **22.** 2 $\times$ 856

Set E *(Lesson 7, pages 182–184)*

Find each product.

1. 3,226 $\times$ 3	**2.** $41.71 $\times$ 2	**3.** $52.34 $\times$ 2	**4.** 8,461 $\times$ 3	**5.** 2,143 $\times$ 7
6. 6,547 $\times$ 4	**7.** 3,469 $\times$ 8	**8.** 1,268 $\times$ 9	**9.** 4,133 $\times$ 4	**10.** $54.63 $\times$ 3

11. 3 $\times$ 7,582   **12.** 4 $\times$ $18.76   **13.** 3 $\times$ 8,459   **14.** 2 $\times$ 9,372

15. 5 $\times$ 14,339   **16.** 7 $\times$ 12,219   **17.** 2 $\times$ 25,962   **18.** 4 $\times$ 33,284

Set F *(Lesson 8, pages 186–187)*

Multiply. Estimate to check.

1. 306 $\times$ 5	**2.** 409 $\times$ 2	**3.** 5,009 $\times$ 4	**4.** 8,050 $\times$ 5	**5.** 2,000 $\times$ 7

6. 3 $\times$ 7,502   **7.** 4 $\times$ 109   **8.** 6 $\times$ 890   **9.** 2 $\times$ 29,070

10. 8 $\times$ 5,308   **11.** 7 $\times$ 6,009   **12.** 9 $\times$ 506   **13.** 4 $\times$ 13,084

Extra Practice

Set G (Lesson 10, pages 192–193)

Use basic facts and patterns to find each product.

1. 4 × 60
40 × 60
40 × 600

2. 9 × 40
90 × 40
90 × 400

3. 3 × 50
30 × 50
30 × 500

4. 8 × 70
80 × 70
80 × 700

5. 50
× 40

6. 40
× 80

7. 300
× 40

8. 700
× 70

9. 30 × 70

10. 60 × 100

11. 30 × 200

12. 80 × 900

Set H (Lesson 11, pages 194–196)

Multiply.

1. 26
× 15

2. 41
× 21

3. 24
× 43

4. 61
× 37

5. 34
× 72

6. 47
× 65

7. 69
× 83

8. 72
× 96

9. 33
× 41

10. 63
× 36

11. 58 × 73

12. 87 × 44

13. 59 × 68

14. 93 × 27

Multiply. Use the Associative Property.

15. 48 × 30

16. 18 × 20

17. 24 × 40

18. 19 × 40

19. 56 × 80

20. 29 × 70

21. 38 × 60

22. 46 × 30

Set I (Lesson 12, pages 198–199)

Multiply.

1. 126
× 50

2. 713
× 27

3. 509
× 34

4. 610
× 73

5. 434
× 27

6. 470
× 65

7. 639
× 85

8. 720
× 96

9. 353
× 41

10. 637
× 36

11. 58 × 903

12. 87 × 484

13. 59 × 698

14. 93 × 289

15. 43 × 519

16. 62 × 950

17. 37 × 408

18. 23 × 965

Extra Practice • Problem Solving

Look at each pattern. What is the likely rule?
Use that rule to find the next number or letter. *(Lesson 5, pages 176–177)*

1 3 6 5 10 9 18 17

2 4 9 5 10 6 11 7

3 Z W T Q N K H

4 1 2 4 5 10 11 22

Tell whether you would add, subtract, multiply, or divide.
Then solve. *(Lesson 9, pages 188–189)*

5 At soccer camp, 280 children have signed up to play. In the morning, 149 children will play. How many will play in the afternoon?

6 Three friends order a large pizza for lunch. The pizza costs $12. If each person pays the same amount, how much will each pay?

7 Nine of the children on a soccer team need new shirts. The shirts cost $14.50 each. How much will their shirts cost altogether?

8 At a grocery store, lettuce costs 99¢. A 5-pound bag of potatoes is $2.00. Tomatoes are 3 for $1.29. What is the total cost of the items?

Use the pictograph to solve each problem. *(Lesson 13, pages 200–201)*

Fourth-Grade Recycle Collection	
Plastic bottles	♺♺♺♺♺♺♺♺♺♺
Aluminum cans	♺♺♺♺♺♺♺♺♺♺♺♺
Glass bottles	♺♺♺♺♺♺♺

♺ = 32 items

9 How many items for recycling were collected by the fourth-grade class in all?

10 Which item did the class collect most of? How many did they collect?

11 The recycling plant pays 23¢ for each glass bottle. How much money did the fourth-graders receive for the glass bottles?

12 John brings in 32 more plastic bottles and 16 more glass bottles. Describe how that changes the pictograph.

Chapter Review

Reviewing Vocabulary

1. What do you call the number that is multiplied?

2. What do you call the answer in multiplication?

3. Show an example of the Associative Property of multiplication.

Reviewing Concepts and Skills

Use basic facts and patterns to find each product. *(pages 166–167)*

4. 5×60

5. 8×30

6. 3×700

7. 9×800

8. 6×300

9. $5 \times 4,000$

10. $7 \times 6,000$

11. $3 \times 9,000$

Multiply. *(pages 170–172)*

12. $\begin{array}{r} 33 \\ \times\ 2 \\ \hline \end{array}$

13. $\begin{array}{r} 41 \\ \times\ 6 \\ \hline \end{array}$

14. $\begin{array}{r} 24 \\ \times\ 3 \\ \hline \end{array}$

15. $\begin{array}{r} 29 \\ \times\ 3 \\ \hline \end{array}$

16. $\begin{array}{r} 82 \\ \times\ 4 \\ \hline \end{array}$

17. 3×72

18. 4×13

19. 9×51

20. 8×11

Estimate each product. *(pages 174–175)*

21. $\begin{array}{r} 78 \\ \times\ 5 \\ \hline \end{array}$

22. $\begin{array}{r} 77 \\ \times\ 2 \\ \hline \end{array}$

23. $\begin{array}{r} 6,493 \\ \times\ \ \ \ 8 \\ \hline \end{array}$

24. $\begin{array}{r} \$86.37 \\ \times\ \ \ \ \ 4 \\ \hline \end{array}$

25. $\begin{array}{r} 127 \\ \times\ \ \ 3 \\ \hline \end{array}$

26. 9×38

27. 6×333

28. $9 \times \$81.59$

29. $3 \times 4,856$

Multiply. Estimate to check. *(pages 180–189)*

30. $\begin{array}{r} 127 \\ \times\ \ \ 3 \\ \hline \end{array}$

31. $\begin{array}{r} 384 \\ \times\ \ \ 2 \\ \hline \end{array}$

32. $\begin{array}{r} \$5.15 \\ \times\ \ \ \ 5 \\ \hline \end{array}$

33. $\begin{array}{r} 4,334 \\ \times\ \ \ \ 2 \\ \hline \end{array}$

34. $\begin{array}{r} 8,621 \\ \times\ \ \ \ 4 \\ \hline \end{array}$

35. $\begin{array}{r} \$53.73 \\ \times\ \ \ \ \ 3 \\ \hline \end{array}$

36. $\begin{array}{r} 12,434 \\ \times\ \ \ \ \ 9 \\ \hline \end{array}$

37. $\begin{array}{r} 207 \\ \times\ \ 8 \\ \hline \end{array}$

38. $\begin{array}{r} 3,008 \\ \times\ \ \ \ 7 \\ \hline \end{array}$

39. $\begin{array}{r} \$70.40 \\ \times\ \ \ \ \ 5 \\ \hline \end{array}$

40. 6×179

41. 4×349

42. $6 \times 2,962$

43. $8 \times 4,721$

44. $4 \times 6,302$

45. 9×306

46. $8 \times 6,003$

47. 7×403

Use basic facts and patterns to find each product. *(pages 192–193)*

48. 500
× 50

49. 60
× 30

50. 700
× 60

51. 800
× 80

52. 80
× 40

53. 90 × 30

54. 40 × 100

55. 30 × 500

56. 70 × 90

Multiply. *(pages 194–199)*

57. 56 × 74

58. 38 × 96

59. 64 × 27

60. 33 × 214

61. 63 × 186

62. 95 × 85

63. 39 × 272

64. 68 × 181

Solve. Use the pictograph for Problems 65–67. *(pages 176–177, 188–189, and 200–201)*

65. Three friends collected books to donate to a thrift shop. Did Molly or Rhea collect more books?

66. How many books did Molly and Rhea collect together?

67. A neighbor gave Luke a box filled with more books to donate. The box contained twice as many books as Rhea had collected. How many books does Luke now have in all?

Books Collected

Molly	📖 📖 📖 📖
Luke	📖 📖 📖
Rhea	📖 📖 📖 📖

📖 = 16 books.

68. Look at this pattern of letters. A D F I K N. What is the next letter likely to be? Describe the rule.

Brain Teasers Math Reasoning

ADD THE DIGITS

Choose a number that is a multiple of 9. Add the digits. What do you notice?

ONE AND ONE IS TWELVE?

Todd multiplied two one-digit factors. Ann added one digit to each of Todd's factors. Her product was 12 greater than Todd's product. What were Todd's factors?

Safe Site

Internet Brain Teasers
Visit **www.eduplace.com/kids/mhm**
for more *Brain Teasers.*

Chapter Test

Use basic facts and patterns to find each product.

1. 6×2 **2.** 6×20 **3.** 6×200 **4.** $6 \times 2,000$

5. 5×60 **6.** 80×300 **7.** 20×90 **8.** 30×900

Multiply.

9. $\begin{array}{r} 85 \\ \times\ 9 \\ \hline \end{array}$
10. $\begin{array}{r} 34 \\ \times\ 2 \\ \hline \end{array}$
11. $\begin{array}{r} 427 \\ \times\ \ \ 2 \\ \hline \end{array}$
12. $\begin{array}{r} 108 \\ \times\ \ \ 6 \\ \hline \end{array}$
13. $\begin{array}{r} \$1.56 \\ \times\ \ \ \ \ 4 \\ \hline \end{array}$

14. $\begin{array}{r} 3,511 \\ \times\ \ \ \ \ 6 \\ \hline \end{array}$
15. $\begin{array}{r} 406 \\ \times\ \ \ 5 \\ \hline \end{array}$
16. $\begin{array}{r} 210 \\ \times\ \ \ 7 \\ \hline \end{array}$
17. $\begin{array}{r} 89 \\ \times\ 6 \\ \hline \end{array}$
18. $\begin{array}{r} 1,406 \\ \times\ \ \ \ \ 8 \\ \hline \end{array}$

19. 3×84 **20.** 2×187 **21.** 3×127 **22.** $5 \times \$4.25$

23. $6 \times 3,841$ **24.** $4 \times 2,040$ **25.** 37×421 **26.** $8 \times \$6.32$

Estimate each product.

27. $\begin{array}{r} 63 \\ \times\ 4 \\ \hline \end{array}$
28. $\begin{array}{r} 421 \\ \times\ \ \ 5 \\ \hline \end{array}$
29. $\begin{array}{r} 2,186 \\ \times\ \ \ \ \ 3 \\ \hline \end{array}$
30. $\begin{array}{r} \$5.95 \\ \times\ \ \ \ \ 4 \\ \hline \end{array}$

Multiply.

31. $\begin{array}{r} 18 \\ \times 16 \\ \hline \end{array}$
32. $\begin{array}{r} 47 \\ \times\ 21 \\ \hline \end{array}$
33. $\begin{array}{r} 131 \\ \times\ 42 \\ \hline \end{array}$
34. $\begin{array}{r} 307 \\ \times\ 25 \\ \hline \end{array}$
35. $\begin{array}{r} 726 \\ \times\ 34 \\ \hline \end{array}$

36. 27×72 **37.** 51×30 **38.** 17×410 **39.** 25×35

40. 20×111 **41.** 44×302 **42.** 94×12 **43.** 77×38

44. 83×356 **45.** 46×19 **46.** 55×201 **47.** 65×909

Solve.

48. Look at the pattern.

    3 4 8 9 18 19

What is the likely rule? Use
that rule to find the next two numbers.

49. Beth is selling jewelry at a craft fair. She sells
293 items. Of these items, 127 are not necklaces.
How many necklaces does she sell?

50. Judy's class is collecting seashells. The pictograph
below shows how many shells Judy, Grace, and Jamie
have collected. Who collected the most shells? How
many shells is that?

 Write About It

**Solve each problem. Use correct math vocabulary to
explain your thinking.**

1. Look at the pictograph.

  a. Jamie says that he collected 22 more
shells than Judy. Do you agree with
Jamie? Why or why not?

  b. Grace says that she and Judy
collected twice as many shells as
Jamie. Judy says they collected more
than that. Who is correct? Explain.

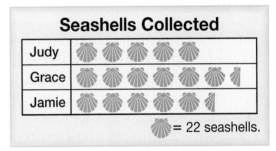

Seashells Collected

Judy	
Grace	
Jamie	

= 22 seashells.

2. Sarah is creating a number pattern. The pattern
begins 5, 9.

  a. Make a rule and describe how Sarah's number
pattern might look.

  b. Make a different rule. Describe how this new
pattern would look and how it is different from
your answer in *a*.

  c. Use the patterns you created for *a*. and *b*. Tell
what the 10th number would be in each
sequence.

Another Look

Use the information in the diagram to answer the questions. You can use what you know about multiplication and estimation.

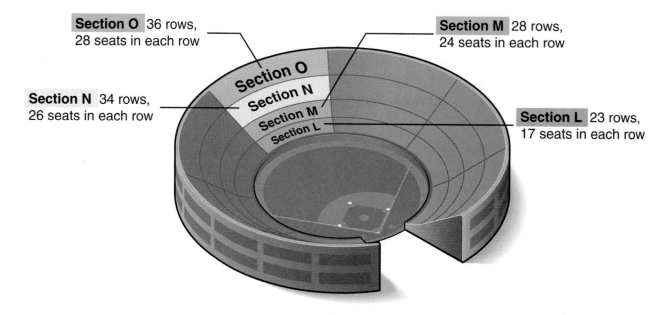

Section O 36 rows, 28 seats in each row

Section M 28 rows, 24 seats in each row

Section N 34 rows, 26 seats in each row

Section L 23 rows, 17 seats in each row

Section O

Section N

Section M

Section L

1. Round both the number of rows and the number of seats in each row to the nearest ten. Estimate the number of seats for each of the sections of the baseball stadium.

2. Write a multiplication expression for the number of seats in each section. Then find the actual number of seats in each section.

3. **Look Back** Compare your estimates from Problem 1 to the actual number of seats from Problem 2. Do your answers seem reasonable? If some estimates are not very close to the actual product, check that you have rounded correctly. Then check that you have multiplied correctly.

4. **Analyze** Suppose you round both the number of rows and the number of seats to the next multiple of ten. How will your estimate compare to the actual number of seats in a section?

Enrichment

Distributive Property

The Distributive Property states that when you multiply two addends by a factor the answer is the same as if you multiply each addend by the factor and then add the products.

Think about the expression **4 × 27.**

Here is one way to evaluate the expression using the Distributive Property.	Here is another way to evaluate the expression.
$4 \times (25 + 2)$ **Think:** $27 = 25 + 2$	$4 \times (20 + 7)$ **Think:** $27 = 20 + 7$
$(4 \times 25) + (4 \times 2)$	$(4 \times 20) + (4 \times 7)$
$100 + 8$	$80 + 28$
108	108

Find the value of *n*.

1. $8 \times (20 + 2) = (8 \times 20) + (8 \times n)$ **2.** $5 \times (10 + 3) = (5 \times n) + (5 \times 3)$

3. $7 \times (25 + 4) = (n \times 25) + (n \times 4)$ **4.** $8 \times (20 + 3) = (n \times 20) + (n \times 3)$

Find each product mentally.

5. 4×29 **Think:** $29 = 25 + 4$ **8.** 8×26

6. 5×32 **Think:** $32 = 30 + 2$ **9.** 7×108

7. 2×56 **Think:** $56 = 50 + 6$ **10.** 6×206

Explain Your Thinking

▶ Which number would you express as a sum to multiply 20×46? Explain.

Standards   AF **1.0**

CHAPTER 5

One-Digit Divisors

Why Learn About Division by One-Digit Divisors?

Division by one-digit divisors helps you to find the number of equal groups or the number in each group when you want to put a number of things in equal groups.

When you bake some cookies and want to share them equally with some friends, you can use division to figure out how many cookies each friend should get.

These children are planting 4 kinds of seeds. They have 24 containers for the project, so they used division to find the number of containers to use for each kind of seed.

Reading Mathematics

Reviewing Vocabulary

Understanding math language helps you become a successful problem solver. Here are some math vocabulary words you should know.

$$6\overline{)54} = 9$$

quotient
divisor
dividend

divide	to separate into equal parts or groups
dividend	the number that is being divided
divisor	the number of equal parts or the number in each part
quotient	the answer in division
remainder	the number left over in division

How do you know that these words are related to dividing?

divide   **dividend**   **divisor**   **division**

Reading Words and Symbols

When you read mathematics, sometimes you read words, sometimes you read words and symbols, and sometimes you read only symbols.

All of these statements represent the same problem.

▶ Fifteen divided by three equals what number?

▶ 15 divided by 3 = ?

▶ $15 \div 3 = n$

▶ $3\overline{)15}$

Try These

1. Write whether n represents the divisor, the dividend, or the quotient. Then find the value of n.

   a. $n\overline{)14}$ with quotient 7

   b. $8\overline{)24}$ with quotient n

   c. $4\overline{)n}$ with quotient 6

   d. $42 \div n = 6$

   e. $n \div 7 = 9$

   f. $72 \div 9 = n$

2. Write *true* or *false* for each sentence.

   a. The answer in division is the quotient.

   b. The quotient can never be greater than the divisor.

   c. You cannot divide by zero.

   d. When you divide whole numbers, the quotient always becomes smaller as the divisor becomes greater if the dividend remains the same.

3. Think about putting division words and symbols together. Replace each ■ with *quotient, dividend,* or *divisor.*

   a. $\blacksquare\overline{)\blacksquare}$ with quotient $\blacksquare$

   b. $\blacksquare \div \blacksquare = \blacksquare$

   c. $\blacksquare \times \blacksquare = \blacksquare$

4. Copy and complete. Use numbers that make the sentence true. If _____ is the dividend and _____ is the divisor, then the quotient is _____, and the remainder is _____.

Upcoming Vocabulary

Write About It **Here are some other vocabulary words** you will learn in this chapter. Watch for these words. Write their definitions in your journal.

prime	**average**
composite	**regroup**
divisible	**even and odd**

Modeling Division

You will learn how to use money to model regrouping in division.

New
Vocabulary
regroup

Learn About It

Use play money to learn how to make equal groups.

Mrs. Raoul pays Jake, Alice, and Cindy $12 each week for taking care of her lawn.

Materials

For each group:
play money
($10 bills and
$1 bills)

The First Week Mrs. Raoul gave the three friends 12 one-dollar bills. How did they share the money so that each friend got the same amount?

Use 12 one-dollar bills to show $12.

- Can you make three equal groups with the 12 one-dollar bills? Why or why not?

- How much will be in each group?

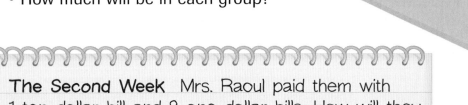

The Second Week Mrs. Raoul paid them with 1 ten-dollar bill and 2 one-dollar bills. How will they share the money this week?

First, use 1 ten-dollar bill and 2 one-dollar bills to show $12.

- Can you make 3 groups of equal value with these bills?

- What can you do with the ten-dollar bill to help you divide the money into 3 equal groups?

Standards NS 3.0, 3.2

Then exchange 1 ten-dollar bill for 10 one-dollar bills.
When you do this, you **regroup** 1 ten as 10 ones.

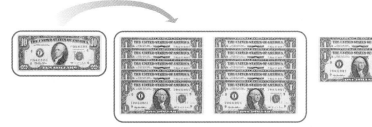

- Now how many one-dollar bills do you have?

- How much money will each friend get this week?

Try It Out

Use play $10 and $1 bills to find the missing information.
Make the greatest number of equal groups you can.

	Amount in All	Number of Equal Groups	Amount in Each Group	Amount Left Over
1.	$10	5	$2	none
2.	$19	9		
3.	$20	8		
4.	$24		$6	
5.	$33		$4	

Divide. Tell if there is a remainder.

6. Divide $24 into 3 equal groups.

7. Divide $29 into 6 equal groups.

8. Divide $37 into groups with $5 in each group.

Write about it!   Talk about it!

Use what you have learned to answer these questions.

9. Why is it possible for 3 friends to share 12 one-dollar bills equally?

10. Why did the friends have to regroup the ten-dollar bill?

Two-Digit Quotients

You will learn that thinking about numbers as tens and ones is necessary when doing long division.

New Vocabulary
remainder

Learn About It

Mrs. King's class is studying Latin music. Her students have collected 38 maracas to put on display. They want to put the same number of maracas on each of 3 shelves. How many maracas should they put on each shelf?

Divide. **38 ÷ 3 = ▪** or **3)38**

Find 38 ÷ 3.

Step 1 You can use base-ten blocks to show 38.

blocks in each group
groups
▪
3)38 ← blocks in all

Step 2 Divide the 3 tens into 3 equal groups. Put 1 ten in each group.

$$\begin{array}{r} 1 \\ 3\overline{)38} \\ -3 \\ \hline 0 \end{array}$$
Multiply. 1 ten × 3
← Subtract. 3 − 3
Compare. 0 < 3

Step 3 Try to divide the 8 ones into 3 groups. Put 2 ones in each group. There are 2 ones left over.

$$\begin{array}{r} 12\ \mathbf{R2} \\ 3\overline{)38} \\ -3\downarrow \\ \hline 08 \\ -6 \\ \hline 2 \end{array}$$
Bring down 8 ones.
Multiply. 2 ones × 3
← Subtract. 8 − 6
Compare. 2 < 3

The amount left over is called the **remainder**. → 2
It should always be less than the divisor.

Solution: They should put 12 maracas on each shelf. There will be 2 maracas left over.

Explain Your Thinking

▶ Why is 38 shown as 3 tens and 8 ones instead of 38 ones?

▶ Can 38 be divided into 3 equal groups? Why or why not?

Another Example

Remainder of Zero
$$\begin{array}{r} 32 \\ 3\overline{)96} \\ -9\downarrow \\ \hline 06 \\ -6 \\ \hline 0 \end{array}$$

Standards NS 3.0, 3.2, 3.4   MR 2.4

Guided Practice

Divide. Tell if there is a remainder.

1. $3\overline{)39}$
2. $2\overline{)85}$
3. $4\overline{)47}$
4. $5\overline{)57}$

5. $66 \div 3$
6. $88 \div 2$
7. $34 \div 3$
8. $94 \div 3$

Ask Yourself

• Can I divide the tens?

• Can I divide the ones?

• Are there any ones left over?

Independent Practice

Divide. Tell if there is a remainder.

9. $2\overline{)28}$
10. $2\overline{)65}$
11. $4\overline{)46}$
12. $4\overline{)87}$
13. $2\overline{)45}$

14. $5\overline{)55}$
15. $2\overline{)63}$
16. $3\overline{)68}$
17. $2\overline{)69}$
18. $4\overline{)48}$

19. $86 \div 2$
20. $97 \div 3$
21. $67 \div 2$
22. $89 \div 4$
23. $37 \div 3$

24. $78 \div 7$
25. $69 \div 6$
26. $26 \div 2$
27. $65 \div 3$
28. $29 \div 2$

Problem Solving • Reasoning

Solve. Whenever you solve problems involving division, the remainder must always be less than the divisor.

29. There are 95 musicians trying to line up in 3 equal rows for a concert. Any musicians that do not fit in the rows will stand in front. How many musicians will stand in front?

30. **Analyze** How many different ways can 16 trumpet players be arranged in equal rows so that there are at least 3 trumpet players in each row and exactly 1 player left over?

31. **Write About It** A marching-band section has 2 rows of 3 saxophones, 3 rows of 4 clarinets, 4 rows of 2 flutes, and 1 row of 3 oboes. How many musicians are in the section? Explain your answer.

MUSIC Maracas are rattlelike instruments made from gourds and seeds. You can use rice, paper cups, and tape to make maracas.

Sam has 24 teaspoons of rice. He needs 2 teaspoons of rice to make 1 maraca. How many maracas can he make?

Mixed Review • Test Prep

Add, subtract, or multiply. *(pages 56–63, 194–197)*

32. $5{,}892 + 4{,}268$
33. $555 - 466$
34. 48×24
35. 29×62

36. What is the product of 216 and 4? *(pages 180–181)*

   A 54   **B** 212   **C** 220   **D** 864

Regrouping in Division

You will learn that in division you sometimes need to regroup.

LESSON 3

Learn About It

Suppose 54 students sign up to play on 4 baseball teams. If each team must have the same number of players, how many students will be on each team? How many students will be left over?

Divide. **54 ÷ 4 = ■** or **4)‾5‾4‾**

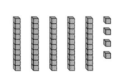

New Vocabulary
quotient
divisor
dividend

Find 54 ÷ 4.

Step 1 You can use base-ten blocks to show 54.

quotient (blocks in each group)

divisor (number of groups) → 4)‾5‾4‾ ← **dividend** (blocks in all)

Step 2 Try to divide the 5 tens into 4 groups. Put 1 ten in each group. There is 1 ten left over.

$$\begin{array}{r} 1 \\ 4{\overline{\smash{\big)}\,54}} \\ \underline{-4} \\ 1 \end{array}$$

Multiply. 1 ten × 4
← Subtract. 5 − 4
Compare. 1 < 4

Step 3 Regroup the 1 ten left over as 10 ones.
10 ones + 4 ones = 14 ones

$$\begin{array}{r} 1 \\ 4{\overline{\smash{\big)}\,54}} \\ \underline{-4\downarrow} \\ 14 \end{array}$$

Bring down
← 4 ones.

Step 4 Divide the 14 ones. Put 3 ones in each group. There are 2 ones left over.

$$\begin{array}{r} 13\ R2 \\ 4{\overline{\smash{\big)}\,54}} \\ \underline{-4} \\ 14 \\ \underline{-12} \\ 2 \end{array}$$

Multiply. 3 ones × 4
← Subtract. 14 − 12
Compare. 2 < 4

The remainder is less than the divisor. →

Solution: There will be 13 students on each team. There will be 2 students left over.

222 **Standards** NS **3.2, 3.4** AF **1.0, 1.1, 1.5** SDP **1.0**

Here's a way to check that an answer is correct.

Check 54 ÷ 4 = 13 R2.

- Multiply the quotient
  by the divisor. $4 \times 13 = 52$

- Add the remainder. $52 + 2 = 54$

$\qquad (4 \times 13) + 2 = 54$

The sum equals the dividend, so the answer is correct.

Other Examples

A. Remainder of Zero

$$
\begin{array}{r}
15 \\
5\overline{)75} \\
-5 \\
\hline
25 \\
-25 \\
\hline
0
\end{array}
$$

Check:
$$
\begin{array}{r}
15 \\
\times\ 5 \\
\hline
75 \\
+\ 0 \\
\hline
75
\end{array}
$$

B. Zero in the Dividend

$$
\begin{array}{r}
12\ \text{R6} \\
7\overline{)90} \\
-7 \\
\hline
20 \\
-14 \\
\hline
6
\end{array}
$$

Check:
$$
\begin{array}{r}
12 \\
\times\ 7 \\
\hline
84 \\
+\ 6 \\
\hline
90
\end{array}
$$

Explain Your Thinking

▶ How are the answer checks for Examples *A* and *B* the same?

▶ When the remainder is zero, what would be a simpler answer check?

Guided Practice

Divide. Check your answers.

1. $5\overline{)74}$ 2. $4\overline{)50}$ 3. $6\overline{)79}$ 4. $3\overline{)72}$

5. $40 \div 3$ 6. $84 \div 5$ 7. $78 \div 6$ 8. $63 \div 4$

Ask Yourself

- When I divide the tens, are there any left over?

- What should I do with any leftover tens?

Independent Practice

Divide. Check your answers.

9. $2\overline{)37}$ 10. $4\overline{)78}$ 11. $3\overline{)51}$ 12. $2\overline{)59}$ 13. $3\overline{)48}$

14. $2\overline{)62}$ 15. $8\overline{)92}$ 16. $6\overline{)74}$ 17. $7\overline{)94}$ 18. $8\overline{)96}$

19. $3\overline{)63}$ 20. $2\overline{)76}$ 21. $5\overline{)81}$ 22. $4\overline{)49}$ 23. $3\overline{)82}$

24. $84 \div 6$ 25. $99 \div 7$ 26. $65 \div 3$ 27. $81 \div 7$ 28. $64 \div 4$

n **Algebra • Functions** Complete each table by following the rule.

Rule: y = x ÷ 3

	x	y
29.	54	
30.	45	
31.	66	
32.	39	

Rule: y = x ÷ 6

	x	y
33.	72	
34.	66	
35.	90	
36.	84	

Rule: y = x ÷ 7

	x	y
37.	7	
38.	91	
39	49	
40.	14	

Problem Solving • Reasoning

Use Data Use the graph for Problems 41–44.

41. Analyze There are 5 teams in the basketball league. Each team has the same number of players. How many players are on each team?

42. How many more players are on the basketball and volleyball teams than are on the football and tennis teams?

43. The volleyball and tennis teams ride in 4 buses to the park. If each bus carries the same number of players, how many players are on each bus? Write an equation to solve.

44. Write Your Own Write a problem by using data from the graph. Give your problem to a classmate to solve.

Mixed Review • Test Prep

Multiply or add. *(pages 56–59, 170–173, 194–196)*

45. 60×4 **46.** 76×2 **47.** $101 + 98$ **48.** $99 + 26$ **49.** 51×42

Choose the letter of the correct answer. *(pages 56–59, 170–173)*

50 $48 \times 2 = n$

A 24   **C** 68
B 50   **D** 96

51 $24 + 36 + 92 = n$

F 142   **H** 512
G 152   **J** 1,412

Extra Practice See Set B on page 264.

Race for the Remainder

Practice division by playing this game with a partner.
Try to be the first person to get 30 points!

What You'll Need

- *a number cube labeled 1 to 6*
- *a number cube labeled 4 to 9*

**Players
2**

Here's What to Do

1. The number cube labeled 4 to 9 is rolled. The number rolled is the divisor for the game.

2. The first player then rolls both number cubes to make a two-digit dividend.

3. The first player divides the dividend by the divisor. The second player checks that the quotient is correct.

4. The remainder is the number of points the first player receives.

   Repeat Steps 1 to 4. The first player to reach a total of 30 or more points wins.

Share Your Thinking Is making the greater two-digit dividend the best strategy for winning the game? Explain why or why not.

Problem-Solving Skill: Interpreting Remainders

You will learn how to solve problems involving remainders.

When you solve a problem that has a remainder, you need to decide how to interpret the remainder.

Look at the situations below.

Sometimes you increase the quotient.

There are 76 girls at a sports camp. If 8 girls are assigned to each cabin, how many cabins are needed?

$$\begin{array}{r} 9\,R4 \\ 8\overline{)76} \\ -72 \\ \hline 4 \end{array}$$

9 cabins will be filled by 72 girls.
Another cabin is needed for the 4 extra girls.
So 10 cabins are needed in all.

Sometimes you drop the remainder.

If 38 girls sign up for swimming, how many 4-person relay teams can there be?

$$\begin{array}{r} 9\,R2 \\ 4\overline{)38} \\ -36 \\ \hline 2 \end{array}$$

There can be 9 relay teams.

Sometimes the remainder is the answer.

All 76 girls play basketball. Each team has 6 members. Anyone not placed on a team will be a referee. How many girls will be referees?

$$\begin{array}{r} 12\,R4 \\ 6\overline{)76} \\ -6 \\ \hline 16 \\ -12 \\ \hline 4 \end{array}$$

Since there are 4 girls not on teams, they will be referees.

Look Back Why does thinking about the question in each situation help you decide what to do with the remainder?

Left: Space camp shows children how astronauts train. Right: Children at a dance camp learn about movement through the use of a human skeleton.

Guided Practice

Solve.

 Each child's astronaut suit requires 3 yards of fabric. How many complete suits can be made if there are 17 yards of fabric?

> **Think:** Can an astronaut suit be made with less than 3 yards of fabric?

2 Fourteen campers try out for a dance act. They will dance in groups of three. How many campers will not be chosen for this dance?

> **Think:** Will the answer tell how many will dance or how many will not dance?

Choose a Strategy

Solve. Use these or other strategies.

Problem-Solving Strategies

- Write an Equation
- Draw a Picture
- Find a Pattern
- Guess and Check

 Thirty girls are playing in a basketball tournament. Two bottles of juice will be given to each player. One carton of juice contains eight bottles. How many cartons of juice should be purchased for the players?

4 Some campers found rocks to display in the nature hut. They brought back 18 rocks. How many different ways can they arrange the rocks in equal rows of 2 or more so that there are no rocks left over?

5 Benjamin is going to space camp for 8 weeks. He plans to spend $6 a week on snacks. Will $50 be enough for all 8 weeks?

6 Together, Ruth and Marco sold 42 tickets to a camp play. Ruth sold 6 more tickets than Marco. How many tickets did each child sell?

7 Seats in the camp auditorium are arranged in 12 rows of 20 seats. If each seat is filled, and there are 9 people standing, how many people are in the audience?

8 On Friday, 67 girls signed up for a trip to a basketball game. Each van can carry 9 girls. What number of vans is needed? Explain your thinking.

Extra Practice See 1–4 on page 267.

Quick ✓ Check

Check Your Understanding of Lessons 1-4

Divide. Tell if there is a remainder.

1. $2\overline{)84}$ **2.** $4\overline{)45}$ **3.** $3\overline{)68}$ **4.** $7\overline{)78}$

Divide. Check your answers.

5. $3\overline{)78}$ **6.** $6\overline{)82}$ **7.** $5\overline{)93}$ **8.** $8\overline{)97}$

Solve.

9. Josh is putting 35 pictures into a photo album.
He is placing 4 pictures on each page.
How many pictures will be on the last page he
uses?

10. Ms. Tate is buying markers for her class.
There are 5 markers in each package. If she needs
23 markers, how many packages should she buy?

How did you do?

If you had difficulty with any items in the Quick Check, you
can use the following pages for review and extra practice.

California Standards	ITEMS	REVIEW THESE PAGES	DO THESE EXTRA PRACTICE ITEMS
Number Sense: **3.0, 3.2**	1–4	pages 220–221	Set A, page 264
Number Sense: **3.0, 3.2**	5–8	pages 222–225	Set B, page 264
Number Sense: **1.4, 3.0, 3.4** Math Reasoning: **2.6, 3.1**	9–10	pages 226–227	1–4, page 267

Test Prep • Cumulative Review

Maintaining the Standards

Choose the letter of the correct answer. If a correct answer is not here, choose NH.

1 Paula has a stamp collection. There are 125 stamps on each page of her stamp book. If Paula has 12 pages, how many stamps does she have in all?

A 365   **C** 1,500

B 1,490   **D** 1,600

2 What is the relationship between the number of gallons of gas and the cost?

Number of Gallons	3	6	9
Cost	$6	$12	$18

F Cost = number of gallons × $1

G Cost = number of gallons × $2

H Cost = number of gallons × $3

J Cost = number of gallons × $4

3
783
× 23

A 3,715   **C** 18,009

B 16,809   **D** NH

4 Sergio scored 5,615 points on a computer game. Patrick scored 4,972 points. How many more points did Sergio score?

F 743   **H** 1,743

G 1,363   **J** NH

5 Ninety-nine students are seated in an auditorium. Each row has the same number of seats. The students fill 6 rows. The seventh row has 3 students. How many students are in each of the other rows?

A 3   **C** 16

B 12   **D** 20

6 The parking garage has 34 rows with 15 spaces in each row. If the lot is filled, how many cars are parked there?

F 184   **H** 510

G 490   **J** NH

7 Mrs. Kennedy has 37 pennies. She wants to give each of 5 children the same number of pennies. What is the greatest number of pennies each child can receive?

A 2

B 5

C 7

D 9

8 Lillian has 56 pine cones. She needs 7 pine cones to make one wreath. How many wreaths can she make in all?

Explain How did you find your answer?

Safe Site

Internet Test Prep
Visit **www.eduplace.com/kids/mhm** for more *Test Prep Practice*.

Mental Math: Divide Multiples of 10, 100, and 1,000

LESSON 5

You will learn how to use basic facts and patterns to divide mentally.

Learn About It

A museum has 1,500 rocks in its collection. All of the rocks are displayed in 3 equal groups. How many rocks are in each group?

Divide. **1,500 ÷ 3 = ▪ or 3)‾1,500**

Find 1,500 ÷ 3.

$$15 \div 3 = 5$$
$$150 \div 3 = 50$$
$$1,500 \div 3 = 500$$

Think: What do you notice about the pattern of zeros?

Solution: There are 500 rocks in each group.

Explain Your Thinking

▶ As the number of zeros in the dividend increases, what happens to the number of zeros in the quotient?

▶ What basic fact can you use to divide 4,000 by 5? How many zeros will there be in the quotient?

Guided Practice

Divide.

1.
$$48 \div 8 = 6$$
$$480 \div 8 = 60$$
$$4,800 \div 8 = ▪$$

2.
$$21 \div 7 = 3$$
$$210 \div 7 = ▪$$
$$2,100 \div 7 = ▪$$

3.
$$80 \div 2 = ▪$$
$$800 \div 2 = ▪$$
$$8,000 \div 2 = ▪$$

4.
$$18 \div 9 = 2$$
$$180 \div 9 = ▪$$
$$1,800 \div 9 = ▪$$

5. $4,500 \div 9 = ▪$ **6.** $900 \div 3 = ▪$ **7.** $2,400 \div 4 = ▪$ **8.** $3,000 \div 3 = ▪$

> **Ask Yourself**
> • What basic fact can I use?
> • How many zeros should be in the quotient?

Standards   NS 3.0, 3.4   AF 1.0, 1.1, 1.2

Independent Practice

Divide.

9. 8 ÷ 4 = ▨
80 ÷ 4 = ▨
800 ÷ 4 = ▨

10. 9 ÷ 3 = ▨
90 ÷ 3 = ▨
900 ÷ 3 = ▨

11. 6 ÷ 2 = ▨
60 ÷ 2 = ▨
600 ÷ 2 = ▨

12. 270 ÷ 3 = ▨

13. 120 ÷ 2 = ▨

14. 160 ÷ 4 = ▨

15. 240 ÷ 8 = ▨

16. 120 ÷ 3 = ▨

17. 350 ÷ 7 = ▨

18. 3,200 ÷ 4 = ▨

19. 5,600 ÷ 8 = ▨

20. 2,500 ÷ 5 = ▨

21. 7,200 ÷ 8 = ▨

22. 6,300 ÷ 9 = ▨

23. 1,400 ÷ 2 = ▨

Problem Solving • Reasoning

24. Fred and Larry have a total of 25 action toys. If Fred has 5 more action toys than Larry, how many toys does each boy have?

25. Tanya has 5 books of stickers. Each book holds 200 stickers. How many stickers does Tanya have altogether?

26. Analyze Stacey has six times as many marbles now as she had 4 months ago. If she has 240 marbles now, how many marbles did she have 4 months ago?

27. Write About It Chad has twice as many rocks as fossils in his collection. If he has 40 rocks, how many fossils does he have? Explain your answer.

Using Algebra

Simplify each expression.

Ⓐ (144 ÷ 4) + 2

Ⓑ 144 ÷ (4 + 2)

Ⓒ 810 ÷ (3 × 2)

Ⓓ (810 ÷ 3) × 2

Ⓔ (52 × 5) + 5

Ⓕ 52 × (5 + 5)

Ⓖ (132 ÷ 6) × (72 × 0)

Ⓗ (0 ÷ 6) × (132 + 72)

Mixed Review • Test Prep

Compare. Use >, <, or = for each ●. *(pages 74–77)*

28. 18 ÷ 6 ● 12 ÷ 4

29. 798 − 332 ● 23 × 19

30. 8 × 7 ● 3 × 6 × 3

31. 17 + 14 ● 4 × 8

32. 49 ÷ 7 ● 103 − 96

33. 63 + 59 ● 5 × 60

Choose the letter of the correct answer. *(pages 144–147)*

㉞ 162 + (630 ÷ 7) = n

A 88   **C** 799

B 252   **D** 5,544

㉟ 183 − (240 ÷ 3) = n

F 263   **H** 175

G 191   **J** 103

Extra Practice See Set C on page 264.

Three-Digit Quotients

You will learn about dividing when the quotient has 3 digits.

Learn About It

Students in the third, fourth, and fifth grades at Hilltop School made 525 origami animals to sell at a craft fair. If each grade made the same number of animals, how many animals did each grade make?

Divide. **525 ÷ 3 = ▢** or **3)525**

Find 525 ÷ 3.

Step 1 Divide the hundreds.

Think: $\dfrac{?\text{ hundreds}}{3)5\text{ hundreds}}$

$$
\begin{array}{r}
1 \\
3)\overline{525} \\
-3 \\
\hline
2
\end{array}
$$
← Multiply. 1 × 3
Subtract. 5 − 3
Compare. 2 < 3

Step 2 Bring down the tens. Divide the tens.

Think: $\dfrac{?\text{ tens}}{3)22\text{ tens}}$

$$
\begin{array}{r}
17 \\
3)\overline{525} \\
-3\downarrow \\
\hline
22 \\
-21 \\
\hline
1
\end{array}
$$
← Multiply. 7 × 3
Subtract. 22 − 21
Compare. 1 < 3

Step 3 Bring down the ones. Divide the ones.

Think: $\dfrac{?\text{ ones}}{3)15\text{ ones}}$

$$
\begin{array}{r}
175 \\
3)\overline{525} \\
-3 \\
\hline
22 \\
-21\downarrow \\
\hline
15 \\
-15 \\
\hline
0
\end{array}
$$
← Multiply. 5 × 3
Subtract. 15 − 15
Compare. 0 < 3

Check your work.
Multiply.

3 × 175 = 525

The product equals the dividend.

Solution: Each grade made 175 origami figures.

Other Examples

A. With a Remainder

$$
\begin{array}{r}
168\ \text{R4} \\
5)\overline{844} \\
-5\downarrow \\
\hline
34 \\
-30\downarrow \\
\hline
44 \\
-40 \\
\hline
4
\end{array}
$$

Check:
$$
\begin{array}{r}
168 \\
\times\ \ 5 \\
\hline
840 \\
+\ \ 4 \\
\hline
844
\end{array}
$$

B. Zero in the Dividend

$$
\begin{array}{r}
117 \\
6)\overline{702} \\
-6\downarrow \\
\hline
10 \\
-6\downarrow \\
\hline
42 \\
-42 \\
\hline
0
\end{array}
$$

Check:
$$
\begin{array}{r}
117 \\
\times\ \ 6 \\
\hline
702
\end{array}
$$

Explain Your Thinking

▶ To check Example *A*, why do you first multiply and then add?

▶ In Example *B*, why must you remember to bring down the zero?

Standards NS **3.2, 3.4** MR **2.4, 2.6**

Guided Practice

Divide.

1. $2\overline{)394}$ 2. $2\overline{)963}$ 3. $4\overline{)450}$ 4. $7\overline{)852}$

Ask Yourself

• Can I divide the hundreds?

• Can I divide the tens?

• Can I divide the ones?

Independent Practice

Divide.

5. $2\overline{)836}$ 6. $4\overline{)709}$ 7. $6\overline{)824}$ 8. $3\overline{)519}$ 9. $3\overline{)404}$

10. $5\overline{)762}$ 11. $6\overline{)918}$ 12. $3\overline{)806}$ 13. $8\overline{)923}$ 14. $8\overline{)889}$

15. $7\overline{)856}$ 16. $5\overline{)913}$ 17. $7\overline{)931}$ 18. $4\overline{)918}$ 19. $6\overline{)762}$

20. $578 \div 3$ 21. $710 \div 5$ 22. $992 \div 8$ 23. $535 \div 2$ 24. $295 \div 2$

25. $438 \div 3$ 26. $685 \div 6$ 27. $945 \div 2$ 28. $775 \div 3$ 29. $864 \div 5$

Problem Solving • Reasoning

Use Data Use the table for Problems 30–32.

30. The turtles are sold in sets of four. How many sets of turtles are there?

31. At the start of the fair, 29 animals were displayed on a table. The rest were divided equally into 4 bags. How many animals were in each bag?

32. **Write About It** Each cat was made with either brown, blue, red, or silver paper. The number of cats in each color was the same. Write and solve an equation to show how many red cats were made. Explain your thinking.

Craft Fair Origami Animals	
Animal	**Number Made**
Crane	234
Turtle	108
Cat	68
Frog	115

Mixed Review • Test Prep

Solve. *(pages 144–147)*

33. $13 - (2 \times 5) = n$ 34. $81 + (9 \times 3) = n$

35. $(81 \div 9) \times 2 = n$ 36. $64 - (8 \div 4) = n$

37. What is the value of the 6 in 246,308? *(pages 4–5)*

    A 600   **B** 6,000   **C** 60,000   **D** 600,000

Place the First Digit of the Quotient

You will learn how to decide where to write the first digit in the quotient.

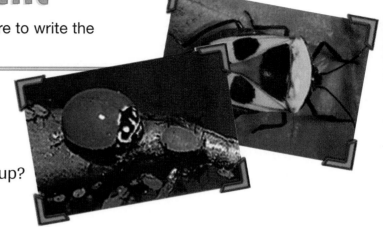

Learn About It

Reggie has 237 photographs of insects. If he puts them into 5 groups of the same size, how many photos will be in each group?

Divide. **237 ÷ 5 = ▇ or 5)237**

Find 237 ÷ 5.

Step 1 Decide where to place the first digit.

$$\text{Think:} \quad 5)\overline{2 \text{ hundreds}}^{\text{? hundreds}}$$

5)237   2 < 5 There are not enough hundreds to divide.

↓

5)237   23 > 5 Place the first digit in the tens place.

Step 2 Divide the tens.

$$\text{Think:} \quad 5)\overline{23 \text{ tens}}^{\text{? tens}}$$

$$\begin{array}{r} 4 \\ 5\overline{)237} \\ -20 \\ \hline 3 \end{array}$$ ← Multiply. 4 × 5
Subtract. 23 − 20
Compare. 3 < 5

Step 3 Bring down the ones. Divide the ones.

$$\text{Think:} \quad 5)\overline{37 \text{ ones}}^{\text{? ones}}$$

$$\begin{array}{r} 47 \text{ R2} \\ 5\overline{)237} \\ -20 \downarrow \\ \hline 37 \\ -35 \\ \hline 2 \end{array}$$ ← Multiply. 7 × 5
Subtract. 37 − 35
Compare. 2 < 5

Solution: There will be 47 photographs in each group. Two photographs will be left over.

Check your work. Multiply. Then add.

$(5 \times 47) + 2 = 237$ ← The sum equals the dividend, so the answer is correct.

Other Examples

A. Multiple of 10

$$\begin{array}{r} 83 \text{ R6} \\ 8\overline{)670} \\ -64 \downarrow \\ \hline 30 \\ -24 \\ \hline 6 \end{array}$$

Check:
$$\begin{array}{r} 83 \\ \times\ 8 \\ \hline 664 \\ +\ 6 \\ \hline 670 \end{array}$$

B. Multiple of 100

$$\begin{array}{r} 85 \text{ R5} \\ 7\overline{)600} \\ -56 \downarrow \\ \hline 40 \\ -35 \\ \hline 5 \end{array}$$

Check:
$$\begin{array}{r} 85 \\ \times\ 7 \\ \hline 595 \\ +\ 5 \\ \hline 600 \end{array}$$

Explain Your Thinking

► When you divide a three-digit dividend by a one-digit divisor, what is the least number of digits that can be in the quotient? Explain your answer.

Guided Practice

Divide. Then check your work.

Ask Yourself

- Can I divide hundreds? If not, what should I do?

- Where should I write the first digit in the quotient?

1. $6\overline{)384}$
2. $8\overline{)672}$
3. $7\overline{)542}$
4. $4\overline{)348}$

5. $437 \div 6$
6. $235 \div 5$
7. $341 \div 9$
8. $473 \div 6$

Independent Practice

Divide. Then check your work.

9. $4\overline{)396}$
10. $8\overline{)272}$
11. $5\overline{)394}$
12. $2\overline{)172}$
13. $5\overline{)485}$

14. $2\overline{)162}$
15. $4\overline{)284}$
16. $6\overline{)532}$
17. $3\overline{)261}$
18. $3\overline{)194}$

19. $3\overline{)154}$
20. $5\overline{)913}$
21. $3\overline{)185}$
22. $7\overline{)638}$
23. $8\overline{)889}$

24. $134 \div 2$
25. $504 \div 7$
26. $317 \div 9$
27. $657 \div 5$

28. $277 \div 2$
29. $619 \div 8$
30. $514 \div 4$
31. $315 \div 4$

Problem Solving • Reasoning

32. **Analyze** Tim sorted 252 butterfly photos into equal groups of small, medium, and large photos. How many photos of each size did he have?

33. On Friday, 135 people visited a nature center's butterfly house. Twice as many people visited on Saturday. How many people visited the butterfly house during the two days?

34. **Write About It** An insect zoo has 365 insects displayed in 5 equal groups. How many insects are in each group? Explain your answer.

SCIENCE North American monarch butterflies migrate the farthest of all monarchs. In the fall they fly from Canada to Mexico.

During this fall migration they travel about 3,000 miles. It takes them about 9 weeks. About how many miles do they travel in each week?

Mixed Review • Test Prep

Write the value of the underlined digit. *(pages 4–5)*

35. 6,<u>3</u>41
36. 8<u>7</u>9
37. 1<u>7</u>3,826
38. 78,96<u>3</u>

Choose the letter of the correct answer. *(pages 56–63)*

39. $3,426 + 6,574 = n$

A 9,000 C 10,000

B 9,900 D 10,900

40. $14,832 - 11,216 = n$

F 3,916 H 3,116

G 3,616 J 2,916

Divide Money

You will learn that dividing money is like dividing whole numbers.

Learn About It

Mrs. Ellis bought 4 key chains as souvenirs while she was on vacation. Each key chain cost the same amount. If she spent a total of $9.80 on the key chains, how much did each one cost?

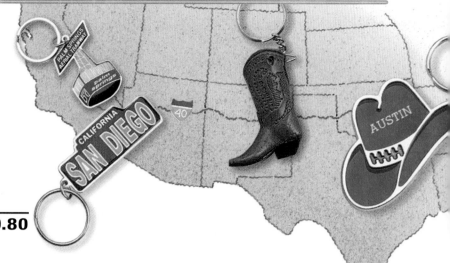

Divide.   **$9.80 ÷ 4 = ■** or **4)$9.80**

Find $9.80 ÷ 4.

Step 1   Divide as if you were dividing whole numbers.

```
        2 45
    4)$9.80
      - 8
        1 8
      - 1 6
          2 0
        - 2 0
            0
```

Step 2   Write the dollar sign and decimal point in the quotient.

Align the decimal point in the quotient with the decimal point in the dividend.

```
         $2.45
     4)$9.80
       - 8
         1 8
       - 1 6
           2 0
         - 2 0
             0
```

Solution: Each key chain cost $2.45.

Explain Your Thinking

▶ Why would an answer of $245 not be reasonable?

▶ How is dividing $8.47 by 7 the same as dividing 847 by 7? How is it different?

Guided Practice

Divide and check.

1. 8)$9.20

2. 3)$756

3. 2)$0.42

4. 4)$7.92

5. 2)$856

6. 3)$0.81

7. 6)$252

8. 5)$1.55

9. 7)$5.39

Ask Yourself

• Where should I place the first digit in the quotient?

• Where should I place the dollar sign and the decimal point in the quotient?

Standards Reviews Grade 3 Standards

Independent Practice

Divide and check.

10. $7\overline{)\$0.91}$ **11.** $6\overline{)\$0.78}$ **12.** $3\overline{)\$0.48}$ **13.** $4\overline{)\$0.64}$

14. $4\overline{)\$88}$ **15.** $8\overline{)\$5.76}$ **16.** $9\overline{)\$8.19}$ **17.** $2\overline{)\$1.34}$

18. $7\overline{)\$4.83}$ **19.** $9\overline{)\$8.46}$ **20.** $5\overline{)\$5.60}$ **21.** $4\overline{)\$7.24}$

22. $3\overline{)\$5.46}$ **23.** $6\overline{)\$6.72}$ **24.** $2\overline{)\$3.32}$ **25.** $3\overline{)\$9.42}$

26. $\$0.45 \div 3$ **27.** $\$0.36 \div 2$ **28.** $\$0.88 \div 8$ **29.** $\$0.72 \div 6$

30. $\$7.56 \div 6$ **31.** $\$5.58 \div 9$ **32.** $\$6.36 \div 3$ **33.** $\$4.64 \div 8$

Problem Solving • Reasoning

Use Data Use the ad for Problems 34 and 36.

34. Estimate What is a good estimate of the total cost of 3 T-shirts at the gift shop?

35. On the way to the Wild Animal Park, Mr. Ellis bought 6 gallons of gasoline for $8.70. How much did he spend on each gallon?

36. Compare Mrs. Ellis needs to buy 6 rolls of film. What is the least amount she might pay? What is the greatest amount she might pay?

37. Analyze Admission to the Wild Animal Park costs $9.50 for each adult and $7.00 for each child. The Ellis family paid $40 for admission. How many adults and children are in the family?

Mixed Review • Test Prep

Add or subtract. *(pages 56–63)*

38. $\begin{array}{r} 3,267 \\ + 4,529 \end{array}$ **39.** $\begin{array}{r} 7,602 \\ - 4,311 \end{array}$ **40.** $\begin{array}{r} 8,264 \\ + 728 \end{array}$ **41.** $\begin{array}{r} 5,281 \\ - 3,105 \end{array}$

42 What is the value of
$(4 \times 1,000) + (6 \times 10) + (9 \times 1)$? *(pages 4–5)*

A 4,600 **B** 4,069 **C** 469 **D** 56

LESSON 9

Zeros in the Quotient

You will learn the importance of placing zeros in the quotient.

Learn About It

Turbo skateboards are shipped in boxes of 8. If a store orders 824 skateboards, how many boxes should the store receive?

Divide.   **824 ÷ 8 = ■ or 8)824**

Find 824 ÷ 8.

Step 1 Decide where to place the first digit. You can divide the hundreds.

$$\overset{\text{? hundreds}}{\textbf{Think: } 8)8 \text{ hundreds}}$$

```
      1
  8)824
  − 8  ← Multiply. 1 × 8
  ———
    0     Subtract. 8 − 8
          Compare. 0 < 8
```

Step 2 Bring down the tens. Divide the tens.

$$\overset{\text{? tens}}{\textbf{Think: } 8)2 \text{ tens}}$$

```
     10
  8)824
  − 8↓
  ———
    02
```
Since 2 < 8, you cannot divide the tens. Write a zero in the tens place.

Step 3 Bring down the ones. Divide the ones.

$$\overset{\text{? ones}}{\textbf{Think: } 8)24 \text{ ones}}$$

```
     103
  8)824
  − 8 ↓
  ———
    024
  − 24  ← Multiply. 3 × 8
  ————
     0     Subtract. 24 − 24
           Compare. 0 < 8
```

Check your work.
Multiply. 8 × 103 = 824

The product equals the dividend.

Solution: The store should receive 103 boxes.

Other Examples

A. Two-Digit Quotient

```
    90 R4        Check:    90
 5)454                   ×  5
 − 45                    ———
 ———                      450
   04                   +  4
 −  0                    ———
 ———                      454
    4
```

B. Multiple of 10

```
    140        Check: 140
 6)840              ×   6
 − 6               ———
 ———                840
   24
 − 24
 ———
   00
```

C. Zero in the Dividend

```
   101 R2      Check:  101
 7)709              ×   7
 − 7               ———
 ———                707
   009             +  2
 −  7              ———
 ———                709
    2
```

Explain Your Thinking

▶ In Example *A*, why is there a zero in the ones place of the quotient?

▶ In Example *B*, why must you remember to write the zero in the quotient?

Standards   NS **3.2, 3.4**   AF **1.1, 1.2**   SDP **1.0, 2.1**   MR **2.4**

Guided Practice

Divide. Then check your work.

1. $3\overline{)924}$ 2. $4\overline{)832}$ 3. $5\overline{)547}$ 4. $7\overline{)729}$

5. $9\overline{)972}$ 6. $8\overline{)863}$ 7. $7\overline{)746}$ 8. $6\overline{)639}$

Ask Yourself

- Can I divide the hundreds? If not, what should I do?
- Can I divide the tens?
- Can I divide the ones?

Independent Practice

Divide. Then check your work.

9. $4\overline{)804}$ 10. $2\overline{)412}$ 11. $7\overline{)\$7.56}$ 12. $6\overline{)361}$

13. $3\overline{)\$9.03}$ 14. $5\overline{)535}$ 15. $6\overline{)648}$ 16. $4\overline{)821}$

17. $8\overline{)565}$ 18. $4\overline{)438}$ 19. $9\overline{)725}$ 20. $2\overline{)\$2.10}$

21. $7\overline{)\$8.40}$ 22. $3\overline{)631}$ 23. $4\overline{)523}$ 24. $8\overline{)965}$

25. $9\overline{)992}$ 26. $2\overline{)\$2.06}$ 27. $2\overline{)613}$ 28. $5\overline{)754}$

29. $162 \div 8$ 30. $529 \div 5$ 31. $\$8.72 \div 8$ 32. $420 \div 3$

33. $637 \div 9$ 34. $\$6.37 \div 7$ 35. $842 \div 4$ 36. $841 \div 2$

n Algebra • Expressions Find the value of each expression when $n = 3$.

37. $66 \div n$ 38. $96 \div n$ 39. $849 \div n$ 40. $342 \div n$

41. $848 \div (n - 1)$ 42. $(8 \times n) \div 2$ 43. $742 \div (n + 4)$ 44. $342 \div (n \times 3)$

Problem Solving • Reasoning

Use Data Use the table for Problems 45–47.

45. The skateboard store sells wheels in sets of 4. How many sets of 4 blue wheels can the store sell?

46. **Compare** How many more sets of 4 red wheels than sets of 4 yellow wheels can the store sell?

47. **Write About It** If 8 green wheels weigh 1 pound, how much do all of the green wheels weigh? Explain how you found your answer.

Skateboard Wheels	
Color	Number of Wheels
Red	428
Yellow	312
Blue	412
Green	480

Use the table for Problems 48–53.

48. Compare Amy, Lisa, and Dwayne skated on different paths. Amy's path was longer than Dwayne's but shorter than Lisa's. Lisa did not skate on Winding Way. Which path did each person take?

49. A third of Speedy Street goes down a hill. How long is the downhill part of Speedy Street?

Flipside Skate Park Paths	
Path	**Length**
Speedy Street	321 yards
Twisty Trail	208 yards
Winding Way	432 yards
Bumpy Boulevard	342 yards

50. When he was halfway down Twisty Trail, Tom stopped to fix his kneepads. How much farther did he have to go to reach the end of the path?

51. Analyze Ty skated all of Speedy Street and Twisty Trail. Ed skated all of Bumpy Boulevard and Winding Way. Decide who skated farther just by looking at the table.

52. Estimate One day, Pete skated Twisty Trail 4 times. About how far did he skate?

53. Write Your Own Using the information in the table, write a division word problem.

Mixed Review • Test Prep

Add, subtract, or multiply. *(pages 56–63, 170–173, 180–181)*

54. 46 + 38   **55.** 4,896 + 3,245   **56.** 324 − 165   **57.** 137 × 6   **58.** 98 × 9

59 How is forty-five thousand, two hundred nine written in standard form? *(pages 4–5)*

  A 450,290   **C** 45,029

  B 45,209   **D** 4,529

Combinations

Turbo skateboards and skateboard wheels are sold in the colors shown. What are all the different ways that the skateboards and wheels could be put together? (The wheels on a skateboard should all be the same color).

Dividing a Different Way

When you lose track of place value in a division problem, you may make mistakes. Here's a way to use columns to help you keep track of the places you are working with.

See how 586 divided by 3 is done here.

Find 586 ÷ 3.

Start with the hundreds place (H).

Think:
5 hundreds ÷ 3

Write 1 in the quotient.
Multiply, subtract, and compare.
There is a remainder of 2 hundreds.

```
    H | T | O
    1 |   |
3)5 | 8 | 6
  - 3 |   |
    2 |   |
```

Next work with the tens place (T).
Regroup the 2 hundreds as 20 tens.
Add the 20 tens and the 8 tens.
Write 28 in the tens column.

Think:
28 tens ÷ 3

Write 9 in the quotient.
Multiply, subtract, and compare.
There is a remainder of 1 ten.

```
    H | T  | O
    1 | 9  |
3)5 | 8  | 6
  - 3 |    |
   -2▶| 20 |
      | 28 |
    - | 27 |
      |  1 |
```

Then work with the ones place (O).
Regroup the 1 ten as 10 ones.
Add the 10 ones and the 6 ones.
Write 16 in the ones column.

Think:
16 ones ÷ 3

Write 5 in the quotient.
Multiply, subtract, and compare.
There is a remainder of 1 one.

```
    H | T  | O
    1 | 9  | 5
3)5 | 8  | 6
  - 3 |    |
   -2▶| 20 |
      | 28 |
    - | 27 |
      | -1▶| 10
      |    | 16
      |  - | 15
      |    |  1
```

Solution: 195 R1

Explain Your Thinking

How is this way of dividing similar to the way you have been using? How is it different?

Problem-Solving Strategy: Work Backward

You will learn how to solve a problem by working backward.

Sometimes in a problem you know the final amount and you need to find the beginning amount. You can start with what you know and work backward.

Problem Lauren rode her bike a certain number of miles on Friday. On Saturday, she rode twice as far as on Friday. On Sunday, she rode 4 miles less than on Saturday. On Monday, she rode 2 miles more than on Sunday. Lauren rode 20 miles on Monday. How many miles did Lauren ride on Friday?

Understand

What is the question?
How many miles did Lauren ride on Friday?

What do you know?
Lauren rode 20 miles on Monday.

Plan

How can you find the answer?
Start with what you know. Work backward and use inverse operations.

> **Remember:**
> Addition and subtraction are inverse operations.
> Multiplication and division are inverse operations.

Solve

Start with the 20 miles Lauren rode on Monday.

Monday		Sunday		Saturday		Friday
20 miles	**− 2**	**18 miles**	**+ 4**	**22 miles**	**÷ 2**	**11 miles**
This is 2 miles more than on Sunday.	Work backward. Subtract 2.	This is 4 miles less than on Saturday.	Work backward. Add 4.	This is twice as far as Friday.	Work backward. Divide by 2.	

Lauren rode 11 miles on Friday.

Look Back

Look back at the problem.
Is your answer reasonable? Explain why or why not.

Standards MR **1.0, 1.1, 1.2, 2.0, 3.0, 3.1, 3.2**

Guided Practice

Use the Work Backward strategy to solve each problem.

1 Tina bought some bottled water for a bike trip. She drank 3 bottles. Then she bought 5 more. After drinking another 2 bottles, she had 4 bottles left. How many bottles of water did Tina start with?

Think: What information should you start with?

2 During a bicycle trip, Lara rode 6 more miles than Spencer. Courtney rode 8 more miles than Lara. Maria rode twice as many miles as Courtney. Maria rode 76 miles. How many miles did Spencer ride?

Think: Should you start with 6 miles or 76 miles? Why?

Choose a Strategy

Solve. Use these or other strategies.

Problem-Solving Strategies

- **Find a Pattern**
- **Guess and Check**
- **Draw a Picture**
- **Work Backward**

3 On Thursday, Mr. Riccio's bicycle shop received its first shipment of bicycle helmets. That day he sold 8 helmets. On Friday, he sold 9 helmets. On Saturday, after 10 more helmets were delivered, he had 18 helmets in his shop. How many helmets were delivered on Thursday?

4 Look at the figures below. Then draw the figure likely to come next in the pattern. Explain your answer.

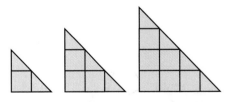

5 Moe is thinking of a number. If he divides his number by 4 and then multiplies the quotient by 5, the result is 135. What number is Moe thinking of?

6 Michael is 5 years older than Elizabeth. Elizabeth is 8 years younger than José. José is 2 years older than Meredith. If Meredith is 12 years old, how old is Michael?

7 Dale buys a pair of bicycle shorts and a shirt. The shirt costs half as much as the shorts. The total cost is $36. How much do the shorts cost?

8 Look at the number pattern. What is the next number likely to be? Why?

8,000   4,000   2,000   1,000

Extra Practice See 5–7 on page 267.

Quick ✓ Check

Check Your Understanding of Lessons 5-10

Divide. Then check your work.

1. $360 \div 4$

2. $4\overline{)525}$

3. $6\overline{)806}$

4. $6\overline{)366}$

5. $7\overline{)394}$

6. $9\overline{)\$2.16}$

7. $7\overline{)\$9.31}$

8. $6\overline{)623}$

9. $7\overline{)212}$

Solve.

10. Danesha is making 3 stacks of coins. The first stack has 3 coins more than the second stack. The second stack has 4 coins less than the third stack. The third stack has 14 coins. How many coins are in the first stack?

How did you do?

If you had difficulty with any items in the Quick Check, you can use the following pages for review and extra practice.

California Standards	ITEMS	REVIEW THESE PAGES	DO THESE EXTRA PRACTICE ITEMS
Number Sense: **3.2, 3.4**	1	pages 230–231	Set C, page 264
Number Sense: **3.2, 3.4**	2–3	pages 232–233	Set D, page 264
Number Sense: **3.2, 3.4**	4–5	pages 234–235	Set E, page 265
Reviews Grade 3 Standards	6–7	pages 236–237	Set F, page 265
Number Sense: **3.2, 3.4**	8–9	pages 238–240	Set G, page 265
Math Reasoning: **1.1, 1.2, 2.6, 3.1**	10	pages 242–243	5–7, page 267

Test Prep • Cumulative Review
Maintaining the Standards

Choose the letter of the correct answer. If a correct answer is not here, choose NH.

1. The zoo has two lions. The male lion weighs 528 pounds. The female lion weighs 452 pounds. About how many more pounds does the male lion weigh?

   A 10   **C** 80

   B 30   **D** 150

2. Which expression does not equal 56?

   F 2×28

   G 8×7

   H 4×14

   J $2 \times 4 \times 9$

3. What should go in the box to make the number sentence true?
   $74 \div 5 = \blacksquare$

   A 14

   B 14 R3

   C 14 R4

   D 14 R5

4. $\begin{array}{r} 145 \\ 378 \\ + 452 \\ \hline \end{array}$

   F 865

   G 965

   H 975

   J NH

5. Which expression does not equal 72?

   A 9×8

   B $3 \times 3 \times 8$

   C 4×18

   D $3 \times 3 \times 3 \times 3$

6. Which expression does not equal 50?

   F 2×25

   G 5×10

   H $2 \times 5 \times 5$

   J 25×25

7. What is the value of n?

   $(32 \times 15) + (96 \div 4) = n$

   A 16

   B 216

   C 480

   D 504

8. Write an expression that is equal to 30. Use two different operations and parentheses in your expression.

   Explain How did you decide where to place the parentheses?

Divisibility Rules

You will learn ways to tell whether a number is divisible by 2, 5, or 10.

New Vocabulary

divisible
even
odd

Learn About It

A whole number is **divisible** by another whole number if the remainder is zero. 18 is divisible by 2 because 18 ÷ 2 = 9, but 18 is not divisible by 4 because 18 ÷ 4 = 4 R2.

Even numbers are divisible by 2.

$\frac{0}{2)0}$	$\frac{1}{2)2}$	$\frac{2}{2)4}$	$\frac{3}{2)6}$	$\frac{4}{2)8}$
$\frac{5}{2)10}$	$\frac{6}{2)12}$	$\frac{7}{2)14}$	$\frac{8}{2)16}$	$\frac{9}{2)18}$

Odd numbers are not divisible by 2.

$\frac{0 \text{ R1}}{2)1}$	$\frac{1 \text{ R1}}{2)3}$	$\frac{2 \text{ R1}}{2)5}$	$\frac{3 \text{ R1}}{2)7}$	$\frac{4 \text{ R1}}{2)9}$
$\frac{5 \text{ R1}}{2)11}$	$\frac{6 \text{ R1}}{2)13}$	$\frac{7 \text{ R1}}{2)15}$	$\frac{8 \text{ R1}}{2)17}$	$\frac{9 \text{ R1}}{2)19}$

A number is divisible by 5 if it can be divided by 5 with a remainder of 0.

$\frac{1}{5)5}$	$\frac{2}{5)10}$	$\frac{3}{5)15}$	$\frac{4}{5)20}$
$\frac{5}{5)25}$	$\frac{6}{5)30}$	$\frac{7}{5)35}$	$\frac{8}{5)40}$

A number is divisible by 10 if it can be divided by 10 with a remainder of 0.

$\frac{1}{10)10}$	$\frac{2}{10)20}$	$\frac{3}{10)30}$	$\frac{4}{10)40}$
$\frac{5}{10)50}$	$\frac{6}{10)60}$	$\frac{7}{10)70}$	$\frac{8}{10)80}$

Explain Your Thinking

▶ What rule could you make to identify a number that is divisible by 2? by 5? by 10?

▶ Name a number that is divisible by 2, 5, and 10. Are there others?

Guided Practice

1. Which numbers are divisible by 2? Tell how you know.

2. Which numbers are divisible by 5? by 10? by both 5 and 10?

28   120

48   75

> **Ask Yourself**
> • Is the ones digit divisible by 2?
> • Is the ones digit 0 or 5?

Standards NS **3.2**, **4.1**   MR **3.0**, **3.3**

Independent Practice

Copy and complete this table. Use a check mark to show divisibility.

		30	45	84	95	130	175
3.	divisible by 2	✓					
4.	divisible by 5	✓					
5.	divisible by 10	✓					

Problem Solving • Reasoning

6. **Analyze** Beth wants to plant 24 flowers. She wants more than 1 flower but the same number in each row. She could plant 1 row of 24 flowers. List all the other ways she could plant her flowers.

7. Find the smallest number that is divisible by 2, 5, and 10. Explain your reasoning.

8. **Write About It** Every number in the pattern at the right is divisible by 2. Record a different pattern in which every number is divisible by both 5 and 10. Tell how you decided on the pattern.

Mixed Review • Test Prep

Estimate each answer. *(pages 64–65)*

9.	10.	11.	12.	13.
49	143	$4.29	898	58
+ 28	− 98	+ $2.72	− 102	+ 67

14 $(136 \div 2) \times 2 = n$ *(pages 144–147)*

   A 68   **B** 136   **C** 272   **D** 544

Logical Thinking

Write *true* or *false*. Give examples to support each answer.

15. All numbers that are divisible by 10 are divisible by 2.

16. Some numbers that are divisible by 2 are divisible by 5.

17. All numbers that are divisible by 5 are divisible by 10.

Prime and Composite Numbers

You will learn how to decide whether a number is prime or composite.

New Vocabulary
prime number
composite number

Learn About It

You can use the factors of a number to tell if it is a prime number or a composite number.

Examples of Prime Numbers	Examples of Composite Numbers
2, 7, 13, and 19 are prime numbers.	4, 8, 15, and 18 are composite numbers.
Notice that each number has exactly two factors:	Notice that each number has more than two factors:

$$2 \rightarrow 1, 2$$
$$7 \rightarrow 1, 7$$
$$13 \rightarrow 1, 13$$
$$19 \rightarrow 1, 19$$

$$4 \rightarrow 1, 2, 4$$
$$8 \rightarrow 1, 2, 4, 8$$
$$15 \rightarrow 1, 3, 5, 15$$
$$18 \rightarrow 1, 2, 3, 6, 9, 18$$

A **prime number** is a whole number that has exactly two factors, 1 and itself.

A **composite number** is a whole number that has more than two factors.

The number 1 is neither prime nor composite.

Explain Your Thinking

▶ Divisibility rules can help you find the factors of a number. Explain why.

Guided Practice

Copy and complete the table.

	Number	Factors	Prime or Composite
	1	1	Neither
	2	1, 2	Prime
1.	3		
2.	4		
3.	5		
4.	6		

Ask Yourself

• Have I found all of the factors?

• How many factors does the number have?

Standards NS **4.2**   MR **3.0, 3.3**

Independent Practice

5. Write the factors for 7 through 30 in a table like the one below. Then decide whether each number is prime or composite.

Number	Factors	Prime or Composite
7		
8		
9		
10		

6. Which numbers from 7 to 30 are prime numbers?

7. Which numbers from 7 to 30 are composite numbers?

8. In how many ways can you write 36 as the product of two numbers?

Problem Solving • Reasoning

9. Is the product of two prime numbers ever a prime number? Explain.

10. Analyze Are any even numbers prime? Are all odd numbers prime? Give examples.

11. Analyze Other than 5 itself, can a whole number ending in 5 be prime? Explain.

12. Write About It What strategy could you use to find all the primes from 1 to 50? Show that your strategy works.

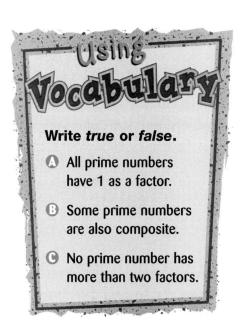

Using Vocabulary

Write *true* or *false*.

A All prime numbers have 1 as a factor.

B Some prime numbers are also composite.

C No prime number has more than two factors.

Mixed Review • Test Prep

Multiply or divide. *(pages 180–185, 234–235)*

13. 342×6 **14.** $276 \div 3$ **15.** $438 \div 6$ **16.** $2{,}903 \times 7$

17. $600 \div 8$ **18.** $497 \div 7$ **19.** 607×5 **20.** 328×9

Choose the letter of the correct answer. *(pages 56–59, 170–173)*

21 What is the sum of 300 and 6?

    A 50   **C** 306

    B 294   **D** 1,800

22 What is the product of 27 and 3?

    F 9   **H** 30

    G 24   **J** 81

Extra Practice See Set I on page 266.

Modeling Averages

You will learn what an average is.

Learn About It

Finding an average is one way to find a number that is typical of the numbers in a group.

Work with a partner to learn about finding an average.

During summer vacation, Anna read 3 books, Marsha read 8 books, and Flo read 7 books. What is the average number of books read?

Materials

For each pair: counters

Step 1 Use counters to stand for the number of books each girl read. Make a column of counters to show how many books each girl read.

- How many columns of counters did you make?
- How many counters are there in each column?

Step 2 To find the average, arrange the counters so that there is the same number of counters in each column.

Move counters from one column to another until the number of counters in each column is the same.

Now the number of counters in each column shows the average.

- What is the average number of books read?

Standards NS 3.0, 3.4 | MR 2.3, 2.4

Try It Out

Use counters to find the average of the numbers in each group.

1. 6, 8

2. 4, 8

3. 2, 2, 5

4. 10, 1, 1

5. 3, 9, 2, 6

6. 4, 1, 1, 1, 3

7. 8, 3, 4, 5

8. 5, 7, 3, 9

9. 6, 3, 4, 1, 1

10. Look back at Exercise 8. List a different group of 4 numbers that have the same average.

Use counters to find the missing number in each group.

Average = 2

11. 3, ▪

Average = 5

12. ▪, 7

Average = 6

13. ▪, 4, 2

Average = 4

14. 1, 9, ▪

Average = 6

15. 5, 5, ▪

Average = 7

16. 12, ▪, 6

17. What is the average of 8, 8, and 8? What is the average of 5, 5, 5, and 5? What do you notice?

18. **Write Your Own** Write a problem for which the answer is an average of 9. Use counters and have your partner check your work.

Write about it! Talk about it!

Use what you have learned to answer these questions.

19. Look at the numbers 2, 5, 14, 1, and 3. Will the average of these numbers be closer to 1 or to 14? Explain your prediction.

20. What operations could you use to find the average of the numbers in a group?

Find Averages

You will learn how to calculate the average of a group of numbers.

Learn About It

During a three-week food drive, Frank collected 15 cans the first week, 21 cans the second week, and 12 cans the third week. What was the average number of cans he collected each week?

To calculate the **average** of the numbers in a group, divide their sum by the number of addends. This average is also called the **mean**.

Find the average of 15, 21, and 12.

Step 1 Find the sum of the numbers. Count the addends.	**Step 2** Divide the sum by the number of addends.
$\begin{array}{r} 15 \\ 21 \\ + 12 \\ \hline 48 \end{array}$ ⟵ 3 addends	$\begin{array}{r} 16 \\ 3\overline{)48} \\ -\underline{3} \\ 18 \\ -\underline{18} \\ 0 \end{array}$

Solution: He collected an average of 16 cans each week.

Week 2

Explain Your Thinking

► Can the average of the numbers in a group be greater than every number in the group? Explain.

► Can the average of the numbers in a group be equal to a number in the group? Explain.

Guided Practice

Find the average of the numbers in each group.

1. 6, 8, 9, 33

2. 34, 45, 26

3. 43, 10, 25, 38

4. 41, 39, 29, 19, 17

5. 124, 157, 214

6. 75, 54, 65, 22, 24

Ask Yourself

• What is the sum of the numbers?

• How many numbers are there in the group?

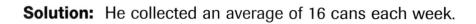

| **Standards** | NS **3.0, 3.4** | AF **1.0, 1.1** | SDP **1.0** | MR **2.4** |

Independent Practice

Find the average of the numbers in each group.

7. 1, 4, 4

8. $3, $4, $8

9. 15, 24, 44, 29

10. $3, $5, $6, $6

11. 11, 12, 16, 17, 19

12. $23, $36, $36, $47, $18

13. 10, 12, 17

14. $22, $31, $55

15. 2, 9, 28, 41

16. 50, 25, 10, 15

17. $62, $67, $104, $155

18. 15, 499, 7, 100, 4

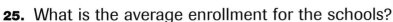 **Algebra • Properties** Write >, < or = for each .

19. 4×1 ⬤ 41

20. $23 \div 1$ ⬤ 23×1

21. $28 - 17$ ⬤ $28 + 17$

22. $47 - 0$ ⬤ 47×0

23. $54 + 32$ ⬤ $32 + 54$

24. 3×7 ⬤ 7×3

Problem Solving • Reasoning

Use Data Use the table for Problems 25–27.

School	Enrollment	Length of School Day
Lakeside	314	7 h 10 min
Eastman	355	5 h 15 min
King	129	6 h 20 min

25. What is the average enrollment for the schools?

26. What is the average length of a school day?

 27. Write About It If Carl transfers from King School to Eastman School will his school day be longer or shorter? Explain.

Mixed Review • Test Prep

Multiply or divide. *(pages 180–185, 232–233, 236–241)*

28. $2.75 \times 3 = $ ▨

29. $3{,}482 \times 7 = $ ▨

30. $4.56 \div 6 = $ ▨

31. $983 \div 4 = $ ▨

32. $7{,}689 \times 3 = $ ▨

33. $6.30 \div 7 = $ ▨

Choose the letter of the correct answer. *(pages 144–146)*

34 $n = (5 + 3) \times (2 + 1)$

   A 11   **C** 16

   B 12   **D** 24

35 $n = (5 \times 3) + (2 \times 1)$

   F 10   **H** 17

   G 16   **J** 30

Extra Practice See Set J on page 266.

253

Estimate Quotients

You will learn how to estimate quotients.

Learn About It

Kaitlyn is making 6 jewelry kits. She has 311 small beads. About how many small beads can she use in each kit?

You can estimate to find about how many beads she can use in each kit.

One way to estimate 311 ÷ 6 is to use basic facts and multiples of 10. Think of a new dividend close to 311 that is divisible by 6.

Estimate $6\overline{)311}$.

Step 1 Use basic facts and multiples of 10 to find a new dividend.

$$6\overline{)311} \longrightarrow 6\overline{)300}$$

Think: $6 \times 5 = 30$
$30 \times 10 = 300$

Step 2 Divide.

$$6\overline{)300} \quad \overset{50}{\phantom{6\overline{)300}}}$$

Look Back.
Is 50 beads a reasonable answer?

Solution: Kaitlyn can use about 50 beads in each kit.

Explain Your Thinking

▶ How does the divisor help you choose your basic fact?

Guided Practice

Estimate. Write the basic fact you used.

1. $8\overline{)50}$

2. $5\overline{)262}$

3. $3\overline{)261}$

4. $4\overline{)19}$

5. $6\overline{)177}$

6. $9\overline{)627}$

Ask Yourself

• Which basic fact can help me choose a new dividend?

Standards NS **3.0**   MR **1.2, 2.0, 2.1**

Independent Practice

Estimate. Write the basic fact you used.

7. 2$\overline{)15}$ **8.** 3$\overline{)25}$ **9.** 6$\overline{)31}$ **10.** 4$\overline{)35}$ **11.** 9$\overline{)61}$

12. 5$\overline{)103}$ **13.** 7$\overline{)409}$ **14.** 3$\overline{)188}$ **15.** 2$\overline{)157}$ **16.** 8$\overline{)735}$

17. 6$\overline{)168}$ **18.** 4$\overline{)251}$ **19.** 7$\overline{)291}$ **20.** 9$\overline{)627}$ **21.** 3$\overline{)114}$

22. 5$\overline{)189}$ **23.** 2$\overline{)123}$ **24.** 8$\overline{)172}$ **25.** 5$\overline{)263}$ **26.** 4$\overline{)149}$

27. 46 ÷ 6 **28.** 22 ÷ 3 **29.** 37 ÷ 6 **30.** 339 ÷ 4 **31.** 396 ÷ 5

Problem Solving • Reasoning

Solve. Choose a method.

Computation Methods

• Mental Math   • Estimation   • Paper and Pencil

32. A jewelry store had sales of $535 for necklaces during a one-day sale. Nine people bought necklaces that day. About how much did each necklace cost?

33. Analyze Joyce and 3 friends spent $44 on jewelry-making supplies. If each person spent the same amount, how much did each person spend on supplies?

34. At a craft store, plastic beads cost $3 per package and glass beads cost $7 per package. On Friday, 38 packages of plastic beads and 12 packages of glass beads were sold. What was the sales amount for beads on Friday?

35. Write About It Beaded belts are sold at a Navajo craft festival. Tell how to write an equation for n in which n is the cost of 3 small belts and 2 large belts.

Small $8.00

Large $25.00

Medium $15.00

Mixed Review • Test Prep

Solve for n. *(pages 82–83, 136–139)*

36. 7 × n = 49   **37.** 24 + 15 + n = 96   **38.** 143 − n = 59   **39.** 72 ÷ 9 = n

Choose the correct value for n. *(pages 6–9)*

40 20 < n < 30

A 32   **B** 23   **C** 19   **D** 2

41 71 > n > 65

F 70   **G** 64   **H** 61   **I** 59

Divide Greater Numbers

You will learn how to divide greater numbers.

Learn About It

Visitors to Mesa Verde National Park can see many cliff dwellings and learn about the people who built them. Guides lead tours through some of the buildings.

One week a total of 1,638 people visited the park. What was the **average** number of visitors each day that week?

Divide. $1,638 \div 7 = \blacksquare$ $7\overline{)1,638}$

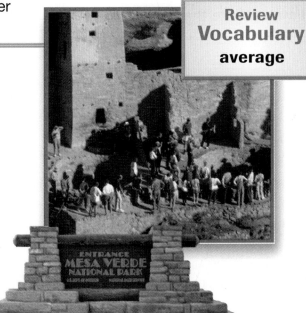

Find 1,638 ÷ 7.

Step 1 Divide the thousands.

Think: $\dfrac{?\ \text{thousands}}{7\overline{)1\ \text{thousand}}}$

$7\overline{)1,638}$
↑
not enough thousands

Step 2 Regroup the thousands as hundreds. Divide the hundreds.

Think: $\dfrac{?\ \text{hundreds}}{7\overline{)16\ \text{hundreds}}}$

$\begin{array}{r} 2 \\ 7\overline{)1,638} \\ -1\,4 \\ \hline 2 \end{array}$ ← Multiply. 2 × 7
Subtract. 16 − 14
Compare. 2 < 7

Step 3 Complete the division.

$\begin{array}{r} 234 \\ 7\overline{)1,638} \\ -1\,4 \\ \hline 23 \\ -\,21 \\ \hline 28 \\ -\,28 \\ \hline 0 \end{array}$

Check your work.
Multiply.

$7 \times 234 = 1,638$

Solution: The average number of visitors each day was 234.

Other Examples

A. Four-Digit Quotient

$\begin{array}{r} 1,675 \\ 3\overline{)5,025} \\ -3 \\ \hline 2\,0 \\ -1\,8 \\ \hline 22 \\ -21 \\ \hline 15 \\ -15 \\ \hline 0 \end{array}$

Check: $\begin{array}{r} 1,675 \\ \times\quad 3 \\ \hline 5,025 \end{array}$

B. Five-Digit Dividend

$\begin{array}{r} 3,184\ \text{R3} \\ 6\overline{)19,107} \\ -\,18 \\ \hline 1\,1 \\ -\,6 \\ \hline 50 \\ -\,48 \\ \hline 27 \\ -\,24 \\ \hline 3 \end{array}$

Check: $\begin{array}{r} 3,184 \\ \times\quad 6 \\ \hline 19,104 \\ +\quad 3 \\ \hline 19,107 \end{array}$

Standards   NS **3.0, 3.2, 3.4**   AF **1.0, 1.1, 1.2**   SDP **1.0**   MR **2.4**

Explain Your Thinking

▶ Think about 9,872 ÷ 7. Without dividing, how many digits are in the quotient? Explain how you know.

▶ How is dividing with 3-digit, 4-digit, and 5-digit dividends the same? How is it different?

Guided Practice

Divide. Check your work.

1. $5\overline{)4,325}$
2. $4\overline{)7,318}$
3. $8\overline{)56,912}$

4. $10,967 \div 9$
5. $3,755 \div 7$
6. $\$15,310 \div 2$

Ask Yourself

- Where do I write the first digit in each quotient?
- What steps should I follow each time I divide?

Independent Practice

Divide. Check your work.

7. $4\overline{)1,356}$
8. $2\overline{)1,704}$
9. $3\overline{)\$2,136}$
10. $6\overline{)6,906}$

11. $8\overline{)9,851}$
12. $5\overline{)6,453}$
13. $8\overline{)\$2,080}$
14. $7\overline{)9,170}$

15. $9\overline{)\$9,072}$
16. $9\overline{)9,160}$
17. $6\overline{)8,022}$
18. $5\overline{)2,338}$

19. $\$1,135 \div 5$
20. $2,991 \div 3$
21. $8,414 \div 7$
22. $\$2,922 \div 6$

23. $39,306 \div 6$
24. $\$31,482 \div 9$
25. $12,020 \div 4$
26. $\$27,081 \div 9$

n **Algebra • Equations** Solve for *n*.

27. $700 \div 7 = n$
28. $(7,896 \div 3) \times 1 = n$

29. $n \div 60 = 10$
30. $(3,544 \div 3) \times 0 = n$

31. $2,500 \div n = 500$
32. $(750 \div 6) - 125 = n$

Mental Math Compare.
Use >, <, or = for each ●.

33. $2,000 \div 4$ ● $2,000 \div 8$

34. $5,000 \div 5$ ● 500×2

35. $3,000 \div 3$ ● $3,000 \times 3$

36. 400×2 ● $800 \div 2$

37. $8,000 \div 4$ ● $4,000 \times 2$

38. $600 \div 2$ ● $1800 \div 3$

Using Vocabulary

Write *true* or *false* for each sentence. Then write an example.

Ⓐ The divisor is always less than the remainder.

Ⓑ The quotient and the divisor can sometimes be equal.

Ⓒ The dividend and the divisor can never be equal.

Problem Solving • Reasoning

Use Data Use the graph for Problems 39 and 40.

39. Half the number of visitors on Wednesday paid a $5.00 "walk-in" fee to enter the park. How much money did the park collect from walk-in visitors on Wednesday?

40. Analyze Six guided tours were given on Friday. If every visitor took only one tour and each tour had the same number of people, how many visitors were in each tour?

Visitors to Mesa Verde National Park in One Week

41. On weekdays, a souvenir center at a state park is open for 14 hours each day. On weekends, it is open for 16 hours each day. For how many hours is the visitor center open each week?

42. During last week's special promotion, a national park's Web site received 10,367 visits. What was the average number of visits the Web site received each day?

43. Estimate The Ramirez family drove 1,815 miles in three days to visit Mesa Verde. About how many miles did the family drive each day?

44. A private campground rents each of its 560 campsites for $8 a day. How much money is collected in one day if every campsite is rented?

Mixed Review • Test Prep

Add, subtract, or multiply. *(pages 56–63, 68–69, 180–181)*

45.
  $14.99
  − 3.28

46.
  $6.59
  ×   4

47.
  $17.98
  + 26.53

48.
  $81.03
  − 43.96

49.
  $4.32
  ×   5

Choose the letter of the correct answer. *(pages 10–11)*

50 Which number when rounded to the nearest thousand is 24,000?

  A 23,450 **C** 24,516

  B 23,509 **D** 123,950

51 Which number when rounded to the nearest hundred is 23,200?

  F 20,188 **H** 22,202

  G 22,188 **J** 23,202

Using Vocabulary

Use the clues to find each number.

1. The divisor is 4.
The dividend is 127.
The quotient is 31.
What is the remainder?

2. The dividend is 363.
The remainder is 3.
The quotient is 90.
What is the divisor?

3. The remainder is 5.
The quotient is 547.
The divisor is 8.
What is the dividend?

4. The dividend is 287.
The remainder is 3.
The divisor is 4.
What is the quotient?

Check It Out

Write and solve a division problem that matches each multiplication check.

1.
$$\begin{array}{r} 39 \\ \times\ 7 \\ \hline 273 \end{array}$$

2.
$$\begin{array}{r} 84 \\ \times\ 7 \\ \hline 588 \\ +\ 5 \\ \hline 593 \end{array}$$

3.
$$\begin{array}{r} 241 \\ \times\ 3 \\ \hline 723 \\ +\ 2 \\ \hline 725 \end{array}$$

4.
$$\begin{array}{r} 103 \\ \times\ 6 \\ \hline 618 \\ +\ 4 \\ \hline 622 \end{array}$$

Digit Detective

Use the digits in each square exactly once to complete each problem.

1. 1 3 R1
$\blacksquare)\overline{\blacksquare\blacksquare}$

3 4 5

2. 1 6 R1
$\blacksquare)\overline{\blacksquare\blacksquare}$

5 4 6

3. 1 2 R2
$\blacksquare)\overline{\blacksquare\blacksquare}$

6 7 8

4. $\blacksquare$ R1
$\blacksquare)\overline{\blacksquare\blacksquare}$

1 2 4 5

Problem-Solving Application: Use Operations

You will learn how to choose an operation to solve a problem.

You need to decide which operations to use to solve word problems.

During the 1999 Rose Parade, a camera on the Baseball Float, shown at right, sent live pictures to a Web site. About 120,000 people visited the site during the first hour of the parade. During the second hour, 85,000 people visited the site. What was the average number of people who visited the site each hour?

Baseball Float in the 1999 Rose Parade. This float was unusual because it was powered solely by electricity.

Understand

What is the question?
What was the average number of people who visited the site each hour?

What do you know?
The number of people who visited each hour.

Plan

What can you do to find the answer?
Add the numbers of people who visited the site the first and second hours. Then divide that sum by 2.

Solve

$$120,000 + 85,000 = 205,000$$
$$205,000 \div 2 = 102,500$$

The average number of people who visited the site each hour was 102,500.

Look Back

Look back at the question. Is your answer reasonable?
Explain how you can use estimation to decide if your answer is reasonable.

Standards MR **1.0, 1.2, 2.0, 2.1, 2.6, 3.0, 3.1, 3.2**

Left: Children from the community help work on pieces of the float throughout the year. Right: This is a view of Colorado Boulevard filmed from the float and sent to the Web site.

Guided Practice

Solve.

1 To decorate the float, 350 people each worked an average of 20 hours. How many hours altogether did the people work to decorate the float?

 Think: Do you multiply or divide to solve this problem? Why?

2 The float weighed 44,650 pounds. A car weighs about 4,000 pounds. The weight of about how many cars is equal to the weight of the float?

 Think: Can you use estimation to solve this problem?

Choose A Strategy

Solve. Use these or other strategies.

Problem-Solving Strategies

| • Draw a Picture | • Guess and Check | • Work Backward | • Write an Equation |

3 A parade had 36 small floats and 24 large floats. Each small float carried 5 people. Each large float carried 15 people. Altogether, how many people were on the floats?

4 A parade grandstand has 6 sections. All of its sections are the same size and are filled with people. If the grandstand holds 1,452 people, how many people are in each section?

5 A float took 8 minutes to travel 1,760 feet. If it always traveled at the same speed, how many feet did the float travel in 1 minute?

6 A souvenir stand sells parade pennants. The pennants come in boxes of 48. About how many pennants are there in 98 boxes?

7 Three floats were decorated with a total of 16,000 roses. One float had twice the number of roses as each of the other two floats. How many roses were on each float?

8 How much longer is the Baseball Float than it is wide?

28 ft

18 ft

55 ft

Quick ✓ Check

Check Your Understanding of Lessons 11–17

Solve.

1. Which of the following numbers are divisible by both 2 and 5?

36, 50, 65, 110, 144

2. Which of the following numbers are prime numbers?

4, 7, 13, 24, 33, 41

Find the average of each group of numbers.

3. 30, 41, 36, 28, 45

4. 132, 212, 175

Estimate. Write the basic fact you used.

5. $6\overline{)57}$

6. $4\overline{)253}$

Divide. Check your work.

7. $6\overline{)9,687}$

8. $3\overline{)1,815}$

9. $9\overline{)31,207}$

Solve.

10. Suppose Mr. Tyson had $55. He bought 3 CDs for $8. He bought 2 CDs for $12. How much money did he have left?

How did you do?

If you had difficulty with any items in the Quick Check, you can use the following pages for review and extra practice.

California Standards	ITEMS	REVIEW THESE PAGES	DO THESE EXTRA PRACTICE ITEMS
Number Sense: **4.1**	1	pages 246–247	Set H, page 265
Number Sense: **4.2**	2	pages 248–249	Set I, page 266
Statistics, Data, Probability: **1.0**	3–4	pages 252–253	Set J, page 266
Number Sense: **3.0, 3.2**	5–6	pages 254–255	Set K, page 266
Number Sense: **3.0, 3.2, 3.4**	7–9	pages 256–258	Set L, page 266
Math Reasoning: **1.1, 1.2, 2.6, 3.2**	10	pages 260–261	8–11, page 267

Test Prep • Cumulative Review
Maintaining the Standards

Choose the letter of the correct answer. If a correct answer is not here, choose NH

1 One hundred eighty-nine senior citizens were planning a trip to the theater. They rented vans for transportation. If each van can seat 9 senior citizens, how many vans do they need in all?

  A 15

  B 21

  C 25

  D NH

2 Which number is a prime number?

  F 9

  G 15

  H 19

  J 21

3 Mr. Harmon pays $659 a month to rent his apartment. How much does Mr. Harmon pay for rent in a year?

  A $7,708

  B $7,798

  C $7,808

  D NH

4 Which number is a composite number?

  F 3

  G 5

  H 7

  J 9

5 Which equation does the table show?

x	y
18	2
27	3
36	4
45	5

  A $y = x \times 2$ **C** $y = x - 16$

  B $y = x \div 9$ **D** $y = x + 3$

6 The bookstore put 256 books on 8 shelves. If the same number of books were on each shelf, how many books were on one shelf?

  F 3 R2

  G 32

  H 302

  J NH

7 What number should go in the box to make the number sentence true?

  $(108 - 49) \times 2 = \blacksquare \times 2$

  A 40

  B 59

  C 61

  D 69

8 List the factors of 42.
  Explain Tell which factors are prime and explain how you know.

Safe Site

Internet Test Prep
Visit **www.eduplace.com/kids/mhm**
for more *Test Prep Practice.*

263

Extra Practice

Set A (Lesson 2, pages 220–221)

Divide. Tell if there is a remainder.

1. $2\overline{)48}$
2. $6\overline{)74}$
3. $8\overline{)89}$
4. $6\overline{)68}$

5. $4\overline{)84}$
6. $3\overline{)65}$
7. $5\overline{)58}$
8. $2\overline{)86}$

9. $64 \div 2$
10. $72 \div 3$
11. $48 \div 4$
12. $88 \div 8$

13. $87 \div 2$
14. $49 \div 2$
15. $57 \div 5$
16. $98 \div 9$

Set B (Lesson 3, pages 222–225)

Divide. Check your answers.

1. $4\overline{)58}$
2. $3\overline{)82}$
3. $6\overline{)92}$
4. $7\overline{)84}$

5. $8\overline{)94}$
6. $5\overline{)89}$
7. $4\overline{)68}$
8. $6\overline{)98}$

9. $37 \div 2$
10. $54 \div 3$
11. $76 \div 4$
12. $95 \div 5$

13. $49 \div 3$
14. $63 \div 4$
15. $87 \div 7$
16. $33 \div 2$

Set C (Lesson 5, pages 230–231)

Divide.

1. $60 \div 6$
2. $80 \div 4$
3. $120 \div 2$
4. $280 \div 7$

5. $300 \div 6$
6. $240 \div 6$
7. $450 \div 5$
8. $120 \div 4$

9. $3,000 \div 5$
10. $3,200 \div 4$
11. $5,500 \div 5$
12. $8,100 \div 9$

13. $2,700 \div 3$
14. $2,800 \div 4$
15. $4,500 \div 9$
16. $2,700 \div 9$

Set D (Lesson 6, pages 232–233)

Divide.

1. $2\overline{)648}$
2. $7\overline{)785}$
3. $5\overline{)564}$
4. $3\overline{)954}$

5. $4\overline{)853}$
6. $6\overline{)682}$
7. $8\overline{)897}$
8. $9\overline{)999}$

9. $444 \div 2$
10. $309 \div 2$
11. $507 \div 4$
12. $703 \div 3$

13. $834 \div 3$
14. $287 \div 2$
15. $695 \div 5$
16. $938 \div 4$

Extra Practice

Set E   *(Lesson 7, pages 234–235)*

Divide. Then check your work.

1. $8\overline{)332}$
2. $3\overline{)298}$
3. $9\overline{)997}$
4. $7\overline{)498}$

5. $5\overline{)575}$
6. $6\overline{)138}$
7. $5\overline{)368}$
8. $9\overline{)658}$

9. $363 \div 8$
10. $495 \div 5$
11. $560 \div 7$
12. $819 \div 9$

13. $426 \div 6$
14. $498 \div 7$
15. $357 \div 5$
16. $916 \div 8$

Set F   *(Lesson 8, pages 236–237)*

Divide and check.

1. $5\overline{)\$5.95}$
2. $3\overline{)\$2.37}$
3. $2\overline{)\$3.48}$
4. $4\overline{)\$3.16}$

5. $4\overline{)\$8.84}$
6. $7\overline{)\$8.26}$
7. $6\overline{)\$9.54}$
8. $3\overline{)\$7.29}$

9. $\$9.36 \div 8$
10. $\$1.60 \div 5$
11. $\$8.37 \div 9$
12. $\$7.98 \div 2$

13. $\$8.88 \div 2$
14. $\$7.92 \div 4$
15. $\$9.36 \div 2$
16. $\$1.47 \div 7$

Set G   *(Lesson 9, pages 238–241)*

Divide. Then check your work.

1. $3\overline{)690}$
2. $7\overline{)721}$
3. $8\overline{)856}$
4. $3\overline{)661}$

5. $4\overline{)839}$
6. $3\overline{)422}$
7. $5\overline{)535}$
8. $2\overline{)615}$

9. $987 \div 9$
10. $214 \div 7$
11. $654 \div 6$
12. $845 \div 7$

13. $429 \div 4$
14. $927 \div 3$
15. $610 \div 2$
16. $962 \div 3$

17. $811 \div 9$
18. $619 \div 3$
19. $655 \div 6$
20. $920 \div 3$

Set H   *(Lesson 11, pages 246–247)*

Is each number divisible by 2, 5, or 10?

1. 15
2. 2
3. 126
4. 405
5. 54

6. 192
7. 762
8. 270
9. 50
10. 100

11. 95
12. 5
13. 36
14. 35
15. 4,536

Extra Practice

Set I (Lesson 12, pages 248–249)

Write whether each number is prime or composite.

1. 13   **2.** 45   **3.** 28   **4.** 29   **5.** 65

6. 34   **7.** 57   **8.** 23   **9.** 67   **10.** 19

11. 81   **12.** 93   **13.** 42   **14.** 63   **15.** 79

16. 58   **17.** 89   **18.** 97   **19.** 102   **20.** 103

Set J (Lesson 14, pages 252–253)

Find the average of the numbers in each group.

1. 9, 11   **2.** 7, 13, 19   **3.** 6, 8, 12, 14   **4.** 6, 9, 10, 10, 15

5. 4, 3, 8   **6.** 6, 9, 9, 12   **7.** 5, 6, 9, 22, 33   **8.** 3, 13, 17, 23, 24

9. 7, 8, 9, 10, 11   **10.** 3, 5, 7, 9, 11   **11.** 8, 8, 8, 8   **12.** 11, 22, 23, 24, 35

13. 12, 20, 16, 4   **14.** 32, 32, 64, 128   **15.** 27, 81, 63   **16.** 35, 35, 25, 15, 5

Set K (Lesson 15, pages 254–255)

Estimate. Write the basic fact you used.

1. $627 \div 9$ **2.** $719 \div 8$ **3.** $242 \div 3$ **4.** $565 \div 7$

5. $303 \div 6$ **6.** $363 \div 6$ **7.** $991 \div 9$ **8.** $633 \div 8$

9. $425 \div 7$ **10.** $407 \div 8$ **11.** $256 \div 5$ **12.** $358 \div 7$

13. $728 \div 9$ **14.** $572 \div 8$ **15.** $205 \div 4$ **16.** $642 \div 9$

Set L (Lesson 16, pages 256–259)

Divide. Check your work.

1. $4\overline{)3,834}$ **2.** $7\overline{)8,543}$ **3.** $9\overline{)6,592}$ **4.** $5\overline{)4,654}$

5. $2\overline{)6,588}$ **6.** $5\overline{)9,266}$ **7.** $4\overline{)6,786}$ **8.** $9\overline{)9,438}$

9. $7,419 \div 6$ **10.** $8,216 \div 3$ **11.** $9,642 \div 8$ **12.** $8,346 \div 6$

13. $11,516 \div 6$ **14.** $12,345 \div 5$ **15.** $27,398 \div 3$ **16.** $56,567 \div 7$

Extra Practice • Problem Solving

Solve. Think about the remainders. *(Lesson 4, pages 226–227)*

1 Tara has 16 carrots. She used 3 carrots for each salad she made. She fed the rest to her rabbit. How many carrots did the rabbit get if she made the greatest possible number of salads?

2 The 76 students in 3 fourth-grade classes are going to visit the post office. They will go in vans that carry 8 students each. How many vans are needed for the trip?

3 Each page of Mike's sticker book has space for 9 stickers. He has 76 stickers to put in the book. How many full pages will he make with the stickers that he has?

4 Mario makes club sandwiches with 3 slices of bread. A loaf of bread has 22 slices. What is the greatest number of club sandwiches that Mario can make with 3 loaves of bread?

Solve. Use the Work Backward or another strategy. *(Lesson 10, pages 242–243)*

5 Latanya arrived home at 6:30 P.M. She was at the library for 2 hours and 15 minutes just before she got home. It took her 45 minutes to get to the library from school. What time did she leave school?

6 Rosa bought 4 stickers, a pen, a set of 64 markers, and a notebook. Her receipt was torn but her change was $2.75. How much money did she give the clerk?

7 Joe said, "Think of a number. Add 3. Multiply by 4. Then divide by 2. Tell me that number and I'll tell you what you started with." What does Joe do to the number you tell him to find the number you started with?

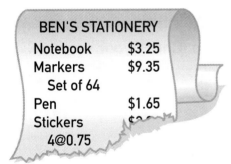

BEN'S STATIONERY
Notebook $3.25
Markers $9.35
  Set of 64
Pen $1.65
Stickers $_____
  4@0.75

Solve. Choose an operation that makes sense. *(Lesson 17, pages 260–261)*

8 After taking 3 math tests, Juan's average was 84. His score on the next test was 96. Did his test average go up or go down? Explain how you know.

9 Brett scored 9 points in his first basketball game. He scored 12 points in the second game and 6 in the third game. How many points did he average in these 3 games?

10 At Sojourner Truth School, all 624 students were assigned to teams of 6 for the interschool field day. How many teams were formed?

11 At McAuliffe Elementary School, 98 teams of 6 students were formed for the field day. How many students will be at the field day?

Chapter Review

Reviewing Vocabulary

Write *always*, *sometimes*, or *never* for each statement.
Give an example to support your answer.

1. The quotient is less than the dividend when dividing whole numbers.

2. The remainder is greater than the divisor.

3. The remainder is less than the quotient when dividing whole numbers.

4. The quotient is greater than the divisor.

Match each word with a definition.

5. **average**

6. **composite number**

7. **prime number**

A. a whole number greater than 1 that has only 2 factors

B. a number that best represents all the numbers in a group

C. a whole number greater than 1 that has more than 2 factors

Reviewing Concepts and Skills

Divide. Check your answers. (*pages 220–225, 230–241*)

8. $3\overline{)96}$

9. $4\overline{)78}$

10. $2\overline{)64}$

11. $5\overline{)47}$

12. $4\overline{)848}$

13. $2\overline{)642}$

14. $6\overline{)894}$

15. $7\overline{)783}$

16. $3\overline{)969}$

17. $9\overline{)999}$

18. $6\overline{)187}$

19. $5\overline{)563}$

20. $927 \div 9$

21. $373 \div 6$

22. $\$6.40 \div 5$

23. $\$8.96 \div 8$

24. $329 \div 9$

25. $423 \div 7$

26. $\$4.20 \div 3$

27. $\$8.48 \div 4$

28. Which of the following numbers are divisible by both 2 and 5? Explain how you know. (*pages 246–247*)

    9, 12, 15, 18, 20, 24, 87, 110

29. Is the product of 8 and 3 a prime or composite number? Explain your answer. (*pages 248–249*)

30. List all prime numbers from 15 to 55. (*pages 248–249*)

Find the average of the numbers in each group. (*pages 252–253*)

31. 44, 24, 36, 56

32. 4, 11, 15, 19, 26

33. 8, 12, 9, 13, 10, 14

34. 137, 141, 139, 147

Estimate. Write the basic fact you used. (*pages 254–255*)

35. $729 \div 9$

36. $500 \div 7$

37. $394 \div 8$

38. $640 \div 7$

Divide. Check your work. (*pages 256–258*)

39. $4\overline{)5,098}$

40. $6\overline{)5,699}$

41. $4\overline{)8,416}$

42. $7\overline{)21,735}$

43. $4,078 \div 3$

44. $7,856 \div 5$

45. $7,352 \div 8$

46. $12,345 \div 6$

Solve. (*pages 226–227, 242–243, 260–261*)

47. Three members of a rock band share equally to pay their expenses. Some new equipment costs $975. What will each member pay?

48. Joey owns 63 CDs. He wants to arrange the CDs on a shelf in equal stacks of more than 2 CDs. What are the ways that he can do this?

49. Mr. Gomez has to buy 326 name tags for Parent's Night. The name tags come in packages of 8. How many packages should Mr. Gomez buy?

50. An elephant eats about 770 lb of hay a week. Is 4,322 lb of hay enough to feed 5 elephants for a week? Explain your thinking.

 Brain Teasers Math Reasoning

SOMETHING IN COMMON

Find 2 odd numbers below that have the same remainder when they are divided by 4.

7 5 ? 19 ? 15 3 9 ?

MISSING DIGITS

Put the digits 4, 6, and 8 in the boxes. What is the greatest possible quotient? What is the least possible quotient?

$\square\overline{)\square\,\square}$

Safe Site

Internet Brain Teasers
Visit **www.eduplace.com/kids/mhm**
for more *Brain Teasers.*

269

Chapter Test

Divide. Check your answer.

1. $3\overline{)69}$ **2.** $4\overline{)86}$ **3.** $2\overline{)72}$ **4.** $5\overline{)65}$

5. $5\overline{)67}$ **6.** $6\overline{)822}$ **7.** $3\overline{)746}$ **8.** $4\overline{)984}$

9. $8\overline{)193}$ **10.** $7\overline{)419}$ **11.** $927 \div 9$ **12.** $508 \div 4$

13. $420 \div 6$ **14.** $5\overline{)\$7.20}$ **15.** $4\overline{)\$0.96}$ **16.** $\$8.19 \div 9$

Complete each of the following exercises.

17. Which of the following numbers are divisible by 2, 5, and 10? Explain how you know.

9, 12, 15, 18, 20, 24, 87, 110

18. Is the product of 17 and 1 a prime or a composite number? Explain your answer.

19. List all prime numbers from 15 to 25.

Find the average of the numbers in each group.

20. 11, 15, 9, 13, 10, 14 **21.** 327, 331, 337, 345 **22.** 984, 875, 718

Estimate. Write the basic fact you need.

23. $629 \div 8$ **24.** $502 \div 7$ **25.** $828 \div 9$

Divide. Check your work.

26. $2\overline{)3,042}$ **27.** $5\overline{)6,876}$ **28.** $8\overline{)9,106}$

29. $9\overline{)8,406}$ **30.** $7\overline{)11,975}$ **31.** $6\overline{)3,817}$

Solve.

32. Alex needs 23 sheets of construction paper for an art project. If construction paper is sold in packages of 5 sheets, how many packages does Alex need to buy?

33. Sam grew 2 inches more than Michael did last year. Michael grew 1 inch less than Sherry. Sherry grew two times as much as Jesse. If Jesse grew 1 inch last year, how much did Sam grow?

 Write About It

Solve each problem. Use correct math vocabulary to explain your thinking.

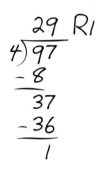

1. John completed this division.

   a. Explain what he did wrong.

   b. Show how to find the correct answer.

2. Alena uses strips of ribbon to decorate picture frames. Each strip is 6 inches long. She needs 4 strips for each picture frame. How many picture frames can she decorate by using a 60-inch strip of ribbon?

   a. Represent the problem with a drawing, with numbers, or in some other way.

   b. Show your work to find the answer.

   c. Explain how you know that your answer is correct.

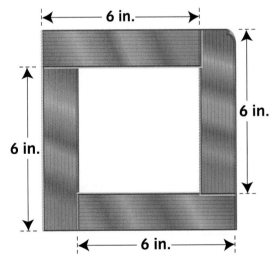

Another Look

Use the newspaper ad to solve each problem. Show your work using base-ten blocks, pictures, numbers, or words.

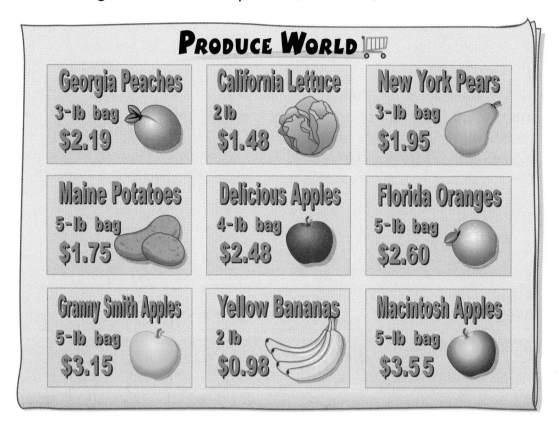

PRODUCE WORLD

Georgia Peaches
3-lb bag
$2.19

California Lettuce
2 lb
$1.48

New York Pears
3-lb bag
$1.95

Maine Potatoes
5-lb bag
$1.75

Delicious Apples
4-lb bag
$2.48

Florida Oranges
5-lb bag
$2.60

Granny Smith Apples
5-lb bag
$3.15

Yellow Bananas
2 lb
$0.98

Macintosh Apples
5-lb bag
$3.55

1. When shoppers read an ad like this one, they often estimate the cost of 1 pound of things they want to buy. Estimate the cost of 1 pound of each food. List your estimates and show the numbers you used.

2. The store manager wants to know the price of 1 pound of each food. Calculate the price for 1 pound of each food. Make a list of the new prices.

3. **Look Back** Find the differences between your estimates and the actual prices for each food. Are your estimates close to the actual prices? If not, first check your division. If it was correct, then look for a way to make a closer estimate.

4. **Analyze** How does knowing the price for 1 pound rather than the price of different-sized packages help shoppers compare prices?

Enrichment

Factor Trees

A composite number can be written as the product of **prime factors**. To find the prime factors of a composite number, you can make a **factor tree**.

Here is how to find the prime factors for 24.

Step 1 Write a pair of factors for 24.	**Step 2** Write a pair of factors for each factor until all of the factors are prime numbers.
24 4 6	24 4 6 2 2 2 3

$2 \times 2 \times 2 \times 3 = 24$, so the prime factors of 24 are 2, 2, 2, 3.

You can often find different ways to make a factor tree for a number.

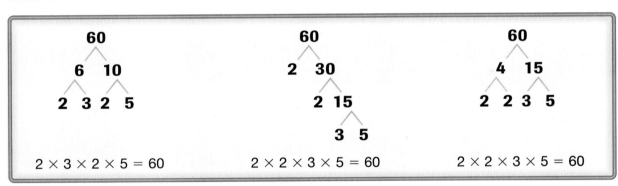

60 6 10 2 3 2 5	60 2 30 2 15 3 5	60 4 15 2 2 3 5
$2 \times 3 \times 2 \times 5 = 60$	$2 \times 2 \times 3 \times 5 = 60$	$2 \times 2 \times 3 \times 5 = 60$

The prime factors for 60 are 2, 2, 3, 5.

Make a factor tree for each number.

1. 12   **2.** 27   **3.** 50   **4.** 48

5. 65   **6.** 90   **7.** 18   **8.** 56

9. Choose one number. See how many different ways you can make its factor tree.

Explain Your Thinking

Chris says that greater numbers have more prime factors than smaller numbers. Is Chris right? Explain your thinking.

Standards | NS 4.0, 4.1, 4.2

CHAPTER 6

Measurement and Negative Numbers

Why Learn About Measurement and Negative Numbers?

You can measure objects in many ways to find out more about them. You can also measure temperature, and understanding negative numbers is helpful for reading a thermometer.

When you use a yardstick to decide whether two posters can fit on a wall, you are using measurement.

These scientists in New Zealand are using special instruments to make measurements that will help them as they carry out their research on active volcanoes.

Reading Mathematics

Reviewing Vocabulary

Understanding math language helps you become a successful problem solver. Here are some units of measurement you should recognize.

Customary Units of Measure

Length

1 foot (ft) = 12 inches (in.)
1 yard (yd) = 3 feet (ft)
1 mile (mi) = 5,280 feet (ft)

Capacity

1 pint (pt) = 2 cups (c)
1 quart (qt) = 2 pints (pt)
1 gallon (gal) = 4 quarts (qt)

Weight

1 pound (lb) = 16 ounces (oz)
1 ton (T) = 2,000 pounds (lb)

Metric Units of Measure

Length

1 meter (m) = 100 centimeters (cm)
1 kilometer (km) = 1,000 meters (m)

Capacity

1 liter (L) = 1,000 milliliters

Mass

1 kilogram (kg) = 1,000 grams (g)

Reading Words and Symbols

When you read mathematics, sometimes you read only words, sometimes you read words and symbols, and sometimes you read only symbols.

You can describe the length and capacity of an object by using customary units or metric units.

Customary Units

▶ The glass is about 4 inches tall.

▶ It holds about 1 cup of lemonade.

Metric Units

▶ The glass is about 10 centimeters tall.

▶ It holds about 250 milliliters of lemonade.

Try These

1. Use the words at the right to complete each sentence.

> **Vocabulary**
> foot
> ounces
> gallons
> inches

   a. The Science Club bought an aquarium that holds twenty ____ of water.

   b. The water is one ____ deep.

   c. The smallest fish in the aquarium is two ____ long.

   d. The biggest fish weighs six ____.

2. Match the tool with the unit it measures. Write *centimeter, kilogram,* or *liter.*

   a.    **b.**   **c.**

3. Write *true* or *false.*

   a. Temperature is measured with a thermometer.

   b. Water freezes at two hundred twelve degrees Fahrenheit.

   c. Ninety degrees Fahrenheit is warmer than ten degrees Fahrenheit.

   d. Water boils at zero degrees Celsius.

Upcoming Vocabulary

 Write About It **Here are some other vocabulary words** you will learn in this chapter. Watch for these words. Write their definitions in your journal.

half inch   **negative temperatures**

quarter inch   **perimeter**

Inch, Half Inch, and Quarter Inch

You will learn how to measure lengths by using an inch ruler.

New Vocabulary
inch
half inch
quarter inch

Learn About It

Use an inch ruler to measure objects to the nearest inch, half inch, and quarter inch.

Materials

inch ruler

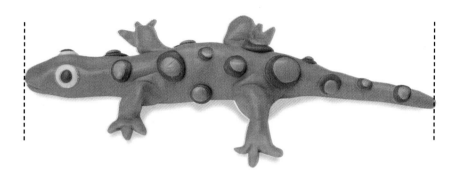

Estimate:	
Nearest inch:	
Nearest half inch:	
Nearest quarter inch:	

Step 1 Estimate the length of the lizard. Record your estimate in a table like the one at the right.

Step 2 Use an **inch** ruler to measure the lizard to the nearest inch. Use a **half-inch** mark to decide which inch mark is closer to the end of the lizard. Record the length.

inches   1

If the end is exactly at the half-inch mark, round to the next inch.

Step 3 Now measure the lizard to the nearest half inch. Use a **quarter-inch** mark to decide which half-inch mark is closer to the end. Record the length.

inches   1

Step 4 Measure the lizard to the nearest quarter inch. Use an eighth-inch mark to decide which quarter-inch mark is closer to the end of the lizard. Record the length.

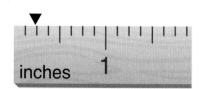

inches   1

The more marks your ruler has, the more accurately you will be able to measure.

- Compare the three measurements of the lizard. Which is closest to the actual length of the lizard?

Standards NS **1.4**   MR **2.4, 2.5**

Step 5 Find 5 objects that are shorter than your ruler. Estimate the length of each object to the nearest inch. Then measure each object to the nearest inch, half inch, and quarter inch. Record your work in a table.

Try It Out

Measure each side to the nearest inch. Add to find the distance around each figure.

1.

2.

Estimate the length of each object to the nearest inch. Then measure to the nearest inch, half inch, and quarter inch.

3.

4.

5.

Write about it! Talk about it!

Use what you have learned to answer the question.

6. One clay iguana is less than 5 inches long, and another is more than 5 inches long. When the iguanas are measured to the nearest inch, both are about 5 inches long. Explain how this is possible.

Perimeter and Customary Units of Length

You will learn how to find the perimeter of a rectangle.

Learn About It

The distance around a figure is called its **perimeter**. To find the perimeter of the rectangular banner, add the lengths of the sides.

6 feet + 9 feet + 6 feet + 9 feet = 30 feet

The perimeter of the banner is 30 feet. What is its perimeter in inches? in yards?

When you change from larger units to smaller units, the number of units increases. So multiply.

Pine Street School
SPORTS DAY
6 feet
9 feet

Changing Feet to Inches

Multiply by the number of inches in 1 foot.

30	×	12	=	360
↑		↑		↑
number of feet		inches in 1 foot		inches in 30 feet

30 feet = 360 inches

When you change from smaller units to larger units, the number of units decreases. So divide.

Customary Units of Length
1 foot (ft) = 12 inches (in.)
1 yard (yd) = 3 feet
1 yard (yd) = 36 inches
1 mile (mi) = 1,760 yards
1 mile (mi) = 5,280 feet

Changing Feet to Yards

Divide by the number of feet in 1 yard.

30	÷	3	=	10
↑		↑		↑
number of feet		feet in 1 yard		yards in 30 feet

30 feet = 10 yards

Solution: The perimeter of the banner is 360 inches or 10 yards.

Explain Your Thinking

▶ Do you need to measure the lengths of all 4 sides of a rectangle to find its perimeter? Why or why not?

Standards NS **3.3, 3.4** AF **1.4** MG **1.0, 1.4** MR **1.1, 2.3**

Guided Practice

Find the perimeter of each rectangle.

1.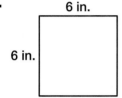
12 ft
5 ft

2.
1 yd
4 yd

Ask Yourself

• Did I add the lengths of all sides?

Independent Practice

Find the perimeter of each rectangle.

3.
6 in.
6 in.

4.
20 mi
8 mi

5.
28 ft
85 ft

n **Algebra • Equations** Find each missing number.

6. 5 yd = ____ ft

7. ____ ft = 3 mi

8. 4 ft = ____ in.

Problem Solving • Reasoning

9. Laura has a rectangular soccer poster that is 3 feet long and 6 feet wide. What is the perimeter of the poster in feet? in inches? in yards?

10. Write About It The sign at the right shows the length of a race in feet, yards, and miles. The labels are hidden! Which unit goes with which number? Explain how you know.

11. A small pool is 12 ft long and 7 ft wide. A big pool is 20 ft long and 15 ft wide. How much greater is the perimeter of the big pool?

Relay Race
Distance:
2
10,560
3,520

Mixed Review • Test Prep

Multiply or divide. *(pages 170–173, 220–221)*

12. 45 × 8

13. 56 ÷ 4

14. 96 ÷ 3

15. 7 × 61

16. 5 × 27

17 Choose the correct value of n. 128 × 4 = n *(pages 180–181)*

A 602   **B** 512   **C** 482   **D** 412

Extra Practice See Set A on page 310.

LESSON 3

Customary Units of Capacity and Weight

You will learn how to change units of capacity and weight.

New
Vocabulary
capacity
weight

Learn About It

This container holds 8 quarts of lemonade. How many cups is that? How many gallons is that?

Gallons, quarts, and cups all measure capacity. **Capacity** is the amount a container can hold.

When you change from larger units to smaller units, the number of units increases. So mulitply.

Changing Quarts to Cups

Multiply by the number of cups in 1 quart.

8	×	4	=	32
↑		↑		↑
number of quarts		cups in 1 quart		cups in 8 quarts

8 quarts = 32 cups

When you change from smaller units to larger units, the number of units decreases. So divide.

Changing Quarts to Gallons

Divide by the number of quarts in 1 gallon.

8	÷	4	=	2
↑		↑		↑
number of quarts		quarts in 1 gallon		gallons in 8 quarts

8 quarts = 2 gallons

Customary Units of Capacity

1 pint (pt)	=	2 cups (c)
1 quart (qt)	=	2 pints
1 quart (qt)	=	4 cups
1 gallon (gal)	=	4 quarts
1 gallon (gal)	=	8 pints
1 gallon (gal)	=	16 cups

Solution: The container holds 32 cups or 2 gallons of lemonade.

Other Examples

A. Changing Cups to Pints

10 cups = ____ pints

Think: Cups are smaller than pints, so divide.

10 ÷ 2 = 5

B. Changing Gallons to Pints

3 gallons = ____ pints

Think: Gallons are larger than pints, so multiply.

3 × 8 = 24

Standards | AF **1.4** | MR **1.1, 1.2, 2.3**

Look at the picture on the right. How many tons of watermelons does the truck carry?

Ounces, pounds, and tons measure **weight**. You can use the table on the right to change units.

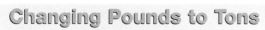

Changing Pounds to Tons

Divide by the number of pounds in 1 ton.

$$4{,}000 \div 2{,}000 = 2$$

| number of pounds | pounds in 1 ton | tons in 4,000 pounds |

4,000 pounds = 2 tons

Solution: The truck carries 2 tons of watermelons.

Customary Units of Weight		
1 pound (lb)	=	16 ounces (oz)
1 ton (T)	=	2,000 pounds

If one watermelon weighs 10 pounds, how many ounces does it weigh?

Changing Pounds to Ounces

Multiply by the number of ounces in 1 pound.

$$10 \times 16 = 160$$

| number of pounds | ounces in 1 pound | ounces in 10 pounds |

10 pounds = 160 ounces

Solution: The watermelon weighs 160 ounces.

Other Examples

A. Changing Ounces to Pounds

64 ounces = _____ pounds

Think: Ounces are smaller than pounds, so divide.

$$64 \div 16 = 4$$

B. Changing Tons to Pounds

5 tons = _____ pounds

Think: Tons are larger than pounds, so multiply.

$$5 \times 2{,}000 = 10{,}000$$

Explain Your Thinking

▶ Do small objects always weigh less than large ones? Give examples to support your answer.

Guided Practice

Find each missing number.

1. 8 c = ____ pt

2. ____ qt = 5 gal

3. 8,000 lb = ____ T

4. 5 lb = ____ oz

Ask Yourself

- Which is the larger unit?

- How many smaller units are equal to one larger unit?

Independent Practice

Copy and complete the table.

Equivalent Measures of Capacity								
gallons	1	2	3	4	5	6	7	8
5. quarts	4							
6. pints	8							
7. cups	16							

n **Algebra • Equations** **Find each missing number.**

8. 14 c = ____ pt

9. 8 gal = ____ qt

10. 9 pt = ____ c

11. ____ qt = 16 pt

12. ____ lb = 2 T

13. 48 oz = ____ lb

n **Algebra • Inequalities** **Compare. Write >, <, or = for each ●.**

14. 28 oz ● 2 lb

15. 5,000 lb ● 3 T

16. 5 lb ● 80 oz

17. 4 pt ● 7 c

18. 8 gal ● 30 qt

19. 13 pt ● 8 qt

Problem Solving • Reasoning

Use the sign for Problems 20–22.

20. Jan bought 4 pints of apple juice. Marla bought the same amount of juice in quarts. How much money did Marla spend on apple juice?

21. Analyze Michael needs to buy 24 cups of apple juice. What is the cheapest way he can buy the juice?

22. Tom bought 12 quart containers of apple juice. How much cheaper would it have been for him to buy the same amount of juice in gallons?

Apple Juice Prices	
Item	**Price**
Pint	$0.75
Quart	$1.25
Half Gallon	$2.25
Gallon	$4.25

23. Estimation An apple weighs about 6 ounces. About how many pounds do 8 apples weigh?

24. One truck from Ollie's Orchards carries 8,000 lb of apples. How many tons is that?

Mixed Review • Test Prep

Solve. *(pages 110–111)*

25. $12 \times (8 + 7)$

26. $(10 \times 4) \times 21$

27. $2 \times (53 - 18)$

Choose the correct value of *n* in each equation. *(pages 232–233, 198–199)*

28 $984 \div 3 = n$

   A 2,952   **C** 328

   B 2,228   **D** 326

29 $574 \times 65 = n$

   F 6,314   **H** 37,290

   G 37,110   **J** 37,310

Logical Thinking

Balancing Act

1. Which containers should you move so that each group has the same amount of juice?

Group A

Group B

2. Which pieces of fruit should you move so that the scale is balanced?

Apple = 6 oz	Peach = 4 oz
Banana = 5 oz	Pear = 6 oz
Orange = 8 oz	Lime = 2 oz

Problem-Solving Skill: Too Much or Too Little Information

You will learn how to find the information you need to solve a problem.

When a problem has too many facts, you must decide which facts are important. When a problem does not have enough facts, you must decide what facts are missing.

A sequoia called the General Sherman Tree is 275 ft tall and measures 103 ft around its trunk. A sequoia called the General Grant Tree is 267 ft tall. The General Grant Tree is more than 1,500 years old!

▲ General Sherman Tree

Sometimes you have too much information.

How much taller is the General Sherman Tree than the General Grant Tree?

What facts do I need?
• the height of the General Sherman Tree (275 ft)

• the height of the General Grant Tree (267 ft)

There is more information in the problem, but it is not needed.

How can I solve the problem?
Subtract to compare the heights.

$$275 \text{ ft} - 267 \text{ ft} = 8 \text{ ft}$$

The General Sherman Tree is 8 feet taller.

Sometimes you have too little information.

How much bigger around is the General Grant Tree than the General Sherman Tree?

What facts do I need?
• the distance around the trunk of the General Grant Tree (not given)

• the distance around the trunk of the General Sherman Tree (103 ft)

The distance around the trunk of the General Grant Tree is not given. You do not have enough information to solve the problem.

Look Back Why is it important to read the question carefully when a problem gives too much information?

Standards MR **1.0, 1.1, 2.0, 3.0, 3.2**

▲ Tule Tree

Guided Practice

Use the information on page 286 to solve each problem.

1 A cypress tree in Mexico called the Tule Tree measures 140 ft around its trunk and is 130 ft tall. How much bigger around is the Tule Tree than the General Sherman Tree?

Think: What information is extra?

2 One day, 800 people visited the General Sherman Tree. How many more people visited the General Sherman Tree that day than visited the General Grant Tree?

Think: What information do I need?

Choose a Strategy

Solve. Use these or other strategies. If not enough information is given, tell what information is needed to solve the problem.

Problem-Solving Strategies

- **Write an Equation**
- **Guess and Check**
- **Draw a Picture**
- **Work Backward**

3 Sequoias grow about 1 in. taller each year. One sequoia lived for 3,200 years. About how many years would it take for a sequoia to grow 139 feet?

4 Five friends are on a log. Dan is at one end. Ellie is at the other end. Eva, Ian, and Joe are equally spaced between them. How far apart from each other are the five friends?

5 Zack took 15 pictures of sequoias. Liz took twice as many pictures of sequoias as Molly did. If Liz and Molly took 36 pictures in all, how many did each girl take?

6 A gift shop sells small and large post cards. Small post cards cost 45¢ each. Ben bought 5 small post cards and 6 large post cards. How much did he spend altogether?

7 Al climbed for an hour and rested. Then he climbed 760 ft more. After resting again, he climbed 430 ft more. If he climbed 1,380 ft in all, how far did he climb before his first rest?

8 Jamie lives 290 miles from Sequoia National Park. It takes 6 hours to drive to the park. About how many miles must he drive to go to the park and home again?

Extra Practice See 1–4 on page 313.

Quick ✓ Check

Check Your Understanding of Lessons 1–4

Find the perimeter of each figure in feet.

1.
15 yd

5 yd

2.
8 in.

10 in.

Find each missing number.

3. 6 yd = ____ ft

4. 3 mi = _____ yd

5. ____ in. = 7 yd

Find each missing number.

6. 7 lb = ____ oz

7. ____ pt = 4 gal

8. 12 qt = ____ c

Solve. If not enough information is given, tell what information is needed to solve the problem.

9. Some bristlecone pine trees are more than 4,000 years old. Their needles are 1 to $1\frac{1}{2}$ inches long. A giant redwood seed measures only about $\frac{1}{16}$ of an inch long. How much longer is a bristlecone pine seed than a giant redwood seed?

10. The General Sherman Tree has a trunk about 37 feet wide. The tree is about 275 feet tall. A Montezuma bald cypress in Mexico has a trunk about 40 feet wide. About how many inches wider is the cypress trunk than the General Sherman Tree trunk?

How did you do?

If you had difficulty with any items in the Quick Check, you can use the following pages for review and extra practice.

California Standards	Items	Review These Pages	Do These Extra Practice Items
Algebra: **1.1** Reasoning: **1.1**	1–5	pages 278–281	Set A, page 310
Algebra: **1.1** Reasoning: **1.1**	6–8	pages 282–285	Set B, page 310
Reasoning: **1.1, 3.2**	9–10	pages 286–287	1–4, page 313

Test Prep • Cumulative Review
Maintaining the Standards

Choose the letter of the correct answer. If a correct answer is not here, choose NH.

1 What is the perimeter of the figure?

32 ft

16 ft

A 48 feet

B 86 feet

C 96 feet

D 108 feet

2 What is the product of 64 × 73?

F 137

G 640

H 4,472

J NH

3 A pool is 65 feet wide. How many inches equals 65 feet?

A 195

B 770

C 780

D 800

4 The baseball diamond is a square. The distance from one base to another is 90 feet. What is the total distance around the diamond?

F 90 feet

G 180 feet

H 270 feet

J 360 feet

5
$$56 \\ \times 24$$

A 336

B 1,324

C 1,344

D NH

6 Which expression is not equivalent to (36 − 10) − 3?

F 26 − 3

G 36 − (10 − 3)

H 36 − (10 + 3)

J 36 − 10 − 3

7 Twenty-six people are on a bus. At the next stop, 4 people get off the bus, and 3 people get on the bus. Which expression would you use to find the number of people on the bus after the stop?

A 26 − (4 + 3)

B (26 − 4) + 3

C 26 + (4 − 3)

D (26 + 4) − 3

8 What is the perimeter of a square with a side measuring 7 inches?

Explain How did you find your answer?

Safe Site

Internet Test Prep
Visit **www.eduplace.com/kids/mhm**
for more *Test Prep Practice.*

289

Centimeter and Millimeter

LESSON 5

Hands-On Activity

You will learn how to measure lengths using a centimeter ruler.

New Vocabulary
centimeter
millimeter

Learn About It

Use a centimeter ruler to measure objects to the nearest centimeter or millimeter.

Materials

centimeter ruler

Step 1 Estimate the length of the clay stick below. Record your estimate in a table like the one below.

Object	Estimate	Nearest Centimeter	Nearest Millimeter
clay stick			

Step 2 Use a centimeter ruler to measure the length of the clay stick to the nearest **centimeter**. Use a half-centimeter mark to decide which centimeter mark is closer to the end of the stick. Record the length in your table.

If the end is exactly halfway between centimeters, round to the next centimeter.

Step 3 Now measure the stick to the nearest **millimeter**. Decide which millimeter mark is closer to the end of the stick. Record the length in millimeters in your table.

There are 10 millimeters in 1 centimeter.

290

Standards NS **1.4**   MR **2.5**

> **Step 4** Find 5 objects that are shorter than your ruler to measure. Estimate the length of each object to the nearest centimeter. Then measure each object to the nearest centimeter and millimeter. Record your work in your table.

Try It Out

Find each perimeter to the nearest centimeter.

1.

2.

Estimate the length of each object below to the nearest centimeter. Then measure each object to the nearest centimeter.

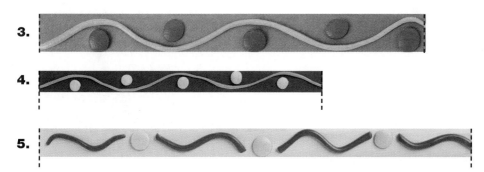

3.

4.

5.

Write about it! Talk about it!

Use what you have learned to answer these questions.

6. If you know how long a shoelace is in centimeters, can you tell how long it is in millimeters without measuring? Explain why or why not.

7. Suppose you are measuring wood for a project. Would it be better to measure in centimeters or in millimeters? Explain your thinking.

Perimeter and Metric Units of Length

You will learn how to determine perimeters in millimeters, centimeters, decimeters, meters, and kilometers.

Learn About It

What is the perimeter of the ranch shown at the right? To find the perimeter, add the lengths of the sides.

1,000 m + 600 m + 1,200 m + 1,200 m = 4,000 m

The perimeter of the ranch is 4,000 meters.

Find the perimeter of the ranch in decimeters and in kilometers.

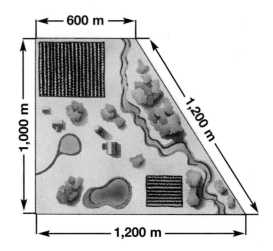

Changing Meters to Decimeters

Multiply by the number of decimeters in 1 meter.

4,000	×	10	=	40,000
↑		↑		↑
number of meters		decimeters in 1 meter		decimeters in 4,000 meters

4,000 meters = 40,000 decimeters

Changing Meters to Kilometers

Divide by the number of meters in 1 kilometer.

4,000	÷	1,000	=	4
↑		↑		↑
number of meters		meters in 1 kilometer		kilometers in 4,000 meters

4,000 meters = 4 kilometers

Metric Units of Length

1 centimeter (cm)	=	10 millimeters (mm)
1 decimeter (dm)	=	10 centimeters
1 meter (m)	=	10 decimeters
1 kilometer (km)	=	1,000 meters

Solution: The perimeter of the ranch is 40,000 decimeters or 4 kilometers.

Explain Your Thinking

▶ Which unit of measure is the best to use to describe the ranch's perimeter? Why?

Standards   NS **3.3, 3.4**   AF **1.4**   MG **1.0, 1.4**   MR **1.2, 2.4**

Guided Practice

Find the perimeter of each figure in m and km.

1.
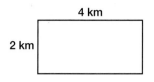
4 km
2 km

2.
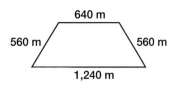
640 m
560 m   560 m
1,240 m

Ask Yourself
• Did I include all of the sides?

Independent Practice

Find the perimeter of each figure.

3.

180 m
410 m

4.
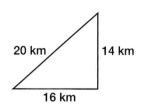
20 km   14 km
16 km

5.
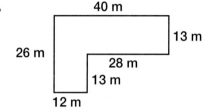
40 m
13 m
26 m
28 m
13 m
12 m

n **Algebra • Equations** Find each missing number.

6. 5 km = ____ m

7. 600 cm = ____ m

8. ____ mm = 9 cm

9. 3 m = ____ cm

10. 4,000 m = ____ km

11. ____ m = 40 dm

Problem Solving • Reasoning

12. A rectangular sign is 2 m high and 4 m wide. What is its perimeter in cm? in mm?

13. Two rectangular fields are each 150 m wide. East Field's perimeter is 1 km. West Field's perimeter is 200 m shorter. How long and wide is West Field?

14. **Analyze** A ranch horse trail 3 km long has signs every 250 m, including both ends, telling the distance. How many signs are there along the trail?

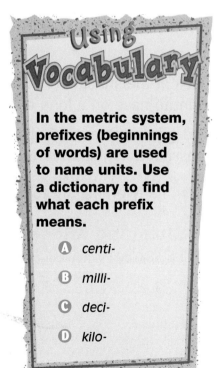

Using Vocabulary

In the metric system, prefixes (beginnings of words) are used to name units. Use a dictionary to find what each prefix means.

Ⓐ *centi-*

Ⓑ *milli-*

Ⓒ *deci-*

Ⓓ *kilo-*

Mixed Review • Test Prep

Multiply or divide. *(pages 194–195, 234–235)*

15. 12 × 43

16. 522 ÷ 6

17. 376 ÷ 4

18 Which shows 74,219 rounded to the nearest thousand? *(pages 24–25)*

    A 70,000   **B** 74,000   **C** 74,220   **D** 74,200

Extra Practice See Set C on page 311.

Metric Units of Capacity and Mass

You will learn how to change from one unit of capacity to another and from one unit of mass to another.

New Vocabulary
milliliter (mL)
liter (L)
gram (g)
kilogram (kg)

Learn About It

Look at these containers of juice. Which would you want to have on a long hike?

The **milliliter (mL)** and **liter (L)** are metric units of capacity. You might want to have a liter of juice. How many milliliters are there in 4 liters?

Changing Liters to Milliliters

Multiply by the number of milliliters in a liter.

$$4 \quad \times \quad 1{,}000 \quad = \quad 4{,}000$$

number of liters	milliliters in 1 liter	milliliters in 4 liters

4 L = 4,000 mL

Metric Units of Capacity

1 liter (L) = 1,000 milliliters (mL)

Solution: There are 4,000 milliliters in 4 liters.

Look at the snacks on the right. Which would you want to have on a long hike?

The **gram (g)** and **kilogram (kg)** are metric units of mass. You might want to have a kilogram of snacks.

How many grams are there in 3 kilograms?

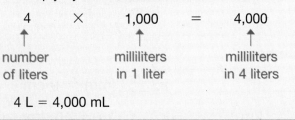

Changing Kilograms to Grams

Multiply by the number of grams in a kilogram.

$$3 \quad \times \quad 1{,}000 \quad = \quad 3{,}000$$

number of kilograms	grams in 1 kilogram	grams in 3 kilograms

3 kg = 3,000 grams

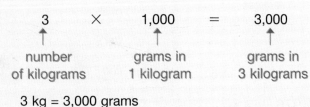

Metric Units of Mass

1 kilogram (kg) = 1,000 grams (g)

Solution: There are 3,000 grams in 3 kilograms.

Standards AF **1.4** MR **2.0**

Explain Your Thinking

▶ Do larger objects always have greater mass than smaller objects? Give examples to support your answer.

Guided Practice

Find each missing number.

Ask Yourself
- Are the units for capacity or mass?
- Should I multiply or divide to change units?

1. 9 L = _____ mL

2. _____ L = 5,000 mL

3. 8 kg = _____ g

4. _____ kg = 2,000 g

Choose the better estimate of the capacity of each.

5.

20 mL or 20 L

6.

400 mL or 400 L

7.

250 mL or 25 L

Choose the better estimate of the mass of each.

8.

20 g or 20 kg

9.

450 g or 45 kg

10.

250 g or 25 kg

Independent Practice

Find each missing number.

11. 4 L = _____ mL

12. _____ L = 6,000 mL

13. _____ mL = 10 L

14. 5,000 g = _____ kg

15. _____ g = 3 kg

16. 44 kg = _____ g

17. 9 L = _____ mL

18. _____ kg = 31,000 g

19. _____ mL = 15 L

n **Algebra • Inequalities** Compare. Write >, <, or = for each ⬤.

20. 6 mL ⬤ 6,000 L

21. 8 L ⬤ 8,000 mL

22. 300 mL ⬤ 3 L

23. 8 kg ⬤ 800 g

24. 4,000 g ⬤ 40 kg

25. 9 kg ⬤ 9,000 g

Choose the better estimate of the measure of each.

26.

| 8 mL or 8 L |

27.

| 400 mL or 40 L |

28.

| 15 mL or 15 L |

29.

| 8 g or 8 kg |

30.

| 100 g or 10 kg |

31.

| 300 g or 300 kg |

Problem Solving • Reasoning

Solve. Choose a method.

Computation Methods

• **Estimation**   • **Mental Math**   • **Pencil and Paper**

32. Carla has 3 water bottles. Each can hold up to 1,900 mL of water. About how many liters can the bottles hold in all?

33. A Super Cooler can hold 20 L, and a Mini Cooler can hold 5 L. How many more milliliters can a Super Cooler hold than a Mini Cooler?

34. Analyze Jared's empty backpack has a mass of 3 kg. He doesn't want to carry more than 7 kg on a trip. How many grams of equipment can Jared pack?

35. Write About It A 500-g bag of granola costs $4, and a 2-kg bag of granola costs $13. What is the cheapest way to buy 5 kg of granola?

Mixed Review • Test Prep

Solve. *(pages 56–58, 60–62, 198–199)*

36. 461
× 14

37. 829
+ 530

38. 581
× 45

39. 758
− 94

40. 468
+ 691

41. 291
× 64

42 Which shows 78,204 in expanded form? *(pages 4–5)*

A 70,000 + 8,000 + 200 + 4

c 70,000 + 8,000 + 20 + 4

B 70,000 + 8,000 + 200 + 40

D 7,000 + 8,000 + 200 + 4

Tick-tack-toe Measurement

Practice using metric units by playing this game with a partner.
Try to get three counters in a row.

What You'll Need

- *5 red and 5 yellow counters*
- *meter stick*
- *game board (Teaching Tool 05)*

**Players
2**

Here's What To Do

1. Each player takes 5 counters of the same color.

2. One player chooses any square on the board. Each player writes an estimate for the item in the square using metric units. Then players work together to measure the item. The player whose estimate comes closest to the actual measurement places his or her counter on the square.

3. Take turns repeating Step 2. The first player to get 3 counters in a row horizontally, vertically, or diagonally wins!

the length of your classroom	the width of the chalkboard	the width of your chair
the width of your desk	the height of your chair	the length of a math book
the length of a new pencil	the length of a chalk eraser	the height of your desk

Share Your Thinking How did you decide which unit to use?

Problem-Solving Strategy: Make a Table

You will learn how to make a table to solve a problem.

Making a table can help you organize information.

Problem Andy is taking a train into the city. The first train leaves at 7:05 A.M. After that a train leaves every 20 minutes. The trip takes 45 minutes. If Andy takes the fourth train, when will he arrive in the city?

Understand

What is the question?
What time will the fourth train arrive in the city?

What do you know?
- A train leaves at 7:05 A.M. and then every 20 minutes after that.
- The trip takes 45 minutes.

Plan

How can you find the answer?
Make a table to find out when the fourth train will arrive.

Solve

First, find when the second train leaves.

7:05 + 20 min = 7:25 A.M.

Continue to fill in the table until you find when the fourth train leaves.

Then find when the fourth train arrives.

8:05 + 45 min = 8:50 A.M.

Andy will arrive in the city at 8:50 A.M.

Train	Leaves	Arrives
First	7:05 A.M.	
Second	7:25 A.M.	
Third	7:45 A.M.	
Fourth	8:05 A.M.	8:50 A.M.

Look Back

Look back at the problem.
How can you use patterns in the table to find when the fifth train will leave and arrive?

Standards MR **1.0, 1.1, 1.2, 2.3, 2.4, 3.0, 3.2**

Guided Practice

Use the information on page 298 to solve each problem.

1 On Mondays the second train is supposed to leave at 7:25 A.M. If that train is 5 minutes late, when will it arrive in the city?

> **Think:** Should I add or subtract 5 minutes?

2 Alex needs to be in the city by 8:25 A.M. If he misses the 7:05 A.M. train, can he still get to the city on time? Explain.

> **Think:** How long does it take for the train to get to the city?

Choose a Strategy

Solve. Use these or other strategies.

Problem-Solving Strategies

- Make a Table
- Use Logical Thinking
- Guess and Check
- Work Backward

3 One day a train stayed 2 extra minutes at each stop. Usually it gets to Sun Station in 45 minutes. If the train makes 7 stops before getting to Sun Station, how long did it take to get to Sun Station that day?

4 Four local subway trains just left Shady Station. The B train left second. The R train left before the G train but after the N train. In what order did the four local trains leave the station?

5 Each hour local trains leave Oaktown Station twice as often as express trains. If 15 trains leave Oaktown Station each hour, how many of them are express trains?

6 A train starts a trip at 4:30 P.M. Its first stop is 5 minutes later. After that it takes 5 minutes longer to reach each stop than the stop before. When will it reach its sixth stop?

7 Rosa rode the subway twice in the first week. Each week after that she rode the subway twice as many times as the week before. How many times altogether did Rosa ride the subway in 4 weeks?

8 A subway sells special passes. Monthly passes cost twice as much as ten-day passes. Ten-day passes cost $8 more than weekly passes. If a weekly pass costs $12, how much does a monthly pass cost?

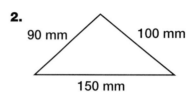

Quick ✓ Check

Check Your Understanding of Lessons 5–8

Find the perimeter of each figure in centimeters.

1. 5 m
3 m

2. 90 mm   100 mm
150 mm

Find each missing number.

3. 6 km = ____ m

4. 35 cm = ____ mm

5. ____ m = 70 dm

6. 8 L = ____ mL

7. ____ kg = 25,000 g

8. 3,000 mL = ____ L

Solve.

9. Janell and her father will take a bus tour of the city. The first tour leaves at 9:34 A.M. After that, a tour bus leaves every 35 minutes. The tour takes 55 minutes. If Janell and her father take the second tour, when will their tour end?

10. Buses for the city tours leave every 35 minutes. On Sundays the first tour leaves at 11:35 A.M. When does the third tour leave?

How did you do?

If you had difficulty with any items in the Quick Check, you can use the following pages for review and extra practice.

California Standards	ITEMS	REVIEW THESE PAGES	DO THESE EXTRA PRACTICE ITEMS
Algebra: **1.1** Reasoning: **1.1**	1–5	pages 292–293	Set C, page 311
Algebra: **1.1** Reasoning: **1.1**	6–8	pages 294–296	Set D, page 311
Reasoning: **1.1, 2.3, 2.6**	9–10	pages 298–299	5–6, page 313

Test Prep • Cumulative Review

Maintaining the Standards

Choose the letter of the correct answer.

1 The length of a book is 18 centimeters. How many millimeters equals 18 centimeters?

A 18   **C** 1,800

B 180   **D** 18,000

2 What is the perimeter of the square?

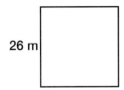

26 m

F 13 meters

G 52 meters

H 104 meters

J 676 meters

3 What number should go in the box to make the number sentence true?

$$(16 \div 8) + 9 = 2 + \blacksquare$$

A 8

B 9

C 15

D 16

4 What is the value of n?

$$(15 \times 12) - (72 \div 9) = n$$

F 108

G 172

H 188

J 200

Use the table to answer Questions 5–6.

5 What number is missing from the table?

x	y
12	3
20	5
28	7
36	▨

A 8   **C** 10

B 9   **D** 11

6 Which equation does the table show?

F $y = x + 2$

G $y = x \div 4$

H $y = x \times 3$

J $y = x - 9$

7 What goes in the box to make the statement true?

If ♥ = ♦ , then ♥ × 5

equals ♦ × ■.

A ♥   **C** 1

B ♦   **D** 5

8 Alyssa wants to put a lace border around an album. If the album is 14 inches long and 10 inches wide, how much lace does Alyssa need?

Explain How did you find your answer?

Safe Site

Internet Test Prep
Visit **www.eduplace.com/kids/mhm**
for more *Test Prep Practice.*

301

Degrees Fahrenheit and Negative Numbers

You will learn how to read and use positive and negative temperatures on a Fahrenheit thermometer.

New
Vocabulary
degrees Fahrenheit (°F)
negative

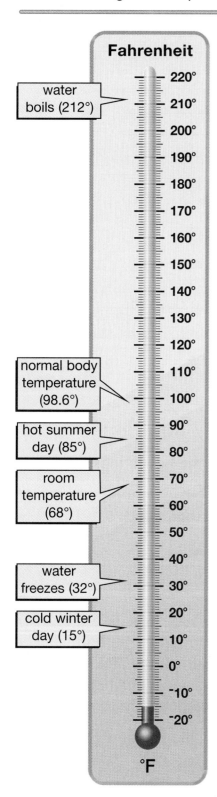

Fahrenheit

water boils (212°) — 220°, 210°, 200°, 190°, 180°, 170°, 160°, 150°, 140°, 130°, 120°

normal body temperature (98.6°) — 110°, 100°

hot summer day (85°) — 90°, 80°

room temperature (68°) — 70°, 60°, 50°, 40°

water freezes (32°) — 30°, 20°

cold winter day (15°) — 10°, 0°, ⁻10°, ⁻20°

°F

Learn About It

A thermometer can be used to measure temperature in **degrees Fahrenheit (°F)**. Temperatures below 0°F are **negative** temperatures. You can think of a thermometer as a vertical number line.

Think: The farther left (or down) you go, the lower the temperature.

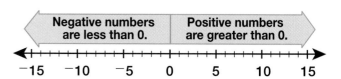

Negative numbers are less than 0.   Positive numbers are greater than 0.

⁻15   ⁻10   ⁻5   0   5   10   15

The temperature shown on this thermometer is ⁻15°F.

Write: ⁻15°F
Say: negative fifteen degrees Fahrenheit or fifteen degrees Fahrenheit below zero

You can use a thermometer to find the difference between two temperatures.

Find the difference between

A. 70°F and 42°F

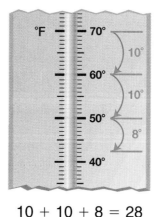

°F — 70°
10°
— 60°
10°
— 50°
8°
— 40°

10 + 10 + 8 = 28
The difference is 28°.

B. ⁻15°F and 8°F

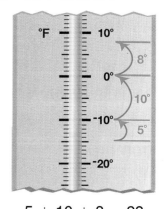

°F — 10°
8°
— 0°
10°
— ⁻10°
5°
— ⁻20°

5 + 10 + 8 = 23
The difference is 23°.

Explain Your Thinking

▶ Which is lower, ⁻5°F or ⁻15°F? How do you know?

Guided Practice

Write each temperature.

1.  °F — 80° / — 70°

2. °F — 50° / — 40°

3. °F — ⁻10° / — ⁻20°

Independent Practice

Write each temperature.

4. °F — 60° / — 50°

5. °F — 20° / — 10°

6. °F — ⁻10° / — ⁻20°

7. °F — 120° / — 110°

Find the difference between the temperatures.

8. 88°F and 110°F

9. ⁻3°F and ⁻10°F

10. 70°F and 46°F

11. 54°F and 19°F

12. 31°F and 67°F

13. ⁻12°F and 23°F

Problem Solving • Reasoning

Use Data Use the table for Problems 14–16.

14. How much higher was the temperature in Houston than in Atlanta on January 21?

15. **Analyze** The low temperature on January 21 was 43°F in Atlanta and 52°F in Houston. What was the difference between the low and high temperatures in Atlanta?

16. **Write Your Own** Write a problem using the data in the table. Then give it to a classmate to solve.

High Temperatures on January 21	
City	**Temperature**
New York	27°F
Atlanta	54°F
Chicago	⁻2°F
Houston	65°F

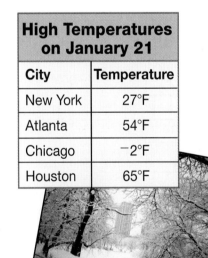

Mixed Review • Test Prep

Solve for n. (pages 180–181, 198–199, 256–259)

17. $184 \times 9 = n$

18. $4{,}683 \div 3 = n$

19. $n = 310 \times 18$

20. $24 \times n = 264$

21. Which number sentence is correct? (pages 124–125)

A $49 \div 7 = 8$

B $64 \div 8 = 9$

C $72 \div 9 = 8$

D $65 \div 5 = 7$

Degrees Celsius and Negative Numbers

You will learn how to read and use positive and negative temperatures on a Celsius thermometer.

New Vocabulary
degrees Celsius (°C)

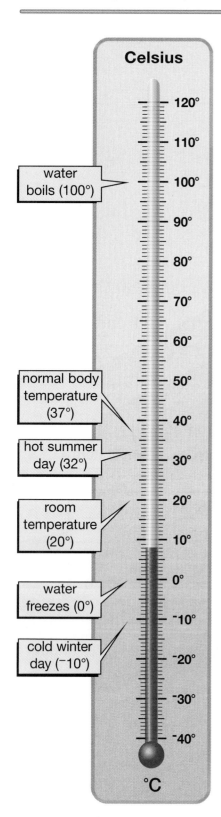

Celsius

water boils (100°) → 100°

normal body temperature (37°)

hot summer day (32°)

room temperature (20°)

water freezes (0°) → 0°

cold winter day (⁻10°)

°C

Learn About It

In the metric system, temperature is measured in **degrees Celsius (°C)**. The temperature shown on this thermometer is 8°C.

Write: 8°C

Say: eight degrees Celsius

Suppose the temperature was 10° lower than shown on this thermometer. What would the temperature be?

Remember to think of the thermometer as a vertical number line. Start at 8 and count back 10.

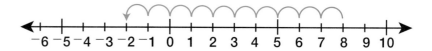

Think: $8 - 10 = {}^-2$

Write: ⁻2°C

Say: negative two degrees Celsius or two degrees Celsius below zero

The temperature would be ⁻2°C.

Explain Your Thinking

▶ Which is farther from 0°F, 5°F or ⁻8°F? How do you know?

▶ Look back at the Fahrenheit thermometer on page 302. Which is cooler, 30°F or 30°C? Explain how you know.

▶ Which statement is true? Explain how you know.

$32°C = 0°F$ $\qquad$ $32°C < 0°F$ $\qquad$ $32°F = 0°C$

Standards NS **1.8**   MR **1.1, 2.3**

Guided Practice

Write each temperature.

1.

2.

3.

Ask Yourself

• What numbers is the temperature between?

• Is the temperature positive or negative?

Independent Practice

Write each temperature.

4.

5.

6.

7.

Find the difference between the temperatures.

8. 18°C and 79°C

9. ⁻10°C and 5°C

10. ⁻15°C and ⁻2°C

Problem Solving • Reasoning

11. Mr. Cordova likes the temperature of his store to be 17°C. How much lower than room temperature does he like the temperature of his store to be?

12. **Analyze** During one day the temperature rose 5°. In the evening the temperature fell 3°. If the temperature was 24°C then, what was the temperature that morning?

13. On Tuesday the temperature was 8°C in Boston and ⁻8°C in Detroit. How many degrees lower was the temperature in Detroit than in Boston?

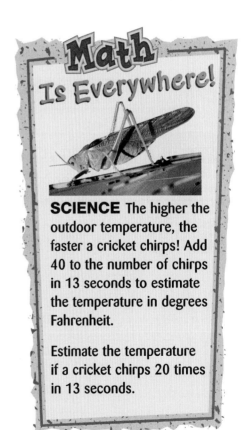

Math Is Everywhere!

SCIENCE The higher the outdoor temperature, the faster a cricket chirps! Add 40 to the number of chirps in 13 seconds to estimate the temperature in degrees Fahrenheit.

Estimate the temperature if a cricket chirps 20 times in 13 seconds.

Mixed Review • Test Prep

Round each to the nearest hundred. *(pages 24–25)*

14. 42,671

15. 714,950

16. 8,413,607

17. Which number sentence is correct? *(pages 234–235)*

    A 243 ÷ 3 = 81   **B** 641 ÷ 7 = 91   **C** 450 ÷ 4 = 11   **D** 942 ÷ 3 = 31

Extra Practice See Set F on page 312.

Problem-Solving Application: Use Temperature

You will learn how to use temperature to solve problems.

You can use what you know about finding temperature to solve problems.

Problem Antarctica is the coldest continent on Earth. The temperature at noon one day is ⁻6°F. The temperature rises 4 degrees over the next two hours. Then by 8:00 P.M. the temperature falls 7 degrees. What is the temperature at 8:00 P.M.?

Understand

What is the question?
What is the temperature at 8:00 P.M.?

What do you know?
• The temperature is ⁻6°F at noon.
• The temperature rises 4 degrees and then falls 7 degrees by 8 P.M.

Plan

How can you find the answer?
Use a thermometer to count up and down.

Solve

Start at ⁻6°F.   Count up 4 degrees.   Count down 7 degrees.

The temperature is ⁻9°F at 8:00 P.M.

Look Back

Look back at the problem.
How can you tell if your answer is reasonable?

Antarctic research stations allow scientists to study the climate near the South Pole. The coldest temperature ever recorded was about $^-130°F$ (about $^-90°C$)

Remember:
► Understand
► Plan
► Solve
► Look Back

Guided Practice

Solve.

 Suppose it is 68°F inside and 24°F outside. How many degrees lower is the temperature outside than inside?

> **Think:** What is the difference between the temperatures?

 A thermometer shows a temperature of 16°F. The wind makes the air feel 10 degrees colder. How cold does it feel?

> **Think:** Should you count up or down?

Choose a Strategy

Solve. Use these or other strategies.

> ### Problem-Solving Strategies
>
> • **Use Logical Thinking** • **Find a Pattern** • **Work Backward** • **Make a Table**

3 Mina recorded the temperature at noon. Then clouds blocked the sun, and the temperature fell 6 degrees. The temperature rose 4 degrees after the clouds moved. If the temperature then was 17°C, what was it at noon?

4 In Antarctica, it is warmer in January than in August. It is warmer in August than in July. November is warmer than August but colder than January. List these months in order from warmest to coldest.

5 One day at 10 A.M. the temperature was $^-14°F$ at a research station in Antarctica. If the temperature rose 2 degrees every hour, what was the temperature at 3 P.M.?

6 The temperature typically falls 1 degree Celsius for every 100 meters you climb. If your thermometer shows 2°C now, what will it show after you climb 400 meters?

7 A researcher in Antarctica found that the temperature at Station B was 4 degrees lower than at Station A. The temperature at Station C was 8°F, which was 12 degrees higher than the temperature at Station B. What was the temperature at Station A?

8 If the pattern shown in the table below continues, what is the next temperature likely to be?

4 P.M.	5 P.M.	6 P.M.	7 P.M.
$^-3°F$	$^-4°F$	$^-6°F$	$^-9°F$

Extra Practice See 7–10 on page 313.

Quick ✓ Check

Check Your Understanding of Lessons 9–11

Find each temperature.

1. 6 degrees colder than ⁻3°F

2. 18 degrees warmer than 5°F

Find the difference between the two temperatures. Use the thermometer below.

3. 2°F and 10°F

4. 15°F and 7° F

5. ⁻4°F and ⁻22°F

6. 6°C and 22°C

7. 7°C and 12°C

8. ⁻3°C and ⁻18°C

Solve. Use the thermometer if you need help.

9. When Jim got up, the temperature was 28°F. An hour later the temperature was 3 degrees warmer. During the next hour, the temperature fell 5 degrees. What was the temperature then?

10. The highest temperature during the winter was 5°C. The lowest temperature was ⁻29°C. How many degrees difference was there between the highest and lowest temperatures?

How did you do?

If you had difficulty with any items in the Quick Check, you can use the following pages for review and extra practice.

California Standards	ITEMS	REVIEW THESE PAGES	DO THESE EXTRA PRACTICE ITEMS
Number Sense: **1.8**	1–5	pages 302–303	Set-E, page 312
Number Sense: **1.8**	6–8	pages 304–305	Set-F, page 312
Number Sense: **1.8** Reasoning: **1.1, 2.3**	9–10	pages 306–307	7–10, page 313

Test Prep • Cumulative Review

Maintaining the Standards

Choose the letter of the correct answer.

1 How is five million, three hundred thousand written in standard form?

A 5,300   **C** 5,000,300

B 53,000   **D** 5,300,000

Use the thermometer to answer Questions 2–3.

2 What temperature is shown on the thermometer?

F ⁻10°F   **H** 10°F

G 0°F   **J** 20°F

3 Suppose the temperature rose 25°F from what is shown above. What would the temperature be then?

A 0°F

B 10°F

C 15°F

D 25°F

---

4 A rectangular pool is 40 feet long, 15 feet wide, and 8 feet deep. What is the distance around the pool?

F 63 feet

G 110 feet

H 120 feet

J 320 feet

---

5 What is the perimeter of the figure?

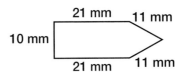

A 42 mm   **C** 64 mm

B 62 mm   **D** 74 mm

---

6 Which lists the numbers in order from least to greatest?

F 17,496; 18,150; 17,412

G 17,496; 17,412; 18,150

H 18,150; 17,496; 17,412

J 17,412; 17,496; 18,150

---

7 In January, the normal temperature for Anchorage, Alaska is 15°F. The normal temperature for Miami, Florida, in January is 67°F. What is the difference between these two temperatures?

A 52 degrees

B 62 degrees

C 72 degrees

D 82 degrees

---

8 A survey was taken of 3,485,557 people. What is 3,485,557 rounded to the nearest hundred thousand?

Explain How did you find your answer?

Extra Practice

Set A *(Lesson 2, pages 280–281)*

Find the perimeter of each figure.

1.

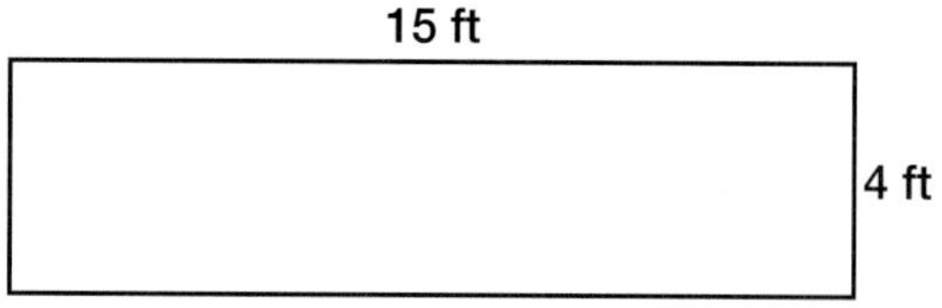

15 ft
4 ft

2.

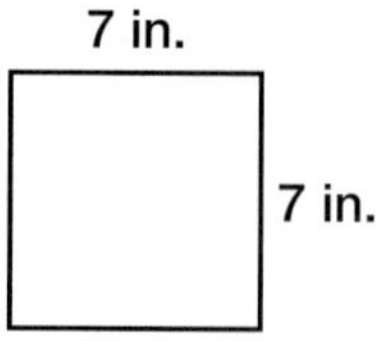

7 in.
7 in.

3.

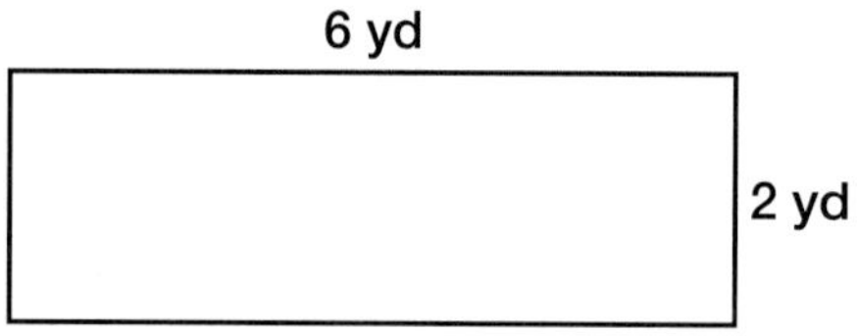

6 yd
2 yd

4.

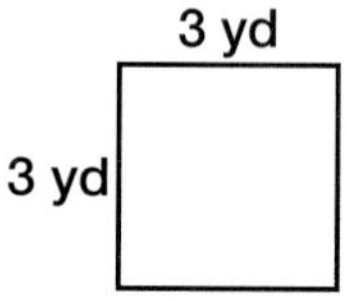

3 yd
3 yd

5.

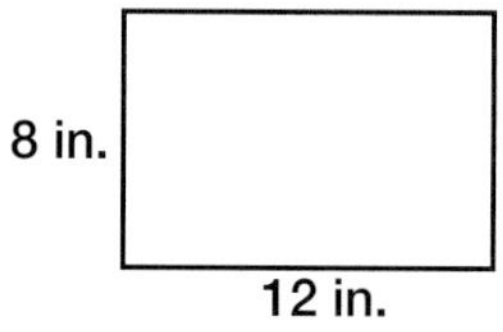

8 in.
12 in.

6.

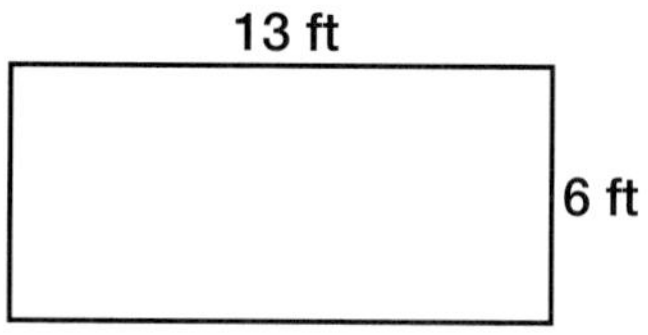

13 ft
6 ft

Find each missing number.

7. 3 yd = ____ in. **8.** 24 in. = ____ ft **9.** ____ in. = 6 ft

10. 2 mi = ____ ft **11.** 4 yd = ____ ft **12.** 2 mi = ____ yd

13. ____ yd = 72 in. **14.** 36 in. = ____ ft **15.** 48 in. = ____ ft

16. 4 mi = ____ yd **17.** 7 ft = ____ in. **18.** 6 mi = ____ yd

Set B *(Lesson 3, pages 282–284)*

Find each missing number.

1. 16 c = ____ pt **2.** 6 gal = ____ qt **3.** ____ pt = 6 qt

4. ____ gal = 12 qt **5.** 11 pt = ____ c **6.** ____ qt = 14 pt

7. 32 c = ____ pt **8.** ____ pt = 5 gal **9.** ____ lb = 2 tons

10. 4 lb = ____ oz **11.** 32 oz = ____ lb **12.** 3 tons = ____ lb

13. 3 lb = ____ oz **14.** 8,000 lb = ____ tons **15.** ____ oz = 5 lb

Extra Practice

Set C (Lesson 6, pages 292–293)

Find the perimeter of each figure.

1.
5 km
3 km

2.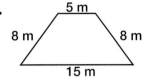
5 m
8 m   8 m
15 m

3.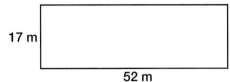
17 m
52 m

4.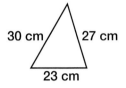
30 cm   27 cm
23 cm

5.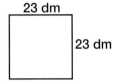
23 dm
23 dm

6.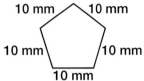
10 mm   10 mm
10 mm   10 mm
10 mm

Set D (Lesson 7, pages 294–296)

Find each missing number.

1. 2 L = ____ mL

2. ____ L = 5,000 mL

3. ____ mL = 10 L

4. 37 kg = ____ g

5. ____ kg = 17,000 g

6. 8 L = ____ mL

Choose the better estimate of the measure of each.

7.
| 200 mL | 200 L |

8.
| 4 mL | 4 L |

9.
| 5 mL | 5 L |

10.
| 1 g | 1 kg |

11.
| 5 g | 5 kg |

12.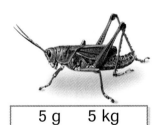
| 5 g | 5 kg |

13.
| 1 g | 1 kg |

14.
| 30 g | 30 kg |

15.
| 200 g | 200 kg |

Extra Practice

Set E   *(Lesson 9, pages 302–303)*

Write each temperature.

1.

2.

3.

Use the thermometer at the right. Find the difference between the two temperatures.

4. 77°F and 102°F

5. ⁻4°F and ⁻10°F

6. 80°F and 57°F

7. 63°F and 28°F

8. 43°F and 89°F

9. ⁻14°F and ⁻2°F

Set F   *(Lesson 10, pages 304–305)*

Write each temperature.

1.

2.

3.

Use the thermometer at the right. Find the difference between the two temperatures.

4. 17°C and 69°C

5. ⁻9°C and ⁻5°C

6. 80°C and 47°C

7. 32°C and 38°C

8. ⁻10°C and 8°C

9. 34°C and ⁻5°C

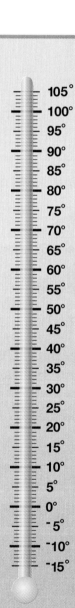

Extra Practice • Problem Solving

Solve each problem. If not enough information is given, tell what information is needed to solve the problems. *(Lesson 4, pages 286–287)*

1 At their inaugurations, Dwight Eisenhower was 62, John Kennedy was 43, and Lyndon Johnson was 55. How much younger was John Kennedy than Lyndon Johnson when he became President?

2 The Dead Sea in the Middle East is the lowest point in the world. The lowest point in the United States is in Death Valley, California. It is 202 feet below sea level. How much lower is the Dead Sea?

3 The Chrysler Building is 1,046 ft tall and has 77 stories. The Woolworth Building is 792 ft tall. How much taller is the Chrysler Building than the Woolworth Building?

4 An elephant lives about 35 years. A hippopotamus lives about 41 years and a baboon about 20 years. About how many fewer years does a baboon live than a hippopotamus?

Solve. Use the Make a Table strategy. *(Lesson 8, pages 298–299)*

5 At what time would the third bus leave Afton on Sunday?

6 Mark takes the fourth bus on Friday. It takes 35 minutes to go to Dixon. At what time does he get to Dixon?

Afton Bus Schedule	
Mon.–Fri. buses leave every 30 minutes	
Sat.–Sun. buses leave every 50 minutes	
First Bus: Monday–Friday	6:45 A.M.
Saturday–Sunday	7:10 A.M.

Solve. *(Lesson 11, pages 306–307)*

7 Gina's thermometer shows a temperature of 14°F. The wind makes the air feel 10 degrees colder. How cold does it feel?

8 The temperature at 8:00 A.M. was 32°F. Then the temperature rose 15 degrees by 5:30 P.M. What was the temperature at 5:30 P.M.?

9 At 7:00 P.M. the temperature was 65°F. At midnight, the temperature was 48°F. How much higher was the temperature at 7:00 P.M.?

10 The temperature inside Lia's house was 72°F. Outdoors, the temperature was 92°F. How much lower was the temperature inside Lia's house?

Chapter Review

Reviewing Vocabulary

Answer each question.

1. A one-foot ruler is divided into 12 equal units. What are the units called?

2. When you measure how much a container can hold, what are you measuring?

3. What do you call the distance around a polygon?

4. What kinds of numbers are used for reading temperatures below zero?

Reviewing Concepts and Skills

Find the perimeter of each figure. *(pages 280–281)*

5.
```
         13 ft
┌─────────────────┐
│                 │ 5 ft
└─────────────────┘
```

6.
```
  3 yd
┌────┐
│    │ 4 yd
│    │
└────┘
```

7.
```
  6 in.
┌────┐
│    │ 6 in.
│    │
└────┘
```

8.
```
   7 km
┌────────┐
│        │ 2 km
└────────┘
```

9.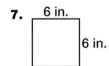

10.
```
      46 cm
┌──────────────┐
│              │ 19 cm
│              │
└──────────────┘
```

11.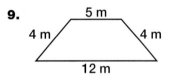

12.
```
  32 m
┌──────┐
│      │ 32 m
│      │
└──────┘
```

13.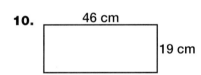

Find each missing number. *(pages 282–285)*

14. 12 c = ___ pt

15. 7 gal = ___ qt

16. ___ pt = 10 qt

17. ___ lb = 7 tons

18. 3 lb = ___ oz

19. 80 oz = ___ lb

Choose the better estimate of the capacity of each. *(pages 294–296)*

20.

5 mL	5 L

21.

2 mL	2 L

22.

5 mL	5 L

Choose the better estimate of the mass of each. (pages 294–296)

23.

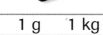

| 20 g | 20 kg |

24.

| 1 g | 1 kg |

25.

| 300 g | 300 kg |

Find the difference between the two temperatures. (pages 302–305)

26. 68°F and 110°F

27. 70°C and 44°C

28. 18°F and 7°F

29. 10°C and 3°C

30. 23°C and 6°C

31. 14°F and 27°F

Solve. If not enough information is given to solve Problems 32–33, tell what information is needed. (pages 286–287, 306–307)

32. In New Mexico, Aztec ruins cover 320 acres, Fort Union covers 721 acres, and the Gita Cliff Dwellings cover 533 acres. How much larger is Fort Union than the Aztec Ruins?

33. Constitution Gardens and the National Mall are in Washington, D.C. The Mall covers 146 acres and includes the Washington Monument. How much larger is the mall than the Gardens?

34. A train leaves Milford at 7:05 A.M. and arrives in Truro 47 minutes later. At what time does it arrive in Truro?

35. The temperature at 5:00 A.M. was 45°F. At noon it was 32°F. How many degrees cooler was it at noon?

Brain Teasers Math Reasoning

SNAIL'S PACE

A snail is climbing a 15-foot fence. Every day it climbs 3 feet, but slides back 1 foot every night. How long does it take the snail to climb to the top of the fence?

TRIANGLES

Can you draw a triangle with a perimeter of 15 inches if the triangle has one side that is 10 inches long? Why or why not?

Safe Site

Internet Brain Teasers
Visit **www.eduplace.com/kids/mhm**
for more *Brain Teasers*.

Chapter Test

Find the perimeter of each figure.

1.
```
        14 ft
┌─────────────────┐
│                 │ 3 ft
└─────────────────┘
```

2.
```
  3 km
┌──────┐
│      │
│      │ 5 km
│      │
└──────┘
```

3.
```
  10 m
┌────────┐
│        │
│        │ 10 m
│        │
└────────┘
```

4.
```
      67 yd
┌──────────────┐
│              │
│              │ 29 yd
│              │
└──────────────┘
```

5.
```
     20 m
┌───────────┐
│           │
│           │ 16 m
│           │
└───────────┘
```

6.
```
   4 mi
┌────────┐
│        │
│        │ 4 mi
│        │
└────────┘
```

Find each missing number.

7. 22 c = ___ pt

8. 8 gal = ___ qt

9. ___ pt = 4 qt

10. 6 lb = ___ oz

11. ___ lb = 64 oz

12. ___ lb = 7 T

13. 8 L = ___ mL

14. ___ L = 9,000 mL

15. ___ mL = 3 L

16. ___ g = 7 kg

17. 3,000 g = ___ kg

18. 5 kg = ___ g

Write each temperature.

19.

20.

21.

Solve. If not enough information is given to solve Problems 22–23, tell what information is needed.

22. The tallest mountain in the world, Mt. Everest, is 29,028 ft high. Aconcagua, in Argentina, is 22,834 ft high. The tallest mountain in the United States is Mt. McKinley, which is 20,320 ft high. How much taller is Everest than Aconcagua?

23. Alaska, Texas, and California are the states with the largest land area. Texas has a population of about 20 million people. California has a population of about 33 million. How many more people live in Texas than in Alaska?

24. Sally will take a bus to Bangor. The first bus leaves at 7:12 A.M. After that, a bus to Bangor leaves every 30 minutes. The trip takes 34 minutes. If Sally takes the third bus, when will she arrive in Bangor?

25. Sally will take the bus home from Bangor. The first bus leaves at 7:46 P.M. After that a bus leaves every 22 minutes. The trip takes 34 minutes. If Sally takes the second bus, when will she arrive home?

 Write About It

Solve each problem. Use correct math vocabulary to explain your thinking.

1. You can choose to use a scale marked in ounces or one marked in pounds.

   a. The scale will be used to weigh letters for mailing. Which scale would you use? Why?

   b. The scale will be used to weigh an apple. Which scale would you use? Why?

   c. The scale will be used to weigh the students in your class. Which scale would you use? Why?

2. You can choose among a teaspoon, a drinking cup, and a small bucket.

   a. You are assigned to change the water in the class aquarium. Which container would you use? Explain your thinking.

   b. You are assigned to fill the water dish for the class gerbil. Which container would you use? Explain your thinking.

   c. The class gerbil needs 5 mL of liquid vitamins. The vitamins are put in its water dish. Which container would you use to measure the vitamins? Explain.

Another Look

The picture gives information about shipping a box. Use the picture and what you know about measurement to answer the questions.

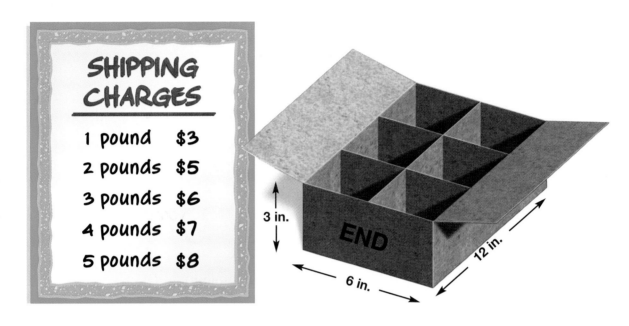

SHIPPING CHARGES

1 pound	$3
2 pounds	$5
3 pounds	$6
4 pounds	$7
5 pounds	$8

3 in.

END

6 in.

12 in.

1. Ship USA will deliver only those packages whose length plus girth is less than 35 inches. The girth is the perimeter of the end of the box. What is the length plus girth of the big box in the picture? Will the company deliver the big box?

2. The big box weighs 6 oz when empty. It holds 6 smaller boxes. Each smaller box weighs 7 ounces. How much does the big box weigh when it is full? How much will it cost to ship the big box?

3. **Look Back** Suppose you were shipping a 1-pound package and a 4-pound package. How much would you save if you put them both in one box?

4. **Analyze** At most, by how many whole inches could you increase the height of the big box and still have Ship USA agree to deliver it? Explain.

Standards MG **1.0**, MR **1.1, 2.0**

Enrichment

Time Lines

A **time line** can be used to show when events happened or when they will happen.

This time line shows when some popular foods were invented.

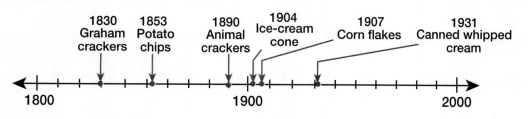

1830 Graham crackers   1853 Potato chips   1890 Animal crackers   1904 Ice-cream cone   1907 Corn flakes   1931 Canned whipped cream

1800   1900   2000

A **century** is 100 years.   A **decade** is 10 years.

Try These

Use the time line for Questions 1–7.

1. What foods were invented in the 1800s? in the 1900s?

2. How many decades are there between the invention of graham crackers and that of animal crackers?

3. Was there more or less than a century between the invention of graham crackers and the invention of canned whipped cream? Explain.

4. There were 3 decades and 7 years between the invention of potato chips and the invention of animal crackers. How many years is that?

Match each invention with the decade in which it was invented.

5. corn flakes   a. 1930–1939

6. graham crackers   b. 1900–1909

7. canned whipped cream c. 1830–1839

CHAPTER 7

Fractions and Mixed Numbers

Why Learn About Fractions and Mixed Numbers?

You can use fractions to describe equal parts of a region or set. You can use mixed numbers to describe a fraction that is greater than one.

When you use a recipe for cooking or baking, you usually use fractions and mixed numbers.

Look at these children competing in a race. They built their own racing cars. They used fractions to measure the wood for parts of their racing cars.

Reading Mathematics

Reviewing Vocabulary

Understanding math language helps you become a successful problem solver. Here are some math vocabulary words you should know.

equal parts	parts that are the same size
fraction	a number that names part of a region or part of a group
denominator	the number written below the bar in a fraction that tells how many equal parts the whole is divided into
numerator	the number written above the bar in a fraction that tells how many equal parts of the whole
mixed number	a number that is made up of a whole number and a fraction less than one

Reading Words and Symbols

When you read mathematics, sometimes you read words, sometimes you read words and symbols, and sometimes you read only symbols.

All of these statements describe the colored parts of the square.

▶ Two fifths of the square is blue.

▶ One fifth of the square is red.

▶ Three fifths of the square is colored.

▶ Two fifths plus one fifth equals three fifths.

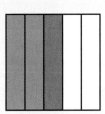

$$\frac{2}{5} + \frac{1}{5} = \frac{3}{5}$$

Try These

1. Tell whether the 6 is the *numerator* or *denominator*.

   a. $\frac{2}{6}$ **b.** $\frac{6}{10}$ **c.** $\frac{6}{3}$ **d.** $4\frac{1}{6}$

2. Write each fraction or mixed number.

   a. one eighth   **b.** nine sixths   **c.** two and one third

   d. twelve thirds   **e.** six and three tenths   **f.** one fifth

3. Tell if each statement is *true* or *false*.

   a. One eighth of the stars are red.

   b. Two eighths of the stars are blue.

   c. One half of the stars are green.

   d. Eight eighths of the stars are white.

4. Write a fraction for each description.

   a. A fraction with a numerator that is two less than the denominator.

   b. A fraction that can be changed to a mixed number.

   c. The denominator is three times greater than the numerator.

   d. The numerator is half the denominator.

Upcoming Vocabulary

Write About It **Here are some other vocabulary words** you will learn in this chapter. Watch for these words. Write their definitions in your journal.

equivalent fractions

simplest form

improper fractions

Represent Fractions

You will learn how to use fractions to describe the parts of a whole.

Review
Vocabulary
fraction
numerator
denominator

Learn About It

A **fraction** is a number that describes a part of a whole.

A fraction can describe part of a collection of things.

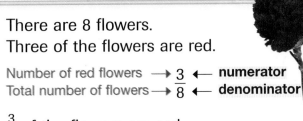

There are 8 flowers.
Three of the flowers are red.

Number of red flowers → $\frac{3}{8}$ ← **numerator**
Total number of flowers → ← **denominator**

$\frac{3}{8}$ of the flowers are red.

A fraction can describe part of a region.

This garden is separated into 3 equal parts.
One of the parts contains yellow marigolds.

Number of yellow parts → $\frac{1}{3}$ ← **numerator**
Total number of equal parts → ← **denominator**

So, $\frac{1}{3}$ of the garden contains yellow marigolds.

| pink petunias |
| yellow marigolds |
| purple violets |

Another Example

Fraction Equal to 1

$\frac{4}{4}$ ← number of shaded parts
 ← total number of parts

$\frac{4}{4} = 1$

Explain Your Thinking

▶ Can the fraction $\frac{2}{5}$ be used to describe the shaded part? Explain why or why not.

 Standards NS **1.0, 1.5, 1.7** MR **2.3**

Guided Practice

Write the fraction for the shaded part.

1.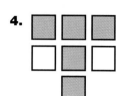
2.
3.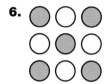

Ask Yourself
- How many parts are shaded?
- How many parts are there in all?

Independent Practice

Write the fraction for the shaded part.

4.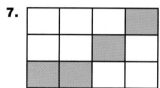

5.

6.

7.

Draw a picture to show each fraction.

8. $\frac{2}{7}$
9. $\frac{4}{5}$
10. $\frac{11}{12}$
11. $\frac{2}{3}$
12. $\frac{1}{8}$
13. $\frac{3}{6}$

Problem Solving • Reasoning

14. If 7 of the 12 flowers are red, what fraction of the flowers are red?

15. **Money** Anna buys 3 large plants for $1.75 each and 2 small plants for $1.25 each. She pays with a ten-dollar bill. How much change should she get?

16. **Patterns** Jo planted 20 rosebushes. The repeating pattern she used was 3 red rosebushes followed by 2 white rosebushes. How many red rosebushes did Jo plant?

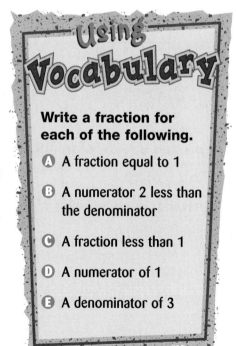

Using Vocabulary

Write a fraction for each of the following.

Ⓐ A fraction equal to 1

Ⓑ A numerator 2 less than the denominator

Ⓒ A fraction less than 1

Ⓓ A numerator of 1

Ⓔ A denominator of 3

Mixed Review • Test Prep

Multiply or divide. *(pages 180–181, 234–235)*

17. $348 \div 7$
18. 142×9
19. $684 \div 5$

20. What is the product of 607 and 3? *(pages 180–181)*

   A 1,821   **C** 1,902

   B 1,861   **D** 2,001

Fractional Parts of a Number

You will learn how to find a fractional part of a number.

Learn About It

Julie used 20 beads to make a necklace. One fourth of the beads were blue and three fourths of the beads were green. How many of the beads were blue? How many of the beads were green?

Different Ways to Find Fractional Parts of a Number

You can use counters to find a fractional part of a number.

Find $\frac{1}{4}$ of 20.

- Separate 20 counters into 4 equal groups.
- Then find the number in 1 group.

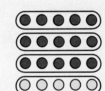

$\frac{1}{4}$ of 20 is 5.

Find $\frac{3}{4}$ of 20.

- Separate 20 counters into 4 equal groups.
- Then find the number in 3 groups.

$\frac{3}{4}$ of 20 is 15.

You can use division and multiplication.

Find $\frac{1}{4}$ of 20.

- Divide 20 by 4 to find the number in each group.

$$20 \div 4 = 5$$

- Multiply the number in each group by 1.

$$1 \times 5 = 5$$

$\frac{1}{4}$ of 20 is 5.

Find $\frac{3}{4}$ of 20.

- Divide 20 by 4 to find the number in each group.

$$20 \div 4 = 5$$

- Multiply the number in each group by 3.

$$3 \times 5 = 15$$

$\frac{3}{4}$ of 20 is 15.

Solution: There were 5 blue beads and 15 green beads.

Standards NS **1.0, 1.5**   MR **2.3, 2.4**

Explain Your Thinking

▶ How does knowing $\frac{1}{3}$ of 12 help you find $\frac{2}{3}$ of 12?

Guided Practice

Find the fractional part of each number.

1.

   $\frac{3}{4}$ of 8

2.

   $\frac{2}{3}$ of 15

3. $\frac{1}{4}$ of 24

4. $\frac{3}{4}$ of 24

5. $\frac{1}{3}$ of 6

Independent Practice

Find the fractional part of each number.

6. $\frac{1}{3}$ of 9

7. $\frac{2}{3}$ of 9

8. $\frac{1}{4}$ of 12

9. $\frac{3}{4}$ of 12

10. $\frac{3}{8}$ of 16

11. $\frac{2}{5}$ of 25

12. $\frac{5}{6}$ of 18

13. $\frac{1}{6}$ of 18

14. $\frac{3}{5}$ of 15

15. $\frac{5}{6}$ of 12

16. $\frac{3}{8}$ of 24

17. $\frac{3}{7}$ of 14

Problem Solving • Reasoning

18. Mia made a bracelet with 21 beads. One third of the beads in the bracelet were orange. How many orange beads were in the bracelet?

19. **Write About It** Show why $\frac{2}{3}$ of 9 and $\frac{1}{3}$ of 18 name the same number. Use counters and draw pictures to help explain your answer.

Mixed Review • Test Prep

Estimate each sum or product. (pages 64–65, 174–175)

20. 307×8

21. $672 + 325$

22. 178×3

23. $534 + 126$

24 Which of the following is a prime number? (pages 248–249)

　　A 25　　C 23

　　B 24　　D 21

Modeling Equivalent Fractions

You will learn about fractions that name the same part of a whole.

New
Vocabulary
equivalent fractions

Learn About It

A fraction can be named in different ways. Work with a partner to find fractions that name the same amount.

Materials

fraction strips

Step 1 Line up $\frac{1}{4}$ fraction strips to fit below a $\frac{1}{2}$ strip.

- How many $\frac{1}{4}$ fraction strips did you use?

- What fraction names the same amount as $\frac{1}{2}$?

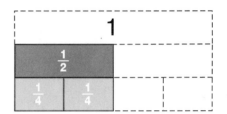

Step 2 Line up $\frac{1}{8}$ fraction strips to fit below the $\frac{1}{4}$ fraction strips.

- How many $\frac{1}{8}$ strips did you use?

- What fraction names the same amount as $\frac{1}{2}$ and $\frac{2}{4}$?

Fractions that name the same part of a whole are called **equivalent fractions** .

$\frac{1}{2}$, $\frac{2}{4}$, and $\frac{4}{8}$ are equivalent fractions.

Step 3 Use fraction strips to find as many other fractions as you can that are equivalent to $\frac{1}{2}$. Make a chart like the one below to record your work.

Fractions Equivalent to $\frac{1}{2}$		
Fraction Strip	How Many?	Equivalent Fraction
$\frac{1}{4}$	2	$\frac{1}{2} = \frac{2}{4}$
$\frac{1}{8}$		$\frac{1}{2} = $ ▆
$\frac{1}{6}$		$\frac{1}{2} = $ ▆

 Standards NS 1.0, 1.5, 1.9   MR 1.1, 2.3

Step 4 Look at the number lines at the right.

- Which fractions are equivalent to $\frac{1}{3}$?
- Which fractions are equivalent to $\frac{2}{3}$?

Use fraction strips to check your answer.

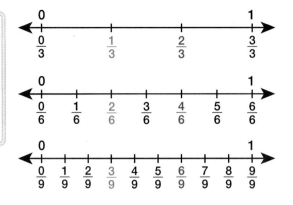

Try It Out

Use fraction strips to find fractions equivalent to $\frac{1}{4}$ and $\frac{3}{4}$. Copy and complete each chart.

1.

Fractions Equivalent to $\frac{1}{4}$		
Fraction Strip	How Many?	Equivalent Fraction
$\frac{1}{8}$		$\frac{1}{4} = \frac{\blacksquare}{\blacksquare}$
$\frac{1}{12}$		$\frac{1}{4} = \frac{\blacksquare}{\blacksquare}$

2.

Fractions Equivalent to $\frac{3}{4}$		
Fraction Strip	How Many?	Equivalent Fraction
$\frac{1}{8}$		$\frac{3}{4} = \frac{\blacksquare}{\blacksquare}$
$\frac{1}{12}$		$\frac{3}{4} = \frac{\blacksquare}{\blacksquare}$

Decide whether the fractions are equivalent.
Write *yes* or *no*. Use fraction strips to help you.

3. $\frac{3}{4}$ and $\frac{6}{8}$ **4.** $\frac{7}{10}$ and $\frac{5}{6}$ **5.** $\frac{8}{12}$ and $\frac{4}{6}$ **6.** $\frac{5}{6}$ and $\frac{10}{12}$

Find a fraction equivalent to each.
Use fraction strips to help you.

7. $\frac{2}{10}$ **8.** $\frac{4}{4}$ **9.** $\frac{3}{4}$ **10.** $\frac{2}{3}$ **11.** $\frac{2}{6}$ **12.** $\frac{4}{12}$

Write about it! Talk about it!

Use what you have learned to answer these questions.

13. Describe the patterns you see in these equivalent fractions. Then use the patterns to find three more equivalent fractions.

$$\frac{1}{3} = \frac{2}{6} = \frac{3}{9} = \frac{4}{12}$$

14. If you know that $\frac{2}{3} = \frac{6}{9}$ and $\frac{6}{9} = \frac{12}{18}$, what can you say about $\frac{2}{3}$ and $\frac{12}{18}$?

Equivalent Fractions

You will learn how to find equivalent fractions.

New
Vocabulary
simplest form

Learn About It

Patti is using a recipe to make fruit shakes to share with her friends. She needs $\frac{2}{4}$ cup of pineapple juice. What are two fractions equivalent to $\frac{2}{4}$?

There are different ways to find equivalent fractions.

Different Ways to Find Equivalent Fractions

You can use fraction strips.

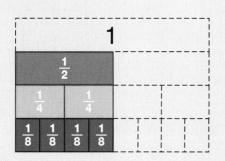

$\frac{1}{2}$, $\frac{2}{4}$, and $\frac{4}{8}$ are equivalent fractions.

You can use number lines.

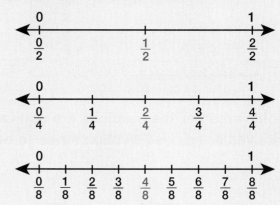

$\frac{1}{2}$, $\frac{2}{4}$, and $\frac{4}{8}$ are equivalent fractions.

You can multiply.

Multiply the numerator and denominator by the same number.

$$\frac{2}{4} = \frac{2 \times 2}{4 \times 2} = \frac{4}{8}$$

$\frac{2}{4}$ and $\frac{4}{8}$ are equivalent fractions.

You can divide.

Divide the numerator and denominator by the same number.

$$\frac{2}{4} = \frac{2 \div 2}{4 \div 2} = \frac{1}{2}$$

$\frac{2}{4}$ and $\frac{1}{2}$ are equivalent fractions.

Solution: $\frac{1}{2}$ and $\frac{4}{8}$ are two fractions equivalent to $\frac{2}{4}$.

Standards NS **1.5, 1.9** AF **2.2** MR **1.1, 2.3, 2.4**

A fraction is in **simplest form** when 1 is the only number that divides both the numerator and the denominator.

These fractions are in simplest form.
$\frac{1}{2}$ $\quad$ $\frac{2}{3}$ $\quad$ $\frac{3}{8}$ $\quad$ $\frac{2}{7}$ $\quad$ $\frac{5}{9}$

These fractions are not in simplest form.
$\frac{2}{4}$ $\quad$ $\frac{4}{8}$ $\quad$ $\frac{3}{15}$ $\quad$ $\frac{6}{9}$ $\quad$ $\frac{8}{12}$

You can write a fraction in simplest form by dividing the numerator and the denominator by their greatest common factor.

Write $\frac{4}{8}$ in simplest form.

• Find the common factors.	Factors of 4: 1, 2, 4 Factors of 8: 1, 2, 4, 8 $\qquad$ Common Factors
• Find the greatest common factor: The greatest common factor of 4 and 8 is 4.	Factors of 4: 1, 2, 4 Factors of 8: 1, 2, 4, 8 $\qquad$ Greatest Common Factor
• Divide the numerator and the denominator by their greatest common factor.	$\frac{4}{8} = \frac{4 \div 4}{8 \div 4} = \frac{1}{2}$

Solution: The simplest form of $\frac{4}{8}$ is $\frac{1}{2}$.

Explain Your Thinking

▶ How could you use multiplication to find a fraction equivalent to $\frac{3}{12}$? How could you use division?

▶ Why is $\frac{3}{4}$ in simplest form?

Guided Practice

Complete. Find the value of each ■.

1. $\frac{3}{4} = \frac{3 \times 4}{4 \times 4} = \frac{\blacksquare}{16}$

2. $\frac{2}{3} = \frac{2 \times 3}{3 \times 3} = \frac{6}{\blacksquare}$

3. $\frac{2}{5} = \frac{2 \times \blacksquare}{5 \times \blacksquare} = \frac{8}{20}$

4. $\frac{1}{4} = \frac{1 \times \blacksquare}{4 \times \blacksquare} = \frac{5}{20}$

5. $\frac{12}{18} = \frac{12 \div 3}{18 \div 3} = \frac{\blacksquare}{\blacksquare}$

6. $\frac{8}{12} = \frac{8 \div 4}{12 \div 4} = \frac{\blacksquare}{\blacksquare}$

> **Ask Yourself**
> • Should I multiply or divide?
> • Which number should I multiply or divide by?

Independent Practice

Complete. Find the value of each ▪.

7. $\frac{2}{4} = \frac{2 \times 3}{4 \times ▪} = \frac{▪}{▪}$

8. $\frac{2}{4} = \frac{2 \div ▪}{4 \div 2} = \frac{▪}{▪}$

9. $\frac{2}{4} = \frac{2 \times 5}{4 \times ▪} = \frac{▪}{▪}$

10. Look at Exercises 7–9. What do you know about the three answers?

Is each fraction in simplest form? Write *yes* or *no*.

11. $\frac{2}{8}$　　**12.** $\frac{5}{7}$　　**13.** $\frac{9}{11}$　　**14.** $\frac{4}{10}$　　**15.** $\frac{1}{3}$　　**16.** $\frac{10}{12}$

Write each fraction in simplest form.

17. $\frac{9}{12}$　　**18.** $\frac{12}{16}$　　**19.** $\frac{6}{10}$　　**20.** $\frac{4}{6}$　　**21.** $\frac{6}{12}$　　**22.** $\frac{12}{18}$

Problem Solving • Reasoning

Use the recipe for Problems 23 and 24.

23. Analyze Patti made 12 servings of her tropical fruit shake for her friends. How much pineapple juice did she use?

24. Another fruit shake recipe uses $\frac{6}{8}$ cup of cranberry juice. Does it use the same amount of cranberry juice as Patti's recipe? Explain how you know.

25. Write About It Justine says that $\frac{2}{3}$ and $\frac{16}{25}$ are equivalent fractions. Is she correct? Explain your thinking.

Patti's Fruit Shake

Makes 3 Servings

1 Large Banana
1 Cup Strawberries
1 Mango Cubed
$\frac{3}{4}$ Cup Cranberry Juice
$\frac{1}{2}$ Cup Pineapple Juice
1 Cup Ice Cubes

Put all ingredients in blender.
Blend until thick and smooth.

Mixed Review • Test Prep

Find the missing numbers. *(pages 280–281, 292–293)*

26. 4 ft = ____ in.

27. 300 cm = ____ m

28. 42 in. = ____ ft ____ in.

29 Which of the following is a likely length for a pencil? *(pages 292–293)*

　A 12 mm　　　**C** 12 m

　B 12 cm　　　**D** 12 km

Fractions in Simplest Form

There are different ways to find a fraction in simplest form.

Here's how Glen finds a fraction in simplest form.

Glen keeps dividing until 1 is the only number that divides both the numerator and the denominator.

First he divides by 3.

$$\frac{12}{18} = \frac{12 \div 3}{18 \div 3} = \frac{4}{6}$$

Then he divides by 2.

$$\frac{4}{6} = \frac{4 \div 2}{6 \div 2} = \frac{2}{3}$$

$\frac{2}{3}$ is in simplest form.

Would Glen's answer be different if he first divided by 2 and then by 3?

Here's how Lisa finds a fraction in simplest form.

Lisa finds the greatest number that is a factor of both the numerator and the denominator. Then she divides the numerator and denominator by that number.

First she lists the factors of 12 and 18.

Factors of 12: 1, 2, 3, 4, 6, 12
Factors of 18: 1, 2, 3, 6, 9, 18
6 is the greatest common factor.

Then she divides 12 and 18 by 6.

$$\frac{12}{18} = \frac{12 \div 6}{18 \div 6} = \frac{2}{3}$$

$\frac{2}{3}$ is in simplest form.

Why does Lisa have to divide only once?

Try These

Use Glen's, Lisa's, or your own strategy to find each fraction in simplest form.

1. $\frac{12}{16}$ 2. $\frac{6}{24}$ 3. $\frac{8}{12}$ 4. $\frac{9}{18}$ 5. $\frac{15}{30}$ 6. $\frac{10}{14}$

Explain Your Thinking

▶ How are Glen's and Lisa's strategies alike? How are they different?

Problem-Solving Strategy: Draw a Picture

You will learn how to draw a picture to help you solve a problem.

Sometimes you can draw a picture to help you solve a problem.

Problem Mrs. Carl's class displayed three kinds of projects. One half of the projects were drawings, $\frac{1}{6}$ were sculptures, and 8 were paintings.

How many art projects were displayed?

Understand

What is the question?
How many art projects were displayed?

What do you know?
$\frac{1}{2}$ of the projects were drawings, $\frac{1}{6}$ of the projects were sculptures, and 8 projects were paintings.

Plan

How can you find the answer?
You can draw a picture to help you find the answer.

Solve

Draw a picture.

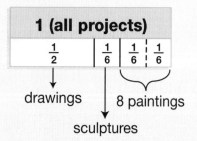

Since $8 = \frac{2}{6}$ of the projects, $\frac{1}{6} = 4$ projects.
To find $\frac{6}{6}$ of the projects, find 6×4.

$6 \times 4 = 24$

There were 24 art projects displayed.

Look Back

Look back at the problem.
How do you know that 8 equals $\frac{2}{6}$ of the projects?

Standards MR 1.0, 1.1, 1.2, 2.0, 2.3, 3.2

Guided Practice

Use the Draw a Picture strategy to solve each problem.

1 Joan collected 3 kinds of items to make a collage. Of the items, $\frac{2}{8}$ were post cards, $\frac{3}{8}$ were photographs, and 9 were stickers. How many items did she collect for her collage?

> **Think:** Into how many equal parts should the picture be divided?

2 After Rodney spent $\frac{1}{2}$ of all of his money on a sketchpad, $\frac{1}{4}$ of it on a drawing pencil, and $2 on erasers, he had no money left. How much money did Rodney spend altogether?

> **Think:** Into how many equal parts should the picture be divided?

Choose a Strategy

Solve. Use these or other strategies.

Problem-Solving Strategies

- **Draw a Picture**
- **Make a Table**
- **Write an Equation**
- **Guess and Check**

3 Mr. Grant brought a bowl of punch to serve at the school's art show. Half of all the punch was orange juice, $\frac{2}{6}$ was cranberry juice, and 12 ounces was ginger ale. How many ounces of punch did he make?

4 Lila spent $35 on beads. She bought the same number of packets of small beads as packets of large beads. A packet of small beads costs $3. A packet of large beads costs $4. How many packets of each did she buy?

5 Franklin just finished drawing the last 2 frames of a comic strip. Yesterday he drew $\frac{1}{2}$ of the comic strip. He drew $\frac{1}{6}$ of it two days ago. How many frames are in his comic strip?

6 Cory used $\frac{1}{2}$ of a piece of ribbon to make a large bow and $\frac{3}{8}$ of it to make a smaller bow. She had 3 inches of ribbon left over. How many inches of ribbon did Cory start with?

7 A total of 44 papier-mâché models and dioramas were displayed at the school's art show. There were 8 more dioramas than papier-mâché models on display. How many of each were displayed at the school's art show?

8 Terence has only markers and crayons in his pencil case. He has 23 more crayons than markers. He has 18 markers. How many crayons and markers does Terence have in his pencil case altogether?

Quick ✓ Check

Check Your Understanding of Lessons 1-5

Find the fractional part of each number.

1. $\frac{3}{4}$ of 20 **2.** $\frac{3}{5}$ of 15 **3.** $\frac{2}{7}$ of 14

Find an equivalent fraction for each.

4. $\frac{3}{5}$ **5.** $\frac{4}{6}$ **6.** $\frac{3}{12}$

Write each fraction in its simplest form.

7. $\frac{9}{15}$ **8.** $\frac{6}{18}$

Use the Draw a Picture strategy to solve each problem.

9. Rico spent $\frac{1}{2}$ of his money on a kite and $\frac{1}{4}$ of his money on kite string. He had $5.00 left. How much money did Rico have when he started?

10. Tina arranged her beads by color. One third of the beads are red, $\frac{5}{12}$ of the beads are green, and 9 of the beads are yellow. How many beads does Tina have?

How did you do?

If you had difficulty with any items in the Quick Check, you can use the following pages for review and extra practice.

California Standards	ITEMS	REVIEW THESE PAGES	DO THESE EXTRA PRACTICE ITEMS
Number Sense: **1.5**	1–3	pages 326–327	Set B, page 358
Number Sense: **1.5**	4–6	pages 330–332	Set C, page 358
Number Sense: **1.5**	7–8	pages 330–332	Set C, page 358
Number Sense: **1.5** Reasoning: **1.1, 1.2, 2.3, 3.2**	9–10	pages 334–335	1– 4, page 361

Test Prep • Cumulative Review
Maintaining the Standards

Choose the letter of the correct answer.

1 What fraction represents the shaded portion of this model?

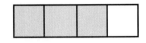

A $\frac{1}{4}$ **C** $\frac{3}{5}$

B $\frac{1}{2}$ **D** $\frac{3}{4}$

2 Which number is a prime number?

F 17

G 27

H 30

J 39

3 Which fraction is not equivalent to $\frac{1}{2}$?

A $\frac{3}{6}$ **C** $\frac{2}{3}$

B $\frac{4}{8}$ **D** $\frac{5}{10}$

4 What fraction of the beads are shaded?

F $\frac{1}{8}$ **H** $\frac{1}{2}$

G $\frac{3}{8}$ **J** $\frac{5}{8}$

5 Which number is a composite number?

A 5 **C** 29

B 21 **D** 37

Use the drawing to answer Questions 6–7.

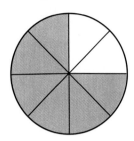

6 What fraction represents the shaded portion of this model?

F $\frac{1}{3}$

G $\frac{2}{3}$

H $\frac{6}{8}$

J $\frac{5}{6}$

7 Which fraction is equivalent to $\frac{6}{8}$?

A $\frac{1}{5}$

B $\frac{1}{2}$

C $\frac{3}{4}$

D $\frac{7}{8}$

8 A pizza is divided into 8 equal slices. Janet eats $\frac{1}{4}$ of the pizza. How many pieces does Janet eat?

Explain How did you find your answer?

Compare and Order Fractions

You will learn how to compare and order fractions.

Learn About It

Bonsai trees are beautiful miniature trees. Look at the trees at the right. Which tree is taller?

If two fractions have the same denominators, or like denominators, you can compare the numerators to find the greater fraction.

Compare. $\frac{3}{4}$ and $\frac{1}{4}$

$\frac{3}{4}$ ft

$\frac{1}{4}$ ft

Compare $\frac{3}{4}$ and $\frac{1}{4}$.

Step 1 Write the fractions.

$\frac{3}{4}$ $\qquad$ $\frac{1}{4}$

Step 2 Compare the numerators.

$\frac{3}{4}$ ← numerators → $\frac{1}{4}$

$3 > 1$, So $\frac{3}{4} > \frac{1}{4}$.

Solution: The $\frac{3}{4}$-foot tree is taller.

To compare two fractions with different denominators, or unlike denominators, first find equivalent fractions.

Compare $\frac{2}{3}$ and $\frac{5}{6}$.

Different Ways to Compare Fractions With Unlike Denominators

You can find equivalent fractions. Then compare the numerators.

- First, find a fraction equivalent to $\frac{2}{3}$ that has a denominator of 6.

$\frac{2}{3} = \frac{2 \times 2}{3 \times 2} = \frac{4}{6}$ $\quad$ So $\frac{2}{3} = \frac{4}{6}$.

- Then compare the numerators.

$\frac{4}{6}$ ←compare→ $\frac{5}{6}$

$\frac{4}{6} < \frac{5}{6}$, so $\frac{2}{3} < \frac{5}{6}$

You can use a number line.

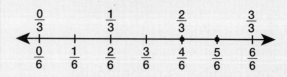

$$\frac{0}{3} \qquad \frac{1}{3} \qquad \frac{2}{3} \qquad \frac{3}{3}$$
$$\frac{0}{6} \quad \frac{1}{6} \quad \frac{2}{6} \quad \frac{3}{6} \quad \frac{4}{6} \quad \frac{5}{6} \quad \frac{6}{6}$$

$\frac{2}{3}$ is to the left of $\frac{5}{6}$.

So $\frac{2}{3} < \frac{5}{6}$.

Solution: $\frac{2}{3}$ is less than $\frac{5}{6}$.

Standards | NS 1.5, 1.9 AF 1.0, 2.2 MR 2.4

You can use what you know about comparing fractions to order $\frac{1}{3}$, $\frac{1}{6}$, and $\frac{5}{6}$ from least to greatest.

Different Ways to Order Fractions

You can find equivalent fractions before comparing the numerators.

- First, find a fraction equivalent to $\frac{1}{3}$ that has a denominator of 6.

$$\frac{1}{3} = \frac{1 \times 2}{3 \times 2} = \frac{2}{6}, \text{ so } \frac{1}{3} = \frac{2}{6}.$$

- Then compare the numerators and order the fractions.

$$\frac{1}{6} < \frac{2}{6} < \frac{5}{6}, \text{ so } \frac{1}{6} < \frac{1}{3} < \frac{5}{6}.$$

You can use a number line.

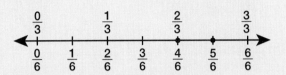

$\frac{1}{6}$ is the farthest to the left.

$\frac{5}{6}$ is the farthest to the right.

So $\frac{1}{6} < \frac{1}{3} < \frac{5}{6}$.

Solution: The order of the fractions from least to greatest is $\frac{1}{6}$, $\frac{1}{3}$, and $\frac{5}{6}$.

Explain Your Thinking

▶ Why is it easier to compare fractions with like denominators than fractions with unlike denominators?

▶ How can you use equivalent fractions to compare $\frac{2}{3}$ and $\frac{4}{12}$?

Growing a bonsai requires careful pruning and a lot of patience.

Guided Practice

Compare. Write >, <, or = for each ⬤.

1.
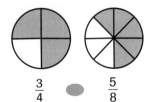

$\frac{3}{4}$ ⬤ $\frac{5}{8}$

2.
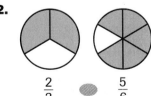

$\frac{2}{3}$ ⬤ $\frac{5}{6}$

Ask Yourself

- Do the fractions have the same denominator? If not, what should I do?

Order each group of fractions from greatest to least.
Draw number lines to help if you wish.

3. $\frac{3}{4}$, $\frac{7}{8}$, $\frac{5}{8}$

4. $\frac{2}{7}$, $\frac{6}{7}$, $\frac{4}{7}$

5. $\frac{2}{5}$, $\frac{3}{10}$, $\frac{7}{10}$

Independent Practice

Compare. Write >, <, or = for each ⚫.

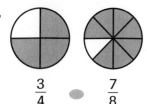

6. $\frac{3}{4}$ ⚫ $\frac{7}{8}$

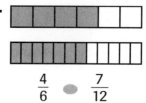

7. $\frac{4}{6}$ ⚫ $\frac{7}{12}$

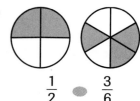

8. $\frac{1}{2}$ ⚫ $\frac{3}{6}$

9. $\frac{5}{7}$ ⚫ $\frac{6}{7}$ **10.** $\frac{2}{3}$ ⚫ $\frac{5}{9}$ **11.** $\frac{3}{8}$ ⚫ $\frac{1}{2}$ **12.** $\frac{2}{2}$ ⚫ $\frac{4}{4}$

13. $\frac{3}{4}$ ⚫ $\frac{5}{8}$ **14.** $\frac{2}{8}$ ⚫ $\frac{1}{4}$ **15.** $\frac{1}{3}$ ⚫ $\frac{3}{9}$ **16.** $\frac{3}{5}$ ⚫ $\frac{7}{10}$

Order each group of fractions from least to greatest. Draw number lines to help you if you wish.

17. $\frac{7}{12}$ $\frac{10}{12}$ $\frac{3}{4}$ **18.** $\frac{4}{9}$ $\frac{2}{3}$ $\frac{5}{9}$ **19.** $\frac{4}{8}$ $\frac{7}{8}$ $\frac{1}{8}$ **20.** $\frac{2}{3}$ $\frac{7}{12}$ $\frac{5}{12}$

21. $\frac{5}{6}$ $\frac{1}{3}$ $\frac{2}{3}$ **22.** $\frac{3}{5}$ $\frac{2}{5}$ $\frac{4}{5}$ **23.** $\frac{1}{2}$ $\frac{3}{8}$ $\frac{5}{8}$ **24.** $\frac{3}{4}$ $\frac{1}{2}$ $\frac{1}{4}$

Problem Solving • Reasoning

Use Data Use the table for Problems 25–27.

25. Measurement Of the bonsai trees described in the table, what is the greatest height a bonsai tree can be in inches? Explain.

26. Analyze Lian has a Mame, a Katade, and a Keishi Tsubo tree. If he is to place the trees from shortest to tallest on a shelf, in what order should he place the trees?

27. Write Your Own Write a problem about comparing heights of bonsai trees. Ask a classmate to solve your problem.

Special Types of Bonsai Trees	
Name	**Height**
Katade	from $\frac{1}{2}$ ft to $\frac{5}{6}$ ft
Keishi Tsubo	less than $\frac{1}{6}$ ft
Mame	from $\frac{1}{6}$ ft to $\frac{1}{2}$ ft

Mixed Review • Test Prep

Estimate each difference or quotient to the nearest hundred. *(pages 64–65, 254–255)*

28. $734 - 285$ **29.** $872 \div 9$ **30.** $432 - 161$ **31.** $598 \div 6$

32 What is the value of 4 in 346,129? *(pages 4–5)*

    A four thousand　**B** forty thousand　**C** four hundred　**D** four hundred thousand

Action Fractions

Practice comparing fractions by playing this game with a partner.
Try to be the player with more points.

What You'll Need

For each pair:

- *4 sets of cards labeled 1, 2, 3, 4, 6, 8*
  (Teaching Tool 6)

**Players
2**

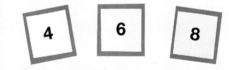

Here's What to Do

1. One player shuffles and deals all cards facedown. Players stack their cards.

2. Players take 3 cards from the top of their stacks. Using 2 of the 3 cards, each player makes a fraction whose numerator is less than or equal to its denominator. The unused card is returned to the bottom of the player's stack.

3. Players compare the fractions. The player with the greater fraction earns 1 point. If the fractions are equivalent, each player earns 1 point.

   Repeat Steps 2 and 3. The player with more points after all the cards have been used is the winner.

Share Your Thinking Is forming a fraction with your two highest cards always the best strategy? Explain why or why not.

Write Mixed Numbers

You will learn how to write improper fractions
and mixed numbers

New
Vocabulary
improper fraction
mixed number

Learn About It

The photo shows 3 whole
juice bars and one half
juice bar. There are
7 halves.

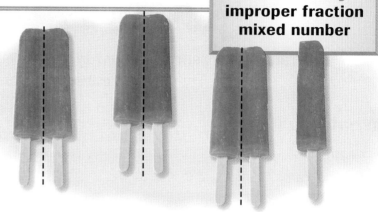

improper fraction → $\dfrac{7}{2} = 3\dfrac{1}{2}$ ← mixed number

An **improper fraction** has a
numerator that is greater than or equal
to the denominator. An improper
fraction is greater than or equal to 1.

$\dfrac{7}{2}$ ← numerator
← denominator

A **mixed number** is made up of a
whole number and a fraction. A mixed
number is a number greater than 1
that is between two whole numbers.

whole
number → $3\dfrac{1}{2}$ ← fraction

There are different ways to change an improper
fraction to a mixed number.

Write $\dfrac{7}{3}$ as a mixed number.

Different Ways to Change an Improper Fraction to a Mixed Number

You can draw a picture.

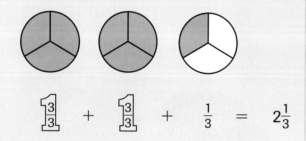

$\boxed{1\dfrac{3}{3}} + \boxed{1\dfrac{3}{3}} + \dfrac{1}{3} = 2\dfrac{1}{3}$

The picture shows that $\dfrac{7}{3}$ equals $2\dfrac{1}{3}$.

You can divide the numerator by the denominator.

The fraction bar stands for "divided
by." So $\dfrac{7}{3}$ means "7 divided by 3."

$\quad\quad 2$ ← number of wholes
$3\overline{)7}$
$\quad\underline{-6}$
$\quad\quad 1$ ← number of thirds

So $\dfrac{7}{3}$ equals $2\dfrac{1}{3}$.

Solution: The improper fraction $\dfrac{7}{3}$ can be written as the mixed number $2\dfrac{1}{3}$.

California **Standards** | NS **1.9** AF **1.1** MR **2.3, 2.4**

To write a mixed number as an improper fraction, you can draw a picture. Divide each whole into fractional parts. Then add all the fractional parts.

Write $2\frac{3}{4}$ as an improper fraction.

Draw a picture showing $2\frac{3}{4}$.

$$\boxed{1}\frac{4}{4} \quad + \quad \boxed{1}\frac{4}{4} \quad + \quad \frac{3}{4} \quad = \quad \frac{11}{4}$$

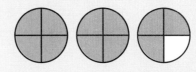

The picture shows that $2\frac{3}{4} = \frac{11}{4}$.

$2\frac{3}{4}$ is the same as $\frac{11}{4}$.

Explain Your Thinking

▶ Why can you write the improper fraction $\frac{9}{3}$ as a whole number?

▶ How can you tell whether a fraction can be rewritten as a mixed number?

Guided Practice

Write an improper fraction and a mixed number for the shaded parts.

1.

2.

3.

4.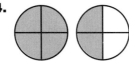

Ask Yourself

• How many equal parts is each figure divided into?

• How many parts are shaded?

Independent Practice

Write an improper fraction and a mixed number for the shaded parts.

5.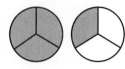

6.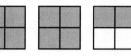

7.

Write the letter from the number line that matches each fraction.

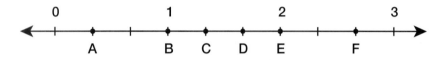

8. $\dfrac{4}{3}$ **9.** $\dfrac{6}{3}$ **10.** $2\dfrac{2}{3}$ **11.** $\dfrac{1}{3}$ **12.** $1\dfrac{2}{3}$ **13.** $\dfrac{3}{3}$

Write an improper fraction and a mixed number to match each letter.

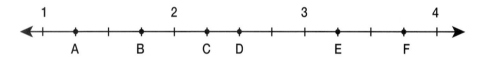

14. A   **15.** C   **16.** F   **17.** D   **18.** B   **19.** E

Write a mixed number or whole number for each improper fraction.

20. $\dfrac{15}{3}$ **21.** $\dfrac{8}{7}$ **22.** $\dfrac{11}{9}$ **23.** $\dfrac{10}{3}$ **24.** $\dfrac{18}{2}$ **25.** $\dfrac{15}{4}$

26. $\dfrac{9}{2}$ **27.** $\dfrac{7}{5}$ **28.** $\dfrac{16}{4}$ **29.** $\dfrac{5}{4}$ **30.** $\dfrac{24}{5}$ **31.** $\dfrac{6}{1}$

Write an improper fraction for each mixed number.

32. $3\dfrac{1}{2}$ **33.** $1\dfrac{2}{3}$ **34.** $2\dfrac{3}{4}$ **35.** $5\dfrac{1}{3}$ **36.** $4\dfrac{2}{5}$ **37.** $2\dfrac{5}{6}$

38. $2\dfrac{5}{8}$ **39.** $6\dfrac{1}{4}$ **40.** $7\dfrac{3}{8}$ **41.** $3\dfrac{4}{5}$ **42.** $2\dfrac{1}{10}$ **43.** $3\dfrac{1}{8}$

𝑛 Algebra • Equations   Find each missing numerator.

44. $\dfrac{\blacksquare}{3} = 2\dfrac{1}{3}$ **45.** $\dfrac{\blacksquare}{2} = 6\dfrac{1}{2}$ **46.** $\dfrac{\blacksquare}{4} = 3$ **47.** $\dfrac{\blacksquare}{5} = 1\dfrac{3}{5}$ **48.** $\dfrac{\blacksquare}{6} = 3\dfrac{1}{6}$

49. $\dfrac{\blacksquare}{8} = 2\dfrac{7}{8}$ **50.** $\dfrac{\blacksquare}{3} = 5\dfrac{2}{3}$ **51.** $\dfrac{\blacksquare}{4} = 1\dfrac{3}{4}$ **52.** $\dfrac{\blacksquare}{2} = 6$ **53.** $\dfrac{\blacksquare}{9} = 4\dfrac{2}{9}$

Problem Solving • Reasoning

Solve. Choose a method.

Computation Methods

• Mental Math • Estimation • Paper and Pencil

54. Analyze Miss Carter made vegetable pies for a picnic. She wanted to make enough so that each of her 20 friends could have $\frac{1}{8}$ pie. How many pies did she need to make?

55. Mr. Alvarez brought 6 oranges to the picnic. The oranges were cut into halves. If all the oranges were eaten and each person ate $\frac{1}{2}$ orange, how many people ate oranges?

56. Money For the pies, Miss Carter spent $10.95 on broccoli and $4.85 on cheese. If she gave the clerk a $20 bill, about how much change should she receive?

57. Measurement A guest brought 3 quarts of fruit salad to the picnic. Was there enough for each of 11 people to have 1 cup? Explain why or why not.

58. The last guest to leave the picnic left at 7:00 P.M. The first guest to arrive at the picnic got there $4\frac{1}{2}$ hours earlier. At what time did the first guest arrive?

59. At the picnic, 21 people played either volleyball or badminton. Twice as many people played volleyball than badminton. How many played volleyball?

Mixed Review • Test Prep

Write each temperature. *(pages 302–305)*

60. 3 degrees colder than 2°F

61. 2 degrees colder than 1°F

62. 1 degree colder than 0°C

63. 4 degrees warmer than 9°C

Choose the letter of the correct answer. *(pages 118–119)*

64 Which expression matches the picture?

A 3 + 5   **C** 3 × 5

B 3 − 5   **D** 3 ÷ 5

65 Which expression matches the picture?

F 12 ÷ 3   **H** 12 × 3

G 12 − 3   **J** 12 + 3

Extra Practice See Set E on page 359.

Problem-Solving Skill: Choose How to Write the Quotient

You will learn how to write a quotient to answer a problem.

When you solve problems by dividing, you need to decide how to write the quotient in order to answer a problem.

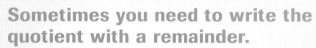

Sometimes you need to write the quotient with a remainder.

A class of 23 students went to the zoo. There was a parent for each group of 4 students. The remaining students were with the teacher. How many groups were with a parent? How many students were with the teacher?

$$\begin{array}{r} 5 \text{ R}3 \\ 4\overline{)23} \\ -20 \\ \hline 3 \end{array}$$

The remainder is the number of students with the teacher. So you should write the quotient and the remainder.

There were 5 groups with a parent.
There were 3 students with the teacher.

Sometimes you need to write the quotient as a mixed number.

A parent gave 5 oranges to the 4 students in his group. If the students shared all of the oranges equally, how many oranges did each student receive?

$$\begin{array}{r} 1\frac{1}{4} \\ 4\overline{)5} \\ -\ 4 \\ \hline 1 \end{array}$$

It is possible to split an orange into parts. So you should write the quotient as a mixed number.

Each student received $1\frac{1}{4}$ oranges.

Look Back How do you decide how to write the quotient when you solve a problem?

  Standards MR **1.0, 2.0, 2.4, 3.2, 3.3**

You can see wild animals up close at zoos and safari parks.

Guided Practice

Solve each problem. Explain why your answer is reasonable.

1. Fred has $10 to ride the camels and elephants at the zoo. Each ride costs $3. How many rides can he take? How much money will he have left?

   Think: What does the remainder represent?

2. For lunch at the zoo, 8 students shared a pizza with 12 slices. Each student ate the same amount. How many slices did each student eat?

   Think: Can you eat a fractional part of a pizza slice?

Choose a Strategy

Solve. Use these or other strategies.

Problem-Solving Strategies

- **Use Logical Thinking**
- **Guess and Check**
- **Work Backward**
- **Draw a Picture**

3. A ticket for the safari ride costs $2. How many tickets can the teacher buy with $25? How much money will the teacher have left over?

4. One group of students saw a total of 24 crocodiles and alligators. They saw 4 more crocodiles than alligators. How many of each animal did they see?

5. A group of students followed a map during their visit to the zoo. They visited the reptile house after visiting the lions and before visiting the seals. They saw the giraffes third and the elephants first. In what order did they see the animals?

6. Some of the students watched a zookeeper feed 5 lions. She told them that she was giving the lions a total of 38 pounds of meat. If the zookeeper gave each lion the same amount, how many pounds of meat did each lion eat?

7. Rusty spent all of the money he brought to the zoo. He spent $\frac{1}{2}$ of the money on lunch, $\frac{1}{4}$ of it on a snack, and $3 on a souvenir toy snake. How much money did Rusty spend?

8. The zoo is one hour away from the school. After spending $5\frac{1}{2}$ hours at the zoo, the class returned to school at 4:00 P.M. At what time did they leave school for the zoo?

Extra Practice See 5–6 on page 361.

Quick ✓ Check

Check Your Understanding of Lessons 6–8

Write >, <, or = for each oval.
Draw number lines to help you if you wish.

1. $\frac{2}{3}$ ⬤ $\frac{5}{12}$

2. $\frac{5}{8}$ ⬤ $\frac{3}{4}$

Order each group of fractions from least to greatest.
Use a number line to help you if you wish.

3. $\frac{5}{6}$, $\frac{2}{6}$, $\frac{2}{3}$

4. $\frac{7}{9}$, $\frac{2}{3}$, $\frac{5}{9}$

Write a mixed number for each improper fraction.

5. $\frac{17}{4}$

6. $\frac{24}{7}$

Write an improper fraction for each mixed number.

7. $3\frac{2}{3}$

8. $4\frac{3}{8}$

Solve. Explain why your answer is reasonable.

9. Jeremy has $10.00 to buy bird seed. The seed costs $3.00 a box. How many boxes of bird seed can he buy? How much money will he have left over?

10. A group of 6 friends shared 15 small bottles of orange juice. Each person drank the same amount of juice. How much orange juice did each person drink?

How did you do?

If you had difficulty with any items in the Quick Check, you can use the following pages for review and extra practice.

California Standards	Items	Review These Pages	Do These Extra Practice Items
Number Sense: **1.5** Algebra: **1.0**	1–4	pages 338–340	Set D, page 359
Number Sense: **1.5**	5–8	pages 342–345	Set E, page 359
Algebra: **1.5** Reasoning: **1.1, 2.3, 2.4, 2.6, 3.2, 3.3**	9–10	pages 346–347	5–6, page 361

Test Prep • Cumulative Review

Maintaining the Standards

Choose the letter of the correct answer.

1 What fraction of the balls are soccer balls?

A $\frac{1}{3}$ **C** $\frac{2}{3}$

B $\frac{2}{5}$ **D** 2

---

2 What mixed number is represented by point *F*?

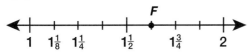

F $1\frac{1}{8}$ **H** $1\frac{3}{8}$

G $1\frac{1}{4}$ **J** $1\frac{5}{8}$

---

3 What are the prime factors of 24?

A 8×3 **C** $2 \times 2 \times 2 \times 3$

B 3×3 **D** $2 \times 3 \times 4$

---

4 What fraction represents the shaded portion of this model?

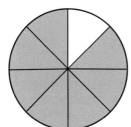

F $\frac{1}{5}$ **H** $\frac{5}{6}$

G $\frac{3}{4}$ **J** $\frac{7}{8}$

Use the number line to answer Questions 5–6.

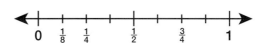

5 Which symbol makes this statement true?

$$\frac{1}{2} \quad \bullet \quad \frac{3}{4}$$

A $>$ **C** $=$

B $<$ **D** $+$

---

6 Which fraction is greater than $\frac{1}{2}$, but less than $\frac{3}{4}$?

F $\frac{1}{4}$ **H** $\frac{5}{8}$

G $\frac{3}{8}$ **J** $\frac{7}{8}$

---

7 One fourth of the class participated in the contest. If there are 20 students in the class, how many participated in the contest?

A 1

B 4

C 5

D 7

---

8 What mixed number represents the shaded portion of this model?

Explain How did you find your answer?

Safe Site

Internet Test Prep
Visit **www.eduplace.com/kids/mhm**
for more *Test Prep Practice.*

349

Add With Like Denominators

You will learn how to add fractions and mixed numbers with like denominators.

Learn About It

Amanda's mother made a beautiful design on Amanda's jacket. She used $\frac{3}{8}$ yard of red cloth and $\frac{1}{8}$ yard of green cloth. What was the total length of cloth used to make the design?

Add. $\frac{3}{8} + \frac{1}{8} = \blacksquare$

Find $\frac{3}{8} + \frac{1}{8}$.

Step 1 Since the denominators are the same, add the numerators.

Then write the sum over the denominator.

$$\begin{array}{r} \frac{3}{8} \\ + \frac{1}{8} \\ \hline \frac{4}{8} \end{array}$$

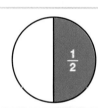

Step 2 Write the sum in **simplest form**.

$$\begin{array}{r} \frac{3}{8} \\ + \frac{1}{8} \\ \hline \frac{4}{8} - \frac{4 \div 4}{8 \div 4} = \frac{1}{2} \end{array}$$

Solution: Amanda's mother used $\frac{1}{2}$ yard of cloth.

You can use what you know about adding fractions to add mixed numbers.

Find $2\frac{3}{5} + 1\frac{4}{5}$.

Step 1 Add the fractions.

$$\begin{array}{r} 2\frac{3}{5} \\ + 1\frac{4}{5} \\ \hline \frac{7}{5} \end{array}$$

Think: $\frac{3+4}{5}$

Step 2 Add the whole numbers.

$$\begin{array}{r} 2\frac{3}{5} \\ + 1\frac{4}{5} \\ \hline 3\frac{7}{5} \end{array}$$

Think: $2 + 1 = 3$

Step 3 Write the sum in simplest form.

$$\begin{array}{r} 2\frac{3}{5} \\ + 1\frac{4}{5} \\ \hline 3\frac{7}{5} = 3 + 1\frac{2}{5} = 4\frac{2}{5} \end{array}$$

Explain Your Thinking

▶ How can the diagram at the right be used to explain how $3\frac{7}{5}$ can be written in simplest form?

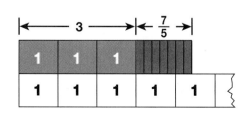

Standards | NS **2.1**, AF **1.1**

Guided Practice

Add. Write each sum in simplest form.

1. $\frac{3}{7} + \frac{1}{7}$
2. $\frac{7}{10} + \frac{1}{10}$
3. $\frac{3}{8} + \frac{5}{8}$
4. $3\frac{11}{12} + 1\frac{5}{12}$
5. $6\frac{3}{8} + 2\frac{3}{8}$
6. $7\frac{2}{5} + 1\frac{1}{5}$

Ask Yourself

• Is the sum in simplest form? If not, what should I do?

Independent Practice

Add. Write each sum in simplest form.

7. $\frac{2}{9}$
    $+ \frac{4}{9}$

8. $2\frac{3}{5}$
    $+ 4\frac{1}{5}$

9. $7\frac{4}{7}$
    $+ 2\frac{2}{7}$

10. $\frac{2}{5}$
    $+ \frac{1}{5}$

11. $3\frac{1}{4}$
    $+ 2\frac{1}{4}$

12. $\frac{4}{12} + \frac{5}{12}$
13. $\frac{3}{10} + \frac{7}{10}$
14. $\frac{1}{6} + \frac{1}{6}$
15. $\frac{4}{9} + \frac{7}{9}$

16. $6\frac{3}{8} + 2\frac{1}{8}$
17. $2\frac{2}{5} + 4\frac{2}{5}$
18. $5\frac{2}{3} + 2\frac{1}{3}$
19. $7\frac{3}{8} + 4\frac{7}{8}$

Problem Solving • Reasoning

20. Justin bought $\frac{3}{8}$ yard of green cloth and $\frac{3}{8}$ yard of blue cloth to make a design on his jacket. What was the total length of cloth he bought?

21. One day, a store sold $6\frac{1}{4}$ yards of blue cloth. If the store sold $5\frac{1}{4}$ yards more red cloth than blue cloth, how many yards of red cloth did it sell?

22. **Write About It** Lee has $\frac{3}{4}$ yard of ribbon. Does she have enough to outline two pockets that take $\frac{1}{8}$ yard each? Explain your thinking.

SOCIAL STUDIES
Kuna Indian women of Panama make molas out of layers of colorful cloth.

If 2 colors are used to make a mola, what combinations of red, black and orange cloth can you use to make a mola?

Mixed Review • Test Prep

Write an algebraic expression for each. *(pages 78–80, 132–134)*

23. 3 more than p
24. 5 times r

25. 2 less than m
26. n divided by 3

27. What is the sum of $45.62 and $17.35? *(pages 56–57)*

   A $62.97   **B** $52.97   **C** $32.33   **D** $28.27

Subtract With Like Denominators

LESSON 10

You will learn how to subtract fractions and mixed numbers with like denominators.

Learn About It

Cora is training for the Run for Hunger race. Each morning she stretches for $\frac{1}{4}$ hour and runs for $\frac{3}{4}$ hour. How much more time does she spend running than stretching each morning?

Subtract. $\quad \frac{3}{4} - \frac{1}{4} = \blacksquare$

Find $\frac{3}{4} - \frac{1}{4}$.

Step 1 Since the denominators are the same, subtract the numerators. Then write the difference over the denominator.

$$\begin{array}{r} \frac{3}{4} \\ - \frac{1}{4} \\ \hline \frac{2}{4} \end{array}$$

1 whole

$$\frac{2}{4}$$

Step 2 Write the difference in simplest form.

$$\begin{array}{r} \frac{3}{4} \\ - \frac{1}{4} \\ \hline \frac{2}{4} \end{array} = \frac{2 \div 2}{4 \div 2} = \frac{1}{2}$$

$$\frac{1}{2}$$

Solution: Cora spends $\frac{1}{2}$ hour more running than stretching.

You can use what you know about subtracting fractions to subtract mixed numbers.

Find $5\frac{7}{8} - 2\frac{3}{8}$.

Step 1 Subtract the fractions.

$$\begin{array}{r} 5\frac{7}{8} \\ - 2\frac{3}{8} \\ \hline \frac{4}{8} \end{array}$$

Think:
$$\frac{7-3}{8} = \frac{4}{8}$$

Step 2 Subtract the whole numbers.

$$\begin{array}{r} 5\frac{7}{8} \\ - 2\frac{3}{8} \\ \hline 3\frac{4}{8} \end{array}$$

Step 3 Write the difference in simplest form.

$$\begin{array}{r} 5\frac{7}{8} \\ - 2\frac{3}{8} \\ \hline 3\frac{4}{8} = 3\frac{4 \div 4}{8 \div 4} = 3\frac{1}{2} \end{array}$$

Solution: $5\frac{7}{8} - 2\frac{3}{8} = 3\frac{1}{2}$

Standards | Extends Grade 4 Standards

Explain Your Thinking

▶ Describe two ways to find $\frac{15}{4} - \frac{9}{4}$.

Guided Practice

Subtract. Write each difference in simplest form.

1. $\frac{7}{9} - \frac{5}{9}$

2. $\frac{4}{7} - \frac{2}{7}$

3. $\frac{4}{5} - \frac{1}{5}$

4. $2\frac{3}{4} - 1\frac{1}{4}$

5. $6\frac{7}{8} - 4\frac{1}{8}$

6. $7\frac{6}{8} - 4\frac{2}{8}$

Ask Yourself
• Is the difference in simplest form? If not, what should I do?

Independent Practice

Subtract. Write each difference in simplest form.

7. $\begin{array}{r} \frac{3}{5} \\ -\frac{2}{5} \end{array}$

8. $\begin{array}{r} 3\frac{5}{8} \\ -1\frac{1}{8} \end{array}$

9. $\begin{array}{r} 6\frac{9}{10} \\ -4\frac{4}{10} \end{array}$

10. $\begin{array}{r} 5\frac{4}{9} \\ -2\frac{2}{9} \end{array}$

11. $\begin{array}{r} \frac{7}{8} \\ -\frac{4}{8} \end{array}$

12. $\frac{7}{12} - \frac{4}{12}$

13. $\frac{6}{7} - \frac{4}{7}$

14. $\frac{5}{8} - \frac{5}{8}$

15. $\frac{7}{9} - \frac{3}{9}$

16. $2\frac{3}{4} - 1\frac{1}{4}$

17. $7\frac{8}{9} - 2\frac{4}{9}$

18. $7\frac{3}{4} - 1\frac{3}{4}$

19. $5\frac{7}{8} - 4\frac{5}{8}$

Problem Solving • Reasoning

Use Data Use the table for Problems 20–21.

20. How many more miles did Cora run on Day 5 than on Day 2?

21. In all how many miles did Cora run during the first three days of training?

22. **Money** Twelve people signed up to donate $1.25 for each mile Cora runs in the race. How much money will Cora raise if she runs 3 miles?

Cora's Training Record	
Day	**Distance Run**
1	1 mile
2	$1\frac{1}{4}$ miles
3	$1\frac{3}{4}$ miles
4	2 miles
5	$2\frac{3}{4}$ miles

Mixed Review • Test Prep

Add or subtract. *(pages 56–62, 68–69)*

23. $23.25 - $11.78

24. $32.40 + $8.35

25. $10.00 - $3.58

26 What is the product of $4.35 and 12? *(pages 198–199)*

   A $5.22   **B** $52.20   **C** $522   **D** $5,220

Extra Practice See Set G on page 360.   **353**

Problem-Solving Application: Use Fractions

You will learn how to use fractions to solve problems.

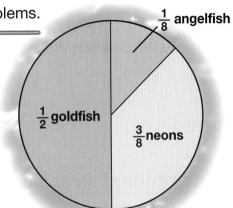

$\frac{1}{8}$ angelfish

$\frac{1}{2}$ goldfish

$\frac{3}{8}$ neons

Sometimes you can use fractions and a circle graph to show a total amount divided into parts.

Problem Cameron has 16 fish in his aquarium. He made a circle graph to show what fractions of the fish are goldfish, neons, and angelfish. How many more goldfish than angelfish are there?

Understand

What is the question?

How many more goldfish than angelfish are there?

What do you know?

• Cameron has 16 fish.

• $\frac{1}{2}$ of the fish are goldfish.

• $\frac{3}{8}$ of the fish are neons.

• $\frac{1}{8}$ of the fish are angelfish.

Plan

How can you find the answer?

You can use the fractions on the circle graph to find the number of goldfish and angelfish. Then subtract to find the difference.

Solve

Find the number of goldfish and angelfish.

$\frac{1}{2}$ of 16 = 8 ←— number of goldfish

$\frac{1}{8}$ of 16 = 2 ←— number of angelfish

Then subtract. $8 - 2 = 6$

There are 6 more goldfish than angelfish.

Look Back

Look back at the problem.

How can you use the circle graph to find the total number of neons and angelfish in Cameron's aquarium?

Standards SDP **1.0** MR **1.0, 1.1, 1.2, 2.0, 2.3, 3.2**

Guided Practice

Use the circle graph on page 354 to solve each problem.

Remember:
► Understand
► Plan
► Solve
► Look Back

1 The number of fish that Ashley has is two more than the number of neons that Cameron has. How many fish does Ashley have?

Think: What part of the circle is neons?

2 Cameron just added 8 fish to his aquarium but his circle graph is the same. How many angelfish are in the aquarium now?

Think: How many fish are in Cameron's aquarium now?

Choose a Strategy

Solve. Use these or other strategies.

Problem-Solving Strategies

• **Use Logical Thinking** • **Work Backward** • **Draw a Picture** • **Make a Table**

3 Timothy helps out at his father's pet shop 6 hours a week. Each week he spends $\frac{2}{3}$ of his time cleaning fish tanks and $\frac{1}{3}$ of his time feeding the fish. How many hours does Timothy spend on each task?

4 Liz put layers of red, blue, and green rocks in her aquarium. The red rocks are not on the bottom. The blue rocks are not in the middle. The top layer is not red or blue. In what order are the rocks layered?

5 After buying fish food for $3.25 and a fish net for $2.25, Cameron had $4.50 left. How much money did Cameron have before he bought the food and the net?

6 A pet store sells neons for $3 each and catfish for $2 each. If Norton buys the same number of each kind of fish, what is the largest number of each he can buy with $20?

7 A large fish tank holds 24 gallons of water. A small tank holds $\frac{2}{3}$ as much water as the large tank. How much water does a small tank hold?

8 There are 3 types of fish in Trisha's aquarium. Four of the fish are neons, $\frac{1}{5}$ are guppies, and $\frac{2}{5}$ are mollies. How many fish are in Trisha's aquarium?

Quick ✓ Check

Check Your Understanding of Lessons 9–11

Find each sum or difference in simplest form.
Use fraction pieces to help you if you wish.

1. $\frac{1}{5} + \frac{3}{5}$

2. $\frac{7}{10} - \frac{3}{10}$

3. $3\frac{1}{6} + 5\frac{1}{6}$

4. $6\frac{7}{12} - 2\frac{5}{12}$

5. $\begin{aligned} &\quad\ \frac{4}{6} \\ &+\ \frac{1}{6} \\ \hline \end{aligned}$

6. $\begin{aligned} &\quad\ \frac{7}{9} \\ &+\ \frac{4}{9} \\ \hline \end{aligned}$

7. $\begin{aligned} &\ 5\frac{7}{8} \\ &-\ 3\frac{3}{8} \\ \hline \end{aligned}$

8. $\begin{aligned} &\ 2\frac{3}{7} \\ &+\ 3\frac{2}{7} \\ \hline \end{aligned}$

Use the circle graph to solve each problem.

9. Jesse has 24 colored tiles. He made a circle graph to show what part of the tiles are red, green, and blue. How many more green tiles does he have than red tiles?

10. Suppose Jesse replaces the blue tiles with red tiles. How many red tiles would he have then?

Jesse's Tiles

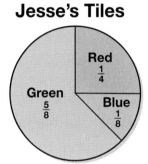

How did you do?

If you had difficulty with any items in the Quick Check, you can use the following pages for review and extra practice.

California Standards	Items	Review These Pages	Do These Extra Practice Items
Extends Grade 4 standards	1–8	pages 350–353	Sets F, G, page 360
Statistics, Data, Probability: **1.0** Math Reasoning: **1.1, 2.3, 2.4, 3.1, 3.2,**	9–10	pages 354–355	7–9, page 361

Test Prep • Cumulative Review

Maintaining the Standards

Choose the letter of the correct answer.

1 Which number is a prime number?

A 7

B 25

C 39

D 51

2 What fraction of the stars are shaded?

F $\frac{1}{4}$ **H** $\frac{3}{4}$

G $\frac{2}{3}$ **J** $\frac{4}{5}$

Use the number line to answer Questions 3–4.

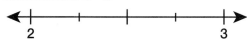

3 Which mixed number is greater than 2, but less than $2\frac{1}{2}$?

A $1\frac{1}{4}$ **C** $2\frac{1}{4}$

B $2\frac{1}{2}$ **D** $2\frac{3}{4}$

4 What mixed number is halfway between 2 and 3?

F $2\frac{1}{4}$

G $2\frac{1}{2}$

H $2\frac{2}{3}$

J $2\frac{3}{4}$

5 What fraction represents the shaded portion of this model?

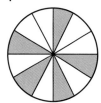

A $\frac{1}{4}$ **C** $\frac{5}{12}$

B $\frac{1}{3}$ **D** $\frac{5}{8}$

Use the models to answer Questions 6–7.

Model A   Model B

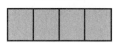

6 If $\frac{1}{2}$ of model A was shaded, how many parts would be shaded?

F 1

G 2

H 3

J 4

7 If $\frac{1}{2}$ of model B was shaded, how many circles would be shaded?

A 1

B 2

C 3

D 4

8 **Explain** What is the sum of $\frac{1}{2}$ and $\frac{1}{4}$? Support your answer by using a drawing.

Extra Practice

Set A (Lesson 1, pages 324–325)

Write the fraction for the shaded parts.

1.

2.

3.

Draw a picture to show each fraction.

4. $\frac{3}{7}$

5. $\frac{1}{8}$

6. $\frac{2}{2}$

7. $\frac{7}{8}$

8. $\frac{2}{3}$

9. $\frac{8}{9}$

10. $\frac{6}{8}$

11. $\frac{4}{4}$

12. $\frac{1}{9}$

13. $\frac{9}{10}$

14. $\frac{3}{5}$

15. $\frac{4}{10}$

Set B (Lesson 2, pages 326–327)

Find the fractional part of each number.

1.

$\frac{2}{4}$ of 16

2.

$\frac{2}{3}$ of 21

3.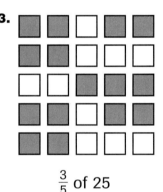

$\frac{3}{5}$ of 25

4. $\frac{1}{3}$ of 15

5. $\frac{3}{5}$ of 10

6. $\frac{4}{7}$ of 14

7. $\frac{1}{4}$ of 28

Set C (Lesson 4, pages 330–332)

Multiply or divide to find each equivalent fraction.

1. $\frac{1}{5} = \frac{1 \times 2}{5 \times 2} = \frac{\blacksquare}{\blacksquare}$

2. $\frac{6}{24} = \frac{6 \div 6}{24 \div 6} = \frac{\blacksquare}{\blacksquare}$

3. $\frac{3}{8} = \frac{3 \times 3}{8 \times \blacksquare} = \frac{\blacksquare}{\blacksquare}$

4. $\frac{8}{14} = \frac{8 \div \blacksquare}{14 \div 2} = \frac{\blacksquare}{\blacksquare}$

5. $\frac{4}{10} = \frac{4 \times 2}{10 \times \blacksquare} = \frac{\blacksquare}{\blacksquare}$

6. $\frac{12}{16} = \frac{12 \div 4}{16 \div \blacksquare} = \frac{\blacksquare}{\blacksquare}$

Write each fraction in simplest form.

7. $\frac{2}{16}$

8. $\frac{6}{12}$

9. $\frac{4}{20}$

10. $\frac{3}{9}$

11. $\frac{10}{15}$

Extra Practice

Set D *(Lesson 6, pages 338–340)*

Compare. Write > , < , or = for each ⬤.
Draw number lines to help you if you wish.

1.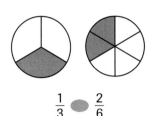
$\frac{1}{3}$ ⬤ $\frac{2}{6}$

2.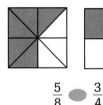
$\frac{5}{8}$ ⬤ $\frac{3}{4}$

3.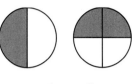
$\frac{1}{2}$ ⬤ $\frac{2}{4}$

4. $\frac{1}{2}$ ⬤ $\frac{1}{6}$

5. $\frac{2}{3}$ ⬤ $\frac{3}{9}$

6. $\frac{5}{8}$ ⬤ $\frac{1}{2}$

7. $\frac{2}{3}$ ⬤ $\frac{3}{4}$

8. $\frac{5}{9}$ ⬤ $\frac{7}{9}$

9. $\frac{2}{5}$ ⬤ $\frac{3}{15}$

10. $\frac{11}{12}$ ⬤ $\frac{3}{4}$

11. $\frac{5}{5}$ ⬤ $\frac{6}{6}$

Order each group of fractions from least to greatest.

12. $\frac{4}{10}$ $\frac{7}{10}$ $\frac{9}{10}$

13. $\frac{6}{10}$ $\frac{1}{10}$ $\frac{1}{5}$

14. $\frac{1}{2}$ $\frac{1}{6}$ $\frac{4}{6}$

15. $\frac{3}{4}$ $\frac{2}{8}$ $\frac{2}{4}$

16. $\frac{1}{8}$ $\frac{3}{8}$ $\frac{1}{4}$

17. $\frac{8}{9}$ $\frac{5}{18}$ $\frac{4}{9}$

18. $\frac{2}{3}$ $\frac{7}{15}$ $\frac{5}{15}$

19. $\frac{6}{12}$ $\frac{1}{12}$ $\frac{1}{3}$

Set E *(Lesson 7, pages 342–345)*

Write an improper fraction and a mixed number or a whole
number for each letter on the number line.

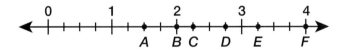

1. *B*

2. *D*

3. *A*

4. *F*

5. *C*

6. *E*

Write a mixed number or whole number for each
improper fraction.

7. $\frac{11}{3}$

8. $\frac{9}{2}$

9. $\frac{21}{6}$

10. $\frac{20}{3}$

11. $\frac{8}{4}$

12. $\frac{16}{5}$

Write an improper fraction for each mixed number.

13. $3\frac{3}{4}$

14. $4\frac{2}{4}$

15. $1\frac{5}{9}$

16. $2\frac{3}{7}$

17. $5\frac{2}{5}$

18. $3\frac{5}{6}$

Extra Practice

Set F *(Lesson 9, pages 350–351)*

Add. Write each sum in simplest form.

1. $\frac{1}{4}$
$+ \frac{2}{4}$

2. $1\frac{7}{9}$
$+ 4\frac{1}{9}$

3. $5\frac{3}{7}$
$+ 1\frac{2}{7}$

4. $4\frac{5}{8}$
$+ 2\frac{1}{8}$

5. $3\frac{1}{3}$
$+ 2\frac{1}{3}$

6. $4\frac{2}{6}$
$+ 3\frac{2}{6}$

7. $2\frac{1}{9}$
$+ 3\frac{2}{9}$

8. $8\frac{1}{4}$
$+ 1\frac{1}{4}$

9. $7\frac{3}{10}$
$+ 2\frac{2}{10}$

10. $6\frac{3}{5}$
$+ 2\frac{1}{5}$

11. $\frac{3}{5} + \frac{1}{5}$

12. $\frac{2}{9} + \frac{5}{9}$

13. $\frac{7}{12} + \frac{9}{12}$

14. $\frac{4}{10} + \frac{1}{10}$

15. $\frac{2}{6} + \frac{2}{6}$

16. $\frac{1}{8} + \frac{5}{8}$

17. $\frac{7}{9} + \frac{4}{9}$

18. $1\frac{2}{3} + 3\frac{1}{3}$

19. $2\frac{5}{8} + 1\frac{1}{8}$

20. $4\frac{2}{5} + 2\frac{2}{5}$

Set G *(Lesson 10, pages 352–353)*

Subtract. Write each difference in simplest form.

1. $\frac{3}{4}$
$- \frac{2}{4}$

2. $3\frac{7}{8}$
$- 1\frac{3}{8}$

3. $5\frac{3}{7}$
$- 1\frac{2}{7}$

4. $4\frac{5}{12}$
$- 3\frac{1}{12}$

5. $7\frac{5}{6}$
$- 2\frac{1}{6}$

6. $4\frac{3}{4}$
$- 3\frac{1}{4}$

7. $8\frac{6}{12}$
$- 6\frac{4}{12}$

8. $7\frac{8}{10}$
$- 5\frac{3}{10}$

9. $4\frac{8}{9}$
$- 2\frac{6}{9}$

10. $8\frac{5}{6}$
$- 7\frac{1}{6}$

11. $\frac{3}{5} - \frac{1}{5}$

12. $\frac{8}{9} - \frac{5}{9}$

13. $\frac{11}{12} - \frac{3}{12}$

14. $\frac{14}{16} - \frac{6}{16}$

15. $\frac{5}{6} - \frac{4}{6}$

16. $\frac{7}{8} - \frac{5}{8}$

17. $3\frac{7}{9} - 1\frac{4}{9}$

18. $5\frac{2}{3} - 3\frac{2}{3}$

19. $2\frac{5}{8} - 1\frac{1}{8}$

20. $4\frac{4}{5} - 2\frac{1}{5}$

Extra Practice • Problem Solving

Solve. Use the Draw a Picture strategy.

(Lesson 5, pages 334–335)

1 After Shelly spent $\frac{1}{2}$ of her money on a hot dog, $\frac{1}{6}$ on a drink, and $1 for popcorn, she had no money left. How much money did Shelly spend altogether?

2 Ted has a stamp collection. $\frac{1}{5}$ of his stamps are from Canada, $\frac{1}{5}$ are from Spain, and 15 are from other countries. How many stamps are in his collection?

3 Ann's art class worked on projects. $\frac{3}{8}$ of the class did paintings, $\frac{1}{4}$ did charcoal sketches, and 12 made pottery. How many students are there in Ann's art class?

4 After Ryan spent $\frac{1}{3}$ of his money on a CD and $\frac{1}{6}$ of it on a poster, he had $15.00 left. How much money did Ryan spend on the CD and poster?

Solve. Explain why your answer is reasonable.

(Lesson 8, pages 346–347)

5 Donna has $11 to buy notebooks. Each notebook costs $3. How many notebooks can she buy? How much money will she have left?

6 Jen has 7 sandwiches to share equally with 3 friends. If each person receives the same amount, how many sandwiches will each of the four persons receive?

Use the circle graph at the right to solve each problem.

(Lesson 11, pages 354–355)

7 If Carl has 18 coins in his pocket, how many of them are pennies?

8 How many more quarters than dimes does Carl have in his pocket?

9 Carl buys a new pen for $1.27. How much money does he have left over in his pocket?

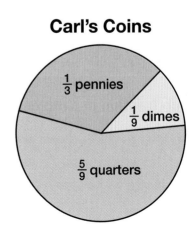

Carl's Coins

$\frac{1}{3}$ pennies

$\frac{1}{9}$ dimes

$\frac{5}{9}$ quarters

Chapter Review

Reviewing Vocabulary

Answer each question.

1. Write a fraction that has 3 in the numerator and 7 in the denominator.

2. Write a fraction that is equivalent to $\frac{3}{4}$.

3. Why is it easier to compare fractions if they have like denominators?

4. How would you use division to write $\frac{4}{8}$ in simplest form?

5. What are the two parts to every mixed number?

Reviewing Concepts and Skills

Draw a picture to show each fraction. *(Lesson 1, pages 324–325)*

6. $\frac{3}{5}$ 7. $\frac{6}{7}$ 8. $\frac{8}{8}$ 9. $\frac{0}{9}$ 10. $\frac{1}{3}$ 11. $\frac{3}{4}$

Find the fractional part of each number.

(Lesson 2, pages 326–327)

12. $\frac{3}{5}$ of 15 13. $\frac{1}{4}$ of 8 14. $\frac{1}{3}$ of 21 15. $\frac{3}{4}$ of 16

16. $\frac{2}{9}$ of 18 17. $\frac{2}{3}$ of 24 18. $\frac{7}{10}$ of 10 19. $\frac{1}{2}$ of 14

Multiply or divide to find each equivalent fraction.

(Lesson 4, pages 330–332)

20. $\frac{6}{12} = \frac{6 \div 6}{12 \div 6} = \frac{\blacksquare}{\blacksquare}$

21. $\frac{8}{9} = \frac{8 \times 2}{9 \times 2} = \frac{\blacksquare}{\blacksquare}$

22. $\frac{3}{4} = \frac{3 \times 3}{4 \times \blacksquare} = \frac{\blacksquare}{\blacksquare}$

23. $\frac{8}{24} = \frac{8 \div \blacksquare}{24 \div 8} = \frac{\blacksquare}{\blacksquare}$

24. $\frac{3}{4} = \frac{3 \times \blacksquare}{4 \times 4} = \frac{\blacksquare}{\blacksquare}$

25. $\frac{12}{20} = \frac{12 \div 4}{20 \div \blacksquare} = \frac{\blacksquare}{\blacksquare}$

Write each fraction in simplest form.

26. $\frac{8}{12}$ 27. $\frac{3}{12}$ 28. $\frac{6}{18}$ 29. $\frac{2}{8}$ 30. $\frac{9}{15}$

Compare. Write $>$, $<$, or $=$ for each $\bullet$. *(Lesson 6, pages 338–340)*

31. $\frac{3}{10} \bullet \frac{7}{20}$ 32. $\frac{5}{25} \bullet \frac{1}{5}$ 33. $\frac{5}{8} \bullet \frac{6}{16}$ 34. $\frac{12}{18} \bullet \frac{5}{9}$

Write an improper fraction and a mixed number or whole number for each letter on the number line. *(Lesson 7, pages 342–345)*

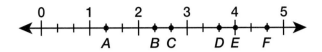

35. *E* **36.** *A* **37.** *B* **38.** *F* **39.** *D* **40.** *C*

Add or subtract. Write each sum or difference in simplest form. *(Lessons 9 –10, pages 350–353)*

41. $\frac{2}{7} + \frac{3}{7}$ **42.** $\frac{7}{16} + \frac{3}{16}$ **43.** $3\frac{2}{11} + 1\frac{8}{11}$ **44.** $6\frac{2}{3} + 2\frac{1}{3}$

45. $2\frac{5}{7} - 1\frac{1}{7}$ **46.** $\frac{6}{10} - \frac{1}{10}$ **47.** $7\frac{4}{5} - 5\frac{2}{5}$ **48.** $5\frac{3}{4} - 1\frac{3}{4}$

Solve. Use the circle graph to solve Problem 49.

49. Ellen has 24 ceramic figures. How many more ceramic cats does she have than dogs?

50. After Jan spent $\frac{2}{5}$ of her money on a cage, $\frac{1}{5}$ of her money on rabbit food, and $10 on a rabbit, she had no money left. How much did she spend altogether?

51. Steve has $19 to buy paints for art class. Each jar of paint costs $2. How many jars can Steve buy? How much money will he have left?

Ellen's Ceramic Figures

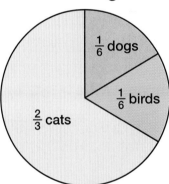

$\frac{1}{6}$ dogs

$\frac{1}{6}$ birds

$\frac{2}{3}$ cats

 Brain Teasers Math Reasoning

How Many Ways?

Choose from 2, 3, 4, 6, 8, or 9 to fill the blanks. How many ways can you fill in the blanks to make the equation true? (You can use the same number twice if you wish.)

$$\frac{\blacksquare}{\blacksquare} = \frac{1}{\blacksquare}$$

Half and Half

List ten words or names where $\frac{1}{2}$ of the letters are vowels.

Safe Site

Internet Brain Teasers
Visit **www.eduplace.com/kids/mhm**
for more *Brain Teasers*.

Chapter Test

Write the fraction for the shaded part.

1.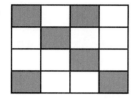

2.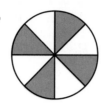

3.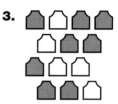

Find the fractional part of each number.

4. $\frac{1}{4}$ of 8

5. $\frac{1}{3}$ of 9

6. $\frac{5}{6}$ of 12

7. $\frac{3}{8}$ of 16

Write each fraction in simplest form.

8. $\frac{9}{27}$

9. $\frac{4}{8}$

10. $\frac{18}{20}$

11. $\frac{9}{12}$

Compare. Write > , < , or = for each ●.

12. $\frac{3}{9}$ ● $\frac{2}{3}$

13. $\frac{5}{6}$ ● $\frac{10}{12}$

14. $\frac{7}{10}$ ● $\frac{3}{5}$

15. $\frac{1}{2}$ ● $\frac{5}{12}$

Multiply or divide to find each equivalent fraction.

16. $\frac{3}{4} = \frac{3 \times 3}{4 \times 3} = \frac{\blacksquare}{\blacksquare}$

17. $\frac{6}{8} = \frac{6 \div \blacksquare}{8 \div 2} = \frac{\blacksquare}{\blacksquare}$

18. $\frac{3}{6} = \frac{3 \times \blacksquare}{6 \times 4} = \frac{\blacksquare}{\blacksquare}$

Write a mixed number or a whole number for each improper fraction.

19. $\frac{14}{2}$

20. $\frac{8}{5}$

21. $\frac{3}{1}$

22. $\frac{11}{3}$

23. $\frac{16}{4}$

Add or subtract. Write each sum or difference in simplest form.

24. $\frac{11}{2} + \frac{3}{2}$

25. $\frac{1}{6} + \frac{5}{6}$

26. $3\frac{1}{8} + 5\frac{5}{8}$

27. $4\frac{2}{15} + 3\frac{7}{15}$

28. $\frac{7}{16} - \frac{3}{16}$

29. $\frac{19}{20} - \frac{3}{20}$

30. $5\frac{7}{8} - 2\frac{1}{8}$

31. $8\frac{2}{3} - 5\frac{1}{3}$

Solve.

32. Cory made sandwiches for a picnic. $\frac{1}{6}$ were cheese sandwiches, $\frac{1}{3}$ were peanut butter sandwiches, and 9 were ham sandwiches. How many sandwiches did Cory make altogether?

33. Five children are going to the movies with Beth's mother. Children's tickets cost $4 each. Adults' tickets cost $8 each. Beth's mother has $30. How much money will she have left over after buying the tickets?

 Write About It

Solve each problem. Use correct math vocabulary to explain your thinking.

1. Alan added the improper fractions shown on the right.

   a. What did Alan do wrong?

   b. How would you tell Alan to correct his mistake?

   c. Solve the problem correctly.

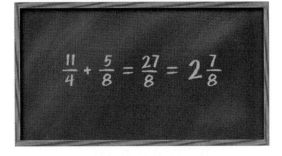

$$\frac{11}{4} + \frac{5}{8} = \frac{27}{8} = 2\frac{7}{8}$$

2. Dan helps his father with yard work a total of 12 hours every week. He spends $\frac{1}{6}$ of his time raking leaves and $\frac{1}{3}$ of his time mowing.

   a. How many hours does Dan rake leaves?

   b. What portion of Dan's time is left for other yard chores after the raking and mowing are done? Write your answer as a fraction.

   c. How many hours does Dan spend doing other yard work with his father each week?

Dan's Yard Chores

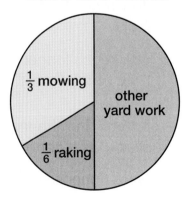

$\frac{1}{3}$ mowing

other yard work

$\frac{1}{6}$ raking

Another Look

Use the map to answer the questions. The Pond Trail and the Forest Trail are paved paths for bicycling or inline skating. Give answers in simplest form.

Pond Trail
$2\frac{3}{4}$ miles

Forest Trail
$3\frac{1}{4}$ miles

1. A lap is one time around a trail. How far would you go if you made

   a. 2 laps of the Pond Trail?

   b. 2 laps of the Forest Trail?

   c. A "figure-8" of 1 lap of the Pond Trail and 1 lap of the Forest Trail?

2. a. How much longer is the Forest Trail than the Pond Trail?

   b. How much longer are 2 laps of the Pond Trail than 1 lap of the Forest Trail?

3. **Look Back** Put the lengths of the three answers from problem 1 in order from least to greatest.

4. **Analyze** Suppose you want to go a whole number of miles. What is the least number of whole laps of the Pond Trail you would have to make?

Enrichment

Fractions and Division

A fraction is a way to show division.
Think about the improper fraction $\frac{12}{6}$ and
the division example $12 \div 6$.

- **You can think of the fraction bar as a division sign.**

  $\frac{12}{6}$ means the same as $12 \div 6$ and $6\overline{)12}$.

- **You can think of the division of the two whole numbers as a fraction.**

  $6\overline{)12} = 12 \div 6 = \frac{12}{6} = 2$.

Now think about the fraction $\frac{6}{12}$ and the division example $6 \div 12$.

- **You can still think of the fraction bar as a division sign.**

  $\frac{6}{12}$ means the same as $6 \div 12$ and $12\overline{)6}$.

- **You can still think of division of two whole numbers as a fraction
  even if you are dividing a lesser number by a greater number.**

  $12\overline{)6} = 6 \div 12 = \frac{6}{12} = \frac{1}{2}$

**That is why you can write the answer to a division problem as a
mixed number instead of a quotient with a remainder.**

  $\frac{15}{6} = 15 \div 6 = 6\overline{)15} = 2R3 = 2\frac{3}{6} = 2\frac{1}{2}$

Try These

Write each division example as a fraction.

1. $3 \div 9$ **2.** $4 \div 6$ **3.** $8 \div 16$ **4.** $5 \div 25$ **5.** $9 \div 12$

Divide. Write each answer as a mixed number.

6. $7\overline{)23}$ **7.** $4\overline{)31}$ **8.** $6\overline{)40}$ **9.** $9\overline{)79}$ **10.** $8\overline{)68}$

Explain Your Thinking

Write $\frac{23}{7}$ as a mixed number. Is your answer the
same as for Exercise 6? Explain why or why not.

Standards   NS **1.5** MR **3.2, 3.3**

CHAPTER

Decimals

Why Learn About Decimals?

Another way to write a fraction is as a decimal. You can calculate with decimals just as you do with whole numbers. You can use decimals to write dollars and cents.

When you use information from labels on foods that show weight and price, you are using decimals.

These girls are competing in a race. Someone is using a stopwatch to measure the time to the nearest tenth of a second that it takes for the winner to finish the race.

Reviewing Vocabulary

Understanding math language helps you become a successful problem solver. Here are some math vocabulary words you should know.

round   to express a number to the nearest ten, hundred, thousand, and so on

estimate   to find an approximate answer rather than an exact answer

tenth   one of ten equal parts of a whole

hundredth   one of one hundred equal parts of a whole

decimal   a number with one or more digits to the right of the decimal point

decimal point   a symbol used to separate ones and tenths in a decimal

Reading Words and Symbols

When you read mathematics, sometimes you read only words, sometimes you read words and symbols, and sometimes you read only symbols.

You can write fractions that have denominators of 10 or 100 as decimals.

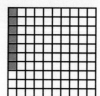

▶ Three tenths is shaded.

▶ $\frac{3}{10}$ is shaded.

▶ 0.3 is shaded.

▶ Seven hundredths is shaded.

▶ $\frac{7}{100}$ is shaded.

▶ 0.07 is shaded.

Try These

1. Write a fraction and a decimal to describe each model.

a.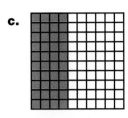

b.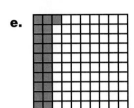

c.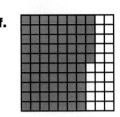

d.

e.

f.

2. Write each as a fraction and a decimal.

a. eight tenths   **b.** seventeen hundredths   **c.** five tenths

d. one tenth   **e.** thirty-one hundredths   **f.** ninety-nine hundredths

3. Tell whether the 9 is in the *ones, tenths,* or *hundredths* place.

a. 0.9   **b.** 0.19   **c.** 9.24   **d.** 0.96

e. 0.69   **f.** 9.82   **g.** 0.95   **h.** 0.09

Upcoming Vocabulary

Write About It Here is vocabulary you will learn in this chapter. Watch for it. Write its definition in your journal.

decimal equivalent

Fractions and Decimals

You will learn that tenths and hundredths can be shown in different ways.

Review
Vocabulary
decimal
decimal point

Learn About It

Use grid paper to learn how fractions and decimals are related.

Materials
grid paper
crayons

Matt has 100 soccer and football cards. He says that $\frac{7}{10}$ are soccer cards. He could also say that $\frac{70}{100}$ are soccer cards.

Soccer Cards $\frac{7}{10}$ or $\frac{70}{100}$ **Football Cards**

A fraction with a denominator of 10 can be written as a **decimal** in tenths.

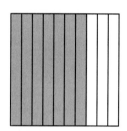

Fraction	Decimal	Words
$\frac{7}{10}$	0.7	seven tenths

decimal point

A fraction with a denominator of 100 can be written as a decimal in hundredths.

Fraction	Decimal	Words
$\frac{70}{100}$	0.70	seventy hundredths

Matt says that $\frac{3}{10}$ of his cards are football cards.

Follow these steps to show how many of Matt's sports cards are football cards.

Step 1 Draw a 10 × 10 square. Divide it into 10 equal parts. Color 3 of the parts to show 0.3.

Step 2 Draw another 10 × 10 square. Divide it into 100 equal parts. Color 30 of the parts to show 0.30.

Standards NS **1.0, 1.6, 1.7** MR **2.3**

Step 3 Compare the squares.

- Is the same area colored on both squares?
- How do you write $\frac{3}{10}$ as a decimal?
- How do you write 0.30 as a fraction?

30 of Matt's 100 cards are football cards.

Repeat Step 2 to show twenty-five hundredths.

- How do you write $\frac{25}{100}$ as a decimal?
- How do you write 0.25 as a fraction?

Try It Out

Write a fraction and a decimal to describe each model.

1.
2.
3.
4.

Use grid paper. Draw a model to show each fraction. Then write each fraction as a decimal.

5. $\frac{9}{10}$ **6.** $\frac{1}{10}$ **7.** $\frac{8}{10}$ **8.** $\frac{6}{10}$ **9.** $\frac{4}{10}$

10. $\frac{20}{100}$ **11.** $\frac{45}{100}$ **12.** $\frac{99}{100}$ **13.** $\frac{7}{100}$ **14.** $\frac{70}{100}$

Use grid paper. Draw a model to show each decimal. Then write each decimal as a fraction.

15. 0.3   **16.** 0.5   **17.** 0.7   **18.** 0.1   **19.** 0.8

20. 0.39   **21.** 0.83   **22.** 0.01   **23.** 0.76   **24.** 0.54

Write about it! Talk about it!

Use what you have learned to answer these questions.

25. How are 0.9 and 0.90 alike? How are they different?

26. Why is 0.1 greater than 0.01?

LESSON 2 Mixed Numbers and Decimals

You will learn how to read, write, and model amounts greater than 1.

Learn About It

Melanie painted tiles in her art class. Each tile had 10 equal sections. What decimal shows how many tiles Melanie painted?

There are different ways to show the amount of tiles Melanie painted.

You can use models.	You can write a mixed number.	You can write a decimal.
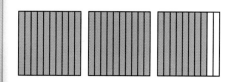	$2\frac{8}{10}$	ones . tenths 2 . 8 **Write:** 2.8 **Read:** two and eight tenths

Solution: Melanie painted 2.8 tiles.

Melanie also painted tiles that had 100 equal sections. She painted one whole tile and 44 sections of another tile. How many tiles did she paint?

You can use models.	You can write a mixed number.	You can write a decimal.
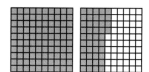	$1\frac{44}{100}$	ones . tenths hundredths 1 . 4 4 **Write:** 1.44 **Read:** one and forty-four hundredths

Solution: Melanie painted 1.44 tiles.

Another Example

Write $10\frac{3}{100}$ as a decimal.

10.03
↑
Write a zero in the tenths place.

Explain Your Thinking

▶ Why isn't $\frac{30}{100}$ a mixed number?

▶ Why is the value of each 4 in 1.44 different?

374 **Standards** NS **1.0, 1.6, 1.7** MR **2.3**

Guided Practice

Write a mixed number and a decimal to describe the shaded part in each problem.

1.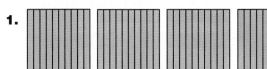

2.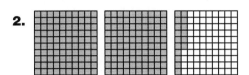

3.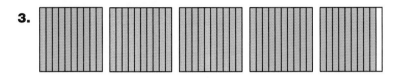

Ask Yourself

- What is the whole-number part?
- What should the numerator be? What should the denominator be?
- Should I write the answer in tenths or hundredths?

Write each mixed number as a decimal.

4. $5\frac{3}{10}$ 5. $9\frac{9}{10}$ 6. $26\frac{7}{10}$ 7. $11\frac{1}{10}$ 8. $15\frac{76}{100}$ 9. $12\frac{5}{100}$

Write each as a decimal.

10. seven tenths 11. twenty-two hundredths 12. one and five hundredths

Independent Practice

Write a mixed number and a decimal to describe the shaded part in each problem.

13. 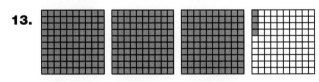 14.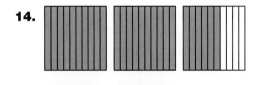

15. 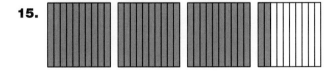 16.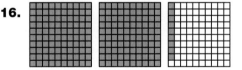

Write each mixed number as a decimal.

17. $1\frac{2}{10}$ 18. $7\frac{7}{100}$ 19. $4\frac{54}{100}$ 20. $5\frac{36}{100}$

21. $4\frac{7}{10}$ 22. $77\frac{77}{100}$ 23. $99\frac{9}{100}$ 24. $158\frac{85}{100}$

25. $34\frac{17}{100}$ 26. $19\frac{88}{100}$ 27. $175\frac{75}{100}$ 28. $202\frac{2}{100}$

Write each as a decimal.

29. sixty-two hundredths

30. five and seven tenths

31. forty and four hundredths

32. six and eleven hundredths

33. ninety-two and fourteen hundredths

34. fifty-six and eighty hundredths

35. three and three tenths

36. twenty-two and four tenths

Write the value of the digit 8 in each number.

37. 4.86   **38.** 6.08   **39.** 28.94   **40.** 856.25   **41.** 8,015.43

Problem Solving • Reasoning

Use Data Use the table for Problems 42–44.

42. Measurement On which day was there less than 1 inch of snow?

43. Analyze A basketball game was canceled on this day because eleven and five tenths inches of snow fell the day before. On which day of the week was the basketball game canceled?

44. Mark is trying to remember when he took his painting home. There was not much new snow the day he took it home, but about 9 inches of snow was already on the ground. There was a big storm the next day. On what day did Mark take his painting home?

Snowfall During a Week	
Day	**Inches of Snow**
Monday	4.0
Tuesday	4.5
Wednesday	0.5
Thursday	10.0
Friday	11.5

Mixed Review • Test Prep

Write the value of the digit 7 in each number. *(pages 4–5)*

45. 1,357   **46.** 37,280   **47.** 702,193   **48.** 153,276   **49.** 987,435

Choose the letter of the correct answer. *(pages 10–11)*

50 What is 15,495 rounded to the nearest thousand?

    A 20,000   **C** 15,500

    B 16,000   **D** 15,000

51 What is 15,495 rounded to the nearest ten?

    F 20,000   **H** 15,490

    G 15,500   **J** 15,000

It All Adds Up

Practice adding money to make whole dollars.

What You'll Need

- *stopwatch or timer*
- *Decimal Table like the one shown (Teaching Tool 9)*
- *two different spinners, like the ones shown (Teaching Tools 10 and 11)*

Players
4 or 6

Here's What to Do

1. Play in teams of 2 or 3. Each team chooses a spinner.

2. A player from the first team spins its spinner. The player has 1 minute to match the amount shown on the spinner with an amount on the table to make $1.00.

3. If the sum is $1.00, the team gets one point.

4. Teams and players take turns repeating Steps 1–3. The team with the most points wins.

$0.90	$0.33	$0.85	$0.51
$0.04	$0.70	$0.22	$0.62
$0.43	$0.01	$0.66	$0.29
$0.15	$0.31	$0.87	$0.50
$0.25	$0.94	$0.19	$0.48
$0.61	$0.76	$0.30	$0.03

Share Your Thinking
Is there anything you can do during the game to be ready for your turn?

Fractions and Decimal Equivalents

You will learn about fractions and decimals that name the same amount.

New
Vocabulary
decimal equivalent

Learn About It

Carrie says that $\frac{1}{2}$ of the grid is red. Jenny says that $\frac{5}{10}$ is red. Rosa says that 0.5 is red, and Marla says that 0.50 of the grid is red. Are all four girls correct?

A decimal that names the same amount as a fraction is the fraction's **decimal equivalent**.

To change a fraction to a decimal, find an equivalent fraction with a denominator of 10 or 100.

Different Ways to Show Equivalent Amounts

You can use models.

 $\frac{1}{2}$

 $\frac{5}{10}$ **or 0.5**

$$\frac{1}{2} = \frac{1 \times 5}{2 \times 5} = \frac{5}{10} = 0.5$$

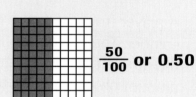 $\frac{50}{100}$ **or 0.50**

$$\frac{1}{2} = \frac{1 \times 50}{2 \times 50} = 0.50$$

You can use number lines.

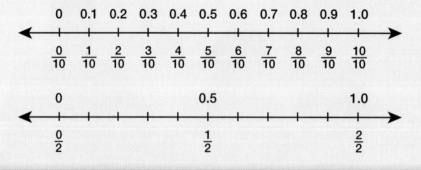

Solution: Yes, all four girls are correct.

Explain Your Thinking

▶ By what steps can you express the fraction $\frac{1}{5}$ as a decimal?

▶ How do models and number lines relate fractions and decimals?

Standards NS **1.0, 1.5, 1.6, 1.7** AF **2.2**

Guided Practice

Write a fraction and a decimal to describe the shaded part of each.

1.
2.
3.

Ask Yourself
- What part of the square is shaded?
- How do I write that amount as a fraction? as a decimal?

Independent Practice

Write a fraction and a decimal to describe the shaded part of each.

4.
5.
6.
7.
8.

9.
10.
11.
12.
13.

Problem Solving • Reasoning

Use the picture for Problems 14 and 15.

14. Write a decimal that tells the part of the total number of hats that is blue.

15. Write a decimal that tells the part of the total number of hats that is not blue.

16. **Analyze** Suppose there are 100 hats, and $\frac{4}{10}$ of them are not red. The rest are red. How many hats are red?

Mixed Review • Test Prep

Solve. (pages 56–63)

17. $532 + 253$
18. $937 - 432$
19. $7,384 - 6,103$
20. $6,294 + 14,295$

Choose the letter of the correct answer. (pages 56–63, 68–69)

21. $539 + 10,583$

   A 1,122   **C** 10,122

   B 2,122   **D** 11,122

22. $20,070 - 16,428$

   F 3,542   **H** 4,542

   G 3,642   **J** 4,652

Extra Practice See Set B on page 403.

Compare and Order Decimals

You will learn how to compare and order decimals.

Review
Vocabulary
tenths

Learn About It

At a diving meet, Sue earned these scores. What are her highest and lowest scores? What is the order of the scores from least to greatest?

4.6   3.9   4.8   4.0

Different Ways to Compare and Order Decimals

You can use a place-value chart.

- Line up the decimal points.
- Start comparing in the ones place.

  $3 < 4$ 3.9 is the least.

- Continue comparing in the **tenths** place.

  $8 > 6 > 0$ 4.8 is the greatest.

ones	tenths
4 .	6
3 .	9
4 .	8
4 .	0

$4.8 > 4.6 > 4.0 > 3.9$

You can use a number line.

- Locate all scores on a number line.

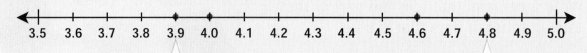
3.5 3.6 3.7 3.8 3.9 4.0 4.1 4.2 4.3 4.4 4.5 4.6 4.7 4.8 4.9 5.0

3.9 is the *least,* because it is farthest to the left.

4.8 is the *greatest,* because it is farthest to the right.

Solution: 4.8 is her highest score and 3.9 is her lowest score. The order of her scores is 3.9, 4.0, 4.6, 4.8.

Another Example

Different Number of Decimal Places

Order 2.59, 2.5, 2.12 from least to greatest.

- Line up the decimal points.
- Start comparing in the ones place.
- Continue until all are ordered.

ones	tenths	hundredths
2 .	5	9
2 .	5	0
2 .	1	2

2.5 = 2.50

same   1 < 5, so   0 < 9, so
2.12 is the least.   2.50 < 2.59

$2.12 < 2.5 < 2.59$

Explain Your Thinking

▶ How is comparing decimals like comparing whole numbers?

Standards | NS **1.0, 1.2, 1.9**   AF **1.0**

Guided Practice

Compare. Write >, <, or = for each ●.

1. 3.2 ● 3.6

2. 9.25 ● 8.93

3. 12.5 ● 12.50

Order the numbers from least to greatest.

4. 2.9   3.5   3.2   2.3

5. 4.7   4.78   4.73   4.67

Ask Yourself

• Where could each decimal be on a number line?

• What should I do if the numbers do not have the same number of decimal places?

Independent Practice

Compare. Write >, <, or = for each ●.

6. 7.8 ● 8.7

7. 24.6 ● 24.58

8. 6.9 ● 6.90

9. 21.03 ● 21.30

10. 4.9 ● 5.1

11. 86.4 ● 86.40

12. 17.25 ● 16.93

13. 13.53 ● 13.59

Order the numbers from greatest to least.

14. 2.13   2.14   2.24   2.42

15. 9.8   6.9   8.29   9.85

16. 4.73   4.82   4.38   4.9

17. 346.9   62.38   327.86

18. 32.87   87.3   82   28.32

19. 32.98   7   7.3   36.38   23.8

Problem Solving • Reasoning

20. Four teams have scores of 49.5, 50.0, 47.6, and 47.8. What is the order of the scores from least to greatest?

21. Analyze A decimal number with two digits is between 7.3 and 7.9. It is less than 7.89 and greater than 7.58. The digit in the tenths place is odd. What is the number?

22. Write Your Own Write a problem that requires comparing or ordering decimals. Give your problem to a classmate to solve.

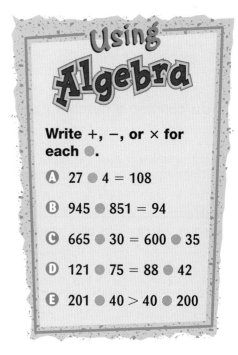

Using Algebra

Write +, −, or × for each ●.

Ⓐ 27 ● 4 = 108

Ⓑ 945 ● 851 = 94

Ⓒ 665 ● 30 = 600 ● 35

Ⓓ 121 ● 75 = 88 ● 42

Ⓔ 201 ● 40 > 40 ● 200

Mixed Review • Test Prep

Solve. *(pages 82–83)*

23. $x - 4 = 9$

24. $x + 3 = 12$

25. $15 - x = 4$

26. $12 + x = 29$

27 **Find *n*.** *(pages 74–77, 82–83)*

$$(5 \times 2) + (4 \times 3) = n$$

A 17   **B** 22   **C** 42   **D** 120

Compare and Order Fractions, Mixed Numbers, and Decimals

You will learn how to use a number line and place value to compare and order fractions, mixed numbers, and decimals.

Learn About It

Kayla and her mom are buying cheese. So far, the deli clerk has sliced Swiss cheese and American cheese. Kayla's mom still needs $1\frac{1}{2}$ pounds of Muenster cheese and $1\frac{1}{4}$ pounds of Cheddar cheese. What is the order of all the weights from least to greatest?

Different Ways to Compare and Order Numbers

You can use a place-value chart.

- Change the fractions to decimals.
- Write the decimals in hundredths.
- Compare.

	ones	tenths	hundredths
$1\frac{1}{2}$ lb	1	5	0
$1\frac{1}{4}$ lb	1	2	5
1.3 lb	1	3	0
1.60 lb	1	6	0

You can use a number line.

$1\frac{1}{4}$ $1\frac{1}{2}$

1	$1\frac{1}{10}$	$1\frac{2}{10}$	$1\frac{3}{10}$	$1\frac{4}{10}$	$1\frac{5}{10}$	$1\frac{6}{10}$	$1\frac{7}{10}$	$1\frac{8}{10}$	$1\frac{9}{10}$	2
1.00	1.10	1.20	1.30	1.40	1.50	1.60	1.70	1.80	1.90	2.00

1.3   1.60

Solution: The order of the weights from least to greatest is $1\frac{1}{4}$ lb, 1.3 lb, $1\frac{1}{2}$ lb, 1.60 lb.

Explain Your Thinking

▶ Would you use a number line or place value to order these numbers? Why?

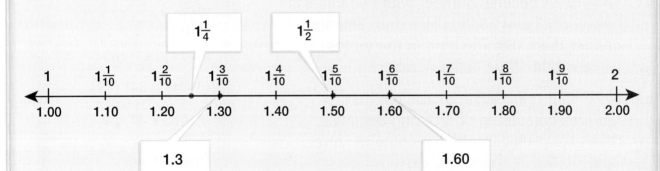

83.38   18.3   83.24

$52\frac{1}{10}$ 79.67 $36\frac{14}{100}$

Standards NS **1.0, 1.2 , 1.9** MR **3.2**

Guided Practice

Order the numbers from least to greatest.

1. 1.4 $1\frac{9}{10}$ 1.05 $1\frac{15}{100}$

2. $\frac{25}{100}$ 6.1 4.26 $5\frac{8}{10}$

3. 63.43 $68\frac{1}{10}$ 60.3 $68\frac{52}{100}$

4. $\frac{2}{5}$ $\frac{25}{100}$ 1.5 $1\frac{1}{10}$

Ask Yourself

• Should I start with the least number or the greatest number?

• Should I use a number line or place value?

Independent Practice

Order the numbers from greatest to least.

5. $1\frac{5}{10}$ 1.9 $1\frac{36}{100}$ 1.63

6. $15\frac{3}{100}$ 18.05 12.9 $19\frac{1}{10}$

7. 123.4 $123\frac{4}{100}$ $124\frac{3}{10}$ 123.34

8. 352.02 293.2 $352\frac{2}{10}$ $293\frac{2}{100}$

Problem Solving • Reasoning

Use the drawings for Problems 9–11.

 A B C D

3.2 lb.   3.7 lb.   3.45 lb.   3.25 lb.

9. May needs cheese for a party. Which package will give her the most cheese?

10. **Measurement** Suppose May wants to buy about $3\frac{1}{2}$ pounds of cheese. Which package is closest to $3\frac{1}{2}$ pounds?

11. **Money** The largest package costs \$11.21 and the smallest cost \$9.57. How much less does the smallest package cost than the largest package?

Math Is Everywhere!

HEALTH Cheese is made from the milk of cows, goats, sheep, and buffalo.

One fourth of Monterey Jack, 0.48 of Cheddar, and 0.45 of Muenster are fat. Write the cheeses in order from the one with the most fat to the one with the least.

Mixed Review • Test Prep

Measure each to the nearest half inch. *(pages 278–279)*

12. ├────────────┤

13. ├──────────────────┤

14 Which expression represents the product of a variable *n* and 9? *(pages 78–79, 132–135)*

A $9n$ **B** $9 - n$ **C** $9 + n$ **D** $\frac{n}{9}$

Extra Practice See Set D on page 404.

Problem-Solving Strategy: Find a Pattern

You will learn that patterns can sometimes help you solve problems.

To find a missing number in a list, you can look for a pattern.

Problem The sign on the right shows the prices of party favors. Nick wants to buy 6 packages of favors to put in a piñata. If the price pattern continues, how much will Nick pay?

Party Favors

1 package	$0.30
2 packages	$0.50
3 packages	$0.70
4 packages	$0.90
5 packages	$
6	

Understand

What is the question?
How much will Nick pay for 6 packages?

What do you know?
- 1 package costs $0.30.
- 3 packages cost $0.70.
- 2 packages cost $0.50.
- 4 packages cost $0.90.

Plan

How can you find the answer?
Find a pattern. Use it to find the cost of 6 packages.

Solve

Find the pattern.

$0.30 $0.50 $0.70 $0.90
  + $0.20   + $0.20   + $0.20

The pattern is to add $0.20.

Now use the pattern to solve the problem.

- First, find the cost of 5 packages.
  Add $0.20 to the cost of 4 packages. $0.90 + $0.20 = $1.10

- Then find the cost of 6 packages.
  Add $0.20 to the cost of 5 packages. $1.10 + $0.20 = $1.30

If this pattern continues, Nick will pay $1.30 for 6 packages.

Look Back

Look back at the problem.
Is your answer reasonable? Tell why.

Standards MR 1.0, 1.1, 2.3, 3.0, 3.2

Guided Practice

Use the Find a Pattern strategy to solve each problem.

1 One photo enlargement costs $3.50, two cost $6.50, three cost $9.50, and four cost $12.50. If the costs follow a pattern, what is likely to be the cost of seven enlargements?

Think: How does the amount change each time?

2 A store owner spilled ink on her order for boxes of beads in different sizes. The sizes on the order follow this pattern: 3.1 oz, 6.2 oz, 9.3 oz, ▇ oz, and 15.5 oz. What size is covered by ink?

Think: What is the difference between each size and the next?

 $3.50
 $6.50
 $9.50
 $12.50

Independent Practice

Solve. Use these or other strategies.

Problem-Solving Strategies

• Work Backward   • Make a Table   • Find a Pattern   • Draw a Picture

3 A shop sells wrapping paper by the yard. One yard sells for $1.00, 2 yards for $1.50, and 3 yards for $2.00. If this pattern continues, how many yards of paper can you buy for $5.00?

4 Mick needs 10 invitations. He likes some that he can buy in boxes of 8 for $3.65 or individually for $0.75 each. What is the least amount Mick can pay for 10 invitations?

5 Kerry bought party hats for $2.00 each and packages of balloons for $1.50 each. She bought a total of 7 items for $11.50. How many of each item did she buy?

6 Daniel is buying 19 packages of party favors. Each package costs $0.98, including tax. Daniel has exactly $19.00. Does he have enough money? Explain.

7 Hannah bought a mouse decoration. It is 12 inches long. The mouse's tail is as long as its head and body together. The mouse's head is half as long as its body. How long is each part of the mouse?

8 Josh began donating to an animal shelter in January. He donated $3.00 in March, $3.50 in April, and $4.00 in May. If his donations followed the same pattern all year, how much did he likely donate in January?

Extra Practice See 1–4 on page 405.

385

Quick ✓ Check

Check Your Understanding of Lessons 1–6

Write a fraction or mixed number and a decimal for each model.

1. 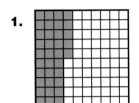   **2.**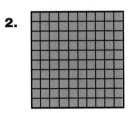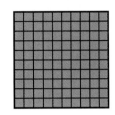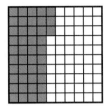

Write each mixed number as a decimal.

3. $55\frac{55}{100}$

4. $7\frac{8}{10}$

5. $162\frac{1}{4}$

Order the numbers from least to greatest.

6. 6.67   6.76   7.66   6.66

7. $3\frac{5}{10}$,   3.9, $3\frac{28}{100}$,   3.45

8. $5\frac{4}{100}$ $4\frac{15}{100}$ 4.6   5.07

Solve. Use the Find a Pattern strategy.

9. A souvenir shop sells 1 post card for $0.50, 2 post cards for $0.75, 3 post cards for $1.00, and 4 post cards for $1.25. If the pattern continues, how much are 6 post cards likely to cost?

10. Teri ordered some dried fruit in different-sized boxes. She ordered an 8-oz size, a 10.5-oz size, and a 13-oz size. If the sizes follow a pattern, what is likely to be the next size in the pattern?

How did you do?

If you had difficulty with any items in the Quick Check, you can use the following pages for review and extra practice.

California Standards	ITEMS	REVIEW THESE PAGES	DO THESE EXTRA PRACTICE ITEMS
Number Sense: **1.5, 1.6**	1–2	pages 374–376	Set A, page 402
Number Sense: **1.6**	3–5	pages 378–379	Set B, page 403
Number Sense: **1.2**	6–8	pages 380–383	Set D, pages 403 and 404
Math Reasoning: **1.1, 2.3, 3.2, 3.3**	9–10	pages 384–385	1–4, page 405

Test Prep • Cumulative Review

Maintaining the Standards

Choose the letter of the correct answer.
If a correct answer is not here, choose NH.

1 What decimal represents the shaded portion of this model?

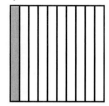

A 1.0   **C** 0.05

B 0.1   **D** 0.01

---

2 Which decimal is between 1.5 and 2?

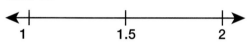

F 1.25   **H** 1.75

G 1.4   **J** 2.2

---

3 Which mixed number is equivalent to 1.75?

A $1\frac{1}{3}$ **C** $1\frac{5}{7}$

B $1\frac{2}{3}$ **D** $1\frac{3}{4}$

---

4 Which decimal is equivalent to $\frac{1}{2}$?

F 0.2   **H** 0.75

G 0.5   **J** 1.2

---

5 Which symbol makes the statement true?

$$\frac{1}{2} \bullet 0.3$$

A >   **C** =

B <   **D** $

Use the thermometer to answer Questions 6–7.

6 The temperature is ⁻5°F. If the temperature rises 10 degrees, what will the temperature be?

F 0°F

G 5°F

H 10°F

J 15°F

---

7 What is the difference between 20°F and ⁻20°F?

A 0 degrees

B 10 degrees

C 20 degrees

D 40 degrees

---

8 Matt and Damon shared a pizza that was divided into 8 equal pieces. Matt ate 3 pieces and Damon ate 4 pieces. What decimal represents the amount eaten by Damon?

Explain How did you find your answer?

Safe Site

Internet Test Prep
Visit **www.eduplace.com/kids/mhm**
for more *Test Prep Practice.*

387

Add and Subtract Decimals

You will learn that adding and subtracting decimals is like adding and subtracting whole numbers.

Learn About It

Sharon is making a dessert. She has one 8.25-ounce can of fruit and one 8.8-ounce can of fruit. How much fruit does she have?

Add. **8.25 + 8.8 = *n***

Find 8.25 + 8.8.

Step 1 Line up the decimal points. Add as you would with whole numbers.

$$\begin{array}{r} {\scriptstyle 1} \\ 8.25 \\ +\ 8.8\underline{0} \\ \hline 17\ 05 \end{array}$$ Place a zero in the hundredths place.

Step 2 Write the decimal point in the answer.

$$\begin{array}{r} {\scriptstyle 1} \\ 8.25 \\ +\ 8.80 \\ \hline 17.05 \end{array}$$
↑
decimal point

Step 3 Estimate to check. Round both numbers and add.

$$\begin{array}{r} 8.25 \rightarrow 8 \\ 8.80 \rightarrow \underline{9} \\ \hline 17 \end{array}$$

17.05 is close to 17.

Solution: Sharon has 17.05 ounces of fruit.

If Sharon uses 14.5 ounces of fruit, how many ounces will be left?

Subtract. **17.05 − 14.5 = *n***

Find 17.05 − 14.5.

Step 1 Line up the decimal points. Subtract as you would with whole numbers.

$$\begin{array}{r} {\scriptstyle 6\ 10} \\ 1\cancel{7}.\cancel{0}5 \\ -\ 14.5\underline{0} \\ \hline 2\ 55 \end{array}$$ Place a zero in the hundredths place.

Step 2 Write the decimal point in the answer.

$$\begin{array}{r} {\scriptstyle 6\ 10} \\ 1\cancel{7}.\cancel{0}5 \\ -\ 14.50 \\ \hline 2.55 \end{array}$$
↑
decimal point

Step 3 Add to check.

$$\begin{array}{r} 14.50 \\ +\ 2.55 \\ \hline 17.05 \end{array}$$

Solution: There will be 2.55 ounces of fruit left.

Standards | NS **2.0, 2.1**   MR **2.3, 2.6**

Explain Your Thinking

▶ In what way are addition and subtraction of decimals like addition and subtraction of whole numbers? In what way are they different?

Guided Practice

Add or subtract.

1.
   8.2
   + 2.5

2.
   2.32
   + 1.71

3.
   83.35
   − 20.67

4. 24.3 + 2.5

5. 14.8 − 6.4

6. 9.31 − 3.45

Ask Yourself

• Should I add or subtract?

• Where do I put the decimal point?

Independent Practice

Add or subtract.

7.
   2.4
   + 7.1

8.
   3.25
   + 3.49

9.
   91.42
   − 35.21

10.
   35.4
   − 34.16

11.
   5.38
   − 0.67

12. 13.3 − 3.8

13. 71 + 31.6

14. 45.36 − 23

15. 35.92 + 63.29

Problem Solving • Reasoning

16. **Compare** Randy bought an 8.8-oz box of crackers and a 7.75-oz box. Compare the number of ounces in each box. Is the difference more or less than 1 ounce?

17. Three pieces of string are 1.9 m, 1.6 m, and 2.7 m long. Which two pieces of string when placed end-to-end would be between 3 m and 4 m long? Explain.

18. **Write Your Own** Write a problem that requires adding or subtracting decimals. Give your problem to a classmate to solve.

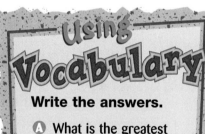

Using Vocabulary

Write the answers.

Ⓐ What is the greatest number that has only ones, tenths, and hundredths places?

Ⓑ Why can a whole number be written with or without a decimal point?

Ⓒ When you say "two and three tenths," what word stands for the decimal point?

Mixed Review • Test Prep

Multiply or divide. *(pages 126–127, 170–173, 234–235)*

19. 78 ÷ 8

20. 94 × 3

21. 329 ÷ 8

㉒ What is the mean of 9, 6, 8, 3, and 4? *(pages 252–253)*

A 4   **B** 5   **C** 6   **D** 30

Extra Practice See Set E on page 404.

Problem-Solving Application: Use Decimals

You will learn how to use decimals to solve problems.

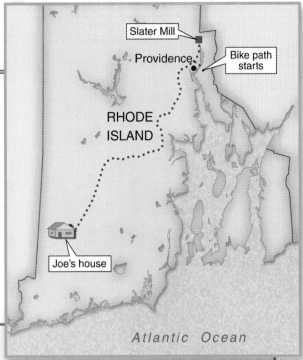

You can add or subtract decimals to solve problems.

Problem Joe lives in Rhode Island, the smallest state in the United States. It is 31.6 miles from his house to Slater Mill. It is 28.7 miles from his house to the East Bay bike path. From Joe's house, how much farther is it to Slater Mill than to the bike path?

 What is the question?

From Joe's house, how much farther is it to Slater Mill than to the bike path?

What do you know?

- It is 31.6 miles from Joe's house to Slater Mill.
- It is 28.7 miles from Joe's house to the bike path.

 **How can you find the answer?**

Subtract the number of miles to the bike path from the number of miles to Slater Mill.

$$\begin{array}{r} 31.6 \\ -\ 28.7 \\ \hline 2.9 \end{array}$$

It is 2.9 miles farther from Joe's house to Slater Mill than to the bike path.

Look back at the problem.

Is your answer reasonable? Explain.

Standards NS **2.0, 2.1** MR **1.0, 1.1, 1.2, 2.6, 3.0, 3.2**

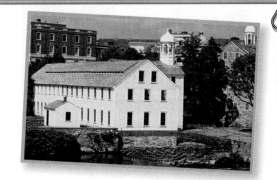

Old Slater Mill was the first factory in the United States to make cotton yarn with machines powered by water.

Remember:
▶ Understand
▶ Plan
▶ Solve
▶ Look Back

Guided Practice

Solve each problem.

1 Joe's family spent 4 hours at Slater Mill. They spent 2.5 hours at a park. How long did they spend altogether at Slater Mill and the park?

Think: What operation should I use?

2 At a salt pond, high tide on March 25 was 2.4 feet. Low tide was 0.2 feet. What was the difference between high tide and low tide?

Think: Do I add or do I subtract?

Independent Practice

Solve. Use these or other strategies.

> **Problem-Solving Strategies**
>
> • Act It Out   • Guess and Check   • Work Backward   • Find a Pattern

3 One cold night in November the temperature dropped 0.2 degrees every 15 minutes for 2 hours. Then the temperature stayed at 15.6°F. What was the temperature when it began to drop?

4 For a trip, each student is charged $10.00, and each adult is charged $18.50. A 10-seat minibus costs $117.00 to rent. How many students and adults need to sign up to pay exactly for 2 buses?

5 Sam likes to jog along the beach. He jogs 1.3 miles each day from Monday to Wednesday. On Thursday and Friday, he jogs 1.8 miles each day. How many miles does he jog in those five days?

6 A hotel room for two people costs $57.95 a night. There is a $5.00 charge for each extra person up to four people. A room for four people costs $69.95 a night. Which is the less expensive room for a family of four?

7 These fractions form a pattern. What do you believe the pattern to be? For this pattern, what are the next two fractions?

$$\frac{1}{5} \quad \frac{2}{10} \quad \frac{4}{20} \quad \frac{8}{40} \quad \frac{16}{80}$$

8 Brooke is making a model of a mill. She wants to cut four 18 in. × 18 in. squares from a 36 in. × 48 in. sheet of posterboard. Is this possible? If so, show how.

Extra Practice See 5–7 on page 405.

391

Round Decimals

You will learn how to use rules or a number line to round decimals.

12.35 POUNDS

Learn About It

Leon's cat Sam weighs 12.35 pounds. What is Sam's weight to the nearest whole pound?

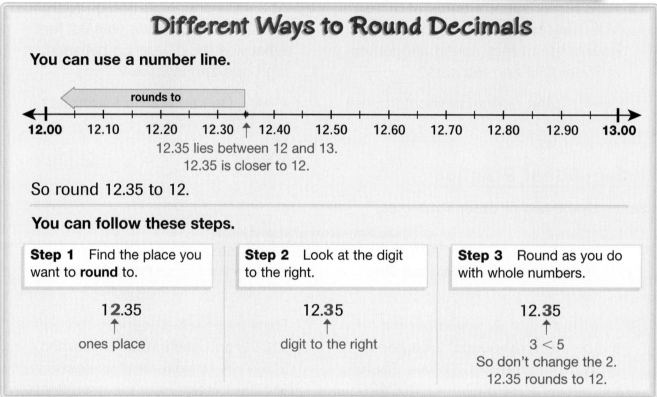

Different Ways to Round Decimals

You can use a number line.

rounds to

12.00 12.10 12.20 12.30 ↑ 12.40 12.50 12.60 12.70 12.80 12.90 13.00

12.35 lies between 12 and 13.
12.35 is closer to 12.

So round 12.35 to 12.

You can follow these steps.

Step 1 Find the place you want to **round** to.	**Step 2** Look at the digit to the right.	**Step 3** Round as you do with whole numbers.
12.35 ↑ ones place	12.35 ↑ digit to the right	12.35 ↑ 3 < 5 So don't change the 2. 12.35 rounds to 12.

Solution: Sam's weight to the nearest whole pound is 12 pounds.

Other Examples

A. Round Tenths Place to the Nearest Whole Number

24.7   7 > 5
ones place ⬆⬆ Change 4 to 5.

24.7 rounds to 25

B. Round Hundredths Place to the Nearest Tenth

52.14   4 < 5
tenths place ⬆⬆ Don't change the 1.

52.14 rounds to 52.1

Explain Your Thinking

▶ Is the solution to the problem about Sam's weight a reasonable answer? Why?

Standards NS 2.2

Guided Practice

Round each decimal to the nearest whole number.

1. 38.6   **2.** 199.5   **3.** 95.05   **4.** 436.36

Round each decimal to the nearest tenth.

5. 7.37   **6.** 16.19   **7.** 153.96   **8.** 501.02

Ask Yourself

• Which digit do I need to look at in order to round this decimal?

• Should the rounding-place digit change or stay the same?

Independent Practice

Round each decimal to the nearest whole number.

9. 2.8   **10.** 9.4   **11.** 16.7   **12.** 89.9   **13.** 135.5   **14.** 118.16

15. 5.91   **16.** 8.05   **17.** 23.77   **18.** 64.36   **19.** 352.75   **20.** 680.98

Round each decimal to the nearest tenth.

21. 7.86   **22.** 6.51   **23.** 73.87   **24.** 90.15   **25.** 183.59   **26.** 236.45

27. 10.01   **28.** 56.35   **29.** 118.26   **30.** 465.64   **31.** 777.77   **32.** 501.98

Problem Solving • Reasoning

Use Data Use the table for Problems 33 and 34.

33. Which cats weigh less than $10\frac{1}{2}$ pounds?

34. For which two cats is the difference in weight about 4 pounds? Why is your answer reasonable?

35. Analyze A cat show will begin at 1:00 P.M. It takes $1\frac{1}{2}$ hours to set up tables that must be ready at least 45 minutes before the show begins. What is the latest time that workers can start setting up tables?

Cat Weights	
Cat	**Weight**
Murphy	10.86 lb
Tiny	10.18 lb
Licorice	15.04 lb
Ginger	10.34 lb

Mixed Review • Test Prep

Add or subtract. *(pages 56–63)*

36. 33,630 + 1,532   **37.** 82,603 + 64,862   **38.** 81,426 − 20,351

39 What is the value of 803 × 4? *(pages 180–181)*

   A 332   **B** 2,412   **C** 3,212   **D** 32,012

Extra Practice See Set F on page 404.

Estimate Decimal Sums and Differences

You will learn how to use rounding to estimate sums and differences.

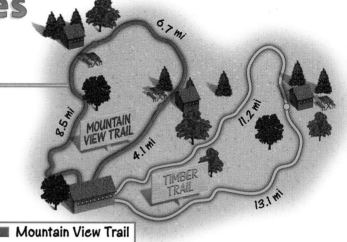

Learn About It

Jacob wants to ride on the shorter trail. Should he pick Mountain View Trail or Timber Trail?

You may not need an exact answer. So try to solve the problem with an estimate.

| ■ Mountain View Trail |
| ■ Timber Trail |

Step 1 Estimate the length of each trail.

- Round each decimal to the nearest whole number.
- Then add the rounded numbers.

Mountain View Trail

8.5	rounds to	9
6.7	rounds to	7
+ 4.1	rounds to	+ 4
		20 miles

Timber Trail

11.2	rounds to	11
+ 13.1	rounds to	+ 13
		24 miles

Step 2 Compare the two estimates.

20 miles < 24 miles
Mountain View Trail seems to be shorter than Timber Trail.

Solution: Based on his estimate, he should pick Mountain View Trail.

Other Examples

A. Estimate Differences

18.5	rounds to	19
−16.9	rounds to	−17
		2

B. Estimate Money

$308.17	rounds to	$308
− 163.82	rounds to	− 164
		$144

Explain Your Thinking

▶ If you round to estimate the sum of 7.8 and 6.5, how would the estimate compare to the actual sum?

▶ Are the estimates that Jacob made reasonable? Why or why not?

Guided Practice

Estimate each sum or difference by rounding each decimal to the nearest whole number.

Ask Yourself

• How do I round each decimal to the nearest whole number?

• Should I add or subtract?

1. 4.7
    2.5
    + 3.1

2. $44.63
    + 14.35

3. 349.29
    + 34.51

4. 5.1
    − 1.7

5. 73.78
    − 32.15

6. $157.93
    − 104.42

7. 984.38
    − 506.23

8. $21.73
    − 19.95

Independent Practice

Estimate each sum or difference by rounding each decimal to the nearest whole number.

9. 8.6
    + 5.2

10. 13.5
    + 15.9

11. 198.1
    + 238.5

12. 579.44
    + 94.15

13. $349.29
    + 34.51

14. 8.2
    − 3.9

15. $23.82
    − 20.49

16. 527.49
    − 248.21

17. $600.46
    − 64.92

18. 902.55
    − 343.72

19. 6.4
    7.1
    + 2.5

20. 4.37
    8.40
    + 2.53

21. $67.17
    31.25
    + 8.24

22. 90.75
    44.58
    + 82.32

23. $615.03
    210.93
    + 414.42

Problem Solving • Reasoning

Solve. Choose a method.

Computation Methods

• Mental Math   • Estimation   • Paper and Pencil

24. A carpenter needs to build a platform to support 8 horses that each weigh between 1,500 and 2,600 pounds. How much weight must the platform be able to hold?

25. **Money** Before going to the trail, Joe needs to buy sunblock for $5.79, a hat for $6.80, and a water bottle for $4.25. Joe has $20. Will that be enough money? Explain.

26. Margaret rode 87.8 miles in one week. She rode 77.6 miles in the first 6 days. How many miles did she ride on the seventh day?

27. **Measurement** One lap around a horse training track is 400 meters. How many laps would you have to ride to go 2 kilometers?

Use the map for problems 28–30.

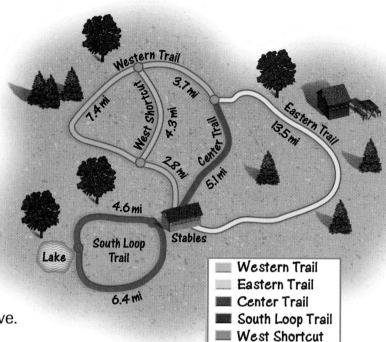

28. Anna rode about 25 miles. She started and ended at the stables. What trails did she take?

29. **Analyze** Mary rode about 5 miles with Alex. Then she rode about 8 miles more and met Dave at a crossing. They rode about 3 miles back to the stables. Which trails did Mary take?

30. **Write Your Own** Use the map to write a problem of your own. Give your problem to a classmate to solve.

Mixed Review • Test Prep

Copy and complete each table. (pages 132–135)

31.
n	3 × n
4	12
6	■
8	■

32.
n	n + 4
5	9
12	■
16	■

33.
n	8n
4	32
9	■
■	104

Choose letter of the correct answer. (pages 294–295)

34 2,000 L = _____ mL

   A 2   C 20,000

   B 20   D 2,000,000

35 2,000 mg = _____ g

   F 2   H 200

   G 20   J 20,000

Logical Thinking

Analogies

See how the first pair of words is related. Choose the letter of the word that forms a similar relationship for the second pair.

36. **Addend** is to **sum** as **factor** is to _____.

   A difference   C quotient

   B product   D divisor

37. **Ounce** is to **weight** as **inch** is to _____.

   F foot   H capacity

   G pound   J length

Using Vocabulary

Write the answer to each question.

1. What is a good estimate of the difference between 46.2 and 42.6?

2. What is a good estimate of the sum of 46.2 and 42.6?

3. What is 4.50 rounded to the nearest whole number?

4. What are two different mixed numbers that are equivalent to 4.8?

Check It Out

Estimate each sum or difference by rounding each number to the greatest place.

1.
$$22.3 + 46.5$$

2.
$$199.86 - 131.42$$

3.
$$538.41 - 113.68$$

4.
$$8,466.73 + 1,501.08$$

5.
$$312.09 + 404.65$$

6.
$$9,247.43 - 2,453.42$$

7.
$$746.6 - 746.5$$

8.
$$28,677.33 + 34,298.78$$

Decimal Roundup

Use what you know about rounding to answer each.

1. What is the least decimal in hundredths that rounds to 56?

2. What is the greatest decimal in tenths that rounds to 83?

3. A number rounded to the nearest tenth is 13.4. What are the greatest and least numbers in hundredths that could have been rounded?

4. When 3.9 and another decimal in tenths are rounded to the nearest whole number, their sum is 9. What could the other decimal be?

Problem-Solving Skill: Choose a Computation Method

You will learn how to decide which method to use to solve a problem.

Before you find an answer, you need to decide if you will use mental math, estimation, or paper and pencil.

Look at the situations below.

Sometimes you can use mental math.

Emma earned $3.25 last week and $1.75 this week walking dogs. How much did Emma earn in all?

Think: $3.25 = $3.00 + $0.25
$1.75 = $1.00 + $0.75
$4.00 + $1.00 = $5.00

Emma earned $5.00 in all.

Sometimes you only need an estimate.

Ben delivered *The Neighborhood News* to 4 stores in town last week. He got $0.98 from each store. Did he earn more or less money than Emma?

$0.98 ⟩ rounds to ⟩ $1.00
× 4   × 4
                 $4.00

Ben earned less than $4.00, so he earned less than Emma.

Sometimes you will want to use paper and pencil.

Emma and Ben want to buy a videotape that costs $31.45. She has $14.68, and he has $15.57. Do they have enough money?

First, add to find
how much they
have.
$14.68
+ 15.57
$30.25

Subtract to find
how much more
they need.
$31.45
− 30.25
$ 1.20

No, they need $1.20 more.

Look Back Why was the paper-and-pencil method used in the third example? Would an estimate have worked as well?

Standards NS **2.1** MR **1.0, 2.6, 3.0, 3.2**

Left: Before dog guides are given to blind people, the dogs learn how to behave with people by living with families.
Right: A woman walks with her dog guide.

Guided Practice

Use mental math, estimation, or paper and pencil.

1. Kelly's family is raising a puppy that will guide a blind person. Last month, Kelly's family spent $24.75 on food, $8.10 on a leash, and $4.95 on a tag. About how much did they spend?

    Think: Is an estimate enough or is an exact answer needed?

2. Jeffrey, Amanda, and William earned $3.50, $2.25, and $3.25 shoveling snow. They divided the money equally. How much money did they each get?

    Think: Are the amounts easy to add without a pencil and paper?

Independent Practice

Solve. Use these or other strategies.

Problem-Solving Strategies

- **Find a Pattern**   - **Work Backward**   - **Solve a Simpler Problem**   - **Write an Equation**

3. Lu earned $6.45 baby-sitting. She earned $5.00 raking leaves. She needs $16.75 to buy a videotape. How much more money does she need to earn?

4. Sasha earned money mowing grass. She used $\frac{5}{8}$ of the money to buy a videotape. She put $\frac{1}{8}$ of the money in her savings. What fraction of her money was left?

5. Look at the prices below. If the pattern continues, what is likely to be the next number in the pattern?

   $21, $35, $49, $63, $77, ▇

6. Mr. Taylor had $125.00. He spent $98.00 on a CD player and $22.25 on CDs. Did he have enough money left to buy a CD case for $5.00? Tell how you found your answer.

7. Brian has read many books this year. If he divides the number of books by 3 and then multiplies the quotient by 2, the answer is 148. How many books has he read this year?

8. Mandy's mother gave her a $20 bill to buy some groceries. Mandy bought items that cost $2.26, $7.49, $1.98, $6.85, and $1.15. How much change did she get?

Extra Practice See 8–11 on page 405.   **399**

Quick ✓ Check

Check Your Understanding of Lessons 7–11

Round each decimal to the nearest tenth.

1. 58.43 **2.** 292.47 **3.** 760.75

Estimate each sum or difference by rounding to the nearest whole number.

4.
```
   362.57
+ 123.46
```

5.
```
   657.08
- 324.51
```

Add or subtract.

6.
```
   7.43
- 0.62
```

7.
```
   62.05
+ 43.76
```

8.
```
   48.7
+ 25.38
```

Solve.

9. Ryan had $12.38. Megan had $14.15. How much more do they need in order to buy a video game that costs $35.85? What computation method did you use?

10. Mike's grandparents live 26.7 miles away. His cousin lives 15.9 miles farther. How many miles away does Mike's cousin live?

How did you do?

If you had difficulty with any items in the Quick Check, you can use the following pages for review and extra practice.

California Standards	Items	Review These Pages	Do These Extra Practice Items
Number Sense: **2.1**	1–3	pages 392–393	Set F, page 404
Number Sense: **2.2**	4–5	pages 394–396	Set G, page 404
Number Sense: **2.1, 2.2**	6–8	pages 388–389	Set E page 404
Number Sense: **2.1** Reasoning: **1.1, 2.2, 2.6, 3.2**	9	pages 398–399	8–11, page 405
Number Sense: **2.1** Reasoning: **1.1, 2.6, 3.2**	10	pages 390–391	5–7, page 405

Test Prep • Cumulative Review

Maintaining the Standards

Choose the letter of the correct answer. If a correct answer is not here, choose NH.

1 What decimal represents the shaded portion of this model?

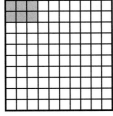

A 6.0   **C** 0.60

B 0.6   **D** 0.06

2 Which decimal is between 0.15 and 0.2?

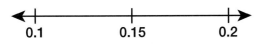

0.1   0.15   0.2

F 0.02   **H** 0.17

G 0.14   **J** 0.3

3
$$\begin{array}{r} 6.15 \\ -\ 2.79 \\ \hline \end{array}$$

A 3.36   **C** 4.64

B 4.46   **D** NH

4 On Monday the high temperature for the day was 15°F. The low temperature for the day was 15 degrees colder than the high temperature. What was the low temperature for the day?

F ⁻15°F

G ⁻5°F

H 0°F

J 5°F

5 What is 7.65 rounded to the nearest tenth?

A 6   **C** 7.6

B 7   **D** 7.7

6 The graduating class lined up in 15 rows. If there were 20 students in each row, how many students were in the class?

A 125   **C** 250

B 200   **D** NH

Use the table to answer Questions 7–8.

Jewelry Sale	
Item	Cost
Earrings (pair)	$17.99
Bracelets	$25.49
Necklaces	$20.59

7 What is the cost of a bracelet rounded to the nearest dollar?

F $24.00   **H** $25.50

G $25.00   **J** $26.00

8 Janet is estimating the cost of a pair of earrings and a bracelet. If she rounds the prices to the nearest dollar, what is the estimated cost?

Explain How did you find your answer?

Extra Practice

Set A *(Lesson 2, pages 374–377)*

Write a mixed number and a decimal to describe
the shaded part in each problem.

1. 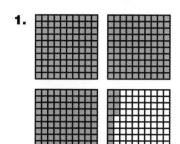 **2.**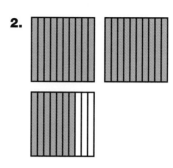

Write each mixed number as a decimal.

3. $5\frac{25}{100}$ **4.** $33\frac{33}{100}$ **5.** $22\frac{2}{10}$ **6.** $136\frac{63}{100}$

7. $9\frac{9}{10}$ **8.** $5\frac{5}{100}$ **9.** $42\frac{84}{100}$ **10.** $24\frac{43}{100}$

11. $25\frac{3}{100}$ **12.** $37\frac{37}{100}$ **13.** $14\frac{41}{100}$ **14.** $20\frac{2}{100}$

15. $2\frac{2}{10}$ **16.** $20\frac{2}{10}$ **17.** $45\frac{67}{100}$ **18.** $98\frac{7}{10}$

Write each as a decimal.

19. twenty-six hundredths

20. two and four tenths

21. thirty-one and forty-two hundredths

22. two and seventy-one hundredths

23. eight and five tenths

24. eight and fifty hundredths

25. one hundred twenty-three and forty-five hundredths

26. six hundred nine and ninety-six hundredths

27. seven hundred seven and seven hundredths

Extra Practice

Set B *(Lesson 3, pages 378–379)*

Write a fraction and a decimal to describe the shaded part of each.

1.   2.   3.   4.

5.   6.   7.   8.

Set C *(Lesson 4, pages 380–381)*

Compare. Write >, <, or = for each ●.

1. 4.3 ● 3.4   2. 1.6 ● 1.60   3. 8.75 ● 7.23   4. 9.05 ● 9.50

5. 2.4 ● 2.7   6. 4.9 ● 4.90   7. 8.14 ● 8.41   8. 5.33 ● 5.3

Order the numbers from least to greatest.

9. 3.24 3.25 3.53 3.35

10. 14.29 9.24 14.19 19.14

11. 8.7 5.8 7.18 8.74

12. 6.04 6.40 4.6 4.4

13. 5.84 5.91 5.49 5.0

14. 32.1 3.21 2.31 2.13

Use the prices for Exercises 15–17.

15. Which is the greatest price?

16. Which is the least price?

17. List the prices in order from greatest to least.

Extra Practice

Set D

Order the numbers from greatest to least. *(Lesson 5, pages 382–383)*

1. 2   2.9 $2\frac{44}{100}$ 2.84

2. $13\frac{5}{100}$ 16.07   11.8 $17\frac{2}{10}$

3. 234.11 $234\frac{1}{100}$ $234\frac{1}{10}$ 234.21

4. 235.03   194.3 $235\frac{3}{10}$ $194\frac{3}{100}$

5. $4\frac{6}{100}$ $3\frac{14}{100}$ 3.7   4.08

6. 17.23 $19\frac{3}{10}$ $13\frac{16}{100}$ 18.7

Set E

Add or subtract. *(Lesson 7, pages 388–389)*

1. 7.8
$+\ 2.1$

2. 4.37
$+\ 4.21$

3. 87.6
$-\ 28.5$

4. 59.3
$-\ 58.23$

5. 53.39
$-\ 30.61$

6. $19.1 + 9.7$ **7.** $25 + 21.47$ **8.** $19.31 - 9.45$ **9.** $48.6 - 27.04$

Set F

Round each decimal to the nearest whole number. *(Lesson 9, pages 392–393)*

1. 1.9   **2.** 8.3   **3.** 5.27   **4.** 13.05   **5.** 14.5   **6.** 33.72

7. 40.8   **8.** 52.83   **9.** 60.2   **10.** 79.81   **11.** 127.6   **12.** 112.25

Round each decimal to the nearest tenth.

13. 6.75   **14.** 5.42   **15.** 11.79   **16.** 7.28   **17.** 9.08   **18.** 14.15

19. 23.71   **20.** 32.19   **21.** 53.31   **22.** 61.79   **23.** 146.67   **24.** 314.04

Set G

Estimate each sum or difference by rounding each decimal to the nearest whole number. *(Lesson 10, pages 394–396)*

1. 6.8
$+\ 2.5$

2. 15.3
$+\ 13.8$

3. 189.1
$+\ 328.5$

4. 459.32
$+\ 83.23$

5. 653.39
$+\ 38.41$

6. 9.1
$-\ 3.7$

7. 25.63
$-\ 20.37$

8. 426.38
$-\ 247.17$

9. 700.58
$-\ 72.99$

10. 56.13
28.38
$+\ 7.96$

Extra Practice • Problem Solving

Use the Find a Pattern strategy to solve each problem. *(Lesson 6, pages 384–385)*

1 Nikki saves money to donate to a wildlife fund. She donated $2.25 in March, $3.00 in April, and $3.75 in May. If she followed the same pattern all year long, what is the likely amount she donated in November?

2 A store manager buys different size bottles. She made a list of the sizes: 1.2 oz, 2.4 oz, ■ oz, 4.8 oz, and 6.0 oz. She knows the sizes follow a pattern, but forgot one. What is that size likely to be?

3 Jay is saving for a new bike. He saves $3.00 in January, $5.00 in February, and $7.00 in March. If Jay's savings follow the same pattern all year, how much is he likely to save in May?

4 At the toy store, two trading cards cost $0.75. Three trading cards cost $0.95, and four trading cards cost $1.15. If the prices follow a pattern, how much are seven trading cards likely to cost?

Solve each problem. *(Lesson 8, pages 390–391)*

5 Tom rode his bike 5.6 miles to Jim's house. Then Tom and Jim rode 1.2 miles to Nathan's house. How many miles did Tom ride?

6 Don spent 3 hours swimming. He spent 1.25 fewer hours reading. How long did he spend swimming and reading?

7 Beth keeps track of the hours she practices piano. How much time will she have to practice on Wednesday if she wants to practice 5.5 hours before Thursday?

Beth's Practice Time	
Day	Hours
Monday	2.5
Tuesday	1.5

Use mental math, estimation, or paper and pencil. *(Lesson 11, pages 398–399)*

8 Tasha has $10.50. Joel has $9.27. If they combine their money, how much more do they need to buy a set of tapes that costs $29.95?

9 Three friends earned $4.00, $3.75, and $4.25. They divided the money equally. How much money did each one get?

10 Sue earned $3.25 a week for 2 weeks of pet sitting. Al earned $0.95 an hour mowing lawns for 6 hours. Who earned more?

11 Tina earned $6.75 doing chores and $7.00 babysitting. She spent $10.00 of the money she earned. How much did she have left?

Chapter Review

Reviewing Vocabulary

Answer each question.

1. What kind of numbers are 0.4, 0.09, 1.25, and 3.7?

2. What is used to separate the ones place from the tenths place?

Reviewing Concepts and Skills

Write a mixed number and a decimal to describe the shaded part in each problem. *(pages 374–376)*

3.   4.

Write each mixed number as a decimal. *(pages 374–376)*

5. $4\frac{3}{10}$ 6. $43\frac{96}{100}$ 7. $54\frac{3}{100}$ 8. $167\frac{76}{100}$

Write each as a decimal. *(pages 374–376)*

9. sixty-six hundredths   10. three and one tenth

Write the value of the digit 6 in each number. *(pages 374–376)*

11. 5.96   12. 7.61   13. 36.47   14. 695.32   15. 2,061.32

Write a fraction and a decimal for the shaded part. *(pages 378–379)*

16.   17.

Use the prices for Exercises 18–20.
(pages 380–381)

18. Which is the greatest price?

19. Which is the least price?

20. List the prices in order from greatest to least.

Burger Menu

Fancy Burger $2.25
Super Burger $2.75
Hamburger $1.50
Cheeseburger $1.85

Order the numbers from greatest to least. *(pages 382–383)*

21. $5\frac{1}{2}$ 5.9 $5\frac{24}{100}$ 5.84

22. $11\frac{52}{100}$ 12.07   12.8 $17\frac{5}{10}$

Add or subtract. *(pages 388–389)*

23. $18.39 + 9.7$ **24.** $32.84 + 21.47$ **25.** $5.81 + 6.1$ **26.** $29.4 - 9.55$

27. $37.62 - 7.43$ **28.** $45.23 - 9.62$ **29.** $54.59 - 32.61$ **30.** $27.4 - 22.64$

Round each decimal to the nearest whole number. *(pages 392–393)*

31. 1.6   **32.** 8.1   **33.** 51.27   **34.** 49.91   **35.** 12.76   **36.** 110.65

Round each decimal to the nearest tenth. *(pages 392–393)*

37. 8.89   **38.** 4.52   **39.** 32.29   **40.** 35.78   **41.** 128.64   **42.** 31.41

Estimate each sum or difference by rounding each decimal to the nearest whole number. *(pages 394–396)*

43. 6.8
      + 2.5

44. 15.3
      + 13.8

45. 28.2
      − 15.6

46. 87.32
      + 6.23

47. 459.32
      − 83.23

Solve. *(pages 384–385, 390–391, and 398–399)*

48. Bea started buying glitter pens each month. She bought 1 in August, 3 in September, and 5 in October. If this pattern continues, how many pens is she likely to buy in December?

49. Kim paid $53.75 for two old bikes. She fixed them and sold them for $75.00 each. How much money did she earn? Did you use mental math, estimation, or paper and pencil to find the answer? Why?

50. Eric spent 2.75 hours at the park. He spent 0.5 hours playing tag. How much time did he spend doing other things?

Brain Teasers Math Reasoning

JUST A PIECE

This is 0.4 of a bigger grid. How many small squares are in the bigger grid?

Chapter Test

Write each mixed number as a decimal.

1. $8\frac{6}{10}$ **2.** $31\frac{41}{100}$ **3.** $29\frac{62}{100}$ **4.** $148\frac{8}{10}$

Write a decimal and a mixed number for each amount.

5. two and thirty-seven hundredths   **6.** four and three tenths

Compare. Write >, <, or = for each ⬤.

7. 7.9 ⬤ 9.7   **8.** 2.5 ⬤ 2.50   **9.** 6.41 ⬤ 6.14

Order the numbers from greatest to least.

10. 7   7.9 $7\frac{64}{100}$ 7.82   **11.** $11\frac{3}{100}$ 11.07   11.7 $11\frac{2}{10}$

Round each decimal to the nearest whole number and to the nearest tenth.

12. 3.61   **13.** 8.17   **14.** 17.72   **15.** 15.27

Estimate each sum or difference. Round to the nearest whole number.

16.   4.8   **17.**   16.6   **18.**   147.1   **19.**   479.32
    + 2.5   − 14.8   + 238.7   − 83.23

Add or subtract.

20.   8.91   **21.**   104.9   **22.**   21.08   **23.**   305.72
    + 3.77   − 99.8   − 17.11   + 193.68

Solve.

24. Jamie earned $5.75. Celia earned $6.75, and Michael earned $7.75 working together last weekend. They combined their earnings and then divided the money equally. How much money did each receive? Did you use mental math, estimation, or paper and pencil to find your answer? Why?

25. Jill visits her cousin once a month. In March she visited during the first week of the month. In April she visited during the second week. In May she visited during the third week. If the pattern continued, during which week of June did Jill likely visit her cousin?

 Write About It

Solve each problem. Use correct math vocabulary to explain your thinking.

1. Elizabeth estimated the answer to this problem.

5.01 + 5.29 + 5.76 + 6.98 is about 21.00

a. Explain what she did wrong.

b. Show how to estimate the answer correctly.

2. Mr. Gold has $30.00 to buy food and party supplies for 28 people.

Food and Party Supplies	
Ice Cream ($\frac{1}{2}$ gal)	$3.89
Lemonade (gal)	$1.98 (serves 16)
Chips	$2.85
Napkins	$2.49
Plastic Spoons	$0.89 (package of 12)
Paper Plates	$2.99 (package of 15)

a. Is there enough money to buy 4 half gallons of ice cream, 3 bags of chips, 1 package of napkins, and enough lemonade, plastic spoons, and paper plates for 28 people?

b. Explain how you found your answer.

c. If your answer to *a* is *no*, explain what Mr. Gold might do so that he does not spend more than $30.00.

Another Look

The Dolphins and the Sea Lions had a swim meet. They had three races. Use the table below to answer the questions. You can use what you know about adding, subtracting, and comparing decimals.

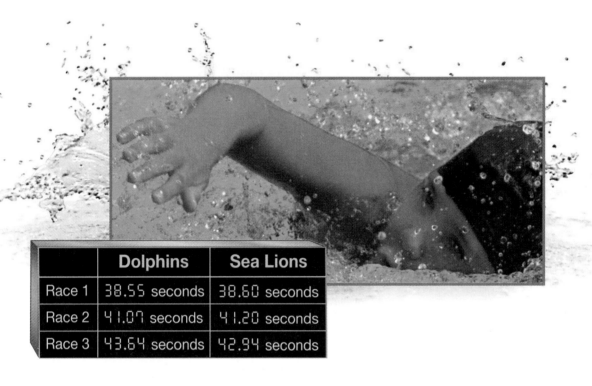

	Dolphins	Sea Lions
Race 1	38.55 seconds	38.60 seconds
Race 2	41.07 seconds	41.20 seconds
Race 3	43.64 seconds	42.94 seconds

1. The team that wins the meet is the team with the lowest total time for all three races. Find the total times for each team. Which team won the meet?

2. Find the difference in the times of the two teams for each race.

3. **Look Back** Which race was won by the greatest difference in the two times? Which race was won by the least difference in the two times?

4. **Analyze** The Dolphins won 2 out of the 3 races but did not win the meet. What is the longest time, in hundredths of a second, that the Dolphins could have had in the third race to have the lowest total time for the three races?

Enrichment

If – then Statements

If it is July, **then** it is summer.

You often hear statements that use the words "if" and "then." Are these statements always true?

> **Here is a way to decide.** Whenever the "if" part is true, the "then" part must also be true for the statement to be true. If the "then" part is false, the entire statement is false.
>
> | These statements are *true*. | These statements are *false*. |
> |---|---|
> | • If today is Thursday, then yesterday was Wednesday. | • If a number is even, then it ends in 0. |
> | • If a number is greater than 10, then it is greater than 5. | • If a fraction is less than $\frac{1}{3}$, then it is less than 0.25. |
> | • If a figure is a square, then it is a quadrilateral. | • If a figure is a quadrilateral, then it is a square. |

Try These

Decide whether each statement is *true* or *false*. If the statement is *false*, give an example that shows why.

1. If today is February 28, then tomorrow is March 1.

2. If a number is odd, then it is prime.

3. If a number is even, then it is composite.

4. If $y = 42$ and $x = 6$, then $y = x + 36$.

5. If $n = 0.06$, then $n + 0.3 = 0.9$.

6. If a number is less than 0, then the number is less than 100.

7. If a number is divisible by 9, then it is divisible by 3.

8. If a number is divisible by 3, then it is divisible by 9.

9. If a rectangle's perimeter is 20 in. then its sides are 5 in. each.

10. If something is longer than a foot, then it is shorter than a yard.

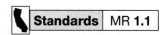

CHAPTER 9

Statistics and Probability

Why Learn About Statistics and Probability?

Learning about statistics and probability helps you collect, organize, and use information and decide how likely it is that an event will happen.

When you keep a record of your times in several races, you are collecting data. You use statistics when you analyze that data to learn more about how you run.

This man is collecting data at a baseball game. He likes to keep his own statistics about the players on his favorite team.

Reading Mathematics

Reviewing Vocabulary

Understanding math language helps you become a successful problem solver. Here are some math vocabulary words you should know.

data	a collection of numbers that give information
bar graph	a graph with bars of different lengths that show data
line plot	a pictorial representation of each item of a set of data on a number line
range	the difference between the greatest and the least number in a set of data
mode	the number that occurs most often in a set of data
probability	the chance that an event will occur
outcome	a result in a probability experiment
predict	to make a reasonable statement about what might happen in an experiment

Reading Words and Symbols

When you read mathematics, sometimes you read words and symbols displayed on graphs.

The line plot shows the ages of students on a soccer team.

▶ Each X stands for 1 student.

▶ Eleven students are on the soccer team.

▶ The range of ages is 9 minus 6, or 3.

▶ The mode age is 8.

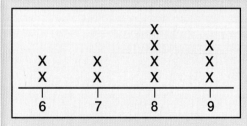

Ages of Soccer Players

Try These

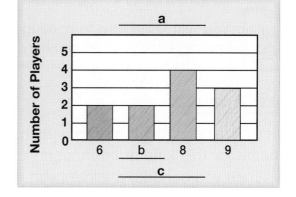

1. The data in the line plot on page 414 are displayed in the bar graph at the right. Write the labels that are missing on the bar graph.

2. Write *true* or *false*. Use the bag of counters on the right.

   a. If you pick a counter without looking, there are four possible outcomes.

   b. It is more likely that you will pick a red counter than a yellow counter.

   c. The chance of picking a purple counter is impossible.

3. Use the words at the right to complete each sentence.

   a. A ____ uses pictures to show data.

   b. Marks like this ⅢⅠ are used in a ____.

   c. You can compare data by looking at the height of the bars on a ____.

   d. A ____ is a good way to show how often something happens.

> **Vocabulary**
> **tally chart**
> **line plot**
> **bar graph**
> **pictograph**

Upcoming Vocabulary

Write About It **Here are some other vocabulary words** you will learn in this chapter. Watch for these words. Write their definitions in your journal.

median **line graph**

outlier **tree diagram**

double bar graph

Collect and Organize Data

You will learn how to conduct a survey and how to collect and organize your information.

Learn About It

A survey is a way to collect information. The name for this kind of information is data. When you conduct a survey, you ask a question and record the answers.

This question was part of a survey: "How many children are in your family?"

Look at the survey results in the tally chart.

- 25 people answered the survey question.

$$2 + 13 + 8 + 2 + 0 = 25$$

- The answer choices were 1, 2, 3, 4, and *more than* 4.

- The number 2 was the answer that was given most often.

How Many Children Are in Your Family?

Answer	Tally	Number
1	II	2
2	HH HH III	13
3	HH III	8
4	II	2
More than 4		0

Work with a partner. Conduct a survey and organize the data you collect.

Step 1 Decide on a survey question that has 3 or 4 possible answers. Then list the possible answers in a tally chart like the one on the right.

Question: _____		
Possible Answers	**Tally**	**Number**

Step 2 Survey 20 people. Allow each person to give only one answer. Make a tally mark for each answer. Then add the tally marks for each answer.

Step 3 Analyze your data.

- Which answer was given most often?
- Which answer was given least often?

Standards SDP **1.0, 1.1**   MR **2.4**

Try It Out

Use the tally chart for Problems 1–5.

1. What is the survey question?

2. Which answer was given most often? least often?

3. How many people answered the survey question?

4. How many people named the two most popular activities?

5. What is the order of the activities from most to least popular?

What Is Your Favorite Summer Activity?		
Activity	Tally	Number
Bicycling	卌 卌 II	12
Going to camp	III	3
Playing video games	卌 I	6
Swimming	卌 卌 卌 I	16
Visiting grandparents	IIII	4

Use the list on the right to make a tally chart. Then use your tally chart for Problems 6–9.

6. What are the possible answers on your tally chart?

7. How many students never bring their lunch?

8. How many students sometimes bring their lunch to school?

9. How many students always bring their lunch to school?

How Often Do You Bring Your Lunch to School?	
Sandy	always
Gina	sometimes
Wilson	never
Paco	sometimes
Joy	sometimes
Rosalie	always
Bob	sometimes
Joanna	sometimes
Will	always

Write about it! Talk about it!

Use what you have learned to answer these questions.

10. What are some ways that students might answer the question "What kinds of books do you like to read?"

11. Can a survey tell you anything about the opinions of people who did not take part in the survey? Explain your answer.

Mean, Median, and Mode

You will learn how to use a one-variable data set.

New
Vocabulary
median
outlier

Learn About It

A line plot is a way to represent data using X's. The line plot below shows the weights of 7 adult badgers. There are different ways to describe the data in this line plot.

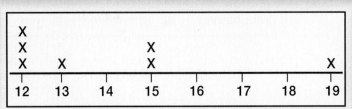

Weights of Seven Adult Badgers (in kg)

Different Ways to Describe Data

The **range** of the data is the difference between the greatest number and the least number.

$$19 - 12 = 7$$

The range is 7 kg.

The number that occurs most often in a data set is called the **mode**. Some data sets do not have a mode. Others have one or more modes.

In the line plot, there are more X's above 12 than above any other number.

The mode is 12 kg.

When a set of numbers is ordered from least to greatest, the middle number is called the **median**.

12 12 12 **13** 15 15 19

The median is 13 kg.

Suppose there was another badger weighing 15 kg. When there are two middle numbers, the median is the mean of these two numbers.

12 12 12 **13 15** 15 15 19

$$13 + 15 = 28$$
$$28 \div 2 = 14$$

The median is 14 kg.

The **mean** is sometimes called the average. To find the mean:

• Find the sum of the numbers: 98

• Divide the sum by the number of addends: $98 \div 7 = 14$

The mean is 14 kg.

An **outlier** is a number that is distant from most of the other data. Some data sets do not have outliers. Other data sets have one or more outliers.

Most of the weights are less than 16 kg. So 19 kg is an outlier.

Standards SDP **1.0, 1.1, 1.2, 1.3** MR **1.1**

Explain Your Thinking

▶ Can the mean and the median of a data set ever be the same? Give an example to support your answer.

▶ What effect do you think an outlier has on the mean?

Guided Practice

Use the line plot to answer Problems 1–3.

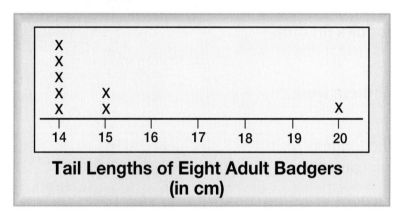

Tail Lengths of Eight Adult Badgers (in cm)

Ask Yourself

• Have I ordered the numbers?

• Is there any number that is distant from most of the numbers?

1. What is the range of the lengths?

2. Find the mode, mean, and median.

3. Which number or numbers are the outliers? Explain your answer.

4. Suppose a tail length of 24 cm is added. Find the mean and median.

Independent Practice

Order the data from least to greatest. Find the range, mode, median, and mean. Then identify any outliers.

5. 24, 49, 23, 24

6. 5, 8, 18, 6, 9, 8

7. 17, 4, 19, 17, 18

Use the line plot for Problems 8–10.

8. What is the range of the data set?

9. What is the mode?

10. Find the median and the mean of this data set.

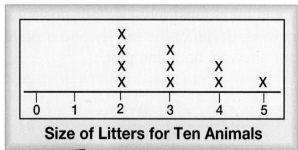

Size of Litters for Ten Animals

Problem Solving • Reasoning

Use Data Use the line plot for Problems 11–12.

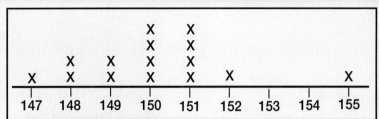

```
                        X     X
                        X     X
            X     X     X     X
      X     X     X     X     X     X           X
      |     |     |     |     |     |     |     |     |
     147   148   149   150   151   152   153   154   155
```

Tail Lengths of 15 Adult Peacocks (in cm)

11. How would the median change if there were 5 more X's above 152?

12. **Compare** How much longer is the longest peacock tail than the shortest peacock tail?

13. The median body length of 4 peacocks is 90 cm. The range is 6 cm. Make two lists of possible body lengths.

14. **Logical Thinking** A scientist studied a group of peacocks. In that group, eighteen peacocks ate cracked corn. Nine peacocks ate wheat. Of these, five peacocks ate both cracked corn and wheat. How many peacocks did the scientist study?

15. **Analyze** Do you think that some other peacocks may have 153-cm tails or 154-cm tails?

16. **Write Your Own** Decide on a survey question for which the answers are numbers. There should be at most three or four possible answers. Conduct the survey and then record your answers on a line plot.

Is Everywhere!

SCIENCE Most adult raccoons weigh between 5 kg and 7 kg. Some large raccoons weigh as much as 18 kg.

Suppose 5 raccoons have these weights in kilograms:

| 6 | 8 | 10 | 7 | 18 |

Are any of the weights outliers? Explain.

Mixed Review • Test Prep

Multiply or divide. *(pages 194–197, 234–235)*

17. $144 \div 2$ **18.** 17×11 **19.** $357 \div 7$ **20.** 24×23 **21.** $490 \div 5$

22 Find the value of t when $t = 224 \div 8$. *(pages 234–235)*

    A 28   **B** 32   **C** 36   **D** 48

Modes of Sets of Data

Sometimes a mode can be found for sets of things grouped by categories.

This set of dog tags is grouped by size. The size that occurs the most number of times is medium. So the mode for size is medium.

Use the picture of dog tags for Problems 1 and 2.

1. What is the mode for dog tag shape—octagon, rectangle, or circle?

2. What is another way to group the tags? What is the mode for that grouping?

The set of animals below is grouped by number of legs. Use the set of animals for Problems 3–4.

3. What is the mode for number of legs?

4. What is another way to group these animals? What is the mode for that grouping?

Explain Your Thinking

▶ How is finding the mode of a set of things similar to finding the mode of a set of numbers? How is it different?

Use Bar Graphs

You will learn how to use graphs that compare data.

New Vocabulary
double bar graph

Learn About It

Robin has a large collection of books. The bar graph shows how many of each type of book Robin has. For which types does she have about the same number of books?

A bar graph may be used to compare data that can be counted. Look for bars that are about the same height to find the types that are about the same in number.

Robin has about the same number of sports books and adventure books.

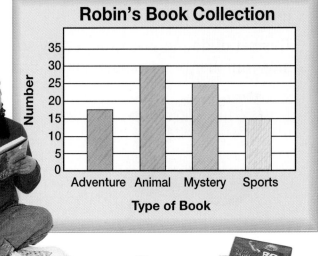

A **double bar graph** compares two sets of data. A key shows what the bars stand for.

This bar graph shows data about Robin's and Phil's book collections.

You can compare the heights of the two bars for each type of book.

- Phil has more adventure books than Robin.

You can also compare both bars for one type of book with both bars for other types of books.

- Robin and Phil both have fewer sports books than any other kind.

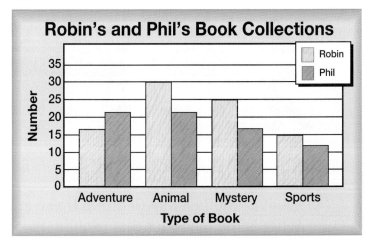

Explain Your Thinking

▶ For the same data, how would the length of the bars change if each number on the vertical scale of the graph was doubled?

Standards SDP **1.0, 1.3**   MR **1.1, 2.3**

Guided Practice

Use the bar graph for Problems 1–4.

Caleb and his dad are ordering books on the Internet.

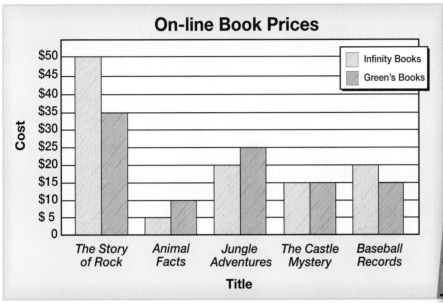

On-line Book Prices

Legend:
- Infinity Books
- Green's Books

Y-axis: Cost — $50, $45, $40, $35, $30, $25, $20, $15, $10, $5, 0

X-axis (Title): The Story of Rock, Animal Facts, Jungle Adventures, The Castle Mystery, Baseball Records

Ask Yourself

• What do the different colors of the bars stand for?

• What do the labels on the side and bottom of the graph stand for?

1. How much does the book *Animal Facts* cost at Green's Books?

2. Which book costs the same at both sites?

3. What is the cost of *Baseball Records* at Infinity Books? at Green's Books? What is the difference in cost?

4. Which book has the greatest difference in cost between Infinity Books and Green's Books?

Independent Practice

Use the graph above for Problems 5–10.

5. **Compare** What is the difference in the prices of *Jungle Adventures* at the two sites?

6. What are the mean and the median costs of the five books at the Infinity Books site?

7. **Logical Thinking** Mr. Chan spent $75 on three books at Infinity Books. Which books do you think he bought?

8. If you bought *The Castle Mystery* and had to pay $2.50 for shipping, how much would you pay in all?

9. **Analyze** Suppose you have $60 to spend, and you want to buy as many different books as possible. Both Infinity Books and Green's Books are offering free shipping. Which books would you buy?

10. **Write About It** If you want to buy *Jungle Adventures* and *Baseball Records*, would you spend more if you buy them at Infinity Books or at Green's Books? Explain your thinking.

Problem Solving • Reasoning

Solve. Choose a method.

Computation Methods

• Mental Math   • Estimation   • Paper and Pencil

11. Ana bought 5 books with a mean cost of $10. Shawn bought 3 books with a mean cost of $20. Did Ana or Shawn spend more?

12. Eight customers each bought an identical backpack. The total sales for the 8 backpacks was $392. About how much did each backpack cost?

13. Mr. Pak ordered two software packages by mail. Each package cost $159.99. The tax was $9.60 and the shipping was $10.95 for his order. What was the total amount Mr. Pak paid for the software packages?

14. A book club plans to order 26 copies of a book. Each copy costs $12.95. A bookstore owner will reduce the cost of each book by $2 if the club orders 30 books. Which number of books is less expensive, 26 or 30?

Mixed Review • Test Prep

Simplify each expression. Let $f = 6$. *(pages 132–133)*

15. $f \times 3$ **16.** $42 \div f$ **17.** $f \div 3$ **18.** $12 \times f$ **19.** $f + 20$

20 Evaluate $y \div 4$ when $y = 12$. *(pages 132–133)*

A 3   **B** 8   **C** 16   **D** 48

Visual Thinking

Which of these bar graphs show the same information?

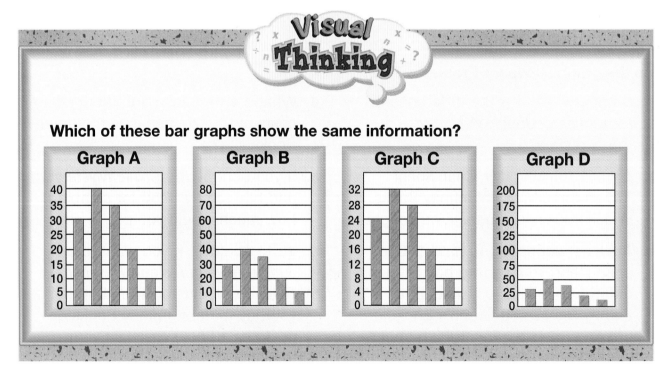

Extra Practice See Set B on page 446.

Even It Out

Practice finding the mean by making a bar graph.

What You'll Need

- *24 squares of paper*
- *a set of cards like the cards shown (Teaching Tool 13)*

Players 2

5, 1, 2, 4

2, 8, 5, 1	6, 3, 1, 2
8, 4, 5, 3	6, 5, 2, 3
1, 2, 3, 2	5, 8, 6, 5

Here's What To Do

1. Place the cards facedown in a pile.

2. Player 1 picks a card and uses paper squares to create a bar graph for the data.

3. When Player 1 finishes the graph, both players work to find the mean of the data. Player 1 finds the mean by rearranging the squares into bars of equal height. Player 2 finds the mean by using paper and pencil or mental math.

   A player earns one point for each correct answer.

4. The players take turns until all the cards are used. The player with the greater number of points wins.

Example:

9, 6, 4, 5

$9 + 6 + 4 + 5 = 24$

$24 \div 4 = 6$

Mean = 6

Share Your Thinking Which way to find the mean do you like better? Why?

Problem-Solving Skill: Interpret a Line Graph

You will learn how to get information from a graph even if it does not give exact information.

Sometimes you can get information from a graph even though it does not have numbers or labels.

Last spring, Bill, Hannah, and their father visited Joshua Tree National Park in California. Bill kept a log of his rock climb and then graphed the data.

You can use the graph to understand what is being compared.

Bill used a line graph to describe the climb. A line graph can be used to show how data changes with time.

The graph compares height and time. It shows the heights Bill reached at different times during his climb.

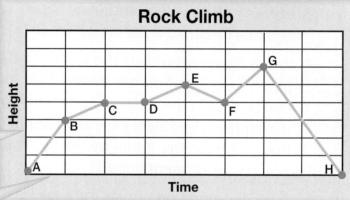

The vertical axis shows the height of the rock climb.

The horizontal axis shows the time spent climbing.

You can use the graph to answer questions.

Which points show when Bill stopped for lunch?

• The line is flat between Points C and D, so that is probably when Bill ate lunch.

Did more time elapse between points A and C or between points C and F?

• There are more divisions on the Time axis between C and F than between A and C, so more time elapsed between C and F.

Look Back Explain why the graph cannot show lines that go straight up or down.

Standards SDP **1.0, 1.3**   MR **2.0, 2.4, 3.0, 3.2**

Joshua Tree National Park, one of the newest national parks, is named for the Joshua trees, which grow in the Mojave Desert.

Guided Practice

Use the graph on page 426 for Problems 1 and 2.

 Explain what happened between points *A* and *B*. Tell how you know.

> **Think:** How are height and time related?

 Between which two points did Bill climb the least distance?

> **Think:** Which part of the graph shows the least distance climbed?

Choose a Strategy

Solve. Use these or other strategies. Use the graph for Problems 3–5.

Problem-Solving Strategies

- Use Logical Thinking
- Find a Pattern
- Choose the Operation

③ Was it colder at the start of the day or at the end of the day?

④ Estimate the time of day when the highest temperature occurred. Explain why your answer is only an estimate.

⑤ Between which two consecutive points did the greatest change in temperature occur? Can you tell how much the temperature changed during that time? Explain.

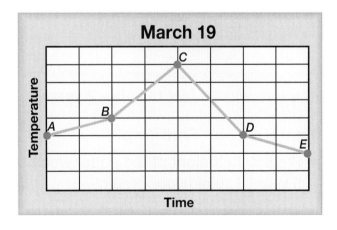

⑥ One day the temperature was 50°F at 6 A.M. The temperature increased 1 degree the first hour, 2 degrees the second hour, and 3 degrees the third hour. If this pattern of temperature change continued, what was the temperature at 12:00 noon?

⑦ Joshua trees can grow to be 4 feet around. Suppose a line graph shows that the distance around a Joshua tree increases as the tree grows taller. From left to right, would the direction of the graph go up or down? Tell how you decided.

Extra Practice See 1–3 on page 449.

Read and Understand Line Graphs

You will learn how to use a line graph.

New **Vocabulary** line graph

Learn About It

A **line graph** can be used to show how data changes over time. A line graph tells a story. This line graph tells the story of how high a cottonwood tree has grown. What was the height of the tree after 2 years?

Find the height.

To find the height of the tree after 2 years,

- Find 2 at the bottom of the graph.

- Move up to the line of the graph.

- Move left and read the height.

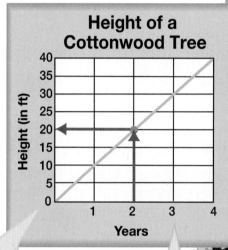

Height of a Cottonwood Tree

These numbers stand for the height of the tree in feet.

These numbers stand for the time in years.

The tree was 20 feet tall after 2 years.

Explain Your Thinking

▶ Predict the height of the cottonwood tree after 5 years. Explain your prediction.

Guided Practice

Use the graph above for Problems 1–3.

1. What was the height of the cottonwood tree after 3 years?

2. According to the graph, how much does the tree grow each year?

3. From left to right the graph is going up. Could its direction ever change? Explain your reasoning.

Ask Yourself

- What do the numbers on the side and bottom of the graph stand for?

 Standards SDP **1.0, 1.3** MR **2.3**

Independent Practice

The graph shows the number of feet that a vine grew between Monday and Friday.

4. How long was the vine on Monday?

5. Between which two days did the vine grow the most?

6. How many feet did the vine grow between Monday and Friday?

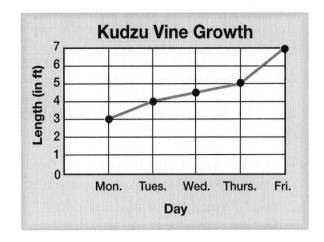

Problem Solving • Reasoning

The graph shows the highest temperature for each day of the week. Use the graph for Problems 7–8.

7. **Analyze** What was the mean high temperature for the week?

8. **Predict** Would you expect the high temperature on the day after Sunday to be 0°F, 20°F, 50°F, or 90°F? Explain your answer.

9. A student records the temperature at 12:00 midnight, 3:00 A.M., 6:00 A.M., and 9:00 A.M. If he continues to record the temperature in 3-hour intervals, when will his 8th reading be recorded?

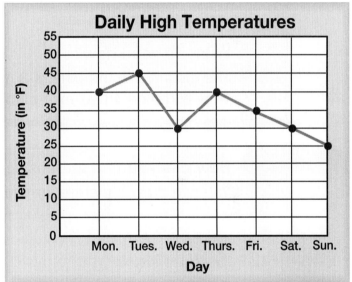

Mixed Review • Test Prep

Find each value for *n*. (pages 82–83, 132–134)

10. $396 \div 3 = n$ 11. $9 \times n = 90$ 12. $144 \div 9 = n$ 13. $418 - 139 = n$

Choose the letter of the correct answer. (pages 30–31)

14. What is the total cost of a $49.95 purchase if shipping is $5.50?

    A $44.45   **C** $54.45

    B $49.95   **D** $55.45

15. What is 20.07 rounded to the nearest tenth?

    F 19.0   **H** 20.1

    G 20.0   **J** 21.0

Extra Practice See Set C on page 446.

Problem-Solving Strategy: Choose a Strategy

You will learn how to choose strategies to solve problems.

Sometimes you can solve a problem in more than one way.

Problem Sadie and her mother biked 3 miles to the park. Then they biked on 4 paths that were each 2 miles long. After that, they biked home. How many miles did Sadie and her mother bike altogether?

Understand

What is the question?
How many miles did Sadie and her mother bike altogether?

What do you know?
The distance to the park is 3 miles.
They biked on 4 two-mile paths.

Plan

How can you find the answer?
You can draw a picture, or you can write an equation.

Solve

Draw a Picture	**Write an Equation**
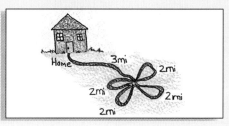	Let m = the number of miles biked.
$3 + 2 + 2 + 2 + 2 + 3 = 14$	$3 + (4 \times 2) + 3 = m$ $3 + 8 + 3 = m$ $14 = m$

Sadie and her mother biked 14 miles.

Look Back

Look back at the problem.
Which strategy would you use? Explain why.

Standards | MR **1.0, 1.1, 2.3, 3.0, 3.2**

Guided Practice

Solve.

Remember:
► Understand
► Plan
► Solve
► Look Back

1 Jon, Ray, Will, and Amy live on the same street. Ray lives 9 houses to the right of Amy. Will lives 3 houses to the right of Ray. Jon lives halfway between Amy and Will. How many houses from Ray does Jon live?

 Think: What kind of picture can I draw?

2 Sadie's mother runs along the beach every afternoon. She can run 1 mile in 8 minutes. If she can continue to run that fast, how long will it take Sadie's mother to run 6 miles along the beach?

 Think: What equation could help me solve this problem?

Choose a Strategy

Solve. Use these or other strategies.

Problem-Solving Strategies

• Use Logical Thinking   • Write an Equation   • Draw a Picture   • Guess and Check

3 Five friends are waiting in a line to buy pool passes. Nancy is in front of Scott but behind Matt. Scott is in front of Jared. Erin is first. In what order are the friends waiting?

4 Miranda, Tanya, and Stephen own dogs named Big Red, Pepper, and Daisy. Miranda's dog is not Daisy. Tanya's dog is not Daisy or Pepper. Who owns each dog?

5 Dan ate 4 energy bars. Then he gave 2 bars to William and 5 to Ellen. Dan had 4 bars left. How many energy bars did Dan start with?

6 Sue, Greg, and Jeff stand in a row to have their picture taken. List all the different ways they can arrange themselves for the picture.

7 The 32 runners in a competition compete two at a time in each round. The winner goes on to compete in the next round. In how many rounds will there be one champion?

8 Two years ago, Mr. Esh spent $290 for walking shoes for his family. Last year he spent $310 for walking shoes. During those years, how much did he spend on walking shoes?

Quick ✓ Check

Check Your Understanding of Lessons 1–6

Find the range, mode, median, and mean.
Then identify any outliers.

1. 24, 21, 39, 24, 20, 22

2. 107, 122, 103, 105, 103

Use the bar graph to answer the questions.

3. How many more nature videos does Jill have than Mark?

4. How many sports videos does Jill have? How many does Mark have?

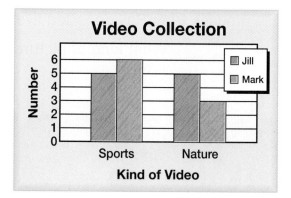

Video Collection

Use the line graph to answer questions 5–6.

5. Which months had the same amount of rainfall?

6. How much rain fell in the wettest month? Which month was it?

7. Zoe walked a half mile from her home to the park. There she hiked $1\frac{1}{2}$ miles and took a $1\frac{1}{4}$ mile trail back to where she started. Then she walked home. How many miles did she cover altogether?

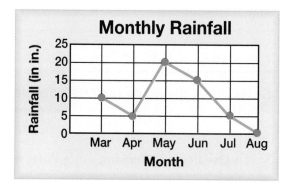

Monthly Rainfall

How did you do?

If you had difficulty with any items in the Quick Check, you can use the following pages for review and extra practice.

California Standards	Items	Review These Pages	Do These Extra Practice Items
Statistics, Data, Probability: **1.2** Math Reasoning: **1.1**	1–2	pages 418–421	Set A, page 446
Statistics, Data, Probability: **1.3** Math Reasoning: **1.1, 2.3**	3–4	pages 422–424	Set B, page 446
Statistics, Data, Probability: **1.0** Math Reasoning: **1.1, 2.3**	5–6	pages 426–429	Set C, page 446
Math Reasoning: **1.1, 2.5, 3.1, 3.2**	7	pages 430–431	4–7, page 449

Test Prep • Cumulative Review
Maintaining the Standards

Choose the letter of the correct answer.

Use the bar graph to answer Questions 1–2.

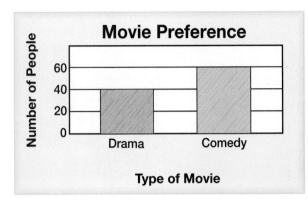

Movie Preference

Number of People / Type of Movie

Drama — Comedy

1 How many people were surveyed?

A 40   **C** 80

B 60   **D** 100

2 How many people preferred comedy over drama?

F 10   **H** 30

G 20   **J** 40

Use the line graph to answer Questions 3–4.

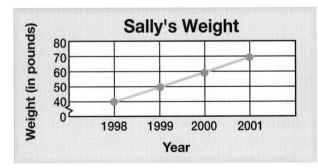

Sally's Weight

Weight (in pounds) / Year

1998 1999 2000 2001

3 How much did Sally weigh in 1998?

A 35 lb   **C** 45 lb

B 40 lb   **D** 50 lb

4 If the pattern continues, how much is Sally likely to weigh in 2002?

F 75 lb   **H** 85 lb

G 80 lb   **J** 90 lb

Use the line plot to answer Questions 5–7.

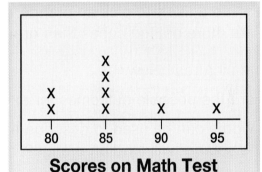

Scores on Math Test

5 How many students took the test?

A 4   **C** 8

B 6   **D** 10

6 What is the mode of the data?

F 80   **H** 90

G 85   **J** 95

7 What is the median of the data?

A 80   **C** 90

B 85   **D** 95

8 Suppose you conducted a survey on favorite kinds of cereal. What type of graph would you use to display your data?

Explain Tell why you chose that type of graph.

Safe Site

Internet Test Prep
Visit **www.eduplace.com/kids/mhm**
for more *Test Prep Practice.*

433

Probability and Outcomes

You will learn how to decide what the probability is that an event will happen.

Learn About It

Probability is a way of describing how likely it is that an event will happen. An **outcome** is a possible result of a probability experiment.

If you pick a cube from the bag without looking, there are two possible outcomes.

- You can pick an orange cube or a green cube.

- You are more likely to pick an orange cube, because there are more orange cubes than green cubes.

Possible outcomes:
orange or green

Look at the pictures below.

- What are the possible outcomes for each spinner?

- What words can be used to describe the probability that the spinner will land on orange?

Possible Outcomes	Orange	Orange, Green	Green, Orange	Green
Probability of Landing on Orange	Certain	Likely	Unlikely	Impossible

Another Example

Equally Likely Outcomes

Each spinner is divided into equally likely regions. The number of orange regions is equal to the number of green regions. So the arrow is equally likely to land on orange or green.

Explain Your Thinking

▶ How would you change each spinner to make it likely that a spin will land on green? Why would your change work?

Standards SDP 2.0

Guided Practice

Look at the bag of marbles. Write *certain*, *likely*, *unlikely*, or *impossible* to describe the probability of picking the color.

1. purple

2. orange

3. pink

4. purple or pink

Ask Yourself

• How many marbles of each color are there?

• Are there more marbles of one color than the other?

Independent Practice

Write *certain*, *likely*, *equally likely*, *unlikely*, or *impossible* to describe the probability of landing on blue.

5.

6.

7.

8.

Problem Solving • Reasoning

Use Data Use the chart for Problems 9–11.

9. Predict Which number of tiles is more likely to be found in the bag: 5 yellow, 5 orange, and 5 brown or 10 yellow, 10 orange, and 5 brown?

10. Write About It Is it likely that the number of orange tiles and yellow tiles in the bag is the same? Explain.

11. Suppose a bag of red tiles and green tiles has 15 tiles in it. If you take out 5 red tiles, there are 2 more green tiles than red tiles left in the bag. How many red tiles and green tiles were in the bag at the start?

Picking Tiles

Outcome	Tally	Number
Brown	|||||		6
Orange	||||| |||||		11
Yellow	||||| ||||| |||	13

The tally chart shows the results of picking tiles from a bag. The tile was replaced after each pick.

Mixed Review • Test Prep

Find x. *(pages 136–138)*

12. $5x = 15$

13. $9 = 54 \div x$

14. $x \div 3 = 9$

15. $12x = 36$

16 What is $\frac{6}{10}$ in simplest form? *(pages 330–332)*

A $\frac{1}{6}$ **B** $\frac{3}{5}$ **C** $\frac{4}{5}$ **D** 6

Extra Practice See Set D on page 447.

435

Find Probability

You will learn how to write the probability of an event in words and as a fraction.

Learn About It

You can use words or fractions to describe the probability of an event.

This spinner has 2 possible outcomes: purple, green.

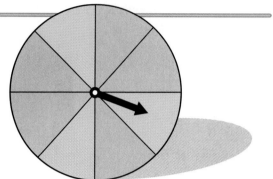

Probability of the Spins Landing on Each Color	
Green	The probability of a spin landing on green is 3 out of 8, or $\frac{3}{8}$. It is **unlikely** that a spin will land on green.
Purple	The probability of a spin landing on purple is 5 out of 8, or $\frac{5}{8}$. It is **likely** that a spin will land on purple.
Orange	The probability of landing on orange is 0 out of 8, or $\frac{0}{8}$. It is **impossible** for a spin to land on orange.
Purple **or** Green	The probability of landing on purple or green is 8 out of 8, or $\frac{8}{8}$. It is **certain** that a spin will land on purple or green.

The number line shows that the probability of an event ranges from 0, or impossible, to 1, or certain.

The closer a fraction is to 1, the more likely the event is to happen.

> You can write a probability in words, 3 out of 8, or as a fraction, $\frac{3}{8}$.

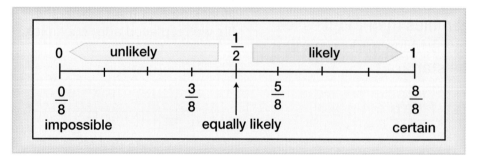

Explain Your Thinking

▶ The probability of spinning purple is $\frac{5}{8}$. Does this mean that you will always spin purple 5 out of 8 times? Explain.

| **Standards** | AF **1.1, 1.2** SDP **2.0, 2.2** MR **2.3** |

Guided Practice

Suppose you pick one of the tiles below without looking. Write the probability of picking each letter as a fraction and in words.

M A T H E M A T I C S

1. M **2.** A **3.** T **4.** H **5.** E **6.** I **7.** C **8.** S

Ask Yourself

• How many tiles are there altogether?

• How many tiles have the letter or letters I am looking for?

Independent Practice

Suppose you pick one tile from this bag without looking. Use a fraction and words to write the probability of each event.

9. picking 1 **10.** picking 3 or 5 **11.** picking a multiple of 3

12. Is the probability of picking an even number greater or less than the probability of picking an odd number? Explain.

Problem Solving • Reasoning

13. A bag holds 5 red marbles and 3 blue marbles. How many and what color marbles would you add to the bag so that the probability of picking a blue marble is $\frac{1}{2}$?

14. Draw a spinner for which the probability of spinning yellow is $\frac{1}{6}$ and it is more likely to spin red than blue.

15. **Write Your Own** You will choose a letter from a list without looking. Make a list of letters for which the probability of choosing a vowel is $\frac{1}{4}$.

Using Algebra

Find the value for *n* in each equation.

Ⓐ $n + 12 = 36$

Ⓑ $88 - n = 77$

Ⓒ $4n = 96$

Ⓓ $72 \div n = 8$

Ⓔ $(13 \times 3) + (4 \times 12) = n$

Ⓕ $4 + n = 8 - n$

Mixed Review • Test Prep

Write another fact in each fact family. *(pages 54–55, 118–119)*

16. $8 + 4 = 12$
$12 - 4 = 8$

17. $15 - 7 = 8$
$7 + 8 = 15$

18. $6 \times 5 = 30$
$30 \div 6 = 5$

19 Which number is greater than 987,451? *(pages 26–27)*

A 978,456 **B** 986,457 **C** 987,450 **D** 988,450

Making Predictions

LESSON 9

You will learn how to predict outcomes in a probability experiment.

Review
Vocabulary
prediction

Learn About It

In some situations you can use probability to make a **prediction** about what is likely to happen.

Materials

paper bag
a set of cards like
the ones shown
(Teaching Tool 14)

Step 1 Make 12 cards like the ones shown and put them in a bag.

Step 2 Predict what will happen if you picked one from the bag without looking.

- What is the probability of picking each kind of card? Write the answer as a fraction in simplest form.

- Suppose you pick a card 48 times and put it back each time. How many times do you predict you would pick a circle? a square? a triangle?

Step 3 Pick a card without looking. Record the result in a tally chart like the one below. Put the card back in the bag. Do this 47 more times.

- Were your predictions close to the number of times you picked each kind of card?

Shape Experiment		
Outcome	**Tally**	**Number**
Triangle		
Square		
Circle		

Standards SDP **1.0, 1.1, 1.3, 2.0, 2.2** MR **2.3, 2.4**

You can use the results of an experiment to make predictions.

The grid shows the results of a card experiment.

- How many times was a blue card picked? a red card picked? a green card picked?

- If there were 12 cards in the bag, how many of each color would you predict there were?

Try It Out

1. Follow these steps to make another prediction.

   - Make 6 cards like the ones on the right. Put the cards in a bag.

   - Predict how many times you will pick an *S* if you pick a card 30 times without looking and put it back each time.

   - Without looking, pick a card. Record the result on a line plot like the one on the right. Put the card back in the bag. Do this 29 more times.

Answer these questions about your experiment.

2. Compare your prediction with your results. Was your prediction accurate? Explain.

3. If you picked a card 600 times, about how many times do you think you would pick an *S* card? Explain.

4. Look at your line plot. Which other letter has about as many marks as the letter *S*? Explain why.

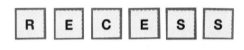

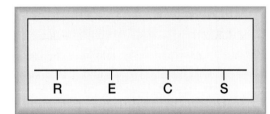

Write about it! Talk about it!

Use what you have learned to answer this question.

5. Suppose you toss a cube with the numbers 1, 2, 3, 4, 5, and 6 on its faces. Why would you predict that a number less than 4 would come up more often than a number greater than 4?

Represent Outcomes

You will learn how to show all the possible outcomes of a probability experiment in a tree diagram.

New **Vocabulary**
tree diagram
grid

Learn About It

A coin is tossed twice. What is the probability that it will land heads up once and tails up once?

Different Ways to Represent Outcomes

You can use a tree diagram.

- Use branches to show the outcomes for the first toss.
- Show the outcomes for the second toss.
- List the outcomes for both tosses.

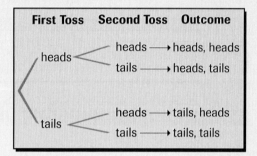

First Toss	Second Toss	Outcome
heads	heads	heads, heads
	tails	heads, tails
tails	heads	tails, heads
	tails	tails, tails

You can use a grid.

- Write the outcomes for the first toss at the left.
- Write the outcomes for the second toss at the top.
- Put the outcomes for both tosses in each part of the grid.

		Second Toss	
		heads	tails
First Toss	heads	heads, heads	heads, tails
	tails	tails, heads	tails, tails

The probability of the coin landing heads up once and tails up once is 2 out of 4, or $\frac{2}{4}$.

Explain Your Thinking

▶ Why is it helpful to use a tree diagram or a grid to organize possible outcomes?

Guided Practice

A bag holds two cards, one with the letter _T_ and one with _Y_. A card is picked twice and put back each time.

1. Make a tree diagram or a grid to show possible outcomes. How many outcomes are there?

2. What is the probability of spelling the word TY?

Ask Yourself

- What are all the possible outcomes?
- How many times does the outcome I want occur?

Standards SDP **1.0, 2.0, 2.1, 2.2** MR **2.0**

Independent Practice

The tree diagram shows the possible outcomes when a coin is tossed and a four-part spinner is spun. Use the tree diagram for Problems 3–5.

3. Make a grid to show the same outcomes.

4. How many possible outcomes show heads and red or blue?

5. What is the probability of heads and yellow or heads and green when a coin is tossed and a spinner is spun?

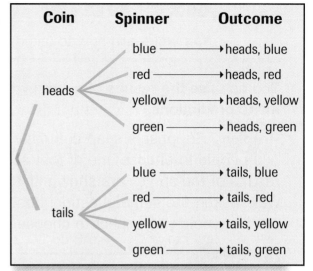

Problem Solving • Reasoning

Use the spinners for Problems 6 and 7.

6. Draw a grid to show all the possible outcomes of spins on both spinners.

7. Find the probability of spins on both spinners landing on red.

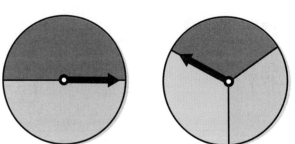

8. Ed will glaze the inside of a mug red or yellow, the outside green or blue, and the handle black or white. What are all the ways the mug can be glazed? Use a tree diagram to show your work.

9. **Analyze** Tim wrote each letter of his name on cards and put the cards in a bag. He picked a card and returned it to the bag. He did this 3 times. What is the probability that Tim spelled his name with the cards he picked?

Mixed Review • Test Prep

Solve. *(pages 54–55, 194–195)*

10. $\begin{array}{r} 28 \\ \times\ 4 \\ \hline \end{array}$

11. $\begin{array}{r} 684 \\ +397 \\ \hline \end{array}$

12. $\begin{array}{r} 42 \\ \times 18 \\ \hline \end{array}$

13. $\begin{array}{r} 1{,}004 \\ -\ 395 \\ \hline \end{array}$

14. $\begin{array}{r} 204 \\ \times\ 61 \\ \hline \end{array}$

15 Which number sentence is correct? *(pages 350–351)*

A $\frac{3}{8} + \frac{5}{8} = 1\frac{2}{8}$ **B** $\frac{1}{8} + \frac{6}{8} = \frac{6}{8}$ **C** $\frac{5}{8} + \frac{6}{8} = 1\frac{3}{8}$ **D** $\frac{2}{8} + \frac{7}{8} = 1$

Extra Practice See Set F on page 448.

Problem-Solving Application: Use Data and Probability

You will learn how to use data and probability to solve problems.

You can use the results of a survey to make predictions.

Problem Suppose a soap company asks 100 people to choose one of four scents. The results of the survey are shown. If 1,000 people were asked the same question, about how many people would you expect to choose lemon?

Scent	Number of People
Cinnamon	26
Lemon	50
Pine	14
Vanilla	10

Understand

What is the question?

If 1,000 people were asked the same question, about how many people would you expect to choose lemon?

What do you know?

100 people were surveyed. 26 chose cinnamon, 50 chose lemon, 14 chose pine, and 10 chose vanilla.

Plan

What can you do to find the answer?

Find the fraction of 100 people who chose lemon. Use the fraction to predict about how many people out of 1,000 you would expect to choose lemon.

Solve

Find the fraction of 100 people who chose lemon.

$$\frac{\text{Number who chose lemon}}{\text{Number of people surveyed}} = \frac{50}{100} = \frac{1}{2}$$

Use the data to predict about how many people out of 1,000 would be expected to choose lemon.

$\frac{1}{2}$ of 1,000 = 500

About 500 people would be expected to choose lemon.

Look Back

Look back at the question.

How could you check if $\frac{1}{2}$ of 1,000 = 500?

Standards SDP **1.0, 2.0, 2.2** MR **1.0, 1.1, 2.0, 3.0, 3.2, 3.3**

Guided Practice

Solve.

Remember:
► Understand
► Plan
► Solve
► Look Back

1 Fifty people took a taste test of fruit drinks. These are the results.

Cherry	Lemon	Lime
卌 卌 卌 卌 卌	卌 卌 IIII	卌 卌 I

Suppose 500 people took the same test. About how many people would you expect to pick cherry?

Think: How many people out of 50 chose cherry?

2 This chart shows the kinds of pets 100 pet owners have.

Cat	Dog	Other
26	54	20

Suppose 400 pet owners were asked what kind of pets they have. About how many would you expect to have dogs?

Think: Out of 100 pet owners, how many have dogs?

Choose a Strategy

Solve. Use these or other strategies.

Problem-Solving Strategies

• Use Logical Thinking   • Write an Equation   • Draw a Picture   • Work Backward

3 A mall opens at 9:30 A.M. Sam takes 45 minutes to set up a taste test which must be ready when the mall opens. If Sam takes 20 minutes to get to the mall, what is the latest time he can leave home?

4 Jeff, Leon, Margie, and Pamela will sit at a square table, with one sitting at each side. Jeff will sit at Pamela's left and Margie will not sit next to Jeff. Between which two people will Margie be seated?

5 A box with 3 bars of soap costs $7.95. A box with 6 bars of the same kind of soap costs $15.95. What is the least expensive way to buy 21 bars of that soap?

6 In a survey, 15 people chose blue paint, 21 chose pink, and 14 chose green. If 500 people were asked the same question, how many would you expect to choose green?

7 These are the results of spinning a spinner 15 times. If the spinner were spun again, which color would you predict the spinner would land on? Explain your answer.

Red	White	Black
IIII	III	卌 III

Extra Practice See 8 and 9 on page 449.   **443**

Quick ✓ Check

Check Your Understanding of Lessons 7–11

Write *certain, likely, unlikely, impossible,* or *equally likely* to describe the probability of spinning red.

1.
2.
3.
4.

Use words and a fraction to write the probability of each outcome.

5. drawing tile 5

6. drawing either tile 7 or 9

7. drawing a number greater than 6

Make a tree diagram or grid to solve.

8. What are all the possible outcomes of tossing 2 coins?

Solve.

9. 100 people were asked what their favorite color was. The results are shown in the table. If 500 people were asked the same question, how many people do you think would be likely to choose red?

Color	Number of People
Red	20
Blue	35
Yellow	15
Green	30

How did you do?

If you had difficulty with any items in the Quick Check, you can use the following pages for review and extra practice.

California Standards	ITEMS	REVIEW THESE PAGES	DO THESE EXTRA PRACTICE ITEMS
Statistics, Data, Probability: **2.0** Math Reasoning: **1.1, 3.1**	1–4	pages 434–435	Set D, page 447
Statistics, Data, Probability: **2.0, 2.2** Math Reasoning: **1.1, 3.1**	5–7	pages 436–437	Set E, page 447
Statistics, Data, Probability: **1.0, 2.1** Math Reasoning: **1.1, 2.3, 3.1**	8	pages 440–441	Set F, page 448
Statistics, Data, Probability: **2.0, 2.2** Math Reasoning: **1.1, 2.3, 3.1**	9	pages 442–443	8–9, page 449

Test Prep • Cumulative Review
Maintaining the Standards

Choose the letter of the correct answer.

1 Which graph best displays data that shows change with time?

   A line plot

   B bar graph

   C double bar graph

   D line graph

2 How many people preferred vanilla ice cream?

Ice Cream Preference

Vanilla	卌 卌 I
Chocolate	卌 卌 卌
Strawberry	卌 II

   F 9   **H** 13

   G 11   **J** 15

Use this set of data to answer Questions 3 and 4.

$$15, 19, 4, 19, 16$$

3 What is the median?

   A 4   **C** 16

   B 15   **D** 19

4 Which number is an outlier?

   F 4   **H** 16

   G 15   **J** 19

5 What is the probability of spinning an 8?

   A $\frac{1}{8}$ **C** $\frac{3}{4}$

   B $\frac{1}{4}$ **D** $\frac{7}{8}$

Three blocks are in a bag. Use this information to answer Questions 6 and 7.

6 If a block is picked without looking, what is the probability of picking block A?

   F 1 out of 3   **H** 2 out of 3

   G 3 out of 5   **J** 3 out of 3

7 Block B is picked and then replaced. What is the probability that block B will be picked again?

   A $\frac{1}{2}$ **C** $\frac{1}{6}$

   B $\frac{1}{3}$ **D** $\frac{1}{9}$

8 Two coins are tossed. What is the probability that both land heads up? **Explain** Draw a tree diagram or grid to support your answer.

Safe Site

Internet Test Prep
Visit **www.eduplace.com/kids/mhm**
for more *Test Prep Practice.*

445

Extra Practice

Set A   *(Lesson 2, pages 418–420)*

Order the data from least to greatest. Find the range, mode, median, and mean. Then identify any outliers.

1. 2, 4, 5, 2, 6, 2, 7

2. 3, 2, 3, 9, 3

3. 10, 13, 23, 11, 14, 13

4. 13, 14, 15, 17, 16

5. 21, 20, 46, 21

6. 27, 29, 14, 27, 28

7. 25, 14, 19, 22, 20

8. 127, 122, 132, 127

9. 84, 93, 27, 88

Set B   *(Lesson 3, pages 422–424)*

Use the graph for Problems 1–4.

1. What is the difference in scores for Team A and Team B on Wednesday?

2. What score is the median of the scores for Team A?

3. On which day was the difference in scores the greatest between Team A and Team B?

4. Which team has the greatest range of scores?

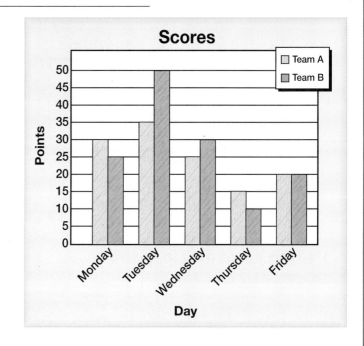

Set C   *(Lesson 5, pages 428–429)*

Use the graph for problems 1–3.

1. What was the temperature at 10 A.M.? at 1:00 P.M.?

2. What does the graph tell you about what happened to the temperature between 9:00 A.M. and 3:00 P.M. ?

3. Why do you think the line goes straight across between 11:00 A.M. and 12 noon?

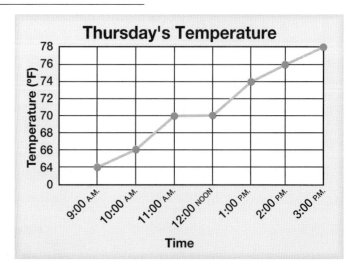

Extra Practice

Set D *(Lesson 7, pages 434–435)*

Look at the bag of tiles. Write *certain*, *likely*, *equally likely*, *unlikely*, or *impossible* to show how likely each outcome is.

1. pick red

2. pick yellow

3. pick pink

4. pick red or yellow

Write *certain*, *likely*, *equally likely*, *unlikely*, or *impossible* to describe the probability of landing on blue.

5.    **6.**    **7.** 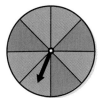   **8.**

Write *certain*, *likely*, *equally likely*, *unlikely*, or *impossible* to describe the probability of landing on red.

9. 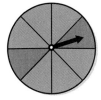   **10.** 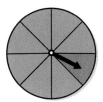   **11.** 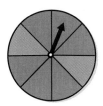   **12.**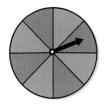

Set E *(Lesson 8, pages 436–437)*

Look at the spinner. Write the probability of each outcome in words and as a fraction.

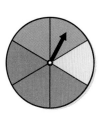

1. blue

2. red

3. yellow

4. yellow or red

Use the bag of tiles for problems 5–8. Write the probability of each outcome in words and as a fraction.

5. 9

6. 11 or 15

7. a multiple of 5

8. an even number

9. an odd number

10. a multiple of 10

Extra Practice

Set F (Lesson 10, pages 440–441)

Use the tree diagram for Problems 1–6.

1. How many possible outcomes are there for picking a star two times?

2. Write all the possible outcomes for two picks.

3. What is the probability of picking the star twice?

4. What is the probability of picking a star and a square?

5. What is the probability of picking the star first and the square second?

6. What is the probability of picking the square first and the star second?

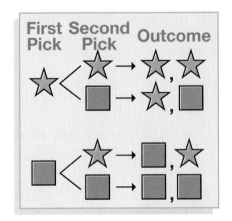

The tree diagram shows the outcomes from spinning two spinners with equally likely regions. Use the tree diagram for Questions 7–13.

7. What are the possible outcomes for spinning the first spinner?

8. What are the possible outcomes for spinning the second spinner?

9. What are the possible outcomes for spinning both spinners?

10. What is the probability of landing on red for both spins?

11. What is the probability of landing on red for the second spin?

12. What is the probability of landing on blue for the first spin?

13. What is the probability of landing on two different colors for both spins?

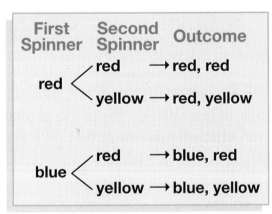

Extra Practice • Problem Solving

Use the graph to solve Problems 1–3. *(Lesson 4, pages 426–427)*

The graph shows the sales of running shoes in Mr. Gomez's store.

1 In which two months were the sales the same?

2 In which month did Mr. Gomez sell 50 pairs of running shoes? Explain how you know.

3 How many more pairs of running shoes did Mr. Gomez sell in August than he did in March?

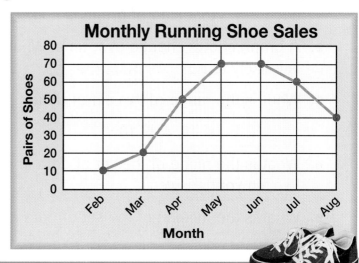

Solve each problem. *(Lesson 6, pages 430–431)*

4 Ike is writing a 5-page book report. He writes the first page in 8 minutes. If he continues to write 1 page every 8 minutes, how long will it take Ike to write the entire book report?

5 Tasha is gluing colorful yarn around the edges of pictures in a collage. One square picture has 4 sides that are each 12 inches long. How much yarn did Tasha glue around the picture?

6 Mrs. Baker makes necklaces. She uses 5 silver beads in each necklace. How many necklaces can she make if she has 105 silver beads?

7 Adam saved $35. He earned $28 doing yard work. He used his savings and earnings to buy soccer shoes that cost $48. How much money does Adam have left?

Solve. *(Lesson 11, pages 442–443)*

8 100 students were asked which color they liked best. The results are shown below.

Red	Blue	Yellow	Green
38	30	14	18

Suppose 500 students were asked for their favorite color. How many would probably choose blue?

9 100 students were asked how they got to school. The results are shown below.

Car	Bus	Walked
30	49	21

Suppose 400 students were asked how they got to school. How many would probably say "walked"?

Chapter Review

Reviewing Vocabulary

1. A graph shows how many fish were caught each day. What kind of graph is it likely to be?

2. A graph shows change over time. What kind of graph is it likely to be?

3. What is the range of this set of data?

    6, 10, 4, 5, 10

4. What is the mode of the set of data in Question 3? Explain your answer.

5. What is the median of the set of data in Question 3?

6. What is the mean of the set of data in Question 3?

7. Write a set of data that has an outlier.

Reviewing Concepts and Skills

Order the data from least to greatest. Find the range, mode, median, and mean. Then identify any outliers. *(pages 424–427)*

8. 6, 10, 8, 10, 8, 6

9. 16, 41, 15, 16

10. 90, 33, 99, 94

11. 35, 25, 35, 95, 35

12. 21, 10, 15, 18, 16

13. 5, 7, 8, 12, 12, 10

Use the graph below for Questions 14–16. *(pages 428–431)*

14. What is the difference of the number of milk cartons and the number of orange juice cartons sold on Wednesday?

15. What is the median number of orange juice cartons sold?

16. Were more milk cartons sold on Monday and Tuesday than orange juice cartons? How many of each were sold altogether on both days?

Use the tree diagram for Problems 17–18. *(pages 446–447)*

17. How many possible outcomes are there?

18. What is the probability of first picking an "X" and then an "O"?

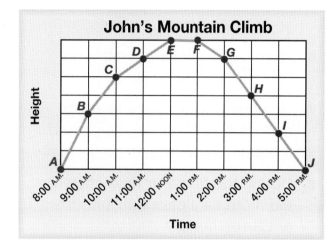

First Pick   Second Pick   Outcome

$$X \begin{cases} X \to X, X \\ O \to X, O \end{cases}$$

$$O \begin{cases} X \to O, X \\ O \to O, O \end{cases}$$

Solve. *(pages 434–435)*

Use the graph to answer Problems 19–21.

John kept a log of his mountain climb and then graphed the climb.

19. When does it seem that John reached the highest point of the climb? Tell how you know.

20. When does it seem that John began heading back down the mountain?

21. During what hour did John climb the fastest?

John's Mountain Climb

Height / Time

(points A, B, C, D, E, F, G, H, I, J; times 8:00 A.M. through 5:00 P.M.)

Brain Teasers Math Reasoning

SPINNER DESIGN

Design a spinner with 3 sections. Put one number in each section so that if you spin the spinner twice and add the numbers you spin, you are more likely to get an even sum than an odd sum.

FAVORITE VOWELS

Is E really the vowel we use the most often? Choose a paragraph in a newspaper. Make a tally chart showing how many times each of the vowels A, E, I, O, and U is used. Try again using other paragraphs. Is E the most frequently used vowel? Why do you think so?

Safe Site

Internet Brain Teasers
Visit **www.eduplace.com/kids/mhm**
for more *Brain Teasers.*

Chapter Test

Order the data from least to greatest. Find the range, mode, median, and mean. Then identify any outliers.

1. 2, 8, 2, 4
2. 2, 7, 8, 5, 9, 5
3. 6, 5, 31, 6
4. 30, 35, 30, 25, 45

Use the graph for Problems 5–8.

5. What is the difference in the number of cars passing Bob's and Carol's houses on Tuesday?

6. What is the median number of cars passing Bob's house?

7. On what day did twice as many cars pass Bob's house as passed there on Wednesday?

8. During the first four days shown, did more cars pass Bob's house or Carol's house?

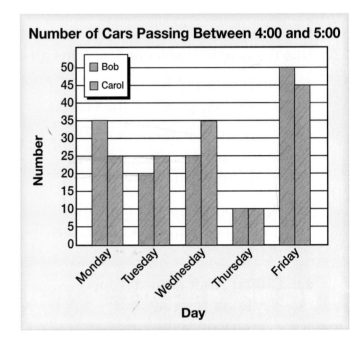

The graph shows the growth of an empress tree over 5 years. Use the graph to solve Problems 9–12.

9. What is the height of the tree after 5 years?

10. How many years did it take the tree to grow to a height of 18 feet?

11. During what year did the tree grow 6 feet?

12. Does the tree grow faster or slower as it gets older? Explain.

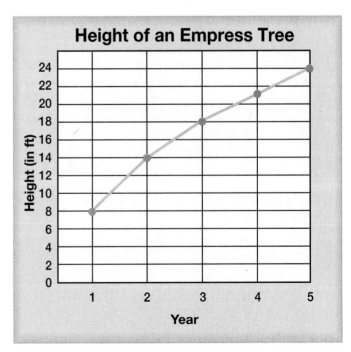

Use the tree diagram for Problems 13–17. *(Lesson 10, pages 442–443)*

13. How many possible outcomes are there when A is spun first?

14. How many possible outcomes are there in all?

15. What is the probability of spinning "A, 2"?

16. What is the probability of spinning the number "3"?

17. What is the probability of spinning the letter "C"?

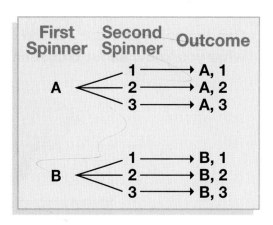

First Spinner	Second Spinner	Outcome
A	1	A, 1
	2	A, 2
	3	A, 3
B	1	B, 1
	2	B, 2
	3	B, 3

Solve.

18. It takes Mark 35 minutes to shovel a driveway. How many minutes would it take him to shovel 4 driveways?

19. Maya charges $5 an hour to rake leaves. If she raked leaves for 36 hours last fall, how much money did she earn?

20. Several children in the neighborhood worked a total of 105 hours. If each child worked 7 hours, how many children were there?

 ## Write About It

Solve the problem. Use correct math vocabulary to explain your thinking.

To use this game spinner, you spin twice and add the numbers. Henry figured that there are three outcomes, 1 + 1, 1 + 2, and 2 + 2. Two of these have even sums and one has an odd sum. Henry said it would be unlikely to get an odd sum.

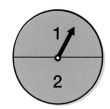

a. Is Henry's reasoning correct? Draw a grid to show whether it is *certain, likely, equally likely, unlikely,* or *impossible* to get an odd sum with 2 spins.

b. Draw a tree diagram to show the outcomes for spinning 3 times and adding the numbers.

Another Look

Use the spinner to answer the questions. You can use what you know about probability.

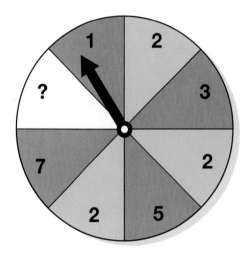

1. The spinner is missing a number. Use these clues to find the missing number: Spinning an even number or an odd number is equally likely. The sum of the odd numbers should be the same as the sum of the even numbers. What is the missing number? Explain your thinking.

2. Make a line plot to organize the data shown below.

Numbers that the Spinner Landed on in 25 Spins
10 2 1 2 10 5 2 1 7 2 3 2 5
5 2 3 7 2 10 7 2 1 2 3 5

   What is the mode of the data?

3. **Look Back** Suppose that landing on a red section for this spinner should be more likely than landing on a blue section. What color should the section for the missing number be? Why?

4. **Analyze** Gary wrote these rules for a game: Team A scores a point if the spinner lands on a number 5 or less. Team B scores a point if the spinner lands on a number greater than 5. Is the game fair? Explain.

Enrichment

Combinations

How many different faces can you draw using the shapes below for faces, eyes, and mouth?

Face		Eyes		Mouth	
Square	□	Triangles	△ △	Happy	‿
Circle	○	Ovals	⬭ ⬭	Sad	⌢

You can make an organized list to find all the combinations, or arrangements, of faces, eyes, and mouths.

Organized List			
Square, triangles, happy	☺	Circle, triangles, happy	☺
Square, triangles, sad	☹	Circle, triangles, sad	☹
Square, ovals, happy	☺	Circle, ovals, happy	☺
Square, ovals, sad	☹	Circle, ovals, sad	☹

There are 8 combinations or different faces that you can draw.

Make an organized list to find all the combinations.

1. **Outfits**

   Shorts: Black, Red

   Shirt: White, Green, Orange

2. **Pizzas with One Topping**

   Crust: Thin, Thick, Stuffed

   Toppings: Mushrooms, Pepperoni

3. **Mixing Paint Colors**

   1st Choice: Red, Blue, Yellow

   2nd Choice: White, Green, Black

4. **Meals**

   Main Course: Beef, Chicken

   Salad: Spinach, Lettuce

Explain Your Thinking

Look back at the example at the top of the page. If you started the organized list with the shape of the eyes first instead of the shape of the face, would you still find 8 combinations? Why or why not?

Standards   SDP **2.1**

CHAPTER 10

Geometry and Measurement

Why Learn About Geometry and Measurement?

You use geometric terms to describe the shapes that you see around you. You use measurement to describe and compare the sizes of these shapes.

When you put together a jigsaw puzzle or draw a geometric design, you are using geometry and measurement.

Look at the geometric shapes in these houses and in the skyscrapers beyond. The architects who designed these buildings used geometry and measurement to create their plans.

Reading Mathematics

Reviewing Vocabulary

Understanding math language helps you become a successful problem solver. Here are some math vocabulary words you should know.

line	a straight path of points that goes on without end in both directions
line segment	a part of a line with two endpoints
polygon	a flat, closed plane figure made up of three or more line segments
angle	two rays with a common endpoint
triangle	a polygon with three sides
right triangle	a triangle with one right angle
quadrilateral	a polygon with four sides
congruent	the same shape and size

Reading Words and Symbols

When you read mathematics, you sometimes read words that name geometric figures.

Look at the different names that polygons have.

triangle	square	rectangle
3 sides	4 equal sides	4 sides

pentagon	hexagon	octagon
5 sides	6 sides	8 sides

Try These

1. Name the polygon that each object looks like.

a.   **b.**   **c.**  **d.**

2. Write *true* or *false*.

a. A right triangle has four sides.

b. An angle is formed by two rays with the same endpoint.

c. Congruent figures are the same shape but not the same size.

d. A pentagon has more than 4 sides.

3. Write *always*, *sometimes*, or *never*.

a. A quadrilateral ____ has three sides.

b. The sides of a square are ____ the same length.

c. An angle is ____ greater than a right angle.

d. A line segment ____ goes on without end in both directions.

Upcoming Vocabulary

 Write About It Here are some other vocabulary words you will learn in this chapter. Watch for these words. Write their definitions in your journal.

parallel lines	**scalene triangle**
intersecting lines	**acute triangle**
perpendicular lines	**obtuse triangle**
trapezoid	**center**
parallelogram	**radius**
rhombus	**diameter**
	rotational symmetry

Points, Lines, and Line Segments

You will learn about geometric figures in the world around you.

New
Vocabulary
point
line
line segment
endpoint
parallel lines
intersecting lines
perpendicular

Learn About It

Many everyday things can model geometric figures. The period at the end of this sentence is a model of a point. A solid painted stripe in the middle of a straight road is a model of a line. A pair of railroad tracks is a model of parallel lines.

Geometric Figures

A **point** is a location in space.

$\bullet$
B

Say: point *B*
Write: *B*

You can draw a **line** through any two points. A line goes on without end in both directions.

C   *D*

Say: line *CD* or line *DC*
Write: $\overleftrightarrow{CD}$ or $\overleftrightarrow{DC}$

A **line segment** is part of a line. It has two **endpoints**.

R
Q

Say: line segment *QR* or line segment *RQ*
Write: $\overline{QR}$ or $\overline{RQ}$

Lines that are always the same distance apart are **parallel lines**.

Say: Line *ZY* is parallel to line *KL*.
Write: $\overleftrightarrow{ZY} \parallel \overleftrightarrow{KL}$

↑
The symbol ∥ means "is parallel to."

Lines that cross each other are **intersecting lines**.

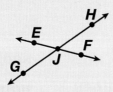

Say: Line *EF* and line *GH* intersect at point *J*.

Two lines that form right angles are **perpendicular** to each other.

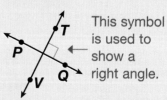

This symbol is used to show a right angle.

Say: Line *PQ* is perpendicular to line *TV*.
Write: $\overleftrightarrow{PQ} \perp \overleftrightarrow{TV}$

↑
The symbol ⊥ means "is perpendicular to."

Standards MG **3.0, 3.1**   MR **2.4**

In the picture at the right, the horizontal line is perpendicular to the vertical line. At their intersection, they form right angles.

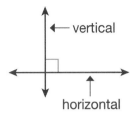

Explain Your Thinking

▶ How are a line and a line segment alike? How are they different?

▶ How are intersecting lines and perpendicular lines alike? How are they different?

Guided Practice

Use words and symbols to name each figure.

1.

2.

3.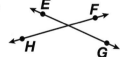

Ask Yourself

• Which point will I write first to name the figure?

• What symbol stands for the figure?

Write *parallel*, *intersecting*, or *perpendicular* to describe the relationship between each pair of lines.

4.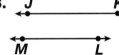

5.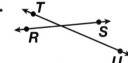

6.

7.

Independent Practice

Use words and symbols to name each figure.

8.

9.

10.

11. •Q

12.

Write *parallel*, *intersecting*, or *perpendicular* to describe the relationship between each pair of lines.

13.

14.

15.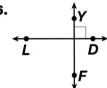

16.

Draw an example of each.

17. line segment *JK*   **18.** line *MN*   **19.** horizontal line segment *WY*

20. $\overleftrightarrow{EF} \parallel \overleftrightarrow{GH}$ **21.** $\overleftrightarrow{AB} \perp \overleftrightarrow{CD}$ **22.** horizontal $\overleftrightarrow{PQ}$ and vertical $\overleftrightarrow{PR}$

Problem Solving • Reasoning

Use the drawing at the right for Problems 23–26.

23. Name a line.

24. Name a pair of perpendicular lines.

25. Name a pair of parallel lines.

26. **Explain** Is $\overleftrightarrow{AB}$ perpendicular to $\overleftrightarrow{FJ}$? Explain your answer.

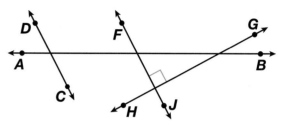

27. **Write About It** Look around your classroom. Describe something that shows a pair of parallel lines. Then describe something that shows a pair of perpendicular lines.

Mixed Review • Test Prep

Write each fraction or mixed number as a decimal. *(pages 374–376)*

28. $\frac{4}{10}$ **29.** $\frac{81}{100}$ **30.** $\frac{1}{2}$ **31.** $6\frac{8}{100}$ **32.** $3\frac{1}{4}$

Choose the letter of the correct answer. *(pages 54–55, 110–111)*

33 Find $(23 + 15) + 85$.

  A 230   **C** 123

  B 185   **D** 113

34 Find $(9 \times 8) \times 6$.

  F 78   **H** 422

  G 102   **J** 432

Write *true* or *false* for each sentence.

1. If a line is horizontal, then it is parallel to a vertical line.

2. If two lines are parallel, then they never meet.

3. If two lines intersect, they are always perpendicular.

4. If two lines are perpendicular, they are also parallel.

Extra Practice See Set A on page 510.

Triple Concentration

Practice recognizing and naming basic
geometric shapes. Try to get the most cards.

What You'll Need

• *18 game cards (Teaching Tool 17)*

Players
2

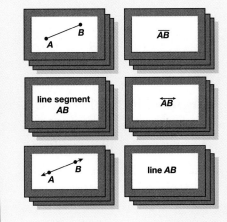

Here's What to Do

1. Shuffle the cards. Place them facedown
   in a 3 by 6 array.

2. • The first player turns up three cards.

   • If all the cards match (picture, word
   name, and symbol), the player collects
   those cards.

   • If the cards do not match, the player
   turns the cards facedown.

   • The next player takes a turn.

3. Continue the game until all matches
   have been made. The player with the
   most cards wins.

Share Your Thinking Would line *AB*
and $\overline{BC}$ be a match? What strategy
did you use to try to win the game?

LESSON 2

Rays and Angles

You will learn how to name and describe rays and angles.

New
Vocabulary
ray
angle
sides
vertex
right angle
obtuse angle
acute angle

Learn About It

So far you have learned about lines and line segments. Rays and angles are also geometric figures.

Rays and Angles

A **ray** is also a part of a line. A ray has only one endpoint and goes on without end in one direction.

Say: ray BA
Write: $\overrightarrow{BA}$

An **angle** is formed by two rays with a common endpoint. The rays are the **sides** of the angle. The common endpoint is the **vertex** of the angle.

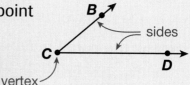

Say	Write
angle C	$\angle C$
angle BCD	$\angle BCD$
angle DCB	$\angle DCB$

←When naming an angle, the vertex is the middle letter.

Angles are classified by the size of the opening between the rays.

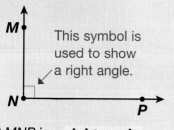

This angle forms a square corner.

This symbol is used to show a right angle.

$\angle MNP$ is a **right angle**.

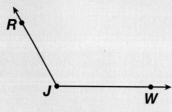

This angle is greater than a right angle.

$\angle RJW$ is an **obtuse angle**.

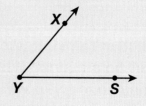

This angle is less than a right angle.

$\angle XYS$ is an **acute angle**.

Explain Your Thinking

▶ Can $\angle PQR$ also be named $\angle PRQ$? Why or why not?

▶ Do perpendicular lines form right angles, obtuse angles, or acute angles?

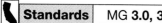
Standards   MG **3.0, 3.5**   MR **1.1, 2.4**

Guided Practice

Name each angle in three ways. Then classify the angle as *acute, obtuse,* or *right*.

1.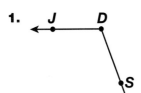

2.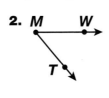

3.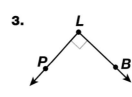

> **Ask Yourself**
> • What point will be the middle letter in the name of the angle?
> • How does the size of the angle compare to the size of a right angle?

Independent Practice

Name each angle in three ways. Then classify the angle as *acute, obtuse,* or *right*.

4.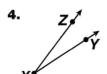

5.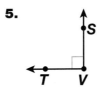

6.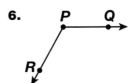

7.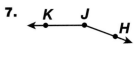

Problem Solving • Reasoning

8. Look at the clocks. What is the time shown on the clock with hands that show
   - a right angle?
   - an obtuse angle?
   - an acute angle?

9. **Analyze** Draw an obtuse angle. Fold your angle so the two sides meet. The fold should go through the vertex of the angle. How many smaller angles are formed? What kind of angles are they?

10. **Write About It** Draw two separate angles. Name your angles ∠*MHP* and ∠*TWZ*. Write a sentence to describe each angle. Use the words *vertex* and *sides* in your description. Classify the angles you drew.

Mixed Review • Test Prep

Estimate each sum or difference. *(pages 64–65)*

11. $13.78 + 5.68$ **12.** $6.94 - 3.17$ **13.** $8.64 + 6.75$ **14.** $10.34 - 6.95$

15 Which of these numbers is a prime number? *(pages 248–249)*

   A 27   **C** 39

   B 31   **D** 49

Polygons and Quadrilaterals

You will learn how to identify geometric figures by the number of sides they have.

New Vocabulary

polygon
sides
rectangle
square
trapezoid
parallelogram
rhombus

Learn About It

A **polygon** is a flat, closed plane figure made up of three or more line segments called **sides**. Look at the polygons below.

triangle
3 sides

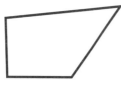

quadrilateral
4 sides

pentagon
5 sides

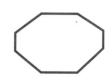

hexagon
6 sides

octagon
8 sides

Some quadrilaterals have special names.

Quadrilaterals That Have Special Names

A **rectangle** has opposite sides parallel and four right angles.

A **square** has four sides of the same length and four right angles.

A **trapezoid** has only one pair of parallel sides.

A **parallelogram** has opposite sides parallel and of the same length.

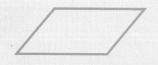

A **rhombus** has opposite sides parallel and four sides all of the same length.

Explain Your Thinking

▶ Why is a circle not a polygon?

▶ Why are rectangles, squares, and rhombuses all parallelograms?

466   **Standards**   MG **3.0, 3.8**   MR **2.4**

Guided Practice

Name each polygon. If the polygon is a quadrilateral, write all names that apply.

1.

2.

3.

Ask Yourself
- How many sides does the polygon have?
- If there are 4 sides, are there any parallel sides or right angles?

Independent Practice

Name each polygon. If the polygon is a quadrilateral, write all names that apply.

4.

5.

6.

7.

Problem Solving • Reasoning

Use the traffic signs below for Problems 8–10.

8. Which traffic sign is shaped like an octagon?

9. Rob saw a sign that showed how far it is to San Jose. Name the kind of quadrilateral he saw.

10. Why is the railroad crossing sign not a polygon?

11. **Analyze** I have an even number of sides. I have more sides than a pentagon, but fewer sides than an octagon. What kind of polygon am I?

Using Vocabulary

Write *true* or *false*. Explain your thinking.

- Ⓐ All squares are rectangles.
- Ⓑ Some polygons are pentagons.
- Ⓒ All octagons are polygons.
- Ⓓ All parallelograms are rectangles.
- Ⓔ Some rectangles are squares.

Mixed Review • Test Prep

Write the value of the underlined digit. *(pages 4–5)*

12. 7<u>5</u>0

13. <u>3</u>,756

14. <u>6</u>75,231

15. 3.<u>2</u>5

16. 13.2<u>5</u>

⓱ What time is shown on the clock? *(pages xvi–ix)*

A 3:37   C 4:37

B 3:42   D 7:18

Extra Practice See Set C on page 510.

LESSON 4

Classify Triangles

You will learn how to identify triangles by the lengths of their sides and the sizes of their angles.

New Vocabulary
equilateral triangle
isosceles triangle
scalene triangle
right triangle
obtuse triangle
acute triangle

Learn About It

If you look at some bridges, you will see many triangles. Triangles can be classified in two ways.

Different Ways to Classify Triangles

You can classify triangles by the lengths of their sides.

Equilateral Triangle

All sides are the same length.

Isosceles Triangle

At least two sides are the same length.

Scalene Triangle

No sides are the same length.

You can classify triangles by the sizes of their angles.

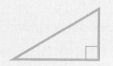

Right Triangle

One angle is a right angle.

Obtuse Triangle

One angle is an obtuse angle.

Acute Triangle

All angles are acute angles.

Explain Your Thinking

▶ Can a triangle be isosceles and obtuse? Explain.

Guided Practice

Classify each triangle as *equilateral, isosceles,* or *scalene* and as *right, obtuse,* or *acute.*

1.

2.

3.

Ask Yourself
• Are any sides the same length?
• What kind of angles does the triangle have?

Standards MG **3.0, 3.7** MR **1.1, 2.4**

Independent Practice

Classify each triangle as *equilateral, isosceles,* or *scalene* and as *right, obtuse,* or *acute*.

4.   **5.**   **6.**   **7.**

8.   **9.**   **10.**    **11.**

Draw one triangle for each exercise.

12. an equilateral triangle that is also an acute triangle

13. an isosceles triangle that is also a right triangle

14. a scalene triangle that is also an obtuse triangle

Problem Solving • Reasoning

15. Measurement April built a model bridge. For one section she built triangles with sides of 4 cm, 3 cm, and 5 cm. Did she build equilateral, isosceles, or scalene triangles?

16. Analyze April made one triangle that measured 3 cm on one side. The other two sides were twice as long as the first side. Did she build an equilateral, an isosceles, or a scalene triangle?

17. Write About It Look at the picture of the bridge on page 468. Make sketches of the triangles you see. Classify each triangle you draw.

SCIENCE The longest suspension bridge in the world is in Japan. It is about 4 kilometers long. The bridge was started in 1988 and finished 10 years later.

About how many meters long is the bridge?

Mixed Review • Test Prep

Write the numbers in order from least to greatest. *(pages 6–7, 382–383)*

18. 112   111   121   211   **19.** 0.07   0.7   0.17   0.1   **20.** 5.2   5.02   2.05   2.5

21 What is the perimeter of a square with sides of 1.2 m? *(pages 280–281)*

A 1.28 m   **B** 2.4 m   **C** 4.8 m   **D** 12.8 m

Extra Practice See Set D on page 510.   **469**

Circles

LESSON 5

You will learn about the parts of a circle.

New Vocabulary
circle
center
radius (radii)
diameter

Learn About It

A **circle** is made up of all points in a plane that are the same distance from a given point in that plane, called the **center**. Point *D* is the center of the circle below.

Circles

A **radius** is any line segment that joins a point on the circle to the center of the circle.

$\overline{DE}$ or $\overline{ED}$ is a radius of this circle.

$\overline{DG}$ and $\overline{DF}$ are also radii of this circle.

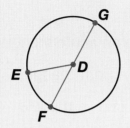

A **diameter** is any line segment that passes through the center of a circle and has its endpoints on the circle.

$\overline{GF}$ or $\overline{FG}$ is a diameter of this circle.

The number of degrees in a full circle is 360. The symbol for degrees is °. You can turn an object around the point that is the center of a circle.

Each turn is measured from the start position. The start position is at the mark for 0°.

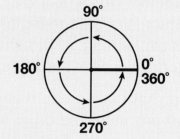

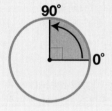

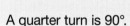

A quarter turn is 90°.

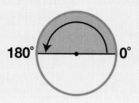

A half turn is 180°.

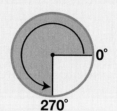

A three-quarter turn is 270°.

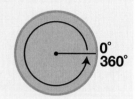

A full turn is 360°.

Explain Your Thinking

▶ If a circle has more than one radius drawn, would each radius be the same length?

▶ How does the length of a diameter of a circle compare to the length of a radius of that same circle?

Standards | AF 1.4   MG 3.0, 3.2, 3.5   MR 2.3

Guided Practice

Name the parts of the circle. Write *center,*
radius, **or** *diameter.*

1. G

2. $\overline{FG}$

3. $\overline{FH}$

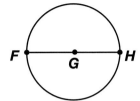

Ask Yourself

• Does the line segment
connect a point on the
circle to the center of
the circle?

• Does it pass through
the center of the circle?

Independent Practice

Name the part of each circle that is shown in red.
Write *center, radius, diameter,* **or** *none of these.*

4.

5.

6.

7.

Problem Solving • Reasoning

8. **Measurement** The radius of a circle is 6 feet.
How long is the diameter of the circle?

9. Between noon and 12:30, the minute hand on a
clock moves from 12 to 6. Has the minute hand
made a quarter turn, a half turn, or a three-
quarter turn? What time will it be when the
minute hand has made a full turn?

10. **Write About It** Trace around a circular object.
Label the center *C.* Draw radius *CS.* Draw
diameter *AB.* Look at $\overline{BC}$. Is $\overline{BC}$ a radius?
Explain how you know.

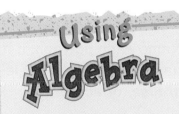

Using Algebra

The equation **d = 2r**
shows that the
diameter (**d**) is
twice the radius (**r**).

Copy and complete
the table.

Rule: d = 2r

d	r
4	2
8	■
12	■
■	30
■	50

Mixed Review • Test Prep

Find each sum or difference. *(pages 56–58, 60–62)*

11. $6,240 - 1,378$

12. $786 + 324$

13. $9,086 - 6,723$

14. $8,576 + 9,423$

15. Which shows $2\frac{3}{4}$ as an improper fraction? *(pages 342–343)*

    A $\frac{11}{4}$ **B** $\frac{6}{4}$ **C** $\frac{10}{4}$ **D** $\frac{12}{2}$

Extra Practice See Set E on page 511.

Check Your Understanding of Lessons 1–5

Write *parallel* or *perpendicular* for each pair of lines.

1.

2.

Name the parts of the circle.

3. the center

4. a diameter

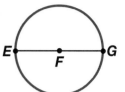

Name each angle three ways. Then write whether the angle is *acute, obtuse,* or *right*.

5.

6.

Name each polygon. If it is a quadrilateral, write all names that apply. If it is a triangle, classify it as *right, obtuse,* or *acute*.

7. ⬡

8. ▱

9. ◺

10. △

How did you do?

If you had difficulty with any items in the Quick Check, you can use the following pages for review and extra practice.

California Standards	ITEMS	REVIEW THESE PAGES	DO THESE EXTRA PRACTICE ITEMS
Geometry: **3.1**	1–2	pages 460–462	Set A, page 510
Geometry: **3.2**	3–4	pages 470–471	Set E, page 511
Geometry: **3.5**	5–6	pages 464–465	Set B, page 510
Geometry: **3.8**	7–8	pages 466–467	Set C, page 510
Geometry: **3.7**	9–10	pages 468–469	Set D, page 510

Test Prep • Cumulative Review

Maintaining the Standards

Choose the letter of the correct answer.
If a correct answer is not here, choose NH.

1 Which model shows lines that are parallel?

Use the model to answer Questions 2–3.

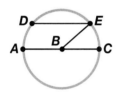

2 Which is not a radius of the circle?

  F $\overline{AB}$ **H** $\overline{DE}$

  G $\overline{BC}$ **J** $\overline{BE}$

3 Which is a diameter of the circle?

  A $\overline{AB}$ **C** $\overline{DE}$

  B $\overline{AC}$ **D** $\overline{BC}$

4 Polly drew a right angle. What is the measure of a right angle?

  F 45°   **H** 180°

  G 90°   **J** 360°

5 Classify this triangle.

  A equilateral

  B isosceles

  C right

  D scalene

6 Which statement is not true?

  F All squares are rectangles.

  G Some trapezoids are parallelograms.

  H All rectangles are parallelograms.

  J Some parallelograms are squares.

7 Which angle is an obtuse angle?

 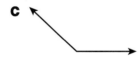

8 Are all squares rectangles? Are all rectangles squares?

Explain Make drawings to support your answers.

Safe Site

Internet Test Prep
Visit **www.eduplace.com/kids/mhm**
for more *Test Prep Practice.*

473

Congruent Figures

You will learn about figures that have the same size and shape.

Learn About It

European mapmakers made the first jigsaw puzzles so children could practice putting maps together. Look at the jigsaw puzzle map on the right.

You can tell that this puzzle piece belongs in the puzzle because it is the same shape and size as the empty space in the puzzle.

Plane figures that have the same shape and the same size are **congruent** figures. Congruent figures do not have to be in the same position.

These figures are congruent.

These figures are not congruent.

These figures are congruent.

One way to tell whether two figures are congruent is to trace one figure and then check whether it matches the other figure.

Sometimes different parts of the same figure are congruent. Look at figure *ABCD*.

$\overline{BC}$ is congruent to $\overline{CD}$.

$\overline{AB}$ is congruent to $\overline{AD}$.

$\angle B$ is congruent to $\angle D$.

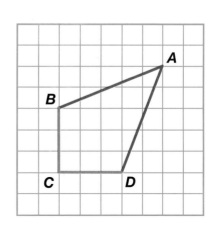

Standards MG 3.0, 3.3, 3.8   MR 1.1, 2.3, 2.4, 3.3

Explain Your Thinking

▶ Are all hexagons congruent? Why or why not?

▶ Are all circles with radii of 4 inches congruent? Why or why not?

Guided Practice

Do the figures in each pair appear to be congruent?

1.

2.

3.

4.

> **Ask Yourself**
> • Are the figures the same shape?
> • Are the figures the same size?

Independent Practice

Do the figures in each pair appear to be congruent?

5.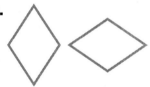

6.

7.

8.

9.

10.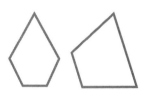

Choose the figure that appears to be congruent to the first figure. Write a, b, or c.

11.

a. b. c.

12.

a. b. c.

Problem Solving • Reasoning

Use Figures *A*, *B*, and *C* for Problems 13 and 14.

13. **Measurement** Parallelograms have opposite sides that are congruent. Use a centimeter ruler. Which of the figures at the right are parallelograms?

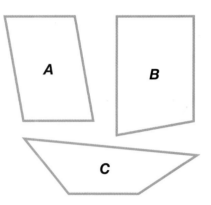

14. **Analyze** Which figure at the right has some right angles? Is it a rectangle or square? Explain.

15. Adam drew a square that had sides of 14 inches. Nancy drew a square that was congruent to Adam's square. What was the perimeter of Nancy's square?

16. **Analyze** Six congruent triangles form the figure shown at the right. What figure is it? Draw a picture of another way to combine the triangles to make a figure with a different shape.

Mixed Review • Test Prep

Solve. *(pages 292–293, 294–296)*

17. 3,000 g = ▧ kg

18. 12,000 mL = ▧ L

19. 50 cm = ▧ mm

20. What is the sum of $\frac{5}{8}$ and $\frac{1}{8}$? *(pages 350–351)*

   A $\frac{4}{8}$ **B** $\frac{6}{16}$ **C** $\frac{1}{2}$ **D** $\frac{3}{4}$

Logical Thinking

Look at the Venn diagram.

The orange area contains all quadrilaterals. The red area contains all parallelograms.

Trapezoid and *Square* need to be added to the diagram. Which one goes in the green area? Which goes in the purple area?

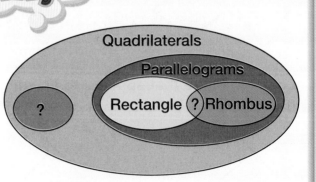

Think: Which quadrilateral has a special name but is not a parallelogram?

Think: What is the name for a rectangle that is also a rhombus?

Similar Figures

Figures that are the same shape, but not necessarily the same size, are similar figures.

Look at the figures below.

These figures are similar.
They are the same shape.
They are not the same size.

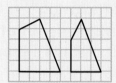

These figures are not similar.
They are not the same shape.

Tell whether the two shapes in each exercise appear to be similar. If the shapes are similar, tell whether they appear to be congruent.

1.

2.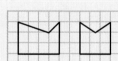

3.

4.

5.

**Write *true* or *false* for each sentence.
Then draw an example to support your answer.**

6. All squares are similar.

7. All hexagons are similar.

8. All parallelograms are similar.

9. All circles are similar.

Explain Your Thinking

► Think about right triangles. Are they all similar?
Are they all congruent? Draw examples to explain
your thinking.

Symmetry

You will learn how to identify figures that can be folded into matching parts.

New
Vocabulary
line symmetry
line of symmetry
rotational symmetry

Learn About It

Dylan made a scrapbook for his summer trip to northern California. He decorated the front of his scrapbook with geometric shapes.

A figure has **line symmetry** if it can be folded so that its two parts match exactly. The fold line is a **line of symmetry**. Line symmetry is also called bilateral symmetry.

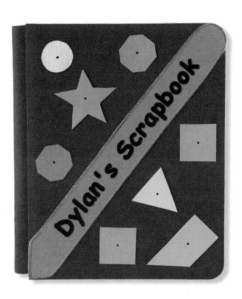

To find out if a figure has a line of symmetry, trace the figure. Then try to fold the figure so both parts match. If both parts match, draw the line of symmetry on the fold line.

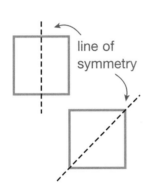

line of symmetry

Some figures do not have a line of symmetry. The green quadrilateral on Dylan's scrapbook does not have line symmetry.

Figures can have one or more than one line of symmetry.

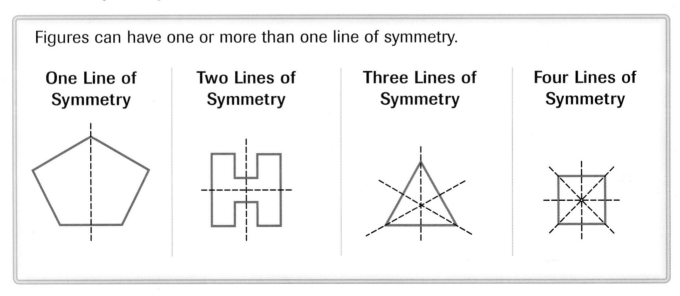

One Line of Symmetry	Two Lines of Symmetry	Three Lines of Symmetry	Four Lines of Symmetry

Standards MG **3.4** MR **2.3, 2.4**

A figure has **rotational symmetry** if you can rotate it less than a full turn about a point to make the figure look the same as it did before the rotation.

quarter turn　　　half turn　　　three-quarter turn

Explain Your Thinking

► Which of the shapes on Dylan's scrapbook have line symmetry? Which have rotational symmetry?

► How can you use a tracing of a figure to find out if it has rotational symmetry?

Guided Practice

Is the dashed line a line of symmetry? Write *yes* or *no*.

1.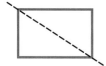

2.

Does the figure have rotational symmetry? Write *yes* or *no*.

3.

4.

5.

Ask Yourself

• Can I fold along the dashed line so the parts match exactly?

• Can I turn the figure less than a full turn and make it look like it did before I turned it?

Independent Practice

Is the dashed line a line of symmetry? Write *yes* or *no*.

6.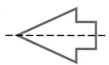

7.

8.

9.

Draw each figure on grid paper. Draw the line of symmetry.
Draw the other half of the figure on your grid paper.

10.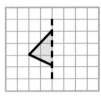

11.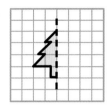

12.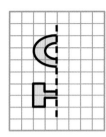

13.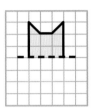

14.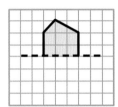

15.

Trace each figure. Does the figure have
rotational symmetry? Write *yes* or *no*.

16.

17.

18.

19.

Problem Solving • Reasoning

20. Analyze Draw the figure below.
Turn it a half turn and draw it again.
Does the figure have rotational
symmetry around the point? Explain.

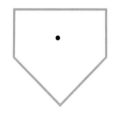

21. Draw the circle below. Cut it out
and fold it on line segment *NP*.
What happens to points *M* and *O*?

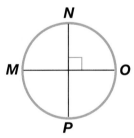

22. Write About it Dylan used the figure at the right to
decorate the back of his scrapbook. How many right
triangles are in the figure? Explain your solution.
Hint: Look for 4 different sizes of triangles.

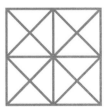

Mixed Review • Test Prep

Use Data Use the graph for Problems 23–26. *(pages 424–426)*
Each student had one vote for his or her favorite season.
The results are shown at the right.

23. Which season did most students choose as their favorite season?

24. How many more students chose summer than chose winter as their favorite season?

25. Which season was chosen by twice as many students as spring was?

26. How many students named their favorite season?

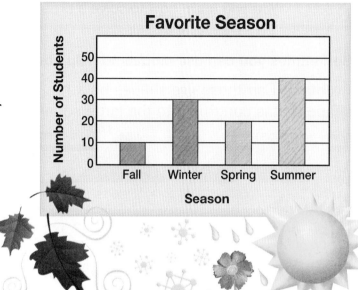

Choose the letter of the correct answer. *(pages 298–299)*

27 Eli started reading a short story at 6:45 P.M. He finished reading the story at 7:25 P.M. How long did it take Eli to read that story?

   A 20 minutes   **C** 1 hour 20 minutes

   B 40 minutes   **D** 1 hour 40 minutes

28 Jill started reading at 3:25 P.M. She finished reading 1 hour and 40 minutes later. At what time did Jill finish reading?

   F 1:45 P.M.   **H** 5:05 P.M.

   G 4:05 P.M.   **J** 6:05 P.M.

Visual Thinking

Turning Letters

Suppose each of these letters is rotated a half turn.
Draw a picture to show what each letter would look like.

1. M   **2.** P   **3.** ⊙   **4.** H

5. Which of the letters above have rotational symmetry? How do you know?

LESSON 8

Problem-Solving Strategy: Use Models to Act It Out

You will learn how to solve a problem by using a model.

Sometimes you can use models to help you solve problems.

Problem Can these five shapes be arranged to form a shape that is congruent to the large square at the right?

Understand

What is the question?
Can these five shapes be arranged to form a shape that is congruent to the large square?

What do you know?
Congruent figures have the same size and shape.

Plan

How can you find the answer?

• First you can make models of the five shapes and the large square above on grid paper.

• Then cut out each shape and try to arrange them to form a square that is congruent to the large square above.

Solve

Try to arrange the shapes so that they fit inside the large square without overlapping.

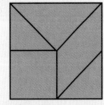

The five shapes can be arranged to form a shape that is congruent to the large square.

Look Back

Look Back
Suppose you arranged the five figures to form a hexagon. Would the hexagon be congruent to the large square? Explain.

Standards MG **3.0, 3.3, 3.8** MR **1.0, 2.0, 3.0, 3.2**

Guided Practice

Use the shapes on page 482 to solve each problem.

Remember:
- ▶ Understand
- ▶ Plan
- ▶ Solve
- ▶ Look Back

1. Arrange the largest triangle, the parallelogram, and one of the small triangles to form a shape congruent to the quadrilateral below. Make a drawing to explain how you did it.

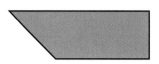

Think: Where must right angles be?

2. Arrange all the shapes except the largest triangle to form a figure congruent to the parallelogram below. Make a drawing to explain how you did it.

Think: How can I move or turn pieces?

Choose a Strategy

Use the shapes on page 482 to solve Problems 3 and 4.
Use these or other strategies.

Problem-Solving Strategies

| • Draw a Picture | • Make a Table | • Use a Model | • Work Backward |

3. Use four of the shapes to form a shape congruent to the pentagon shown below. Make a drawing to explain how you did it.

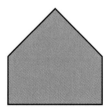

4. Use all five of the shapes to form a shape congruent to the triangle shown below. Make a drawing to explain how you did it.

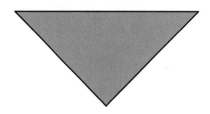

5. Al draws 20 circles in a row. Each circle has a diameter of 25 mm. Each circle touches the next circle at only one point. What is the length of the row of circles?

6. Amber draws rows of congruent shapes. The number of shapes doubles in each row. The sixth row has 96 shapes. How many shapes are in the first row?

7. Can 12 toothpicks be used to form 4 congruent squares? If so, draw the figures.

8. Can 9 toothpicks be used to form 4 congruent triangles? If so, draw the figures.

Extra Practice See 1–2 on page 513.

Quick ✓ Check

Check Your Understanding of Lessons 6–8

Are the figures congruent? Write *yes* or *no*.

1.

2.

Tell whether each line is a line of symmetry.

3.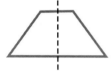

4.

Tell whether each figure has rotational symmetry.

5.

6.

Solve.

7. Arrange twelve toothpicks like this to make 4 squares. Then remove 2 of the toothpicks so that only 2 squares remain.

8. Make a parallelogram like this. Then make one cut so you can put the two pieces together to make a rectangle.

How did you do?

If you had difficulty with any items in the Quick Check, you can use the following pages for review and extra practice.

California Standards	Items	Review These Pages	Do These Extra Practice Items
Geometry: **3.3**	1–2	pages 474–476	Set F, page 511
Geometry: **3.4**	3–6	pages 478–481	Set G, page 511
Reasoning: **1.1, 2.3**	7–8	pages 482–483	1–2, page 513

Test Prep • Cumulative Review
Maintaining the Standards

Choose the letter of the correct answer.

1 Which figure has a line of symmetry?

A

C

B

D

2 Which angle is an acute angle?

F

H

G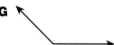

J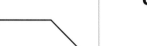

3 Which shows lines that are perpendicular?

A

B

C

D

4 If an isosceles triangle is divided into two congruent parts, what are the two parts?

F squares   **H** triangles

G rectangles   **J** trapezoids

5 Which statement about a radius of a circle is not true?

A It has an endpoint on the circle.

B It is $\frac{1}{2}$ the length of a diameter.

C It has an endpoint at the center of the circle.

D It has both endpoints on the circle.

6 Which figure has rotational symmetry?

F

H

G

J

7 In which pair are the figures congruent?

A

B

C

D

8 Can a right triangle have 3 sides that are the same length?
Explain Support your answer with a drawing.

Modeling Perimeter and Area

You will learn how to find perimeter and area.

New Vocabulary
perimeter
area

Learn About It

Does the **perimeter**, or distance around a figure, determine the number of square units needed to cover the figure?

Use grid paper to find out.

Materials

grid paper or Teaching Tool 25

Step 1 Look at the figures at the right. Find the perimeter of each figure by counting the number of units around the outside of the figure.

Record your answers in a table like the one below.

Shape	Perimeter	Area
Square A	▦ units	▦ square units
Rectangle B	▦ units	▦ square units

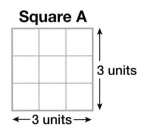

Square A

3 units

3 units

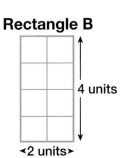

Rectangle B

4 units

2 units

Step 2 Now find the number of square units needed to cover each of the figures.

> The number of square units needed to cover a figure is called the **area** of the figure.

Count to find the area of each figure. Record your answers in your table.

Step 3 Look at your table.

- Can a square have the same perimeter as a rectangle?

- Can rectangles and squares with the same perimeter have different areas?

Standards MG **1.0, 1.2, 1.3, 3.8** SDP **1.0** MR **2.3**

Try It Out

Find the perimeter and area of each figure.
Record your answers in a table like this one.

	Shape	Perimeter	Area
1.	Rectangle C	▦ units	▦ square units
2.	Square D	▦ units	▦ square units
3.	Rectangle E	▦ units	▦ square units

Rectangle C

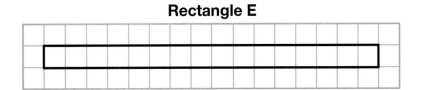

Square D

Rectangle E

Use your table to answer these questions.

4. Can a square have the same area as a rectangle?

5. Can rectangles and squares with the same area have different perimeters?

Use grid paper for Problems 6–8.

6. Draw a rectangle with an area of 20 square units and a perimeter greater than 20 units.

7. Draw a rectangle with an area of 18 square units and a perimeter of 18 units.

8. Draw a rectangle with an area of 24 square units and a perimeter less than 24 units.

Write about it! Talk about it!

Use what you have learned to answer these questions.

9. How are perimeter and area different?

10. Two figures have different shapes. If one figure has a greater perimeter than the other, does it also have a greater area? Explain.

Use Formulas for Perimeter and Area

LESSON 10

You will learn how to use formulas to find the perimeters or areas of polygons.

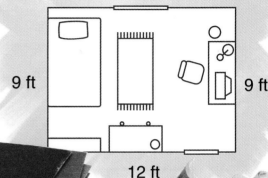

Sherri's Bedroom
12 ft
9 ft   9 ft
12 ft

Learn About It

Sherri's bedroom is 12 ft long and 9 ft wide. She wants to put a border around the room. She also needs a new tile floor. How many feet of border does she need? How many square feet of tile does she need?

In order to find the length of the border she needs, find the perimeter of the room.

Different Ways to Find Perimeter

You can add the lengths of the sides.

Perimeter $= l + w + l + w$

$P = 12 \text{ ft} + 9 \text{ ft} + 12 \text{ ft} + 9 \text{ ft}$

$P = 42 \text{ ft}$

You can use the formula to find the perimeter of a rectangle.

Perimeter $= (2 \times l) + (2 \times w)$

$P = (2 \times 12 \text{ ft}) + (2 \times 9 \text{ ft})$

$P = 24 \text{ ft} + 18 \text{ ft}$

$P = 42 \text{ ft}$

Remember: Do what is in parentheses first.

Solution: Sherri needs 42 feet of border.

To find how much tile is needed for the floor, find the area of the floor. You can also do this in two ways.

Different Ways to Find Area

You can draw a model and count the squares.

1 2 3 ...

Each square is 1 square foot or 1 ft².

You can use this formula to find the area of a rectangle.

Area = length × width

Area $= l \bullet w$

$A = 12 \text{ ft} \bullet 9 \text{ ft}$

$A = 108 \text{ ft}^2$

$l \bullet w$ is another way to write $l \times w$.

Solution: Sherri needs 108 square feet of tile.

Standards AF **1.0, 1.2, 1.4** MG **1.1, 1.4** MR **2.0**

Other Examples

A. Perimeter of a Square

Since all sides (s) of a square are the same length, you can use this formula.

9 in.

9 in.

Perimeter = $4 \cdot s$
$P = 4 \cdot 9$ in.
$P = 36$ in.

The perimeter is 36 inches or 36 in.

B. Area of a Square

Since all sides (s) of a square are the same length, you can use this formula.

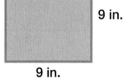

9 in.

9 in.

Area = $s \cdot s$
$A = 9$ in. $\cdot 9$ in.
$A = 81$ in.^{2}

The area is 81 square inches or 81 in.^{2}

Explain Your Thinking

► When you use a formula to find the perimeter of a rectangle, why do you multiply the length by 2 and the width by 2?

► When finding area, why is the answer in square units?

Guided Practice

Find the perimeter of each polygon.

1.
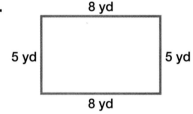
8 yd
5 yd   5 yd
8 yd

2.
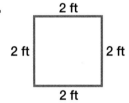
2 ft
2 ft   2 ft
2 ft

Ask Yourself

- What formula can I use to find the perimeter?

- What formula can I use to find the area?

3.

7 mi
3 mi   3 mi
7 mi

4.
10 in.   10 in.
10 in.

5.
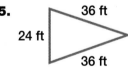
36 ft
24 ft
36 ft

Use a formula to find the area of each rectangle.

6.
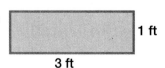
1 ft
3 ft

7.
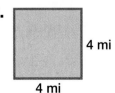
4 mi
4 mi

8.
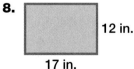
12 in.
17 in.

Independent Practice

Find the perimeter of each polygon.

9.

10 ft
30 ft

10.

3 mi
3 mi

11.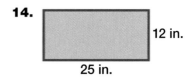

30 in.   50 in.
40 in.

Find the area of each rectangle.

12.

2 mi
3 mi

13.

16 ft
13 ft

14.

12 in.
25 in.

Problem Solving • Reasoning

Solve. Choose a method. Use the information on page 488 for Problems 15–18.

Computation Methods

• **Mental Math**   • **Estimation**   • **Paper and Pencil**

15. Measurement Sherri wants to put ribbon around a square mirror. Each side of the mirror is 20 inches long. What is the least amount of ribbon she will need?

16. Money The tiles that Sherri wants for the floor of her bedroom cost $30 per box. A box of tiles will cover 9 square feet. Can the floor be tiled for less than $350?

17. Compare Sherri was given 2 square wall hangings for her room. The blue wall hanging has sides of 1 yard each. The green wall hanging has sides of 1 meter each. Which wall hanging is larger? Explain how you know.

18. Analyze Sherri bought a rectangular rug for her bedroom. The rug is 2 yards wide and 3 yards long. What is the area of the rug in square feet? How much of her floor will not be covered by the rug?

Mixed Review • Test Prep

Find the average of each set of numbers. *(pages 252–253)*

19. 28, 44, 36, 20

20. 58, 66, 50

21. 121, 219, 225, 130, 170

22 What is the product of 24 and 163? *(pages 198–199)*

A 4,012   **B** 3,912   **C** 3,812   **D** 978

Number Sense

The Length and Width of It

If you know the length and width of a rectangle, you can find the perimeter and area of that rectangle in different units.

Customary Units of Measurement

12 inches = 1 foot (ft)
3 feet = 1 yard (yd)

1-foot-by-1-foot square	**1-yard-by-1-yard square**
1 ft ☐ 1 ft	1 yd ▢ 1 yd
$P = 4$ ft $A = 1$ ft^2	$P = 4$ yd $A = 1$ yd^2

Work together.

1. Use a large sheet of paper or tape on the floor to show a 1-yard-by-1-yard square.

2. Cut out twelve 1-foot-by-1-foot squares from large sheets of paper or from newspapers.

3. Use the 1-foot squares with your 1-yard square to find how many square feet are equal to 1 square yard.

4. Suppose you want to carpet a floor that is 12 feet wide and 15 feet long.

   a. How many square feet of carpeting do you need?

   b. How many square yards of carpeting do you need?

Explain Your Thinking

▶ Explain how you answered the questions in Exercise 4. Did you make a drawing? Did you use addition? Did you use a formula?

Perimeter and Area of Complex Figures

You will learn how to find the perimeters and the areas of figures that are not squares or rectangles.

Learn About It

Dee wants to put a fence around her garden. The space she can use is shown at the right. How much fence should she buy? What is the area of her garden?

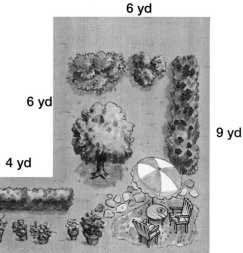

Find the perimeter.

Add the lengths of the sides.

Perimeter = 10 yd + 3 yd + 4 yd + 6 yd + 6 yd + 9 yd

$P = 38$ yd

Solution: She should buy 38 yards of fence.

Find the area.

Step 1 Separate the figure into a rectangle and a square.

3 yd | 10 yd
rectangle

6 yd | 6 yd
square

Step 2 Use a formula to find the area of each polygon. $A = l \times w$ can be written $A = lw$.

Area of the Rectangle
Area = lw
$A = 10$ yd $\times 3$ yd
$A = 30$ yd^2

Area of the Square
Area = $s \times s$
$A = 6$ yd $\times 6$ yd
$A = 36$ yd^2

Step 3 Add both areas to find the area of the whole figure.

30 yd^2 + 36 yd^2 = 66 yd^2

Solution: The area of Dee's garden is 66 square yards.

Explain Your Thinking

▶ Suppose the garden above is separated into a 9 yd by 6 yd rectangle and a 3 yd by 4 yd rectangle. Will the perimeter of the garden be the same? Will the area of the garden be the same?

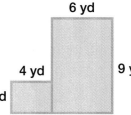

Standards AF **1.0, 1.4** MG **1.0, 1.1, 1.4** MR **1.1, 1.2, 2.4**

Guided Practice

Find the perimeter and area of each figure.

1.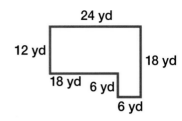

2.

Independent Practice

Find the perimeter and area of each figure.

3.

4.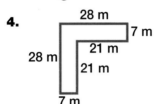

5.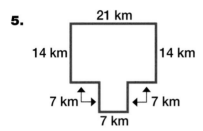

Problem Solving • Reasoning

Use Data Use the drawing and the table at the right for Problems 6–8.

6. Patrick needs to put a fence around this yard. Fencing costs $2 per foot. How many feet of fencing does he need? How much will it cost?

7. **Analyze** Patrick wants to put grass seed on the yard. How many pounds of grass seed will he need?

8. **Write Your Own** Use the data in the table to write a problem. Give your problem to a classmate to solve.

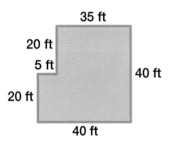

How Much Grass Seed to Buy	
Area (ft²)	**Pounds of Seed**
1,000	1
1,500	2
2,000	3
2,500	4

Mixed Review • Test Prep

Find the product or quotient. *(pages 180–181, 236–237)*

9. $1.55 × 5   10. $7.11 ÷ 3   11. $6.84 × 6   12. $3.75 ÷ 5

13. How many inches are there in 5 feet? *(pages 280–281)*

    A 15 in.   **B** 50 in.   **C** 60 in.   **D** 60 ft

Problem-Solving Skill: Analyze Visual Problems

You will learn how to solve problems that require visual thinking.

Some problems can be solved by finding visual patterns.

Problem Sakura is using tiles to design a mural. If she continues the pattern, which group of tiles should she use for the unfinished section?

First, find the pattern.

• Look at the color of the tiles from top to bottom.

• Then look from left to right.

• Then look at the diagonal rows.

If you look from top to bottom, you see a column of red, green, red followed by a column of yellow, blue, yellow, blue. This pattern repeats.

Then decide which of the choices below completes the pattern.

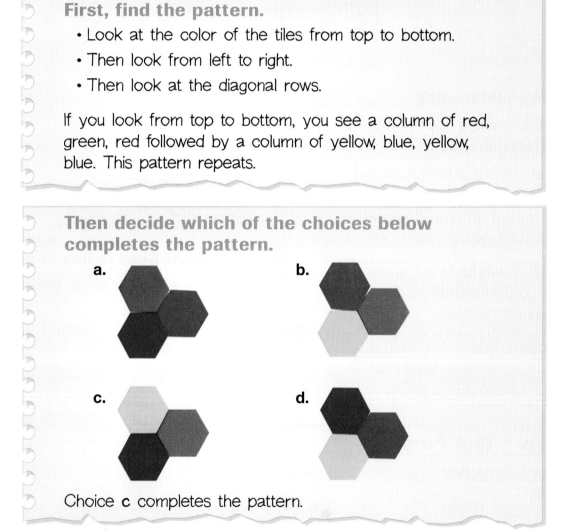

a.

b.

c.

d.

Choice **c** completes the pattern.

Look Back Why would the other choices not complete the pattern?

Standards | MR **1.0, 1.1, 2.0, 2.3, 3.0, 3.2**

Guided Practice

Choose a letter for the missing piece that could complete the pattern.

1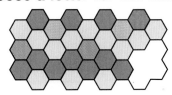

a.   **b.**

c.   **d.**

Think: Look at the rows to find the pattern.

2

a.    **b.**

c. ◥▱◣   **d.** ◥▱◣

Think: Look at the columns to find the pattern.

Choose a Strategy

Solve. Use these or other strategies.

Problem-Solving Strategies

• **Use Logical Thinking**   • **Find a Pattern**   • **Act It Out**   • **Draw a Picture**

3 A border has a repeating design that shows a triangle, a circle, and a pentagon in a row. The triangle is just before the pentagon. The circle is first. Draw the first 8 figures in the border design.

4 Sue Ellen made a design in which 3 out of every 7 quadrilaterals were green. In all, Sue Ellen colored 56 quadrilaterals. How many quadrilaterals did Sue Ellen color green?

Choose a letter for the missing piece that could complete the pattern.

5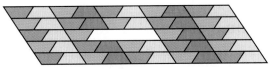

a. ◸▱◿   **b.** ◣▱◸

c. ◢▱◿   **d.** ◸▱◿

6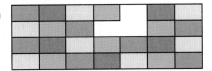

a. ▢▢   **b.** ▢▢

c. ▢▢   **d.** ▢▢

Extra Practice See 3–4 on page 513.

Quick ✓ Check

Check Your Understanding of Lessons 9–12

Find the perimeter and area of each rectangle.

1.

7 in.
7 in.

2.

7 mi
12 mi

3.

10 yd
12 yd

Find the perimeter and area of each figure.

4.

7 cm
8 cm
20 cm
13 cm
20 cm
28 cm

5.

33 m
15 m
21 m
9 m
6 m
24 m

6.

18 cm
25 cm
13 cm
9 cm
6 cm
18 cm
9 cm
6 cm

Solve.

7. Marsha was tiling her wall. If she continues the pattern, how should she fill the missing unfinished section?

a.   b.   c.   d.

8. A border has a triangle, a circle, a rectangle, and a pentagon in a row. The circle is not next to a shape with an even number of sides. The pentagon is just before a shape with an even number of sides. The triangle is first. Draw the border design.

How did you do?

If you had difficulty with any items in the Quick Check, you can use the following pages for review and extra practice.

California Standards	Items	Review These Pages	Do These Extra Practice Items
Geometry: **1.1, 1.4**	1–3	pages 488–490	Set H, page 511
Geometry: **1.1, 1.4**	4–6	pages 492–493	Set I, page 512
Reasoning: **1.1, 2.3, 3.1**	7–8	pages 494–495	3–4, page 513

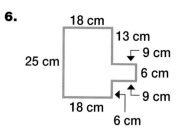

Test Prep • Cumulative Review

Maintaining the Standards

Choose the letter of the correct answer.

1 What is the area of this figure?

3 m

4 m

A 12 m   **C** 12 m³

B 12 m²   **D** 14 m

2 Which figures are congruent?

F

G

H

J

3 What is the median of this set of data?

3, 9, 5, 7, 9

A 3   **C** 7

B 5   **D** 9

4 Which figure has rotational symmetry?

F   **H**

G   **J**

5 There are 8 counters in a bag. Five counters are blue, and 3 counters are green. If you pick a counter without looking, what is the probability that the counter will be green?

A $\frac{3}{8}$ **C** $\frac{5}{8}$

B $\frac{1}{2}$ **D** $\frac{8}{8}$

6 Kathy's bedroom is 12 feet long and 9 feet wide. If she wants to carpet the entire floor, how much carpeting will she need?

F 42 feet   **H** 96 square feet

G 108 feet   **J** 108 square feet

7 How many nonfiction books does the library have?

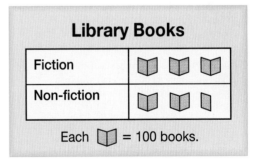

Library Books

Fiction	
Non-fiction	

Each = 100 books.

A 100   **C** 250

B 200   **D** 300

8 Can figures with the same area have different perimeters? **Explain** Give examples to support your answer.

Safe Site

Internet Test Prep
Visit **www.eduplace.com/kids/mhm** for more *Test Prep Practice*.

Solid Figures and Nets

You will learn how to identify and make solid figures.

New
Vocabulary
face
edge
vertex (vertices)
net

Learn About It

Sandcastles are fun to make. You create solid figures when you build sandcastles. Solid figures are figures that take up space. This solid figure is called a cube.

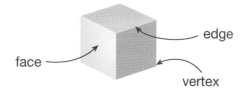

face — edge — vertex

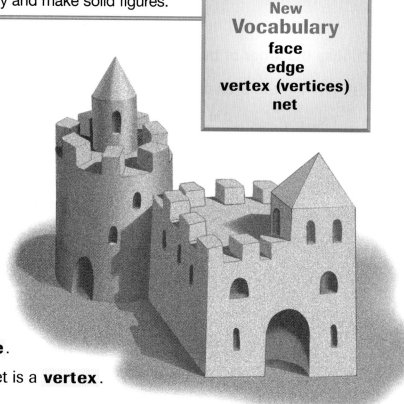

- A cube has 6 **faces**.
- Two faces meet to form an **edge**.
- The point where three edges meet is a **vertex**.

Look at these solid figures.

Solid Figures

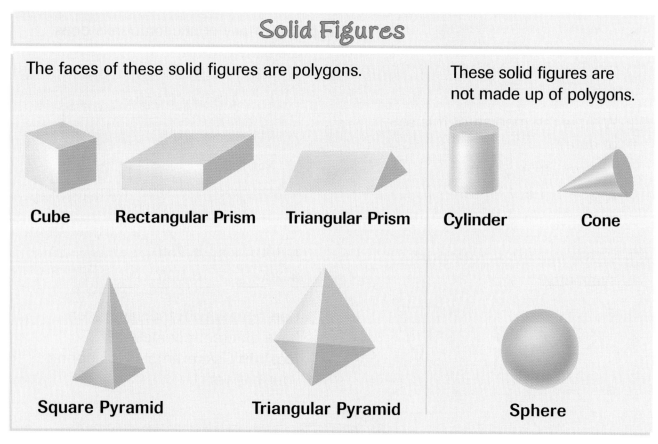

The faces of these solid figures are polygons.

Cube   **Rectangular Prism**   **Triangular Prism**

Square Pyramid   **Triangular Pyramid**

These solid figures are not made up of polygons.

Cylinder   **Cone**

Sphere

Standards MG 3.0, 3.6

These patterns are **nets**. If you cut out a net and fold it on the dotted lines, you can make a solid figure.

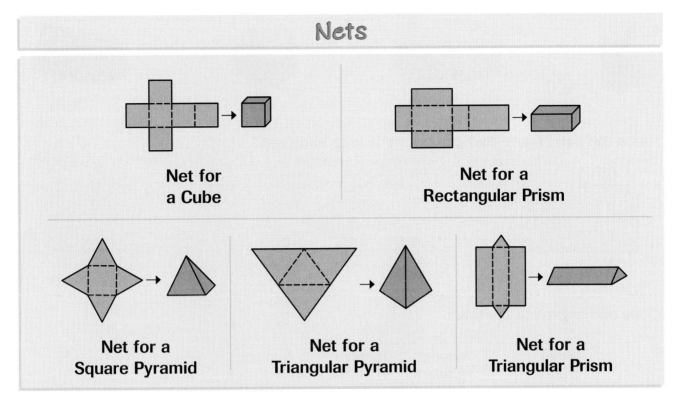

Nets

Net for a Cube

Net for a Rectangular Prism

Net for a Square Pyramid

Net for a Triangular Pyramid

Net for a Triangular Prism

Explain Your Thinking

▶ Which solid figure has faces that are all squares?

▶ Which solid figures can you find in the sandcastle?

Guided Practice

Name each solid figure.

1.

2.

3.

> ### Ask Yourself
> • Are the faces of the solid figure polygons or circles?
> • How many faces will the solid figure have when the net is folded?

4. Which net can be folded to make a cube?

a.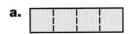

b.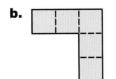

c.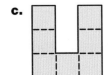

d.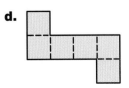

499

Independent Practice

Name the solid figure each object looks like.

5.

6.

7.

8.

Name the solid figure that can be made with each net.

9.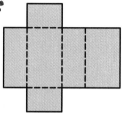

10.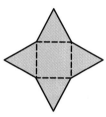

11.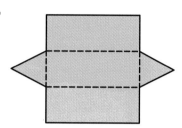

Copy and complete the table.

	Solid Figure	Number of Faces	Number of Edges	Number of Vertices
12.	Cube			
13.	Triangular prism			
14.	Rectangular prism			
15.	Triangular pyramid			

Problem Solving • Reasoning

16. Which solid figures shown on page 498 have curved surfaces?

17. Name a solid figure that has only four faces. Draw a picture of it.

18. Analyze Sarah built a pyramid out of sand. The bottom of the pyramid was a square. What shape were the other faces of the pyramid? How many other faces were there?

19. Explain Jessica got $4.02 in change. She bought items that cost $3.25 and $2.34. Tax was $0.39. How much money did Jessica give the clerk?

Mixed Review • Test Prep

Write each sum or difference. *(page 390–391)*

20. 2.34 + 1.78

21. 8.73 − 2.06

22. 17.8 − 6.9

23. 25.6 + 1.9

24 How many degrees warmer than 3°F is 12°F? *(pages 302–303)*

   A 36 degrees   **B** 15 degrees   **C** 9 degrees   **D** 6 degrees

Extra Practice See Set J on page 512.

Making Solid Figures

Below are three incomplete nets for solid figures.

- Draw each pattern on grid paper or dot paper.

- Draw lines to complete the net for each figure.

- Then cut out and fold to make each solid figure.

- Finally, write the name of the solid figure and tell how many faces, edges, and vertices each has.

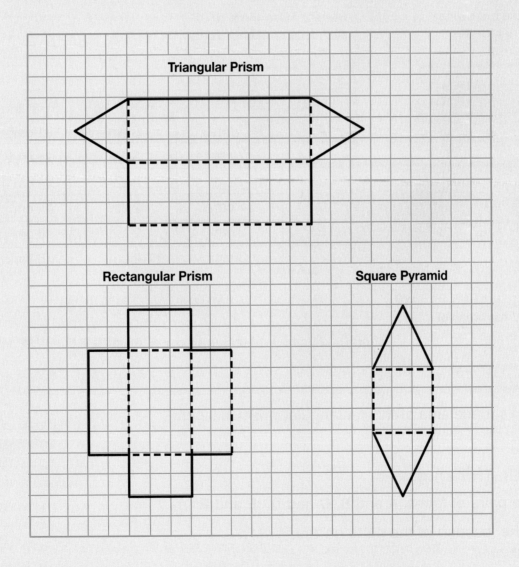

Triangular Prism

Rectangular Prism

Square Pyramid

Surface Area

You will learn how to find the number of square units needed to cover the outside of a solid figure.

New Vocabulary
surface area

Learn About It

The **surface area** of a solid figure is the sum of the areas of all the faces of the figure.

You can follow these steps to find the surface area of the rectangular prism at the right.

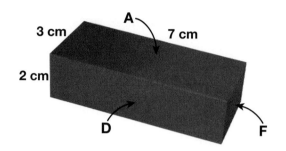

3 cm · A · 7 cm
2 cm
D · F

Step 1 Make a drawing to show the net for this rectangular prism.

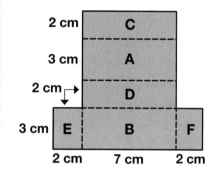

2 cm · C
3 cm · A
2 cm
3 cm · E · B · F
2 cm · 7 cm · 2 cm

Step 2 Find the area of each face of the net using the formula $A = l \times w$.

Face	Length (l)	Width (w)	Area (A)
A	7 cm	3 cm	21 cm^2
B	7 cm	3 cm	21 cm^2
C	7 cm	2 cm	14 cm^2
D	7 cm	2 cm	14 cm^2
E	3 cm	2 cm	6 cm^2
F	3 cm	2 cm	6 cm^2

Step 3 Add the areas of all the faces.

21 cm^2 + 21 cm^2 + 14 cm^2 + 14 cm^2 + 6 cm^2 + 6 cm^2 = 82 cm^2

Solution: The surface area of this rectangular prism is 82 cm^2.

Explain Your Thinking

Look at these pairs of faces: A and B, C and D, E and F.

▶ Describe the location of the pairs on the rectangular prism.

▶ What is true about the areas of the faces in each pair? Explain.

Standards MG 1.1, 1.4, 3.0, 3.6   AF 1.0, 1.4   MR 2.3

Guided Practice

Use the net to find the surface area of this solid figure.

1.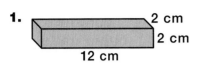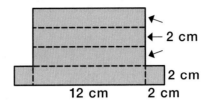

Independent Practice

Use the net to find the surface area of each solid figure.

2.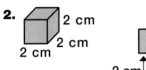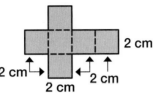

3.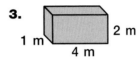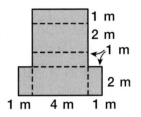

Problem Solving • Reasoning

4. A cube has edges that each measure 10 in. What is the surface area of the cube?

5. **Measurement** A square pyramid has a bottom with an area of 16 in.^{2}. Each of the triangular faces has an area of 6 in.^{2}. What is the surface area of that pyramid?

6. **Analyze** Beth is painting the outside of a rectangular box. She must paint all six faces. The box is 7 ft tall, 4 ft wide, and 2 ft deep. A gallon of paint covers 120 ft^2. Will 1 gallon be enough to paint the outside of the container?

7. **Write Your Own** On grid paper, draw a net for a rectangular prism. Find the surface area of your prism.

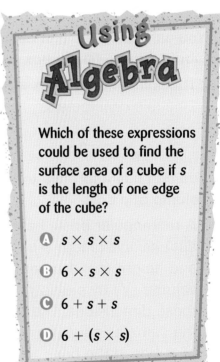

Using Algebra

Which of these expressions could be used to find the surface area of a cube if s is the length of one edge of the cube?

A $s \times s \times s$

B $6 \times s \times s$

C $6 + s + s$

D $6 + (s \times s)$

Mixed Review • Test Prep

Find each product or quotient. *(pages 194–196, 220–221)*

8. 24×12 **9.** 36×11 **10.** $392 \div 14$ **11.** $437 \div 23$

12 What is the sum of $4,526 + 3,339$? *(pages 56–57)*

A 7,955   **B** 7,865   **C** 7,855   **D** 1,187

Volume

You will learn how to find the number of cubes needed to fill the inside of a solid figure.

New Vocabulary
volume
cubic units
cubic centimeter

Learn About It

Suppose you need to know how much a box can hold. You need to find the volume of the box.

Volume (V) is the amount of space inside a solid figure. Volume is measured in **cubic units**.

One standard unit used for measuring volume is a cube with each edge 1 centimeter long. This unit is called a **cubic centimeter**.

1 cm   1 cm

1 cm

Different Ways to Find Volume

You can count the unit cubes it would take to fill the box.

The volume of this box is 24 cubic centimeters.

You can use a formula to find the volume of a box.

A rectangular prism has three dimensions: length (l), width (w), and height (h). You can find its volume (V) by multiplying these dimensions. The result is the same as counting the number of cubes in the box.

The volume of the box is 24 cubic centimeters.

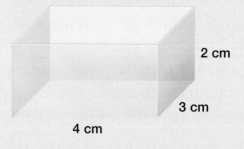

2 cm

3 cm

4 cm

Volume = length × width × height

$$V = l \times w \times h$$
$$V = 4 \text{ cm} \times 3 \text{ cm} \times 2 \text{ cm}$$
$$V = 24 \text{ cubic centimeters}$$

Explain Your Thinking

▶ If the dimensions of a cube are in inches, in what units would the volume be given?

Guided Practice

Find the volume of each figure.

1.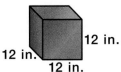
12 in.
12 in.
12 in.

2.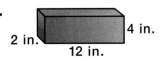
4 in.
2 in.
12 in.

Independent Practice

Find the volume of each figure.

3.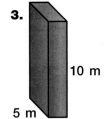
10 m
5 m
2 m

4.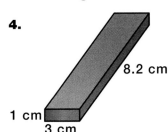
8.2 cm
1 cm
3 cm

5.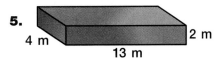
2 m
4 m
13 m

6.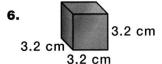
3.2 cm
3.2 cm
3.2 cm

Problem Solving • Reasoning

7. An animal watering tank has dimensions of 5 ft by 3 ft by 8 ft. Find the volume of that tank.

8. Measurement Matt has a cube-shaped box that measures 3 inches on each edge. Penny has a cube-shaped box that measures 6 inches on each edge. What is the volume of Matt's box? What is the volume of Penny's box?

9. Analyze Look at your answers for Problem 8. What happens to the volume of a box when the length of an edge doubles?

Mixed Review • Test Prep

Find each sum or difference. (pages 34–35)

10. $7.68 + $1.44   **11.** $9.09 − $5.55

12 On the spinner base at the right, which outcome is least likely? (pages 436–437)

   A a number less than 5

   B a number greater than 4

   C an even number

   D an odd number

Using Vocabulary

Copy and complete. Use *perimeter, area,* or *volume*.

A To find how much carpeting to buy, you find the _____.

B To find how much fence to buy, you find the _____.

C To find how much water in a container, you find the _____.

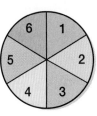

LESSON 16

Problem-Solving Application: Using Formulas

You will learn how to use a formula to solve a problem.

You can use formulas for perimeter, area, surface area, and volume to solve word problems.

Mr. Brown's class is creating a terrarium. The tank for the terrarium is 12 inches long, 8 inches wide, and 9 inches high. They will fill one third of the tank with soil. Then they will put plants in the terrarium. How much soil will they need?

Understand

What is the question?

How much soil is needed to fill one third of the tank?

What do you know?

the length, width, and height of the tank

Plan

How can you find the answer?

- To find the volume of the tank, use this formula:
  $$\text{Volume } (V) = l \times w \times h$$

- Put the known values in the formula and solve.

- Find one third of that volume.

Solve

$$\text{Volume } = l \times w \times h \qquad V = 12 \times 8 \times 9$$
$$V = 864$$

The volume of the tank is 864 cubic inches.
Divide to find how much soil is needed. $\qquad 864 \div 3 = 288$

They will need 288 cubic inches of soil.

Look Back

Estimate to check that your solution is reasonable. Round each measure and estimate the volume.

$$10 \times 10 \times 10 = 1{,}000$$

One third of 1,000 is about 333, which is close to 288.
The answer is reasonable.

| **Standards** | AF **1.4**   MG **1.0, 1.4**   MR **1.0, 1.2, 2.1, 3.0, 3.2**

Guided Practice

Use the terrarium on page 506 for Problems 1 and 2.

1 The terrarium Mr. Brown's class is creating is made from glass. The terrarium will have a glass lid. How many square inches of glass are needed to make the terrarium?

> **Think:** How do I find the surface area of a rectangular prism?

2 Mr. Brown's class took a class vote and decided to put a special multicolored glass lid on the terrarium. What will the area of that lid be?

> **Think:** What is the shape of the lid? How do I find the area?

Choose a Strategy

Use the terrarium on page 506 to solve Problems 3 and 4. Use these or other strategies.

Problem-Solving Strategies

- **Draw a Picture**
- **Write an Equation**
- **Use Logical Thinking**

3 Suppose Mr. Brown's class had decided to fill the terrarium half full with soil. How much soil would the class have used?

4 Draw the net for the terrarium that Mr. Brown's class is creating. Label the top, bottom, and all of the sides.

5 Mark drew a square with a perimeter of 36 inches. Tina drew a square with a perimeter of 32 inches. Beth drew a square with an area of 64 square inches. Which two students drew congruent squares?

6 A terrarium is 3 feet long, 2 feet wide, and 1 feet tall. How much space will the terrarium take on a table? Do you need to find perimeter, area, or volume? What is the answer to the problem?

7 Mr. Brown's class put 3 small plants and 2 large plants in the terrarium. The small plants cost $1.49 each. The large plants cost $2.95 each. How much did the 5 plants cost?

8 Jennifer made a bulletin board about terrariums. The bulletin board is 5 feet long and 4 feet tall. What is the area of the bulletin board that Jennifer made?

 $ 1.49
 $ 2.95
 $ 1.49
 $ 2.95
 $ 1.49

Extra Practice See 5–6 on page 513.

Remember:
► Understand
► Plan
► Solve
► Look Back

Check Your Understanding of Lessons 13–16

Name each solid figure.

1.

2.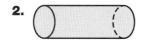

3.

Use the solid figure and its net to answer Exercises 4 and 5.

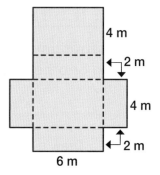

4. Find the surface area of the solid figure at the right.

5. Find the volume of the solid figure at the right.

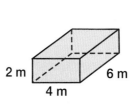

Solve. Use the drawing of the terrarium.

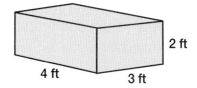

6. Mason wants to find the volume of this terrarium. What formula can he use? What is the volume of the terrarium?

How did you do?

If you had difficulty with any items in the Quick Check, you can use the following pages for review and extra practice.

California Standards	Items	Review These Pages	Do These Extra Practice Items
Geometry: **3.6**	1–3	pages 498–500	Set J, page 512
Algebra: **1.4** Geometry: **1.4, 3.6**	4	pages 502–503	Set K, page 512
Algebra: **1.4** Geometry: **3.6**	5	pages 504–505	Set L, page 512
Algebra: **1.4** Geometry: **3.6** Reasoning: **1.1, 2.4**	6	pages 506–507	5–6, page 513

Test Prep • Cumulative Review
Maintaining the Standards

Choose the letter of the correct answer.

1 What solid can be made from this net?

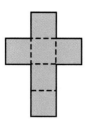

A cube   **C** pyramid

B cylinder   **D** cone

2 Which symbol is not a model of perpendicular line segments?

F +

G L

H =

J T

3 Which figure is an equilateral triangle?

A

C

B

D

4 Which solid has no faces, edges, or vertices?

F cone

G cylinder

H rectangular prism

J sphere

5 What is the area of this figure?

8 in.

4 in.

A 24 square inches

B 32 inches

C 32 square inches

D 32 cubic inches

6 What is the name of this figure?

F rectangle

G rhombus

H trapezoid

J parallelogram

7 How many vertices does a cube have?

A 4

B 6

C 8

D 10

8 Can figures with the same perimeters have different areas?

Explain Give examples to support your answer.

Extra Practice

Set A *(Lesson 1, pages 460–462)*

Use words and symbols to name each figure.

1. K   F

2. M

3. B L

Write *parallel, intersecting,* or *perpendicular* to describe the relationship between lines.

4. H P O N

5. W Y X Z

6. A F D G

Draw an example of each.

7. line segment *LM*

8. line *QR*

9. horizontal line segment *XZ*

10. $\overleftrightarrow{AB} \parallel \overleftrightarrow{CD}$

11. $\overleftrightarrow{EF} \perp \overleftrightarrow{GH}$

12. horizontal $\overleftrightarrow{JK}$ and vertical $\overleftrightarrow{LM}$

Set B *(Lesson 2, pages 464–465)*

Name each angle in three ways. Then classify as *acute, obtuse,* or *right*.

1. M L N

2. S R T

3. W V X

4. M O N

Set C *(Lesson 3, pages 466–467)*

Name each polygon. If the polygon is a quadrilateral, write all names that apply.

1.

2.

3.

4.

Set D *(Lesson 4, pages 468–469)*

Classify each triangle as *equilateral, isosceles,* or *scalene*. Then classify it as *right, obtuse,* or *acute*.

1.

2.

3.

4.

5.

Extra Practice

Set E (Lesson 5, pages 476–477)

Name the part of the circle that is shown in color. Write *center*, *radius*, *diameter*, or *none of these*.

1.   **2.**   **3.**   **4.**   **5.**

Set F (Lesson 6, pages 480–483)

Are the figures in each pair congruent? Write *yes* or *no*.

1.  **2.**  **3.**

Set G (Lesson 7, pages 484–487)

Is the dashed line a line of symmetry? Write *yes* or *no*.

1. 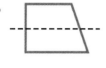 **2.**  **3.**   **4.**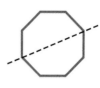

Does each figure have rotational symmetry? Write *yes* or *no*.

5.   **6.**   **7.**   **8.**

Set H (Lesson 10, pages 494–497)

Use a formula to find the perimeter and area of each polygon.

1.
20 in.
30 in.

2.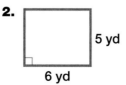
5 yd
6 yd

3.
3 mi
5 mi

Extra Practice

Set I (Lesson 11, pages 492–493)

Find the perimeter and area of each figure.

1.

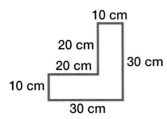

10 cm
20 cm
20 cm
30 cm
10 cm
30 cm

2.

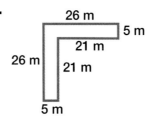

26 m
5 m
21 m
26 m
21 m
5 m

3.

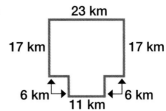

23 km
17 km
17 km
6 km
11 km
6 km

Set J (Lesson 13, pages 498–500)

Name the solid figure each object looks like.

1.

2.

3.

4.

Name the solid figure that can be made with each net.

5.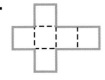

6.

7.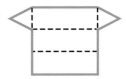

Set K (Lesson 14, pages 502–503)

Use the net to find the surface area of each figure.

1.

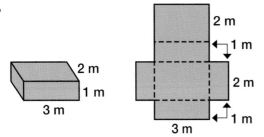

2 m
1 m
3 m
2 m
1 m
2 m
2 m
1 m
3 m

2.

2 m
2 m
2 m
2 m
2 m
2 m
2 m
2 m

Set L (Lesson 15, pages 504–505)

Find the volume of each figure.

1.

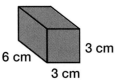

6 cm
3 cm
3 cm

2.

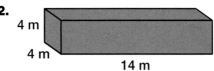

4 m
4 m
14 m

3.

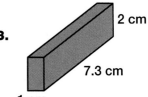

2 cm
7.3 cm
1 cm

Extra Practice • Problem Solving

Use the shapes below for Problems 1–2. *(Lesson 8, pages 482–483)*

1 Arrange the three triangles to form a figure congruent to the rectangle below. Make a drawing to explain how you did it.

2 Arrange all the shapes to form a figure congruent to the shape below. Make a drawing to explain how you did it.

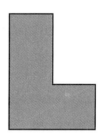

Choose the correct letter of the missing piece. *(Lesson 12, pages 494–495)*

3

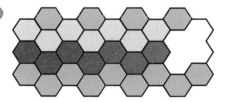

a.

b.

c.

d.

4

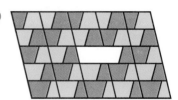

a.

b.

c.

d.

Solve. Use the picture. *(Lesson 16, pages 506–507)*

5 All six faces of the terrarium are made of glass. How many square inches of glass were needed to build the terrarium?

6 What is the volume of the terrarium?

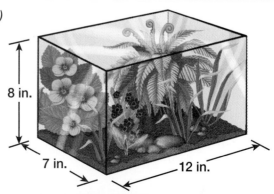

8 in.

7 in.

12 in.

Chapter Review

Reviewing Vocabulary

Answer each question.

1. What is the meaning of each symbol? $\overline{AB}$ $\overleftrightarrow{AB}$

2. Is a circle a polygon? Explain why or why not.

3. Is a square a rectangle? Explain.

4. What is a diameter?

5. How can you tell if a figure has rotational symmetry?

6. What kind of quadrilaterals are the faces of a cube?

Reviewing Concepts and Skills

Write *parallel*, *intersecting*, or *perpendicular* to describe the relationship between each pair of figures. *(pages 460–462)*

7.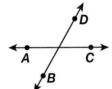

8.

9.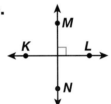

10.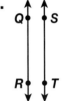

Name each figure. If the figure is a quadrilateral, write all names that apply. *(pages 466–467)*

11.

12.

13.

14.

Draw one triangle for each exercise. *(pages 468–469)*

15. an isosceles triangle that is also an acute triangle

16. a scalene triangle that is also an obtuse triangle

Are the figures in each pair congruent? *(pages 474–476)*

17.

18.

Find the perimeter and area of each figure. (pages 488–493)

19.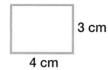
3 cm
4 cm

20.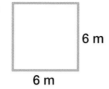
6 m
6 m

21.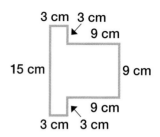
3 cm 3 cm
9 cm
15 cm   9 cm
9 cm
3 cm   3 cm

Name the solid figure that can be made with each net. Then use the net to find the surface area of each figure. (pages 498–503)

22.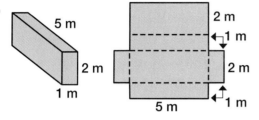
5 m
2 m
2 m
1 m
1 m
2 m
2 m
5 m
1 m

23.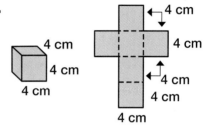
4 cm
4 cm
4 cm
4 cm
4 cm
4 cm
4 cm

Find the volume of each figure. (pages 504–505)

24.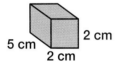
2 cm
5 cm   2 cm
2 cm

25.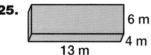
6 m
4 m
13 m

Brain Teasers Math Reasoning

SYMMETRY
Put together 4 equilateral triangles, so that they make a shape that has symmetry. Then put them together a different way to make a shape without symmetry.

TOOTHPICK TRIANGLES
Keith had 12 toothpicks. What was the greatest number of triangles that he can make with all of his toothpicks?

Safe Site

Internet Brain Teasers
Visit **www.eduplace.com/kids/mhm**
for more *Brain Teasers.*

Chapter Test

Write *parallel, intersecting,* or *perpendicular* to describe the relationship between each pair of lines.

1.

2.

3.

Name each figure. If the figure is a quadrilateral, write all names that apply.

4.

5.

6.

7.

Draw one triangle for each exercise.

8. an isosceles triangle that is also a right triangle

9. a scalene triangle that is also an acute triangle

Find the perimeter and area of each figure.

10.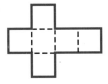
7 m
7 m

11.
10 m
5 m

12.
6 cm
4 cm
4 cm
4 cm
4 cm
14 cm

Name the solid figure that can be made with each net.

13.

14.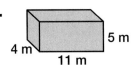

15.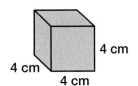

Find the volume of each figure.

16.
4 m
3 m
2 m

17.
5 m
4 m
11 m

18.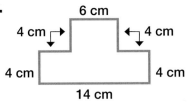
4 cm
4 cm
4 cm

Solve.

19. Choose the two shapes you can use to form a figure congruent to the one below. Make a drawing to explain how you did it.

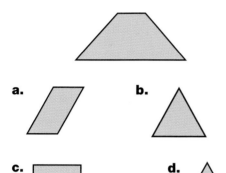

a.

b.

c.

d.

20. Choose the correct letter of the missing piece.

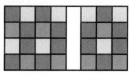

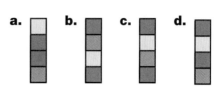

a. b. c. d.

 Write About It

Solve each problem. Use correct math vocabulary to explain your thinking.

1. Copy the figure at the right.

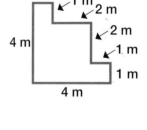

1 m 1 m 2 m

4 m 2 m

1 m

1 m

4 m

   a. Divide the figure in a way that will let you find the area of the figure. Find the area.

   b. Are there other ways to divide the figure to help you find its area? If so, show at least one other way to divide the figure. Will you get the same area by using that way to divide it? Explain. Show your work.

2. The chalkboard shows how Brian found the perimeter of the pentagon.

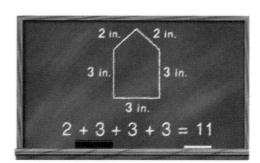

2 in. 2 in.

3 in. 3 in.

3 in.

2 + 3 + 3 + 3 = 11

   a. What did Brian do wrong?

   b. What is the perimeter of the pentagon? What advice would you give Brian so that he does not make the same mistake again?

Another Look

The net below is for making a box. Use the net to answer the questions. You can use formulas to help you solve the problems.

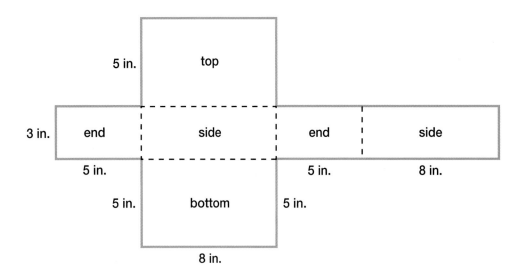

1. Find the perimeter and area of each face. Include appropriate units for each. Make a list of your perimeters and areas and show the numbers you used.

2. What is the surface area of the box?

3. Write a multiplication expression for the volume of the box. What will be the volume of the box?

4. **Look Back** Which parts of the box are congruent? How can you tell?

5. **Analyze** Suppose each side of the bottom was made 2 inches longer. How should the other dimensions of the box be changed in order to make a box? What would be the volume of the new box?

Enrichment

Reflections

Alison is using a stencil to make patterns. She paints
a figure and then flips the stencil over and paints the
figure again.

The second figure she paints is called a reflection.
The dotted line is called the line of reflection.

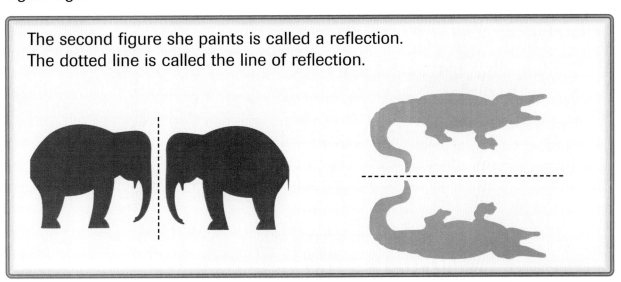

Tell whether the pair of figures shows a reflection.

1.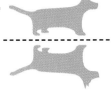

2.

3.

Copy each figure and line of reflection on graph paper.
Draw the reflection of each figure.

4.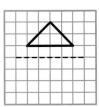

5.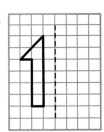

6.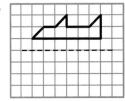

Explain Your Thinking

► How is a reflection like a reflection in a mirror?

Standards | MG 3.4

CHAPTER 11

Graphing and Algebra

Why Learn About Graphing and Algebra?

Graphing helps you organize and display data in a way that makes it easy for you to analyze the information. Algebra is an important part of mathematics that you are just beginning to study.

When you plot points on a graph that are named by ordered pairs, you are beginning to see how graphing and algebra are related.

This woman uses both algebra and graphing in her job of creating special maps of towns and cities.

Reading Mathematics

Reviewing Vocabulary

Understanding math language helps you become a successful problem solver. Here are some math vocabulary words you should know.

ordered pair	a pair of numbers used to locate a point on a grid
positive numbers	numbers that are greater than zero
negative numbers	numbers that are less than zero

Reading Words and Symbols

When you read mathematics, sometimes you read only words, sometimes you read words and symbols, and sometimes you read only symbols.

Here is how to describe the location of the points on the grid at the right.

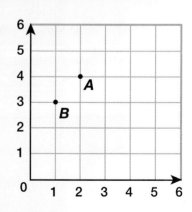

Point A

▶ Start at 0.

▶ Move right 2 units.

▶ Move up 4 units.

▶ The ordered pair for point A is (2, 4).

Point B

▶ Start at 0.

▶ Move right 1 unit.

▶ Move up 3 units.

▶ The ordered pair for point B is (1, 3).

Try These

1. Write *true* or *false*.

   a. The first number in an ordered pair tells how far to move right.

   b. The second number in an ordered pair tells how far to move up.

   c. The ordered pair (2, 3) describes the same location as the ordered pair (3, 2).

   d. The first number in an ordered pair can never be the same as the second number in an ordered pair.

2. Copy and complete the directions for each location.

   a. **Library:** Start at ____.

      Move right ____ units.

      Move ____ 4 units.

   b. **Office:** ____ at 0.

      Move ____ 3 units.

      Move up ____ unit.

   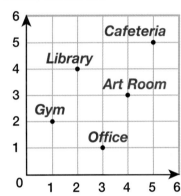

3. Write the ordered pair that describes each location on the grid.

   a. Gym   b. Cafeteria   c. Art Room

Upcoming Vocabulary

Write About It Here are some other vocabulary words you will learn in this chapter. Watch for these words. Write their definitions in your journal.

coordinate	***x*-axis**
integers	***y*-axis**
opposites	***x*-coordinate**
origin	***y*-coordinate**

Locate Points on a Grid Using Whole Numbers

You will learn how to use ordered pairs to name points on a grid.

New
Vocabulary
coordinate

Learn About It

Jana is looking at a map of her town. How can Jana describe where the school is on the map?

Describe the location of the school.

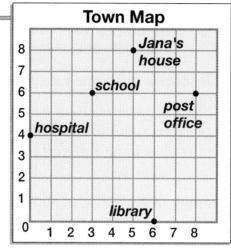

Town Map

Different Ways to Locate a Point

You can use directions in words.

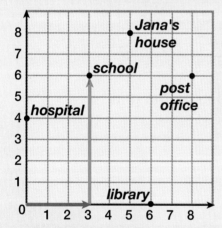

- Start at 0.
- Move right 3 units.
- Then move up 6 units.

You can use an ordered pair.

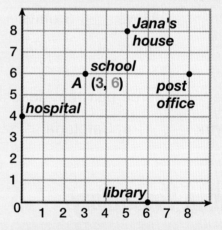

- The ordered pair for point A is (3, 6).
- The numbers in an ordered pair are called **coordinates**. right up

---

Solution: (3, 6) is the ordered pair that names the location of the school.

Other Examples

A. Zero as the First Coordinate

The location of the hospital is (0, 4).

Start at 0. Move 0 units to the right. Then move up 4 units.

B. Zero as the Second Coordinate

The location of the library is (6, 0).

Start at 0. Move right 6 units. Then move up 0 units.

Standards | MG **2.0** MR **2.4**

Explain Your Thinking

▶ Why does knowing both coordinates of an ordered pair help you locate a point?

Guided Practice

Use the town map on page 524 to complete each.

1. Which building location do the following directions describe?

   • Start at 0.
   • Move right 5 units.
   • Then move up 8 units.

2. Complete the directions for the post office.

   • Start at ■.
   • Move right ■ units.
   • Then move up ■ units.

Ask Yourself

• Did I start at zero?

• Did I move to the right first?

Independent Practice

Use the graph to the right for Exercises 3–8.
Write the letter of the point for each ordered pair.

3. $(1, 1)$ 4. $(7, 0)$ 5. $(5, 5)$

Write the ordered pair for each point.

6. Q 7. M 8. N

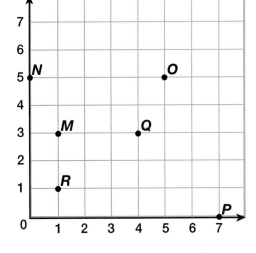

Problem Solving • Reasoning

Use the graph for Problems 9–12.

9. **Compare** Which coordinates of M and Q are the same? Which are different?

10. Which coordinates of M and R are the same? Which are different?

11. Name the ordered pairs for N, O, and P. What do N and P have in common?

12. **Write About It** Does the ordered pair $(3, 4)$ name point Q? Explain.

Mixed Review • Test Prep

Add or subtract. *(pages 350–353)*

13. $\frac{5}{12} + \frac{1}{12}$ 14. $3\frac{3}{4} - 1\frac{1}{4}$ 15. $2\frac{2}{5} + 5\frac{1}{5}$ 16. $\frac{7}{8} - \frac{3}{8}$

Choose the letter of the correct answer. *(pages 330–333)*

17 Which is not in simplest form?

A $\frac{5}{7}$ B $\frac{2}{3}$ C $\frac{6}{11}$ D $\frac{4}{12}$

18 Which fraction is equal to $\frac{1}{2}$?

F $\frac{2}{6}$ G $\frac{4}{10}$ H $\frac{5}{12}$ J $\frac{4}{8}$

Extra Practice See Set A on page 554.

LESSON 2 Graph Ordered Pairs

You will learn how to use ordered pairs to plot points on a graph.

Learn About It

Dana and Maria are playing *Hit the Target*. They take turns naming the coordinates of a point that they think will be inside the target.

Then they **plot** the point on the grid. The first coordinate tells the distance to the right. The second coordinate tells the distance up.

Maria names (5, 7). Is she correct?

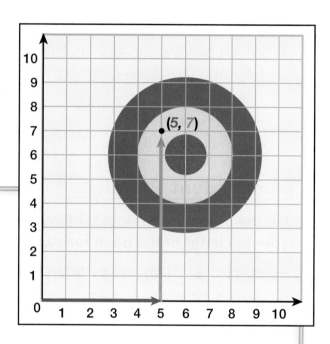

Plot the point named by (5, 7).

• Start at 0.

• Move 5 units to the right.

• Next, move 7 units up.

• Then make a dot on the point.

• Label the point (5, 7).

Solution: The point named by (5, 7) is in the target. Maria is correct.

Another Example: Point Outside Target

Is the point named by (7, 2) in the target?

• Start at 0.
• Move 7 units to the right.
• Then move up 2 units.

The point named by (7, 2) is not in the target.

Explain Your Thinking

▶ Do (3, 5) and (5, 3) name the same point? Why or why not?

Guided Practice

Is the point named by each ordered pair in the target?

1. (5, 2)   **2.** (8, 4)   **3.** (3, 6)

4. (9, 9)   **5.** (3, 4)   **6.** (6, 9)

Ask Yourself

• Did I move to the right the correct number of units?

• Did I move up the correct number of units?

Standards MG **2.0** MR **2.4**

Independent Practice

Copy the grid. Plot each point and label it with the correct letter.

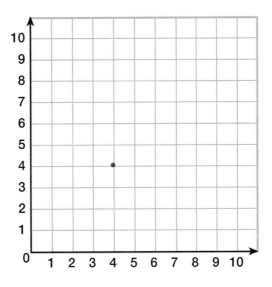

7. E (1, 5)

8. R (3, 5)

9. W (0, 2)

10. L (4, 4)

11. T (0, 5)

12. M (7, 8)

13. X (4, 1)

14. S (4, 7)

15. Z (5, 3)

16. P (8, 7)

Problem Solving • Reasoning

17. Plot the points A (2, 2), B (2, 5), C (8, 5), and D (8, 2) on a grid like the one shown above. Connect the points to form a rectangle.

18. **Analyze** What can you say about the points that have the same first coordinate? What can you say about the points that have the same second coordinate?

19. Look at the target on page 526. Name the ordered pair that describes its center. Maria thinks that the center of the target is at (5, 6). Dan thinks that the center is at (6, 7). Which point is closer to the center? Explain.

20. **Write About It** If one of the coordinates of a point is 0, what do you know about the location of that point?

The famous astronomer who discovered Halley's comet was also a mapmaker.

Edmund Halley made the first map with grid lines in 1701. How many years ago was that?

Mixed Review • Test Prep

Estimate each sum or difference. *(pages 64–65)*

21. $17.25 − $9.98

22. $37.62 + $11.03

23. $299.87 − $87.21

Choose the letter of the correct answer. *(pages 342–343)*

24 What mixed number is equal to $\frac{11}{5}$?

A $1\frac{2}{5}$

C $2\frac{2}{5}$

B $2\frac{1}{5}$

D $5\frac{1}{2}$

25 Which of the following is $3\frac{1}{4}$ written as an improper fraction?

F $\frac{7}{4}$

H $\frac{8}{3}$

G $\frac{7}{3}$

J $\frac{13}{4}$

Extra Practice See Set B on page 554.

Graphs of Functions

You will learn how to plot ordered pairs from a function table and draw a line to help you solve problems.

Learn About It

Josie is buying some gliders. Each package has 2 gliders. She wants to know how many gliders are in 5 packages.

Although Josie could find the answer by extending the table or solving the equation, she could also find the answer by graphing points.

Packages of Gliders	
Equation: $y = 2x$	
x (Number of Packages)	y (Number of Gliders)
1	2
2	4
3	6

Find the number of gliders in 5 packages.

▶ **Plot** and connect the points to show the information from the function table.

▶ **Extend** the line segment.

▶ **Observe** that the points appear to lie on a line.

▶ **Find** the point on the line for 5 packages.

 • Start at 0.

 • Move 5 units to the right.

 • Then move up to meet the line at (5, 10).

The point named by (5, 10) appears to lie on the same line.

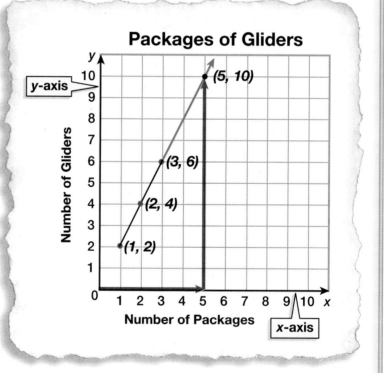

This suggests that continuing the table would lead to more points that lie on the same line.

Solution: There are 10 gliders in 5 packages.

Explain Your Thinking

▶ Why would you show 10 packages with 20 gliders as (10, 20) and not (20, 10)?

▶ Do you think the point named by (8, 18) lies on the line? Explain.

 Standards MG **2.0, 2.1** SDP **1.3** MR **2.3**

Bags of Badminton Birdies

Ask Yourself

• Did I record ordered pairs in the correct order?

• Are all points on a line?

Bags of Badminton Birdies	
Equation: $y = 3x$	
x (Number of Bags)	y (Number of Birdies)
1	3
2	6
3	9

Guided Practice

1. Write the pairs of data in the table as ordered pairs. Use the number of bags as the first coordinate.

2. Copy the grid and the point named by the first ordered pair. Plot the other points and connect them. Extend the line segment. Check that the points lie on a line.

3. Use the graph to decide how many birdies you would expect to find in 4 bags.

Independent Practice

4. Copy the table and extend it to 10 boxes. Then write the pairs of data as ordered pairs. Record the number of boxes as the first coordinate.

5. Make a grid. Number the x-axis to 15 and the y-axis to 30. Plot and connect the points named by the ordered pairs. Check that the points lie on a line.

6. Extend the line segment. Find the number of flying discs that would be in 14 boxes.

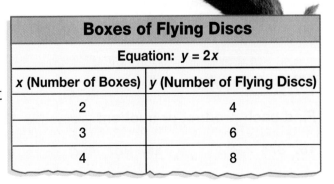

Boxes of Flying Discs	
Equation: $y = 2x$	
x (Number of Boxes)	y (Number of Flying Discs)
2	4
3	6
4	8

Use the table to complete Exercises 7–10.

7. There are 5 flying stars in each box. Copy and complete the table.

8. Make a grid. Number the *x*-axis to 7 and the *y*-axis to 35. Plot ordered pairs from the table. Use the number of boxes as the first coordinate and the number of stars as the second coordinate.

9. Check that the ordered pairs lie on the same line.

10. Extend the line. How many flying stars would you expect to be in 6 boxes?

Boxes of Flying Stars	
Equation: $y = 5x$	
x (Number of Boxes)	y (Number of Stars)
1	5
2	
3	
4	

Problem Solving • Reasoning

Use Data Use the graph for Problems 11–14. Assume that the graph consists of points that lie on the same line.

11. How many dragonflies are in 3 bags?

12. **Compare** How many more dragonflies are in 3 bags than in 1 bag?

13. How many bags would hold 10 dragonflies? How can you tell from the graph?

14. **Analyze** Let *x* stand for the number of bags. Let *y* stand for the number of dragonflies. Write a rule of the form "*y* = " for calculating the number of dragonflies in *x* bags.

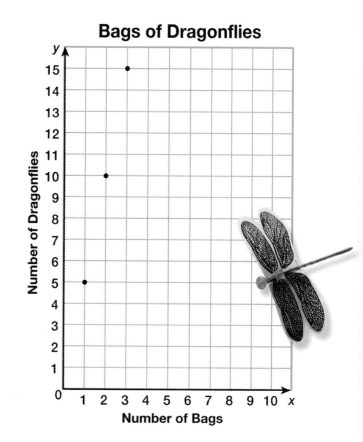

Bags of Dragonflies

Number of Dragonflies / Number of Bags

Mixed Review • Test Prep

Find each product or quotient. *(pages 198–199; 232–233)*

15. 374×82

16. $987 \div 2$

17. 623×12

18. $652 \div 3$

19. Which of these numbers is not divisible by 5? *(pages 246–247)*

   A 35   **B** 40   **C** 45   **D** 52

   Extra Practice See Set C on page 554.

Show What You Know

Using Vocabulary

Use the clues to find each ordered pair.

1. The first coordinate is 3 more than 6. The second coordinate is 8 more than 2.

2. The first coordinate is the product of 4 and 5. The second coordinate is the sum of 4 and 9.

3. The first coordinate is exactly halfway between 4 and 8. The second coordinate is 3 more than the first coordinate.

4. The first coordinate is 4 more than the second coordinate. The sum of the coordinates is the product of 2 and 7.

What's My Rule?

Choose the equation that shows the rule for each graph. Let x stand for the first coordinate and let y stand for the second coordinate.

1.

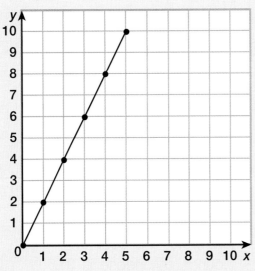

a. $y = x + 2$ **b.** $y = 2x$

2.

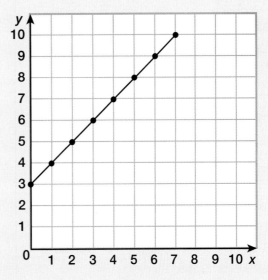

a. $y = x + 3$ **b.** $y = 3x$

Problem-Solving Skill: Use a Graph

You will learn how to solve problems using graphs.

When you see a line graph, you should think about what the points on the line mean.

Problem Students and their parents are planning for Family Night at school. They need to know how much snacks will cost.

Look at the graphs below.

Sometimes only some of the points on a line have meaning.	**Sometimes every point on a line has meaning.**
You can use this graph to find the cost of 1 box, 2 boxes, 3 boxes, and so on.	You can use this graph to find the cost of any amount of cheese.

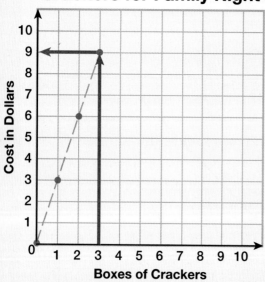

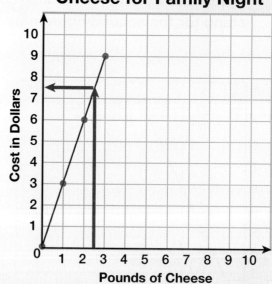

For example, the cost of 3 boxes of crackers is $9.

For example, the cost of $2\frac{1}{2}$ pounds of cheese is $7.50.

Look Back Why doesn't it make sense to use the graph to find the cost of $2\frac{1}{2}$ boxes of crackers?

Standards SDP **1.3**   MR **1.0, 2.0, 3.0, 3.2**

Guided Practice

Solve. Use the graph at the right.

Recipe For Fruit Punch

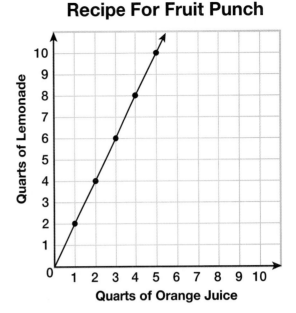

Quarts of Lemonade (y-axis, 0 to 10)
Quarts of Orange Juice (x-axis, 0 to 10)

1. Some students made fruit punch with orange juice and lemonade for Family Night. If they used 4 quarts of orange juice, how many quarts of lemonade did they use?

   Think: Can you use one of the points marked to help you?

2. Suppose the students use 4 $\frac{1}{2}$ quarts of orange juice. How many quarts of lemonade should they use?

   Think: Is there a point on the line that you can mark to use?

Choose a Strategy

Solve. Use the graph above for Problems 3–6. Use these or other strategies.

Problem-Solving Strategies

- **Guess and Check**
- **Find a Pattern**
- **Write an Equation**
- **Use Logical Thinking**

3. The first batch of fruit punch was made with 10 quarts of lemonade. How many quarts of orange juice were used?

4. The second batch of fruit punch was made with 7 quarts of lemonade. How many quarts of orange juice were used?

5. Are more than 4 quarts of orange juice needed to make 3 gallons of fruit punch? Explain your thinking.

6. Let x stand for quarts of orange juice. Let y stand for quarts of lemonade. Write a rule to show the relationship.

7. The fruit the school bought for Family Night cost twice as much as the nuts. The nuts cost twice as much as the vegetables. If the school spent a total of $84 on fruit, nuts, and vegetables, how much did it spend on fruit?

8. First-graders sent up 1 balloon at Family Night. The second-graders sent up 4 balloons. Third-graders sent up 9 balloons. If this pattern continued, how many balloons did the fourth-graders likely send up?

Extra Practice See Set 1–2 on page 557.

Quick ✓ Check

Check Your Understanding of Lessons 1–4

Use the graph. Write the letter of the point for each ordered pair.

1. (4, 4) **2.** (3, 1) **3.** (1, 3)

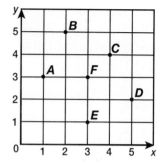

Plot each point on a grid. Label the point with the letter.

4. *L* (1, 4) **5.** *M* (5, 2) **6.** *N* (2, 1)

Use the table for Problems 7–9.

7. Write the pairs of data as ordered pairs. Record the number of boxes as the first coordinate.

8. Draw a grid. Plot the points named by the ordered pairs. Connect the points.

9. Extend the line. Find the number of kites that would be in 5 boxes.

Boxes of Kites	
Number of Boxes	Number of Kites
1	2
2	4
3	6

Solve.

10. Use the graph at the right. Find the cost for 2 pounds of sauce and for $2\frac{1}{2}$ pounds of sauce.

How did you do?

If you had difficulty with any items in the Quick Check, you can use the following pages for review and extra practice.

California Standards	ITEMS	REVIEW THESE PAGES	DO THESE EXTRA PRACTICE ITEMS
Measurement and Geometry: **2.0**	1–3	pages 524–525	Set A, page 554
Measurement and Geometry: **2.1**	4–6	pages 526–527	Set B, page 554
Measurement and Geometry: **2.1**	7–9	pages 528–530	Set C, page 554
Measurement and Geometry: **2.0** Math Reasoning: **1.1, 2.3, 3.2**	10	pages 532–534	1–2, page 557

Test Prep • Cumulative Review

Maintaining the Standards

Choose the letter of the correct answer. If a correct answer is not here, choose NH.

1 Jamie's hamster weighs 1.25 pounds. What is 1.25 rounded to the nearest tenth?

A 1　　　　**C** 1.3

B 1.2　　　**D** 1.35

2 Which shows this figure turned 180°?

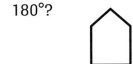

3 Two lines intersect and form four right angles. What are these lines called?

A parallel　　　**C** perpendicular

B skew　　　　**D** diagonal

4 Which is a diameter of the circle?

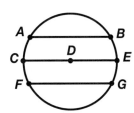

F $\overline{AB}$　　　**H** $\overline{FG}$

G $\overline{CD}$　　　**J** $\overline{CE}$

5 $5\overline{)137}$

A 27　　　　**C** 28

B 27 R2　　**D** NH

6 Mr. Harris fenced in a rectangular dog run in his backyard. The dog run measures 50 feet long and 25 feet wide. What is the area of the dog run?

F 150 ft　　　**H** 1,250 ft^2

G 150 ft^2　　**J** 1,250 ft

7 Which figure has a line of symmetry?

A

B

C

D

8 If all circles are the same shape, are all circles congruent?

Explain Tell why or why not.

Safe Site

Internet Test Prep
Visit **www.eduplace.com/kids/mhm**
for more *Test Prep Practice*.

535

LESSON 5

Integers

You will learn about integers.

New Vocabulary
integers
opposites
negative integers
positive integers

Learn About It

David and Sara are playing a game. In the first round, David lost 4 points and Sara won 5 points. How will David and Sara record their scores?

The numbers ⁻4 and ⁺5 are **integers**. ⁻4 is a negative integer. 5 is a positive integer. We can write ⁺5 instead of 5. They are the same. The opposite of the negative integer ⁻4 is the positive integer 4. The opposite of the positive integer ⁺5 is ⁻5.

The **opposites** of the positive integers (1, 2, 3, 4, …), are the negative integers (⁻1, ⁻2, ⁻3, ⁻4, …). Integers include 0, the positive integers, and the negative integers.

Score Card

	David	Sara
Round 1	⁻4	⁺5
Round 2		
Round 3		

David can write ⁻4 to show his score is 4 points less than 0. The number is read "negative 4."

Sara can write ⁺5 or 5 to show she has 5 points more than 0. The number is read "positive 5."

Integers can be shown on a number line.

| Negative integers are less than 0. | Positive integers are greater than 0. |

$$-8 \quad -7 \quad -6 \quad -5 \quad -4 \quad -3 \quad -2 \quad -1 \quad 0 \quad +1 \quad +2 \quad +3 \quad +4 \quad +5 \quad +6 \quad +7 \quad +8$$

Zero is neither positive nor negative. It is its own opposite.

Other Examples

A. Positive Integers
- 17 feet above sea level   ⁺17
- 50 degrees above zero   ⁺50
- 4 minutes after blast off   ⁺4

B. Negative Integers
- 5 feet below sea level   ⁻5
- 14 degrees below zero   ⁻14
- 3 floors below street level   ⁻3

Explain Your Thinking

▶ Locate ⁺3 and ⁻3 on the number line. Why are these numbers called opposites?

Standards NS **1.8**   AF **1.0**   MR **2.3**

Guided Practice

Write the integer for each letter on the number line.

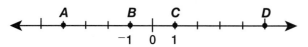

1. A **2.** B **3.** C **4.** D

Ask Yourself

• Is the number greater than 0?

• Is the number less than 0?

Independent Practice

Write the integer for each situation.

5. 3 minutes before blast off

6. 9 degrees below zero

7. 2 stories above street level

8. $4 overdrawn in an account

For each letter, write the integer from the number line.

9. E **10.** I **11.** J **12.** L **13.** G **14.** F **15.** K **16.** H

Problem Solving • Reasoning

17. Draw a number line. Show the integers $^-12$ through $^+12$.

18. Suzy's checking account balance was $50. She wrote a check for $55. What integer represents her checking account balance?

19. **Write About It** On a number line, Jill started at zero, moved 4 spaces to the right, and then moved 9 spaces to the left. On what number did she end? Explain your thinking.

Using Algebra

Compare. Use >, <, or = for each ⬤ .

Ⓐ $^-3$ ⬤ $^+3$

Ⓑ 7 ⬤ $^+7$

Ⓒ $^-2$ ⬤ $^-5$

Ⓓ $^-8$ ⬤ $^-4$

Ⓔ $^+6$ ⬤ 3

Mixed Review • Test Prep

Find the mean, median, and mode for each group of numbers. *(pages 420–421)*

20. 6, 8, 7, 6, 3   **21.** 41, 28, 72   **22.** 14, 10, 10, 18   **23.** 31, 38, 43, 36

24 What is $\frac{3}{4}$ of 12? *(pages 326–327)*

A 3   **B** 6   **C** 9   **D** 16

Extra Practice See Set D on page 555.

Identify Points on a Coordinate Plane

You will learn how to use ordered pairs of integers to name points on a coordinate plane.

Learn About It

Students at Carter School used a grid to make this treasure map. The **coordinate plane** is formed by two perpendicular number lines. What is the location of the treasure trunk?

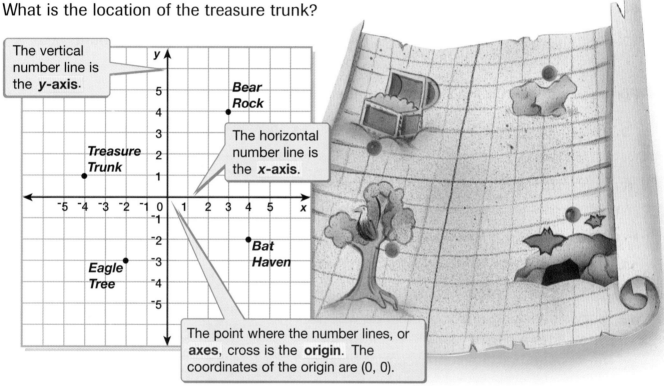

The vertical number line is the **y-axis**.

Bear Rock

The horizontal number line is the **x-axis**.

Treasure Trunk

Eagle Tree

Bat Haven

The point where the number lines, or **axes**, cross is the **origin**. The coordinates of the origin are (0, 0).

Different Ways to Locate a Point

You can use directions in words.

To find the treasure trunk:

• Start at 0.

• Move left 4 units.

• Move up 1 unit.

You can use an ordered pair.

The treasure trunk is located at (⁻4, 1).

The first coordinate, ⁻4, is called the **x-coordinate**. If the x-coordinate is positive, move to the right. If it is negative, move to the left.

The second coordinate, 1, is called the **y-coordinate**. If the y-coordinate is positive, move up. If it is negative, move down.

Standards AF **1.1** MG **2.0** MR **2.0, 3.3**

Other Examples

A. Negative y-coordinate

Locate Bat Haven.

- Start at the origin.
- Move right 4 units.
- Then move down 2 units.

The ordered pair is (4, ⁻2).

B. Negative x- and y-coordinates

Locate Eagle Tree.

- Start at the origin.
- Move left 2 units.
- Then move down 3 units.

The ordered pair is (⁻2, ⁻3).

Explain Your Thinking

▶ In the ordered pair, (4, 3), which number is the *x*-coordinate? What does it tell you?

▶ In the ordered pair (5, ⁻6), which number is the *y*-coordinate? What does it tell you?

▶ Why do you need two coordinates to name a point?

Ask Yourself

- If I move right, is the x-coordinate positive or negative?

- If I move down, is the y-coordinate positive or negative?

Guided Practice

Use the graph at the right. Follow the directions. Write the letter and the coordinates of each point.

1. • Start at the origin.
   • Move right 5 units.
   • Then move up 4 units.

2. • Start at the origin.
   • Move left 4 units.
   • Then move up 2 units.

3. • Start at the origin.
   • Move left 5 units.
   • Then move down 4 units.

4. • Start at the origin.
   • Move left 1 unit.
   • Then move down 2 units.

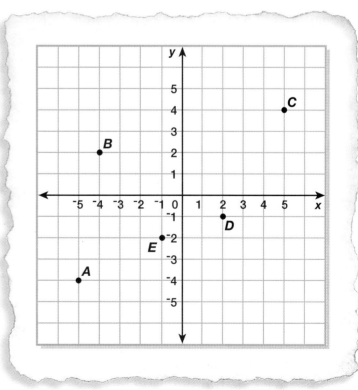

Independent Practice

Use the graph at the right. Follow the directions. Write the letter and the coordinates of each point.

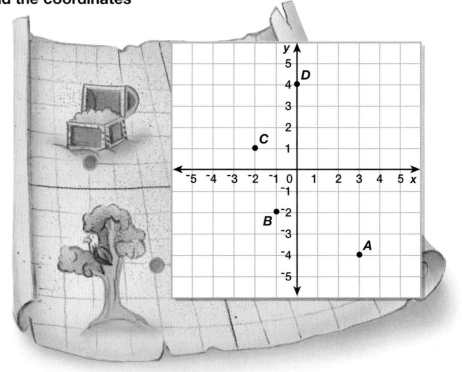

5. • Start at the origin.
   • Move right 3 units.
   • Then move down 4 units.

6. • Start at the origin.
   • Move left 2 units.
   • Then move up 1 unit.

7. • Start at the origin.
   • Move right 0 units.
   • Then move up 4 units.

8. • Start at the origin.
   • Move left 1 unit.
   • Then move down 2 units.

**Use the graph at the right.
Name the letter for each ordered pair.**

9. $(3, ^-1)$

10. $(1, 2)$

11. $(^-3, ^-1)$

12. $(^-3, 3)$

13. $(^-2, ^-2)$

14. $(0, 2)$

15. $(^-3, ^-3)$

16. $(5, 1)$

n **Algebra • Expressions Let *n* = 5.**
Write the coordinates for each ordered pair.

17. $(n, n + 4)$

18. $(n, n - 4)$

19. $(n, 5n)$

20. $(n, n + 12)$

21. $(n, 8n)$

22. $(n, 8n + 1)$

23. If the *x*-coordinate of a point is negative, will the point be to left or right of the *y*-axis?

24. If the *y*-coordinate of a point is positive, will the point be above or below the *x*-axis?

Problem Solving • Reasoning

Solve. Choose a method.

Computation Methods

- Mental Math
- Estimation
- Paper and Pencil

25. Analyze A point is exactly 3 units away from the origin on one of the axes. Where can it be?

26. At Carter School, 195 students are boys and 198 are girls. About how many students are there?

27. On a town map, Carter School is located at (4, 0). The library is located at (0, 4). The post office is at the origin. What do you know about the distance from the post office to the library and the school?

28. The number of fourth-grade students at Carter School is 4 greater than the number of third-grade students. There are 48 third- and fourth-graders in all. How many students are in each grade?

Mixed Review • Test Prep

Find the area and perimeter of each rectangle. *(pages 490–493)*

29. $l = 3$ in.
$w = 4$ in.

30. $l = 12$ m
$w = 23$ m

31. $l = 28$ ft
$w - 16$ ft

32. $l = 11$ cm
$w = 12$ cm

Choose the letter of the correct answer. *(pages 78–81; 132–135)*

33 Which expression stands for 4 more than p?

A $p - 4$
B $4 - p$
C $p + 4$
D $p \times 4$

34 Which expression stands for the product of 3 and w?

F $w + 3$
G $3w$
H $w \div 3$
J $w - 3$

Write *true* or *false* for each statement.

35. A point on the x-axis has a y-coordinate of 0.

36. Every point on the y-axis has a y-coordinate of 0.

37. The point (0, 3) is on the x-axis.

38. The origin is on both the x-axis and the y-axis.

Extra Practice See Set E on page 555.

Graph Ordered Pairs on the Coordinate Plane

You will learn how to plot points with integer coordinates.

Learn About It

Harriet made a shape on grid paper. She told her friend Karl how to make the shape.

Harriet said, "The four corners of my shape are *A*, *B*, *C*, and *D*. *A* is at (5, 4). *B* is at (⁻4, 4). *C* is at (⁻5, ⁻3). *D* is at (4, ⁻3). Connect *A* to *B*, *B* to *C*, *C* to *D*, and *D* to *A* to make the shape." What is the shape Harriet made?

Plot and connect points on a grid to make the shape Harriet made.

Step 1 Plot *A* (5, 4).

- Start at the origin.
- Move 5 units to the right.
- Then move 4 units up.
- Make a dot on the point.
- Label the point *A* (5, 4).

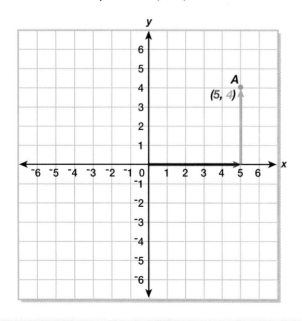

Step 2 Plot *B* (⁻4, 4).

- Start at the origin.
- Move 4 units to the left.
- Then move 4 units up.
- Make a dot on the point.
- Label the point *B* (⁻4, 4).

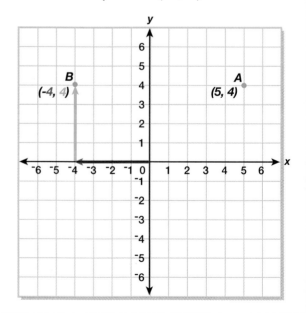

Standards   MG **2.0**   MR **2.3**

Step 3 Plot C (⁻5, ⁻3).	**Step 4** Plot D (4, ⁻3).
• Start at the origin.	• Start at the origin.
• Move 5 units to the left.	• Move 4 units to the right.
• Then move 3 units down.	• Then move 3 units down.
• Make a dot on the point.	• Make a dot on the point.
• Label the point C (⁻5, ⁻3).	• Label the point D (4, ⁻3)
	• Connect A to B, B to C, C to D, and D to A.

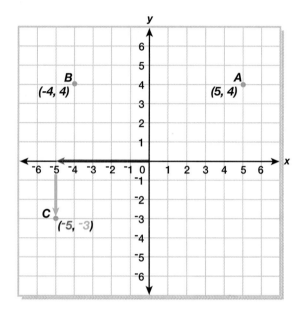 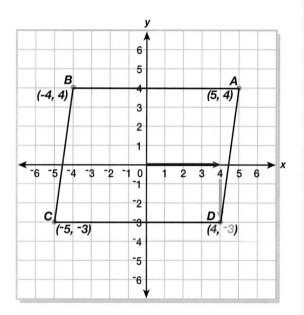

Solution: The shape Harriet made is a parallelogram.

Explain Your Thinking

▶ If both numbers in an ordered pair are greater than zero, in what part of the coordinate plane will the point be?

▶ If both numbers in an ordered pair are less than zero, in what part of the coordinate plane will the point be?

Guided Practice

Complete the sentence for each point.

    a. First move ____ units to the ____.

    b. Then move ____ units ____.

1. (3, ⁻4)

2. (⁻6, 3)

3. (8, 5)

4. (⁻2, ⁻7)

Ask Yourself

• Did I start at the origin?

• Did I move left or right first?

• Did I move up or down second?

Independent Practice

Draw an *x*-axis and a *y*-axis on graph paper. Number each axis as shown in the graph below. Find, mark, and label each point.

5. *R* (2, ⁻4)

6. *U* (⁻4, 2)

7. *S* (⁻1, ⁻3)

8. *W* (3, 6)

9. *T* (4, 5)

10. *Y* (⁻7, 2)

Use your graph to answer these questions.

11. List the points that are above the *x*-axis. List the points that are below the *x*-axis.

12. Predict How can you tell from an ordered pair whether a point will be above or below the *x*-axis?

13. Which points are to the left of the *y*-axis? Which points are to the right of the *y*-axis?

14. How can you tell from an ordered pair whether a point will be to the left or to the right of the *y*-axis?

Problem Solving • Reasoning

Use the graph on the right.

15. Write the ordered pairs for *A*, *B*, *C*, and *D*.

16. Compare How are the ordered pairs alike? What do you notice? How are the ordered pairs different? What do you notice?

17. Write About It Record the ordered pairs for three other points you know are on this graph. Tell how you decided what the coordinates should be.

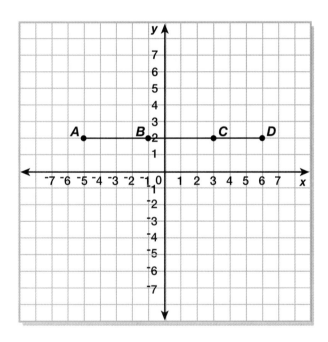

Mixed Review • Test Prep

Write a fraction for each decimal. Write a decimal for each fraction. *(pages 380–381)*

18. 0.1

19. $\frac{3}{100}$

20. 0.75

21. $\frac{8}{10}$

22. 0.02

23. $\frac{44}{100}$

24 Which number is divisible by 2 and 5? *(pages 246–247)*

A 12   **B** 15   **C** 20   **D** 25

        Extra Practice See Set F on page 555.

Graph Tick-tack-toe

Practice plotting points by playing this game with a partner.
Try to be the first to get four in a row!

What You'll Need

- *Playing board made on graph paper with x and y axes as shown. (Teaching Tool 21)*

**Players
2**

Here's What To Do

1. One player uses *X* and the other uses *O*.

2. Players take turns choosing a point by naming its coordinates and marking the point with *X* or *O*.

3. If a point has already been marked, the player loses a turn.

4. The winner is the first player to get four *X*'s or four *O*'s together in a line—horizontally, vertically, or diagonally.

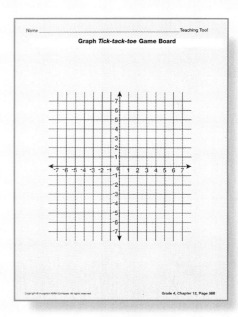

Share Your Thinking Explain a strategy you used when playing the game.

Problem-Solving Strategy: Choose a Strategy

You will learn how to choose a strategy to solve a problem.

When you have a problem to solve, you need to decide which strategy to use.

Problem Andrew's sister is his "home banker." His account was at ⁻7 because he owed her $7. She agreed to give him a credit of $5 because he gave her his old hockey stick. What integer now represents the balance of Andrew's account?

Understand

What is the question?
What integer shows the balance of Andrew's account?

What do you know?
- Andrew's balance was ⁻7 .
- His sister gave him a credit of $5.

Plan

How can you solve this problem?
Use either the Use a Model or the Draw a Picture strategy.

Solve

Make a Model

+5

```
←—+—+—+—+—+—+—+—+—+—+—+—+—+—+—+—+—→
  ⁻8 ⁻7 ⁻6 ⁻5 ⁻4 ⁻3 ⁻2 ⁻1  0  1  2  3  4  5  6  7  8
```

Draw a Picture

| -$1 | | -$1 | | -$1 | | -$1 | | -$1 | | -$1 | | -$1 |

The balance of Andrew's account now is ⁻2.

Look Back

Look back at the problem.
Which strategy would you use? Explain why.

Standards NS **1.8**   MR **1.0, 2.0, 2.3, 3.0, 3.2**

Guided Practice

Use a strategy to solve each problem.

1 Ed's account with his mother was at ⁻5. He borrowed $10 more to buy kneepads. What integer represents Ed's account with his mother now?

Think: Can I use a model to solve this problem?

2 Beth's account with her father was at ⁻8. Then she earned $8, which she gave to her father for her account. What integer represents her account now?

Think: Can I draw a picture to solve this problem?

Choose a Strategy

Solve. Use these or other strategies.

Problem-Solving Strategies

- **Make a Table**
- **Guess and Check**
- **Draw a Picture**
- **Use Logical Thinking**

3 The Blue Team and the Red Team played a game. Fourteen goals were scored in all. The Red Team scored 2 fewer goals than the Blue Team. How many goals did the Blue Team score?

4 Megan's mother brought enough oranges to hockey practice so that each of the 12 players on the team could have 3 orange quarters. How many oranges did she bring?

5 The balance of Tim's account with his sister Rita went to 0 when he paid her back $10. What was his balance before he paid her the $10?

6 Lea owes $5 to her cousin. She earned $8 baby-sitting for 2 hours. How much money will she have after she pays what she owes?

7 The Blue Team ordered 4 pizzas after the game. Each pizza cost $6, and the delivery charge was $5. The manager gave the delivery person a $50 bill. How much change did the manager receive?

8 During the season, the Red Team won two fewer games than the Blue Team. The Green Team won 5 more games than the Blue Team. How many more games did the Green Team win than the Red Team?

Extra Practice See 3–6 on page 557.

Find Lengths on a Coordinate Plane

You will learn how to use coordinates to find the lengths of line segments.

Learn About It

Diane plotted the points *A* (1, 2) and *B* (7, 2). Then she drew a horizontal line segment to connect the points. Carla plotted the points *C* (9, 3) and *D* (9, 8). She connected these points with a vertical line segment. How many units long is each segment?

To find the length, you can count units. Another way is to find the difference between coordinates.

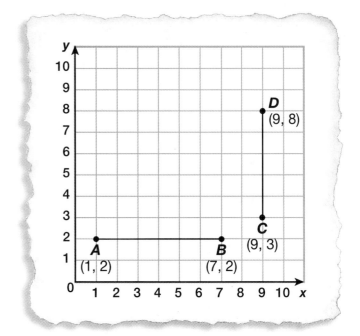

To find the length of a horizontal line segment, find the difference between the x-coordinates.

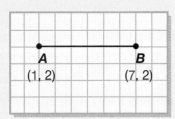

$$7 - 1 = 6$$

To find the length of a vertical line segment, find the difference between the y-coordinates.

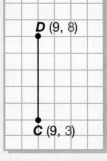

$$8 - 3 = 5$$

Solution: The distance from *A* to *B* is 6 units. The distance from *C* to *D* is 5 units.

Explain Your Thinking

▶ If you connect the points named by (2, 3) and (2, 8) with a line segment, will the line segment be horizontal or vertical? How can you tell without plotting the points?

Standards MG **2.2, 2.3** MR **2.3**

Guided Practice

Find the length of each line segment.

1. $\overline{AB}$ 2. $\overline{BC}$ 3. $\overline{CD}$

4. How many units long is the line segment that connects the points whose ordered pairs are (7, 2) and (7, 5)?

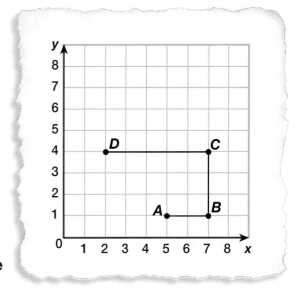

Independent Practice

Graph each pair of points. Find the length of the segment that connects each pair of points.

5. (2, 4) (2, 9) 6. (3, ⁻5) (10, ⁻5) 7. (4, 0) (4, 2) 8. (4, 6) (8, 6)

Find the length of the line segment that connects each pair of points.

9. (6, 0) (9, 0) 10. (⁻2, 1) (⁻2, 7) 11. (6, ⁻1) (1, ⁻1) 12. (⁻8, 4) (⁻8, 13)

Problem Solving • Reasoning

13. **Analyze** The length of segment XY is 5 units. If X is named by (3, 6), and Y is named by (3, ■), then what are the possible values for ■?

14. **Logical Thinking** A rectangle is 6 units long and 4 units wide. Two of the corners of the rectangle are at points named by (10, 7) and (6, 7). Draw a graph showing the ordered pairs for the other two corners.

15. Plot the points A (1, 6), B (8, 6), C (8, 1) and D (1, 1). Connect the points to form a rectangle. What are the length and width of the rectangle?

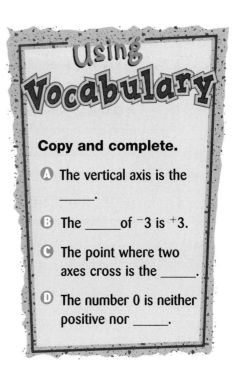

Using Vocabulary

Copy and complete.

Ⓐ The vertical axis is the _____.

Ⓑ The _____ of ⁻3 is ⁺3.

Ⓒ The point where two axes cross is the _____.

Ⓓ The number 0 is neither positive nor _____.

Mixed Review • Test Prep

Find each sum or difference. *(pages 56–63)*

16. $3,010 - 1,893$ 17. $78,123 + 5,675$ 18. $\$22.34 - \$11.99$

19. Which is equal to 0.06? *(pages 380–381)*

A $\frac{6}{10}$ **B** $\frac{1}{6}$ **C** $\frac{6}{100}$ **D** $\frac{1}{60}$

Extra Practice See Set G on page 556.

Problem-Solving Application: Use a Graph

You will learn how to solve a problem by extending a line graph.

When data can be represented by points that lie on a line, you can sometimes solve a problem by extending the line.

Problem Ace Sports Shop rents out bicycles. The table shows some hourly costs for renting a bicycle. The graph shows the relationship between the amount of time and the cost. How much does it cost to rent a bicycle for 4 hours?

 **Understand**

What is the question?
How much will it cost to rent a bicycle for 4 hours?

What does the graph show?
The red line shows the cost to rent a bicycle for times from 1 hour to 3 hours.

Ace Bicycle Rental Fees

Time	Cost
1 hr	$ 7
2 hr	$ 9
3 hr	$ 11

 Plan

How can you find the answer?
You can extend the line.

 Solve

Extend the line on the graph.
Use a ruler to extend the line. The point named by (4, 13) is on the graph.

So it should cost $13 to rent a bicycle for 4 hours if the pattern continues.

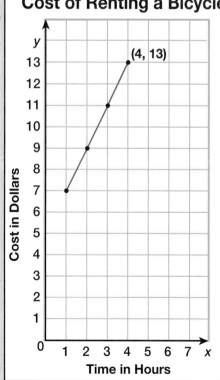

**Ace Rentals
Cost of Renting a Bicycle**

Look Back

Look back at the problem.
How does the graph relate to the table?

Standards MG **2.1** SDP **1.1, 1.3** MR **1.0, 2.0, 3.0, 3.1, 3.2**

Bicyclists in Austin, Texas, ride in a road race to raise money for cancer research.

Remember:
▶ Understand
▶ Plan
▶ Solve
▶ Look Back

Guided Practice

Solve. Use the graph at the right.

1 How much will it cost to rent a bicycle from Star Sports for 2 hours?

Think: Is the information you need shown on the graph?

2 How much will it cost to rent a bicycle from Star Sports for 5 hours?

Think: Can you extend the line to help find the answer?

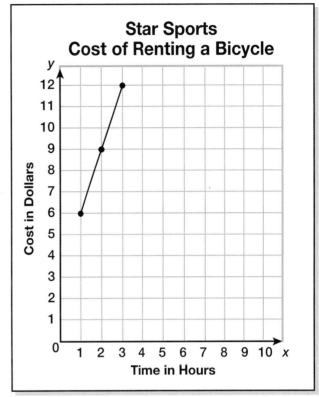

**Star Sports
Cost of Renting a Bicycle**

Cost in Dollars

Time in Hours

Choose a Strategy

Use the graph above for Problems 3–5 and 7–8. Use these or other strategies.

Problem-Solving Strategies

- Draw a Picture
- Find a Pattern
- Write an Equation
- Use Logical Thinking

3 If you extend the line down, the graph will include the point (0, 3). Does that point have any meaning for this graph? Explain.

4 Let *x* stand for the number of hours. Let *y* stand for the cost of the bike rental. Write a rule to show the relationship.

5 Use your rule from Problem 4. How much will it cost to rent a bicycle from Star Sports for 12 hours? for 15 hours?

6 Al's used bike cost $3 more than Joy's. Ed's bike cost $2 less than Joy's. If Ed's bike cost $24, how much did Al's bike cost?

7 How much will it cost to rent a bicycle from Star Sports for 6 hours?

8 If you extend the line, will the point (7, 29) be on it?

Extra Practice See 7–8 on page 557.

551

Quick ✓ Check

Check Your Understanding of Lessons 5–10

Use the graph at the right. Name the letter for each ordered pair.

1. (3, 2)   **2.** (⁻4, ⁻2)   **3.** (5, ⁻1)

Draw a graph like the one at the right. Then locate, mark, and label each point.

4. P (3, ⁻5)   **5.** Q (2, 6)   **6.** R (⁻2, ⁻4)

Find the length of the line segment that connects each pair of points.

7. F (3, 0) and G (3, 4)   **8.** J (2, ⁻3) and K (7, ⁻3)

Solve. Use the graph for Problem 9.

9. Paco and his father want to rent a boat. How much will it cost to rent a boat from Walter's Boat Rentals for 5 hours?

10. Ellen wants to buy sneakers that cost $39. She has $15 and can save $4 more each week. In how many weeks will she have enough money to buy the sneakers?

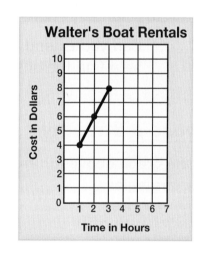

Walter's Boat Rentals

How did you do?

If you had difficulty with any items in the Quick Check, you can use the following pages for review and extra practice.

California Standards	ITEMS	REVIEW THESE PAGES	DO THESE EXTRA PRACTICE ITEMS
Number Sense: **1.8** Geometry: **2.0**	1–3	pages 538–541	Set E, page 555
Number Sense: **1.8** Geometry: **2.1**	4–6	pages 542–544	Set F, page 555
Number Sense: **1.8** Geometry: **2.2, 2.3**	7–8	pages 548–549	Set G, page 556
Geometry: **2.1** Reasoning: **1.1, 2.3**	9	pages 550–551	7–8, page 557
Reasoning: **1.1, 2.3**	10	pages 546–547	3–6, page 557

Test Prep • Cumulative Review
Maintaining the Standards

Choose the letter of the correct answer. If a correct answer is not here, choose NH.

1 Two hundred sixty-four students were assigned to 8 same-size classes. How many students were in each class?

A 32 R2   **C** 38

B 33   **D** NH

2 Which triangle is a scalene triangle?

3 How many vertices does a cylinder have?

A 0   **C** 4

B 1   **D** 7

4 Which equation shows the relationship between the diameter (*d*) and the radius (*r*) of a circle?

F $d = 2r$

G $d = \frac{1}{2}r$

H $d = 3r$

J $d = r \cdot r$

5 Which statement is not true?

A All rectangles are parallelograms.

B Some rectangles are squares.

C No squares are parallelograms.

D No trapezoids are parallelograms.

6 What is the estimated sum of 16.7 and 13.39 if both addends are rounded to the nearest whole number?

F 29   **H** 30.1

G 30   **J** 30.09

7 Two lines are in the same plane but never intersect. What are these lines called?

A perpendicular

B parallel

C skew

D diagonal

8 Carpet squares are being placed on the floor of a closet that is 4 feet long and 3 feet wide. If the carpet squares measure 1 foot on each side, how many carpet squares are needed?

Explain How did you find your answer?

Safe Site

Internet Test Prep
Visit **www.eduplace.com/kids/mhm**
for more *Test Prep Practice.*

553

Extra Practice

Set A *(Lesson 1, pages 524–525)*

Use the grid at the right for Exercises 1–6.
Write the letter of the point for each ordered pair.

1. (2, 2) **2.** (7, 5) **3.** (6, 3)

Write the ordered pair for each point.

4. *E* **5.** *F* **6.** *D*

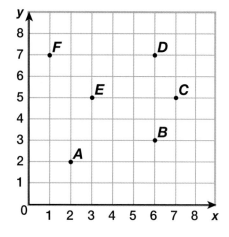

Set B *(Lesson 2, pages 526–527)*

Copy the grid. Plot each point.
Label the point with the letter.

1. *A* (2, 3) **2.** *C* (1, 4) **3.** *E* (5, 2)

4. *D* (3, 0) **5.** *F* (3, 3) **6.** *B* (2, 5)

7. *H* (0, 4) **8.** *J* (5, 1) **9.** *I* (3, 4)

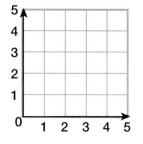

Set C *(Lesson 3, pages 528–530)*

1. Write the pairs of data in the table as ordered pairs. Use the number of packages as the first coordinate.

Packages of Tomatoes

Number of Packages	1	2	3	4	5
Number of Tomatoes	3	6	9	12	15

2. Copy the grid and plot the points named by the ordered pairs. Connect the points.

3. Use your graph to predict how many tomatoes you would expect to be in

a. 6 packages

b. 8 packages

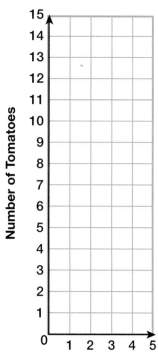

Packages of Tomatoes

Extra Practice

Set D *(Lesson 5, pages 536–537)*

Write the integer for each situation.

1. 4 minutes before blast off
2. 7 degrees below zero
3. score after earning 3 points
4. a balance of $4 in an account

For each letter, write the integer from the number line.

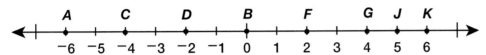

1. A
2. D
3. B
4. F
5. K
6. C
7. J
8. G

9. Draw a number line. Show the integers ⁻15 through ⁺15.

Set E *(Lesson 6, pages 538–541)*

**Use the graph at the right. Follow the directions.
Write the letter and coordinates of each point.**

1. • Start at the origin.
   • Move right 2 units.
   • Then move down 3 units.

2. • Start at the origin.
   • Move left 4 units.
   • Then move up 2 units.

3. • Start at the origin.
   • Move 0 units.
   • Then move down 3 units.

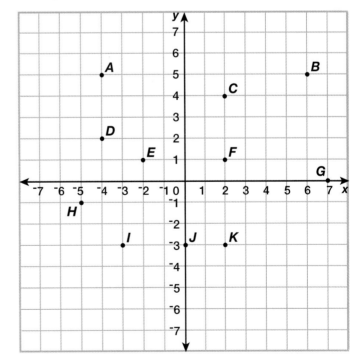

Use the graph above. Name the letter for each ordered pair.

4. (6, 5)
5. (2, 4)
6. (⁻4, 5)
7. (-2,1)
8. (⁻5, ⁻1)
9. (7, 0)

Extra Practice

Set F *(Lesson 7, pages 542–544)*

Draw an *x*-axis and a *y*-axis
on grid paper. Number each
axis as shown at the right.
Find, mark, and label each point.

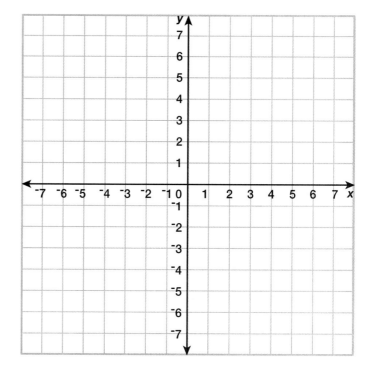

1. $P\,(^-4,\,2)$

2. $Q\,(3,\,^-1)$

3. $R\,(5,\,4)$

4. $S\,(^-2,\,^-4)$

5. $T\,(6,\,3)$

**Use your graph to answer
these questions.**

6. Which points are above
   the *x*-axis?

7. Which points are to the
   right of the *y*-axis?

Set G *(Lesson 9, pages 548–549)*

**Make a grid like the one above. Graph each pair of points.
Find the length of the line segment that connects each
pair of points.**

1. $(1,\,3)$ and $(1,\,8)$ 2. $(3,\,^-2)$ and $(8,\,^-2)$ 3. $(^-5,\,0)$ and $(^-5,\,4)$

4. $(2,\,1)$ and $(7,\,1)$ 5. $(^-4,\,^-5)$ and $(^-4,\,^-8)$ 6. $(0,\,0)$ and $(0,\,8)$

**Find the length of the line segment that connects each
pair of points.**

7. $(4,\,8)$ and $(13,\,8)$ 8. $(^-7,\,6)$ and $(^-7,\,12)$ 9. $(0,\,0)$ and $(5,\,0)$

Extra Practice • Problem Solving

Solve. Use the graph at the right. *(Lesson 4, pages 532–533)*

1 You are in charge of mixing the plaster for art class. The mixing instructions at the right tell how much water to mix with the plaster. If you use 6 cups of plaster mix, how much water should you use?

2 Suppose you want to use 2 cups of water. How many cups of plaster mix should you use?

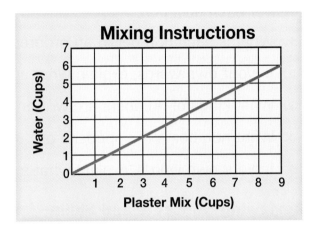

Mixing Instructions

Use a strategy to solve each problem. *(Lesson 8, pages 546–547)*

3 Kevin collects baseball cards. He has an album that will hold 64 cards. He has 23 cards in the album now. If he collects 6 cards each week, how many weeks will it take to fill the album?

4 Sue wants to buy a new coat that costs $54. Sue delivers newspapers to earn money. She earns $9 per week. She has $15 saved now. How many weeks from now will it take for her to have $54?

5 Notebooks cost $1 each. If you buy 2 notebooks, you get a third notebook free. How much will it cost for 6 notebooks?

6 Ned's father is buying shirts. The shirts cost $15 each. If you buy 3 shirts, you get two free. How much will it cost for 5 shirts?

Solve. Use the graph at the right. *(Lesson 10, pages 550–551)*

7 Amy is helping the Read-A-Thon. Every time Amy reads a book, money is donated to the library. How much money will be donated to the library if Amy reads 3 books?

8 Write a rule that shows how much money is donated for each book read.

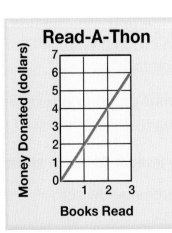

Read-A-Thon

Chapter Review

Reviewing Vocabulary

Answer each question.

1. What is each number in an ordered pair called?

2. In your own words, explain what an integer is.

3. What kinds of numbers are written with a $^+$?

4. What number is the opposite of $^-8$?

5. In your own words, explain what a negative number is.

Reviewing Concepts and Skills

Write the letter or the ordered pair for each point.
(pages 524–525)

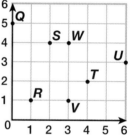

6. (4, 2)   7. (0, 5)   8. (6, 3)

9. *V*   10. *R*   11. *W*

Plot each point on a grid. Label the point with the letter. *(pages 526–527)*

12. *A* (5, 2)   13. *M* (0, 3)   14. *C* (3, 5)

Solve.

15. Write the data in the table as ordered pairs. Use the number of cans as the first coordinate.

Cans of Tennis Balls			
Number of Cans	1	2	3
Number of Balls	3	6	9

16. Copy the grid. Plot the first three points named by the ordered pairs in Exercise 15. Connect the points.

17. Use your graph from Exercise 16 to predict how many balls you would expect to be in 5 cans.

Write the integer for each situation. *(pages 536–537)*

18. 3 degrees below zero   19. 3 feet above sea level

Cans of Tennis Balls

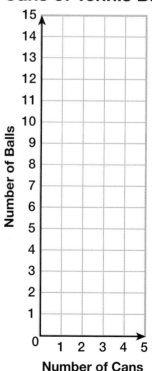

Let _n_ = 3. Write the coordinates for each ordered pair. *(pages 548–551)*

20. $(n, n + 2)$ **21.** $(n, n - 3)$ **22.** $(n, 4n)$ **23.** $(n, 6n + 1)$

Draw an _x_-axis and a _y_-axis on graph paper. Number each axis as shown at the right. Find, mark, and label each point.

24. $P\,(^-3, 3)$ **25.** $L\,(^-3, ^-1)$

26. $M\,(4, ^-1)$ **27.** $T\,(4, 3)$

Find the length of the line segment that connects each pair of points. *(pages 554–555)*

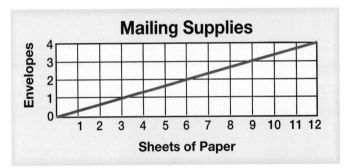

28. $(3, 7)$ and $(12, 7)$ **29.** $(^-7, 1)$ and $(^-7, 7)$ **30.** $(0, 0)$ and $(6, 0)$

Solve. Use the graph for Problems 31–32.

(pages 538–539; 552–555; 556–557)

31. 3 envelopes are used. How many sheets of paper are used?

32. How many envelopes are used when 6 sheets of paper are used?

33. A shirt costs $12. Greg has $5. He saves $2 a week. In how many weeks will he have enough money to buy the shirt?

Mailing Supplies

Envelopes / Sheets of Paper

 Brain Teasers Math Reasoning

A TRICKY TRIO

The sum of 3 numbers is the same as the product of the 3 numbers. What are the numbers?

3, 2, 1

Use the digits 1, 2, and 3 to form all the possible 3-digit numbers in which each digit is used once. What is the average of these numbers?

Safe Site

Internet Brain Teasers
Visit **www.eduplace.com/kids/mhm**
for more *Brain Teasers.*

Chapter Test

Write the letter of the point named by each ordered pair.

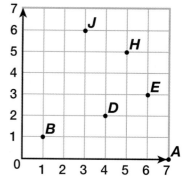

1. (1, 1) **2.** (7, 0) **3.** (3, 6)

Make a grid. Plot each point. Label each point with the letter.

4. Q (2, 5) **5.** R (3, 7) **6.** S (4, 4)

7. Write the pairs of data in the table as ordered pairs. Use the number of packages as the first coordinate.

Packages of Game Cards			
Number of Packages	3	4	5
Number of Cards	15	20	25

For each letter, write the integer from the number line.

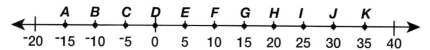

8. B **9.** E **10.** C **11.** H

Let *n* = 4. Write the coordinates for each ordered pair.

12. (*n*, *n* + 3) **13.** (*n*, *n* − 3) **14.** (*n*, 2*n*) **15.** (*n*, *n* + 5)

Draw an *x*-axis and a *y*-axis on graph paper. Number each axis as shown at the right. Find, mark, and label each point.

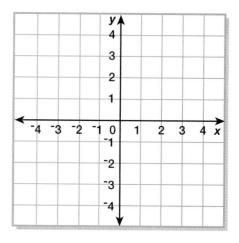

16. Point P (3, 3)

17. Point L (0, ⁻2)

18. Point O (⁻2, ⁻1)

19. Point T (⁻3, 3)

Find the length of the line segment that connects each pair of points.

20. (1, 1) and (1, 5)

21. (⁻3, 3) and (⁻3, 8)

22. (4, 3) and (10, 3)

23. (⁻2, 1) and (⁻2, 7)

Solve. Use the graph for Problem 24.

24. How much water will flow out of the pipe in 3 minutes?

25. Tickets to the science museum cost $4. On Mondays, every third person is admitted free. How much would it cost for 12 people to go to the science museum on a Monday?

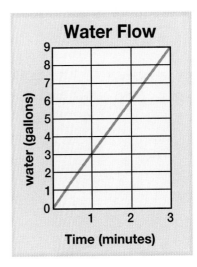

Water Flow

water (gallons) / *Time (minutes)*

Write About It

Solve the problem. Use correct math vocabulary to explain your thinking.

1. Julie does yard work for neighbors. She earns $4 an hour.

   a. Make a data table that shows Julie's hours and total pay for 1–6 hours.

   b. Write the data as ordered pairs. Use hours worked as the first number in each ordered pair.

   c. Make a grid. Plot the ordered pairs on graph paper. Use hours worked for the *x*-axis.

   d. Describe how to use a graph to predict what Julie can earn in 8 hours.

Another Look

Use the graph to solve the problems.
Each square is one square mile.

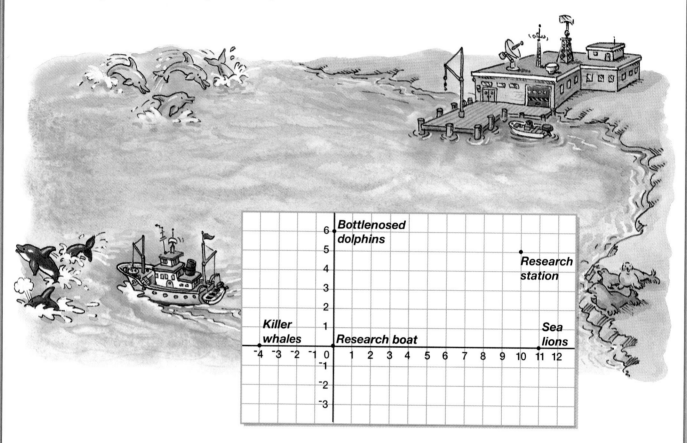

1. Write the coordinates of each of the points that locate something on the graph.

2. Find the distance between the Research boat and each of the marine animals.

3. **Look Back** How could you use the answers to problem 2 to find the distance between the Killer whales and the Sea lions? Explain why this works.

4. **Analyze** Write the ordered pairs whose points lie on a straight line segment that connects the Research boat to the Research station.

Standards MG **2.2, 2.3**

Enrichment

Slides

A **slide** moves a figure up, down, or over along a line. When you slide a figure, its size and shape do not change.

See what happens when the original figure *ABC* slides 5 units to the right.

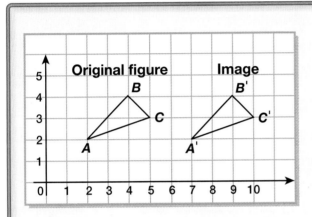

	Ordered Pairs
Original figure	A(2, 2) B(4, 4) C(5, 3)
Image	A'(7, 2) B'(9, 4) C'(10, 3)

Notice that after the slide:

- *A* becomes *A'*, *B* becomes *B'*, and *C* becomes *C'*.
- the first coordinate of each point increases by 5.
- the second coordinate of each point does not change.

Suppose you were to slide figure *ABC* the number of units given in the exercises below. Write the ordered pairs of the points *A'*, *B'*, *C'* on the image after the slide.

1. 1 unit left

2. 2 units down

3. 2 units up

4. 4 units to the right

Explain Your Thinking

Which coordinate of the point changed when the figure was moved left or right? Which coordinate of the point changed when the figure was moved up or down?

Standards | MG **2.0**

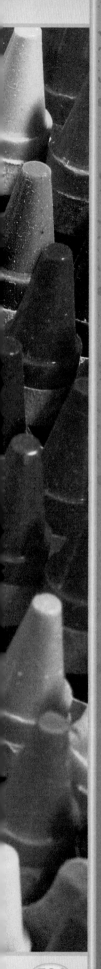

Two-Digit Divisors

Why Learn About Division By Two-Digit Divisors?

Division with two-digit divisors is a very important skill. Calculating batting averages and finding the number of miles a car can drive on one gallon of gasoline are just two ways of using division.

When the members of your softball team sell something to raise money for new equipment, you can use division to figure out the average amount sold by each member.

Look at all these crayons. They are at the factory ready to be placed into crayon boxes. The people who do the packaging use division to determine how many crayon boxes will be needed.

Reading Mathematics

Reviewing Vocabulary

Understanding math language helps you become a successful problem solver. Here are some math vocabulary words you should know.

dividend	a number that is divided
divisor	a number that a dividend is divided by
quotient	the answer in division
remainder	the number left over after dividing
divisible	when a number can be divided by another number and the remainder is zero

Reading Words and Symbols

When you read mathematics, sometimes you read words, sometimes you read words and symbols, and sometimes you read only symbols.

Here are examples of division with and without remainders.

$$
\begin{array}{r}
21 \\
4\overline{)84} \\
-8 \\
\hline
04 \\
-4 \\
\hline
0
\end{array}
\qquad
\begin{array}{r}
16\ \text{R4} \\
5\overline{)84} \\
-5 \\
\hline
34 \\
-30 \\
\hline
4
\end{array}
$$

► When 84 is divided by 4, there is no remainder.

► When 84 is divided by 5, there is a remainder.

Try These

1. Tell if each sentence describes division. Write *yes* or *no*.

   a. Thirty-two marbles are in two bags. Sixteen marbles are in each bag.

   b. Erin shared nineteen stickers with four friends. Each friend got four stickers. Erin kept three stickers.

   c. Ryan spent $27 at the sporting goods store. He paid $10 for a baseball cap and $17 for a T-shirt.

   d. Twenty-four students are members of The Book Club. Thirteen members are boys. Eleven members are girls.

2. Write a division example for each situation.

   a. The quotient has one digit.
   The dividend has two digits.
   The divisor has one digit.
   There is a remainder.

   b. The divisor has one digit.
   The quotient has two digits.
   The dividend has two digits.
   There is no remainder.

   c. The quotient has one digit.
   The dividend has two digits.
   The divisor has one digit.
   There is no remainder.

   d. The divisor has one digit.
   The quotient has two digits.
   The dividend has two digits.
   There is a remainder.

   e. The quotient has two digits.
   The dividend has three digits.
   The divisor has one digit.
   There is a remainder.

   f. The divisor has one digit.
   The quotient has three digits.
   The dividend has three digits.
   There is no remainder.

   g. The quotient has two digits.
   The dividend has three digits.
   The divisor has one digit.
   There is no remainder.

   h. The divisor has one digit.
   The quotient has three digits.
   The dividend has three digits.
   There is a remainder.

Mental Math: Divide by Multiples of 10

You will learn how to use division facts to help you divide by multiples of 10.

Learn About It

A group of students swam a total of 80 laps at a swim-a-thon. If each student swam 20 laps, how many students were in the group?

Divide. **80 ÷ 20 = ▪**

Find 80 ÷ 20.

You can use basic facts to help you divide.

$8 ÷ 2 = 4$ ← basic fact

$80 ÷ 20 = 4$ ← **Think:** 8 tens ÷ 2 tens = 4

$80 ÷ 20 = 4$ because $4 × 20 = 80$

Solution: There were 4 students in the group.

Other Examples

A. Using the Basic Fact $21 ÷ 7 = 3$

$210 ÷ 70 = 3$

$2,100 ÷ 70 = 30$

$21,000 ÷ 70 = 300$

B. Using the Basic Fact $20 ÷ 4 = 5$

$200 ÷ 40 = 5$

$2,000 ÷ 40 = 50$

$20,000 ÷ 40 = 500$

Explain Your Thinking

▶ In Examples *A* and *B*, how do the number of zeros in the quotients compare to the number of zeros in the dividends? Why is the pattern of zeros not the same in the two examples?

Guided Practice

Use basic facts to help you divide.

1. $72 ÷ 8$	**2.** $56 ÷ 7$	**3.** $40 ÷ 8$
$720 ÷ 80$	$560 ÷ 70$	$400 ÷ 80$
$7,200 ÷ 80$	$5,600 ÷ 70$	$4,000 ÷ 80$
$72,000 ÷ 80$	$56,000 ÷ 70$	$40,000 ÷ 80$

Ask Yourself

• How many digits will the quotient have?

Standards NS 3.0   AF 1.1   MR 1.1, 2.3

Independent Practice

Use basic facts to help you divide.

4. 25 ÷ 5
250 ÷ 50

5. 14 ÷ 2
140 ÷ 20

6. 50 ÷ 5
500 ÷ 50

7. 6 ÷ 2
600 ÷ 20

8. 10 ÷ 5
1,000 ÷ 50

9. 81 ÷ 9
8,100 ÷ 90

10. 54 ÷ 6
5,400 ÷ 60

11. 12 ÷ 4
12,000 ÷ 40

12. 80$\overline{)640}$

13. 10$\overline{)900}$

14. 70$\overline{)490}$

15. 30$\overline{)1,500}$

16. 60$\overline{)4,200}$

17. 30$\overline{)9,000}$

18. 50$\overline{)40,000}$

19. 90$\overline{)63,000}$

n **Algebra • Equations Find each value of *n*.**

20. $2,800 \div n = 70$

21. $5,400 \div n = 60$

22. $n \div 80 = 50$

23. $n \div 60 = 600$

24. $16,000 \div n = 800$

25. $n \div 70 = 700$

Problem Solving • Reasoning

26. Marty swims 10 laps in a 50-meter pool each day. How many meters does he swim in 6 days?

27. Twenty schools sent 180 swimmers to compete in a swim meet. If each school sent the same number of swimmers, how many swimmers did each school send?

28. Analyze During the swim-a-thon, Ann swims 1,800 meters in 1 hour. At that rate, how many meters does she swim in 1 minute?

29. Logical Thinking Four teams competed in a relay race. Team *D* finished ahead of Team *A* but after Team *B*. Team *C* finished ahead of Team *B*. Which team won?

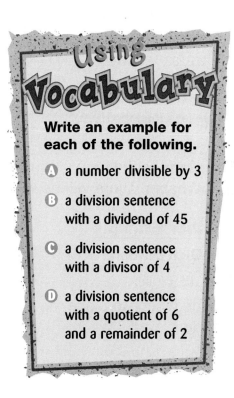

Using Vocabulary

Write an example for each of the following.

A a number divisible by 3

B a division sentence with a dividend of 45

C a division sentence with a divisor of 4

D a division sentence with a quotient of 6 and a remainder of 2

Mixed Review • Test Prep

Round each decimal to the nearest tenth. *(pages 392–393)*

30. 1.23   **31.** 12.49   **32.** 1.01   **33.** 4.99   **34.** 6.84   **35.** 5.75

36 What is the product of 122 and 46? *(pages 198–199)*

A 168   **B** 1,220   **C** 5,512   **D** 5,612

Extra Practice See Set A on page 594.

LESSON 2

One-Digit Quotients

You will learn how to divide by a two-digit divisor.

Learn About It

Isabel's art class is making tissue-paper art. The art teacher has 235 sheets of tissue paper. If 28 students share the tissue paper equally, how many sheets can each student use? How many sheets will be left over?

Divide.   **235 ÷ 28 = ■   28)235**

Find 235 ÷ 28.

Step 1   Decide where to place the first digit in the quotient.

28)235	28 > 2	not enough hundreds
28)235	28 > 23	not enough tens
28)235	28 < 235	There are enough ones.

The remainder should always be less than the divisor.

Step 2   Divide the ones.

$$\begin{array}{r} 8\ R11 \\ 28)\overline{235} \\ -\ 224 \\ \hline 11 \end{array}$$

Multiply. 8 × 28
Subtract. 235 − 224
Compare. 11 < 28

Solution: Each student can use 8 sheets of tissue paper. There will be 11 sheets left over.

Check your answer.

Multiply, then add.

(28 × 8) + 11 = 235

The sum equals the dividend.

Another Example

Two-Digit Dividend

Find 43 ÷ 19.

Decide where to place the first digit.

19)43 → 19 > 4

not enough tens

So 43 ÷ 19 = 2 R5.

Divide ones.

$$\begin{array}{r} 2\ R5 \\ 19)\overline{43} \\ -38 \\ \hline 5 \end{array}$$

Check your answer.

$$\begin{array}{r} 19 \\ \times\ 2 \\ \hline 38 \\ +\ 5 \\ \hline 43 \end{array}$$

Explain Your Thinking

▶ How do you know that 7 is not the correct quotient in the example on the right?

$$\begin{array}{r} 7 \\ 28)\overline{176} \\ -\ 196 \end{array}$$

▶ What does it mean if the remainder is greater than or equal to the divisor?

Standards | NS 3.0   AF 1.0   MR 2.0

Guided Practice

Copy and complete each division problem.

1.
```
      7 R9
19)142
   -1██
      9
```

2.
```
      6 R█
41)249
   -2█6
     ██
```

3.
```
      3 R1█
76)239
   -██8
     1█
```

Ask Yourself
- How can I estimate the quotient?
- How do I check my answer?

Divide. Whenever you divide, the remainder must always be less than the divisor.

4. $17\overline{)62}$

5. $23\overline{)59}$

6. $37\overline{)124}$

7. $92 \div 27$

8. $147 \div 28$

9. $353 \div 48$

Independent Practice

Divide. Check your answer.

10. $42\overline{)88}$

11. $32\overline{)99}$

12. $21\overline{)91}$

13. $46\overline{)55}$

14. $19\overline{)146}$

15. $27\overline{)177}$

16. $61\overline{)250}$

17. $89\overline{)725}$

18. $54\overline{)335}$

19. $76\overline{)512}$

20. $48\overline{)234}$

21. $57\overline{)553}$

22. $73 \div 22$

23. $81 \div 19$

24. $34 \div 11$

25. $74 \div 34$

26. $89 \div 36$

27. $197 \div 36$

28. $422 \div 83$

29. $413 \div 62$

30. $429 \div 71$

31. $826 \div 89$

32. $481 \div 59$

33. $522 \div 85$

n **Algebra • Expressions** Compare.
Use >, <, or = for each ●.

34. $305 \div 48$ ● $300 \div 48$

35. $795 \div 37$ ● $785 \div 37$

36. $400 \div 80$ ● $200 \div 40$

37. $800 \div 20$ ● $80 \div 2$

38. $614 \div 18$ ● $614 \div 12$

39. $516 \div 19$ ● $517 \div 19$

Write the division problem that goes with each of the checks below.

40.
```
    44
  ×  3
   132
  +  8
   140
```

41.
```
    34
  ×  7
   238
  + 16
   254
```

42.
```
    17
  ×  5
    85
  +  3
    88
```

43.
```
    29
  ×  2
    58
  +24
    82
```

Problem Solving • Reasoning

Solve. Choose a method.

Computation Methods

• Mental Math   • Estimation   • Paper and Pencil

44. Measurement Eighteen of the students wanted to decorate their tissue art with yarn. If the students shared 42 yards of yarn equally, how many feet of yarn did each student receive?

46. All of the tissue art was hung in the art classroom. If the 28 pictures were hung 7 pictures across, how many rows of pictures were there?

48. Money The art class sold 28 pictures at the school craft fair. Each picture cost $4. About how much money did the class make?

45. Analyze For a collage, Ramon needs 40 sheets of tissue paper and a bottle of glue. A 25-sheet package of tissue paper costs $3.95. Glue costs $2.95. If Ramon has $10, can he buy all he needs? Explain.

47. Measurement A tissue flower collage is glued on a square board. Each side of the board is 2 feet long. What is the perimeter of the board?

49. There were 8 pictures with 6 flowers each and 11 pictures with 7 flowers each. Find the total number of flowers in all the pictures.

Mixed Review • Test Prep

Use the line plot at the right for Exercises 50–54. (pages 418–420)

50. What is the range?

51. What is the mode?

52. What is the median?

53. What is the mean?

54. Is there an outlier? If so, what is it?

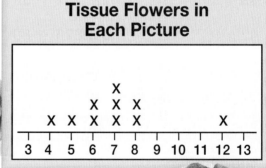

Tissue Flowers in Each Picture

```
                        X
                  X     X     X
            X     X     X     X     X                 X
      ┬─────┬─────┬─────┬─────┬─────┬─────┬─────┬─────┬─────┬─────┬
      3     4     5     6     7     8     9    10    11    12    13
```

Choose the letter of the correct answer. (pages 194–199)

55 Which is the best estimate for 28 × 53?

   A 80   **C** 1,000

   B 150   **D** 1,500

56 Which is the best estimate for 73 × 384?

   F 470   **H** 2,800

   G 500   **J** 28,000

Extra Practice See Set B on page 595.

Dividing in a Different Way

You can use many different strategies to find the answer to a division problem. One strategy is to use repeated subtraction.

Find 224 ÷ 56.

Think: How many groups of 56 are there in 224?

Start with 224.
Subtract 56 repeatedly.

```
   224
 −  56  ❶
   168
 −  56  ❷
   112
 −  56  ❸
    56
 −  56  ❹
     0
```

Count how many times you subtracted 56.

You subtracted 56 four times, so there are 4 groups of 56 in 224.

56 + 56 + 56 + 56 = 224
4 × 56 = 224
and 224 ÷ 56 = 4

Find 296 ÷ 98.

Think: How many groups of 98 are there in 296?

Start with 296.
Subtract 98 repeatedly.

```
   296
 −  98  ❶
   198
 −  98  ❷
   100
 −  98  ❸
     2
```

Count how many times you subtracted 98.

You subtracted 98 three times, so there are 3 groups of 98 in 296. The remainder is 2.

98 + 98 + 98 + 2 = 296
3 × 98 + 2 = 296
and 296 ÷ 98 = 3 R2

Try These

Use repeated subtraction or any other method to find each quotient.

1. 328 ÷ 82   **2.** 350 ÷ 70   **3.** 204 ÷ 54

4. 125 ÷ 25   **5.** 450 ÷ 50   **6.** 188 ÷ 60

Explain Your Thinking

► Why does repeated subtraction work?

► What advantages are there in using repeated subtraction to find the quotient? What disadvantages are there?

Estimate the Quotient

You will **learn** how to estimate quotients.

Learn About It

Sarah's family reenacted the pioneers' trip along the Oregon Trail. They spent 19 days traveling 184 miles. About how many miles did they travel each day?

You can estimate to find out how many miles they traveled each day. One way to estimate 184 ÷ 19 is to use basic facts and multiples of 10. Think of a new **dividend** and a new **divisor** that are close to 184 and 19 and will divide evenly.

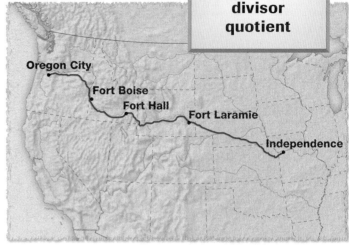

Oregon City
Fort Boise
Fort Hall
Fort Laramie
Independence

Beginning in 1842, pioneers traveled west on the Oregon Trail from Independence, Missouri, to Oregon City, Oregon.

Estimate $19\overline{)184}$.

Step 1 Use basic facts and multiples of 10 to find a new dividend and a new divisor.

$$19\overline{)184}$$
$$\downarrow \quad \downarrow$$
$$20\overline{)180}$$

The basic fact **18 ÷ 2 = 9** helps you find the numbers.

Step 2 Divide.

$$20\overline{)180}^{\,9}$$

So $19\overline{)184}$ is about 9.

Solution: Sarah's family traveled about 9 miles each day.

Another Example

Two-Digit Dividend
Estimate 63 ÷ 29.

$$63 \div 29$$
$$\downarrow \quad \downarrow$$
$$60 \div 30 = 2$$

The basic fact **6 ÷ 3 = 2** helps you find the numbers.

63 ÷ 29 is about 2.

Explain Your Thinking

▶ How can an estimate help you decide where to place the first digit in the quotient?

▶ How can an estimate help you decide if an answer is reasonable?

Standards NS **3.0**   MR **2.3**

Guided Practice

Copy and complete each exercise. Use a new dividend and a new divisor to estimate.

Ask Yourself

- What basic fact can I use?

- What is the quotient of the new dividend and divisor?

1. $82 \div 18$
$80 \div \blacksquare = \blacksquare$

2. $62 \div 27$
$\blacksquare \div 30 = \blacksquare$

3. $52 \div 49$
$\blacksquare \div \blacksquare = \blacksquare$

4. $488 \div 67$
$490 \div \blacksquare = \blacksquare$

5. $158 \div 42$
$\blacksquare \div 40 = \blacksquare$

6. $318 \div 63$
$\blacksquare \div \blacksquare = \blacksquare$

Independent Practice

Estimate each quotient.

7. $98 \div 52$

8. $42 \div 18$

9. $562 \div 81$

10. $308 \div 52$

11. $48\overline{)96}$

12. $19\overline{)83}$

13. $63\overline{)379}$

14. $71\overline{)223}$

15. $89\overline{)448}$

16. $68\overline{)559}$

17. $78\overline{)637}$

18. $18\overline{)138}$

Problem Solving • Reasoning

Use Data Use the map on page 574 and the table at right for Problems 19 and 20.

19. A pioneer family traveled from Fort Boise to Oregon City in 59 days. If they traveled the same distance each day, about how many miles did they travel each day?

20. **Measurement** The distance from Fort Laramie to Fort Hall is 297 more miles than the distance from Fort Hall to Fort Boise. What is the distance between each of the forts?

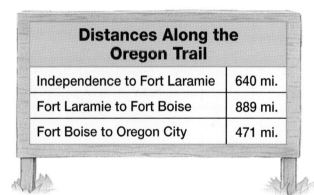

Distances Along the Oregon Trail	
Independence to Fort Laramie	640 mi.
Fort Laramie to Fort Boise	889 mi.
Fort Boise to Oregon City	471 mi.

21. **Analyze** There are 88 people and 11 wagons in the wagon train. Each wagon carries the same number of people. Sarah says that number is 6. Is she right? Explain.

Mixed Review • Test Prep

Solve each equation when $y = 8$. *(pages 82–83, 136–137)*

22. $y + 5 = x$

23. $x = 19 - y$

24. $y \times 7 = x$

25. $48 \div y = x$

26 What is the value of the expression $s + 15$ if $s = 12$? *(pages 78–79)*

A 180   **B** 30   **C** 27   **D** 3

Extra Practice See Set C on page 595.

Problem-Solving Skill: Multistep Problems

You will learn how to solve problems that involve more than one step.

Sometimes it takes more than one step to solve a problem. You must decide *what the steps are* and *in what order* to do them.

Problem Each year, Lucia and her dad volunteer to cook at the Firefighters' Dinner. This year they are in charge of preparing corn on the cob. There are 3 bags of corn. Each bag holds 32 ears of corn. If 16 ears of corn fit in a pot, what is the least number of pots needed to cook all of the corn at the same time?

Decide what the steps are and in what order to do them.

You know that 16 ears of corn fit in each pot.

- First, find how many ears of corn there are in all.

- Then find how many pots are needed.

Do each step in order.

Step 1 Find the total number of ears of corn.

$$3 \times 32 = 96 \leftarrow \text{total number of ears of corn}$$

$\uparrow$ number of bags $\uparrow$ number in each bag

There are 96 ears of corn in all.

Step 2 Find the number of pots needed for all of the corn.

$$96 \div 16 = 6 \leftarrow \text{total number of pots needed}$$

$\uparrow$ number of ears of corn $\uparrow$ number of ears of corn in each pot

Six pots are needed.

Six pots are needed to cook all the corn at the same time.

Look Back Could you have done the steps in a different order? Explain why or why not.

Standards MR **1.0, 1.1, 1.2, 2.0, 3.0, 3.2**

Left: At a visit to a fire station you can find out how fire-fighting equipment works.

Right: A group of children learns about fire safety from Smokey Bear.

Guided Practice

Solve.

1 Lucia's dad bought 10 dozen tomatoes for the dinner. The tomatoes were equally divided among 20 bags. How many tomatoes did each bag have?

 Think: How many tomatoes did Lucia's dad buy?

2 The firehouse pantry has 144 cans of vegetables and 220 cans of soup. Each pantry shelf holds up to 52 cans. How many shelves are needed to store all of the cans?

 Think: How many cans are there in all?

Choose a Strategy

Solve. Use these or other strategies.

Problem-Solving Strategies

| • Draw a Picture | • Make a Table | • Guess and Check | • Write an Equation |

3 Each dining table at the Firefighters' Dinner is twice as long as it is wide. If each table is 12 feet long, what is the area of a table in square yards?

4 Mrs. Ruiz started baking pies at 3 P.M. Pies take 75 minutes to bake. If 2 pies can be baked at a time, how many pies can Mrs. Ruiz bake by 6 P.M.?

5 A child's dinner ticket costs $3 less than an adult's ticket. A family of 2 adults and 2 children paid $26 for tickets. How much does a child's ticket cost?

6 There are 45 more people who want meatballs with their spaghetti than people who do not. If there are 125 servings of spaghetti in all, how many need to include meatballs?

7 Greg, Eric, Kay, and Dave are sitting in a row at dinner. Eric is next to Greg. Kay is not next to Eric or Greg. Greg is farthest to the right. In what order are the four friends sitting?

8 After the dinner, Shana collected 92 cans and 48 bottles for recycling. If she received 5¢ for each can or bottle, about how much money did Shana receive?

Extra Practice See 1–4 on page 597.

577

Quick ✓ Check

Check Your Understanding of Lessons 1–4

Use basic facts to find each quotient.

1. $60\overline{)420}$ **2.** $40\overline{)2,400}$ **3.** $70\overline{)56,000}$

Divide.

4. $26\overline{)87}$ **5.** $49\overline{)447}$ **6.** $86\overline{)716}$

Estimate each quotient.

7. $23\overline{)84}$ **8.** $77\overline{)722}$ **9.** $59\overline{)489}$

Solve.

10. Yoko is a volunteer at a local food pantry. Today she needs to divide all of the oranges equally into 18 bags. If there are 4 crates with 36 oranges each, how many oranges will be in each bag?

How did you do?

If you had difficulty with any items in the Quick Check, you can use the following pages for review and extra practice.

California Standards	Items	Review These Pages	Do These Extra Practice Items
Number Sense: **3.0** Math Reasoning: **1.1**	1–3	pages 568–569	Set A, page 594
Number Sense: **3.0**	4–6	pages 570–572	Set B, page 595
Number Sense: **3.0**	7–9	pages 574–575	Set C, page 595
Math Reasoning: **1.1, 1.2**	10	pages 576–577	1–4, page 597

Test Prep • Cumulative Review

Maintaining the Standards

Choose the letter of the correct answer.

1 Which point is on the line?

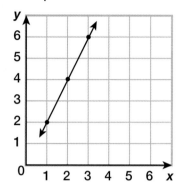

A (1, 3)   **C** (2, 4)

B (2, 2)   **D** (4, 2)

4 Which point is on the line?

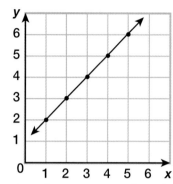

A (4, 5)   **C** (4, 3)

B (4, 4)   **D** (4, 2)

Use the graph to answer Questions 2–3.

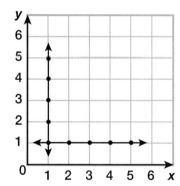

2 What is the length of the line segment joining point (1, 1) to point (5, 1)?

F 0 units   **H** 4 units

G 2 units   **J** 6 units

3 What is the length of the line segment joining point (1, 1) to point (1, 5)?

A 1 unit   **C** 3 units

B 2 units   **D** 4 units

Use the graph to answer Questions 5–6.

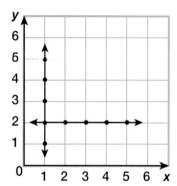

5 What is the length of the line segment joining point (2, 2) to point (5, 2)?

F 0 units   **H** 3 units

G 2 units   **J** 4 units

6 What is the length of the line segment joining point (1, 3) to point (1, 5)?

Explain How did you find your answer?

Safe Site

Internet Test Prep
Visit **www.eduplace.com/kids/mhm**
for more *Test Prep Practice*.

Two-Digit Quotients

You will learn about dividing when the quotient has two digits.

Learn About It

The students at Riverside School have created 1,230 crossword puzzles. The puzzles will be made into 27 books and used in a crossword-puzzle contest. If each book will have the same number of puzzles, how many puzzles will each book have? Will any puzzles be left over?

Divide.　**1,230 ÷ 27 = ▇　27)1,230**

Find 27)1,230.

Step 1　Estimate to decide where to place the first digit in the quotient.

$$27\overline{)1,230} \longrightarrow \overset{40}{30\overline{)1,200}}$$

Step 2　Try the estimate. Divide.

$$\begin{array}{r} 4 \\ 27\overline{)1,230} \\ -1\,08 \\ \hline 15 \end{array}$$

Think: $\overset{4 \text{ tens}}{30\overline{)120 \text{ tens}}}$

← Multiply. 4×27
Subtract. $123 - 108$
Compare. $15 < 27$

Step 3　Bring down the ones. Estimate. Divide.

$$\begin{array}{r} 45 \text{ R15} \\ 27\overline{)1,230} \\ -1\,08\downarrow \\ \hline 150 \\ -135 \\ \hline 15 \end{array}$$

Think: $30\overline{)150}^{\,5}$

← Multiply. 5×27
Subtract. $150 - 135$
Compare. $15 < 27$

Step 4　Check your answer. Multiply. Then add.

$$\begin{array}{r} 45 \\ \times\ 27 \\ \hline 315 \\ +\ 900 \\ \hline 1,215 \\ +\ 15 \\ \hline 1,230 \end{array}$$

← The sum equals the dividend, so the quotient is correct.

Solution: There will be 45 crossword puzzles in each book. There will be 15 puzzles left over.

Standards NS 3.0

You can use the same steps to divide a three-digit dividend.

Divide. $437 \div 19 =$ ■ $19\overline{)437}$

Find $19\overline{)437}$.

Step 1 Estimate to decide where to place the first digit in the quotient.

$$19\overline{)437} \rightarrow \begin{array}{r} 20 \\ 20\overline{)400} \end{array}$$

Step 2 Try the estimate. Divide.

$$\begin{array}{r} 2 \\ 19\overline{)437} \\ -38 \\ \hline 5 \end{array}$$

Think: $\begin{array}{r} 2 \text{ tens} \\ 20\overline{)40 \text{ tens}} \end{array}$

← Multiply. 2×19
Subtract. $43 - 38$
Compare. $5 < 19$

Step 3 Bring down the ones. Estimate. Divide.

$$\begin{array}{r} 23 \\ 19\overline{)437} \\ -38\downarrow \\ \hline 57 \\ -57 \\ \hline 0 \end{array}$$

Think: $20\overline{)60}^{\,3}$

← Multiply. 3×19
Subtract. $57 - 57$
Compare. $0 < 19$

Step 4 Check your answer.

$$\begin{array}{r} 23 \\ \times\ 19 \\ \hline 207 \\ +230 \\ \hline 437 \end{array}$$

← The product equals the dividend, so the quotient is correct.

Solution: $437 \div 19 = 23$

Explain Your Thinking

▶ Explain why it is helpful to know the number of digits in a quotient before you divide.

▶ Explain why you can use multiplication to check an answer to a division problem. Why do you need to add when the answer has a remainder?

Guided Practice

Divide.

1. $28\overline{)647}$

2. $42\overline{)886}$

3. $19\overline{)603}$

4. $26\overline{)562}$

5. $41\overline{)911}$

6. $36\overline{)423}$

7. $47\overline{)2,589}$

8. $55\overline{)4,769}$

9. $81\overline{)6,643}$

10. $61\overline{)4,377}$

11. $38\overline{)2,128}$

12. $94\overline{)7,654}$

Ask Yourself

• How many digits will the quotient have?

• Where do I place the first digit of the quotient?

Independent Practice

Divide. Then check your answer.

13. $18\overline{)582}$

14. $33\overline{)769}$

15. $28\overline{)915}$

16. $45\overline{)547}$

17. $38\overline{)3,459}$

18. $69\overline{)2,218}$

19. $77\overline{)6,319}$

20. $86\overline{)8,123}$

21. $657 \div 21$

22. $966 \div 31$

23. $296 \div 19$

24. $672 \div 48$

25. $3,526 \div 68$

26. $1,527 \div 28$

27. $4,797 \div 52$

28. $4,596 \div 89$

Problem Solving • Reasoning

Use Data Use the bar graph at the right for Problems 29 and 30.

29. At the crossword-puzzle contest, the puzzles about animals and history were given to 52 student teams. If each team received the same number of puzzles, how many puzzles did each team receive?

30. **Estimate** To the nearest hundred, how many more sports puzzles than geography puzzles are there?

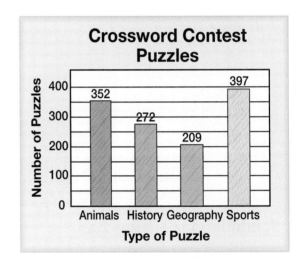

31. The first crossword puzzle ever published appeared in a New York newspaper on December 21, 1913. In what year will the 100th anniversary of the first published crossword puzzle be celebrated?

32. **Write About It** A crossword puzzle is usually symmetrical. Is the crossword puzzle at the right symmetrical? Explain why or why not.

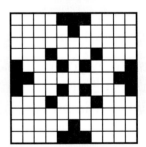

Mixed Review • Test Prep

Evaluate each expression. *(pages 144–146)*

33. $(9 \div 3) + 6$

34. $15 - (36 \div 6) + 0$

35. $(12 \times 2) \div 6$

36. $64 \div (4 \times 2)$

37. $(72 \div 9) + 9$

38. $(10 \times 5) \div (2 + 8)$

39 What is the sum of $3\frac{3}{8}$ and $1\frac{5}{8}$? *(pages 350–351)*

    A 4   **B** $4\frac{3}{8}$ **C** $4\frac{5}{8}$ **D** 5

Extra Practice See Set D on page 596.

Mix and Match

Practice division by playing this game with a partner.
Try to get the greatest number of correct matches.

What You'll Need

For each pair:

- *36 index cards (or Teaching Tool 22)*
- *stopwatch*
- *paper and pencil*

Players 2

792 ÷ 18

34

Here's What to Do

1. Each player makes up nine 3-digit by 2-digit division problems and writes them on index cards. Each player also writes the answers to each of the nine problems on nine other index cards.

2. Players exchange both sets of cards. Each player places the answer cards faceup in one or two rows.

3. Each player tries to match the cards with the division problems with the correct answer cards. The player with the greatest number of correct matches after 3 minutes wins.

Share Your Thinking What strategy did you use to find the correct matches? Would estimation or paper-and-pencil computation be the better strategy?

Adjusting the Quotient

You will learn how to adjust your estimate of the quotient as you divide.

Learn About It

Sometimes your first estimate of the quotient will be too large or too small. You will then need to adjust your estimate.

Estimate Too Large

Find 23)368.

Estimate first. $23\overline{)368}$ → $20\overline{)400}$ (20)

Step 1 Place the first digit in the quotient.	**Step 2** Adjust the estimate. Try 1.
$\begin{array}{r} 2 \\ 23\overline{)368} \\ -46 \end{array}$ 46 > 36 2 is too large.	$\begin{array}{r} 1 \\ 23\overline{)368} \\ -23 \\ \hline 13 \end{array}$ 13 < 23 1 is correct.
Step 3 Bring down the next digit. Try 7.	**Step 4** Try 6.
$\begin{array}{r} 17 \\ 23\overline{)368} \\ -23\downarrow \\ \hline 138 \\ -161 \end{array}$ 161 > 138 7 is too large.	$\begin{array}{r} 16 \\ 23\overline{)368} \\ -23\downarrow \\ \hline 138 \\ -138 \\ \hline 0 \end{array}$ 0 < 23 6 is correct.

Solution: $368 \div 23 = 16$

Estimate Too Small

Find 16)849.

Estimate first. $16\overline{)849}$ → $20\overline{)800}$ (40)

Step 1 Place the first digit in the quotient.	**Step 2** Adjust the quotient. Try 5.
$\begin{array}{r} 4 \\ 16\overline{)849} \\ -64 \\ \hline 20 \end{array}$ 20 > 16 4 is too small.	$\begin{array}{r} 5 \\ 16\overline{)849} \\ -80 \\ \hline 4 \end{array}$ 4 < 16 5 is correct.
Step 3 Bring down the next digit. Try 2.	**Step 4** Try 3.
$\begin{array}{r} 52 \\ 16\overline{)849} \\ -80\downarrow \\ \hline 49 \\ -32 \\ \hline 17 \end{array}$ 17 > 16 2 is too small.	$\begin{array}{r} 53\ R1 \\ 16\overline{)849} \\ -80\downarrow \\ \hline 49 \\ -48 \\ \hline 1 \end{array}$ 1 < 16 3 is correct.

Solution: $849 \div 16 = 53\ R1$

Explain Your Thinking

▶ What should you do if your estimate is too large?
  What should you do if it is too small?

Standards NS 3.0

Guided Practice

Write *too large* or *too small* for each first estimate of the quotient. Then find the correct answer.

1. 12)150 — 13
2. 17)916 — 49
3. 26)543 — 22
4. 35)736 — 19

Ask Yourself
- How many digits will the quotient have?
- Do I need to adjust my estimate?

Independent Practice

Estimate. Then divide. Write whether you needed to adjust any estimates.

5. 18)619
6. 84)943
7. 19)422
8. 31)392
9. 25)672

10. 42)994
11. 28)731
12. 26)626
13. 48)577
14. 19)564

15. 880 ÷ 24
16. 611 ÷ 36
17. 456 ÷ 13
18. 671 ÷ 44

Problem Solving • Reasoning

Use Data Use the list for Problems 19–22.

19. For a time capsule, 14 students recorded messages on audiotapes. How long is each message if each message is the same length?

20. The coins have a value of 91¢. If each coin has a different value, what are the coins?

21. **Analyze** The essays fill a 41-page journal. All essays are the same number of pages except for one essay that is 2 pages longer than each of the other essays. How many pages long is each of the other essays?

22. **Write Your Own** Using the information in the list, write a division problem. Give your problem to a classmate to solve.

Time Capsule Items
- one 360 minute video
- 5 new coins
- 13 student essays
- two 120-minute audio tapes

Mixed Review • Test Prep

Multiply or divide. *(pages 180–181, 234–235)*

23. 102 × 6
24. 205 ÷ 5
25. 420 × 7
26. 650 ÷ 8
27. 501 × 4

28. Which is the best estimate of 725 divided by 6? *(pages 254–255)*

   A 120   **B** 90   **C** 12   **D** 9

Problem-Solving Strategy:
Solve a Simpler Problem

You will learn how to use a simpler problem to help you solve word problems.

Sometimes you can solve a problem by first thinking about a simpler problem.

Problem There are 8 teams in a bike relay race. Each team must race against each of the other teams once. How many races are needed?

What is the question?
How many races are needed?

What do you know?
- There are 8 teams.
- Each team must race against each of the other teams.

How can you find the answer?
Solve a simpler problem. Look for a pattern to use.

Solve the problem for fewer teams.

2 Teams	3 Teams	4 Teams	5 Teams

A ⟷ B
1 race

3 races

6 races

10 races

Look for a pattern you can use.

Number of Teams:	2	3	4	5	6	7	8
Number of Races:	1	3	6	10	15	21	28

+2   +3   +4   +5   +6   +7

- The differences increase by 1 each time.
- Continue the pattern.

28 races are needed for 8 teams.

Look back at the problem.
How does solving the problem for fewer teams help you?

Standards MR **1.0, 1.1, 1.2, 2.0, 2.2, 2.4, 3.0, 3.2**

Guided Practice

Remember:
► Understand
► Plan
► Solve
► Look Back

Solve these problems, using the Solve a Simpler Problem strategy.

1 In a bicycle race, there are judges posted at the beginning and end of each mile. If the race is 20 miles, how many judges are needed?

Think: How many judges would be needed if the race were 2 miles? 3 miles?

2 Bicycle helmet boxes are labeled on the top and front of each box. How many labels can be seen if there are 5 rows of 4 boxes?

Think: How many labels could be seen if there is 1 row of 4 boxes? 2 rows of 4 boxes?

Choose a Strategy

Solve. Use these or other strategies.

Problem-Solving Strategies

• Draw a Picture   • Write an Equation   • Solve a Simpler Problem   • Guess and Check

3 A swimming pool holds 2,640 cubic feet of water. The swimming pool is 12 feet wide and 55 feet long. How deep is the pool?

4 Six friends at a party shake hands with each other. How many handshakes is that? (Hint: Try solving the problem for fewer people.)

5 The bikers eat lunch at a long table made up of 14 small tables placed end to end. One small table seats 1 person on each side. How many people can sit at the long table?

6 Skip used 13 rolls of film during a Florida bike trip. Three of the rolls of film had 24 photos each. Ten of the rolls of film had 12 photos each. How many photos did he take in all?

7 Tara and her grandma shopped for bicycle supplies. They bought 4 bicycle pads for $1.85 each and 2 water bottles for $1.19 each. To the nearest dollar, how much money did Tara and her grandma spend?

8 Jim spent 54 minutes riding 3 laps around a bike path. He rode the first lap in the same amount of time as the second lap. He spent 6 minutes less riding the third lap. How much time did Jim spend on each lap?

Zeros in Two-Digit Quotients

You will learn the importance of placing zeros in the quotient.

Learn About It

The Flying Tigers won the double-dutch competition at the jump-rope tournament. They completed 2,816 jumps in 40 minutes. If they jumped about an equal number of times each minute, about how many jumps a minute did the Flying Tigers jump?

Divide. $2,816 \div 40 = $ ▩ $40\overline{)2,816}$

Find $40\overline{)2,816}$.

Step 1 Estimate to decide where to place the first digit in the quotation.

$$40\overline{)2,816} \rightarrow \begin{array}{r} 70 \\ 40\overline{)2,800} \end{array}$$

Step 2 Try the estimate. Divide.

$$\begin{array}{r} 7 \\ 40\overline{)2,816} \\ -2\,80 \\ \hline 1 \end{array}$$

Think: $\begin{array}{r}7\text{ tens}\\40\overline{)280\text{ tens}}\end{array}$
Multiply. 7×40
Subtract. $281 - 280$
← Compare. $1 < 40$

Step 3 Bring down the ones. Estimate. Divide.

$$\begin{array}{r} 7 \\ 40\overline{)2,816} \\ -2\,80\downarrow \\ \hline 16 \end{array}$$

$16 < 40$
There are not enough ones to divide.

Step 4 Write a 0 in the ones place. Write the remainder.

$$\begin{array}{r} 70\text{ R}16 \\ 40\overline{)2,816} \\ -2\,80 \\ \hline 16 \end{array}$$

Check your answer.

Multiply. Then add.
$(70 \times 40) + 16 = 2,816$
The sum equals the dividend.

Solution: The Flying Tigers jumped about 70 jumps per minute.

Another Example

Three-Digit Dividend

Find $23\overline{)935}$.

$$\begin{array}{r} 40\text{ R}15 \\ 23\overline{)935} \\ -92\downarrow \\ \hline 15 \\ -0 \\ \hline 15 \end{array}$$

Check: $\begin{array}{r} 23 \\ \times\,40 \\ \hline 920 \\ +\,15 \\ \hline 935 \end{array}$

Explain Your Thinking

▶ How do you know when to write a zero in the quotient?

▶ Look at the example at the left. Why is there a zero in the ones place?

Standards NS **3.0** MG **2.2, 2.3** MR **2.3**

Guided Practice

Divide.

1. $19\overline{)390}$
2. $34\overline{)700}$
3. $36\overline{)1,459}$
4. $51\overline{)4,598}$

5. $691 \div 34$
6. $577 \div 28$
7. $3,382 \div 42$

Ask Yourself
- Where do I place the first digit in the quotient?
- Can I divide the tens?
- Can I divide the ones?

Independent Practice

Divide.

8. $22\overline{)451}$
9. $12\overline{)730}$
10. $21\overline{)849}$
11. $56\overline{)601}$

12. $44\overline{)2,222}$
13. $63\overline{)1,278}$
14. $28\overline{)2,537}$
15. $73\overline{)2,217}$

16. $258 \div 24$
17. $778 \div 19$
18. $765 \div 25$
19. $740 \div 36$

20. $4,160 \div 52$
21. $3,164 \div 35$
22. $4,932 \div 61$
23. $4,518 \div 89$

Problem Solving • Reasoning

24. In the double-dutch competition, 680 students competed in 17 rounds. If an equal number of students competed in each round, how many students competed in each round?

25. **Analyze** Teams from 36 schools took part in the jump-rope tournament. There were 1,078 students in all. One team had 2 fewer students than each of the other teams. How many students were on each of the other teams?

26. **Measurement** The world record for fast jumping is 425 jumps in one minute. About how many jumps is that per second?

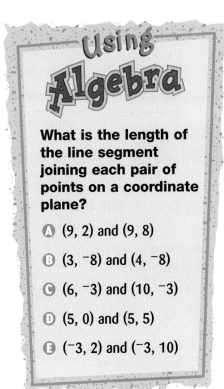

Using Algebra

What is the length of the line segment joining each pair of points on a coordinate plane?

Ⓐ (9, 2) and (9, 8)

Ⓑ (3, ⁻8) and (4, ⁻8)

Ⓒ (6, ⁻3) and (10, ⁻3)

Ⓓ (5, 0) and (5, 5)

Ⓔ (⁻3, 2) and (⁻3, 10)

Mixed Review • Test Prep

Write the number of sides each polygon has. *(pages 466–467)*

27. quadrilateral
28. triangle
29. hexagon
30. octagon
31. pentagon

32. How many centimeters are there in 50 meters? *(pages 292–293)*

    A 5 cm
    B 500 cm
    C 5,000 cm
    D 50,000 cm

Extra Practice See Set F on page 596.

Problem-Solving Application: Use Operations

You will learn how to solve problems using addition, subtraction, multiplication, and division.

You need to decide which operations to use to solve word problems.

Problem Students at Falcon School collected toys to make friendship boxes for children in local hospitals. Each of the 72 students brought 3 toys. If each box contained 12 toys, how many boxes were made?

Understand

What do you need to find?

You need to find how many friendship boxes were made.

What do you know?

- There were 72 students.
- Each student brought 3 toys.
- Each box contained 12 toys.

Plan

How can you find the answer?

First, multiply to find the total number of toys. Then divide the total number of toys by the number in each box.

Solve

Step 1	Step 2
$\begin{array}{r} 72 \\ \times 3 \\ \hline 216 \end{array}$	$\begin{array}{r} 18 \\ 12\overline{)216} \\ -12 \\ \hline 96 \\ -96 \\ \hline 0 \end{array}$

The students made 18 friendship boxes.

Look Back

Look back at the problem.

Could you have solved the problem by dividing first and then multiplying? Explain.

Standards MR 1.0, 1.1, 1.2, 2.0, 3.0, 3.2

School children collect toys for needy children.

Remember:
► Understand
► Plan
► Solve
► Look Back

Guided Practice

Solve. Use the information on page 590 to help you.

1 The students decided to include 5 stuffed animals in each box. Each student brought in one stuffed animal. How many more stuffed animals were needed?

Think: What operation should I do first? What operation should I do next?

2 A bookstore is donating 2 books for each of the boxes made by the students. The price of each book is $1.19. What is the total value of the donated books?

Think: What operation or operations do I need to do to solve this problem?

Choose a Strategy

Solve. Try these or other strategies.

Problem-Solving Strategies

- Solve a Simpler Problem
- Guess and Check
- Draw a Picture
- Write an Equation

3 Mrs. Kantrell's class wants to collect $250 to donate to a local charity. So far the class has collected $17, $18, $25, and $24. How much more money does the class need to collect?

4 Last year, students from 32 schools made 1,472 friendship boxes. If each school made the same number of boxes, about how many boxes were made by each school?

5 Each of the 26 students in Mindy's class brought in 3 cans of food to be given to 2 local charities. If each charity is to receive the same number of cans of food, how many cans will be given to each charity?

6 A third-grade class donated 19 items of clothing for a clothing drive. A fourth-grade class donated 26 items, and a fifth-grade class, 18 items. What is the average number of items each class donated?

7 There is a fence around the donation area at the local school. The fence is a rectangle that is 12 yards long and 6 yards wide. There are posts every 3 yards along the fence and at every corner. How many posts are there?

8 Two elementary schools collected a total of 80 toys for a children's charity. One of the schools collected 4 times as many toys as the other school. How many toys did each school collect?

Quick ✓ Check

Check Your Understanding of Lessons 5–9

Divide.

1. 16)392 **2.** 38)659 **3.** 73)2,635 **4.** 54)3,374

5. 31)637 **6.** 82)3,298 **7.** 56)3,387 **8.** 47)2,372

Solve.

9. In a necklace, every other bead is white. All the other beads are blue. The first bead and the last bead are blue. If the necklace has 25 beads in all, how many beads are blue?

10. Carmen is putting 4 apples in each of 22 fruit baskets. She has 6 boxes of 12 apples each. How many more apples does she need?

11. Mr. Tyler buys 2 pairs of socks and a shirt. The socks cost $5.25 a pair and the shirt costs $24.95. How much change should Mr. Tyler receive if he gives the clerk $50?

How did you do?

If you had difficulty with any items in the Quick Check, you can use the following pages for review and extra practice.

California Standards	Items	Review These Pages	Do These Extra Practice Items
Number Sense: **3.0**	1–4	pages 580–585	Sets D–E, page 596
Number Sense: **3.0**	5–8	pages 588–589	Set F, page 596
Math Reasoning: **1.1, 1.2, 2.2**	9	pages 586–587	5–7, page 597
Math Reasoning: **1.1, 1.2**	10–11	pages 590–591	8–9, page 597

Test Prep • Cumulative Review

Maintaining the Standards

Choose the letter of the correct answer.

Use the graph to answer Questions 1–2.

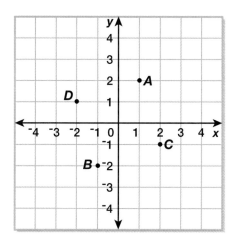

1 Which point is at (⁻2, 1)?

  A *A*   **C** *C*

  B *B*   **D** *D*

2 Which are the coordinates of point *B*?

  F (⁻2, ⁻1)

  G (⁻1, ⁻2)

  H (⁻1, 2)

  J (1, ⁻2)

3 What is the length of the line segment joining point (6, ⁻4) to point (21, ⁻4)?

  A 0 units   **C** 15 units

  B 6 units   **D** 21 units

4 What is the length of the line segment joining point (7, 4) to point (7, 10)?

  F 0 units   **H** 6 units

  G 4 units   **J** 10 units

Use the graph to answer Questions 5–7.

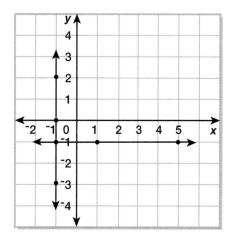

5 What is the length of the line segment joining point (1, ⁻1) to point (5, ⁻1)?

  A 2 units

  B 4 units

  C 6 units

  D 8 units

6 What is the length of the line segment joining point (⁻1, 2) to point (⁻1, ⁻3)?

  F 1 units

  G 3 units

  H 5 units

  J 7 units

7 Are the points (1, 1), (3, 1), and (5, 1) on a straight line?

Explain Tell why or why not.

Safe Site

Internet Test Prep
Visit **www.eduplace.com/kids/mhm**
for more *Test Prep Practice.*

593

Extra Practice

Use basic facts to find each quotient.

1. $30 \div 6$
   $300 \div 60$

2. $18 \div 3$
   $180 \div 30$

3. $36 \div 4$
   $360 \div 40$

4. $40 \div 5$
   $400 \div 50$

5. $63 \div 9$
   $6{,}300 \div 90$

6. $12 \div 2$
   $1{,}200 \div 20$

7. $32 \div 8$
   $3{,}200 \div 80$

8. $56 \div 7$
   $5{,}600 \div 70$

9. $81 \div 9$
   $8{,}100 \div 90$

10. $27 \div 3$
    $2{,}700 \div 30$

11. $28 \div 4$
    $2{,}800 \div 40$

12. $48 \div 8$
    $4{,}800 \div 80$

13. $45 \div 9$
    $450 \div 90$
    $4{,}500 \div 90$
    $45{,}000 \div 90$

14. $35 \div 5$
    $350 \div 50$
    $3{,}500 \div 50$
    $35{,}000 \div 50$

15. $42 \div 7$
    $420 \div 70$
    $4{,}200 \div 70$
    $42{,}000 \div 70$

16. $64 \div 8$
    $640 \div 80$
    $6{,}400 \div 80$
    $64{,}000 \div 80$

17. $49 \div 7$
    $490 \div 70$
    $4{,}900 \div 70$
    $49{,}000 \div 70$

18. $54 \div 6$
    $540 \div 60$
    $5{,}400 \div 60$
    $54{,}000 \div 60$

19. $70\overline{)420}$

20. $20\overline{)160}$

21. $50\overline{)250}$

22. $80\overline{)720}$

23. $40\overline{)2{,}400}$

24. $60\overline{)4{,}200}$

25. $30\overline{)27{,}000}$

26. $90\overline{)54{,}000}$

27. $30\overline{)24{,}000}$

28. $70\overline{)35{,}000}$

29. $20\overline{)18{,}000}$

30. $80\overline{)48{,}000}$

31. $40\overline{)12{,}000}$

32. $50\overline{)45{,}000}$

33. $30\overline{)15{,}000}$

34. $20\overline{)60{,}000}$

35. $90\overline{)72{,}000}$

36. $60\overline{)48{,}000}$

37. $80\overline{)80{,}000}$

38. $70\overline{)63{,}000}$

39. $20\overline{)16{,}000}$

40. $70\overline{)14{,}000}$

41. $40\overline{)20{,}000}$

42. $60\overline{)36{,}000}$

43. $70\overline{)28{,}000}$

44. $30\overline{)90{,}000}$

45. $60\overline{)12{,}000}$

46. $20\overline{)80{,}000}$

Extra Practice

Set B (Lesson 2, pages 570–572)

Divide. Check your answer.

1. $26\overline{)69}$
2. $34\overline{)71}$
3. $67\overline{)488}$
4. $89\overline{)597}$

5. $91\overline{)637}$
6. $27\overline{)214}$
7. $51\overline{)318}$
8. $45\overline{)398}$

9. $424 \div 52$
10. $163 \div 32$
11. $295 \div 72$
12. $448 \div 87$

13. $838 \div 92$
14. $359 \div 59$
15. $497 \div 61$
16. $353 \div 49$

17. $142 \div 19$
18. $164 \div 82$
19. $211 \div 68$
20. $274 \div 88$

21. $219 \div 43$
22. $483 \div 69$
23. $239 \div 76$
24. $372 \div 62$

Set C (Lesson 3, pages 574–575)

Copy and complete each exercise. Use a new dividend and a new divisor.

1. $39 \div 18$
   $\downarrow \quad \downarrow$
   $40 \div \blacksquare = \blacksquare$

2. $88 \div 26$
   $\downarrow \quad \downarrow$
   $\blacksquare \div 30 = \blacksquare$

3. $36 \div 11$
   $\downarrow \quad \downarrow$
   $\blacksquare \div 10 = \blacksquare$

4. $49 \div 11$
   $\downarrow \quad \downarrow$
   $\blacksquare \div 10 = \blacksquare$

5. $638 \div 81$
   $\downarrow \quad \downarrow$
   $640 \div \blacksquare = \blacksquare$

6. $139 \div 24$
   $\downarrow \quad \downarrow$
   $\blacksquare \div 20 = \blacksquare$

7. $268 \div 31$
   $\downarrow \quad \downarrow$
   $270 \div \blacksquare = \blacksquare$

8. $563 \div 72$
   $\downarrow \quad \downarrow$
   $\blacksquare \div \blacksquare = \blacksquare$

9. $283 \div 42$
   $\downarrow \quad \downarrow$
   $\blacksquare \div \blacksquare = \blacksquare$

10. $398 \div 52$
    $\downarrow \quad \downarrow$
    $\blacksquare \div \blacksquare = \blacksquare$

11. $723 \div 88$
    $\downarrow \quad \downarrow$
    $\blacksquare \div \blacksquare = \blacksquare$

12. $243 \div 62$
    $\downarrow \quad \downarrow$
    $\blacksquare \div \blacksquare = \blacksquare$

Estimate each quotient.

13. $59\overline{)543}$
14. $39\overline{)361}$
15. $62\overline{)482}$
16. $87\overline{)808}$

17. $82\overline{)643}$
18. $28\overline{)118}$
19. $53\overline{)254}$
20. $41\overline{)284}$

21. $58\overline{)112}$
22. $74\overline{)351}$
23. $22\overline{)179}$
24. $82\overline{)478}$

25. $31\overline{)269}$
26. $47\overline{)303}$
27. $71\overline{)486}$
28. $28\overline{)178}$

Extra Practice

Set D (Lesson 5, pages 580–582)

Divide. Check your answer.

1. $22\overline{)532}$ 2. $35\overline{)819}$ 3. $71\overline{)934}$ 4. $62\overline{)868}$

5. $87\overline{)4,454}$ 6. $51\overline{)3,639}$ 7. $39\overline{)3,728}$ 8. $93\overline{)8,483}$

9. $2,453 \div 30$ 10. $7,367 \div 85$ 11. $4,299 \div 68$ 12. $5,211 \div 67$

13. $6,814 \div 92$ 14. $2,719 \div 76$ 15. $3,697 \div 51$ 16. $1,353 \div 49$

17. $1,987 \div 81$ 18. $3,908 \div 63$ 19. $2,695 \div 35$ 20. $3,822 \div 42$

Set E (Lesson 6, pages 584–585)

Estimate. Then divide. Write whether you needed to adjust any estimates.

1. $19\overline{)813}$ 2. $34\overline{)784}$ 3. $29\overline{)568}$ 4. $41\overline{)798}$

5. $32\overline{)911}$ 6. $54\overline{)847}$ 7. $82\overline{)989}$ 8. $73\overline{)869}$

9. $645 \div 34$ 10. $924 \div 28$ 11. $948 \div 53$ 12. $851 \div 45$

13. $983 \div 41$ 14. $988 \div 76$ 15. $703 \div 26$ 16. $713 \div 42$

17. $694 \div 31$ 18. $557 \div 43$ 19. $481 \div 25$ 20. $768 \div 35$

21. $455 \div 12$ 22. $618 \div 28$ 23. $546 \div 23$ 24. $837 \div 28$

Set F (Lesson 8, pages 588–589)

Divide.

1. $29\overline{)584}$ 2. $37\overline{)748}$ 3. $19\overline{)580}$ 4. $31\overline{)935}$

5. $71\overline{)4,269}$ 6. $35\overline{)2,470}$ 7. $82\overline{)3,291}$ 8. $93\overline{)3,737}$

9. $360 \div 34$ 10. $973 \div 96$ 11. $984 \div 49$ 12. $916 \div 45$

13. $3,806 \div 93$ 14. $4,344 \div 72$ 15. $5,593 \div 62$ 16. $2,355 \div 47$

17. $6,871 \div 85$ 18. $3,351 \div 67$ 19. $3,745 \div 53$ 20. $6,080 \div 76$

Extra Practice • Problem Solving

Solve. *(Lesson 4, pages 576–577)*

1 Bob helps out at his uncle's farm stand. He is dividing 24 dozen peaches equally into 36 baskets. How many peaches should Bob put into each basket?

2 A store ordered 15 cartons of pencils. There were 50 boxes of pencils in each cartoon. There were 20 pencils in each box. How many pencils did the store order?

3 Fifty-five third-grade students and 65 fourth-grade students at Hilltop School are going on a trip to the planetarium. If each bus can carry 24 students, what is the least number of buses needed?

4 Of the 735 books bought by a library, 335 were children's books. The rest of the books were fiction. If the fiction books were divided equally among 20 shelves, how many books were on each shelf?

Solve these problems, using the Solve a Simpler Problem strategy. *(Lesson 7, pages 586–587)*

5 Seven teams are competing in a mathematics tournament. Each team must compete against each of the other teams once. How many rounds of competition are needed?

6 A sports storc has a sale on soccer balls. If you buy two balls, you get a third one free. One ball costs $9.75. Mr. Jones buys soccer balls for the school team. How many balls can he get for $100?

7 Look at the 5 × 5 square board at the right. How many squares can you see? (**Hint:** remember to include squares made up of smaller squares.)

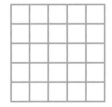

Solve. *(Lesson 9, pages 590–591)*

8 Sixty-eight students brought in cans for a food drive. Each student brought in 6 cans. The cans will be packed 16 to a box. What is the least number of boxes needed to hold all the cans?

9 At a theme park, a gift shop sells mugs for $4.95 each and hats for $8.95 each. During a weekend, 18 mugs and 23 hats were sold. What is the total value of the mugs and hats sold?

Chapter Review

Reviewing Vocabulary

1. When you divide, what do you call the answer?

2. Write a division sentence and circle the divisor.

3. How do you check a division problem?

4. Show an example of division using estimation.

Reviewing Concepts and Skills

Use basic facts to help you divide. *(pages 568–569)*

5. $40 \div 5$
   $400 \div 50$

6. $16 \div 4$
   $160 \div 40$

7. $36 \div 9$
   $360 \div 90$

8. $70\overline{)490}$

9. $20\overline{)120}$

10. $40\overline{)2,400}$

11. $30\overline{)24,000}$

Divide. Check your answer. *(pages 570–572)*

12. $29\overline{)178}$

13. $31\overline{)281}$

14. $65\overline{)492}$

15. $88\overline{)537}$

Estimate each quotient. *(pages 574–575)*

16. $57\overline{)298}$

17. $38\overline{)357}$

18. $64\overline{)479}$

19. $92\overline{)812}$

Divide. Check your answer. *(pages 580–582)*

20. $21\overline{)526}$

21. $33\overline{)828}$

22. $68\overline{)936}$

23. $72\overline{)893}$

24. $1,243 \div 28$

25. $7,268 \div 79$

26. $4,299 \div 68$

27. $5,341 \div 57$

Estimate. Then divide. *(pages 584–585)*

28. $21\overline{)822}$

29. $32\overline{)778}$

30. $31\overline{)573}$

31. $33\overline{)797}$

32. $358 \div 18$

33. $941 \div 73$

34. $948 \div 48$

35. $765 \div 45$

Divide. *(pages 588–589)*

36. $38\overline{)391}$

37. $44\overline{)897}$

38. $16\overline{)492}$

39. $18\overline{)549}$

40. $73\overline{)4,399}$

41. $65\overline{)2,642}$

42. $82\overline{)6,578}$

43. $95\overline{)4,769}$

44. $6,798 \div 97$

45. $1,253 \div 62$

46. $3,160 \div 63$

47. $1,356 \div 27$

Solve. *(pages 576–577, 586–587, 590–591)*

48. There are 9 boxes of books in a bookstore. Each box contains 2 dozen books. How many books do the boxes contain in all?

49. Ten pounds of rice needs to be divided equally into jars. If each jar can hold 20 ounces of rice, how many jars are needed?

50. Last year, 52 students each donated 25 pennies to a charity. This year, $11 more was donated. How much money was donated in all last year and this year?

51. There are 15 1-pound bags and 23 2-pound bags of pears for sale at a grocery store. If there are 6 pears to a pound, what is the total number of pears in all the bags?

52. Forty-five scouts collected old newspapers for recycling. Each scout collected 14 pounds of paper. The papers will be tied into 35-pound bundles. How many bundles will there be?

53. Ms. Green ordered 3 dozen boxes of pads of paper for the school. Each box contained 1 dozen pads. If 72 teachers shared the pads equally, how many pads did each teacher receive?

54. There are 10 players at a checkers tournament. Each player plays one game against each of the other players. How many games will be played at the tournament?

55. A watch alarm chimes every hour on the hour. If the alarm was set at 7:30 A.M. on a Monday, how many times will it have chimed by 7:45 P.M. the following Wednesday?

Brain Teasers Math Reasoning

GUESS AND CHECK
Place one or more pairs of parentheses to make each equation true.

$$70 \div 2 \times 93 + 7 = 3,500$$

$$15 \times 3 - 15 \div 3 = 40$$

FILL THEM IN
Put the digits 1, 2, 3, 4, and 5 in the boxes to make the division sentence true.

$$\overline{\quad)\quad} \; 2\_5 \; R9$$

Safe Site

Internet Brain Teasers
Visit **www.eduplace.com/kids/mhm**
for more *Brain Teasers*.

599

Chapter Test

Use basic facts to help you divide.

1. $80\overline{)320}$ **2.** $30\overline{)120}$ **3.** $50\overline{)450}$ **4.** $60\overline{)480}$

5. $50\overline{)25,000}$ **6.** $40\overline{)3,600}$ **7.** $30\overline{)27,000}$ **8.** $90\overline{)63,000}$

Divide. Check your answer.

9. $22\overline{)49}$ **10.** $31\overline{)83}$ **11.** $19\overline{)74}$ **12.** $42\overline{)92}$

13. $88\overline{)626}$ **14.** $28\overline{)118}$ **15.** $39\overline{)356}$ **16.** $46\overline{)153}$

17. $181 \div 43$ **18.** $341 \div 62$ **19.** $691 \div 74$ **20.** $684 \div 87$

21. $512 \div 95$ **22.** $235 \div 29$ **23.** $510 \div 65$ **24.** $496 \div 54$

Divide.

25. $83\overline{)917}$ **26.** $48\overline{)768}$ **27.** $37\overline{)584}$ **28.** $33\overline{)799}$

29. $54\overline{)2,470}$ **30.** $53\overline{)2,675}$ **31.** $84\overline{)2,557}$ **32.** $67\overline{)5,963}$

33. $78\overline{)4,299}$ **34.** $54\overline{)3,132}$ **35.** $74\overline{)5,933}$ **36.** $35\overline{)1,412}$

37. $3,206 \div 35$ **38.** $4,276 \div 71$ **39.** $2,948 \div 44$ **40.** $1,688 \div 56$

41. $246 \div 22$ **42.** $973 \div 86$ **43.** $602 \div 15$ **44.** $641 \div 38$

45. $4,866 \div 76$ **46.** $3,827 \div 76$ **47.** $3,546 \div 88$ **48.** $3,697 \div 63$

Solve.

49. Mr. Wilson baked 24 dozen muffins to sell in his store. He put all the muffins on trays. If each tray can hold 18 muffins, what is the least number of trays that Mr. Wilson will need?

50. In the school library, there are 173 nature books, 218 history books, 92 reference books, and 487 children's books. If each bookshelf can hold 25 books, what is the least number of shelves needed to hold all the books?

 Write About It

Solve each problem. Use correct math vocabulary to explain your thinking.

1. Alberta completed the division shown on the board.

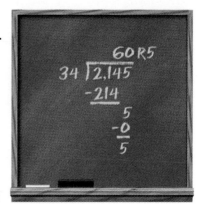

  a. Explain what she did wrong.

  b. Show how to find the correct answer.

  c. Explain how Alberta could have known that her answer was incorrect.

2. The school cafeteria uses 416 gallons of milk each week. One gallon of milk equals 16 cups. Each cup equals 8 fluid ounces.

  a. Half of the milk is used for cooking. Students drink the rest. How many cups of milk do the students drink in a week?

  b. What step would you take next if you wanted to find out how many ounces of milk the students drink each week?

  c. Explain how your answer to *b* can help you find how many ounces of milk in all the school cafeteria uses in one week.

Another Look

Mr. Jacobs is planting tulip bulbs in his flowerbeds. Use the picture below to solve the problems.

1. Find the cost of a tulip bulb in each size bag.

2. Mr. Jacobs wants to fill his flowerbeds with tulips. How many bulbs will he need? How many small bags would it take to fill the flower beds? How many large bags would it take to fill the flower beds?

3. **Look Back** How can you use multiplication to check your answers in problems 1 and 2?

4. **Analyze** Mr. Jacobs wants to buy the tulip bulbs he needs to fill his flower beds at the lowest possible cost, so that no bulbs are left over. How many large bags and how many small bags should he buy?

Enrichment

Order of Operations

Many expressions have more than one operation. Mathematicians have rules for simplifying these expressions. The rules tell you the order in which you must do the operations.

Order of Operations
1. Do the operations inside parentheses.
2. Do the multiplication and division in order from left to right.
3. Do the addition and subtraction in order from left to right.

Simplify $16 - (8 \div 2) \times 2 + 1$.

Step 1 First do the operations inside parentheses.

Step 2 Then start at the left. Do the multiplication and division in order.

Step 3 Start at the left again. Do the addition and subtraction in order.

$$16 - (8 \div 2) \times 2 + 1$$
$$16 - 4 \times 2 + 1$$
$$16 - 8 + 1$$
$$8 + 1$$
$$9$$

Solution: $16 - (8 \div 2) \times 2 + 1 = 9$.

Simplify each expression.

1. $(16 - 10) \times (8 - 3) - 1$

2. $20 - (8 + 2) \div 2$

3. $5 \times 3 - 18 \div 3 + 4 \times 3$

4. $4 + 3 \times 5 - 16 \div 4 + 2$

Evaluate each expression for $m = 6$.

5. $2 + 3m$

6. $4m - 1$

7. $3m + 9m$

Explain Your Thinking

Jamie simplified $15 - 3 + 9$ and got 3. What mistake did he make? What is the correct answer?

Standards AF 1.2

603

Table of Measures

Customary Units of Measure

Length

1 foot (ft) = 12 inches (in.)

1 yard (yd) = 36 inches

1 yard (yd) = 3 feet

1 mile (mi) = 5,280 feet

1 mile (mi) = 1,760 yards

Capacity

1 pint (pt) = 2 cups (c)

1 quart (qt) = 2 pints

1 quart (qt) = 4 cups

1 gallon (gal) = 4 quarts

1 gallon (gal) = 8 pints

1 gallon (gal) = 16 cups

Weight

1 pound (lb) = 16 ounces (oz)

1 ton (T) = 2,000 pounds (lb)

Metric Units of Measure

Length

1 meter (m) = 100 centimeters (cm)

1 meter (m) = 10 decimeters (dm)

1 decimeter (dm) = 10 centimeters

1 kilometer (km) = 1,000 meters

1 centimeter (cm) = 10 millimeters

Capacity

1 liter (L) = 1,000 milliliters (mL)

Mass

1 kilogram (kg) = 1,000 grams (g)

Units of Time

1 minute (min) = 60 seconds (s)

1 hour (h) = 60 minutes

1 day (d) = 24 hours

1 week (wk) = 7 days

1 year (yr) = 12 months (mo)

1 year = 52 weeks

1 year = 365 days

1 leap year = 366 days

1 decade = 10 years

1 century = 100 years

1 millennium = 1,000 years

Glossary

acute angle An angle with a measure less than that of a right angle.

acute triangle A triangle in which each of the three angles is acute.

addend A number to be added in an addition expression. In $7 + 4 + 8$, the numbers 7, 4, and 8 are addends.

algebraic expression An expression that consists of one or more variables. It could contain some constants and some operations.
Example: $2x + 3y + 6$

angle An angle is formed by two rays with the same endpoint.

area The number of square units in a region.

array An arrangement of objects, pictures, or numbers in columns and rows.

Associative Property of Addition The property which states that the way in which addends are grouped does not change the sum. It is also called the Grouping Property of Addition.

Associative Property of Multiplication The property which states that the way in which factors are grouped does not change the product. It is also called the Grouping Property of Multiplication.

average The number found by dividing the sum of a group of numbers by the number of addends.

bar graph A graph in which information is shown by means of rectangular bars.

capacity The amount a container can hold.

Celsius The metric temperature scale. It is also called *centigrade*.

centimeter (cm) A metric unit used to measure length.
100 centimeters = 1 meter

circle A closed figure in which every point is the same distance from a given point called the center of the circle.

Glossary

Commutative Property of Addition
The property which states that the order of addends does not change the sum. It is also called the Order Property of Addition.

Commutative Property of Multiplication The property which states that the order of factors does not change the product. It is also called the Order Property of Multiplication.

composite number A whole number that has more than two factors.

cone A solid that has a circular base and a surface from a boundary of the base to the vertex.

congruent figures Figures that have the same size and the same shape.

coordinates An ordered pair of numbers that locates a point in the coordinate plane with reference to the x- and y-axes.

cube A solid figure that has six square faces of equal size.

cubic centimeter A metric unit for measuring volume. It is the volume of a cube with each edge 1 centimeter long.

cylinder A solid with two circular faces that are congruent and a cylindrical surface connecting the two faces.

decimal A number with one or more digits to the right of a decimal point.

denominator The number below the bar in a fraction.

diameter of a circle A segment that connects two points on the circle and passes through the center.

dividend The number that is divided in a division problem.

divisible One number is divisible by another if the quotient is a whole number and the remainder is 0. For example, 10 is divisible by 2, since $10 \div 2 = 5$ R0.

divisor The number by which a number is being divided. In $6 \div 3 = 2$, the divisor is 3.

double bar graph A graph in which data is compared by means of pairs of rectangular bars drawn next to each other.

Glossary

edge The segment where two faces of a solid figure meet.

endpoint The point at either end of a line segment. The beginning point of a ray.

equation A mathematical sentence with an equals sign.
Examples: $3 + 1 = 4$ and $2x + 5 = 9$ are equations.

equilateral triangle A triangle that has three congruent sides.

equivalent fractions Fractions that show different numbers with the same value.
Example: $\frac{1}{2}$ and $\frac{4}{8}$ are equivalent fractions.

estimate A number close to an exact amount. An estimate tells *about* how much or *about* how many.

evaluating an expression Substituting the values given for the variables and performing the operations to find the value of the expression.

even number A whole number that is a multiple of 2. The ones digit in an even number is 0, 2, 4, 6, or 8. The numbers 56 and 48 are examples of even numbers.

event In probability, a result of an experiment that can be classified as certain, likely, unlikely, or impossible to occur.

face A flat surface of a solid figure.

fact family Facts that are related, using the same numbers.
Examples: $1 + 4 = 5$; $4 + 1 = 5$; $6 - 4 = 2$; $6 - 2 = 4$; $3 \times 5 = 15$; $5 \times 3 = 15$; $15 \div 3 = 5$; $15 \div 5 = 3$

factor One of two or more numbers that are multiplied to give a product.

factor of a number A number that divides evenly into a given number.

Fahrenheit The customary temperature scale.

fraction A number that names a part of a whole, a part of a collection, or a part of a region.
Examples: $\frac{1}{2}$, $\frac{3}{4}$, and $\frac{2}{3}$.

horizontal axis The *x*-axis in a coordinate system. It is a number line that locates points to the left or to the right of the origin.

Glossary

improper fraction A fraction that is greater than or equal to 1. The numerator in an improper fraction is greater than or equal to the denominator.

inch (in.) A customary unit used to measure length.

12 inches = 1 foot

inequality A sentence that contains > (is greater than) or < (is less than).

Examples: 8 > 2, 5 < 6

integers The set of positive whole numbers and their opposites (negative numbers) and 0.

..., ⁻3, ⁻2, ⁻1, 0, ⁺1, ⁺2, ⁺3,...

intersecting lines Lines that meet or cross at a common point.

isosceles triangle A triangle that has two congruent sides.

like denominators Denominators in two or more fractions that are the same.

line A straight path that goes on without end in opposite directions.

line graph A graph that uses a broken line to show changes in data.

line of symmetry The line along which a figure can be folded so that the two halves match exactly.

line plot A diagram that organizes data using a number line.

line segment Part of a line. A line segment has two endpoints.

mean Arithmetic mean, also called *average*. The number found by dividing the sum of a group of numbers by the number of addends.

median The middle number when a set of numbers is arranged in order from least to greatest.

Examples: The median of 2, 5, 7, 9 and 10 is 7. For an even number of numbers, it is the average of the two middle numbers. The median of 2, 5, 7, and 12 is $\frac{(5 + 7)}{2}$ or 6.

milliliter (mL) A metric unit used to measure capacity.

1,000 milliliters = 1 liter

mixed number A number containing a whole number part and a fraction part.

mode The number or numbers that occur most often in a set of data.

negative number A number that is less than 0.

Examples: $^-2$, $^-5$, and $^-26$ are negative numbers.

net A flat pattern that can be folded to make a solid.

numerator The number above the bar in a fraction.

obtuse angle An angle with a measure greater than that of a right angle and less than 180°.

obtuse triangle A triangle that has one obtuse angle.

odd number A whole number that is not a multiple of 2. The ones digit in an odd number is 1, 3, 5, 7, or 9. The numbers 67 and 493 are examples of odd numbers.

opposite of a number The same number but of opposite sign. Examples of opposite numbers are $^+2$ and $^-2$, $^-7$ and $^+7$, and $^-12$ and $^+12$. The opposite of a number is also called its additive inverse.

ordered pairs A pair of numbers in which one number is considered to be first and the other number second.

origin A point assigned to zero on the number line or the point where the x- and y-axes intersect in a coordinate system.

outcome A result in a probability experiment.

outlier A number or numbers that are at one or the other end of a set of data, arranged in order, where there is a gap between the end numbers and the rest of the data.

parallel lines Lines that lie in the same plane and do not intersect. They are everywhere the same distance apart.

Glossary

parallelogram A quadrilateral in which both pairs of opposite sides are parallel.

perimeter The distance around a figure.

perpendicular Two lines or line segments that cross or meet to form right angles.

point An exact location in space represented by a dot.

polygon A simple closed plane figure made up of three or more line segments.

positive numbers Numbers that are greater than zero.

prime number A whole number that has only itself and 1 as factors.

probability The chance of an event occurring. A probability can be any number from 0 through 1.

product The answer in a multiplication problem.

Property of One for Multiplication The property which states that the product of 1 and any number is that number.

Property of Zero for Addition The property which states that if 0 is added to a number, the sum equals that number.

Property of Zero for Multiplication The property which states that if 0 is a factor, the product is 0.

pyramid A solid figure whose base can be any polygon and whose faces are triangles.

quadrilateral A polygon with four sides.

quotient The answer in a division problem.

radius A segment that connects the center of a circle to any point on the circle.

range The difference between the greatest and least numbers in a set of data.

ray Part of a line that starts at an endpoint and goes on forever in one direction.

rectangle A polygon with opposite sides parallel and four right angles.

rectangular prism A solid figure with six faces that are rectangles.

rectangular pyramid A solid figure whose base is a rectangle and whose faces are triangles.

remainder The number that is left after one whole number is divided by another.

rhombus A parallelogram with all four sides the same length.

right angle An angle that measures 90°.

right triangle A triangle that has one right angle.

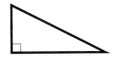

rotational symmetry A figure has rotational symmetry if, after the figure is rotated about a point, the figure is the same as when in its original position.

rounding To find about how many or how much by expressing a number to the nearest ten, hundred, thousand, and so on.

scalene triangle A triangle with all sides of different lengths.

side of a polygon One of the line segments that make up a polygon.

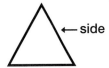

similar figures Figures that have the same shape but not necessarily the same size.

simplest form of a fraction A fraction whose numerator and denominator have the number 1 as the only common factor.

simplest form of an algebraic expression An algebraic expression is in simplest form if no terms can be combined.

solution of an equation A number or numbers that, when substituted for the variable or variables in an equation, give a true statement.

sphere A solid figure that is shaped like a round ball.

Glossary

square A polygon with four right angles and four congruent sides.

surface area The total area of the surface of a solid.

symmetric figure A figure that has symmetry.

trapezoid A quadrilateral with exactly one pair of parallel sides.

tree diagram A diagram that shows combinations of outcomes of an event.

triangular prism A prism whose bases are triangles.

triangular pyramid A pyramid whose base is a triangle.

two-variable equation An equation that has two different variables.

variable A letter or a symbol that represents a number in an algebraic expression.

vertex of an angle A point common to the two sides of an angle.

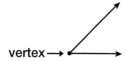

vertex →

vertex of a polygon A point common to two sides of a polygon.

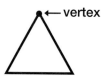

← vertex

vertex of a prism A point common to three edges of a prism.

vertical axis The *y*-axis in the coordinate system. It is a number line that locates points up or down from the origin.

volume The number of cubic units that make up a solid figure.

weight The measure of how heavy something is.

***x*-axis** The horizontal number line in a coordinate system.

***x*-coordinate** The first number of an ordered pair of numbers that names a point in a coordinate system.

***y*-axis** The vertical number line in a coordinate system.

***y*-coordinate** The second number of an ordered pair of numbers that names a point in a coordinate system.

Index

Index

Index

Index

decimals and, 372–373, 378–379, 382–383

definition of, 322

equivalent, 328–333

game, 341

improper, 342–345

mixed numbers and, 342–345, 382–383

ordering, 338–341, 382–383

part of a number, 326–327

probability and, 436–437

representing, 324–325

showing division as, 367

simplest form, 330–333

subtracting, 352–353

Function(s), 58, 87, 94, 97, 114, 131, 146, 147, 150, 224, 396, 529, 530

graphing, 528–530, 550–552

two step, 144–146

Gallon, 282–285

Game

Action Fractions, 341

Dollar Dunk, 33

Even It Out, 425

Expression Matchup, 135

Get the Least, 63

Graph Tick-tack-toe, 545

It All Adds Up, 377

Mix and Match, 583

Multiplying Does It!, 197

Race for the Remainder, 225

Tick-tack-toe Measurement, 297

Triple Concentration, 463

Geometry

angles, 458, 464–465

circles, 470–471

congruent figures, 458, 474–477

game, 463

hexagons, 458, 466–467

intersecting lines, 460–463

lines, 458, 460–463

line segments, 458, 460–463

line symmetry, 478–481

nets, 498–501

octagons, 458, 466–467

parallel lines, 460–463

parallelograms, 466–467

pentagons, 458, 466–467

perpendicular lines, 460–463

points, 460–463

polygons, 458, 466–467

quadrilaterals, 458, 466–467

rays, 464–465

rectangles, 458, 466–467

rhombus, 466–467

right triangles, 458, 468–469

rotational symmetry, 479–481

similar figures, 477

solid figures, 498–501

squares, 458, 466–467

symmetry, 478–481

triangles, 458, 466, 468–469

Gram, 294–295

Graph, *See also* Functions.

bar, 83, 121, 196, 224, 258, 414–415, 422–425, 439, 481, 582

circle, 354–355, 356, 363, 365

coordinate, 522–533, 538–545

double bar, 422–423, 446, 450, 452

line, 426–429, 446, 449, 451, 452

line plot, 414, 418–420, 439, 572

pictograph, 114, 200–201, 497

Greatest common factor, 331, 333

Guess and check, strategy, 88–89

Hands-On Activity

Centimeter and Millimeter, 290–291

Collect and Organize Data, 416–417

Fractions and Decimals, 372–373

How Big is 1 Million?, 16–17

Inch, Half Inch, and Quarter Inch, 278–279

Making Predictions, 438–439

Modeling Averages, 250–251

Modeling Division, 218–219

Modeling Equivalent Fractions, 328–329

Modeling Multiplication by One-Digit Numbers, 168–169

Modeling Perimeter and Area, 486–487

Solve Multiplication Equations, 142–143

Solving Addition Equations, 84–85

Hexagon, 458, 466–467

Hundredths, meaning of, 370

Identity Property

for addition, 54–55

for multiplication, 110–111, 164–165

If-then statements, 411

Impossible outcome, 434–435

Improper fraction, 342–345

Inch, 278–281

Inequalities, 75–77

Input/Output table, 58, 87, 94, 97, 114, 131, 146, 147, 150, 224, 396

Index

Index

Index

Excerpts from MATHEMATICS CONTENT STANDARDS FOR CALIFORNIA PUBLIC SCHOOLS, copyright © December 1997 are reprinted by permission of the California Department of Education.

PHOTOGRAPHY

All photographs by Houghton Mifflin Company (HMCo.) unless otherwise noted.

Coin photography by Mike Tesi for HMCo. xii: Martin Fox for HMCo. xxi: James L. Amos/Corbis. 1: Index Stock Imagery. 4: University of Michigan Athletic Department. 5: Parker/Boon Productions for HMCo. 8: Carl Roessler/FPG International. 11: *t.* Michele Burgess/Stock Boston; *b.* E.R. Degginger/Bruce Coleman Inc. 12: Associated Press Keystone. 13: Philippe Desmazes/AFP Photo. 17: Richard Hutchings for HMCo. 21: *t.* Dusty Perin/Dembinsky Photo Associates; *b.* Gary A. Conner/Index Stock Imagery. 24: David Young-Wolff/PhotoEdit. 27: Mike Tesi for HMCo. 50–51: Richard Hutchings/Stock Boston. 55: PhotoDisc, Inc. 56–57: Kevin Fleming/Corbis. 60: Quarto, Inc./Artville Stock Images. 62: *t.l.* Ron Kimball Photography; *t.r.* Ron Kimball Photography; *b.l.* Ralph Reinhold/Index Stock Imagery; *b.r.* Ron Kimball Photography. 66: *bkgd.* Bill Horsman/Stock Boston/Picture Quest Network International/PNI. 69: PhotoDisc, Inc. 70: Ric Ergenbright/Corbis. 71: Neil Gilchrist/Panoramic Images. 78: American Images Inc./FPG International. 88: Frans Lanting/Minden Pictures. 112: Richard Hutchings for HMCo. 113: Lawrence Migdale/Pix. 119: *t.* Royal Mint; *b.* Uniphoto Pictor. 128: Lawrence Migdale/Stock Boston. 129: *l.* David Young-Wolff/PhotoEdit; *m.l.* Kevin R. Morris/Corbis; *m.r.* Ulf Sjostedt /FPG International; *r.* Patrick Ward/Stock Boston. 140: *b.* Ed Bock/The Stock Market. 141: Martin Fox for HMCo. 144: *r.* PhotoDisc, Inc. 145: John Paul Endress for HMCo. 148: *t.* Barry Lewis/Corbis; *b.* Michael Gaffney for HMCo. 162–163: Richard Hutchings Photography. 166: Zefa/Index Stock Imagery. 167: Bob Daemmrich/Stock Boston. 174: Jose Carrillo/PhotoEdit. 180: Tony Freeman/PhotoEdit. 182: Peter Menzel/Stock Boston. 188: *t.* Tony Freeman/PhotoEdit; *b.* Steven Frame/Stock Boston. 189: *l.* Photomondo/FPG International; *r.* J.R. Holland/Stock Boston. 192: *l.* Lynn M. Stone/Bruce Coleman Inc.; *r.* PhotoDisc, Inc. 193: H. Reinhard/Bruce Coleman Inc. 194: James L. Fly/Unicorn Stock Photos. 196: *l.* Marianne Haas/Corbis; *m.* PhotoDisc, Inc.; *r.* Benjamin Rondel/The Stock Market. 198: *l.* Bob Daemmrich/Stock Boston/Picture Quest Network International/PNI. 201: *l.* Adam Jones/Dembinsky Photo Associates; *m.l.* Hubert Klein/Peter Arnold, Inc.; *m.* Robert Maier/Animals Animals/Earth Scenes; *m.r.* Robert Maier/Animals Animals/Earth Scenes; *r.* Andrew Odum/Peter Arnold, Inc. 223: Frank Siteman/PhotoEdit. 227: *l.* Richard Nowitz Photography; *r.* Lawrence Migdale/Pix. 234: *l.* Brian Kenney/Natural Selection Stock Photography, Inc.; *r.* Art Wolfe. 235: © 1998 Bob London/The Stock Market. 240: Mark Bolster/International Stock Photography Ltd. 242: Michael Newman/PhotoEdit. 256: *t.* Joseph Sohm/ChromoSohm/Corbis; *b.* Courtesy, National Park Service. 258: Jerry Jacka Photography. 260: Pasadena Tournament of Roses. 261: Edison International. 274–275: Kim Westerkov/Tony Stone Images. 277: *l.* Corbis. 282: Richard Hutchings for HMCo. 283: PhotoDisc, Inc. 286: Index Stock Imagery. 287: Arvind Garg/Corbis. 295: *t.m.* PhotoDisc, Inc.; *b.l.* Richard Hutchings for HMCo. 296: *t.l.* Mike Tesi for HMCo.; *b.r.* Cyril Ruoso/BIOS/Peter Arnold, Inc. 298: Helga Lade/Peter Arnold, Inc. 299: Superstock. 303: Dembinsky Photo Associates. 305: Peter Baumann/Animals Animals/Earth Scenes. 306: Dembinsky Photo Associates. 307: Robert Fried/Stock Boston. 311: *m.* Quarto, Inc./Artville Stock Images; *m.r.* Gary Meszaros/Dembinsky Photo Associates; *b.m.* PhotoDisc, Inc.; *b.r.* PhotoDisc, Inc. 314: *l.* Mike Tesi for HMCo. 315: *r.* PhotoDisc, Inc. 320–321: Richard Kasmier/Index Stock Imagery. 324: Michael Gaffney for HMCo. 332: Michael Gaffney for HMCo. 334: Charles Gupton/The Stock Market. 338: Phillip Roullard/Roullard Photography. 339: Jeannie Couch Photographic Arts. 343: Michael Gaffney for HMCo. 346: © Michael Newman/PhotoEdit. 347: *l.* Jeff Greenberg/The Image Works Inc.; *r.* © Ralph Reinhold/Animals Animals/Earth Scenes. 349: *r.* Ken Karp for HMCo. 351: Elizabeth Zuckerman/PhotoEdit. 352: Richard Hutchings for HMCo. 353: Mike Tesi for HMCo. 355: Michael Gaffney for HMCo. 368–369: Bob Daemmrich Photography. 380: Duomo Photography. 383: George Bernard/Animals Animals/Earth Scenes. 384: PhotoDisc, Inc. 385: Bob Daemmrich/Stock Boston. 391: Leonard Harris/Stock Boston. 392: Mark Burnett/Stock Boston. 393: Norman Owen Tomalin/Bruce Coleman Inc. 394: Bob Daemmrich/The Image Works Inc. 398: Paul Barton/The Stock Market. 399: *l.* Lawrence Migdale/Pix; *r.* Stephen McBrady/PhotoEdit/Picture Quest Network International/PNI. 410: © Syracuse Newspapers/Tim Reese/The Image Works Inc. 412–413: John A. Coletti/Stock Boston. 416: *t.l.* SW Productions/PhotoDisc, Inc.; *t.m.* Laurens Roth. 418: Yann Arthus-Bertrand/Corbis. 419: *l.* Schafer & Hill/Tony Stone Images; *m.* Jim Brandenburg/Minden Pictures; *r.* Johan Elzenga/Tony Stone Images. 420: *t.* CMCD/PhotoDisc, Inc.; *b.* Seide Press/PhotoDisc, Inc. 423: Jose L. Pelaez/The Stock Market. 426: Neil Rabinowitz/Corbis. 427: Terry Donnelly/Dembinsky Photo Associates. 430: Index Stock Imagery. 438: *m.* Richard Hutchings for HMCo.; *b.* Richard Hutchings for HMCo. 456–457: Greg Gawlowski/Dembinsky Photo Associates. 460: J. Gleiter/H. Armstrong Roberts, Inc. 467: *l.* PhotoDisc, Inc.; *m.* PhotoDisc, Inc.; *r.* Corbis. 468: Tim Page/Corbis. 469: Honshu-Shikoku Bridge Authority. 474: PhotoDisc, Inc. 500: *m.r.* PhotoDisc, Inc. 512: *m.l.* Mike Tesi for HMCo. 520–521: Bob Daemmrich/Stock Boston. 527: *bkgd.* The Granger Collection; *inset* The Granger Collection. 529: *t.* Mike Tesi for HMCo.; *b.* © Norbert Wu. 530: Mike Tesi for HMCo. 532: Richard Hutchings for HMCo. 546: Michael Gaffney for HMCo. 550: Michael Newman/PhotoEdit. 551: Bob Daemmrich Photography. 564–565: Richard Nowitz Photography. 568: David Madison Photography. 574: James L. Amos/Corbis. 576: Richard Hutchings Photography for HMCo. 577: *l.* Bob Daemmrich Photography; *r.* Unicorn Stock Photos. 586: Scott S. Warren Photography. 588: © Aaron Haupt/Photo Researchers, Inc. 591: Myrleen Ferguson Cate/PhotoEdit/Picture Quest Network International/PNI.

Credits